psalms

the book of

psalms

authorised king james version

printed by authority

published by canongate

---

with an introduction by | bono

First published in Great Britain in 1999
by Canongate Books Ltd
14 High Street, Edinburgh EH1 1TE

10 9 8 7 6 5 4 3 2 1

Introduction copyright © Bono 1999
The moral right of the author has been asserted

British Library Cataloguing-in-Publication Data
A catalogue record is available on request from
the British Library

ISBN 0 86241 969 7

Typeset by Palimpsest Book Production
Book design by Paddy Cramsie at et al
Printed and bound in Great Britain
by Caledonian International, Bishopbriggs

a note about pocket canons

The Authorised King James Version of the Bible, translated between 1603–11, coincided with an extraordinary flowering of English literature. This version, more than any other, and possibly more than any other work in history, has had an influence in shaping the language we speak and write today.

Twenty-four of the eighty original books of the King James Bible are brought to you in this series. They encompass categories as diverse as history, philosophy, law, poetry and fiction. Each Pocket Canon also has its own introduction, specially commissioned from an impressive range of writers, to provide a personal interpretation of the text and explore its contemporary relevance.

introduction by bono

Bono was born (Paul David Hewson) in Dublin in 1960. At seventeen he joined the embryonic U2 with three school-friends. U2 released their first record with Island Records in April 1980 and have gone on to sell 87 million albums worldwide, gathering seven Grammies in the US and five Brit Awards in the UK along the way. In 1992 their ground-breaking Zoo TV tour was hailed as the most innovative spectacle ever staged. The follow-up, 1997's Pop-Mart tour, built on that inventiveness, and played to a record-breaking four million people worldwide. In 1994 Bono was invited to present the Lifetime Achievement Award to Frank Sinatra at the Grammies. He was the guest speaker at the UK International Year of Literature in 1995. The Million Dollar Hotel, a film based on a story co-written by Bono, is currently in production starring Mel Gibson and directed by Wim Wenders. Bono lives in Dublin with his wife and three children.

Explaining belief has always been difficult. How do you explain a love and logic at the heart of the universe when the world is so out of whack? How about the poetic versus the actual truth found in the scriptures? Has free will got *us* crucified? And what about the dodgy characters who inhabit the tome, known as the bible, who claim to hear the voice of God?

You have to be interested, but is God?

Explaining faith is impossible … Vision over visibility … Instinct over intellect … A songwriter plays a chord with the faith that he will hear the next one in his head.

One of the writers of the psalms was a musician, a harp-player whose talents were required at 'the palace' as the only medicine that would still the demons of the moody and insecure King Saul of Israel; a thought that still inspires, if not quite explaining Marilyn singing for Kennedy, or the Spice Girls in the court of Prince Charles …

At age 12, I was a fan of David, he felt familiar … like a pop star could feel familiar. The words of the psalms were as poetic as they were religious and he was a star. A dramatic character, because before David could fulfil the prophecy and become the king of Israel, he had to take quite a beating. He was forced into exile and ended up in a cave in some no-name border town facing the collapse of his ego and abandonment by God. But this is where the soap opera got interesting, this is where David was said to have composed his first psalm – a blues. That's what a lot of the psalms feel like to me, the blues. Man shouting at God – 'My God, my God why hast thou forsaken me? Why art thou so far from helping me?' (Psalm 22).

I hear echoes of this holy row when un-holy bluesman Robert Johnson howls 'There's a hellhound on my trail' or Van Morrison sings 'Sometimes I feel like a motherless child'. Texas Alexander mimics the psalms in 'Justice Blues':

'I cried Lord my father, Lord eh Kingdom come. Send me back my woman, then thy will be done'. Humorous, sometimes blasphemous, the blues was backslidin' music; but by its very opposition, flattered the subject of its perfect cousin Gospel.

Abandonment, displacement, is the stuff of my favourite psalms. The Psalter may be a font of gospel music, but for me it's in his despair that the psalmist really reveals the nature of his special relationship with God. Honesty, even to the point of anger. 'How long, Lord? Wilt thou hide thyself forever?' (Psalm 89) or 'Answer me when I call' (Psalm 5).

Psalms and hymns were my first taste of inspirational music. I liked the words but I wasn't sure about the tunes – with the exception of Psalm 23, 'The Lord is my Shepherd'. I remember them as droned and chanted rather than sung. Still, in an odd way, they prepared me for the honesty of John Lennon, the baroque language of Bob Dylan and Leonard Cohen, the open throat of Al Green and Stevie Wonder – when I hear these singers, I am reconnected to a part of me I have no explanation for … my 'soul' I guess.

Words and music did for me what solid, even rigorous, religious argument could never do, they introduced me to God, not belief in God, more an experiential sense of GOD. Over art, literature, reason, the way in to my spirit was a combination of words and music. As a result the Book of *Psalms* always felt open to me and led me to the poetry of *Ecclesiastes*, the *Song of Solomon*, the book of *John* … My religion could not be fiction but it had to transcend facts. It could be mystical, but not mythical and definitely not ritual …

bono

My mother was Protestant, my father Catholic; anywhere other than Ireland that would be unremarkable. The 'Prods' at that time had the better tunes and the Catholics had the better stage-gear. My mate Gavin Friday used to say: 'Roman Catholicism is the Glamrock of religion' with its candles and psychedelic colours ... Cardinal blues, scarlets and purples, smoke bombs of incense and the ring of the little bell. The Prods were better at the bigger bells, they could afford them. In Ireland wealth and Protestantism went together; to have either, was to have collaborated with the enemy, i.e. Britain. This did not fly in our house.

After going to Mass at the top of the hill, in Finglas on the north side of Dublin, my father waited outside the little Church of Ireland chapel at the bottom of the hill, where my mother had brought her two sons ...

I kept myself awake thinking of the clergyman's daughter and let my eyes dive into the cinema of the stained glass. These Christian artisans had invented the movies ... light projected through colour to tell their story. In the '70s the story was 'the Troubles' and the Troubles came through the stained glass; with rocks thrown more in mischief than in anger, but the message was the same; the country was to be divided along sectarian lines. I had a foot in both camps, so my Goliath became religion itself; I began to see religion as the perversion of faith. As to the five smooth stones for the sling ... I began to see God everywhere else. In girls, fun, music, justice but still – despite the lofty King James translation – the scriptures ...

I loved these stories for the basest reasons, not just the

New Testament with its mind-altering concept that God might reveal himself as a baby born in straw poverty – but even the Old Testament. These were action movies, with some hardcore men and women ... the car chases, the casualties, the blood and guts; there was very little kissing ...

David was a star, the Elvis of the bible, if we can believe the chiselling of Michelangelo (check the face – but I still can't figure out this most famous Jew's foreskin). And unusually for such a 'rock star', with his lust for power, lust for women, lust for life, he had the humility of one who knew his gift worked harder than he ever would. He even danced naked in front of his troops ... the biblical equivalent of the royal walkabout. David was definitely more performance artist than politician.

Anyway, I stopped going to churches and got myself into a different kind of religion. Don't laugh, that's what being in a rock 'n' roll band is, not pseudo-religion either ... Show-business is Shamanism: Music is Worship; whether it's worship of women or their designer, the world or its destroyer, whether it comes from that ancient place we call soul or simply the spinal cortex, whether the prayers are on fire with a dumb rage or dove-like desire ... the smoke goes upwards ... to God or something you replace God with ... usually yourself.

Years ago, lost for words and forty minutes of recording time left before the end of our studio time, we were still looking for a song to close our third album, *War*. We wanted to put something explicitly spiritual on the record to balance the politics and the romance of it; like Bob Marley or Marvin

Gaye would. We thought about the psalms … 'Psalm 40' … There was some squirming. We were a very 'white' rock group, and such plundering of the scriptures was taboo for a white rock group unless it was in the 'service of Satan'. Or worse, Goth.

'Psalm 40' is interesting in that it suggests a time in which grace will replace karma, and love replace the very strict laws of Moses (i.e. fulfil them). I love that thought. David, who committed some of the most selfish as well as selfless acts, was depending on it. That the scriptures are brim full of hustlers, murderers, cowards, adulterers and mercenaries used to shock me; now it is a source of great comfort.

'40' became the closing song at U2 shows and on hundreds of occasions, literally hundreds of thousands of people of every size and shape t-shirt have shouted back the refrain, pinched from 'Psalm 6': "'How long' (to sing this song)". I had thought of it as a nagging question – pulling at the hem of an invisible deity whose presence we glimpse only when we act in love. How long … hunger? How long … hatred? How long until creation grows up and the chaos of its precocious, hell-bent adolescence has been discarded? I thought it odd that the vocalising of such questions could bring such comfort; to me too.

But to get back to David, it is not clear how many, if any, of these psalms David or his son Solomon really wrote. Some scholars suggest the royals never dampened their nibs and that there was a host of Holy Ghost writers … Who cares? I didn't buy Leiber and Stoller … they were just his songwriters … I bought Elvis.

introduction

the book of psalms

1
Blessed is the man that walketh not
    in the counsel of the ungodly,
nor standeth in the way of sinners,
    nor sitteth in the seat of the scornful.
² But his delight is in the law of the Lord;
    and in his law doth he meditate day and night.
³ And he shall be like a tree planted
    by the rivers of water,
        that bringeth forth his fruit in his season;
    his leaf also shall not wither;
        and whatsoever he doeth shall prosper.
⁴ The ungodly are not so, but are like the chaff
    which the wind driveth away.
⁵ Therefore the ungodly shall not stand
    in the judgment,
        nor sinners in the congregation
    of the righteous.
⁶ For the Lord knoweth the way of the righteous;
    but the way of the ungodly shall perish.

2
Why do the heathen rage,
    and the people imagine a vain thing?

[2] The kings of the earth set themselves, and the rulers
    take counsel together, against the Lord,
        and against his anointed, saying,
[3] 'Let us break their bands asunder,
    and cast away their cords from us.'
[4] He that sitteth in the heavens shall laugh:
    the Lord shall have them in derision.
[5] Then shall he speak unto them in his wrath,
    and vex them in his sore displeasure.
[6] Yet have I set my king
    upon my holy hill of Zion.
[7] I will declare the decree:
    the Lord hath said unto me,
        'Thou art my Son;
    this day have I begotten thee.
[8] Ask of me, and I shall give thee the heathen
    for thine inheritance,
        and the uttermost parts of the earth
    for thy possession.
[9] Thou shalt break them with a rod of iron;
    thou shalt dash them in pieces
        like a potter's vessel.'
[10] Be wise now therefore, O ye kings:
    be instructed, ye judges of the earth.
[11] Serve the Lord with fear,
    and rejoice with trembling.
[12] Kiss the Son, lest he be angry,
    and ye perish from the way,
        when his wrath is kindled but a little.

Blessed are all they
that put their trust in him.

3 A psalm of David, when he fled
from Absalom his son.

Lord, how are they increased that trouble me!
Many are they that rise up against me.
² Many there be which say of my soul,
'There is no help for him in God.' Selah.
³ But thou, O Lord, art a shield for me;
my glory, and the lifter up of mine head.
⁴ I cried unto the Lord with my voice,
and he heard me out of his holy hill. Selah.
⁵ I laid me down and slept;
I awaked; for the Lord sustained me.
⁶ I will not be afraid of ten thousands of people,
that have set themselves against me round about.
⁷ Arise, O Lord; save me, O my God,
for thou hast smitten all mine enemies
upon the cheek bone;
thou hast broken the teeth of the ungodly.
⁸ Salvation belongeth unto the Lord:
thy blessing is upon thy people. Selah.

4 To the chief musician on Neginoth,
a psalm of David.

Hear me when I call, O God of my righteousness:

thou hast enlarged me when I was in distress;
have mercy upon me, and hear my prayer.
² O ye sons of men, how long will ye turn
my glory into shame?
How long will ye love vanity,
and seek after leasing? Selah.
³ But know that the Lord hath set apart him
that is godly for himself:
the Lord will hear when I call unto him.
⁴ Stand in awe, and sin not:
commune with your own heart upon your bed,
and be still. Selah.
⁵ Offer the sacrifices of righteousness,
and put your trust in the Lord.
⁶ There be many that say,
'Who will shew us any good?
Lord, lift thou up the light
of thy countenance upon us.'
⁷ Thou hast put gladness in my heart,
more than in the time that their corn
and their wine increased.
⁸ I will both lay me down in peace, and sleep,
for thou, Lord, only makest me dwell in safety.

5

To the chief musician upon Nehiloth,
a psalm of David.

Give ear to my words, O Lord,

consider my meditation.

² Hearken unto the voice of my cry, my King,
    and my God, for unto thee will I pray.

³ My voice shalt thou hear in the morning, O Lord;
    in the morning will I direct my prayer unto thee,
        and will look up.

⁴ For thou art not a God
    that hath pleasure in wickedness;
        neither shall evil dwell with thee.

⁵ The foolish shall not stand in thy sight:
    thou hatest all workers of iniquity.

⁶ Thou shalt destroy them that speak leasing:
    the Lord will abhor the bloody and deceitful man.

⁷ But as for me, I will come into thy house
    in the multitude of thy mercy:
        and in thy fear will I worship
    toward thy holy temple.

⁸ Lead me, O Lord, in thy righteousness
    because of mine enemies;
        make thy way straight before my face.

⁹ For there is no faithfulness in their mouth;
    their inward part is very wickedness;
        their throat is an open sepulchre;
    they flatter with their tongue.

¹⁰ Destroy thou them, O God;
    let them fall by their own counsels;
        cast them out in the multitude
    of their transgressions;

for they have rebelled against thee.

¹¹But let all those that put their trust in thee rejoice:
   let them ever shout for joy,
      because thou defendest them:
   let them also that love thy name
      be joyful in thee.

¹²For thou, Lord, wilt bless the righteous;
   with favour wilt thou compass him
      as with a shield.

6

To the chief musician on Neginoth upon Sheminith,
   a psalm of David.

O Lord, rebuke me not in thine anger,
   neither chasten me in thy hot displeasure.

²Have mercy upon me,
   O Lord; for I am weak:
      O Lord, heal me; for my bones are vexed.

³My soul is also sore vexed;
   but thou, O Lord, how long?

⁴Return, O Lord, deliver my soul:
   oh save me for thy mercies' sake.

⁵For in death there is no remembrance of thee:
   in the grave who shall give thee thanks?

⁶I am weary with my groaning;
   all the night make I my bed to swim;
      I water my couch with my tears.

⁷Mine eye is consumed because of grief;

it waxeth old because of all mine enemies.
⁸ Depart from me, all ye workers of iniquity;
    for the Lord hath heard the voice of my weeping.
⁹ The Lord hath heard my supplication;
    the Lord will receive my prayer.
¹⁰ Let all mine enemies be ashamed and sore vexed:
    let them return and be ashamed suddenly.

7 Shiggaion of David, which he sang unto the Lord,
    concerning the words of Cush the Benjamite.

O Lord my God, in thee do I put my trust:
    save me from all them that persecute me,
        and deliver me,
² lest he tear my soul like a lion, rending it in pieces,
    while there is none to deliver.
³ O Lord my God, if I have done this;
    if there be iniquity in my hands;
⁴ if I have rewarded evil unto him
    that was at peace with me
        (yea, I have delivered him
    that without cause is mine enemy),
⁵ let the enemy persecute my soul, and take it;
    yea, let him tread down my life upon the earth,
        and lay mine honour in the dust. Selah.
⁶ Arise, O Lord, in thine anger, lift up thyself
    because of the rage of mine enemies:
        and awake for me to the judgment
    that thou hast commanded.

⁷ So shall the congregation of the people
  compass thee about:
    for their sakes therefore return thou on high.
⁸ The Lord shall judge the people: judge me, O Lord,
  according to my righteousness,
    and according to mine integrity that is in me.
⁹ Oh let the wickedness of the wicked come to an end;
    but establish the just:
  for the righteous God trieth the hearts and reins.
¹⁰ My defence is of God, which saveth
  the upright in heart.
¹¹ God judgeth the righteous,
  and God is angry with the wicked every day.
¹² If he turn not, he will whet his sword;
  he hath bent his bow, and made it ready.
¹³ He hath also prepared for him
  the instruments of death; he ordaineth his arrows
    against the persecutors.
¹⁴ Behold, he travaileth with iniquity,
  and hath conceived mischief,
    and brought forth falsehood.
¹⁵ He made a pit, and digged it,
  and is fallen into the ditch which he made.
¹⁶ His mischief shall return upon his own head,
  and his violent dealing shall come down
    upon his own pate.
¹⁷ I will praise the Lord
  according to his righteousness,

and will sing praise to the name
of the Lord most high.

8

To the chief musician upon Gittith,
a psalm of David.

O Lord our Lord, how excellent is thy name
in all the earth,
who hast set thy glory above the heavens!
2 Out of the mouth of babes and sucklings hast thou
ordained strength because of thine enemies,
that thou mightest still the enemy
and the avenger.
3 When I consider thy heavens,
the work of thy fingers, the moon and the stars,
which thou hast ordained;
4 what is man, that thou art mindful of him?
And the son of man, that thou visitest him?
5 For thou hast made him a little lower
than the angels,
and hast crowned him with glory and honour.
6 Thou madest him to have dominion over
the works of thy hands;
thou hast put all things under his feet:
7 all sheep and oxen, yea,
and the beasts of the field;
8 the fowl of the air, and the fish of the sea,
and whatsoever passeth through
the paths of the seas.

⁹ O Lord our Lord, how excellent is thy name
  in all the earth!

9 To the chief musician upon Muth-labben, a psalm of
  David.

I will praise thee, O Lord, with my whole heart;
  I will shew forth all thy marvellous works.
² I will be glad and rejoice in thee:
  I will sing praise to thy name, O thou most High.
³ When mine enemies are turned back,
  they shall fall and perish at thy presence.
⁴ For thou hast maintained my right and my cause;
  thou satest in the throne judging right.
⁵ Thou hast rebuked the heathen,
  thou hast destroyed the wicked,
    thou hast put out their name for ever and ever.
⁶ O thou enemy, destructions are come
  to a perpetual end: and thou hast destroyed cities;
    their memorial is perished with them.
⁷ But the Lord shall endure for ever:
  he hath prepared his throne for judgment.
⁸ And he shall judge the world in righteousness,
  he shall minister judgment
    to the people in uprightness.
⁹ The Lord also will be a refuge for the oppressed,
  a refuge in times of trouble.

¹⁰And they that know thy name
  will put their trust in thee,
      for thou, Lord, hast not forsaken them
    that seek thee.
¹¹Sing praises to the Lord, which dwelleth in Zion:
  declare among the people his doings.
¹²When he maketh inquisition for blood,
  he remembereth them:
      he forgetteth not the cry of the humble.
¹³Have mercy upon me, O Lord;
  consider my trouble which I suffer
      of them that hate me,
  thou that liftest me up from the gates of death,
¹⁴that I may shew forth all thy praise
  in the gates of the daughter of Zion:
      I will rejoice in thy salvation.
¹⁵The heathen are sunk down
  in the pit that they made:
      in the net which they hid
  is their own foot taken.
¹⁶The Lord is known by the judgment
  which he executeth: the wicked is snared
      in the work of his own hands. Higgaion. Selah.
¹⁷The wicked shall be turned into hell,
  and all the nations that forget God.
¹⁸For the needy shall not alway be forgotten:
  the expectation of the poor
    shall not perish for ever.

¹⁹Arise, O Lord; let not man prevail:
>   let the heathen be judged in thy sight.
²⁰Put them in fear, O Lord:
>   that the nations may know themselves
>   to be but men. Selah.

10

Why standest thou afar off, O Lord?
>   Why hidest thou thyself in times of trouble?
²The wicked in his pride doth persecute the poor:
>   let them be taken in the devices
>   that they have imagined.
³For the wicked boasteth of his heart's desire,
>   and blesseth the covetous,
>   whom the Lord abhorreth.
⁴The wicked, through the pride of his countenance,
>   will not seek after God:
>   God is not in all his thoughts.
⁵His ways are always grievous;
>   thy judgments are far above out of his sight:
>   as for all his enemies, he puffeth at them.
⁶He hath said in his heart, 'I shall not be moved:
>   for I shall never be in adversity.'
⁷His mouth is full of cursing and deceit and fraud:
>   under his tongue is mischief and vanity.
⁸He sitteth in the lurking places of the villages:
>   in the secret places doth he murder the innocent:
>   his eyes are privily set against the poor.

⁹He lieth in wait secretly as a lion in his den:
    he lieth in wait to catch the poor:
        he doth catch the poor,
    when he draweth him into his net.
¹⁰He croucheth, and humbleth himself,
    that the poor may fall by his strong ones.
¹¹He hath said in his heart, God hath forgotten;
    he hideth his face; he will never see it.
¹²Arise, O Lord; O God, lift up thine hand:
    forget not the humble.
¹³Wherefore doth the wicked contemn God?
    He hath said in his heart,
        'Thou wilt not require it.'
¹⁴Thou hast seen it;
    for thou beholdest mischief and spite,
        to requite it with thy hand;
    the poor committeth himself unto thee;
        thou art the helper of the fatherless.
¹⁵Break thou the arm of the wicked and the evil man:
    seek out his wickedness till thou find none.
¹⁶The Lord is King for ever and ever:
    the heathen are perished out of his land.
¹⁷Lord, thou hast heard the desire of the humble:
    thou wilt prepare their heart,
        thou wilt cause thine ear to hear:
¹⁸to judge the fatherless and the oppressed,
    that the man of the earth
        may no more oppress.

11
To the chief musician, a psalm of David.

In the Lord put I my trust: how say ye to my soul,
   'Flee as a bird to your mountain.
² For, lo, the wicked bend their bow,
   they make ready their arrow upon the string,
      that they may privily shoot
   at the upright in heart.
³ If the foundations be destroyed,
   what can the righteous do?'
⁴ The Lord is in his holy temple,
   the Lord's throne is in heaven:
      his eyes behold, his eyelids try,
   the children of men.
⁵ The Lord trieth the righteous; but the wicked
   and him that loveth violence his soul hateth.
⁶ Upon the wicked he shall rain snares,
   fire and brimstone, and an horrible tempest:
      this shall be the portion of their cup.
⁷ For the righteous Lord loveth righteousness;
   his countenance doth behold the upright.

12
To the chief musician upon Sheminith,
   a psalm of David.

Help, Lord; for the godly man ceaseth;
   for the faithful fail from among
      the children of men.

² They speak vanity every one with his neighbour:
  with flattering lips and with a double heart
    do they speak.
³ The Lord shall cut off all flattering lips,
  and the tongue that speaketh proud things:
⁴ who have said, 'With our tongue will we prevail;
  our lips are our own: who is lord over us?'
⁵ 'For the oppression of the poor,
  for the sighing of the needy,
    now will I arise,' saith the Lord;
  I will set him in safety from him
    that puffeth at him.
⁶ The words of the Lord are pure words:
  as silver tried in a furnace of earth,
    purified seven times.
⁷ Thou shalt keep them, O Lord,
  thou shalt preserve them
    from this generation for ever.
⁸ The wicked walk on every side,
  when the vilest men are exalted.

13 To the chief musician, a psalm of David.

How long wilt thou forget me,
  O Lord? For ever?
    How long wilt thou hide
    thy face from me?
² How long shall I take counsel in my soul,
  having sorrow in my heart daily?

How long shall mine enemy
   be exalted over me?
³ Consider and hear me, O Lord my God:
   lighten mine eyes, lest I sleep the sleep of death;
⁴ lest mine enemy say,
   'I have prevailed against him';
      and those that trouble me rejoice
   when I am moved.
⁵ But I have trusted in thy mercy;
   my heart shall rejoice in thy salvation.
⁶ I will sing unto the Lord,
   because he hath dealt bountifully with me.

14

To the chief musician, a psalm of David.

The fool hath said in his heart, 'There is no God.'
   They are corrupt, they have done
      abominable works,
   there is none that doeth good.
² The Lord looked down from heaven
   upon the children of men, to see if there were
      any that did understand, and seek God.
³ They are all gone aside, they are all together
   become filthy: there is none that doeth good,
   no, not one.
⁴ Have all the workers of iniquity no knowledge?
   Who eat up my people as they eat bread,
      and call not upon the Lord.

⁵ There were they in great fear:
　　for God is in the generation of the righteous.
⁶ Ye have shamed the counsel of the poor,
　　because the Lord is his refuge.
⁷ Oh that the salvation of Israel
　　were come out of Zion!
　　　　When the Lord bringeth back
　　the captivity of his people,
　　　　Jacob shall rejoice, and Israel shall be glad.

15

A psalm of David.

Lord, who shall abide in thy tabernacle?
　　Who shall dwell in thy holy hill?
² He that walketh uprightly,
　　and worketh righteousness,
　　　　and speaketh the truth in his heart.
³ He that backbiteth not with his tongue,
　　nor doeth evil to his neighbour, nor taketh up
　　　　a reproach against his neighbour.
⁴ In whose eyes a vile person is contemned;
　　but he honoureth them that fear the Lord.
　　　　He that sweareth to his own hurt,
　　and changeth not.
⁵ He that putteth not out his money to usury,
　　nor taketh reward against the innocent.
　　　　He that doeth these things
　　shall never be moved.

16

Michtam of David.

Preserve me, O God, for in thee
    do I put my trust.
² O my soul, thou hast said unto the Lord
      'Thou art my Lord: my goodness extendeth
        not to thee,
³ but to the saints that are in the earth,
    and to the excellent,
      in whom is all my delight.'
⁴ Their sorrows shall be multiplied
    that hasten after another god:
      their drink offerings of blood will I not offer,
    nor take up their names into my lips.
⁵ The Lord is the portion of mine inheritance
    and of my cup: thou maintainest my lot.
⁶ The lines are fallen unto me in pleasant places;
    yea, I have a goodly heritage.
⁷ I will bless the Lord, who hath given me counsel:
    my reins also instruct me in the night seasons.
⁸ I have set the Lord always before me:
    because he is at my right hand,
      I shall not be moved.
⁹ Therefore my heart is glad, and my glory rejoiceth:
    my flesh also shall rest in hope.
¹⁰ For thou wilt not leave my soul in hell;
    neither wilt thou suffer thine Holy One
      to see corruption.

"Thou wilt shew me the path of life:
  in thy presence is fulness of joy;
    at thy right hand there are pleasures
  for evermore.

17

A prayer of David.

Hear the right, O Lord, attend unto my cry,
  give ear unto my prayer,
    that goeth not out of feigned lips.
² Let my sentence come forth from thy presence;
  let thine eyes behold
    the things that are equal.
³ Thou hast proved mine heart;
  thou hast visited me in the night;
    thou hast tried me, and shalt find nothing;
  I am purposed that my mouth
    shall not transgress.
⁴ Concerning the works of men,
  by the word of thy lips I have kept me
    from the paths of the destroyer.
⁵ Hold up my goings in thy paths,
  that my footsteps slip not.
⁶ I have called upon thee, for thou wilt hear me,
  O God: incline thine ear unto me,
    and hear my speech.
⁷ Shew thy marvellous lovingkindness,
  O thou that savest by thy right hand

them which put their trust in thee
from those that rise up against them.

8 Keep me as the apple of the eye,
hide me under the shadow of thy wings,

9 from the wicked that oppress me,
from my deadly enemies,
who compass me about.

10 They are inclosed in their own fat:
with their mouth they speak proudly.

11 They have now compassed us in our steps:
they have set their eyes bowing down
to the earth,

12 like as a lion that is greedy of his prey,
and as it were a young lion
lurking in secret places.

13 Arise, O Lord, disappoint him, cast him down:
deliver my soul from the wicked,
which is thy sword:

14 from men which are thy hand, O Lord,
from men of the world,
which have their portion in this life,
and whose belly thou fillest
with thy hid treasure: they are full of children,
and leave the rest of their substance
to their babes.

15 As for me, I will behold thy face in righteousness:
I shall be satisfied, when I awake,
with thy likeness.

18 To the chief musician, a psalm of David, the servant of the Lord, who spake unto the Lord the words of this song in the day that the Lord delivered him from the hand of all his enemies, and from the hand of Saul: and he said,

I will love thee, O Lord, my strength.
² The Lord is my rock, and my fortress,
    and my deliverer;
        my God, my strength, in whom I will trust;
    my buckler, and the horn of my salvation,
        and my high tower.
³ I will call upon the Lord, who is worthy
    to be praised:
        so shall I be saved from mine enemies.
⁴ The sorrows of death compassed me,
    and the floods of ungodly men made me afraid.
⁵ The sorrows of hell compassed me
    about: the snares of death prevented me.
⁶ In my distress I called upon the Lord,
    and cried unto my God:
        he heard my voice out of his temple,
    and my cry came before him, even into his ears.
⁷ Then the earth shook and trembled;
    the foundations also of the hills moved
        and were shaken, because he was wroth.
⁸ There went up a smoke out of his nostrils,
    and fire out of his mouth devoured:
        coals were kindled by it.

⁹ He bowed the heavens also, and came down:
    and darkness was under his feet.

¹⁰ And he rode upon a cherub, and did fly:
    yea, he did fly upon the wings of the wind.

¹¹ He made darkness his secret place;
    his pavilion round about him were dark waters
        and thick clouds of the skies.

¹² At the brightness that was before him
    his thick clouds passed,
        hail stones and coals of fire.

¹³ The Lord also thundered in the heavens,
    and the Highest gave his voice;
        hail stones and coals of fire.

¹⁴ Yea, he sent out his arrows, and scattered them;
    and he shot out lightnings,
        and discomfited them.

¹⁵ Then the channels of waters were seen,
    and the foundations of the world
        were discovered at thy rebuke, O Lord,
    at the blast of the breath of thy nostrils.

¹⁶ He sent from above, he took me,
    he drew me out of many waters.

¹⁷ He delivered me from my strong enemy,
    and from them which hated me:
        for they were too strong for me.

¹⁸ They prevented me in the day of my calamity;
    but the Lord was my stay.

¹⁹ He brought me forth also into a large place;

he delivered me, because he delighted in me.
²⁰ The Lord rewarded me
    according to my righteousness;
        according to the cleanness of my hands
    hath he recompensed me.
²¹ For I have kept the ways of the Lord,
    and have not wickedly departed from my God.
²² For all his judgments were before me,
    and I did not put away his statutes from me.
²³ I was also upright before him,
    and I kept myself from mine iniquity.
²⁴ Therefore hath the Lord recompensed me
    according to my righteousness,
        according to the cleanness of my hands
    in his eyesight.
²⁵ With the merciful thou wilt shew thyself merciful;
    with an upright man
        thou wilt shew thyself upright;
²⁶ with the pure thou wilt shew thyself pure;
    and with the froward
        thou wilt shew thyself froward.
²⁷ For thou wilt save the afflicted people;
    but wilt bring down high looks.
²⁸ For thou wilt light my candle:
    the Lord my God will enlighten my darkness.
²⁹ For by thee I have run through a troop;
    and by my God have I leaped over a wall.
³⁰ As for God, his way is perfect:

the word of the Lord is tried:

he is a buckler to all those that trust in him.

³¹ For who is God save the Lord?

Or who is a rock save our God?

³² It is God that girdeth me with strength,

and maketh my way perfect.

³³ He maketh my feet like hinds' feet,

and setteth me upon my high places.

³⁴ He teacheth my hands to war,

so that a bow of steel is broken by mine arms.

³⁵ Thou hast also given me the shield of thy salvation:

and thy right hand hath holden me up,

and thy gentleness hath made me great.

³⁶ Thou hast enlarged my steps under me,

that my feet did not slip.

³⁷ I have pursued mine enemies, and overtaken them:

neither did I turn again till they were consumed.

³⁸ I have wounded them that they were not able

to rise: they are fallen under my feet.

³⁹ For thou hast girded me with strength

unto the battle: thou hast subdued under me

those that rose up against me.

⁴⁰ Thou hast also given me the necks of mine enemies;

that I might destroy them that hate me.

⁴¹ They cried, but there was none to save them:

even unto the Lord, but he answered them not.

⁴² Then did I beat them small as the dust

before the wind:

I did cast them out as the dirt in the streets.
⁴³ Thou hast delivered me
from the strivings of the people;
and thou hast made me
the head of the heathen: a people whom
I have not known shall serve me.
⁴⁴ As soon as they hear of me, they shall obey me:
the strangers shall submit themselves unto me.
⁴⁵ The strangers shall fade away,
and be afraid out of their close places.
⁴⁶ The Lord liveth; and blessed be my rock;
and let the God of my salvation be exalted.
⁴⁷ It is God that avengeth me,
and subdueth the people under me.
⁴⁸ He delivereth me from mine enemies:
yea, thou liftest me up above
those that rise up against me:
thou hast delivered me from the violent man.
⁴⁹ Therefore will I give thanks unto thee,
O Lord, among the heathen,
and sing praises unto thy name.
⁵⁰ Great deliverance giveth he to his king;
and sheweth mercy to his anointed, to David,
and to his seed for evermore.

19

To the chief musician, a psalm of David.

The heavens declare the glory of God;

and the firmament sheweth his handywork.
² Day unto day uttereth speech,
and night unto night sheweth knowledge.
³ There is no speech nor language,
where their voice is not heard.
⁴ Their line is gone out through all the earth,
and their words to the end of the world.
In them hath he set a tabernacle for the sun,
⁵ which is as a bridegroom
coming out of his chamber,
and rejoiceth as a strong man to run a race.
⁶ His going forth is from the end of the heaven,
and his circuit unto the ends of it;
and there is nothing hid
from the heat thereof.
⁷ The law of the Lord is perfect, converting the soul:
the testimony of the Lord is sure,
making wise the simple.
⁸ The statutes of the Lord are right,
rejoicing the heart:
the commandment of the Lord is pure,
enlightening the eyes.
⁹ The fear of the Lord is clean, enduring for ever:
the judgments of the Lord are true
and righteous altogether.
¹⁰ More to be desired are they than gold,
yea, than much fine gold:
sweeter also than honey and the honeycomb.

¹¹ Moreover by them is thy servant warned;
and in keeping of them there is great reward.
¹² Who can understand his errors?
Cleanse thou me from secret faults.
¹³ Keep back thy servant also
from presumptuous sins;
let them not have dominion over me:
then shall I be upright, and I shall be innocent
from the great transgression.
¹⁴ Let the words of my mouth,
and the meditation of my heart,
be acceptable in thy sight, O Lord,
my strength, and my redeemer.

20

To the chief musician, a psalm of David.

The Lord hear thee in the day of trouble;
the name of the God of Jacob defend thee;
² send thee help from the sanctuary,
and strengthen thee out of Zion;
³ remember all thy offerings,
and accept thy burnt sacrifice; Selah.
⁴ Grant thee according to thine own heart,
and fulfil all thy counsel.
⁵ We will rejoice in thy salvation,
and in the name of our God
we will set up our banners:
the Lord fulfil all thy petitions.

⁶ Now know I that the Lord saveth his anointed;
  he will hear him from his holy heaven with the
    saving strength of his right hand.
⁷ Some trust in chariots, and some in horses;
  but we will remember the name
    of the Lord our God.
⁸ They are brought down and fallen;
  but we are risen, and stand upright.
⁹ Save, Lord: let the king hear us when we call.

21 To the chief musician, a psalm of David.

The king shall joy in thy strength, O Lord;
  and in thy salvation how greatly shall he rejoice!
² Thou hast given him his heart's desire, and hast not
    withholden the request of his lips. Selah.
³ For thou preventest him
  with the blessings of goodness:
    thou settest a crown of pure gold on his head.
⁴ He asked life of thee, and thou gavest it him,
  even length of days for ever and ever.
⁵ His glory is great in thy salvation:
  honour and majesty hast thou laid upon him.
⁶ For thou hast made him most blessed for ever:
  thou hast made him exceeding glad
    with thy countenance.
⁷ For the king trusteth in the Lord,
  and through the mercy of the most High
    he shall not be moved.

⁸ Thine hand shall find out all thine enemies:
    thy right hand shall find out those that hate thee.
⁹ Thou shalt make them as a fiery oven
    in the time of thine anger:
        the Lord shall swallow them up in his wrath,
    and the fire shall devour them.
¹⁰ Their fruit shalt thou destroy from the earth,
    and their seed from among the children of men.
¹¹ For they intended evil against thee:
    they imagined a mischievous device,
        which they are not able to perform.
¹² Therefore shalt thou make them turn their back,
    when thou shalt make ready thine arrows
        upon thy strings against the face of them.
¹³ Be thou exalted, Lord, in thine own strength:
    so will we sing and praise thy power.

22 To the chief musician upon Aijeleth Shahar,
    a psalm of David.

My God, my God, why hast thou forsaken me?
    Why art thou so far from helping me,
        and from the words of my roaring?
² O my God, I cry in the daytime,
    but thou hearest not;
        and in the night season, and am not silent.
³ But thou art holy,
    O thou that inhabitest the praises of Israel.

⁴ Our fathers trusted in thee:
   they trusted, and thou didst deliver them.
⁵ They cried unto thee, and were delivered:
   they trusted in thee, and were not confounded.
⁶ But I am a worm, and no man;
   a reproach of men, and despised of the people.
⁷ All they that see me laugh me to scorn:
   they shoot out the lip,
      they shake the head, saying,
⁸ 'He trusted on the Lord that he would deliver him:
   let him deliver him,
      seeing he delighted in him.'
⁹ But thou art he that took me out of the womb:
   thou didst make me hope when I was upon
      my mother's breasts.
¹⁰ I was cast upon thee from the womb:
   thou art my God from my mother's belly.
¹¹ Be not far from me;
   for trouble is near;
      for there is none to help.
¹² Many bulls have compassed me:
   strong bulls of Bashan have beset me round.
¹³ They gaped upon me with their mouths,
   as a ravening and a roaring lion.
¹⁴ I am poured out like water,
   and all my bones are out of joint:
      my heart is like wax; it is melted
   in the midst of my bowels.

¹⁵ My strength is dried up like a potsherd;
and my tongue cleaveth to my jaws;
and thou hast brought me
into the dust of death.
¹⁶ For dogs have compassed me:
the assembly of the wicked have inclosed me:
they pierced my hands and my feet.
¹⁷ I may tell all my bones:
they look and stare upon me.
¹⁸ They part my garments among them,
and cast lots upon my vesture.
¹⁹ But be not thou far from me, O Lord:
O my strength, haste thee to help me.
²⁰ Deliver my soul from the sword;
my darling from the power of the dog.
²¹ Save me from the lion's mouth,
for thou hast heard me from the horns
of the unicorns.
²² I will declare thy name unto my brethren:
in the midst of the congregation
will I praise thee.
²³ Ye that fear the Lord, praise him;
all ye the seed of Jacob, glorify him;
and fear him, all ye the seed of Israel.
²⁴ For he hath not despised nor abhorred
the affliction of the afflicted;
neither hath he hid his face from him;
but when he cried unto him, he heard.

²⁵ My praise shall be of thee
in the great congregation:
I will pay my vows before them
that fear him.
²⁶ The meek shall eat and be satisfied:
they shall praise the Lord that seek him:
your heart shall live for ever.
²⁷ All the ends of the world shall remember
and turn unto the Lord:
and all the kindreds of the nations
shall worship before thee.
²⁸ For the kingdom is the Lord's:
and he is the governor among the nations.
²⁹ All they that be fat upon earth shall eat
and worship: all they that go down to the dust
shall bow before him:
and none can keep alive his own soul.
³⁰ A seed shall serve him; it shall be accounted
to the Lord for a generation.
³¹ They shall come, and shall declare
his righteousness unto a people
that shall be born, that he hath done this.

23

A psalm of David.

The Lord is my shepherd; I shall not want.
² He maketh me to lie down in green pastures:
he leadeth me beside the still waters.

³ He restoreth my soul:
> he leadeth me in the paths of righteousness
>> for his name's sake.

⁴ Yea, though I walk
> through the valley of
>> the shadow of death,
> I will fear no evil;
>> for thou art with me;
> thy rod and thy staff they comfort me.

⁵ Thou preparest a table before me
> in the presence of mine enemies;
>> thou anointest my head with oil;
> my cup runneth over.

⁶ Surely goodness and mercy shall follow me
> all the days of my life;
>> and I will dwell
> in the house of the Lord for ever.

24

A psalm of David.

The earth is the Lord's, and the fulness thereof;
> the world, and they that dwell therein.

² For he hath founded it upon the seas,
> and established it upon the floods.

³ Who shall ascend into the hill of the Lord?
> Or who shall stand in his holy place?

⁴ He that hath clean hands, and a pure heart;
> who hath not lifted up his soul unto vanity,
>> nor sworn deceitfully.

⁵ He shall receive the blessing from the Lord,
   and righteousness from the God
      of his salvation.
⁶ This is the generation of them that seek him,
   that seek thy face, O Jacob. Selah.
⁷ Lift up your heads, O ye gates;
   and be ye lift up, ye everlasting doors;
      and the King of glory shall come in.
⁸ Who is this King of glory?
   The Lord strong and mighty,
      the Lord mighty in battle.
⁹ Lift up your heads, O ye gates;
   even lift them up, ye everlasting doors;
      and the King of glory shall come in.
¹⁰ Who is this King of glory?
   The Lord of hosts, he is the King of glory. Selah.

25 A psalm of David.

Unto thee, O Lord, do I lift up my soul.
² O my God, I trust in thee: let me not be ashamed,
   let not mine enemies triumph over me.
³ Yea, let none that wait on thee be ashamed:
   let them be ashamed
      which transgress without cause.
⁴ Shew me thy ways, O Lord;
   teach me thy paths.

⁵ Lead me in thy truth, and teach me:
>   for thou art the God of my salvation;
> > on thee do I wait all the day.

⁶ Remember, O Lord,
>   thy tender mercies and thy lovingkindnesses;
> > for they have been ever of old.

⁷ Remember not the sins of my youth,
>   nor my transgressions:
> > according to thy mercy, remember thou me
> > for thy goodness' sake, O Lord.

⁸ Good and upright is the Lord;
>   therefore will he teach sinners in the way.

⁹ The meek will he guide in judgment;
>   and the meek will he teach his way.

¹⁰ All the paths of the Lord are mercy and truth
>   unto such as keep his covenant
> > and his testimonies.

¹¹ For thy name's sake, O Lord,
>   pardon mine iniquity; for it is great.

¹² What man is he that feareth the Lord?
>   Him shall he teach in the way
> > that he shall choose.

¹³ His soul shall dwell at ease;
>   and his seed shall inherit the earth.

¹⁴ The secret of the Lord is with them that fear him;
>   and he will shew them his covenant.

¹⁵ Mine eyes are ever toward the Lord;
>   for he shall pluck my feet out of the net.

¹⁶ Turn thee unto me, and have mercy upon me;
　　for I am desolate and afflicted.
¹⁷ The troubles of my heart are enlarged:
　　O bring thou me out of my distresses.
¹⁸ Look upon mine affliction and my pain;
　　and forgive all my sins.
¹⁹ Consider mine enemies; for they are many;
　　and they hate me with cruel hatred.
²⁰ O keep my soul, and deliver me:
　　let me not be ashamed;
　　　for I put my trust in thee.
²¹ Let integrity and uprightness preserve me;
　　for I wait on thee.
²² Redeem Israel, O God, out of all his troubles.

26

A psalm of David.

Judge me, O Lord; for I have walked in mine integrity:
　　I have trusted also in the Lord;
　　　therefore I shall not slide.
² Examine me, O Lord, and prove me;
　　try my reins and my heart.
³ For thy lovingkindness is before mine eyes:
　　and I have walked in thy truth.
⁴ I have not sat with vain persons,
　　neither will I go in with dissemblers.
⁵ I have hated the congregation of evil doers;
　　and will not sit with the wicked.

⁶ I will wash mine hands in innocency:
　　so will I compass thine altar, O Lord,
⁷ that I may publish with the voice of thanksgiving,
　　and tell of all thy wondrous works.
⁸ Lord, I have loved the habitation of thy house,
　　and the place where thine honour dwelleth.
⁹ Gather not my soul with sinners,
　　nor my life with bloody men,
¹⁰ In whose hands is mischief,
　　and their right hand is full of bribes.
¹¹ But as for me, I will walk in mine integrity:
　　redeem me, and be merciful unto me.
¹² My foot standeth in an even place:
　　in the congregations will I bless the Lord.

27

A psalm of David.

The Lord is my light and my salvation;
　　whom shall I fear?
　　　　The Lord is the strength of my life;
　　of whom shall I be afraid?
² When the wicked, even mine enemies and my foes,
　　came upon me to eat up my flesh,
　　　　they stumbled and fell.
³ Though an host should encamp against me,
　　my heart shall not fear:
　　　　though war should rise against me,
　　in this will I be confident.

⁴ One thing have I desired of the Lord,
    that will I seek after;
        that I may dwell in the house of the Lord
    all the days of my life,
        to behold the beauty of the Lord,
    and to enquire in his temple.
⁵ For in the time of trouble he shall hide me
    in his pavilion:
        in the secret of his tabernacle
    shall he hide me;
        he shall set me up upon a rock.
⁶ And now shall mine head be lifted up
    above mine enemies round about me:
        therefore will I offer in his tabernacle
    sacrifices of joy; I will sing,
        yea, I will sing praises unto the Lord.
⁷ Hear, O Lord, when I cry with my voice:
    have mercy also upon me, and answer me.
⁸ When thou saidst, 'Seek ye my face',
    my heart said unto thee,
        'Thy face, Lord, will I seek.'
⁹ Hide not thy face far from me;
    put not thy servant away in anger:
        thou hast been my help;
    leave me not, neither forsake me,
        O God of my salvation.
¹⁰ When my father and my mother forsake me,
    then the Lord will take me up.

¹¹ Teach me thy way, O Lord,
  and lead me in a plain path,
   because of mine enemies.
¹² Deliver me not over unto the will of mine enemies:
  for false witnesses are risen up against me,
   and such as breathe out cruelty.
¹³ I had fainted, unless I had believed
  to see the goodness of the Lord
   in the land of the living.
¹⁴ Wait on the Lord: be of good courage,
  and he shall strengthen thine heart:
   wait, I say, on the Lord.

28

A psalm of David.

Unto thee will I cry, O Lord my rock;
  be not silent to me:
   lest, if thou be silent to me,
I become like them
  that go down into the pit.
² Hear the voice of my supplications,
  when I cry unto thee,
   when I lift up my hands toward thy holy oracle.
³ Draw me not away with the wicked,
  and with the workers of iniquity,
   which speak peace to their neighbours,
but mischief is in their hearts.

⁴ Give them according to their deeds,
    and according to the wickedness
        of their endeavours;
    give them after the work of their hands;
        render to them their desert.
⁵ Because they regard not the works of the Lord,
    nor the operation of his hands,
        he shall destroy them, and not build them up.
⁶ Blessed be the Lord, because he hath heard
    the voice of my supplications.
⁷ The Lord is my strength and my shield;
    my heart trusted in him, and I am helped:
        therefore my heart greatly rejoiceth;
    and with my song will I praise him.
⁸ The Lord is their strength, and he is the saving
    strength of his anointed.
⁹ Save thy people, and bless thine inheritance:
    feed them also, and lift them up for ever.

29   A psalm of David.

Give unto the Lord, O ye mighty,
    give unto the Lord glory and strength.
² Give unto the Lord the glory due unto his name;
    worship the Lord in the beauty of holiness.
³ The voice of the Lord is upon the waters:
    the God of glory thundereth:
        the Lord is upon many waters.

⁴ The voice of the Lord is powerful;
    the voice of the Lord is full of majesty.
⁵ The voice of the Lord breaketh the cedars;
    yea, the Lord breaketh the cedars of Lebanon.
⁶ He maketh them also to skip like a calf;
    Lebanon and Sirion like a young unicorn.
⁷ The voice of the Lord divideth the flames of fire.
⁸ The voice of the Lord shaketh the wilderness;
    the Lord shaketh the wilderness of Kadesh.
⁹ The voice of the Lord maketh the hinds to calve,
    and discovereth the forests:
        and in his temple doth every one speak
    of his glory.
¹⁰ The Lord sitteth upon the flood;
    yea, the Lord sitteth King for ever.
¹¹ The Lord will give strength unto his people;
    the Lord will bless his people with peace.

30 A psalm and song at the dedication of the house
    of David.

I will extol thee, O Lord;
    for thou hast lifted me up,
        and hast not made my foes to rejoice over me.
² O Lord my God, I cried unto thee,
    and thou hast healed me.
³ O Lord, thou hast brought up my soul
    from the grave: thou hast kept me alive,
        that I should not go down to the pit.

⁴ Sing unto the Lord, O ye saints of his,
   and give thanks at the remembrance
      of his holiness.
⁵ For his anger endureth but a moment;
   in his favour is life:
      weeping may endure for a night,
   but joy cometh in the morning.
⁶ And in my prosperity I said,
   'I shall never be moved.'
⁷ Lord, by thy favour thou hast made my mountain
   to stand strong: thou didst hide thy face,
      and I was troubled.
⁸ I cried to thee, O Lord;
   and unto the Lord I made supplication.
⁹ What profit is there in my blood,
   when I go down to the pit?
      Shall the dust praise thee?
      Shall it declare thy truth?
¹⁰ Hear, O Lord, and have mercy upon me:
   Lord, be thou my helper.
¹¹ Thou hast turned for me my mourning
   into dancing:
      thou hast put off my sackcloth,
   and girded me with gladness;
¹² to the end that my glory may sing praise to thee,
   and not be silent.
      O Lord my God,
   I will give thanks unto thee for ever.

31

To the chief musician, a psalm of David.

In thee, O Lord, do I put my trust;
    let me never be ashamed;
        deliver me in thy righteousness.
2 Bow down thine ear to me;
    deliver me speedily:
        be thou my strong rock,
    for an house of defence to save me.
3 For thou art my rock and my fortress;
    therefore for thy name's sake lead me,
        and guide me.
4 Pull me out of the net that they have laid
    privily for me; for thou art my strength.
5 Into thine hand I commit my spirit:
    thou hast redeemed me,
        O Lord God of truth.
6 I have hated them that regard lying vanities;
    but I trust in the Lord.
7 I will be glad and rejoice in thy mercy;
    for thou hast considered my trouble;
        thou hast known my soul in adversities,
8 and hast not shut me up into the hand of the enemy:
    thou hast set my feet in a large room.
9 Have mercy upon me, O Lord,
    for I am in trouble:
        mine eye is consumed with grief,
    yea, my soul and my belly.

¹⁰ For my life is spent with grief,
   and my years with sighing:
      my strength faileth because of mine iniquity,
      and my bones are consumed.
¹¹ I was a reproach among all mine enemies,
   but especially among my neighbours,
      and a fear to mine acquaintance:
      they that did see me without fled from me.
¹² I am forgotten as a dead man out of mind:
   I am like a broken vessel.
¹³ For I have heard the slander of many:
   fear was on every side:
      while they took counsel together against me,
      they devised to take away my life.
¹⁴ But I trusted in thee, O Lord:
   I said, 'Thou art my God.'
¹⁵ My times are in thy hand:
   deliver me from the hand of mine enemies,
      and from them that persecute me.
¹⁶ Make thy face to shine upon thy servant:
   save me for thy mercies' sake.
¹⁷ Let me not be ashamed, O Lord;
   for I have called upon thee:
      let the wicked be ashamed,
      and let them be silent in the grave.
¹⁸ Let the lying lips be put to silence,
   which speak grievous things proudly
      and contemptuously against the righteous.

¹⁹ Oh how great is thy goodness,
   which thou hast laid up for them that fear thee;
      which thou hast wrought for them
      that trust in thee before the sons of men!
²⁰ Thou shalt hide them in the secret of thy presence
   from the pride of man:
      thou shalt keep them secretly in a pavilion
      from the strife of tongues.
²¹ Blessed be the Lord;
   for he hath shewed me his marvellous kindness
      in a strong city.
²² For I said in my haste,
   'I am cut off from before thine eyes':
      nevertheless thou heardest the voice
      of my supplications when I cried unto thee.
²³ O love the Lord, all ye his saints;
   for the Lord preserveth the faithful,
      and plentifully rewardeth the proud doer.
²⁴ Be of good courage, and he shall strengthen
   your heart, all ye that hope in the Lord.

32

A psalm of David, Maschil.

Blessed is he whose transgression is forgiven,
   whose sin is covered.
² Blessed is the man unto whom
   the Lord imputeth not iniquity,
      and in whose spirit there is no guile.

³ When I kept silence, my bones waxed old
   through my roaring all the day long.
⁴ For day and night thy hand was heavy upon me:
   my moisture is turned
      into the drought of summer. Selah.
⁵ I acknowledged my sin unto thee,
   and mine iniquity have I not hid.
      I said, 'I will confess my transgressions
   unto the Lord'; and thou forgavest the iniquity
      of my sin. Selah.
⁶ For this shall every one that is godly pray
   unto thee in a time when thou mayest be found:
      surely in the floods of great waters
   they shall not come nigh unto him.
⁷ Thou art my hiding place;
   thou shalt preserve me from trouble;
      thou shalt compass me about
   with songs of deliverance. Selah.
⁸ I will instruct thee and teach thee in the way
   which thou shalt go:
      I will guide thee with mine eye.
⁹ Be ye not as the horse, or as the mule,
   which have no understanding:
      whose mouth must be held in with bit
   and bridle, lest they come near unto thee.
¹⁰ Many sorrows shall be to the wicked:
   but he that trusteth in the Lord,
      mercy shall compass him about.

[11] Be glad in the Lord, and rejoice, ye righteous:
>   and shout for joy, all ye that are upright in heart.

33

Rejoice in the Lord, O ye righteous;
>   for praise is comely for the upright.

[2] Praise the Lord with harp:
>   sing unto him with the psaltery
>   and an instrument of ten strings.

[3] Sing unto him a new song;
>   play skilfully with a loud noise.

[4] For the word of the Lord is right;
>   and all his works are done in truth.

[5] He loveth righteousness and judgment:
>   the earth is full of the goodness of the Lord.

[6] By the word of the Lord were the heavens made;
>   and all the host of them
>   by the breath of his mouth.

[7] He gathereth the waters of the sea together
>   as an heap:
>   he layeth up the depth in storehouses.

[8] Let all the earth fear the Lord:
>   let all the inhabitants of the world
>   stand in awe of him.

[9] For he spake, and it was done;
>   he commanded, and it stood fast.

[10] The Lord bringeth the counsel of the heathen
>   to nought:
>   he maketh the devices of the people
>   of none effect.

¹¹ The counsel of the Lord standeth for ever,
the thoughts of his heart to all generations.
¹² Blessed is the nation whose God is the Lord;
and the people whom he hath chosen
for his own inheritance.
¹³ The Lord looketh from heaven;
he beholdeth all the sons of men.
¹⁴ From the place of his habitation
he looketh upon all the inhabitants of the earth.
¹⁵ He fashioneth their hearts alike;
he considereth all their works.
¹⁶ There is no king saved
by the multitude of an host:
a mighty man
is not delivered by much strength.
¹⁷ An horse is a vain thing for safety:
neither shall he deliver any
by his great strength.
¹⁸ Behold, the eye of the Lord is upon them that
fear him, upon them that hope in his mercy;
¹⁹ to deliver their soul from death,
and to keep them alive in famine.
²⁰ Our soul waiteth for the Lord:
he is our help and our shield.
²¹ For our heart shall rejoice in him,
because we have trusted in his holy name.
²² Let thy mercy, O Lord,
be upon us, according as we hope in thee.

34

A psalm of David, when he changed his behaviour
before Abimelech, who drove him away,
and he departed.

I will bless the Lord at all times:
  his praise shall continually be in my mouth.
² My soul shall make her boast in the Lord:
  the humble shall hear thereof, and be glad.
³ O magnify the Lord with me,
  and let us exalt his name together.
⁴ I sought the Lord, and he heard me,
  and delivered me from all my fears.
⁵ They looked unto him, and were lightened:
  and their faces were not ashamed.
⁶ This poor man cried, and the Lord heard him,
  and saved him out of all his troubles.
⁷ The angel of the Lord encampeth round about
  them that fear him, and delivereth them.
⁸ O taste and see that the Lord is good:
  blessed is the man that trusteth in him.
⁹ O fear the Lord, ye his saints;
  for there is no want to them that fear him.
¹⁰ The young lions do lack, and suffer hunger;
  but they that seek the Lord shall not want
    any good thing.
¹¹ Come, ye children, hearken unto me:
  I will teach you the fear of the Lord.
¹² What man is he that desireth life,
  and loveth many days, that he may see good?

¹³ Keep thy tongue from evil,
  and thy lips from speaking guile.
¹⁴ Depart from evil, and do good;
  seek peace, and pursue it.
¹⁵ The eyes of the Lord are upon the righteous,
  and his ears are open unto their cry.
¹⁶ The face of the Lord is against them that do evil,
  to cut off the remembrance of them
    from the earth.
¹⁷ The righteous cry, and the Lord heareth,
  and delivereth them out of all their troubles.
¹⁸ The Lord is nigh unto them
  that are of a broken heart;
    and saveth such as be of a contrite spirit.
¹⁹ Many are the afflictions of the righteous;
  but the Lord delivereth him out of them all.
²⁰ He keepeth all his bones:
  not one of them is broken.
²¹ Evil shall slay the wicked:
  and they that hate the righteous shall be desolate.
²² The Lord redeemeth the soul of his servants:
  and none of them that trust in him
    shall be desolate.

35

A psalm of David.

Plead my cause, O Lord,
  with them that strive with me:
    fight against them that fight against me.

² Take hold of shield and buckler,
   and stand up for mine help.
³ Draw out also the spear, and stop the way
   against them that persecute me:
      say unto my soul, 'I am thy salvation.'
⁴ Let them be confounded and put to shame
   that seek after my soul:
      let them be turned back
   and brought to confusion that devise my hurt.
⁵ Let them be as chaff before the wind;
   and let the angel of the Lord chase them.
⁶ Let their way be dark and slippery;
   and let the angel of the Lord persecute them.
⁷ For without cause have they hid for me their net
   in a pit, which without cause
      they have digged for my soul.
⁸ Let destruction come upon him at unawares;
   and let his net that he hath hid catch himself:
      into that very destruction let him fall.
⁹ And my soul shall be joyful in the Lord:
   it shall rejoice in his salvation.
¹⁰ All my bones shall say, 'Lord, who is like unto thee,
   which deliverest the poor from him
      that is too strong for him,
   yea, the poor and the needy from him
      that spoileth him?'
¹¹ False witnesses did rise up;
   they laid to my charge things that I knew not.

^{12} They rewarded me evil for good
to the spoiling of my soul.
^{13} But as for me, when they were sick,
my clothing was sackcloth:
I humbled my soul with fasting;
and my prayer returned into mine own bosom.
^{14} I behaved myself as though he had been my friend
or brother: I bowed down heavily,
as one that mourneth for his mother.
^{15} But in mine adversity they rejoiced,
and gathered themselves together:
yea, the abjects gathered themselves together
against me, and I knew it not;
they did tear me, and ceased not:
^{16} with hypocritical mockers in feasts,
they gnashed upon me with their teeth.
^{17} Lord, how long wilt thou look on?
Rescue my soul from their destructions,
my darling from the lions.
^{18} I will give thee thanks in the great congregation:
I will praise thee among much people.
^{19} Let not them that are mine enemies
wrongfully rejoice over me:
neither let them wink with the eye
that hate me without a cause.
^{20} For they speak not peace: but they devise
deceitful matters against them
that are quiet in the land.
^{21} Yea, they opened their mouth wide against me,

and said, 'Aha, aha, our eye hath seen it.'
²² This thou hast seen, O Lord: keep not silence:
  O Lord, be not far from me.
²³ Stir up thyself, and awake to my judgment,
  even unto my cause, my God and my Lord.
²⁴ Judge me, O Lord my God,
  according to thy righteousness;
    and let them not rejoice over me.
²⁵ Let them not say in their hearts,
  'Ah, so would we have it': let them not say,
    'We have swallowed him up.'
²⁶ Let them be ashamed and brought to confusion
  together that rejoice at mine hurt:
    let them be clothed with shame and
  dishonour that magnify themselves against me.
²⁷ Let them shout for joy, and be glad,
  that favour my righteous cause:
    yea, let them say continually,
  'Let the Lord be magnified,
    which hath pleasure in the prosperity
  of his servant.'
²⁸ And my tongue shall speak of thy righteousness
  and of thy praise all the day long.

36

To the chief musician, a psalm of David the servant
  of the Lord.

The transgression of the wicked
  saith within my heart, that there is
    no fear of God before his eyes.

² For he flattereth himself in his own eyes,
  until his iniquity be found to be hateful.
³ The words of his mouth are iniquity and deceit:
  he hath left off to be wise, and to do good.
⁴ He deviseth mischief upon his bed;
  he setteth himself in a way that is not good;
    he abhorreth not evil.
⁵ Thy mercy, O Lord, is in the heavens;
  and thy faithfulness reacheth
    unto the clouds.
⁶ Thy righteousness is like the great mountains;
  thy judgments are a great deep:
    O Lord, thou preservest man and beast.
⁷ How excellent is thy lovingkindness, O God!
  Therefore the children of men put their trust
    under the shadow of thy wings.
⁸ They shall be abundantly satisfied with the fatness
  of thy house; and thou shalt make them drink
    of the river of thy pleasures.
⁹ For with thee is the fountain of life:
  in thy light shall we see light.
¹⁰ O continue thy lovingkindness
  unto them that know thee;
    and thy righteousness
    to the upright in heart.
¹¹ Let not the foot of pride come against me,
  and let not the hand of the wicked remove me.
¹² There are the workers of iniquity fallen:

they are cast down,
and shall not be able to rise.

37 A psalm of David.

Fret not thyself because of evildoers,
neither be thou envious
against the workers of iniquity.
2 For they shall soon be cut down like the grass,
and wither as the green herb.
3 Trust in the Lord, and do good;
so shalt thou dwell in the land,
and verily thou shalt be fed.
4 Delight thyself also in the Lord;
and he shall give thee the desires of thine heart.
5 Commit thy way unto the Lord;
trust also in him; and he shall bring it to pass.
6 And he shall bring forth thy righteousness
as the light, and thy judgment as the noonday.
7 Rest in the Lord, and wait patiently for him:
fret not thyself because of him who prospereth
in his way, because of the man who bringeth
wicked devices to pass.
8 Cease from anger, and forsake wrath:
fret not thyself in any wise to do evil.
9 For evildoers shall be cut off:
but those that wait upon the Lord,
they shall inherit the earth.

¹⁰ For yet a little while, and the wicked shall not be:
  yea, thou shalt diligently consider his place,
    and it shall not be.
¹¹ But the meek shall inherit the earth;
  and shall delight themselves
    in the abundance of peace.
¹² The wicked plotteth against the just,
  and gnasheth upon him with his teeth.
¹³ The Lord shall laugh at him:
  for he seeth that his day is coming.
¹⁴ The wicked have drawn out the sword,
  and have bent their bow,
    to cast down the poor and needy,
  and to slay such as be of upright conversation.
¹⁵ Their sword shall enter into their own heart,
  and their bows shall be broken.
¹⁶ A little that a righteous man hath
  is better than the riches of many wicked.
¹⁷ For the arms of the wicked shall be broken;
  but the Lord upholdeth the righteous.
¹⁸ The Lord knoweth the days of the upright:
  and their inheritance shall be for ever.
¹⁹ They shall not be ashamed in the evil time:
  and in the days of famine they shall be satisfied.
²⁰ But the wicked shall perish, and the enemies
  of the Lord shall be as the fat of lambs;
    they shall consume;
  into smoke shall they consume away.

²¹ The wicked borroweth, and payeth not again;
   but the righteous sheweth mercy, and giveth.
²² For such as be blessed of him
   shall inherit the earth;
      and they that be cursed of him
   shall be cut off.
²³ The steps of a good man are ordered by the Lord,
   and he delighteth in his way.
²⁴ Though he fall, he shall not be utterly cast down;
   for the Lord upholdeth him with his hand.
²⁵ I have been young, and now am old;
   yet have I not seen the righteous forsaken,
      nor his seed begging bread.
²⁶ He is ever merciful, and lendeth;
   and his seed is blessed.
²⁷ Depart from evil, and do good;
   and dwell for evermore.
²⁸ For the Lord loveth judgment,
   and forsaketh not his saints;
      they are preserved for ever;
   but the seed of the wicked shall be cut off.
²⁹ The righteous shall inherit the land,
   and dwell therein for ever.
³⁰ The mouth of the righteous speaketh wisdom,
   and his tongue talketh of judgment.
³¹ The law of his God is in his heart;
   none of his steps shall slide.
³² The wicked watcheth the righteous,
   and seeketh to slay him.

³³ The Lord will not leave him in his hand,
　　nor condemn him when he is judged.
³⁴ Wait on the Lord, and keep his way,
　　and he shall exalt thee to inherit the land:
　　　　when the wicked are cut off,
　　thou shalt see it.
³⁵ I have seen the wicked in great power,
　　and spreading himself like a green bay tree.
³⁶ Yet he passed away, and, lo, he was not:
　　yea, I sought him, but he could not be found.
³⁷ Mark the perfect man, and behold the upright;
　　for the end of that man is peace.
³⁸ But the transgressors shall be destroyed together:
　　the end of the wicked shall be cut off.
³⁹ But the salvation of the righteous is of the Lord:
　　he is their strength in the time of trouble.
⁴⁰ And the Lord shall help them, and deliver them:
　　he shall deliver them from the wicked, and save
　　　　them, because they trust in him.

38

A psalm of David, to bring to remembrance.

O Lord, rebuke me not in thy wrath:
　　neither chasten me in thy hot displeasure.
² For thine arrows stick fast in me,
　　and thy hand presseth me sore.
³ There is no soundness in my flesh
　　because of thine anger;

neither is there any rest in my bones
because of my sin.

⁴ For mine iniquities are gone over mine head:
as an heavy burden
they are too heavy for me.

⁵ My wounds stink and are corrupt
because of my foolishness.

⁶ I am troubled; I am bowed down greatly;
I go mourning all the day long.

⁷ For my loins are filled with a loathsome disease:
and there is no soundness in my flesh.

⁸ I am feeble and sore broken:
I have roared by reason of the disquietness
of my heart.

⁹ Lord, all my desire is before thee;
and my groaning is not hid from thee.

¹⁰ My heart panteth, my strength faileth me:
as for the light of mine eyes,
it also is gone from me.

¹¹ My lovers and my friends stand aloof from my sore;
and my kinsmen stand afar off.

¹² They also that seek after my life lay snares for me:
and they that seek my hurt
speak mischievous things,
and imagine deceits all the day long.

¹³ But I, as a deaf man, heard not;
and I was as a dumb man that openeth not
his mouth.

¹⁴ Thus I was as a man that heareth not,
and in whose mouth are no reproofs.
¹⁵ For in thee, O Lord, do I hope:
thou wilt hear, O Lord my God.
¹⁶ For I said, 'Hear me, lest otherwise they should
rejoice over me: when my foot slippeth,
they magnify themselves against me.'
¹⁷ For I am ready to halt,
and my sorrow is continually before me.
¹⁸ For I will declare mine iniquity;
I will be sorry for my sin.
¹⁹ But mine enemies are lively, and they are strong:
and they that hate me wrongfully
are multiplied.
²⁰ They also that render evil for good
are mine adversaries;
because I follow the thing that good is.
²¹ Forsake me not, O Lord:
O my God, be not far from me.
²² Make haste to help me, O Lord my salvation.

39

To the chief musician, even to Jeduthun,
a psalm of David.

I said, I will take heed to my ways,
that I sin not with my tongue:
I will keep my mouth with a bridle,
while the wicked is before me.

²I was dumb with silence, I held my peace,
  even from good;
    and my sorrow was stirred.
³My heart was hot within me, while I was musing
  the fire burned: then spake I with my tongue,
⁴'Lord, make me to know mine end,
  and the measure of my days, what it is;
    that I may know how frail I am.
⁵Behold, thou hast made my days
  as an handbreadth;
    and mine age is as nothing before thee:
  verily every man at his best state
    is altogether vanity. Selah.
⁶Surely every man walketh in a vain shew:
  surely they are disquieted in vain:
    he heapeth up riches,
  and knoweth not who shall gather them.
⁷And now, Lord, what wait I for?
  My hope is in thee.
⁸Deliver me from all my transgressions:
  make me not the reproach of the foolish.
⁹I was dumb, I opened not my mouth;
  because thou didst it.
¹⁰Remove thy stroke away from me:
  I am consumed by the blow of thine hand.
¹¹When thou with rebukes
  dost correct man for iniquity,
    thou makest his beauty to consume away
  like a moth: surely every man is vanity, Selah.

[12] Hear my prayer, O Lord, and give ear unto my cry;
hold not thy peace at my tears;
for I am a stranger with thee, and a sojourner,
as all my fathers were.
[13] O spare me, that I may recover strength,
before I go hence, and be no more.'

40 To the chief musician, a psalm of David.

I waited patiently for the Lord;
and he inclined unto me, and heard my cry.
[2] He brought me up also out of an horrible pit,
out of the miry clay,
and set my feet upon a rock,
and established my goings.
[3] And he hath put a new song in my mouth,
even praise unto our God:
many shall see it, and fear,
and shall trust in the Lord.
[4] Blessed is that man that maketh the Lord his trust,
and respecteth not the proud,
nor such as turn aside to lies.
[5] Many, O Lord my God, are thy wonderful works
which thou hast done,
and thy thoughts which are to us-ward:
they cannot be reckoned up in order unto thee:
if I would declare and speak of them,
they are more than can be numbered.

⁶ Sacrifice and offering thou didst not desire;
  mine ears hast thou opened:
    burnt offering and sin offering
  hast thou not required.
⁷ Then said I, 'Lo, I come:
  in the volume of the book
    it is written of me,
⁸ I delight to do thy will, O my God:
  yea, thy law is within my heart.'
⁹ I have preached righteousness in the great
  congregation: lo, I have not refrained my lips,
    O Lord, thou knowest.
¹⁰ I have not hid thy righteousness within my heart;
  I have declared thy faithfulness
    and thy salvation;
  I have not concealed thy lovingkindness
    and thy truth from the
  great congregation.
¹¹ Withhold not thou thy tender mercies from me,
  O Lord: let thy lovingkindness
    and thy truth continually preserve me.
¹² For innumerable evils have compassed me about:
  mine iniquities have taken hold upon me,
    so that I am not able to look up;
  they are more than the hairs of mine head;
    therefore my heart faileth me.
¹³ Be pleased, O Lord, to deliver me:
  O Lord, make haste to help me.

¹⁴ Let them be ashamed and confounded together
    that seek after my soul to destroy it;
        let them be driven backward
    and put to shame that wish me evil.
¹⁵ Let them be desolate for a reward of their shame
    that say unto me, 'Aha, aha.'
¹⁶ Let all those that seek thee rejoice
    and be glad in thee:
        let such as love thy salvation say continually,
    'The Lord be magnified.'
¹⁷ But I am poor and needy;
    yet the Lord thinketh upon me:
        thou art my help and my deliverer;
    make no tarrying, O my God.

41 To the chief musician, a psalm of David.

Blessed is he that considereth the poor:
    the Lord will deliver him in time of trouble.
² The Lord will preserve him, and keep him alive;
    and he shall be blessed upon the earth;
        and thou wilt not deliver him
    unto the will of his enemies.
³ The Lord will strengthen him
    upon the bed of languishing:
        thou wilt make all his bed in his sickness.
⁴ I said, 'Lord, be merciful unto me:
    heal my soul; for I have sinned against thee.'

⁵Mine enemies speak evil of me,
  'When shall he die, and his name perish?'
⁶And if he come to see me, he speaketh vanity:
  his heart gathereth iniquity to itself;
    when he goeth abroad, he telleth it.
⁷All that hate me whisper together against me:
  against me do they devise my hurt.
⁸An evil disease, say they, cleaveth fast unto him:
  and now that he lieth he shall rise up no more.
⁹Yea, mine own familiar friend, in whom I trusted,
  which did eat of my bread,
    hath lifted up his heel against me.
¹⁰But thou, O Lord, be merciful unto me,
  and raise me up, that I may requite them.
¹¹By this I know that thou favourest me,
  because mine enemy doth not triumph over me.
¹²And as for me, thou upholdest me in mine integrity,
  and settest me before thy face for ever.
¹³Blessed be the Lord God of Israel from everlasting,
  and to everlasting. Amen, and Amen.

42 To the chief musician, Maschil, for the sons
  of Korah.

As the hart panteth after the water brooks,
  so panteth my soul after thee, O God.
²My soul thirsteth for God, for the living God:
  when shall I come and appear before God?

³ My tears have been my meat day and night,
    while they continually say unto me,
        'Where is thy God?'
⁴ When I remember these things,
    I pour out my soul in me;
        for I had gone with the multitude,
    I went with them to the house of God,
        with the voice of joy and praise,
    with a multitude that kept holyday.
⁵ Why art thou cast down, O my soul?
    And why art thou disquieted in me?
        Hope thou in God;
    for I shall yet praise him for the help of his
        countenance.
⁶ O my God, my soul is cast down within me;
    therefore will I remember thee
        from the land of Jordan,
    and of the Hermonites, from the hill Mizar.
⁷ Deep calleth unto deep at the noise
    of thy waterspouts: all thy waves and thy billows
        are gone over me.
⁸ Yet the Lord will command his lovingkindness
    in the daytime,
        and in the night his song shall be with me,
    and my prayer unto the God of my life.
⁹ I will say unto God my rock,
    'Why hast thou forgotten me?
        Why go I mourning because of

the oppression of the enemy?'
¹⁰As with a sword in my bones,
    mine enemies reproach me;
        while they say daily unto me,
    'Where is thy God?'
¹¹Why art thou cast down, O my soul?
    And why art thou disquieted within me?
        Hope thou in God;
    for I shall yet praise him, who is the health
        of my countenance, and my God.

43 Judge me, O God, and plead my cause
    against an ungodly nation:
        O deliver me from the deceitful
    and unjust man.
²For thou art the God of my strength:
    why dost thou cast me off?
        Why go I mourning because of
    the oppression of the enemy?
³O send out thy light and thy truth:
    let them lead me;
        let them bring me unto thy holy hill,
    and to thy tabernacles.
⁴Then will I go unto the altar of God,
    unto God my exceeding joy:
        yea, upon the harp will I praise thee,
    O God my God.

⁵ Why art thou cast down, O my soul?
   And why art thou disquieted within me?
      Hope in God; for I shall yet praise him,
   who is the health of my countenance,
      and my God.

44 To the chief musician, for the sons of Korah,
   Maschil.

We have heard with our ears, O God,
   our fathers have told us, what work thou didst
      in their days, in the times of old.
² How thou didst drive out the heathen with thy
   hand, and plantedst them;
      how thou didst afflict the people,
   and cast them out.
³ For they got not the land in possession
   by their own sword,
      neither did their own arm save them;
   but thy right hand, and thine arm,
      and the light of thy countenance,
   because thou hadst a favour unto them.
⁴ Thou art my King, O God:
   command deliverances for Jacob.
⁵ Through thee will we push down our enemies:
   through thy name will we tread them under
      that rise up against us.
⁶ For I will not trust in my bow,

neither shall my sword save me.

7 But thou hast saved us from our enemies,
  and hast put them to shame that hated us.

8 In God we boast all the day long,
  and praise thy name for ever. Selah.

9 But thou hast cast off, and put us to shame;
  and goest not forth with our armies.

10 Thou makest us to turn back from the enemy:
  and they which hate us spoil for themselves.

11 Thou hast given us like sheep appointed for meat;
  and hast scattered us among the heathen.

12 Thou sellest thy people for nought,
  and dost not increase thy wealth by their price.

13 Thou makest us a reproach to our neighbours,
  a scorn and a derision to them
    that are round about us.

14 Thou makest us a byword among the heathen,
  a shaking of the head among the people.

15 My confusion is continually before me,
  and the shame of my face hath covered me,

16 for the voice of him that reproacheth
  and blasphemeth;
    by reason of the enemy and avenger.

17 All this is come upon us;
  yet have we not forgotten thee,
    neither have we dealt falsely in thy covenant.

18 Our heart is not turned back,
  neither have our steps declined from thy way;

¹⁹ though thou hast sore broken us
    in the place of dragons,
        and covered us with the shadow of death.
²⁰ If we have forgotten the name of our God,
    or stretched out our hands to a strange god,
²¹ shall not God search this out?
    For he knoweth the secrets of the heart.
²² Yea, for thy sake are we killed all the day long;
    we are counted as sheep for the slaughter.
²³ Awake, why sleepest thou, O Lord?
    Arise, cast us not off for ever.
²⁴ Wherefore hidest thou thy face,
    and forgettest our affliction and our oppression?
²⁵ For our soul is bowed down to the dust:
    our belly cleaveth unto the earth.
²⁶ Arise for our help,
    and redeem us for thy mercies' sake.

45

To the chief musician upon Shoshannim,
    for the sons of Korah, Maschil, a song of loves.

My heart is inditing a good matter:
    I speak of the things which I have made
        touching the king:
    my tongue is the pen of a ready writer.
² Thou art fairer than the children of men:
    grace is poured into thy lips;

therefore God hath blessed thee for ever.
³ Gird thy sword upon thy thigh, O most mighty,
   with thy glory and thy majesty.
⁴ And in thy majesty ride prosperously
   because of truth and meekness
      and righteousness;
   and thy right hand shall teach thee
      terrible things.
⁵ Thine arrows are sharp in the heart
   of the king's enemies;
      whereby the people fall under thee.
⁶ Thy throne, O God, is for ever and ever:
   the sceptre of thy kingdom is a right sceptre.
⁷ Thou lovest righteousness, and hatest wickedness;
   therefore God, thy God, hath anointed thee
      with the oil of gladness above thy fellows.
⁸ All thy garments smell of myrrh, and aloes,
   and cassia, out of the ivory palaces,
      whereby they have made thee glad.
⁹ Kings' daughters were among
   thy honourable women:
      upon thy right hand did stand the queen
   in gold of Ophir.
¹⁰ Hearken, O daughter, and consider, and incline
   thine ear; forget also thine own people,
      and thy father's house;
¹¹ so shall the king greatly desire thy beauty;
   for he is thy Lord; and worship thou him.

¹²And the daughter of Tyre shall be there with a gift;
even the rich among the people
shall intreat thy favour.
¹³The king's daughter is all glorious within;
her clothing is of wrought gold.
¹⁴She shall be brought unto the king
in raiment of needlework:
the virgins her companions that follow her
shall be brought unto thee.
¹⁵With gladness and rejoicing shall they be brought:
they shall enter into the king's palace.
¹⁶Instead of thy fathers shall be thy children,
whom thou mayest make princes
in all the earth.
¹⁷I will make thy name to be remembered
in all generations; therefore shall the people
praise thee for ever and ever.

46 To the chief musician for the sons of Korah,
a song upon Alamoth.

God is our refuge and strength,
a very present help in trouble.
²Therefore will not we fear,
though the earth be removed,
and though the mountains be carried
into the midst of the sea;
³though the waters thereof roar and be troubled,

though the mountains shake
  with the swelling thereof. Selah.
⁴ There is a river, the streams whereof
  shall make glad the city of God, the holy place
    of the tabernacles of the most High.
⁵ God is in the midst of her; she shall not be moved:
    God shall help her, and that right early.
⁶ The heathen raged, the kingdoms were moved:
  he uttered his voice, the earth melted.
⁷ The Lord of hosts is with us;
  the God of Jacob is our refuge. Selah.
⁸ Come, behold the works of the Lord,
  what desolations he hath made in the earth.
⁹ He maketh wars to cease unto the end of the earth;
  he breaketh the bow,
    and cutteth the spear in sunder;
  he burneth the chariot in the fire.
¹⁰ Be still, and know that I am God:
  I will be exalted among the heathen,
    I will be exalted in the earth.
¹¹ The Lord of hosts is with us;
  the God of Jacob is our refuge. Selah.

47 To the chief musician, a psalm for
  the sons of Korah.

O clap your hands, all ye people;
  shout unto God with the voice of triumph.

² For the Lord most high is terrible;
  he is a great King over all the earth.
³ He shall subdue the people under us,
  and the nations under our feet.
⁴ He shall choose our inheritance for us,
  the excellency of Jacob whom he loved. Selah.
⁵ God is gone up with a shout,
  the Lord with the sound of a trumpet.
⁶ Sing praises to God, sing praises:
  sing praises unto our King, sing praises.
⁷ For God is the King of all the earth:
  sing ye praises with understanding.
⁸ God reigneth over the heathen:
  God sitteth upon the throne of his holiness.
⁹ The princes of the people are gathered together,
  even the people of the God of Abraham:
    for the shields of the earth belong unto God:
  he is greatly exalted.

48

A song and psalm for the sons of Korah.

Great is the Lord, and greatly to be praised
  in the city of our God,
    in the mountain of his holiness.
² Beautiful for situation, the joy of the whole earth,
  is mount Zion, on the sides of the north,
    the city of the great King.

³ God is known in her palaces for a refuge.
⁴ For, lo, the kings were assembled,
    they passed by together.
⁵ They saw it, and so they marvelled;
    they were troubled, and hasted away.
⁶ Fear took hold upon them there, and pain,
    as of a woman in travail.
⁷ Thou breakest the ships of Tarshish
    with an east wind.
⁸ As we have heard, so have we seen
    in the city of the Lord of hosts,
        in the city of our God:
    God will establish it for ever. Selah.
⁹ We have thought of thy lovingkindness, O God,
    in the midst of thy temple.
¹⁰ According to thy name, O God,
    so is thy praise unto the ends of the earth:
        thy right hand is full of righteousness.
¹¹ Let mount Zion rejoice,
    let the daughters of Judah be glad,
        because of thy judgments.
¹² Walk about Zion, and go round about her:
    tell the towers thereof.
¹³ Mark ye well her bulwarks, consider her palaces;
    that ye may tell it to the
        generation following.
¹⁴ For this God is our God for ever and ever:
    he will be our guide even unto death.

49

To the chief musician, a psalm for the sons of Korah.

Hear this, all ye people;
give ear, all ye inhabitants of the world:
² both low and high, rich and poor,
together.
³ My mouth shall speak of wisdom;
and the meditation of my heart
shall be of understanding.
⁴ I will incline mine ear to a parable:
I will open my dark saying upon the harp.
⁵ Wherefore should I fear in the days of evil,
when the iniquity of my heels
shall compass me about?
⁶ They that trust in their wealth,
and boast themselves in the multitude
of their riches;
⁷ none of them can by any means
redeem his brother,
nor give to God a ransom for him
⁸ (for the redemption of their soul is precious,
and it ceaseth for ever);
⁹ that he should still live for ever,
and not see corruption.
¹⁰ For he seeth that wise men die,
likewise the fool and the brutish person perish,
and leave their wealth to others.

¹¹ Their inward thought is,
    that their houses shall continue for ever,
        and their dwelling places to all generations;
    they call their lands after their own names.
¹² Nevertheless man being in honour abideth not:
    he is like the beasts that perish.
¹³ This their way is their folly:
    yet their posterity approve their sayings. Selah.
¹⁴ Like sheep they are laid in the grave;
    death shall feed on them;
        and the upright shall have dominion over
    them in the morning;
        and their beauty shall consume in the grave
    from their dwelling.
¹⁵ But God will redeem my soul from the power
    of the grave:
        for he shall receive me. Selah.
¹⁶ Be not thou afraid when one is made rich,
    when the glory of his house is increased;
¹⁷ for when he dieth he shall carry nothing away:
    his glory shall not descend after him.
¹⁸ Though while he lived he blessed his soul:
    and men will praise thee,
        when thou doest well to thyself.
¹⁹ He shall go to the generation of his fathers;
    they shall never see light.
²⁰ Man that is in honour, and understandeth not,
    is like the beasts that perish.

50

A psalm of Asaph.

The mighty God, even the Lord, hath spoken,
   and called the earth from the rising of the sun
      unto the going down thereof.
² Out of Zion, the perfection of beauty,
   God hath shined.
³ Our God shall come, and shall not keep silence:
   a fire shall devour before him,
      and it shall be very tempestuous
   round about him.
⁴ He shall call to the heavens from above,
   and to the earth,
      that he may judge his people.
⁵ Gather my saints together unto me;
   those that have made a covenant with me
      by sacrifice.
⁶ And the heavens shall declare his righteousness;
   for God is judge himself. Selah.
⁷ Hear, O my people, and I will speak;
   O Israel, and I will testify against thee:
      I am God, even thy God.
⁸ I will not reprove thee for thy sacrifices
   or thy burnt offerings,
      to have been continually before me.
⁹ I will take no bullock out of thy house,
   nor he goats out of thy folds.
¹⁰ For every beast of the forest is mine,
   and the cattle upon a thousand hills.

¹¹ I know all the fowls of the mountains:
   and the wild beasts of the field are mine.
¹² If I were hungry, I would not tell thee;
   for the world is mine, and the fulness thereof.
¹³ Will I eat the flesh of bulls,
   or drink the blood of goats?
¹⁴ Offer unto God thanksgiving;
   and pay thy vows unto the most High;
¹⁵ and call upon me in the day of trouble:
   I will deliver thee,
      and thou shalt glorify me.
¹⁶ But unto the wicked God saith,
   'What hast thou to do to declare my statutes,
      or that thou shouldest take my covenant in
   thy mouth?
¹⁷ Seeing thou hatest instruction,
   and castest my words behind thee.
¹⁸ When thou sawest a thief,
   then thou consentedst with him,
      and hast been partaker with adulterers.
¹⁹ Thou givest thy mouth to evil,
   and thy tongue frameth deceit.
²⁰ Thou sittest and speakest against thy brother;
   thou slanderest thine own mother's son.
²¹ These things hast thu done, and I kept silence;
   thou thoughtest that I was altogether
      such an one as thyself; but I will reprove thee,
   and set them in order before thine eyes.

²² Now consider this, ye that forget God,
    lest I tear you in pieces,
        and there be none to deliver.
²³ Whoso offereth praise glorifieth me;
    and to him that ordereth his conversation aright
        will I shew the salvation of God.'

51

To the chief musician, a psalm of David,
    when Nathan the prophet came unto him,
    after he had gone in to Bath-sheba.

Have mercy upon me, O God,
    according to thy lovingkindness:
        according unto the multitude
    of thy tender mercies blot out my transgressions.
² Wash me throughly from mine iniquity,
    and cleanse me from my sin.
³ For I acknowledge my transgressions:
    and my sin is ever before me.
⁴Against thee, thee only, have I sinned,
    and done this evil in thy sight:
        that thou mightest be justified
    when thou speakest,
        and be clear when thou judgest.
⁵ Behold, I was shapen in iniquity;
    and in sin did my mother conceive me.
⁶ Behold, thou desirest truth in the inward parts;
    and in the hidden part thou shalt make me

to know wisdom.

7 Purge me with hyssop, and I shall be clean:
    wash me, and I shall be whiter than snow.

8 Make me to hear joy and gladness;
    that the bones which thou hast broken
        may rejoice.

9 Hide thy face from my sins,
    and blot out all mine iniquities.

10 Create in me a clean heart, O God;
    and renew a right spirit within me.

11 Cast me not away from thy presence;
    and take not thy holy spirit from me.

12 Restore unto me the joy of thy salvation;
    and uphold me with thy free spirit.

13 Then will I teach transgressors thy ways;
    and sinners shall be converted unto thee.

14 Deliver me from bloodguiltiness, O God,
    thou God of my salvation;
        and my tongue shall sing aloud
    of thy righteousness.

15 O Lord, open thou my lips;
    and my mouth shall shew forth thy praise.

16 For thou desirest not sacrifice;
    else would I give it:
        thou delightest not in burnt offering.

17 The sacrifices of God are a broken spirit:
    a broken and a contrite heart, O God,
        thou wilt not despise.

¹⁸ Do good in thy good pleasure unto Zion:
   build thou the walls of Jerusalem.
¹⁹ Then shalt thou be pleased with the sacrifices
   of righteousness,
      with burnt offering and whole burnt offering:
   then shall they offer bullocks upon thine altar.

52

To the chief musician, Maschil, a psalm of David,
   when Doeg the Edomite came and told Saul,
   and said unto him,

'David is come to the house of Ahimelech.'
Why boastest thou thyself in mischief,
   O mighty man?
      The goodness of God
      endureth continually.
² Thy tongue deviseth mischiefs;
   like a sharp razor, working deceitfully.
³ Thou lovest evil more than good;
   and lying rather than to speak
      righteousness. Selah.
⁴ Thou lovest all devouring words,
   O thou deceitful tongue.
⁵ God shall likewise destroy thee for ever,
   he shall take thee away, and pluck thee out of
      thy dwelling place,
   and root thee out of the land
      of the living. Selah.

⁶ The righteous also shall see, and fear,
and shall laugh at him:
⁷ Lo, this is the man that made not God his strength;
but trusted in the abundance of his riches,
and strengthened himself
in his wickedness.'
⁸ But I am like a green olive tree in the house of God:
I trust in the mercy of God for ever and ever.
⁹ I will praise thee for ever, because thou hast done it:
and I will wait on thy name;
for it is good before thy saints.

53

To the chief musician upon Mahalath, Maschil,
a psalm of David.

The fool hath said in his heart, 'There is no God.'
Corrupt are they, and have done abominable
iniquity: there is none that doeth good.
² God looked down from heaven upon
the children of men,
to see if there were any that did understand,
that did seek God.
³ Every one of them is gone back;
they are altogether become filthy;
there is none that doeth good, no, not one.
⁴ Have the workers of iniquity no knowledge?
Who eat up my people as they eat bread:
they have not called upon God.

⁵There were they in great fear, where no fear was;
　　for God hath scattered the bones of him
　　　　that encampeth against thee:
thou hast put them to shame,
　　because God hath despised them.
⁶Oh that the salvation of Israel
　　were come out of Zion!
　　　　When God bringeth back the captivity
of his people,
　　　　Jacob shall rejoice, and Israel shall be glad.

54 To the chief musician on Neginoth, Maschil,
a psalm of David, when the Ziphims
came and said to Saul,
'Doth not David hide himself with us?'

Save me, O God, by thy name,
　　and judge me by thy strength.
²Hear my prayer, O God;
　　give ear to the words of my mouth.
³For strangers are risen up against me,
　　and oppressors seek after my soul:
　　　　they have not set God before them. Selah.
⁴Behold, God is mine helper:
　　the Lord is with them that uphold my soul.
⁵He shall reward evil unto mine enemies,
　　cut them off in thy truth.
⁶I will freely sacrifice unto thee:

I will praise thy name, O Lord; for it is good.
⁷ For he hath delivered me out of all trouble;
   and mine eye hath seen his desire
      upon mine enemies.

55 To the chief musician on Neginoth, Maschil, a psalm
of David.

Give ear to my prayer, O God;
   and hide not thyself from my supplication.
² Attend unto me, and hear me:
   I mourn in my complaint, and make a noise;
³ because of the voice of the enemy,
   because of the oppression of the wicked;
      for they cast iniquity upon me,
   and in wrath they hate me.
⁴ My heart is sore pained within me;
   and the terrors of death are fallen upon me.
⁵ Fearfulness and trembling are come upon me,
   and horror hath overwhelmed me.
⁶ And I said, 'Oh that I had wings like a dove!
   For then would I fly away, and be at rest.
⁷ Lo, then would I wander far off,
   and remain in the wilderness. Selah.
⁸ I would hasten my escape from the windy storm
   and tempest.'
⁹ Destroy, O Lord, and divide their tongues;
   for I have seen violence and strife in the city.

¹⁰ Day and night they go about it
  upon the walls thereof: mischief also and sorrow
    are in the midst of it.
¹¹ Wickedness is in the midst thereof:
  deceit and guile depart not from her streets.
¹² For it was not an enemy that reproached me;
  then I could have borne it:
    neither was it he that hated me that did
  magnify himself against me;
    then I would have hid myself from him.
¹³ But it was thou, a man mine equal,
  my guide, and mine acquaintance.
¹⁴ We took sweet counsel together, and walked
  unto the house of God in company.
¹⁵ Let death seize upon them,
  and let them go down quick into hell;
    for wickedness is in their dwellings,
  and among them.
¹⁶ As for me, I will call upon God;
  and the Lord shall save me.
¹⁷ Evening, and morning, and at noon,
  will I pray, and cry aloud;
    and he shall hear my voice.
¹⁸ He hath delivered my soul in peace
  from the battle that was against me;
    for there were many with me.
¹⁹ God shall hear, and afflict them,
  even he that abideth of old. Selah.

Because they have no changes,
therefore they fear not God.
²⁰ He hath put forth his hands against such as
be at peace with him:
he hath broken his covenant.
²¹ The words of his mouth were smoother than butter,
but war was in his heart:
his words were softer than oil,
yet were they drawn swords.
²² Cast thy burden upon the Lord,
and he shall sustain thee: he shall
never suffer the righteous to be moved.
²³ But thou, O God, shalt bring them down
into the pit of destruction:
bloody and deceitful men shall not live out
half their days; but I will trust in thee.

56 To the chief musician upon Jonath-elem-rechokim,
Michtam of David, when the Philistines
took him in Gath.

Be merciful unto me, O God;
for man would swallow me up;
he fighting daily oppresseth me.
² Mine enemies would daily swallow me up;
for they be many that fight against me,
O thou most High.

³ What time I am afraid, I will trust in thee.
⁴ In God I will praise his word,
    in God I have put my trust;
        I will not fear what flesh can do unto me.
⁵ Every day they wrest my words:
    all their thoughts are against me for evil.
⁶ They gather themselves together,
    they hide themselves, they mark my steps,
        when they wait for my soul.
⁷ Shall they escape by iniquity?
    In thine anger cast down the people, O God.
⁸ Thou tellest my wanderings:
    put thou my tears into thy bottle:
        are they not in thy book?
⁹ When I cry unto thee,
        then shall mine enemies turn back:
    this I know; for God is for me.
¹⁰ In God will I praise his word:
    in the Lord will I praise his word.
¹¹ In God have I put my trust:
    I will not be afraid
        what man can do unto me.
¹² Thy vows are upon me, O God:
    I will render praises unto thee.
¹³ For thou hast delivered my soul from death:
    wilt not thou deliver my feet from falling,
        that I may walk before God
    in the light of the living?

57 To the chief musician, Al-taschith, Michtam
of David, when he fled from Saul in the cave.

Be merciful unto me, O God,
be merciful unto me; for my soul trusteth in thee:
yea, in the shadow of thy wings
will I make my refuge,
until these calamities be overpast.
² I will cry unto God most high;
unto God that performeth all things for me.
³ He shall send from heaven,
and save me from the reproach of him
that would swallow me up. Selah.
God shall send forth his mercy and his truth.
⁴ My soul is among lions;
and I lie even among them that are set on fire,
even the sons of men,
whose teeth are spears and arrows,
and their tongue a sharp sword.
⁵ Be thou exalted, O God, above the heavens;
let thy glory be above all the earth.
⁶ They have prepared a net for my steps;
my soul is bowed down;
they have digged a pit before me,
into the midst whereof they are fallen
themselves. Selah.
⁷ My heart is fixed, O God, my heart is fixed;
I will sing and give praise.

[8] Awake up, my glory;
    awake, psaltery and harp:
        I myself will awake early.
[9] I will praise thee, O Lord, among the people:
    I will sing unto thee among the nations.
[10] For thy mercy is great unto the heavens,
    and thy truth unto the clouds.
[11] Be thou exalted, O God, above the heavens:
    let thy glory be above all the earth.

58

To the chief musician, Al-taschith, Michtam
of David.

Do ye indeed speak righteousness, O congregation?
    Do ye judge uprightly, O ye sons of men?
[2] Yea, in heart ye work wickedness;
    ye weigh the violence of your hands
        in the earth.
[3] The wicked are estranged from the womb:
    they go astray as soon as they be born,
        speaking lies.
[4] Their poison is like the poison of a serpent:
    they are like the deaf adder that stoppeth her ear,
[5] which will not hearken to the voice of charmers,
    charming never so wisely.
[6] Break their teeth, O God, in their mouth:
    break out the great teeth of the young lions,
        O Lord.

⁷ Let them melt away as waters
   which run continually:
        when he bendeth his bow to shoot his arrows,
     let them be as cut in pieces.
⁸As a snail which melteth,
   let every one of them pass away:
        like the untimely birth of a woman,
     that they may not see the sun.
⁹ Before your pots can feel the thorns,
   he shall take them away as with a whirlwind,
        both living, and in his wrath.
¹⁰ The righteous shall rejoice
   when he seeth the vengeance:
        he shall wash his feet in the blood
     of the wicked.
¹¹ So that a man shall say,
   'Verily there is a reward for the righteous:
        verily he is a God that judgeth in the earth.'

59

To the chief musician, Al-taschith, Michtam
of David; when Saul sent, and they watched
the house to kill him.

Deliver me from mine enemies, O my God:
   defend me from them that rise up against me.
² Deliver me from the workers of iniquity,
   and save me from bloody men.

³ For, lo, they lie in wait for my soul:
    the mighty are gathered against me;
        not for my transgression,
    nor for my sin, O Lord.
⁴ They run and prepare themselves without my fault:
    awake to help me, and behold.
⁵ Thou therefore, O Lord God of hosts,
    the God of Israel, awake to visit all the heathen:
        be not merciful
    to any wicked transgressors. Selah.
⁶ They return at evening:
    they make a noise like a dog,
        and go round about the city.
⁷ Behold, they belch out with their mouth;
    swords are in their lips;
        for 'Who,' say they, 'doth hear?'
⁸ But thou, O Lord, shalt laugh at them;
    thou shalt have all the heathen in derision.
⁹ Because of his strength will I wait upon thee;
    for God is my defence.
¹⁰ The God of my mercy shall prevent me:
    God shall let me see my desire
        upon mine enemies.
¹¹ Slay them not, lest my people forget:
    scatter them by thy power;
        and bring them down, O Lord our shield.
¹² For the sin of their mouth
    and the words of their lips

let them even be taken in their pride;
and for cursing and lying which they speak.
¹³ Consume them in wrath, consume them,
that they may not be;
and let them know that God ruleth in Jacob
unto the ends of the earth. Selah.
¹⁴And at evening let them return;
and let them make a noise like a dog,
and go round about the city.
¹⁵ Let them wander up and down for meat,
and grudge if they be not satisfied.
¹⁶ But I will sing of thy power;
yea, I will sing aloud of thy mercy
in the morning;
for thou hast been my defence and refuge in the
day of my trouble.
¹⁷ Unto thee, O my strength, will I sing;
for God is my defence, and the God of my mercy.

60 To the chief musician upon Shushan-eduth,
Michtam of David, to teach; when he strove
with Aram-naharaim and with Aram-zobah,
when Joab returned, and smote of Edom
in the valley of salt twelve thousand.

O God, thou hast cast us off, thou hast scattered us,
thou hast been displeased;
O turn thyself to us again.

² Thou hast made the earth to tremble;
  thou hast broken it:
    heal the breaches thereof, for it shaketh.
³ Thou hast shewed thy people hard things:
  thou hast made us to drink
    the wine of astonishment.
⁴ Thou hast given a banner to them that fear thee,
  that it may be displayed
    because of the truth. Selah.
⁵ That thy beloved may be delivered;
  save with thy right hand, and hear me.
⁶ God hath spoken in his holiness:
  'I will rejoice, I will divide Shechem,
    and mete out the valley of Succoth.
⁷ Gilead is mine, and Manasseh is mine;
  Ephraim also is the strength of mine head;
    Judah is my lawgiver;
⁸ Moab is my washpot;
  over Edom will I cast out my shoe;
    Philistia, triumph thou because of me.'
⁹ Who will bring me into the strong city?
  Who will lead me into Edom?
¹⁰ Wilt not thou, O God, which hadst cast us off?
  And thou, O God, which didst not go out
    with our armies?
¹¹ Give us help from trouble;
  for vain is the help of man.
¹² Through God we shall do valiantly;
  for he it is that shall tread down our enemies.

61 To the chief musician upon Neginah,
a psalm of David.

Hear my cry, O God; attend unto my prayer.
² From the end of the earth will I cry unto thee,
when my heart is overwhelmed:
lead me to the rock that is higher than I.
³ For thou hast been a shelter for me,
and a strong tower from the enemy.
⁴ I will abide in thy tabernacle for ever:
I will trust in the covert of thy wings. Selah.
⁵ For thou, O God, hast heard my vows:
thou hast given me the heritage
of those that fear thy name.
⁶ Thou wilt prolong the king's life;
and his years as many generations.
⁷ He shall abide before God for ever:
O prepare mercy and truth,
which may preserve him.
⁸ So will I sing praise unto thy name for ever,
that I may daily perform my vows.

62 To the chief musician, to Jeduthun,
a psalm of David.

Truly my soul waiteth upon God:
from him cometh my salvation.
² He only is my rock and my salvation;
he is my defence; I shall not be greatly moved.

³ How long will ye imagine mischief against a man?
   Ye shall be slain all of you:
         as a bowing wall shall ye be,
      and as a tottering fence.
⁴ They only consult to cast him down
      from his excellency: they delight in lies:
            they bless with their mouth,
      but they curse inwardly. Selah.
⁵ My soul, wait thou only upon God;
      for my expectation is from him.
⁶ He only is my rock and my salvation;
      he is my defence; I shall not be moved.
⁷ In God is my salvation and my glory:
      the rock of my strength,
            and my refuge, is in God.
⁸ Trust in him at all times;
      ye people, pour out your heart before him:
            God is a refuge for us. Selah.
⁹ Surely men of low degree are vanity,
      and men of high degree are a lie:
            to be laid in the balance,
      they are altogether lighter than vanity.
¹⁰ Trust not in oppression,
      and become not vain in robbery:
            if riches increase, set not your heart upon them.
¹¹ God hath spoken once; twice have I heard this;
      that power belongeth unto God.
¹² Also unto thee, O Lord, belongeth mercy:

for thou renderest to every man
according to his work.

63 A psalm of David, when he was in the wilderness
of Judah.

O God, thou art my God; early will I seek thee:
 my soul thirsteth for thee,
  my flesh longeth for thee
 in a dry and thirsty land,
  where no water is,
² to see thy power and thy glory,
 so as I have seen thee in the sanctuary.
³ Because thy lovingkindness is better than life,
 my lips shall praise thee.
⁴ Thus will I bless thee while I live:
 I will lift up my hands in thy name.
⁵ My soul shall be satisfied as with marrow
 and fatness; and my mouth shall praise thee
  with joyful lips:
⁶ when I remember thee upon my bed,
 and meditate on thee in the night watches.
⁷ Because thou hast been my help,
 therefore in the shadow of thy wings
  will I rejoice.
⁸ My soul followeth hard after thee:
 thy right hand upholdeth me.

⁹ But those that seek my soul, to destroy it,
  shall go into the lower parts of the earth.
¹⁰ They shall fall by the sword:
  they shall be a portion for foxes.
¹¹ But the king shall rejoice in God;
  every one that sweareth by him shall glory:
    but the mouth of them that speak lies
  shall be stopped.

64

To the chief musician, a psalm of David.

Hear my voice, O God, in my prayer:
  preserve my life from fear of the enemy.
² Hide me from the secret counsel of the wicked;
  from the insurrection
    of the workers of iniquity,
³ who whet their tongue like a sword,
  and bend their bows to shoot their arrows,
    even bitter words,
⁴ that they may shoot in secret at the perfect:
  suddenly do they shoot at him, and fear not.
⁵ They encourage themselves in an evil matter:
  they commune of laying snares privily;
    they say, 'Who shall see them?'
⁶ They search out iniquities;
  they accomplish a diligent search:
    both the inward thought of every one of them,

and the heart, is deep.
⁷ But God shall shoot at them with an arrow;
    suddenly shall they be wounded.
⁸ So they shall make their own tongue
    to fall upon themselves:
        all that see them shall flee away.
⁹ And all men shall fear, and shall declare
    the work of God;
        for they shall wisely consider of his doing.
¹⁰ The righteous shall be glad in the Lord,
    and shall trust in him;
        and all the upright in heart shall glory.

65

To the chief musician, a psalm and song of David.

Praise waiteth for thee, O God, in Sion:
    and unto thee shall the vow be performed.
² O thou that hearest prayer,
    unto thee shall all flesh come.
³ Iniquities prevail against me:
    as for our transgressions,
        thou shalt purge them away.
⁴ Blessed is the man whom thou choosest,
    and causest to approach unto thee,
        that he may dwell in thy courts:
    we shall be satisfied with the goodness
        of thy house, even of thy holy temple.

⁵ By terrible things in righteousness
   wilt thou answer us,
      O God of our salvation;
   who art the confidence of all the ends
      of the earth,
   and of them that are afar off upon the sea;
⁶ Which by his strength setteth fast the mountains;
   being girded with power;
⁷ Which stilleth the noise of the seas,
   the noise of their waves,
      and the tumult of the people.
⁸ They also that dwell in the uttermost parts
   are afraid at thy tokens:
      thou makest the outgoings of the morning
   and evening to rejoice.
⁹ Thou visitest the earth, and waterest it:
   thou greatly enrichest it with the river of God,
      which is full of water:
   thou preparest them corn,
      when thou hast so provided for it.
¹⁰ Thou waterest the ridges thereof abundantly:
   thou settlest the furrows thereof:
      thou makest it soft with showers:
   thou blessest the springing thereof.
¹¹ Thou crownest the year with thy goodness;
   and thy paths drop fatness.
¹² They drop upon the pastures of the wilderness:
   and the little hills rejoice on every side.

¹³ The pastures are clothed with flocks;
    the valleys also are covered over with corn;
      they shout for joy, they also sing.

66 To the chief musician, a song or psalm.

Make a joyful noise unto God, all ye lands:
² sing forth the honour of his name:
    make his praise glorious.
³ Say unto God,
    'How terrible art thou in thy works!
      Through the greatness of thy power
    shall thine enemies submit
      themselves unto thee.
⁴ All the earth shall worship thee,
    and shall sing unto thee;
      they shall sing to thy name.' Selah.
⁵ Come and see the works of God:
    he is terrible in his doing toward
      the children of men.
⁶ He turned the sea into dry land:
    they went through the flood on foot:
      there did we rejoice in him.
⁷ He ruleth by his power for ever;
    his eyes behold the nations: let not
      the rebellious exalt themselves. Selah.
⁸ O bless our God, ye people,
    and make the voice of his praise to be heard,

⁹ Which holdeth our soul in life,
    and suffereth not our feet to be moved.
¹⁰ For thou, O God, hast proved us:
    thou hast tried us, as silver is tried.
¹¹ Thou broughtest us into the net;
    thou laidst affliction upon our loins.
¹² Thou hast caused men to ride over our heads;
    we went through fire and through water:
        but thou broughtest us out
    into a wealthy place.
¹³ I will go into thy house with burnt offerings:
    I will pay thee my vows,
¹⁴ which my lips have uttered, and my mouth hath
    spoken, when I was in trouble.
¹⁵ I will offer unto thee burnt sacrifices of fatlings,
    with the incense of rams;
        I will offer bullocks with goats. Selah.
¹⁶ Come and hear, all ye that fear God,
    and I will declare what he hath done
        for my soul.
¹⁷ I cried unto him with my mouth,
    and he was extolled with my tongue.
¹⁸ If I regard iniquity in my heart,
    the Lord will not hear me:
¹⁹ but verily God hath heard me;
    he hath attended to the voice of my prayer.
²⁰ Blessed be God, which hath not turned away
    my prayer, nor his mercy from me.

67 To the chief musician on Neginoth, a psalm or song.

God be merciful unto us, and bless us;
    and cause his face to shine upon us; Selah.
² That thy way may be known upon earth,
    thy saving health among all nations.
³ Let the people praise thee, O God;
    let all the people praise thee.
⁴ O let the nations be glad and sing for joy:
    for thou shalt judge the people righteously,
        and govern the nations upon earth. Selah.
⁵ Let the people praise thee, O God;
    let all the people praise thee.
⁶ Then shall the earth yield her increase;
    and God, even our own God, shall bless us.
⁷ God shall bless us; and all the ends of the earth
    shall fear him.

68 To the chief musician, a psalm or song of David.

Let God arise, let his enemies be scattered:
    let them also that hate him flee before him.
² As smoke is driven away, so drive them away:
    as wax melteth before the fire,
        so let the wicked perish
    at the presence of God.
³ But let the righteous be glad;
    let them rejoice before God;
        yea, let them exceedingly rejoice.

⁴ Sing unto God, sing praises to his name:
    extol him that rideth upon the heavens
        by his name JAH, and rejoice before him.
⁵ A father of the fatherless, and a judge
    of the widows, is God in his holy habitation.
⁶ God setteth the solitary in families:
    he bringeth out those which are bound
        with chains:
    but the rebellious dwell in a dry land.
⁷ O God, when thou wentest forth before thy people,
    when thou didst march through
        the wilderness; Selah;
⁸ the earth shook, the heavens also dropped
    at the presence of God;
        even Sinai itself was moved at the presence
    of God, the God of Israel.
⁹ Thou, O God, didst send a plentiful rain,
    whereby thou didst confirm thine inheritance,
        when it was weary.
¹⁰ Thy congregation hath dwelt therein:
    thou, O God, hast prepared of thy goodness
        for the poor.
¹¹ The Lord gave the word:
    great was the company of those that published it.
¹² Kings of armies did flee apace:
    and she that tarried at home divided the spoil.
¹³ Though ye have lien among the pots, yet shall ye be
    as the wings of a dove covered with silver,
        and her feathers with yellow gold.

¹⁴ When the Almighty scattered kings in it,
   it was white as snow in Salmon.
¹⁵ The hill of God is as the hill of Bashan;
   an high hill as the hill of Bashan.
¹⁶ Why leap ye, ye high hills?
   This is the hill which God desireth to dwell in;
      yea, the Lord will dwell in it for ever.
¹⁷ The chariots of God are twenty thousand,
   even thousands of angels:
      the Lord is among them, as in Sinai,
   in the holy place.
¹⁸ Thou hast ascended on high,
   thou hast led captivity captive;
      thou hast received gifts for men;
   yea, for the rebellious also,
      that the Lord God might dwell among them.
¹⁹ Blessed be the Lord, who daily loadeth us
   with benefits,
      even the God of our salvation. Selah.
²⁰ He that is our God is the God of salvation;
   and unto God the Lord belong the issues
      from death.
²¹ But God shall wound the head of his enemies,
   and the hairy scalp of such an one as goeth
      on still in his trespasses.
²² The Lord said,
   'I will bring again from Bashan,
   I will bring my people again
   from the depths of the sea,

²³ that thy foot may be dipped
    in the blood of thine enemies,
        and the tongue of thy dogs in the same.'
²⁴ They have seen thy goings, O God;
    even the goings of my God, my King,
        in the sanctuary.
²⁵ The singers went before,
    the players on instruments followed after;
        among them were the damsels
    playing with timbrels.
²⁶ Bless ye God in the congregations,
    even the Lord, from the fountain of Israel.
²⁷ There is little Benjamin with their ruler,
    the princes of Judah and their council,
        the princes of Zebulun,
    and the princes of Naphtali.
²⁸ Thy God hath commanded thy strength:
    strengthen, O God, that which thou hast
        wrought for us.
²⁹ Because of thy temple at Jerusalem shall kings
    bring presents unto thee.
³⁰ Rebuke the company of spearmen,
    the multitude of the bulls,
        with the calves of the people, till every one
    submit himself with pieces of silver:
        scatter thou the people that delight in war.
³¹ Princes shall come out of Egypt;
    Ethiopia shall soon stretch out her hands
        unto God.

³² Sing unto God, ye kingdoms of the earth;
O sing praises unto the Lord; Selah;
³³ to him that rideth upon the heavens of heavens,
which were of old;

lo, he doth send out his voice, and that a
mighty voice.
³⁴ Ascribe ye strength unto God:
his excellency is over Israel,
and his strength is in the clouds.
³⁵ O God, thou art terrible out of thy holy places:
the God of Israel is he that giveth strength
and power unto his people.
Blessed be God.

69

To the chief musician upon Shoshannim,
a psalm of David.

Save me, O God; for the waters are come in
unto my soul.
² I sink in deep mire, where there is no standing:
I am come into deep waters,
where the floods overflow me.
³ I am weary of my crying: my throat is dried:
mine eyes fail while I wait for my God.
⁴ They that hate me without a cause are
more than the hairs of mine head:
they that would destroy me,
being mine enemies wrongfully, are mighty:
then I restored that which I took not away.

⁵ O God, thou knowest my foolishness;
   and my sins are not hid from thee.
⁶ Let not them that wait on thee, O Lord God of hosts,
   be ashamed for my sake: let not those that seek thee
      be confounded for my sake, O God of Israel.
⁷ Because for thy sake I have borne reproach;
   shame hath covered my face.
⁸ I am become a stranger unto my brethren,
   and an alien unto my mother's children.
⁹ For the zeal of thine house hath eaten me up;
   and the reproaches of them that reproached thee
      are fallen upon me.
¹⁰ When I wept, and chastened my soul with fasting,
   that was to my reproach.
¹¹ I made sackcloth also my garment;
   and I became a proverb to them.
¹² They that sit in the gate speak against me;
   and I was the song of the drunkards.
¹³ But as for me, my prayer is unto thee, O Lord,
   in an acceptable time: O God,
      in the multitude of thy mercy hear me,
      in the truth of thy salvation.
¹⁴ Deliver me out of the mire, and let me not sink:
   let me be delivered from them that hate me,
      and out of the deep waters.
¹⁵ Let not the waterflood overflow me,
   neither let the deep swallow me up,
      and let not the pit shut her mouth upon me.

¹⁶ Hear me, O Lord; for thy loving-kindness is good:
      turn unto me according to the multitude
   of thy tender mercies.
¹⁷ And hide not thy face from thy servant;
      for I am in trouble: hear me speedily.
¹⁸ Draw nigh unto my soul, and redeem it:
      deliver me because of mine enemies.
¹⁹ Thou hast known my reproach,
      and my shame, and my dishonour:
         mine adversaries are all before thee.
²⁰ Reproach hath broken my heart;
      and I am full of heaviness;
         and I looked for some to take pity,
      but there was none;
         and for comforters, but I found none.
²¹ They gave me also gall for my meat;
      and in my thirst they gave me vinegar to drink.
²² Let their table become a snare before them:
      and that which should have been for their welfare,
         let it become a trap.
²³ Let their eyes be darkened, that they see not;
      and make their loins continually to shake.
²⁴ Pour out thine indignation upon them,
      and let thy wrathful anger take hold of them.
²⁵ Let their habitation be desolate;
      and let none dwell in their tents.
²⁶ For they persecute him whom thou hast smitten;
      and they talk to the grief of those
         whom thou hast wounded.

[27] Add iniquity unto their iniquity:
and let them not come into thy righteousness.
[28] Let them be blotted out of the book of the living,
and not be written with the righteous.
[29] But I am poor and sorrowful:
let thy salvation, O God, set me up on high.
[30] I will praise the name of God with a song,
and will magnify him with thanksgiving.
[31] This also shall please the Lord better than an ox
or bullock that hath horns and hoofs.
[32] The humble shall see this, and be glad;
and your heart shall live that seek God.
[33] For the Lord heareth the poor,
and despiseth not his prisoners.
[34] Let the heaven and earth praise him,
the seas, and every thing that moveth therein.
[35] For God will save Zion, and will build
the cities of Judah: that they may dwell there,
and have it in possession.
[36] The seed also of his servants shall inherit it:
and they that love his name shall dwell therein.

70

To the chief musician, a psalm of David,
to bring to remembrance.

Make haste, O God, to deliver me;
make haste to help me, O Lord.

² Let them be ashamed and confounded
    that seek after my soul:
        let them be turned backward,
    and put to confusion, that desire my hurt.
³ Let them be turned back for a reward
    of their shame that say, 'Aha, aha.'
⁴ Let all those that seek thee rejoice
    and be glad in thee:
        and let such as love thy salvation
    say continually, 'Let God be magnified.'
⁵ But I am poor and needy:
    make haste unto me, O God:
        thou art my help and my deliverer;
    O Lord, make no tarrying.

71 In thee, O Lord, do I put my trust:
    let me never be put to confusion.
² Deliver me in thy righteousness,
    and cause me to escape:
        incline thine ear unto me, and save me.
³ Be thou my strong habitation,
    where-unto I may continually resort:
        thou hast given commandment to save me;
    for thou art my rock and my fortress.
⁴ Deliver me, O my God, out of the hand
    of the wicked, out of the hand of the unrighteous
        and cruel man.

⁵ For thou art my hope, O Lord God:
  thou art my trust from my youth.
⁶ By thee have I been holden up from the womb:
  thou art he that took me out
    of my mother's bowels:
  my praise shall be continually of thee.
⁷ I am as a wonder unto many;
  but thou art my strong refuge.
⁸ Let my mouth be filled with thy praise
  and with thy honour all the day.
⁹ Cast me not off in the time of old age;
  forsake me not when my strength faileth.
¹⁰ For mine enemies speak against me;
  and they that lay wait for my soul
    take counsel together,
¹¹ Saying, 'God hath forsaken him:
  persecute and take him;
    for there is none to deliver him.'
¹² O God, be not far from me:
  O my God, make haste for my help.
¹³ Let them be confounded and consumed
  that are adversaries to my soul;
    let them be covered with reproach
  and dishonour that seek my hurt.
¹⁴ But I will hope continually,
  and will yet praise thee more and more.
¹⁵ My mouth shall shew forth thy righteousness
  and thy salvation all the day;
    for I know not the numbers thereof.

¹⁶ I will go in the strength of the Lord God:
    I will make mention of thy righteousness,
      even of thine only.
¹⁷ O God, thou hast taught me from my youth;
    and hitherto have I declared thy wondrous works.
¹⁸ Now also when I am old and gray-headed,
    O God, forsake me not;
      until I have shewed thy strength
    unto this generation,
      and thy power to every one that is to come.
¹⁹ Thy righteousness also, O God,
    is very high, who hast done great things:
      O God, who is like unto thee!
²⁰ Thou, which hast shewed me great
    and sore troubles, shalt quicken me again,
      and shalt bring me up again from the depths
    of the earth.
²¹ Thou shalt increase my greatness,
    and comfort me on every side.
²² I will also praise thee with the psaltery,
    even thy truth, O my God:
      unto thee will I sing with the harp,
    O thou Holy One of Israel.
²³ My lips shall greatly rejoice when I sing unto thee;
    and my soul, which thou hast redeemed.
²⁴ My tongue also shall talk of thy righteousness
    all the day long: for they are confounded,
      for they are brought unto shame,
    that seek my hurt.

72

A psalm for Solomon.

Give the king thy judgments, O God,
   and thy righteousness unto the king's son.
² He shall judge thy people with righteousness,
   and thy poor with judgment.
³ The mountains shall bring peace to the people,
   and the little hills, by righteousness.
⁴ He shall judge the poor of the people,
   he shall save the children of the needy,
     and shall break in pieces the oppressor.
⁵ They shall fear thee as long as the sun
   and moon endure,
     throughout all generations.
⁶ He shall come down like rain upon the mown grass,
   as showers that water the earth.
⁷ In his days shall the righteous flourish;
   and abundance of peace
     so long as the moon endureth.
⁸ He shall have dominion also from sea to sea,
   and from the river unto the ends of the earth.
⁹ They that dwell in the wilderness shall bow
   before him;
     and his enemies shall lick the dust.
¹⁰ The kings of Tarshish and of the isles
   shall bring presents:
     the kings of Sheba and Seba
   shall offer gifts.

¹¹ Yea, all kings shall fall down before him:
     all nations shall serve him.
¹² For he shall deliver the needy when he crieth;
     the poor also, and him that hath no helper.
¹³ He shall spare the poor and needy,
     and shall save the souls of the needy.
¹⁴ He shall redeem their soul from deceit
     and violence: and precious
          shall their blood be in his sight.
¹⁵ And he shall live, and to him shall be given
     of the gold of Sheba:
          prayer also shall be made for him continually;
     and daily shall he be praised.
¹⁶ There shall be an handful of corn in the earth
     upon the top of the mountains;
          the fruit thereof shall shake like Lebanon:
     and they of the city shall flourish
          like grass of the earth.
¹⁷ His name shall endure for ever:
     his name shall be continued as long as the sun:
          and men shall be blessed in him:
     all nations shall call him blessed.
¹⁸ Blessed be the Lord God, the God of Israel,
     who only doeth wondrous things.
¹⁹ And blessed be his glorious name for ever:
     and let the whole earth be filled with his glory;
          Amen, and Amen.
²⁰ The prayers of David the son of Jesse are ended.

73 A psalm of Asaph.

Truly God is good to Israel,
>even to such as are of a clean heart.
2 But as for me, my feet were almost gone;
>my steps had well nigh slipped.
3 For I was envious at the foolish,
>when I saw the prosperity of the wicked.
4 For there are no bands in their death;
>but their strength is firm.
5 They are not in trouble as other men;
>neither are they plagued like other men.
6 Therefore pride compasseth them about as a chain;
>violence covereth them as a garment.
7 Their eyes stand out with fatness:
>they have more than heart could wish.
8 They are corrupt, and speak wickedly
>concerning oppression: they speak loftily.
9 They set their mouth against the heavens,
>and their tongue walketh through the earth.
10 Therefore his people return hither:
>and waters of a full cup are wrung out to them.
11 And they say, 'How doth God know?
>And is there knowledge in the most High?'
12 Behold, these are the ungodly,
>who prosper in the world; they increase in riches.
13 Verily I have cleansed my heart in vain,
>and washed my hands in innocency.

[14] For all the day long have I been plagued,
and chastened every morning.
[15] If I say, 'I will speak thus',
behold, I should offend against
the generation of thy children.
[16] When I thought to know this,
it was too painful for me,
[17] until I went into the sanctuary of God;
then understood I their end.
[18] Surely thou didst set them in slippery places:
thou castedst them down into destruction.
[19] How are they brought into desolation,
as in a moment!
They are utterly consumed with terrors.
[20] As a dream when one awaketh;
so, O Lord, when thou awakest,
thou shalt despise their image.
[21] Thus my heart was grieved,
and I was pricked in my reins.
[22] So foolish was I, and ignorant:
I was as a beast before thee.
[23] Nevertheless I am continually with thee:
thou hast holden me by my right hand.
[24] Thou shalt guide me with thy counsel,
and afterward receive me to glory.
[25] Whom have I in heaven but thee?
And there is none upon earth
that I desire beside thee.

²⁶ My flesh and my heart faileth;
    but God is the strength of my heart,
      and my portion for ever.
²⁷ For, lo, they that are far from thee shall perish:
    thou hast destroyed all them
      that go a whoring from thee.
²⁸ But it is good for me to draw near to God:
    I have put my trust in the Lord God,
      that I may declare all thy works.

74

Maschil of Asaph.

O God, why hast thou cast us off for ever?
    Why doth thine anger smoke
      against the sheep of thy pasture?
² Remember thy congregation,
    which thou hast purchased of old;
      the rod of thine inheritance,
    which thou hast redeemed;
      this mount Zion, wherein thou hast dwelt.
³ Lift up thy feet unto the perpetual desolations;
    even all that the enemy hath done
      wickedly in the sanctuary.
⁴ Thine enemies roar in the midst
    of thy congregations;
      they set up their ensigns for signs.
⁵ A man was famous according as he had lifted up
    axes upon the thick trees.

⁶ But now they break down the carved work thereof
 at once with axes and hammers.
⁷ They have cast fire into thy sanctuary,
 they have defiled by casting down
 the dwelling place of thy name to the ground.
⁸ They said in their hearts,
 'Let us destroy them together';
 they have burned up all the synagogues
 of God in the land.
⁹ We see not our signs: there is no more any prophet:
 neither is there among us
 any that knoweth how long.
¹⁰ O God, how long shall the adversary reproach?
 Shall the enemy blaspheme thy name for ever?
¹¹ Why withdrawest thou thy hand, even thy right hand?
 Pluck it out of thy bosom.
¹² For God is my King of old,
 working salvation in the midst of the earth.
¹³ Thou didst divide the sea by thy strength:
 thou brakest the heads of the dragons
 in the waters.
¹⁴ Thou brakest the heads of leviathan in pieces,
 and gavest him to be meat to the people
 inhabiting the wilderness.
¹⁵ Thou didst cleave the fountain and the flood:
 thou driedst up mighty rivers.
¹⁶ The day is thine, the night also is thine:
 thou hast prepared the light and the sun.

[17] Thou hast set all the borders of the earth:
　　thou hast made summer and winter.
[18] Remember this, that the enemy hath reproached,
　　O Lord, and that the foolish people
　　　have blasphemed thy name.
[19] O deliver not the soul of thy turtledove
　　unto the multitude of the wicked:
　　　forget not the congregation
　　of thy poor for ever.
[20] Have respect unto the covenant:
　　for the dark places of the earth are full
　　　of the habitations of cruelty.
[21] O let not the oppressed return ashamed:
　　let the poor and needy praise thy name.
[22] Arise, O God, plead thine own cause:
　　remember how the foolish man
　　　reproacheth thee daily.
[23] Forget not the voice of thine enemies:
　　the tumult of those that rise up against thee
　　　increaseth continually.

75

To the chief musician, Al-taschith,
　　a psalm or song of Asaph.

Unto thee, O God, do we give thanks,
　　unto thee do we give thanks;
　　　for that thy name is near
　　thy wondrous works declare.

² When I shall receive the congregation
    I will judge uprightly.
³ The earth and all the inhabitants thereof are dissolved:
        I bear up the pillars of it. Selah.
⁴ I said unto the fools, 'Deal not foolishly,
        and to the wicked, 'Lift not up the horn;
⁵ lift not up your horn on high:
    speak not with a stiff neck.'
⁶ For promotion cometh neither from the east,
    nor from the west, nor from the south.
⁷ But God is the judge:
    he putteth down one, and setteth up another.
⁸ For in the hand of the Lord there is a cup,
    and the wine is red; it is full of mixture;
        and he poureth out of the same:
    but the dregs thereof, all the wicked
        of the earth shall wring them out,
    and drink them.
⁹ But I will declare for ever;
    I will sing praises to the God of Jacob.
¹⁰ All the horns of the wicked also will I cut off;
    but the horns of the righteous shall be exalted.

76 To the chief musician on Neginoth,
        a psalm or song of Asaph.

In Judah is God known: his name is great in Israel.

² In Salem also is his tabernacle,
  and his dwelling place in Zion.
³ There brake he the arrows of the bow,
  the shield and the sword, and the battle. Selah.
⁴ Thou art more glorious and excellent than
  the mountains of prey.
⁵ The stouthearted are spoiled,
  they have slept their sleep;
    and none of the men of might
    have found their hands.
⁶ At thy rebuke, O God of Jacob,
  both the chariot and horse are cast
    into a dead sleep.
⁷ Thou, even thou, art to be feared;
  and who may stand in thy sight
    when once thou art angry?
⁸ Thou didst cause judgment
  to be heard from heaven;
    the earth feared, and was still,
⁹ when God arose to judgment,
  to save all the meek of the earth. Selah.
¹⁰ Surely the wrath of man shall praise thee:
  the remainder of wrath shalt thou restrain.
¹¹ Vow, and pay unto the Lord your God:
  let all that be round about him bring presents
    unto him that ought to be feared.
¹² He shall cut off the spirit of princes:
  he is terrible to the kings of the earth.

77 To the chief musician, to Jeduthun,
a psalm of Asaph.

I cried unto God with my voice,
even unto God with my voice;
and he gave ear unto me.
² In the day of my trouble I sought the Lord:
my sore ran in the night, and ceased not:
my soul refused to be comforted.
³ I remembered God,
and was troubled:
I complained, and my spirit
was overwhelmed. Selah.
⁴ Thou holdest mine eyes waking;
I am so troubled
that I cannot speak.
⁵ I have considered the days of old,
the years of ancient times.
⁶ I call to remembrance my song in the night:
I commune with mine own heart:
and my spirit made diligent search.
⁷ Will the Lord cast off for ever?
And will he be favourable no more?
⁸ Is his mercy clean gone for ever?
Doth his promise fail for evermore?
⁹ Hath God forgotten to be gracious?
Hath he in anger shut up
his tender mercies? Selah.

¹⁰And I said, 'This is my infirmity;
    but I will remember the years of the right hand
        of the most High.'
¹¹I will remember the works of the Lord:
    surely I will remember thy wonders of old.
¹²I will meditate also of all thy work,
    and talk of thy doings.
¹³Thy way, O God, is in the sanctuary:
    who is so great a God as our God?
¹⁴Thou art the God that doest wonders:
    thou hast declared thy strength among
        the people.
¹⁵Thou hast with thine arm redeemed thy people,
    the sons of Jacob and Joseph. Selah.
¹⁶The waters saw thee, O God,
    the waters saw thee; they were afraid;
        the depths also were troubled.
¹⁷The clouds poured out water:
    the skies sent out a sound:
        thine arrows also went abroad.
¹⁸The voice of thy thunder was in the heaven:
    the lightnings lightened the world:
        the earth trembled and shook.
¹⁹Thy way is in the sea, and thy path
    in the great waters,
        and thy footsteps are not known.
²⁰Thou leddest thy people like a flock
    by the hand of Moses and Aaron.

78

Maschil of Asaph.

Give ear, O my people, to my law:
  incline your ears to the words of my mouth.
² I will open my mouth in a parable:
  I will utter dark sayings of old,
³ which we have heard and known,
  and our fathers have told us.
⁴ We will not hide them from their children,
  shewing to the generation to come the praises of
    the Lord, and his strength,
  and his wonderful works that he hath done.
⁵ For he established a testimony in Jacob,
  and appointed a law in Israel,
    which he commanded our fathers,
  that they should make them known
    to their children;
⁶ that the generation to come might know them,
  even the children which should be born;
    who should arise and declare them
  to their children;
⁷ that they might set their hope in God,
  and not forget the works of God,
    but keep his commandments;
⁸ and might not be as their fathers,
  a stubborn and rebellious generation;
    a generation that set not their heart aright,
  and whose spirit was not stedfast with God.

⁹ The children of Ephraim,
   being armed, and carrying bows,
      turned back in the day of battle.
¹⁰ They kept not the covenant of God,
   and refused to walk in his law;
¹¹ and forgat his works,
   and his wonders that he had shewed them.
¹² Marvellous things did he
   in the sight of their fathers,
      in the land of Egypt, in the field of Zoan.
¹³ He divided the sea,
   and caused them to pass through;
      and he made the waters to stand as an heap.
¹⁴ In the daytime also he led them with a cloud,
   and all the night with a light of fire.
¹⁵ He clave the rocks in the wilderness,
   and gave them drink as out of the great depths.
¹⁶ He brought streams also out of the rock,
   and caused waters to run down like rivers.
¹⁷ And they sinned yet more against him
   by provoking the most High in the wilderness.
¹⁸ And they tempted God in their heart
   by asking meat for their lust.
¹⁹ Yea, they spake against God; they said,
   'Can God furnish a table in the wilderness?'
²⁰ Behold, he smote the rock, that the waters gushed out,
   and the streams overflowed;
      can he give bread also?
   Can he provide flesh for his people?

²¹ Therefore the Lord heard this, and was wroth:
    so a fire was kindled against Jacob,
        and anger also came up against Israel;
²² because they believed not in God,
    and trusted not in his salvation,
²³ though he had commanded the clouds from above,
    and opened the doors of heaven,
²⁴ and had rained down manna upon them to eat,
    and had given them of the corn of heaven.
²⁵ Man did eat angels' food:
    he sent them meat to the full.
²⁶ He caused an east wind to blow in the heaven:
    and by his power he brought in the south wind.
²⁷ He rained flesh also upon them as dust,
    and feathered fowls like as the sand of the sea;
²⁸ and he let it fall in the midst of their camp,
    round about their habitations.
²⁹ So they did eat, and were well filled;
    for he gave them their own desire;
³⁰ they were not estranged from their lust.
    But while their meat was yet in their mouths,
³¹ the wrath of God came upon them,
    and slew the fattest of them,
        and smote down the chosen men of Israel.
³² For all this they sinned still,
    and believed not for his wondrous works.
³³ Therefore their days did he consume in vanity,
    and their years in trouble.

³⁴ When he slew them, then they sought him;
    and they returned and enquired early after God.
³⁵ And they remembered that God was their rock,
    and the high God their redeemer.
³⁶ Nevertheless they did flatter him with their mouth,
    and they lied unto him with their tongues.
³⁷ For their heart was not right with him,
    neither were they stedfast in his covenant.
³⁸ But he, being full of compassion, forgave
    their iniquity, and destroyed them not:
        yea, many a time turned he his anger away,
    and did not stir up all his wrath.
³⁹ For he remembered that they were but flesh;
    a wind that passeth away, and cometh not again.
⁴⁰ How oft did they provoke him in the wilderness,
    and grieve him in the desert!
⁴¹ Yea, they turned back and tempted God,
    and limited the Holy One of Israel.
⁴² They remembered not his hand,
    nor the day when he delivered them
        from the enemy.
⁴³ How he had wrought his signs in Egypt,
    and his wonders in the field of Zoan;
⁴⁴ and had turned their rivers into blood;
    and their floods, that they could not drink.
⁴⁵ He sent divers sorts of flies among them,
    which devoured them;
        and frogs, which destroyed them.

⁴⁶ He gave also their increase unto the caterpiller,
    and their labour unto the locust.
⁴⁷ He destroyed their vines with hail,
    and their sycomore trees with frost.
⁴⁸ He gave up their cattle also to the hail,
    and their flocks to hot thunderbolts.
⁴⁹ He cast upon them the fierceness of his anger,
    wrath, and indignation, and trouble,
        by sending evil angels among them.
⁵⁰ He made a way to his anger;
    he spared not their soul from death,
        but gave their life over to the pestilence;
⁵¹ and smote all the firstborn in Egypt;
    the chief of their strength in the tabernacles
        of Ham;
⁵² but made his own people to go forth like sheep,
    and guided them in the wilderness like a flock.
⁵³ And he led them on safely, so that they feared not;
    but the sea overwhelmed their enemies.
⁵⁴ And he brought them to the border
    of his sanctuary, even to this mountain,
        which his right hand had purchased.
⁵⁵ He cast out the heathen also before them,
    and divided them an inheritance by line,
        and made the tribes of Israel
    to dwell in their tents.
⁵⁶ Yet they tempted and provoked
    the most high God, and kept not his testimonies;

⁵⁷ but turned back,
>> and dealt unfaithfully like their fathers:
>>> they were turned aside like a deceitful bow.
⁵⁸ For they provoked him to anger
>> with their high places,
>>> and moved him to jealousy
>> with their graven images.
⁵⁹ When God heard this, he was wroth,
>> and greatly abhorred Israel,
⁶⁰ so that he forsook the tabernacle of Shiloh,
>> the tent which he placed among men;
⁶¹ and delivered his strength into captivity,
>> and his glory into the enemy's hand.
⁶² He gave his people over also unto the sword;
>> and was wroth with his inheritance.
⁶³ The fire consumed their young men;
>> and their maidens were not given to marriage.
⁶⁴ Their priests fell by the sword;
>> and their widows made no lamentation.
⁶⁵ Then the Lord awaked as one out of sleep,
>> and like a mighty man that shouteth
>>> by reason of wine.
⁶⁶ And he smote his enemies in the hinder parts:
>> he put them to a perpetual reproach.
⁶⁷ Moreover he refused the tabernacle of Joseph,
>> and chose not the tribe of Ephraim,
⁶⁸ but chose the tribe of Judah,
>> the mount Zion which he loved.

⁶⁹And he built his sanctuary like high palaces,
   like the earth which he hath
      established for ever.
⁷⁰He chose David also his servant,
   and took him from the sheepfolds:
⁷¹from following the ewes great with young
   he brought him to feed Jacob his people,
      and Israel his inheritance.
⁷²So he fed them according to the integrity
   of his heart; and guided them
      by the skilfulness of his hands.

79

A psalm of Asaph.

O God, the heathen are come into thine inheritance;
   thy holy temple have they defiled;
      they have laid Jerusalem on heaps.
²The dead bodies of thy servants have they given
   to be meat unto the fowls of the heaven,
      the flesh of thy saints
   unto the beasts of the earth.
³Their blood have they shed like water
   round about Jerusalem;
      and there was none to bury them.
⁴We are become a reproach to our neighbours,
   a scorn and derision to them
      that are round about us.

⁵ How long, Lord? Wilt thou be angry for ever?
    Shall thy jealousy burn like fire?
⁶ Pour out thy wrath upon the heathen
    that have not known thee, and upon the kingdoms
        that have not called upon thy name.
⁷ For they have devoured Jacob,
    and laid waste his dwelling place.
⁸ O remember not against us former iniquities:
    let thy tender mercies speedily prevent us,
        for we are brought very low.
⁹ Help us, O God of our salvation,
    for the glory of thy name:
        and deliver us, and purge away our sins,
    for thy name's sake.
¹⁰ Wherefore should the heathen say,
    'Where is their God?'
        Let him be known among the heathen
    in our sight by the revenging of the blood
        of thy servants which is shed.
¹¹ Let the sighing of the prisoner come before thee;
    according to the greatness of thy power
        preserve thou those that are appointed to die;
¹² and render unto our neighbours sevenfold
    into their bosom their reproach,
        wherewith they have reproached thee, O Lord.
¹³ So we thy people and sheep of thy pasture
    will give thee thanks for ever:
        we will shew forth thy praise to all generations.

80 To the chief musician upon Shoshannim-Eduth,
a psalm of Asaph.

Give ear, O Shepherd of Israel,
thou that leadest Joseph like a flock;
thou that dwellest between the cherubims,
shine forth.
2 Before Ephraim and Benjamin and Manasseh
stir up thy strength, and come and save us.
3 Turn us again, O God, and cause thy face to shine;
and we shall be saved.
4 O Lord God of hosts, how long wilt thou be angry
against the prayer of thy people.
5 Thou feedest them with the bread of tears;
and givest them tears to drink in great measure.
6 Thou makest us a strife unto our neighbours;
and our enemies laugh among themselves.
7 Turn us again, O God of hosts,
and cause thy face to shine; and we shall be saved.
8 Thou hast brought a vine out of Egypt:
thou hast cast out the heathen, and planted it.
9 Thou preparedst room before it,
and didst cause it to take deep root,
and it filled the land.
10 The hills were covered with the shadow of it,
and the boughs thereof were
like the goodly cedars.
11 She sent out her boughs unto the sea,
and her branches unto the river.

¹² Why hast thou then broken down her hedges,
    so that all they which pass by the way
        do pluck her?
¹³ The boar out of the wood doth waste it,
    and the wild beast of the field doth devour it.
¹⁴ Return, we beseech thee, O God of hosts:
    look down from heaven, and behold,
        and visit this vine;
¹⁵ and the vineyard which thy right hand
    hath planted, and the branch
        that thou madest strong for thyself.
¹⁶ It is burned with fire, it is cut down:
    they perish at the rebuke of thy countenance.
¹⁷ Let thy hand be upon the man of thy right hand,
    upon the son of man
        whom thou madest strong for thyself.
¹⁸ So will not we go back from thee:
    quicken us, and we will call upon thy name.
¹⁹ Turn us again, O Lord God of hosts,
    cause thy face to shine;
        and we shall be saved.

81 To the chief musician upon Gittith,
    a psalm of Asaph.

Sing aloud unto God our strength:
    make a joyful noise unto the God of Jacob.
² Take a psalm, and bring hither the timbrel,
    the pleasant harp with the psaltery.

³ Blow up the trumpet in the new moon,
in the time appointed,
on our solemn feast day.
⁴ For this was a statute for Israel,
and a law of the God of Jacob.
⁵ This he ordained in Joseph for a testimony,
when he went out through the land of Egypt,
where I heard a language that I understood not.
⁶ I removed his shoulder from the burden:
his hands were delivered from the pots.
⁷ Thou calledst in trouble, and I delivered thee;
I answered thee in the secret place of thunder;
I proved thee at the waters of Meribah. Selah.
⁸ Hear, O my people, and I will testify unto thee:
O Israel, if thou wilt hearken unto me;
⁹ there shall no strange god be in thee;
neither shalt thou worship any strange god.
¹⁰ I am the Lord thy God,
which brought thee out of the land of Egypt:
open thy mouth wide, and I will fill it.
¹¹ But my people would not hearken to my voice;
and Israel would none of me.
¹² So I gave them up unto their own hearts' lust;
and they walked in their own counsels.
¹³ Oh that my people had hearkened unto me,
and Israel had walked in my ways!
¹⁴ I should soon have subdued their enemies,
and turned my hand against their adversaries.

¹⁵ The haters of the Lord should have submitted
  themselves unto him;
    but their time should have endured for ever.
¹⁶ He should have fed them also with
  the finest of the wheat;
    and with honey out of the rock
    should I have satisfied thee.

82

A psalm of Asaph.

God standeth in the congregation of the mighty;
  he judgeth among the gods.
² How long will ye judge unjustly,
  and accept the persons of the wicked? Selah.
³ Defend the poor and fatherless:
  do justice to the afflicted and needy.
⁴ Deliver the poor and needy:
  rid them out of the hand of the wicked.
⁵ They know not, neither will they understand;
  they walk on in darkness:
    all the foundations of the earth
    are out of course.
⁶ I have said, 'Ye are gods;
  and all of you are children of the most High.
⁷ But ye shall die like men,
  and fall like one of the princes.'
⁸ Arise, O God, judge the earth:
  for thou shalt inherit all nations.

83

A song or psalm of Asaph.

Keep not thou silence, O God: hold not thy peace,
   and be not still, O God.
² For, lo, thine enemies make a tumult;
   and they that hate thee have lifted up the head.
³ They have taken crafty counsel against thy people,
   and consulted against thy hidden ones.
⁴ They have said, 'Come, and let us
   cut them off from being a nation;
      that the name of Israel may be
   no more in remembrance.'
⁵ For they have consulted together with one consent:
   they are confederate against thee:
⁶ the tabernacles of Edom, and the Ishmaelites;
   of Moab, and the Hagarenes;
⁷ Gebal, and Ammon, and Amalek;
   the Philistines with the inhabitants of Tyre;
⁸ Assur also is joined with them:
   they have holpen the children of Lot. Selah.
⁹ Do unto them as unto the Midianites;
   as to Sisera, as to Jabin, at the brook of Kison,
¹⁰ which perished at En-dor:
   they became as dung for the earth.
¹¹ Make their nobles like Oreb, and like Zeeb:
   yea, all their princes as Zebah, and as Zalmunna,
¹² who said, Let us take to ourselves
   the houses of God in possession.

¹³ O my God, make them like a wheel;
    as the stubble before the wind.
¹⁴ As the fire burneth a wood,
    and as the flame setteth the mountains on fire;
¹⁵ so persecute them with thy tempest,
    and make them afraid with thy storm.
¹⁶ Fill their faces with shame;
    that they may seek thy name, O Lord.
¹⁷ Let them be confounded and troubled for ever;
    yea, let them be put to shame, and perish,
¹⁸ that men may know that thou,
    whose name alone is Jehovah,
        art the most high over all the earth.

84 To the chief musician upon Gittith, a psalm for the sons of Korah.

How amiable are thy tabernacles, O Lord of hosts!
² My soul longeth, yea, even fainteth
    for the courts of the Lord:
        my heart and my flesh crieth out
    for the living God.
³ Yea, the sparrow hath found an house,
    and the swallow a nest for herself,
        where she may lay her young,
    even thine altars, O Lord of hosts,
        my King, and my God.
⁴ Blessed are they that dwell in thy house:

they will be still praising thee. Selah.
⁵ Blessed is the man whose strength is in thee:
   in whose heart are the ways of them.
⁶ Who passing through the valley of Baca
   make it a well;
      the rain also filleth the pools.
⁷ They go from strength to strength,
   every one of them in Zion appeareth before God.
⁸ O Lord God of hosts, hear my prayer:
   give ear, O God of Jacob. Selah.
⁹ Behold, O God our shield,
   and look upon the face of thine anointed.
¹⁰ For a day in thy courts is better than a thousand.
   I had rather be a doorkeeper
      in the house of my God,
   than to dwell in the tents of wickedness.
¹¹ For the Lord God is a sun and shield:
   the Lord will give grace and glory:
      no good thing will he withhold
   from them that walk uprightly.
¹² O Lord of hosts,
   blessed is the man that trusteth in thee.

85   To the chief musician, a psalm for the sons
     of Korah.

Lord, thou hast been favourable unto thy land:
   thou hast brought back the captivity of Jacob.

² Thou hast forgiven the iniquity of thy people,
    thou hast covered all their sin. Selah.
³ Thou hast taken away all thy wrath:
    thou hast turned thyself from the fierceness
        of thine anger.
⁴ Turn us, O God of our salvation,
    and cause thine anger toward us to cease.
⁵ Wilt thou be angry with us for ever?
    Wilt thou draw out thine anger
        to all generations?
⁶ Wilt thou not revive us again,
    that thy people may rejoice in thee?
⁷ Shew us thy mercy, O Lord,
    and grant us thy salvation.
⁸ I will hear what God the Lord will speak,
    for he will speak peace unto his people,
        and to his saints;
    but let them not turn again to folly.
⁹ Surely his salvation is nigh them that fear him;
    that glory may dwell in our land.
¹⁰ Mercy and truth are met together;
    righteousness and peace have kissed each other.
¹¹ Truth shall spring out of the earth;
    and righteousness shall look down
        from heaven.
¹² Yea, the Lord shall give that which is good;
    and our land shall yield her increase.
¹³ Righteousness shall go before him;
    and shall set us in the way of his steps.

86

A prayer of David.

Bow down thine ear, O Lord, hear me;
    for I am poor and needy.
² Preserve my soul; for I am holy:
    O thou my God, save thy servant
        that trusteth in thee.
³ Be merciful unto me, O Lord;
    for I cry unto thee daily.
⁴ Rejoice the soul of thy servant;
    for unto thee, O Lord, do I lift up my soul.
⁵ For thou, Lord, art good, and ready to forgive;
    and plenteous in mercy unto all them
        that call upon thee.
⁶ Give ear, O Lord, unto my prayer;
    and attend to the voice of my supplications.
⁷ In the day of my trouble I will call upon thee:
    for thou wilt answer me.
⁸ Among the gods there is none like unto thee,
    O Lord;
        neither are there any works
        like unto thy works.
⁹ All nations whom thou hast made
    shall come and worship before thee, O Lord;
        and shall glorify thy name.
¹⁰ For thou art great, and doest wondrous things:
    thou art God alone.
¹¹ Teach me thy way, O Lord; I will walk in thy truth:
    unite my heart to fear thy name.

¹² I will praise thee, O Lord my God, with all my heart:
    and I will glorify thy name for evermore.
¹³ For great is thy mercy toward me: and thou hast
    delivered my soul from the lowest hell.
¹⁴ O God, the proud are risen against me,
    and the assemblies of violent men
        have sought after my soul;
    and have not set thee before them.
¹⁵ But thou, O Lord, art a God full of compassion,
    and gracious, longsuffering, and plenteous
        in mercy and truth.
¹⁶ O turn unto me, and have mercy upon me;
    give thy strength unto thy servant,
        and save the son of thine handmaid.
¹⁷ Shew me a token for good;
    that they which hate me may see it,
        and be ashamed, because thou, Lord,
    hast holpen me, and comforted me.

87

A psalm or song for the sons of Korah.

His foundation is in the holy mountains.
² The Lord loveth the gates of Zion
    more than all the dwellings of Jacob.
³ Glorious things are spoken of thee,
    O city of God. Selah.
⁴ I will make mention of Rahab and Babylon
    to them that know me: behold Philistia,

and Tyre, with Ethiopia;
this man was born there.
⁵And of Zion it shall be said,
'This and that man was born in her':
and the highest himself shall establish her.
⁶The Lord shall count,
when he writeth up the people,
that this man was born there. Selah.
⁷As well the singers as the players on instruments
shall be there: all my springs are in thee.

88 A song or psalm for the sons of Korah,
to the chief Musician upon Mahalath Leannoth,
Maschil of Heman the Ezrahite.

O Lord God of my salvation,
I have cried day and night before thee:
²let my prayer come before thee:
incline thine ear unto my cry,
³for my soul is full of troubles;
and my life draweth nigh unto the grave.
⁴I am counted with them that go down into the pit:
I am as a man that hath no strength;
⁵free among the dead, like the slain
that lie in the grave,
whom thou rememberest no more;
and they are cut off from thy hand.

⁶ Thou hast laid me in the lowest pit,
    in darkness, in the deeps.
⁷ Thy wrath lieth hard upon me,
    and thou hast afflicted me
        with all thy waves. Selah.
⁸ Thou hast put a way mine acquaintance
    far from me;
        thou hast made me an abomination
    unto them: I am shut up,
        and I cannot come forth.
⁹ Mine eye mourneth by reason of affliction:
    Lord, I have called daily upon thee,
        I have stretched out my hands unto thee.
¹⁰ Wilt thou shew wonders to the dead?
    Shall the dead arise and praise thee? Selah.
¹¹ Shall thy lovingkindness be declared in the grave?
    Or thy faithfulness in destruction?
¹² Shall thy wonders be known in the dark?
    And thy righteousness in the land
        of forgetfulness?
¹³ But unto thee have I cried, O Lord;
    and in the morning shall my prayer prevent thee.
¹⁴ Lord, why castest thou off my soul?
    Why hidest thou thy face from me?
¹⁵ I am afflicted and ready to die from my youth up:
    while I suffer thy terrors I am distracted.
¹⁶ Thy fierce wrath goeth over me;
    thy terrors have cut me off.

[17] They came round about me daily like water;
    they compassed me about together.
[18] Lover and friend hast thou put far from me,
    and mine acquaintance into darkness.

89

Maschil of Ethan the Ezrahite.

    I will sing of the mercies of the Lord for ever:
        with my mouth will I make known
    thy faithfulness to all generations.
[2] For I have said, 'Mercy shall be built up for ever:
    thy faithfulness shalt thou establish
        in the very heavens.'
[3] I have made a covenant with my chosen,
    I have sworn unto David my servant,
[4] 'Thy seed will I establish for ever,
    and build up thy throne to all generations.' Selah.
[5] And the heavens shall praise thy wonders, O Lord:
    thy faithfulness also in the congregation
        of the saints.
[6] For who in the heaven can be compared
    unto the Lord?
        Who among the sons of the mighty
    can be likened unto the Lord?
[7] God is greatly to be feared in the assembly
    of the saints, and to be had in reverence
        of all them that are about him.

8 O Lord God of hosts, who is a strong Lord
    like unto thee?
        Or to thy faithfulness round about thee?
9 Thou rulest the raging of the sea:
    when the waves thereof arise, thou stillest them.
10 Thou hast broken Rahab in pieces,
    as one that is slain;
        thou hast scattered thine enemies
    with thy strong arm.
11 The heavens are thine, the earth also is thine:
    as for the world and the fulness thereof,
        thou hast founded them.
12 The north and the south thou hast created them:
    Tabor and Hermon shall rejoice in thy name.
13 Thou hast a mighty arm:
    strong is thy hand, and high is thy right hand.
14 Justice and judgment are the habitation
    of thy throne:
        mercy and truth shall go before thy face.
15 Blessed is the people that know the joyful sound:
    they shall walk, O Lord,
        in the light of thy countenance.
16 In thy name shall they rejoice all the day;
    and in thy righteousness shall they be exalted.
17 For thou art the glory of their strength;
    and in thy favour our horn shall be exalted.
18 For the Lord is our defence;
    and the Holy One of Israel is our king.

¹⁹ Then thou spakest in vision to thy holy one,
 and saidst,

 'I have laid help upon one that is mighty;
 I have exalted one chosen out of the people.
²⁰ I have found David my servant;
 with my holy oil have I anointed him,
²¹ with whom my hand shall be established:
 mine arm also shall strengthen him.
²² The enemy shall not exact upon him;
 nor the son of wickedness afflict him.
²³ And I will beat down his foes before his face,
 and plague them that hate him.
²⁴ But my faithfulness and my mercy
 shall be with him;

 and in my name shall his horn be exalted.
²⁵ I will set his hand also in the sea,
 and his right hand in the rivers.
²⁶ He shall cry unto me,

 "Thou art my father, my God,
 and the rock of my salvation."
²⁷ Also I will make him my firstborn,
 higher than the kings of the earth.
²⁸ My mercy will I keep for him for evermore,
 and my covenant shall stand fast with him.
²⁹ His seed also will I make to endure for ever,
 and his throne as the days of heaven.
³⁰ If his children forsake my law,
 and walk not in my judgments;

³¹ if they break my statutes,
and keep not my commandments;
³² then will I visit their transgression with the rod,
and their iniquity with stripes.
³³ Nevertheless my lovingkindness will I not
utterly take from him,
nor suffer my faithfulness to fail.
³⁴ My covenant will I not break,
nor alter the thing that is gone out of my lips.
³⁵ Once have I sworn by my holiness
that I will not lie unto David.
³⁶ His seed shall endure for ever,
and his throne as the sun before me.
³⁷ It shall be established for ever as the moon,
and as a faithful witness in heaven.' Selah.
³⁸ But thou hast cast off and abhorred,
thou hast been wroth with thine anointed.
³⁹ Thou hast made void the covenant of thy servant:
thou hast profaned his crown
by casting it to the ground.
⁴⁰ Thou hast broken down all his hedges;
thou hast brought his strong holds to ruin.
⁴¹ All that pass by the way spoil him:
he is a reproach to his neighbours.
⁴² Thou hast set up the right hand of his adversaries;
thou hast made all his enemies to rejoice.
⁴³ Thou hast also turned the edge of his sword,
and hast not made him to stand in the battle.

⁴⁴ Thou hast made his glory to cease,
and cast his throne down to the ground.
⁴⁵ The days of his youth hast thou shortened:
thou hast covered him with shame. Selah.
⁴⁶ How long, Lord?
Wilt thou hide thyself for ever?
Shall thy wrath burn like fire?
⁴⁷ Remember how short my time is:
wherefore hast thou made all men in vain?
⁴⁸ What man is he that liveth, and shall not see death?
Shall he deliver his soul from the hand
of the grave? Selah.
⁴⁹ Lord, where are thy former lovingkindnesses,
which thou swarest unto David in thy truth?
⁵⁰ Remember, Lord, the reproach of thy servants;
how I do bear in my bosom the reproach
of all the mighty people;
⁵¹ wherewith thine enemies have reproached, O Lord;
wherewith they have reproached the footsteps
of thine anointed.
⁵² Blessed be the Lord for evermore.
Amen, and Amen.

90

A prayer of Moses the man of God.

Lord, thou hast been our dwelling place
in all generations.

² Before the mountains were brought forth,
or ever thou hadst formed the earth
and the world,
even from everlasting
to everlasting, thou art God.
³ Thou turnest man to destruction; and sayest,
'Return, ye children of men.'
⁴ For a thousand years in thy sight
are but as yesterday when it is past,
and as a watch in the night.
⁵ Thou carriest them away as with a flood;
they are as a sleep: in the morning they are like grass
which groweth up.
⁶ In the morning it flourisheth, and groweth up;
in the evening it is cut down, and withereth.
⁷ For we are consumed by thine anger,
and by thy wrath are we troubled.
⁸ Thou hast set our iniquities before thee,
our secret sins in the light of thy countenance.
⁹ For all our days are passed away in thy wrath:
we spend our years as a tale that is told.
¹⁰ The days of our years are three-score years and ten;
and if by reason of strength
they be fourscore years,
yet is their strength labour and sorrow;
for it is soon cut off, and we fly away.
¹¹ Who knoweth the power of thine anger?
Even according to thy fear, so is thy wrath.

¹² So teach us to number our days,
  that we may apply our hearts unto wisdom.
¹³ Return, O Lord, how long?
  And let it repent thee concerning thy servants.
¹⁴ O satisfy us early with thy mercy;
  that we may rejoice and be glad all our days.
¹⁵ Make us glad according to the days
  wherein thou hast afflicted us,
    and the years wherein we have seen evil.
¹⁶ Let thy work appear unto thy servants,
  and thy glory unto their children.
¹⁷ And let the beauty of the Lord our God be upon us;
  and establish thou the work of our hands upon us;
    yea, the work of our hands establish thou it.

91 He that dwelleth in the secret place of the most High
  shall abide under the shadow of the Almighty.
² I will say of the Lord,
  'He is my refuge and my fortress:
    my God; in him will I trust.'
³ Surely he shall deliver thee from the snare
  of the fowler,
    and from the noisome pestilence.
⁴ He shall cover thee with his feathers,
  and under his wings shalt thou trust:
    his truth shall be thy shield and buckler.
⁵ Thou shalt not be afraid for the terror by night;
  nor for the arrow that flieth by day;

⁶ nor for the pestilence that walketh in darkness;
  nor for the destruction that wasteth at noonday.
⁷ A thousand shall fall at thy side,
  and ten thousand at thy right hand;
    but it shall not come nigh thee.
⁸ Only with thine eyes shalt thou behold
  and see the reward of the wicked.
⁹ Because thou hast made the Lord,
  which is my refuge,
    even the most High, thy habitation;
¹⁰ there shall no evil befall thee,
  neither shall any plague come nigh thy dwelling.
¹¹ For he shall give his angels charge over thee,
  to keep thee in all thy ways.
¹² They shall bear thee up in their hands,
  lest thou dash thy foot against a stone.
¹³ Thou shalt tread upon the lion and adder:
  the young lion and the dragon
    shalt thou trample under feet.
¹⁴ Because he hath set his love upon me,
  therefore will I deliver him:
    I will set him on high,
  because he hath known my name.
¹⁵ He shall call upon me,
  and I will answer him;
    I will be with him in trouble;
  I will deliver him, and honour him.
¹⁶ With long life will I satisfy him,
  and shew him my salvation.

92

A psalm or song for the sabbath day.

It is a good thing to give thanks unto the Lord,
and to sing praises unto thy name,
O most High,
2 to shew forth thy lovingkindness in the morning,
and thy faithfulness every night,
3 upon an instrument of ten strings,
and upon the psaltery;
upon the harp with a solemn sound.
4 For thou, Lord, hast made me glad
through thy work:
I will triumph in the works of thy hands.
5 O Lord, how great are thy works!
And thy thoughts are very deep.
6 A brutish man knoweth not;
neither doth a fool understand this.
7 When the wicked spring as the grass,
and when all the workers of iniquity do flourish;
it is that they shall be destroyed for ever;
8 but thou, Lord, art most high for evermore.
9 For, lo, thine enemies, O Lord,
for, lo, thine enemies shall perish;
all the workers of iniquity
shall be scattered.
10 But my horn shalt thou exalt like the horn
of an unicorn:
I shall be anointed with fresh oil.

¹¹ Mine eye also shall see my desire on mine enemies,
    and mine ears shall hear my desire
        of the wicked that rise up against me.
¹² The righteous shall flourish like the palm tree:
    he shall grow like a cedar in Lebanon.
¹³ Those that be planted in the house of the Lord
    shall flourish in the courts of our God.
¹⁴ They shall still bring forth fruit in old age;
    they shall be fat and flourishing;
¹⁵ to shew that the Lord is upright: he is my rock,
    and there is no unrighteousness in him.

93 The Lord reigneth, he is clothed with majesty;
    the Lord is clothed with strength,
        wherewith he hath girded himself:
    the world also is stablished,
        that it cannot be moved.
² Thy throne is established of old:
    thou art from everlasting.
³ The floods have lifted up, O Lord,
    the floods have lifted up their voice;
        the floods lift up their waves.
⁴ The Lord on high is mightier than the noise
    of many waters,
        yea, than the mighty waves of the sea.
⁵ Thy testimonies are very sure:
    holiness becometh thine house, O Lord, for ever.

94 O Lord God, to whom vengeance belongeth;
O God, to whom vengeance belongeth,
shew thyself.
2 Lift up thyself, thou judge of the earth:
render a reward to the proud.
3 Lord, how long shall the wicked,
how long shall the wicked triumph?
4 How long shall they utter and speak hard things?
And all the workers of iniquity boast themselves?
5 They break in pieces thy people, O Lord,
and afflict thine heritage.
6 They slay the widow and the stranger,
and murder the fatherless.
7 Yet they say, 'The Lord shall not see,
neither shall the God of Jacob regard it.'
8 Understand, ye brutish among the people;
and ye fools, when will ye be wise?
9 He that planted the ear, shall he not hear?
He that formed the eye, shall he not see?
10 He that chastiseth the heathen,
shall not he correct?
He that teacheth man knowledge,
shall not he know?
11 The Lord knoweth the thoughts of man,
that they are vanity.
12 Blessed is the man whom thou chastenest,
O Lord,
and teachest him out of thy law;

¹³ that thou mayest give him rest
from the days of adversity,
until the pit be digged for the wicked.
¹⁴ For the Lord will not cast off his people,
neither will he forsake his inheritance.
¹⁵ But judgment shall return unto righteousness;
and all the upright in heart
shall follow it.
¹⁶ Who will rise up for me against the evildoers?
Or who will stand up for me
against the workers of iniquity?
¹⁷ Unless the Lord had been my help,
my soul had almost dwelt in silence.
¹⁸ When I said, 'My foot slippeth';
thy mercy, O Lord, held me up.
¹⁹ In the multitude of my thoughts
within me thy comforts delight my soul.
²⁰ Shall the throne of iniquity have fellowship
with thee, which frameth mischief by a law?
²¹ They gather themselves together
against the soul of the righteous,
and condemn the innocent blood.
²² But the Lord is my defence;
and my God is the rock of my refuge.
²³ And he shall bring upon them their own iniquity,
and shall cut them off in their own wickedness;
yea, the Lord our God
shall cut them off.

95 O come, let us sing unto the Lord:
    let us make a joyful noise to the rock
        of our salvation.
² Let us come before his presence with thanksgiving,
    and make a joyful noise
        unto him with psalms.
³ For the Lord is a great God,
    and a great King above all gods.
⁴ In his hand are the deep places of the earth:
    the strength of the hills is his also.
⁵ The sea is his, and he made it;
    and his hands formed the dry land.
⁶ O come, let us worship and bow down:
    let us kneel before the Lord our maker.
⁷ For he is our God;
    and we are the people of his pasture,
        and the sheep of his hand.
    To day if ye will hear his voice,
⁸ harden not your heart, as in the provocation,
    and as in the day of temptation in the wilderness;
⁹ when your fathers tempted me,
    proved me, and saw my work.
¹⁰ Forty years long was I grieved with this generation,
    and said,
        'It is a people that do err in their heart,
        and they have not known my ways,'
¹¹ unto whom I sware in my wrath that they should
    not enter into my rest.

96

O sing unto the Lord a new song:
   sing unto the Lord, all the earth.
2 Sing unto the Lord, bless his name;
   shew forth his salvation from day to day.
3 Declare his glory among the heathen,
   his wonders among all people.
4 For the Lord is great, and greatly to be praised:
   he is to be feared above all gods.
5 For all the gods of the nations are idols;
   but the Lord made the heavens.
6 Honour and majesty are before him:
   strength and beauty are in his sanctuary.
7 Give unto the Lord, O ye kindreds of the people,
   give unto the Lord glory and strength.
8 Give unto the Lord the glory due unto his name:
   bring an offering, and come into his courts.
9 O worship the Lord in the beauty of holiness:
   fear before him, all the earth.
10 Say among the heathen that the Lord reigneth:
   the world also shall be established
      that it shall not be moved:
   he shall judge the people righteously.
11 Let the heavens rejoice, and let the earth be glad;
   let the sea roar, and the fulness thereof.
12 Let the field be joyful, and all that is therein;
   then shall all the trees of the wood rejoice
13 before the Lord; for he cometh,
   for he cometh to judge the earth:

he shall judge the world with righteousness,
and the people with his truth.

97 The Lord reigneth; let the earth rejoice;
let the multitude of isles be glad thereof.
[2] Clouds and darkness are round about him:
righteousness and judgment are the habitation
of his throne.
[3] A fire goeth before him,
and burneth up his enemies round about.
[4] His lightnings enlightened the world:
the earth saw, and trembled.
[5] The hills melted like wax at the presence of the Lord,
at the presence of the Lord of the whole earth.
[6] The heavens declare his righteousness,
and all the people see his glory.
[7] Confounded be all they that serve graven images,
that boast themselves of idols:
worship him, all ye gods.
[8] Zion heard, and was glad;
and the daughters of Judah rejoiced
because of thy judgments, O Lord.
[9] For thou, Lord, art high above all the earth:
thou art exalted far above all gods.
[10] Ye that love the Lord, hate evil;
he preserveth the souls of his saints;
he delivereth them out of the hand
of the wicked.

¹¹ Light is sown for the righteous,
    and gladness for the upright in heart.
¹² Rejoice in the Lord, ye righteous;
    and give thanks at the remembrance
        of his holiness.

98

A psalm.

O sing unto the Lord a new song;
    for he hath done marvellous things:
his right hand, and his holy arm,
    hath gotten him the victory.
² The Lord hath made known his salvation:
    his righteousness hath he openly shewed
        in the sight of the heathen.
³ He hath remembered his mercy and his truth
    toward the house of Israel:
        all the ends of the earth have seen
    the salvation of our God.
⁴ Make a joyful noise unto the Lord,
    all the earth: make a loud noise,
        and rejoice, and sing praise.
⁵ Sing unto the Lord with the harp;
    with the harp, and the voice of a psalm.
⁶ With trumpets and sound of cornet
    make a joyful noise before the Lord, the King.
⁷ Let the sea roar, and the fulness thereof;

the world, and they that dwell therein.
8 Let the floods clap their hands;
   let the hills be joyful together
9 Before the Lord; for he cometh to judge the earth;
   with righteousness shall he judge the world,
      and the people with equity.

99 The Lord reigneth; let the people tremble:
   he sitteth between the cherubims;
      let the earth be moved.
2 The Lord is great in Zion;
   and he is high above all the people.
3 Let them praise thy great and terrible name;
   for it is holy.
4 The king's strength also loveth judgment;
   thou dost establish equity,
      thou executest judgment
   and righteousness in Jacob.
5 Exalt ye the Lord our God,
   and worship at his footstool; for he is holy.
6 Moses and Aaron among his priests,
   and Samuel among them that call upon his name;
      they called upon the Lord,
   and he answered them.
7 He spake unto them in the cloudy pillar:
   they kept his testimonies,
      and the ordinance that he gave them.

[8] Thou answeredst them, O Lord our God:
   thou wast a God that forgavest them,
      though thou tookest vengeance of their inven-
tions.
[9] Exalt the Lord our God, and worship at his holy
   hill; for the Lord our God is holy.

100

A psalm of praise.

Make a joyful noise unto the Lord, all ye lands.
[2] Serve the Lord with gladness:
   come before his presence with singing.
[3] Know ye that the Lord he is God;
   it is he that hath made us, and not we ourselves;
      we are his people,
   and the sheep of his pasture.
[4] Enter into his gates with thanksgiving,
   and into his courts with praise:
      be thankful unto him, and bless his name.
[5] For the Lord is good; his mercy is everlasting;
      and his truth endureth to all generations.

101

A psalm of David.

I will sing of mercy and judgment:
   unto thee, O Lord, will I sing.
[2] I will behave myself wisely in a perfect way.
   O when wilt thou come unto me?

I will walk within my house
with a perfect heart.
³ I will set no wicked thing before mine eyes;
I hate the work of them that turn aside;
it shall not cleave to me.
⁴ A froward heart shall depart from me:
I will not know a wicked person.
⁵ Whoso privily slandereth his neighbour,
him will I cut off:
him that hath an high look
and a proud heart will not I suffer.
⁶ Mine eyes shall be upon the faithful of the land,
that they may dwell with me:
he that walketh in a perfect way,
he shall serve me.
⁷ He that worketh deceit shall not dwell
within my house:
he that telleth lies shall not tarry in my sight.
⁸ I will early destroy all the wicked of the land;
that I may cut off all wicked doers
from the city of the Lord.

102 A prayer of the afflicted, when he is overwhelmed, and poureth out his complaint before the Lord.

Hear my prayer, O Lord,
and let my cry come unto thee.

² Hide not thy face from me in the day
   when I am in trouble; incline thine ear unto me:
      in the day when I call answer me speedily.
³ For my days are consumed like smoke,
   and my bones are burned as an hearth.
⁴ My heart is smitten, and withered like grass;
   so that I forget to eat my bread.
⁵ By reason of the voice of my groaning my bones
   cleave to my skin.
⁶ I am like a pelican of the wilderness:
   I am like an owl of the desert.
⁷ I watch, and am as a sparrow
   alone upon the house top.
⁸ Mine enemies reproach me all the day;
   and they that are mad against me are sworn
      against me.
⁹ For I have eaten ashes like bread,
   and mingled my drink with weeping,
¹⁰ because of thine indignation and thy wrath;
   for thou hast lifted me up, and cast me down.
¹¹ My days are like a shadow that declineth;
   and I am withered like grass.
¹² But thou, O Lord, shalt endure for ever;
   and thy remembrance unto all generations.
¹³ Thou shalt arise, and have mercy upon Zion;
   for the time to favour her, yea,
      the set time, is come.
¹⁴ For thy servants take pleasure in her stones,
   and favour the dust thereof.

¹⁵ So the heathen shall fear the name of the Lord,
and all the kings of the earth thy glory.
¹⁶ When the Lord shall build up Zion,
he shall appear in his glory.
¹⁷ He will regard the prayer of the destitute,
and not despise their prayer.
¹⁸ This shall be written for the generation to come;
and the people which shall be created
shall praise the Lord.
¹⁹ For he hath looked down from the height
of his sanctuary;
from heaven did the Lord behold the earth;
²⁰ to hear the groaning of the prisoner;
to loose those that are appointed to death;
²¹ to declare the name of the Lord in Zion,
and his praise in Jerusalem;
²² when the people are gathered together,
and the kingdoms, to serve the Lord.
²³ He weakened my strength in the way;
he shortened my days.
²⁴ I said, 'O my God, take me not away
in the midst of my days;
thy years are throughout all generations.'
²⁵ Of old hast thou laid the foundation of the earth;
and the heavens are the work of thy hands.
²⁶ They shall perish, but thou shalt endure:
yea, all of them shall wax old like a garment;
as a vesture shalt thou change them,
and they shall be changed;

²⁷ but thou art the same,
and thy years shall have no end.
²⁸ The children of thy servants shall continue,
and their seed shall be established before thee.

103

A psalm of David.

Bless the Lord, O my soul;
and all that is within me, bless his holy name.
² Bless the Lord, O my soul,
and forget not all his benefits;
³ who forgiveth all thine iniquities;
who healeth all thy diseases;
⁴ who redeemeth thy life from destruction;
who crowneth thee with lovingkindness
and tender mercies;
⁵ who satisfieth thy mouth with good things;
so that thy youth is renewed like the eagle's.
⁶ The Lord executeth righteousness
and judgment for all that are oppressed.
⁷ He made known his ways unto Moses,
his acts unto the children of Israel.
⁸ The Lord is merciful and gracious,
slow to anger, and plenteous in mercy.
⁹ He will not always chide;
neither will he keep his anger for ever.
¹⁰ He hath not dealt with us after our sins;
nor rewarded us according to our iniquities.

¹¹ For as the heaven is high above the earth,
  so great is his mercy toward them that fear him.
¹² As far as the east is from the west,
  so far hath he removed our transgressions
    from us.
¹³ Like as a father pitieth his children,
  so the Lord pitieth them that fear him.
¹⁴ For he knoweth our frame;
  he remembereth that we are dust.
¹⁵ As for man, his days are as grass:
  as a flower of the field, so he flourisheth.
¹⁶ For the wind passeth over it, and it is gone;
  and the place thereof shall know it no more.
¹⁷ But the mercy of the Lord is from everlasting
  to everlasting upon them that fear him,
    and his righteousness unto children's children;
¹⁸ to such as keep his covenant,
  and to those that remember his commandments
    to do them.
¹⁹ The Lord hath prepared his throne in the heavens;
  and his kingdom ruleth over all.
²⁰ Bless the Lord, ye his angels, that excel in strength,
  that do his commandments,
    hearkening unto the voice of his word.
²¹ Bless ye the Lord, all ye his hosts;
  ye ministers of his, that do his pleasure.
²² Bless the Lord, all his works in all places
  of his dominion: bless the Lord, O my soul.

104

Bless the Lord, O my soul.
O Lord my God, thou art very great;
　　thou art clothed with honour and majesty.
² Who coverest thyself with light as with a garment;
　who stretchest out the heavens like a curtain;
³ who layeth the beams of his chambers
　　in the waters;
　　　who maketh the clouds his chariot;
　who walketh upon the wings of the wind;
⁴ who maketh his angels spirits;
　his ministers a flaming fire;
⁵ who laid the foundations of the earth,
　that it should not be removed for ever.
⁶ Thou coveredst it with the deep as with a garment:
　the waters stood above the mountains.
⁷ At thy rebuke they fled;
　at the voice of thy thunder they hasted away.
⁸ They go up by the mountains;
　they go down by the valleys unto the place
　　　which thou hast founded for them.
⁹ Thou hast set a bound that they may not pass over;
　that they turn not again to cover the earth.
¹⁰ He sendeth the springs into the valleys,
　which run among the hills.
¹¹ They give drink to every beast of the field:
　the wild asses quench their thirst.
¹² By them shall the fowls of the heaven
　have their habitation,

which sing among the branches.
¹³ He watereth the hills from his chambers:
    the earth is satisfied with the fruit of thy works.
¹⁴ He causeth the grass to grow for the cattle,
    and herb for the service of man,
        that he may bring forth food out of the earth;
¹⁵ and wine that maketh glad the heart of man,
    and oil to make his face to shine,
        and bread which strengtheneth man's heart.
¹⁶ The trees of the Lord are full of sap;
    the cedars of Lebanon, which he hath planted;
¹⁷ where the birds make their nests:
    as for the stork, the fir trees are her house.
¹⁸ The high hills are a refuge for the wild goats;
    and the rocks for the conies.
¹⁹ He appointed the moon for seasons;
    the sun knoweth his going down.
²⁰ Thou makest darkness, and it is night;
    wherein all the beasts of the forest do creep forth.
²¹ The young lions roar after their prey,
    and seek their meat from God.
²² The sun ariseth, they gather themselves together,
    and lay them down in their dens.
²³ Man goeth forth unto his work and to his labour
    until the evening.
²⁴ O Lord, how manifold are thy works!
    In wisdom hast thou made them all;
        the earth is full of thy riches.

²⁵ So is this great and wide sea,
     wherein are things creeping innumerable,
          both small and great beasts.
²⁶ There go the ships;
     there is that leviathan,
          whom thou hast made to play therein.
²⁷ These wait all upon thee,
     that thou mayest give them their meat
          in due season.
²⁸ That thou givest them they gather:
     thou openest thine hand,
          they are filled with good.
²⁹ Thou hidest thy face, they are troubled:
     thou takest away their breath,
          they die, and return to their dust.
³⁰ Thou sendest forth thy spirit, they are created:
     and thou renewest the face of the earth.
³¹ The glory of the Lord shall endure for ever:
     the Lord shall rejoice in his works.
³² He looketh on the earth, and it trembleth:
     he toucheth the hills, and they smoke.
³³ I will sing unto the Lord as long as I live:
     I will sing praise to my God
          while I have my being.
³⁴ My meditation of him shall be sweet:
     I will be glad in the Lord.
³⁵ Let the sinners be consumed out of the earth,
     and let the wicked be no more.

Bless thou the Lord, O my soul.
Praise ye the Lord.

105

O give thanks unto the Lord;
call upon his name;
make known his deeds among the people.
2 Sing unto him, sing psalms unto him;
talk ye of all his wondrous works.
3 Glory ye in his holy name;
let the heart of them rejoice that seek the Lord.
4 Seek the Lord, and his strength;
seek his face evermore.
5 Remember his marvellous works that he hath done;
his wonders, and the judgments of his mouth;
6 O ye seed of Abraham his servant,
ye children of Jacob his chosen.
7 He is the Lord our God;
his judgments are in all the earth.
8 He hath remembered his covenant for ever,
the word which he commanded
to a thousand generations.
9 Which covenant he made with Abraham,
and his oath unto Isaac;
10 and confirmed the same unto Jacob for a law,
and to Israel for an everlasting covenant,
11 saying, 'Unto thee will I give the land of Canaan,
the lot of your inheritance,'

¹² when they were but a few men in number;
  yea, very few, and strangers in it.
¹³ When they went from one nation to another,
  from one kingdom to another people;
¹⁴ he suffered no man to do them wrong:
  yea, he reproved kings for their sakes,
¹⁵ saying, 'Touch not mine anointed,
  and do my prophets no harm.'
¹⁶ Moreover he called for a famine upon the land:
  he brake the whole staff of bread.
¹⁷ He sent a man before them,
  even Joseph, who was sold for a servant,
¹⁸ whose feet they hurt with fetters:
  he was laid in iron:
¹⁹ until the time that his word came:
  the word of the Lord tried him.
²⁰ The king sent and loosed him;
  even the ruler of the people, and let him go free.
²¹ He made him lord of his house,
  and ruler of all his substance:
²² to bind his princes at his pleasure;
  and teach his senators wisdom.
²³ Israel also came into Egypt;
  and Jacob sojourned in the land of Ham.
²⁴ And he increased his people greatly;
  and made them stronger than their enemies.
²⁵ He turned their heart to hate his people,
  to deal subtilly with his servants.

²⁶ He sent Moses his servant;
   and Aaron whom he had chosen.
²⁷ They shewed his signs among them,
   and wonders in the land of Ham.
²⁸ He sent darkness, and made it dark;
   and they rebelled not against his word.
²⁹ He turned their waters into blood,
   and slew their fish.
³⁰ Their land brought forth frogs in abundance,
   in the chambers of their kings.
³¹ He spake, and there came divers sorts of flies,
   and lice in all their coasts.
³² He gave them hail for rain,
   and flaming fire in their land.
³³ He smote their vines also and their fig trees;
   and brake the trees of their coasts.
³⁴ He spake, and the locusts came,
   and caterpillers, and that without number,
³⁵ and did eat up all the herbs in their land,
   and devoured the fruit of their ground.
³⁶ He smote also all the firstborn in their land,
   the chief of all their strength.
³⁷ He brought them forth also with silver and gold;
   and there was not one feeble person
      among their tribes.
³⁸ Egypt was glad when they departed,
   for the fear of them fell upon them.
³⁹ He spread a cloud for a covering;
   and fire to give light in the night.

⁴⁰ The people asked, and he brought quails,
　　and satisfied them with the bread of heaven.
⁴¹ He opened the rock, and the waters gushed out;
　　they ran in the dry places like a river.
⁴² For he remembered his holy promise,
　　and Abraham his servant.
⁴³ And he brought forth his people with joy,
　　and his chosen with gladness;
⁴⁴ and gave them the lands of the heathen;
　　and they inherited the labour of the people;
⁴⁵ that they might observe his statutes,
　　and keep his laws. Praise ye the Lord.

106

Praise ye the Lord.
　　O give thanks unto the Lord; for he is good;
　　for his mercy endureth for ever.
² Who can utter the mighty acts of the Lord?
　　Who can shew forth all his praise?
³ Blessed are they that keep judgment,
　　and he that doeth righteousness at all times.
⁴ Remember me, O Lord, with the favour
　　that thou bearest unto thy people:
　　　　O visit me with thy salvation,
⁵ that I may see the good of thy chosen,
　　that I may rejoice in the gladness of thy nation,
　　　　that I may glory with thine inheritance.
⁶ We have sinned with our fathers,

we have committed iniquity,
    we have done wickedly.
⁷Our fathers understood not thy wonders in Egypt;
    they remembered not the multitude
        of thy mercies;
    but provoked him at the sea,
        even at the Red sea.
⁸Nevertheless he saved them for his name's sake,
    that he might make his mighty power
        to be known.
⁹He rebuked the Red sea also, and it was dried up:
    so he led them through the depths,
        as through the wilderness.
¹⁰And he saved them from the hand of him
    that hated them, and redeemed them
        from the hand of the enemy.
¹¹And the waters covered their enemies:
    there was not one of them left.
¹²Then believed they his words;
    they sang his praise.
¹³They soon forgat his works;
    they waited not for his counsel,
¹⁴but lusted exceedingly in the wilderness,
    and tempted God in the desert.
¹⁵And he gave them their request;
    but sent leanness into their soul.
¹⁶They envied Moses also in the camp,
    and Aaron the saint of the Lord.

¹⁷ The earth opened and swallowed up Dathan,
   and covered the company of Abiram.
¹⁸ And a fire was kindled in their company;
   the flame burned up the wicked.
¹⁹ They made a calf in Horeb,
   and worshipped the molten image.
²⁰ Thus they changed their glory
   into the similitude of an ox that eateth grass.
²¹ They forgat God their saviour,
   which had done great things in Egypt;
²² wondrous works in the land of Ham,
   and terrible things by the Red sea.
²³ Therefore he said that he would destroy them,
   had not Moses his chosen stood before him
      in the breach, to turn away his wrath,
   lest he should destroy them.
²⁴ Yea, they despised the pleasant land,
   they believed not his word,
²⁵ but murmured in their tents,
   and hearkened not unto the voice of the Lord.
²⁶ Therefore he lifted up his hand against them,
   to overthrow them in the wilderness,
²⁷ to overthrow their seed also among the nations,
   and to scatter them in the lands.
²⁸ They joined themselves also unto Baal-peor,
   and ate the sacrifices of the dead.
²⁹ Thus they provoked him to anger
   with their inventions;
      and the plague brake in upon them.

³⁰ Then stood up Phinehas, and executed judgment;
and so the plague was stayed.
³¹ And that was counted unto him for righteousness
unto all generations for evermore.
³² They angered him also at the waters of strife,
so that it went ill with Moses for their sakes,
³³ because they provoked his spirit,
so that he spake unadvisedly with his lips.
³⁴ They did not destroy the nations,
concerning whom the Lord commanded them;
³⁵ but were mingled among the heathen,
and learned their works.
³⁶ And they served their idols,
which were a snare unto them.
³⁷ Yea, they sacrificed their sons
and their daughters unto devils,
³⁸ and shed innocent blood,
even the blood of their sons
and of their daughters,
whom they sacrificed unto the idols of Canaan;
and the land was polluted with blood.
³⁹ Thus were they defiled with their own works,
and went a whoring with their own inventions.
⁴⁰ Therefore was the wrath of the Lord
kindled against his people, insomuch
that he abhorred his own inheritance.
⁴¹ And he gave them into the hand of the heathen;
and they that hated them ruled over them.

⁴²Their enemies also oppressed them,
   and they were brought into subjection
      under their hand.
⁴³Many times did he deliver them;
   but they provoked him with their counsel,
      and were brought low for their iniquity.
⁴⁴Nevertheless he regarded their affliction,
   when he heard their cry;
⁴⁵and he remembered for them his covenant,
   and repented according to the multitude
      of his mercies.
⁴⁶He made them also to be pitied of all those
   that carried them captives.
⁴⁷Save us, O Lord our God,
   and gather us from among the heathen,
      to give thanks unto thy holy name,
   and to triumph in thy praise.
⁴⁸Blessed be the Lord God of Israel from everlasting
   to everlasting;
      and let all the people say, 'Amen.'
   Praise ye the Lord.

107

O Give thanks unto the Lord,
   for he is good, for his mercy endureth for ever.
²Let the redeemed of the Lord say so,
   whom he hath redeemed from the hand
      of the enemy;

³and gathered them out of the lands,
  from the east, and from the west,
    from the north, and from the south.
⁴They wandered in the wilderness in a solitary way;
  they found no city to dwell in.
⁵Hungry and thirsty,
  their soul fainted in them.
⁶Then they cried unto the Lord in their trouble,
  and he delivered them out of their distresses.
⁷And he led them forth by the right way,
  that they might go to a city of habitation.
⁸Oh that men would praise the Lord
  for his goodness,
    and for his wonderful works
  to the children of men!
⁹For he satisfieth the longing soul,
  and filleth the hungry soul with goodness.
¹⁰Such as sit in darkness and in the shadow of death,
  being bound in affliction and iron,
¹¹because they rebelled against the words of God,
  and contemned the counsel of the most High;
¹²therefore he brought down their heart with labour;
  they fell down, and there was none to help.
¹³Then they cried unto the Lord in their trouble,
  and he saved them out of their distresses.
¹⁴He brought them out of darkness
  and the shadow of death,
    and brake their bands in sunder.

[15] Oh that men would praise the Lord
   for his goodness, and for his wonderful works
      to the children of men!
[16] For he hath broken the gates of brass,
   and cut the bars of iron in sunder.
[17] Fools because of their transgression,
   and because of their iniquities, are afflicted.
[18] Their soul abhorreth all manner of meat;
   and they draw near unto the gates of death.
[19] Then they cry unto the Lord in their trouble,
   and he saveth them out of their distresses.
[20] He sent his word, and healed them,
   and delivered them from their destructions.
[21] Oh that men would praise the Lord
   for his goodness, and for his wonderful works
      to the children of men!
[22] And let them sacrifice the sacrifices
   of thanksgiving,
      and declare his works with rejoicing.
[23] They that go down to the sea in ships,
   that do business in great waters;
[24] these see the works of the Lord,
   and his wonders in the deep.
[25] For he commandeth, and raiseth the stormy wind,
   which lifteth up the waves thereof.
[26] They mount up to the heaven,
   they go down again to the depths:
      their soul is melted because of trouble.

²⁷ They reel to and fro, and stagger
  like a drunken man, and are at their wits' end.
²⁸ Then they cry unto the Lord in their trouble,
  and he bringeth them out of their distresses.
²⁹ He maketh the storm a calm,
  so that the waves thereof are still.
³⁰ Then are they glad because they be quiet;
  so he bringeth them unto their desired haven.
³¹ Oh that men would praise the Lord
  for his goodness, and for his wonderful works
    to the children of men!
³² Let them exalt him also in the congregation
  of the people, and praise him
    in the assembly of the elders.
³³ He turneth rivers into a wilderness,
  and the watersprings into dry ground,
³⁴ a fruitful land into barrenness,
  for the wickedness of them that dwell therein.
³⁵ He turneth the wilderness into a standing water,
  and dry ground into watersprings.
³⁶ And there he maketh the hungry to dwell,
  that they may prepare a city for habitation,
³⁷ and sow the fields, and plant vineyards,
  which may yield fruits of increase.
³⁸ He blesseth them also,
  so that they are multiplied greatly;
    and suffereth not their cattle to decrease.
³⁹ Again, they are minished and brought low
  through oppression, affliction, and sorrow.

⁴⁰ He poureth contempt upon princes,
  and causeth them to wander in the wilderness,
   where there is no way.
⁴¹ Yet setteth he the poor on high from affliction,
  and maketh him families like a flock.
⁴² The righteous shall see it, and rejoice;
  and all inquity shall stop her mouth.
⁴³ Whoso is wise, and will observe these things,
  even they shall understand the lovingkindness
   of the Lord.

108

A song or psalm of David.

O God, my heart is fixed;
I will sing and give praise, even with my glory.
² Awake, psaltery and harp:
  I myself will awake early.
³ I will praise thee, O Lord, among the people;
  and I will sing praises unto thee
   among the nations.
⁴ For thy mercy is great above the heavens;
  and thy truth reacheth unto the clouds.
⁵ Be thou exalted, O God, above the heavens;
  and thy glory above all the earth,
⁶ that thy beloved may be delivered:
  save with thy right hand, and answer me.
⁷ God hath spoken in his holiness;
  I will rejoice, I will divide Shechem,
   and mete out the valley of Succoth.

⁸ Gilead is mine; Manasseh is mine;
 Ephraim also is the strength of mine head;
  Judah is my lawgiver;
⁹ Moab is my washpot;
 over Edom will I cast out my shoe;
  over Philistia will I triumph.
¹⁰ Who will bring me into the strong city?
 Who will lead me into Edom?
¹¹ Wilt not thou, O God, who hast cast us off?
 And wilt not thou, O God, go forth
  with our hosts?
¹² Give us help from trouble;
 for vain is the help of man.
¹³ Through God we shall do valiantly;
 for he it is that shall tread down our enemies.

109 To the chief musician, a psalm of David.

Hold not thy peace, O God of my praise;
² for the mouth of the wicked and the mouth of the
 deceitful are opened against me:
  they have spoken against me
 with a lying tongue.
³ They compassed me about also
 with words of hatred;
  and fought against me without a cause.
⁴ For my love they are my adversaries;
 but I give myself unto prayer.

⁵And they have rewarded me evil for good,
   and hatred for my love.
⁶Set thou a wicked man over him;
   and let Satan stand at his right hand.
⁷When he shall be judged,
   let him be condemned;
      and let his prayer become sin.
⁸Let his days be few;
   and let another take his office.
⁹Let his children be fatherless;
   and his wife a widow.
¹⁰Let his children be continually vagabonds, and beg;
   let them seek their bread also
      out of their desolate places.
¹¹Let the extortioner catch all that he hath;
   and let the strangers spoil his labour.
¹²Let there be none to extend mercy unto him:
   neither let there be any to favour
      his fatherless children.
¹³Let his posterity be cut off;
   and in the generation following
      let their name be blotted out.
¹⁴Let the iniquity of his fathers be remembered
   with the Lord;
      and let not the sin of his mother
   be blotted out.
¹⁵Let them be before the Lord continually,
   that he may cut off the memory of them
      from the earth.

¹⁶ Because that he remembered not to shew mercy,
　　but persecuted the poor and needy man,
　　　　that he might even slay the broken in heart.
¹⁷ As he loved cursing, so let it come unto him:
　　as he delighted not in blessing,
　　　　so let it be far from him.
¹⁸ As he clothed himself with cursing like
　　as with his garment,
　　　　so let it come into his bowels like water,
　　and like oil into his bones.
¹⁹ Let it be unto him as the garment
　　which covereth him,
　　　　and for a girdle wherewith
　　he is girded continually.
²⁰ Let this be the reward of mine adversaries
　　from the Lord,
　　　　and of them that speak evil against my soul.
²¹ But do thou for me, O God the Lord,
　　for thy name's sake,
　　　　because thy mercy is good, deliver thou me.
²² For I am poor and needy,
　　and my heart is wounded within me.
²³ I am gone like the shadow when it declineth:
　　I am tossed up and down as the locust.
²⁴ My knees are weak through fasting;
　　and my flesh faileth of fatness.
²⁵ I became also a reproach unto them;
　　when they looked upon me
　　　　they shaked their heads.

²⁶ Help me, O Lord my God:

O save me according to thy mercy,
²⁷ that they may know that this is thy hand;

that thou, Lord, hast done it.
²⁸ Let them curse, but bless thou:

when they arise, let them be ashamed;

but let thy servant rejoice.
²⁹ Let mine adversaries be clothed with shame,

and let them cover themselves

with their own confusion, as with a mantle.
³⁰ I will greatly praise the Lord with my mouth;

yea, I will praise him among the multitude.
³¹ For he shall stand at the right hand of the poor,

to save him from those that condemn his soul.

110

A psalm of David.

The Lord said unto my Lord,

'Sit thou at my right hand,

until I make thine enemies thy footstool.'
² The Lord shall send the rod of thy strength

out of Zion: rule thou in the midst

of thine enemies.
³ Thy people shall be willing in the day of thy power,

in the beauties of holiness from the womb

of the morning:

thou hast the dew of thy youth.
⁴ The Lord hath sworn, and will not repent,

'Thou art a priest for ever after
    the order of Melchizedek.'
⁵ The Lord at thy right hand
    shall strike through kings in the day of his wrath.
⁶ He shall judge among the heathen,
    he shall fill the places with the dead bodies;
        he shall wound the heads over many countries.
⁷ He shall drink of the brook in the way;
    therefore shall he lift up the head.

111 Praise ye the Lord.
    I will praise the Lord with my whole heart,
        in the assembly of the upright,
    and in the congregation.
² The works of the Lord are great, sought out
    of all them that have pleasure therein.
³ His work is honourable and glorious;
    and his righteousness endureth for ever.
⁴ He hath made his wonderful works
    to be remembered:
        the Lord is gracious and full of compassion.
⁵ He hath given meat unto them that fear him:
    he will ever be mindful of his covenant.
⁶ He hath shewed his people the power of his works,
    that he may give them the heritage
        of the heathen.
⁷ The works of his hands are verity and judgment;
    all his commandments are sure.

⁸ They stand fast for ever and ever,
and are done in truth and uprightness.
⁹ He sent redemption unto his people:
he hath commanded his covenant for ever:
holy and reverend is his name.
¹⁰ The fear of the Lord is the beginning of wisdom:
a good understanding have all they
that do his commandments:
his praise endureth for ever.

112 Praise ye the Lord.
Blessed is the man that feareth the Lord,
that delighteth greatly in his commandments.
² His seed shall be mighty upon earth:
the generation of the upright shall be blessed.
³ Wealth and riches shall be in his house;
and his righteousness endureth for ever.
⁴ Unto the upright there ariseth light in the darkness:
he is gracious, and full of compassion,
and righteous.
⁵ A good man sheweth favour, and lendeth:
he will guide his affairs with discretion.
⁶ Surely he shall not be moved for ever:
the righteous shall be in everlasting
remembrance.
⁷ He shall not be afraid of evil tidings:
his heart is fixed, trusting in the Lord.

⁸ His heart is established, he shall not be afraid,
   until he see his desire
      upon his enemies.
⁹ He hath dispersed, he hath given to the poor;
   his righteousness endureth for ever;
      his horn shall be exalted with honour.
¹⁰ The wicked shall see it, and be grieved;
   he shall gnash with his teeth, and melt away:
      the desire of the wicked shall perish.

113

Praise ye the Lord.
   Praise, O ye servants of the Lord,
      praise the name of the Lord.
² Blessed be the name of the Lord
   from this time forth and for evermore.
³ From the rising of the sun unto the going down
   of the same the Lord's name is to be praised.
⁴ The Lord is high above all nations,
   and his glory above the heavens.
⁵ Who is like unto the Lord our God,
   who dwelleth on high,
⁶ who humbleth himself to behold the things
   that are in heaven, and in the earth!
⁷ He raiseth up the poor out of the dust,
   and lifteth the needy out of the dunghill,
⁸ that he may set him with princes,
   even with the princes of his people.

⁹ He maketh the barren woman to keep house,
    and to be a joyful mother of children.
        Praise ye the Lord.

114   When Israel went out of Egypt,
    the house of Jacob from a people
        of strange language,
² Judah was his sanctuary,
    and Israel his dominion.
³ The sea saw it, and fled:
    Jordan was driven back.
⁴ The mountains skipped like rams,
    and the little hills like lambs.
⁵ What ailed thee, O thou sea, that thou fleddest?
    Thou Jordan, that thou wast driven back?
⁶ Ye mountains, that ye skipped like rams;
    and ye little hills, like lambs?
⁷ Tremble, thou earth, at the presence of the Lord,
    at the presence of the God of Jacob,
⁸ which turned the rock into a standing water,
    the flint into a fountain of waters.

115   Not unto us, O Lord, not unto us,
    but unto thy name give glory, for thy mercy,
        and for thy truth's sake.
² Wherefore should the heathen say,
    'Where is now their God?'
³ But our God is in the heavens:

he hath done whatsoever he hath pleased.

⁴ Their idols are silver and gold,
　　the work of men's hands.

⁵ They have mouths, but they speak not:
　　eyes have they, but they see not:

⁶ they have ears, but they hear not:
　　noses have they, but they smell not:

⁷ they have hands, but they handle not:
　　feet have they, but they walk not:
　　　　neither speak they through their throat.

⁸ They that make them are like unto them;
　　so is every one that trusteth in them.

⁹ O Israel, trust thou in the Lord:
　　he is their help and their shield.

¹⁰ O house of Aaron, trust in the Lord:
　　he is their help and their shield.

¹¹ Ye that fear the Lord; trust in the Lord:
　　he is their help and their shield.

¹² The Lord hath been mindful of us:
　　he will bless us;
　　　　he will bless the house of Israel;
　　he will bless the house of Aaron.

¹³ He will bless them that fear the Lord,
　　both small and great.

¹⁴ The Lord shall increase you more and more,
　　you and your children.

¹⁵ Ye are blessed of the Lord
　　which made heaven and earth.

¹⁶ The heaven, even the heavens, are the Lord's:
　　　but the earth hath he given to the children
　　　　　of men.
¹⁷ The dead praise not the Lord,
　　　neither any that go down into silence.
¹⁸ But we will bless the Lord from this time forth
　　　and for evermore. Praise the Lord.

116

I love the Lord, because he hath heard
　　　my voice and my supplications.
² Because he hath inclined his ear unto me,
　　　therefore will I call upon him as long as I live.
³ The sorrows of death compassed me,
　　　and the pains of hell gat hold upon me:
　　　　　I found trouble and sorrow.
⁴ Then called I upon the name of the Lord:
　　　'O Lord, I beseech thee, deliver my soul.'
⁵ Gracious is the Lord, and righteous;
　　　yea, our God is merciful.
⁶ The Lord preserveth the simple:
　　　I was brought low, and he helped me.
⁷ Return unto thy rest, O my soul;
　　　for the Lord hath dealt bountifully with thee.
⁸ For thou hast delivered my soul from death,
　　　mine eyes from tears, and my feet from falling.
⁹ I will walk before the Lord
　　　in the land of the living.

¹⁰ I believed, therefore have I spoken:
    I was greatly afflicted:
¹¹ I said in my haste, 'All men are liars.'
¹² What shall I render unto the Lord
    for all his benefits toward me?
¹³ I will take the cup of salvation,
    and call upon the name of the Lord.
¹⁴ I will pay my vows unto the Lord
    now in the presence of all his people.
¹⁵ Precious in the sight of the Lord
    is the death of his saints.
¹⁶ O Lord, truly I am thy servant;
    I am thy servant, and the son of thine handmaid:
      thou hast loosed my bonds.
¹⁷ I will offer to thee the sacrifice of thanksgiving,
    and will call upon the name of the Lord.
¹⁸ I will pay my vows unto the Lord,
    now in the presence of all his people,
¹⁹ in the courts of the Lord's house,
    in the midst of thee, O Jerusalem.
      Praise ye the Lord.

117

O praise the Lord, all ye nations:
    praise him, all ye people.
² For his merciful kindness is great toward us:
    and the truth of the Lord endureth for ever.
      Praise ye the Lord.

118

O give thanks unto the Lord; for he is good,
   because his mercy endureth for ever.
2 Let Israel now say
   that his mercy endureth for ever.
3 Let the house of Aaron now say
   that his mercy endureth for ever.
4 Let them now that fear the Lord say
   that his mercy endureth for ever.
5 I called upon the Lord in distress:
   the Lord answered me,
      and set me in a large place.
6 The Lord is on my side;
   I will not fear: what can man do unto me?
7 The Lord taketh my part with them that help me;
   therefore shall I see my desire
      upon them that hate me.
8 It is better to trust in the Lord
   than to put confidence in man.
9 It is better to trust in the Lord
   than to put confidence in princes.
10 All nations compassed me about;
   but in the name of the Lord will I destroy them.
11 They compassed me about;
   yea, they compassed me about;
      but in the name of the Lord I will destroy them.
12 They compassed me about like bees;
   they are quenched as the fire of thorns,
      for in the name of the Lord

I will destroy them.
¹³ Thou hast thrust sore at me that I might fall;
   but the Lord helped me.
¹⁴ The Lord is my strength and song,
   and is become my salvation.
¹⁵ The voice of rejoicing and salvation is in the
   tabernacles of the righteous:
      the right hand of the Lord doeth valiantly.
¹⁶ The right hand of the Lord is exalted:
   the right hand of the Lord doeth valiantly.
¹⁷ I shall not die, but live,
   and declare the works of the Lord.
¹⁸ The Lord hath chastened me sore;
   but he hath not given me over unto death.
¹⁹ Open to me the gates of righteousness:
   I will go into them, and I will praise the Lord:
²⁰ this gate of the Lord, into which
   the righteous shall enter.
²¹ I will praise thee; for thou hast heard me,
   and art become my salvation.
²² The stone which the builders refused
   is become the head stone of the corner.
²³ This is the Lord's doing;
   it is marvellous in our eyes.
²⁴ This is the day which the Lord hath made;
   we will rejoice and be glad in it.
²⁵ Save now, I beseech thee, O Lord:
   O Lord, I beseech thee, send now prosperity.

²⁶ Blessed be he that cometh in the name of the Lord:
   we have blessed you out of the house of the Lord.
²⁷ God is the Lord, which hath shewed us light:
   bind the sacrifice with cords, even unto the horns
      of the altar.
²⁸ Thou art my God, and I will praise thee:
   thou art my God, I will exalt thee.
²⁹ O give thanks unto the Lord; for he is good;
   for his mercy endureth for ever.

119

ALEPH

Blessed are the undefiled in the way,
   who walk in the law of the Lord.
² Blessed are they that keep his testimonies,
   and that seek him with the whole heart.
³ They also do no iniquity: they walk in his ways.
⁴ Thou hast commanded us to keep
   thy precepts diligently.
⁵ O that my ways were directed to keep thy statutes!
⁶ Then shall I not be ashamed,
   when I have respect unto all thy commandments.
⁷ I will praise thee with uprightness of heart,
   when I shall have learned
      thy righteous judgments.
⁸ I will keep thy statutes;
   O forsake me not utterly.

BETH

9 Wherewithal shall a young man cleanse his way?
   By taking heed thereto according to thy word.
10 With my whole heart have I sought thee;
   O let me not wander from thy commandments.
11 Thy word have I hid in mine heart,
   that I might not sin against thee.
12 Blessed art thou, O Lord: teach me thy statutes.
13 With my lips have I declared
   all the judgments of thy mouth.
14 I have rejoiced in the way of thy testimonies,
   as much as in all riches.
15 I will meditate in thy precepts,
   and have respect unto thy ways.
16 I will delight myself in thy statutes;
   I will not forget thy word.

GIMEL

17 Deal bountifully with thy servant,
   that I may live, and keep thy word.
18 Open thou mine eyes, that I may behold
   wondrous things out of thy law.
19 I am a stranger in the earth:
   hide not thy commandments from me.
20 My soul breaketh for the longing that it hath unto
   thy judgments at all times.
21 Thou hast rebuked the proud that are cursed,
   which do err from thy commandments.

²² Remove from me reproach and contempt,
for I have kept thy testimonies.
²³ Princes also did sit and speak against me;
but thy servant did meditate in thy statutes.
²⁴ Thy testimonies also are my delight
and my counsellors.

DALETH

²⁵ My soul cleaveth unto the dust;
quicken thou me according to thy word.
²⁶ I have declared my ways, and thou heardest me:
teach me thy statutes.
²⁷ Make me to understand the way of thy precepts;
so shall I talk of thy wondrous works.
²⁸ My soul melteth for heaviness:
strengthen thou me according unto thy word.
²⁹ Remove from me the way of lying;
and grant me thy law graciously.
³⁰ I have chosen the way of truth:
thy judgments have I laid before me.
³¹ I have stuck unto thy testimonies:
O Lord, put me not to shame.
³² I will run the way of thy commandments,
when thou shalt enlarge my heart.

HE

³³ Teach me, O Lord, the way of thy statutes;
and I shall keep it unto the end.

[34] Give me understanding, and I shall keep thy law;
   yea, I shall observe it with my whole heart.
[35] Make me to go in the path of thy commandments;
   for therein do I delight.
[36] Incline my heart unto thy testimonies,
   and not to covetousness.
[37] Turn away mine eyes from beholding vanity;
   and quicken thou me in thy way.
[38] Stablish thy word unto thy servant,
   who is devoted to thy fear.
[39] Turn away my reproach which I fear;
   for thy judgments are good.
[40] Behold, I have longed after thy precepts:
   quicken me in thy righteousness.

VAU

[41] Let thy mercies come also unto me, O Lord,
   even thy salvation, according to thy word.
[42] So shall I have wherewith to answer him
   that reproacheth me; for I trust in thy word.
[43] And take not the word of truth utterly
   out of my mouth;
      for I have hoped in thy judgments.
[44] So shall I keep thy law continually
   for ever and ever.
[45] And I will walk at liberty; for I seek thy precepts.
[46] I will speak of thy testimonies also before kings,
   and will not be ashamed.

⁴⁷And I will delight myself in thy commandments,
  which I have loved.
⁴⁸ My hands also will I lift up
  unto thy commandments, which I have loved;
    and I will meditate in thy statutes.

ZAIN

⁴⁹ Remember the word unto thy servant,
  upon which thou hast caused me to hope.
⁵⁰ This is my comfort in my affliction;
  for thy word hath quickened me.
⁵¹ The proud have had me greatly in derision;
  yet have I not declined from thy law.
⁵² I remembered thy judgments of old, O Lord;
  and have comforted myself.
⁵³ Horror hath taken hold upon me
  because of the wicked that forsake thy law.
⁵⁴ Thy statutes have been my songs
  in the house of my pilgrimage.
⁵⁵ I have remembered thy name, O Lord,
  in the night, and have kept thy law.
⁵⁶ This I had, because I kept thy precepts.

CHETH

⁵⁷ Thou art my portion, O Lord:
  I have said that I would keep thy words.
⁵⁸ I intreated thy favour with my whole heart:
  be merciful unto me according to thy word.

⁵⁹ I thought on my ways,
    and turned my feet unto thy testimonies.
⁶⁰ I made haste,
    and delayed not to keep thy commandments.
⁶¹ The bands of the wicked have robbed me;
    but I have not forgotten thy law.
⁶² At midnight I will rise to give thanks unto thee
    because of thy righteous judgments.
⁶³ I am a companion of all them that fear thee,
    and of them that keep thy precepts.
⁶⁴ The earth, O Lord, is full of thy mercy:
    teach me thy statutes.

TETH

⁶⁵ Thou hast dealt well with thy servant, O Lord,
    according unto thy word.
⁶⁶ Teach me good judgment and knowledge;
    for I have believed thy commandments.
⁶⁷ Before I was afflicted I went astray;
    but now have I kept thy word.
⁶⁸ Thou art good, and doest good;
    teach me thy statutes.
⁶⁹ The proud have forged a lie against me;
    but I will keep thy precepts with my whole heart.
⁷⁰ Their heart is as fat as grease;
    but I delight in thy law.
⁷¹ It is good for me that I have been afflicted;
    that I might learn thy statutes.

⁷² The law of thy mouth is better unto me
     than thousands of gold and silver.

JOD

⁷³ Thy hands have made me and fashioned me:
     give me understanding,
          that I may learn thy commandments.
⁷⁴ They that fear thee will be glad when they see me;
     because I have hoped in thy word.
⁷⁵ I know, O Lord, that thy judgments are right,
     and that thou in faithfulness hast afflicted me.
⁷⁶ Let, I pray thee, thy merciful kindness
     be for my comfort,
          according to thy word unto thy servant.
⁷⁷ Let thy tender mercies come unto me,
     that I may live; for thy law is my delight.
⁷⁸ Let the proud be ashamed;
     for they dealt perversely with me
          without a cause;
     but I will meditate in thy precepts.
⁷⁹ Let those that fear thee turn unto me,
     and those that have known thy testimonies.
⁸⁰ Let my heart be sound in thy statutes;
     that I be not ashamed.

CAPH

⁸¹ My soul fainteth for thy salvation;
     but I hope in thy word.

82 Mine eyes fail for thy word, saying,
'When wilt thou comfort me?'
83 For I am become like a bottle in the smoke;
yet do I not forget thy statutes.
84 How many are the days of thy servant?
When wilt thou execute judgment on them
that persecute me?
85 The proud have digged pits for me,
which are not after thy law.
86 All thy commandments are faithful;
they persecute me wrongfully;
help thou me.
87 They had almost consumed me upon earth;
but I forsook not thy precepts.
88 Quicken me after thy lovingkindness;
so shall I keep the testimony of thy mouth.

LAMED

89 For ever, O Lord, thy word is settled in heaven.
90 Thy faithfulness is unto all generations:
thou hast established the earth, and it abideth.
91 They continue this day according to
thine ordinances; for all are thy servants.
92 Unless thy law had been my delights,
I should then have perished in mine affliction.
93 I will never forget thy precepts;
for with them thou hast quickened me.
94 I am thine, save me;
for I have sought thy precepts.

⁹⁵ The wicked have waited for me to destroy me;
  but I will consider thy testimonies.
⁹⁶ I have seen an end of all perfection;
  but thy commandment is exceeding broad.

MEM

⁹⁷ O how love I thy law!
  It is my meditation all the day.
⁹⁸ Thou through thy commandments hast made
  me wiser than mine enemies;
    for they are ever with me.
⁹⁹ I have more understanding than all my teachers;
  for thy testimonies are my meditation.
¹⁰⁰ I understand more than the ancients,
  because I keep thy precepts.
¹⁰¹ I have refrained my feet from every evil way,
  that I might keep thy word.
¹⁰² I have not departed from thy judgments;
  for thou hast taught me.
¹⁰³ How sweet are thy words unto my taste!
  Yea, sweeter than honey to my mouth!
¹⁰⁴ Through thy precepts I get understanding;
  therefore I hate every false way.

NUN

¹⁰⁵ Thy word is a lamp unto my feet,
  and a light unto my path.
¹⁰⁶ I have sworn, and I will perform it,
  that I will keep thy righteous judgments.

¹⁰⁷ I am afflicted very much: quicken me, O Lord,
   according unto thy word.
¹⁰⁸ Accept, I beseech thee,
     the freewill offerings of my mouth, O Lord,
       and teach me thy judgments.
¹⁰⁹ My soul is continually in my hand;
     yet do I not forget thy law.
¹¹⁰ The wicked have laid a snare for me;
     yet I erred not from thy precepts.
¹¹¹ Thy testimonies have I taken as an heritage for ever;
     for they are the rejoicing of my heart.
¹¹² I have inclined mine heart to perform thy statutes
     alway, even unto the end.

SAMECH

¹¹³ I hate vain thoughts; but thy law do I love.
¹¹⁴ Thou art my hiding place and my shield:
     I hope in thy word.
¹¹⁵ Depart from me, ye evildoers;
     for I will keep the commandments of my God.
¹¹⁶ Uphold me according unto thy word,
     that I may live;
       and let me not be ashamed of my hope.
¹¹⁷ Hold thou me up, and I shall be safe;
     and I will have respect unto thy statutes
       continually.
¹¹⁸ Thou hast trodden down all them that err
     from thy statutes; for their deceit is falsehood.

119 Thou puttest away all the wicked of the earth
    like dross; therefore I love thy testimonies.
120 My flesh trembleth for fear of thee;
    and I am afraid of thy judgments.

AIN

121 I have done judgment and justice:
    leave me not to mine oppressors.
122 Be surety for thy servant for good:
    let not the proud oppress me.
123 Mine eyes fail for thy salvation,
    and for the word of thy righteousness.
124 Deal with thy servant according unto thy mercy,
    and teach me thy statutes.
125 I am thy servant; give me understanding,
    that I may know thy testimonies.
126 It is time for thee, Lord, to work;
    for they have made void thy law.
127 Therefore I love thy commandments above gold;
    yea, above fine gold.
128 Therefore I esteem all thy precepts concerning
    all things to be right;
        and I hate every false way.

PE

129 Thy testimonies are wonderful;
    therefore doth my soul keep them.
130 The entrance of thy words giveth light;

it giveth understanding unto the simple.

¹³¹ I opened my mouth, and panted;
for I longed for thy commandments.

¹³² Look thou upon me, and be merciful unto me,
as thou usest to do unto those
that love thy name.

¹³³ Order my steps in thy word;
and let not any iniquity have dominion over me.

¹³⁴ Deliver me from the oppression of man:
so will I keep thy precepts.

¹³⁵ Make thy face to shine upon thy servant;
and teach me thy statutes.

¹³⁶ Rivers of waters run down mine eyes,
because they keep not thy law.

TZADDI

¹³⁷ Righteous art thou, O Lord,
and upright are thy judgments.

¹³⁸ Thy testimonies that thou hast commanded
are righteous and very faithful.

¹³⁹ My zeal hath consumed me,
because mine enemies have forgotten thy words.

¹⁴⁰ Thy word is very pure;
therefore thy servant loveth it.

¹⁴¹ I am small and despised;
yet do not I forget thy precepts.

¹⁴² Thy righteousness is an everlasting righteousness,
and thy law is the truth.

¹⁴³ Trouble and anguish have taken hold on me;
　　yet thy commandments are my delights.
¹⁴⁴ The righteousness of thy testimonies is everlasting:
　　give me understanding, and I shall live.

KOPH

¹⁴⁵ I cried with my whole heart;
　　hear me, O Lord: I will keep thy statutes.
¹⁴⁶ I cried unto thee;
　　save me, and I shall keep thy testimonies.
¹⁴⁷ I prevented the dawning of the morning,
　　and cried: 'I hoped in thy word.'
¹⁴⁸ Mine eyes prevent the night watches,
　　that I might meditate in thy word.
¹⁴⁹ Hear my voice according unto thy lovingkindness:
　　'O Lord, quicken me according to thy judgment.'
¹⁵⁰ They draw nigh that follow after mischief:
　　they are far from thy law.
¹⁵¹ Thou art near, O Lord;
　　and all thy commandments are truth.
¹⁵² Concerning thy testimonies,
　　I have known of old that thou hast founded
　　　them for ever.

RESH

¹⁵³ Consider mine affliction, and deliver me;
　　for I do not forget thy law.
¹⁵⁴ Plead my cause, and deliver me:
　　quicken me according to thy word.

¹⁵⁵ Salvation is far from the wicked;
    for they seek not thy statutes.
¹⁵⁶ Great are thy tender mercies, O Lord:
    quicken me according to thy judgments.
¹⁵⁷ Many are my persecutors and mine enemies;
    yet do I not decline from thy testimonies.
¹⁵⁸ I beheld the transgressors, and was grieved;
    because they kept not thy word.
¹⁵⁹ Consider how I love thy precepts:
    quicken me, O Lord, according to thy
        lovingkindness.
¹⁶⁰ Thy word is true from the beginning;
    and every one of thy righteous judgments
        endureth for ever.

SCHIN

¹⁶¹ Princes have persecuted me without a cause;
    but my heart standeth in awe of thy word.
¹⁶² I rejoice at thy word,
    as one that findeth great spoil.
¹⁶³ I hate and abhor lying;
    but thy law do I love.
¹⁶⁴ Seven times a day do I praise thee
    because of thy righteous judgments.
¹⁶⁵ Great peace have they which love thy law;
    and nothing shall offend them.
¹⁶⁶ Lord, I have hoped for thy salvation,
    and done thy commandments.

¹⁶⁷ My soul hath kept thy testimonies;
and I love them exceedingly.
¹⁶⁸ I have kept thy precepts and thy testimonies;
for all my ways are before thee.

TAU

¹⁶⁹ Let my cry come near before thee, O Lord:
give me understanding according to thy word.
¹⁷⁰ Let my supplication come before thee:
deliver me according to thy word.
¹⁷¹ My lips shall utter praise,
when thou hast taught me thy statutes.
¹⁷² My tongue shall speak of thy word;
for all thy commandments are righteousness.
¹⁷³ Let thine hand help me;
for I have chosen thy precepts.
¹⁷⁴ I have longed for thy salvation, O Lord;
and thy law is my delight.
¹⁷⁵ Let my soul live, and it shall praise thee;
and let thy judgments help me.
¹⁷⁶ I have gone astray like a lost sheep;
seek thy servant;
for I do not forget thy commandments.

120

A song of degrees.

In my distress I cried unto the Lord,
and he heard me,

² 'Deliver my soul, O Lord,
   from lying lips, and from a deceitful tongue.'
³ What shall be given unto thee?
   Or what shall be done unto thee,
      thou false tongue?
⁴ Sharp arrows of the mighty,
   with coals of juniper.
⁵ Woe is me, that I sojourn in Mesech,
   that I dwell in the tents of Kedar!
⁶ My soul hath long dwelt with him
   that hateth peace.
⁷ I am for peace;
   but when I speak, they are for war.

121

A song of degrees.

I will lift up mine eyes unto the hills,
   from whence cometh my help.
² My help cometh from the Lord,
   which made heaven and earth.
³ He will not suffer thy foot to be moved:
   he that keepeth thee will not slumber.
⁴ Behold, he that keepeth Israel shall neither
   slumber nor sleep.
⁵ The Lord is thy keeper:
   the Lord is thy shade upon thy right hand.
⁶ The sun shall not smite thee by day,
   nor the moon by night.

⁷ The Lord shall preserve thee from all evil:
    he shall preserve thy soul.
⁸ The Lord shall preserve thy going out
    and thy coming in from this time forth,
        and even for evermore.

122

A song of degrees of David.

I was glad when they said unto me,
    'Let us go into the house of the Lord.'
² Our feet shall stand within thy gates,
    O Jerusalem.
³ Jerusalem is builded as a city
    that is compact together.
⁴ Whither the tribes go up, the tribes of the Lord,
    unto the testimony of Israel,
        to give thanks unto the name of the Lord.
⁵ For there are set thrones of judgment,
    the thrones of the house of David.
⁶ Pray for the peace of Jerusalem:
    they shall prosper that love thee.
⁷ Peace be within thy walls,
    and prosperity within thy palaces.
⁸ For my brethren and companions' sakes,
    I will now say, 'Peace be within thee.'
⁹ Because of the house of the Lord our God
    I will seek thy good.

123

A song of degrees.

Unto thee lift I up mine eyes,
 O thou that dwellest
in the heavens.
² Behold, as the eyes of servants look
 unto the hand of their masters,
  and as the eyes of a maiden
 unto the hand of her mistress;
  so our eyes wait upon the Lord our God,
 until that he have mercy upon us.
³ Have mercy upon us, O Lord,
 have mercy upon us;
  for we are exceedingly filled with contempt.
⁴ Our soul is exceedingly filled with
 the scorning of those that are at ease,
  and with the contempt of the proud.

124

A song of degrees of David.

If it had not been the Lord who was on our side,
 now may Israel say;
² if it had not been the Lord who was on our side,
 when men rose up against us,
³ then they had swallowed us up quick,
 when their wrath was kindled against us;
⁴ then the waters had overwhelmed us,
 the stream had gone over our soul;

⁵ then the proud waters had gone over our soul.
⁶ Blessed be the Lord,
　　who hath not given us as a prey to their teeth.
⁷ Our soul is escaped as a bird out of the snare
　　of the fowlers:
　　　　the snare is broken, and we are escaped.
⁸ Our help is in the name of the Lord,
　　who made heaven and earth.

125

A song of degrees.

They that trust in the Lord shall be as mount Zion,
which cannot be removed,
　　but abideth for ever.
² As the mountains are round about Jerusalem,
　　so the Lord is round about his people
　　from henceforth even for ever.
³ For the rod of the wicked shall not rest
　　upon the lot of the righteous;
　　　　lest the righteous put forth their hands
　　unto iniquity.
⁴ Do good, O Lord, unto those that be good,
　　and to them that are upright in their hearts.
⁵ As for such as turn aside unto their crooked ways,
　　the Lord shall lead them forth
　　　　with the workers of iniquity;
　　but peace shall be upon Israel.

126 A song of degrees.

When the Lord turned again the captivity of Zion,
we were like them that dream.
² Then was our mouth filled with laughter,
and our tongue with singing;
then said they among the heathen,
'The Lord hath done great things for them.'
³ The Lord hath done great things for us;
whereof we are glad.
⁴ Turn again our captivity, O Lord,
as the streams in the south.
⁵ They that sow in tears shall reap in joy.
⁶ He that goeth forth and weepeth,
bearing precious seed,
shall doubtless come again with rejoicing,
bringing his sheaves with him.

127 A song of degrees for Solomon.

Except the Lord build the house,
they labour in vain that build it;
except the Lord keep the city,
the watchman waketh but in vain.
² It is vain for you to rise up early,
to sit up late, to eat the bread of sorrows;
for so he giveth his beloved sleep.

³ Lo, children are an heritage of the Lord;
    and the fruit of the womb
        is his reward.
⁴ As arrows are in the hand of a mighty man;
    so are children of the youth.
⁵ Happy is the man that hath his quiver full of them:
    they shall not be ashamed,
        but they shall speak with the enemies
    in the gate.

128

A song of degrees.

Blessed is every one that feareth the Lord;
    that walketh in his ways.
² For thou shalt eat the labour of thine hands:
    happy shalt thou be,
        and it shall be well with thee.
³ Thy wife shall be as a fruitful vine by the sides
    of thine house: thy children like olive plants
        round about thy table.
⁴ Behold, that thus shall the man be blessed
    that feareth the Lord.
⁵ The Lord shall bless thee out of Zion;
    and thou shalt see the good of Jerusalem
        all the days of thy life.
⁶ Yea, thou shalt see thy children's children,
    and peace upon Israel.

129

A song of degrees.

'Many a time have they afflicted me
   from my youth,'
may Israel now say:

2 'Many a time have they afflicted me
   from my youth;
      yet they have not prevailed against me.

3 The plowers plowed upon my back:
   they made long their furrows.'

4 The Lord is righteous:
   he hath cut asunder the cords of the wicked.

5 Let them all be confounded and turned back
   that hate Zion.

6 Let them be as the grass upon the housetops,
   which withereth afore it groweth up;

7 wherewith the mower filleth not his hand;
   nor he that bindeth sheaves his bosom.

8 Neither do they which go by say,
   'The blessing of the Lord be upon you:
      we bless you in the name of the Lord.'

130

A song of degrees.

Out of the depths have I cried unto thee, O Lord.

2 Lord, hear my voice: let thine ears be attentive
   to the voice of my supplications.

³ If thou, Lord, shouldest mark inquities,
    O Lord, who shall stand?
⁴ But there is forgiveness with thee,
    that thou mayest be feared.
⁵ I wait for the Lord, my soul doth wait,
    and in his word do I hope.
⁶ My soul waiteth for the Lord more than they that
    watch for the morning:
        I say, more than they that watch
    for the morning.
⁷ Let Israel hope in the Lord;
    for with the Lord there is mercy,
        and with him is plenteous redemption.
⁸ And he shall redeem Israel
    from all his iniquities.

131

A song of degrees of David.

Lord, my heart is not haughty, nor mine eyes lofty;
    neither do I exercise myself in great matters,
or in things too high for me.
² Surely I have behaved and quieted myself,
    as a child that is weaned of his mother:
        my soul is even as a weaned child.
³ Let Israel hope in the Lord from henceforth
    and for ever.

132

A song of degrees.

Lord, remember David, and all his afflictions:
2 how he sware unto the Lord,
    and vowed unto the mighty God of Jacob;
3 surely I will not come into the tabernacle
    of my house, nor go up into my bed;
4 I will not give sleep to mine eyes,
    or slumber to mine eyelids,
5 until I find out a place for the Lord,
    an habitation for the mighty God of Jacob.
6 Lo, we heard of it at Ephratah:
    we found it in the fields of the wood.
7 'We will go into his tabernacles:
    we will worship at his footstool.'
8 Arise, O Lord, into thy rest;
    thou, and the ark of thy strength.
9 Let thy priests be clothed with righteousness;
    and let thy saints shout for joy.
10 For thy servant David's sake
    turn not away the face of thine anointed.
11 The Lord hath sworn in truth unto David;
    he will not turn from it:
        'Of the fruit of thy body will I set upon
    thy throne.
12 If thy children will keep my covenant
    and my testimony that I shall teach them,
        their children shall also sit upon
    thy throne for evermore.'

¹³ For the Lord hath chosen Zion;
  he hath desired it for his habitation.
¹⁴ This is my rest for ever:
  here will I dwell;
    for I have desired it.
¹⁵ I will abundantly bless her provision:
  I will satisfy her poor with bread.
¹⁶ I will also clothe her priests with salvation;
  and her saints shall shout aloud for joy.
¹⁷ There will I make the horn of David to bud:
  I have ordained a lamp for mine anointed.
¹⁸ His enemies will I clothe with shame;
  but upon himself
    shall his crown flourish.

133

A song of degrees of David.

Behold, how good and how pleasant it is
  for brethren to dwell together in unity!
² It is like the precious ointment upon the head,
  that ran down upon the beard,
    even Aaron's beard;
  that went down to the skirts of his garments;
³ as the dew of Hermon,
  and as the dew that descended upon
    the mountains of Zion;
  for there the Lord commanded the blessing,
    even life for evermore.

134

A song of degrees.

Behold, bless ye the Lord,
　　all ye servants of the Lord,
　which by night stand in the house of the Lord.
² Lift up your hands in the sanctuary,
　　and bless the Lord.
³ The Lord that made heaven and earth
　　bless thee out of Zion.

135

Praise ye the Lord.
　　Praise ye the name of the Lord; praise him,
　O ye servants of the Lord.
² Ye that stand in the house of the Lord,
　　in the courts of the house of our God,
³ praise the Lord, for the Lord is good;
　　sing praises unto his name, for it is pleasant.
⁴ For the Lord hath chosen Jacob unto himself,
　　and Israel for his peculiar treasure.
⁵ For I know that the Lord is great,
　　and that our Lord is above all gods.
⁶ Whatsoever the Lord pleased,
　　that did he in heaven, and in earth,
　　　in the seas, and all deep places.
⁷ He causeth the vapours to ascend from
　　the ends of the earth;
　　　he maketh lightnings for the rain;
　　he bringeth the wind out of his treasuries.

⁸ Who smote the firstborn of Egypt,
   both of man and beast.

⁹ Who sent tokens and wonders into the midst
   of thee, O Egypt, upon Pharaoh,
      and upon all his servants.

¹⁰ Who smote great nations, and slew mighty kings;

¹¹ Sihon king of the Amorites, and Og king of Bashan,
   and all the kingdoms of Canaan;

¹² and gave their land for an heritage,
   an heritage unto Israel his people.

¹³ Thy name, O Lord, endureth for ever;
   and thy memorial, O Lord,
      throughout all generations.

¹⁴ For the Lord will judge his people,
   and he will repent himself concerning
      his servants.

¹⁵ The idols of the heathen are silver and gold,
   the work of men's hands.

¹⁶ They have mouths, but they speak not;
   eyes have they, but they see not;

¹⁷ they have ears, but they hear not;
   neither is there any breath in their mouths.

¹⁸ They that make them are like unto them:
   so is every one that trusteth in them.

¹⁹ Bless the Lord, O house of Israel;
   bless the Lord, O house of Aaron;

²⁰ bless the Lord, O house of Levi;
   ye that fear the Lord, bless the Lord.

²¹ Blessed be the Lord out of Zion,
>> which dwelleth at Jerusalem.
>>> Praise ye the Lord.

136

O Give thanks unto the Lord; for he is good;
> for his mercy endureth for ever.
² O give thanks unto the God of gods;
> for his mercy endureth for ever.
³ O give thanks to the Lord of lords;
> for his mercy endureth for ever.
⁴ To him who alone doeth great wonders;
> for his mercy endureth for ever.
⁵ To him that by wisdom made the heavens;
> for his mercy endureth for ever.
⁶ To him that stretched out the earth
> above the waters;
>> for his mercy endureth for ever.
⁷ To him that made great lights;
> for his mercy endureth for ever:
⁸ the sun to rule by day;
> for his mercy endureth for ever:
⁹ the moon and stars to rule by night;
> for his mercy endureth for ever.
¹⁰ To him that smote Egypt in their firstborn;
> for his mercy endureth for ever;
¹¹ and brought out Israel from among them;
> for his mercy endureth for ever;

¹² with a strong hand, and with a stretched out arm;
   for his mercy endureth for ever.
¹³ To him which divided the Red sea into parts;
   for his mercy endureth for ever;
¹⁴ and made Israel to pass through the midst of it;
   for his mercy endureth for ever;
¹⁵ but overthrew Pharaoh and his host in the Red sea;
   for his mercy endureth for ever.
¹⁶ To him which led his people
   through the wilderness;
      for his mercy endureth for ever.
¹⁷ To him which smote great kings;
   for his mercy endureth for ever;
¹⁸ and slew famous kings;
   for his mercy endureth for ever;
¹⁹ Sihon king of the Amorites;
   for his mercy endureth for ever;
²⁰ and Og the king of Bashan;
   for his mercy endureth for ever;
²¹ and gave their land for an heritage;
   for his mercy endureth for ever;
²² even an heritage unto Israel his servant;
   for his mercy endureth for ever.
²³ Who remembered us in our low estate;
   for his mercy endureth for ever;
²⁴ and hath redeemed us from our enemies;
   for his mercy endureth for ever.
²⁵ Who giveth food to all flesh;

for his mercy endureth for ever.
²⁶ O give thanks unto the God of heaven;
for his mercy endureth for ever.

137 By the rivers of Babylon, there we sat down,
yea, we wept, when we remembered Zion.
² We hanged our harps upon the willows
in the midst thereof.
³ For there they that carried us away captive
required of us a song;
and they that wasted us required of us mirth,
saying, 'Sing us one of the songs of Zion.'
⁴ How shall we sing the Lord's song
in a strange land?
⁵ If I forget thee, O Jerusalem,
let my right hand forget her cunning.
⁶ If I do not remember thee,
let my tongue cleave to the roof of my mouth;
if I prefer not Jerusalem above my chief joy.
⁷ Remember, O Lord,
the children of Edom in the day of Jerusalem;
who said, 'Rase it, rase it,
even to the foundation thereof.'
⁸ O daughter of Babylon, who art to be destroyed;
happy shall he be, that rewardeth thee
as thou hast served us.

⁹Happy shall he be,
 that taketh and dasheth thy little ones
  against the stones.

138   A psalm of David.

I will praise thee with my whole heart:
 before the gods will I sing praise unto thee.
²I will worship toward thy holy temple,
 and praise thy name for thy loving-kindness
  and for thy truth;
 for thou hast magnified thy word above
  all thy name.
³In the day when I cried thou answeredst me,
 and strengthenedst me with strength
  in my soul.
⁴All the kings of the earth shall praise thee, O Lord,
 when they hear the words of thy mouth.
⁵Yea, they shall sing in the ways of the Lord;
 for great is the glory of the Lord.
⁶Though the Lord be high,
 yet hath he respect unto the lowly;
  but the proud he knoweth afar off.
⁷Though I walk in the midst of trouble,
 thou wilt revive me;
  thou shalt stretch forth thine hand
 against the wrath of mine enemies,
  and thy right hand shall save me.

⁸ The Lord will perfect that which concerneth me:
thy mercy, O Lord, endureth for ever:
forsake not the works of thine own hands.

139

To the chief musician, a psalm of David.

O Lord, thou hast searched me,
and known me.
² Thou knowest my downsitting and mine uprising,
thou understandest my thought afar off.
³ Thou compassest my path and my lying down,
and art acquainted with all my ways.
⁴ For there is not a word in my tongue,
but, lo, O Lord, thou knowest it altogether.
⁵ Thou hast beset me behind and before,
and laid thine hand upon me.
⁶ Such knowledge is too wonderful for me;
it is high, I cannot attain unto it.
⁷ Whither shall I go from thy spirit?
Or whither shall I flee from thy presence?
⁸ If I ascend up into heaven, thou art there:
if I make my bed in hell, behold, thou art there.
⁹ If I take the wings of the morning,
and dwell in the uttermost parts of the sea;
¹⁰ even there shall thy hand lead me,
and thy right hand shall hold me.
¹¹ If I say, 'Surely the darkness shall cover me;
even the night shall be light about me.'

¹² Yea, the darkness hideth not from thee;
　　but the night shineth as the day;
　　　　the darkness and the light are both
　　alike to thee.
¹³ For thou hast possessed my reins:
　　thou hast covered me in my mother's womb.
¹⁴ I will praise thee;
　　for I am fearfully and wonderfully made;
　　　　marvellous are thy works;
　　and that my soul knoweth right well.
¹⁵ My substance was not hid from thee,
　　when I was made in secret,
　　　　and curiously wrought in the lowest parts
　　of the earth.
¹⁶ Thine eyes did see my substance,
　　yet being unperfect; and in thy book
　　　　all my members were written,
　　which in continuance were fashioned when as
　　　　yet there was none of them.
¹⁷ How precious also are thy thoughts unto me,
　　O God! How great is the sum of them!
¹⁸ If I should count them, they are more in number
　　than the sand:
　　　　when I awake, I am still with thee.
¹⁹ Surely thou wilt slay the wicked, O God:
　　depart from me therefore, ye bloody men.
²⁰ For they speak against thee wickedly,
　　and thine enemies take thy name in vain.

²¹ Do not I hate them, O Lord, that hate thee?
  And am not I grieved with those that rise up
    against thee?
²² I hate them with perfect hatred:
  I count them mine enemies.
²³ Search me, O God, and know my heart:
  try me, and know my thoughts:
²⁴ and see if there be any wicked way in me,
  and lead me in the way everlasting.

140

To the chief musician, a psalm of David.

Deliver me, O Lord, from the evil man:
  preserve me from the violent man;
² which imagine mischiefs in their heart;
  continually are they gathered together for war.
³ They have sharpened their tongues like a serpent;
  adders' poison is under their lips. Selah.
⁴ Keep me, O Lord, from the hands of the wicked;
  preserve me from the violent man;
    who have purposed to overthrow my goings.
⁵ The proud have hid a snare for me, and cords;
  they have spread a net by the wayside;
    they have set gins for me. Selah.
⁶ I said unto the Lord, 'Thou art my God:
    hear the voice of my supplications, O Lord.'
⁷ O God the Lord, the strength of my salvation,
  thou hast covered my head
    in the day of battle.

⁸ Grant not, O Lord, the desires of the wicked:
　　further not his wicked device;
　　　　lest they exalt themselves. Selah.
⁹ As for the head of those that compass me about,
　　let the mischief of their own lips cover them.
¹⁰ Let burning coals fall upon them;
　　let them be cast into the fire;
　　　　into deep pits, that they rise not up again.
¹¹ Let not an evil speaker be established in the earth:
　　evil shall hunt the violent man to overthrow him.
¹² I know that the Lord will maintain
　　the cause of the afflicted, and the right
　　　　of the poor.
¹³ Surely the righteous shall give thanks
　　unto thy name:
　　　　the upright shall dwell in thy presence.

141

A psalm of David.

Lord, I cry unto thee: make haste unto me;
　　give ear unto my voice,
when I cry unto thee.
² Let my prayer be set forth before thee as incense;
　　and the lifting up of my hands
　　　　as the evening sacrifice.
³ Set a watch, O Lord, before my mouth;
　　keep the door of my lips.
⁴ Incline not my heart to any evil thing,

to practise wicked works with men
that work iniquity;
and let me not eat of their dainties.

⁵ Let the righteous smite me;
it shall be a kindness; and let him reprove me;
it shall be an excellent oil,
which shall not break my head;
for yet my prayer also
shall be in their calamities.

⁶ When their judges are overthrown in stony places,
they shall hear my words; for they are sweet.

⁷ Our bones are scattered at the grave's mouth,
as when one cutteth and cleaveth wood
upon the earth.

⁸ But mine eyes are unto thee, O God the Lord:
in thee is my trust; leave not my soul destitute.

⁹ Keep me from the snares
which they have laid for me,
and the gins of the workers of iniquity.

¹⁰ Let the wicked fall into their own nets,
whilst that I withal escape.

142

Maschil of David; a prayer when he was
in the cave.

I cried unto the Lord with my voice;
with my voice unto the Lord
did I make my supplication.

² I poured out my complaint before him;
   I shewed before him my trouble.
³ When my spirit was overwhelmed within me,
   then thou knewest my path.
      In the way wherein I walked
      have they privily laid a snare for me.
⁴ I looked on my right hand, and beheld,
   but there was no man that would know me;
      refuge failed me;
      no man cared for my soul.
⁵ I cried unto thee, O Lord; I said,
   'Thou art my refuge and my portion
      in the land of the living.'
⁶ Attend unto my cry; for I am brought very low;
   deliver me from my persecutors;
      for they are stronger than I.
⁷ Bring my soul out of prison, that I may praise
   thy name;
      the righteous shall compass me about;
      for thou shalt deal bountifully with me.

143 A psalm of David.

Hear my prayer, O Lord,
   give ear to my supplications:
in thy faithfulness answer me,
   and in thy righteousness.

²And enter not into judgment with thy servant;
    for in thy sight shall no man living
        be justified.
³For the enemy hath persecuted my soul;
    he hath smitten my life down to the ground;
        he hath made me to dwell in darkness,
    as those that have been long dead.
⁴Therefore is my spirit overwhelmed within me;
    my heart within me is desolate.
⁵I remember the days of old;
    I meditate on all thy works;
        I muse on the work of thy hands.
⁶I stretch forth my hands unto thee:
    my soul thirsteth after thee,
        as a thirsty land. Selah.
⁷Hear me speedily, O Lord: my spirit faileth:
    hide not thy face from me, lest I be like unto
        them that go down into the pit.
⁸Cause me to hear thy lovingkindness in
    the morning; for in thee do I trust:
        cause me to know the way wherein
    I should walk; for I lift up my soul
        unto thee.
⁹Deliver me, O Lord, from mine enemies:
    I flee unto thee to hide me.
¹⁰Teach me to do thy will;
    for thou art my God: thy spirit is good;
        lead me into the land of uprightness.

¹¹ Quicken me, O Lord, for thy name's sake;
    for thy righteousness' sake bring my soul
        out of trouble.
¹² And of thy mercy cut off mine enemies,
    and destroy all them that afflict my soul;
        for I am thy servant.

144

A psalm of David.

Blessed be the Lord my strength,
    which teacheth my hands to war,
and my fingers to fight:
² my goodness, and my fortress;
    my high tower, and my deliverer;
        my shield, and he in whom I trust;
who subdueth my people under me.
³ Lord, what is man,
    that thou takest knowledge of him!
        Or the son of man, that thou makest
account of him!
⁴ Man is like to vanity:
    his days are as a shadow
        that passeth away.
⁵ Bow thy heavens, O Lord, and come down:
    touch the mountains, and they shall smoke.
⁶ Cast forth lightning, and scatter them:
    shoot out thine arrows, and destroy them.

⁷ Send thine hand from above;
   rid me, and deliver me out of great waters,
      from the hand of strange children;
⁸ whose mouth speaketh vanity,
   and their right hand is a right hand of falsehood.
⁹ I will sing a new song unto thee, O God:
   upon a psaltery and an instrument of ten strings
      will I sing praises unto thee.
¹⁰ It is he that giveth salvation unto kings,
   who delivereth David his servant from
      the hurtful sword.
¹¹ Rid me, and deliver me from the hand
   of strange children, whose mouth speaketh vanity,
      and their right hand is a right hand of
   falsehood.
¹² That our sons may be as plants grown up
   in their youth;
      that our daughters may be as corner stones,
   polished after the similitude of a palace;
¹³ that our garners may be full,
   affording all manner of store;
      that our sheep may bring forth thousands
   and ten thousands in our streets;
¹⁴ that our oxen may be strong to labour;
   that there be no breaking in, nor going out;
      that there be no complaining in our streets.
¹⁵ Happy is that people, that is in such a case;
   yea, happy is that people, whose God is the Lord.

145

David's psalm of praise.

I will extol thee, my God, O king;
  and I will bless thy name for ever and ever.
[2] Every day will I bless thee;
  and I will praise thy name for ever and ever.
[3] Great is the Lord, and greatly to be praised;
  and his greatness is unsearchable.
[4] One generation shall praise thy works to another,
  and shall declare thy mighty acts.
[5] I will speak of the glorious honour of thy majesty,
  and of thy wondrous works.
[6] And men shall speak of the might
  of thy terrible acts;
    and I will declare thy greatness.
[7] They shall abundantly utter the memory
  of thy great goodness,
    and shall sing of thy righteousness.
[8] The Lord is gracious, and full of compassion;
  slow to anger, and of great mercy.
[9] The Lord is good to all;
  and his tender mercies are over all his works.
[10] All thy works shall praise thee, O Lord;
  and thy saints shall bless thee.
[11] They shall speak of the glory of thy kingdom,
  and talk of thy power;
[12] to make known to the sons of men his mighty acts,
  and the glorious majesty of his kingdom.

[13] Thy kingdom is an everlasting kingdom,
and thy dominion endureth throughout
all generations.
[14] The Lord upholdeth all that fall,
and raiseth up all those that be bowed down.
[15] The eyes of all wait upon thee;
and thou givest them their meat in due season.
[16] Thou openest thine hand,
and satisfiest the desire of every living thing.
[17] The Lord is righteous in all his ways,
and holy in all his works.
[18] The Lord is nigh unto all them that call upon him,
to all that call upon him in truth.
[19] He will fulfil the desire of them that fear him;
he also will hear their cry, and will save them.
[20] The Lord preserveth all them that love him;
but all the wicked will he destroy.
[21] My mouth shall speak the praise of the Lord;
and let all flesh bless his holy name
for ever and ever.

146

Praise ye the Lord. Praise the Lord, O my soul.
[2] While I live will I praise the Lord:
I will sing praises unto my God while I have
any being.
[3] Put not your trust in princes, nor in
the son of man, in whom there is no help.

⁴ His breath goeth forth, he returneth to his earth;
in that very day his thoughts perish.
⁵ Happy is he that hath the God of Jacob for his help,
whose hope is in the Lord his God,
⁶ which made heaven, and earth, the sea,
and all that therein is;
which keepeth truth for ever;
⁷ which executeth judgment for the oppressed;
which giveth food to the hungry.
The Lord looseth the prisoners.
⁸ The Lord openeth the eyes of the blind;
the Lord raiseth them that are bowed down;
the Lord loveth the righteous;
⁹ the Lord preserveth the strangers;
he relieveth the fatherless and widow;
but the way of the wicked
he turneth upside down.
¹⁰ The Lord shall reign for ever,
even thy God, O Zion, unto all generations.
Praise ye the Lord.

147

Praise ye the Lord;
for it is good to sing praises unto our God;
for it is pleasant; and praise is comely.
² The Lord doth build up Jerusalem:
he gathereth together the outcasts of Israel.
³ He healeth the broken in heart,
and bindeth up their wounds.

⁴ He telleth the number of the stars;
   he calleth them all by their names.
⁵ Great is our Lord, and of great power:
   his understanding is infinite.
⁶ The Lord lifteth up the meek:
   he casteth the wicked down to the ground.
⁷ Sing unto the Lord with thanksgiving;
   sing praise upon the harp unto our God,
⁸ who covereth the heaven with clouds,
   who prepareth rain for the earth,
      who maketh grass to grow upon
      the mountains.
⁹ He giveth to the beast his food,
   and to the young ravens which cry.
¹⁰ He delighteth not in the strength of the horse:
   he taketh not pleasure in the legs of a man.
¹¹ The Lord taketh pleasure in them that fear him,
   in those that hope in his mercy.
¹² Praise the Lord, O Jerusalem;
   praise thy God, O Zion.
¹³ For he hath strengthened the bars of thy gates;
   he hath blessed thy children within thee.
¹⁴ He maketh peace in thy borders,
   and filleth thee with the finest of the wheat.
¹⁵ He sendeth forth his commandment upon earth:
   his word runneth very swiftly.
¹⁶ He giveth snow like wool:
   he scattereth the hoarfrost like ashes.

¹⁷ He casteth forth his ice like morsels.
   Who can stand before his cold?
¹⁸ He sendeth out his word, and melteth them:
   he causeth his wind to blow, and the waters flow.
¹⁹ He sheweth his word unto Jacob,
   his statutes and his judgments
      unto Israel.
²⁰ He hath not dealt so with any nation;
   and as for his judgments,
      they have not known them.
   Praise ye the Lord.

148 Praise ye the Lord.
   Praise ye the Lord from the heavens:
   praise him in the heights.
² Praise ye him, all his angels:
   praise ye him, all his hosts.
³ Praise ye him, sun and moon:
   praise him, all ye stars of light.
⁴ Praise him, ye heavens of heavens,
   and ye waters that be above the heavens.
⁵ Let them praise the name of the Lord;
   for he commanded, and they were created.
⁶ He hath also stablished them for ever and ever:
   he hath made a decree which shall not pass.
⁷ Praise the Lord from the earth,
   ye dragons, and all deeps;

⁸ fire, and hail; snow, and vapour;
   stormy wind fulfilling his word.
⁹ Mountains, and all hills;
   fruitful trees, and all cedars;
¹⁰ beasts, and all cattle;
   creeping things, and flying fowl.
¹¹ Kings of the earth, and all people;
   princes, and all judges of the earth;
¹² both young men, and maidens;
   old men, and children.
¹³ Let them praise the name of the Lord;
   for his name alone is excellent;
      his glory is above the earth and heaven.
¹⁴ He also exalteth the horn of his people,
   the praise of all his saints;
      even of the children of Israel,
a people near unto him. Praise ye the Lord.

149

Praise ye the Lord.
   Sing unto the Lord a new song,
and his praise in the congregation of saints.
² Let Israel rejoice in him that made him:
   let the children of Zion be joyful in their King.
³ Let them praise his name in the dance:
   let them sing praises unto him
      with the timbrel and harp.
⁴ For the Lord taketh pleasure in his people:
   he will beautify the meek with salvation.

⁵ Let the saints be joyful in glory:
    let them sing aloud upon their beds.
⁶ Let the high praises of God be in their mouth,
    and a twoedged sword in their hand;
⁷ to execute vengeance upon the heathen,
    and punishments upon the people;
⁸ to bind their kings with chains,
    and their nobles with fetters of iron;
⁹ to execute upon them the judgment written:
    this honour have all his saints.
        Praise ye the Lord.

150

Praise ye the Lord.
    Praise God in his sanctuary:
praise him in the firmament of his power.
² Praise him for his mighty acts:
    praise him according to his excellent greatness.
³ Praise him with the sound of the trumpet:
    praise him with the psaltery and harp.
⁴ Praise him with the timbrel and dance:
    praise him with stringed instruments and organs.
⁵ Praise him upon the loud cymbals:
    praise him upon the high sounding cymbals.
⁶ Let every thing that hath breath praise the Lord.
    Praise ye the Lord.

Praise for **Ice Road**

"Slovo describes the death of an
her book moving and memorable

— ...elegraph

"This is a novel that explores the moti...   ...nd consequences of
political events on ordinary lives . . . *Ice Road* brilliantly depicts,
from the emotional inside, the most politically disastrous
assassination in Russian history . . . Slovo achieves a depth of
psychological realism through the minds of victim and assassin
that is her most accomplished to date"
— Rachel Holmes, *The Times*

"A novel which is demanding, bold and brave."
— Charlie Lee-Potter, *Observer*

"A beautifully composed, expertly structured and wonderfully
evocative masterpiece—Gillian Slovo's greatest achievement to
date. . . . This book deserves a massive and enduring readership."
— David Shukman, *Daily Mail*

"*Ice Road* is an intelligent novel, written with care and feeling and
imagination"   — Allan Massie, *The Scotsman*

"An unrivalled background. . . . A moving and perceptive epic of
utopia in darkness."   — Catherine Merridale, *The Independent*

"I shall never forget Natasha and Kolya's love story or twelve-
year-old Anya, that polite, obedient, wolfish child, orphaned in
her country's wars, or Irina, whose sturdy self-respect and
determination to survive, seems, at times, to speak for an entire
people."   — Pat Barker

"In this capacious and moving story, Gillian Slovo brings a great
deal of personal experience of the weight of history to bear. Her
novel of Russia during the era of Stalin, building up the siege of
Leningrad, is a masterfully orchestrated work, one that deserves
an honorable place on the shelf of fine contemporary fiction."
— Jay Parini

Also by Gillian Slovo

Ice Road

Gillian Slovo

W. W. Norton & Company
New York London

For information about permission to reproduce selections from
this book, write to Permissions, W. W. Norton & Company, Inc.,
500 Fifth Avenue, New York, NY, 10110

Manufacturing by The Haddon Craftsmen, Inc.
Production manager: Amanda Morrison

Library of Congress Cataloging-in-Publication Data

Slovo, Gillian, 1952–
Ice road / Gillian Slovo.—1st American ed.
p. cm.
ISBN 0-393-32720-5 (pbk.)
1. World War, 1939–1945—Russia (Federation)—Saint
Petersburg—Fiction. 2. Saint Petersburg (Russia)—History—
Siege, 1941–1944—Fiction. 3. Conflict of generations—Fiction.
4. Fathers and daughters—Fiction. 5. Sieges—Fiction. I. Title.
PR6069.L56I27 2005
823'.914—dc22
2004030983

W. W. Norton & Company, Inc.
500 Fifth Avenue, New York, N.Y. 10110
www.wwnorton.com

W. W. Norton & Company Ltd.
Castle House, 75/76 Wells Street, London W1T 3QT

1 2 3 4 5 6 7 8 9 0

To Andy. For everything. Always.

Contents

Part Six: What Lies Ahead

Part One

Beginnings

No path to see: the snow has drifted
across each bush, across each steep,
and all the world is buried deep.

(Aleksander Pushkin, *Eugene Onegin*)

The *Chelyuskin*

Out here on deck my breath is turned to ice but I won't go in, at least not yet. It's good to be alone. Away from all the others. It's quiet. And cold, of course, but that goes without saying in the Arctic.

I know I'm risking frostbite and I know I should go in and I will soon, but I am trying to make sense out of what it is that has happened to me. I'm no storyteller. I look only to the facts. Or, if not to the facts, at least to the essentials.

My name is Ira, Irina Davydovna Arbatova to be exact. Davyd after my father, Arbatov after my husband, although the less said about him the better.

My father's name was Davyd Grigoryevich Pashin. He's dead. He died twenty-nine years ago when I was still a child. He didn't die alone. The menfolk in my family hardly ever do. They always follow trends. In my father's case this meant he breathed his last in 1905 on Bloody Sunday, in Winter Palace Square in the city of Petrograd (as it was then called).

My father was only one of many killed that day, that's why I say he didn't die alone. But maybe he was alone – at least in spirit.

I know he wouldn't have been singing hymns like the

rest of them. He never sang in public. He had an off-key singing voice of which he was ashamed. I know, as well, that he didn't set out from home that day with the intention of taking part in any kind of demonstration. My father wasn't political. He wasn't much of a joiner of any kind, or so my mother tells it. She further says – to anyone who bothers to stick around and listen – that my father was an ineffective man who often got himself caught up in urges he didn't really understand. He liked crowds, my mother says; by all accounts he was a little simple, and he must have got carried along with this one. The way my mother tells it – although I don't know how she knows, she wasn't there – is that on this, his last day on earth, my father was clumsy – like every other day, my mother always adds. Having lived through the gunfire, he tripped on the cobbles, falling into the path of an army detachment which, satisfied by the blood they'd spilled, was just then riding out.

The horses' hooves caved in my father's skull and passed by and so he died, this unimportant man who was born, and who lived, and who perished, all before the onset of our revolution. His death was a trifling thing, a part of a past now so completely done away with that it cannot be got back (and a good thing too or so they say). But it was also an unnecessary death, careless in fact – which was just like him, my mother always says – and it left my family fatherless when I was five.

I am now thirty-four years old. As old as our century. I was born at the moment of its birth although, come to think of it, now that they've moved over to the Gregorian calendar, that's no longer true. Well, never mind. Many other things are also no longer true and the commonplace that I was born at the turn of the century will do.

And now I find myself in the Arctic, on the *Chelyuskin*.

There was no design to my coming here. That's the way

it always goes with the likes of me: things either happen or else they don't. Usually the second. So while the others on the boat might have had to compete for their places (they probably even had to take a test), I didn't. No, with me, it was an accidental meeting in the Smolny that brought me to this place. This set of places.

It started with a man, which is often the way.

In this case, the man's name was Boris Aleksandrovich – Boris Aleksandrovich Ivanov – and he came upon me in the broom cupboard.

I had every reason to be in that cupboard. I'm a cleaner: I'm in and out of there all day. I never did find out, though, what it was that could have brought Boris Aleksandrovich Ivanov there.

A man and a woman in a cupboard must sound suspicious. It isn't. Nothing irregular happened, nothing that could have caused a scandal. 'Course it didn't: Boris Aleksandrovich is a true gentleman.

Hold on a minute – I'm not thinking straight. What I really meant to say was that Boris Aleksandrovich is a true revolutionary and, besides, he has his hands full with his important job, that brainy wife of his, his children and his mistress: why would he even look at me? In fact, until the moment when he came upon me in that cupboard, Boris Aleksandrovich and I had had little contact. We nodded to each other, of course, when we passed in the corridor, but that's just what everybody does. We had no reason to do anything else, not until that day at the Smolny, when fate made him open the door so unexpectedly that I had no chance to wipe my face.

I hardly ever cry. Crying is a luxury. I don't have time for tears. And I certainly wouldn't have chosen to cry in front of an important man like Boris Aleksandrovich.

Not that he was harsh. Not at all. That's not Boris

Aleksandrovich's way. He's a kind man. A controlled one. He wasn't cross, he was embarrassed: that big bear of a man standing there, looking at his feet. I wasn't surprised. Our leaders have confidence enough to put the whole world in their scales and weigh each separate part of it, but shove a tearful woman in their path and they always turn to jelly. Which is what happened to Boris Aleksandrovich.

I'm not an educated woman but this I do know: no good can come from the softening up of someone who's in power. So seeing him standing there like that I thought: trouble.

I grabbed my bucket and made to go.

But before I could make good my escape, Boris Aleksandrovich told me (without lifting his eyes) that it had fallen to him to find stewardesses for the *Chelyuskin* expedition (the many different things that cross our leaders' desks!) and did I want to be one?

'The *Chelyuskin*,' I said. 'What's that?'

'It's a ship,' he said, 'a scientific expedition, that will travel along the coast of Siberia and through the Arctic Circle and round, the first time this has ever been achieved. You must have read about it in *Pravda*, haven't you?'

Well, you know, I didn't like to say I couldn't read, I didn't want to make it worse. So I said something like:

'Oh yes, now you mention it,' and he asked me again.

It was an offer, not an order. I could have turned it down. At any other time, I would have done. One thing life has taught me: it's best to keep out of the limelight and away from crowds – if you don't a horse might run you down. I should have made some excuse, said no, thanks but no, and quickly walked away. I didn't though. I suppose the thought of getting away if only for a short time, both from home and from the endless polishing at the Smolny, was too tempting. Before I had time to come to my senses I heard myself saying yes.

That was all it took, that one, stupid 'yes', and I had to carry through. I couldn't make my way upstairs, the central stairs at that, all the way to the third floor, and walk along that creaking corridor, and knock on Boris Aleksandrovich's door all to tell him that I'd changed my mind. 'Course I couldn't. For a man as important as Boris Aleksandrovich to put my name on the list was dangerous enough: asking him to go to the trouble of explaining why he was removing it would really be tempting fate.

And so I found myself standing on the *Chelyuskin* as the bridges of Leningrad were lifted to let us pass.

I am not a woman given to much enthusiasm, and I have never expected life to have its high points, but that day in July 1933 and that moment when we steamed down the Neva heading for the gulf will always be my summit.

They opened up the bridges in the day. Even now, I can hardly credit it. The bridges opening up for me! Me who had never left the city! I smiled that day, I have to say, I really did smile.

And it wasn't just the bridges that saluted us. There were sailing boats as well – tiny, white sheathed things they were, dipping and rising as our ugly *Chelyuskin* ploughed through the waters of the Neva and out to sea. There were horns that sounded, other ships honouring us. There were ceremonies. Slogans. Speeches. Crowds cheering. There were ribbons and garlands and hands uplifted. I saw Boris Aleksandrovich and his daughter in the crowd and I even saw my husband.

That pleased me. My husband, Fyodor Maksimovich Arbatov, having to watch me leaving him. That brute, Fyodor, powerless, as I sailed away.

And it got even better. Out on the ocean our political commander, Comrade Schmidt, called us together to make a speech. I've heard a lot of those in my time, and I can't promise to remember everything he said. But one thing did stick. We are all equal, he said: each of us matters; together we will make history. I've heard those words before – who hasn't? – but this time they felt real. And they weren't grand words spoken about far more important people. They were about me.

It was far-fetched, unbelievable, but I did find myself half-believing it. Why not believe a man who believes himself so well? Whether this makes any difference in the long run is not for me to say, but I took advantage of his goodness and went to the Red Corner where, along with some illiterate sailors who'd come on board in Murmansk, I learned what it is to read. And almost what it is to write.

I, Ira – Irina Davydovna Arbatova – halfway educated. My husband won't like it. If, that is, we get out of here alive.

Oh dear: that 'if' is part of what's forbidden. I heard so yesterday. Through the walls of the cabin I was wiping down I heard Comrade Schmidt say as much. 'Comrades,' I heard him saying, 'we must guard against defeatism.' I knew exactly what that means. It means no ifs allowed and here I am, a few hours later, bringing one out. My husband's right. I am a stubborn woman. I might be able to read but I still can't learn.

Far away as he now is, my husband still manages to exert his influence. It's as if, even standing here, I can hear his voice. I certainly know what he'd be saying. He'd be jeering at me, asking if I think that when the ice field takes us down, as it most surely will, it will give a toss about whether I can read or write. And, of course, he's got a point. The ice doesn't care. It just is.

If we do go down, though, and if I do die, I know that my last moments will be spent thinking about the things I've learned on board. Thinking about those first days. Those long summer days. The smooth seas. The green coast of

Norway. The noisy welcome when we docked in Murmansk. The speeches delivered in our honour. We were to pass through seas I'd never even heard of. Now, of course, I can both name and almost spell those seas. So many of them: the Barents, the Kara, the Laptev, the East Siberian, the Chukchi, the Bering Strait, the Sea of Okhotsk, the Sea of Japan and finally to Vladivostok. Oh, we had ambitions.

Or maybe we were just bewitched.

The likes of Comrade Schmidt don't believe in magic. They're practical men, persuaded by their material world, their facts and figures, their quotas and their targets. If there's one thing they know, it's that men break boundaries and not boundaries that break men. Their thinking power is what drives them forward – or so they think.

But I know differently. I've watched them. That's what I do: I watch. And I was watching as winter drew in, the ice escalating, the horizon lengthening, I saw the Arctic courting them, offering herself up, and I saw them carried away by her scale and beauty. In short, I saw them fall for her.

Before deep winter set in, I would come across them standing out on deck as I am doing now and I could tell by their faraway gazes that they had been hypnotised by those sunsets the colour of amber and sunrises the colour of blood. Watching, I began to see what they could not: that they, like me, were changing. The points, and dots, and the numbers, and who knows what else, they put down in their notebooks no longer had the same effect. I knew that by the way they looked, the things they said and, more importantly, the things they didn't say. They didn't talk about the shortening of the days, the darkening of the nights, the hissing of the ice as it pressed against our bow. They couldn't talk of these. They were enchanted. The Arctic had got them prisoner. And so it was that they didn't even think of turning back. Not until it was too late.

They don't know any of this. Clever they may be, but they're also dreamers who plan to change the world but who, on waking, say they never dreamed a thing. We are men of action is what they always say: duty drives us on. We have scientists to relieve, they said; supplies to offload; measurements to take, we can't turn back. And so they tore themselves away from the view and took their measurements and offloaded their supplies. But ignorant as I know I am, I knew they were really only halfway present. And then, as if to prove me right, we suddenly got stuck.

That was some time ago and we are still stranded. Surrounded by ice which keeps on moving in. We can't push through: not until winter's over and that's some three months off.

To save power, the heat is on for two hours and off for two. That's lesson number one: without fuel you die. Without food as well. Our cooks are careful. Counting all the time. Checking how much it is that we're allowed to eat.

But I trust Comrade Schmidt and I believe him. So *when* we are rescued and *when* we return, will I say that I enjoyed myself?

Have I enjoyed myself? Hard to say. Enjoy is not a word that comes easily to me. And, to be honest, it has been a bit icy.

But despite the cold, I continue to stand out here on deck, and now I find myself thinking about Leningrad and about Boris Aleksandrovich who was the one to bring me here, and I can't help but wonder whether Boris Aleksandrovich ever thinks of me.

A Pretty Girl

If Boris Aleksandrovich Ivanov was asleep before, he now finds himself suddenly awake. His head is full of images of ice, and of destruction. He must have been dreaming, he realises guiltily, about Irina Davydovna, stuck there on the *Chelyuskin*, but even as he thinks this he is simultaneously coming up to consciousness, and the image of Irina Davydovna slips away so that now he is only conscious of his pounding head, his thick tongue and the bile that is welling in his throat, and none of this because he's ill. He's got a hangover, that's all; that has awakened him in the early hours of the morning before the real hangover has time to begin.

Lying on his back, gazing up into the darkness, Boris Aleksandrovich knows that this biliousness is all his own fault. At forty-four, he must have at least twenty years on the American, Jack Brandon, and he certainly has many more cares: he should have known better than to start a drinking competition. He conjures up a picture of Jack tucked up, comfortably, in the Astoria hotel, sleeping soundly while Boris Aleksandrovich lies awake. Stupid Borya. Vain Borya. He pushes the heavy quilt aside.

11

The cold, kept at bay during the day, has once again set in. Groping blindly for something to put on over his underwear, it takes him a while to extract his clothes from Lina's. Separating his trousers from some female undergarment, he thinks how wonderful it would be to have a wife, someone like Tanya, who put away his clothes (and hers), but then, pulling on the trousers, he tells himself he's being unfair and that Polina Konstantinovna, who works as hard as he does, probably also wishes he was tidier. And besides, he must not compare Lina to Tanya, for that breaks his resolve never to think of his mistress while he is with his wife.

Slippers – fur-lined: they at least are where they ought to be, tucked under the bed. He puts them on and then, his eyes having by now grown acclimatised to the dark, he looks across the bed.

Only part of Lina's face is visible: the rest she's covered with the quilt. She looks terribly pale, he thinks, and – and he thinks this before he can block the thought from pushing through – she also looks almost ugly. She's lying still, still as a plank, this capacity of hers to stay so quiet in slumber (in contrast to his own grunting, snoring, almost exhibitionist unconscious) that once delighted him has now become just another indication of her infuriating detachment.

It's freezing. As quietly as he can, although he never does anything completely quietly, he leaves the room, stopping first at the toilet (their own, private toilet as befits the family of a member of the *nomenklatura*, that small band of the new select who are eligible for responsible jobs) and then heading into the living room, passes those other symbols of privilege – the Bakelite wireless, the telephone, the gramophone propped up in the corner and the grand piano scaled to match the tall windows overlooking Nevsky – until he is finally by the samovar where he pours himself a succession of cups of warm water which he thirstily downs. There. Much better. He even feels warmer.

Back in the bedroom, he rubs away the sheen of newly crusting ice that has smeared itself across the windowpane. He looks out on to Leningrad's premier street, Nevsky Prospect. The wide and whitened road is empty: the only time in this growing city that it ever is. Soon, Boris knows, bundled shadows will appear from inside the catacomb of courtyards and shuffle over the quilted layers of snow, those sleepy workers bent almost double against the freezing wind, as, high up on the roof tops, someone will most likely be chipping away at a series of sharp stalactites that nightly form on every ledge. Now, however, is the time of silence – soft and cold – that Boris loves.

Gazing out at emptiness, he wishes he could do as he used to when a student, and stay up all night to watch the darkness changing. Oh to be young again, he thinks, and even as the thought occurs he knows that what he's really wishing back is neither his youth, nor the time he then possessed, but something much more precious, that something that he might call possibility.

All those possibilities in which they once believed: all those dreams, ambitions and ideals. All that hope and that fear and that courage poured into their project that was, by the theory they had all imbibed, impossible, and yet they made it happen, their revolution, the old order not fighting as they thought it would, but dissolving and there, in their hands: state power. How hopeful they were then: how sure of themselves.

Seventeen years later, Boris Aleksandrovich looks out of the window, and he thinks that although he did help to change the world, what he hadn't realised then was how much he would also be changing himself.

That first step, the seizing of state power, was easy or it

was certainly easy when compared with what came after. Measures taken to counter the invasions from outside and the enemies within, as their youth bled away into their new reality. No longer barricades to man, arms to distribute, pamphlets to write: no, now what absorbed their time was a mountain of paper and of compromises, some immense, others trivial, each creating a different set of circumstances that also needed dealing with until, one day, you wake up and you're not sure where you are, save for the fact that you have an almost grown-up family and a job in the Smolny that qualifies you for this grand apartment on Nevsky. All of which, he thinks, means you also need your sleep.

Heading back to the bed, he looks down on Lina and realises he was wrong before: she's not ugly. On the contrary, even though her face has lined and sagged, she's still a handsome woman. And it's not as if he's so untouched by time himself. What would once have been a clean run from his chest to his genitals is now interrupted by a mound of doughy flesh – more of it now than there was this time last year. Sucking in his stomach, he side-chops his midriff and is pleased to feel that there's still some muscle there. Maybe he should make more of an effort to join the others in the Smolny for their morning exercise session, he thinks as he climbs into bed.

Lina is not asleep. As he pulls the cover up, her voice sounds out calm, clear, wide awake, and delivered on that undercurrent of accusation that seems to be present whenever she says anything to him these days, and in particular when she talks about their youngest child and only daughter.

'You still think of Natasha as a child, don't you?' she says.

He answers mildly: 'In many ways, she is still a child.'

'Your child perhaps.'

Gritting his teeth, he forces himself into stillness, hoping that way to silence her.

But Polina Konstantinovna will not be silenced, especially when it comes to Natasha.

'You didn't notice the way they looked at her?'

'Who's they?'

'Well, Kolya for a start.'

He shrugs. 'Kolya always looks at her like that.'

'And the American.'

That makes him smile. 'If Jack Brandon looked at Natasha,' he says, 'it's because Jack's got an eye for the ladies. He doesn't have designs on Natasha. His hands are already full with a certain young lady who has taken to visiting his hotel room,' and saying this, Boris wonders whether he should find a way to warn the American that the girl is bound to be reporting to the police, a thought that is driven out by Lina's:

'And Dmitry Fedorovich as well.'

Dmitry Fedorovich. Now that's a different matter. Boris pulls the covers tighter. Dmitry Fedorovich Anninsky's presence, and the presence of men like him, might be a safeguard, a necessary evil, but Boris would never want such a man interested in his daughter.

But is Lina right?

Thinking back, Boris Aleksandrovich remembers a moment that unfolded after dinner. Natasha, the centre of attention as she so often is, was up on a chair over by the window. She was singing a popular ditty of love spurned and a lover betrayed, her eyes shining as she joyfully teased out the words, and all of them had turned to watch her, save Dmitry Fedorovich who had been out the room. It was a carefree moment, full of joy until, Boris Aleksandrovich remembers, two things had happened almost simultaneously: Natasha had come to the end of the song and Dmitry Fedorovich had returned. That's what Boris Aleksandrovich can now recall, the sight of Dmitry Fedorovich frozen in the line of Natasha's laughing gaze, as Jack Brandon had begun to clap and the rest of the company had joined in, and Natasha had bowed and then, still laughing, had looked around for a hand to help her off the table where she'd been standing. Dmitry Fedorovich was so fast that even though he was furthest away he got there first, his hand reaching out for Natasha's, and for a moment, lying in bed, Boris Aleksandrovich wonders if Lina is right, and Dmitry Fedorovich could have designs on Natasha. But then he remembers what happened next, Dmitry Fedorovich backing away as Kolya took over, Kolya catching Natasha round the waist and swinging her down, she, carefree, in his embrace while Dmitry Fedorovich retreats so Boris Aleksandrovich knows Lina is wrong, that Dmitry Fedorovich, a normally persistent man, can't be interested in Natasha. He isn't interested in any girl. His kind doesn't believe in love and mostly not even in sex. Their passion is politics and politics alone. And even if Dmitry Fedorovich was interested in Natasha, well, Boris Aleksandrovich knows his daughter. She's a romantic. She would never fall for an apparatchik like Dmitry Fedorovich. Lina's just over-reacting. As always.

'They were *all* watching her,' Lina says.

'It's normal, Lina: she's a pretty girl.'

'Yes, Borya, of course. I know that. What's not normal is that *she* didn't notice.'

When was it, Boris wonders, that Lina first started talking in italics?

'She doesn't notice anybody except *Kolya*.'

'Kolya is her friend.' Boris yawns – he really must get some sleep.

'He's more than that, Borya. He has been for a while. If we're not careful, she'll end up marrying him.'

'Would that be so bad? He's a sweet boy. '

'He's not *right* for her.'

'Because he works in a factory?'

'Because *he*'s not interested in the things that interest *her*.' The sharp edge in Polina Konstantinovna's voice is there to remind Boris Aleksandrovich she's not just his wife but a professional as well, and a scientist, pre-eminent in her field.

'Kolya will limit her horizons,' she's saying now. 'And she'll end up making him unhappy.'

She'll make him unhappy, Boris Aleksandrovich notes, and thinks: Lina couldn't be more wrong. Doesn't she know that there isn't a malicious bone in their daughter's body?

'You really *should* try and make her see sense.'

'Why don't you?'

'She doesn't take any notice of what I say.'

Which is true. What lies between Lina and Natasha is less a passing difficulty than a mutual and inalterable incomprehension, a clash of world views. Mother and daughter are so very different. Natasha's imagination is driven by colours, shapes and texture whereas Lina prefers the known, the mathematical and the organisms that only she and a handful of other experts can pin down in the lenses of her powerful microscope. In fact, Boris Aleksandrovich thinks, of their three children Natasha is most like him while their eldest, Misha, now in Moscow, is like Lina. As for Ilya, well, he's like nobody else on earth.

'*Talk* to her, please, Borya.'

'All right, Lina.'

He leans over, meaning to kiss her goodnight, but when she says:

'Please, Borya. This is *important*. Make the time,' he drops back, abruptly, on to his side of the bed and she turns over. Looking at his wife's back, he is suffused with anger. Her complex world of microbes, he thinks, is turning her into a simpleton.

'Bring her to her senses,' she says.

He closes his eyes.

'Will you, Borya?'

'Yes, Lina. I'll talk to her,' he says and, turning over, forces himself into sleep.

Irina

I can count off my life by the things that have so far happened in this century.

I was five when my father died in 1905; seventeen, in 1917, when Lenin, standing in our own Smolny Institute, announced the birth of the Bolshevik state; twenty-four, in 1924, when they swapped the signs to Petrograd with our city's new name, Leningrad; twenty-eight in 1928, the beginning of our iron age; and thirty-two when they tarred the Winter Palace Square in 1932. If they'd done that earlier my father might still be alive, although, since in my experience people don't ever escape their fate, my father would most likely have found another way to exit early from this world. It doesn't really matter. The fact is: he's long dead.

Until now, I have lived an uneventful life. And a lucky one.

I have been handed three separate pieces of good fortune: I have survived (unlike my three brothers) into adulthood; I have always earned enough to get by; and, probably most important of all, nobody powerful ever interested themselves in me.

Until recently, that is.

I've kept the same job, cleaning in the Smolny Institute, that I got when I turned thirteen. It wasn't hard to keep. Rules and rulers may come and go, but dirt never changes. Not that I'm complaining. Who I clean for is all the same to me. My brother, the idealist in our family when he was still alive, used to go on about the glory of our common humanity, but life has taught me that what common humanity really means is that most people, be they red or white, will leap at the chance to get someone else to sweep away their dirt.

I am a good cleaner. Not brilliant, but good enough.

I have lived my whole life in the city we must now call Leningrad. My home is in one of the buildings overlooking the Moika canal. It's one of the most beautiful parts of the city, or so they say. I don't much notice it: you don't when you know a place so well, and when your life is all work, and queueing for food, and cooking, and sleep. 'Course you don't. What I do notice though – probably because you can't miss it – is the way the canal freezes up in winter. So solid is the ice that I could, if I wanted to, cross over to visit a neighbour on the other side without using any of the bridges, if, that is, I had a neighbour worth visiting, and there were stairs down on our section of the stone-lined canal.

Ours is a grand building, four storeys high, one in a curved row of stone constructions of which our city's founder, Peter the Great, was so proud. From outside they say the building looks exactly as it did in 1705 (except dirtier) but, like all the others in the crescent, inside it has been subdivided and redivided again.

Our allocated space sits on the second floor. The signal for us to answer the door – should anybody come visiting – is two long presses and one short. There are three Primuses in our communal kitchen – ours and the two belonging to the two other families. We don't have much to do with them apart from queueing for the toilet and sticking to the rota for kitchen use and kitchen cleaning. We like to keep ourselves to ourselves: it saves trouble.

We – my family – is me, my husband, his mother and his two unmarried sisters, five of us in the one room that we have partitioned off for privacy.

That I should live in a family where there is only one man (if, that is, my husband can be included in the world of men) is nothing new. It's part of my tradition that stretches way back. My father's end I've already described. As for the rest: my maternal grandfather and my paternal grandfather were both carried away in the famine of 1891. Of their grandchildren, my brothers born to my father's loins, one of them died during the famine of 1906 and another in the typhus epidemic that followed. My only remaining brother, Andrei, the idealist, well, he died in 1917 in the mud of the battlefields just before our glorious revolution put an end to the war.

Andrei was my lovely, my favourite brother. Such an easy-going, kind, devoted boy. Sometimes in the dead of night I find myself wondering if he still stuck to his grand ideas of common humanity even while a German soldier used a bayonet to make tripe out of his guts.

Wait a minute: I didn't mean to lay out this multitude of my dead. They, like me, are unimportant. They lived, that's all, and now they don't. If I am different it is only because I am a survivor, or at least I so far have been one. That, apart from cleaning, is what I do: survive. And watch, of course: I like that.

So here I stand. Irina Davydovna Arbatova, plain and simple. There's nothing else to me except the facts.

The facts like where are we? Now, that's a tricky one. There are around me here people not only clever but also highly educated which, I've been told, is not always the same thing. But these people are both. The elite of our society. Not only the commander of our expedition, Comrade Schmidt, but also the ship's captain, its engineers, helmsmen and radio operators as well as a whole lot of experts who do things I've not heard of nor can hardly pronounce: a physicist, there is, and an ichthyologist, a hydrologist, a meteorologist, a geodesist . . . and more than that as well. At night the talk is all of Freud and Einstein and other grand subjects, my companions being some of the most advanced minds of our age. So much knowledge in such a confined space. But should I want, at any given moment, to pin down exactly where we are, then I might as well ask the artist Reshetnikov or the cine-operator Troyanovsky, or even the baby Karina, born as we entered the Kara Sea, for all the good it would do me.

The fact is that we are nowhere and we are everywhere. We are in the Arctic, somewhere between the Chukchi Sea and the Bering Strait at the mercy of the ice.

When we first set out we were supposed to use the miracle of flight and radio to guide us through uncharted waters from Leningrad via Murmansk through the Arctic Circle and to Vladivostok, thousands of miles' worth of the coldest, most inhospitable region on the planet. But now, with our reconnaissance plane crashed, our radio more a source of morale than help, and the ice locked on to us, our goals are much smaller – and, at the same time, much bigger.

What we must now strive to do is to survive. All one hundred and five of us who are at the mercy of an ice mass that is aimless and unstoppable.

We passed Cape Stone Heart the other day.

For the fourth time.

And soon, we know, although we do not speak of it, the ice will squeeze our ship to death.

An Understanding

Natasha's fingers are freezing. As for her toes: well, although reason tells her that they must still be pressing against the edge of her *valenki*, which are slightly too small, she can no longer feel them.

Oh to be somewhere else! Anywhere else. Anywhere warm. But she can't go, at least not yet, not until Kolya has reached the bridge's other end. It's a promise she made to him.

'Please, Natyushka, don't turn away until I get to the other side,' he'd said with such sweet intensity that she'd laughed out loud and said of course she wouldn't.

He hadn't returned her laughter: he'd stayed solemn as he sometimes does for no reason she can understand, repeating it then as a question, saying:

'Promise?' twice, pleadingly, as if he was afraid she might refuse. And so, of course, she'd promised, and now she must stand here, at one end of the bridge, as he steadily makes his way towards the other.

The light is dwindling and a grey mist has overlaid the day so she can only just make out the sight of Kolya, now halfway over, as he stops and turns to look at her. He's checking she's still there and then, seeing that she is, he waves. She also lifts an arm. Even though she can't quite make out his features, she knows he must be smiling. He has such a lovely smile: it's infectious even in memory. She finds herself returning it.

Kolya's so solid, she thinks: so dependable. So archetypical. In fact, with his blue padded jacket hugging his well-developed shoulders, and with his blond hair hidden by a blue peaked cap, what he most resembles is a poster. An uplifting poster of a healthy man. The Happy Worker Heading to His Factory perhaps?

Yes. A fitting description. It's what he is. A worker. A happy worker. Happy to have her as his girl, that's undoubtedly number one, but happy also to live at home, and to be part of a production line making components for tractors, and happy also to work as many extra shifts as are required because, that way, he knows he can further contribute to the successful fulfilment of the five-year plan. In fact, Natasha thinks, as she watches him setting off again, this is the thing that most characterises Kolya: his contentment with the order of things. With duty. With necessity. That's part of the reason she loves him so: because he's impervious to that longing that can sometimes come over her. That longing to break with ritual, to risk censure, to act spontaneously – to do something, anything, just because she feels like it, rather than because her mother, her Komsomol group, her leader, or her motherland has told her that she should.

Thoughts like these are alien to Kolya: he's far too well adjusted. He even gets on with his difficult mother. Nothing ruffles his equanimity: that's what makes him her perfect match. He stands to one side of her moods. That's what makes him special, that when she falls into one of those states her mother disdainfully calls 'Natasha's frenzies', her father might grow flustered and her mother disapproving but not Kolya – while what he does is he looks at her and laughs in genuine amusement, and this is always enough to make her realise that whatever it is she thinks is annoying her doesn't really matter.

With Kolya she feels herself grounded: with him she feels normal.

No, it's more than that. With him she *is* normal.

He's at the other end of the bridge now; he turns to give one last wave. She waves right back, still waving as he launches himself out into the falling gloom, walking as stolidly as he always does. He is Kolya. And he loves her. Lucky Natasha. Lucky life: it makes her want to call out, to dance, to give a final whirl of joy.

Instead she gazes down the straight section of the Neva just before it winds itself round the bend. Winter has taken hold, the ice forming a thick crust along the river banks while in its centre tiny, grey ice floes dot the syrupy water. For the moment the floes are still on the move, granulated waves heading, slowly, out towards the Gulf of Finland, but it's so cold that soon, Natasha knows, they will multiply and pile up, and form an ice garden of preposterous, needle-pointed shapes.

Like every child of Leningrad, she loves midsummer with its glorious white nights. How could anyone not fall then for the viscous Neva, a contrast to the glistening of the bayonets of Admiralty and the burnished dome of St Isaac's across the water? But for Natasha winter is also precious, for in winter there's an added bonus: mystery and delight. She loves the way this season changes texture, and great snowflakes keep floating down, and falling, mute sound. She loves the lie of them, as well, one flake upon the other until they form an interlocking series of undulating beds of dazzling white that, after a particularly vivid sunset, will turn an almost electric blue. And she never ceases to be entranced by the way that the combination of alabaster snow and the blue light of a full moon somehow combine to cover the earth in an unworldly glow.

It is this that makes winter so special: what it does to colour. Take the red scarf on that child over there in the distance, the one tobogganing down a slope. She can hardly see the child itself – she can't tell how old it is or whether it's a girl or a boy – but the scarf cuts across the whiteness, vividly, brighter than a stain of blood.

As the thought crosses her mind, she shivers.

Two Men

To cater to their tsar's whim, the men whose job it was to build this new city of bridges and islands, this St Petersburg, first had to reclaim most of the land from marshes. Not so, however, in the district of Smolny, for Smolny, formerly the site of the tar yards for Peter's warships and then the favourite choice of residence for the Russian nobility, stands four metres above sea level from where it can look down on the mist and damp and fog that persecute the rest of Leningrad.

At the Smolny's apex, overlooking the Bolshaya Neva, sits the Smolny Institute. In this complex of buildings is history writ large: what started life as an orphan's convent championed by an empress was turned first into a school for the daughters of the nobility, then into the headquarters of the Petrograd Soviet, and finally it became the site of the second all-Russian Congress of Socialists and Workers and Soldiers Deputies. It is here that, in 1917, Lenin and Trotsky and Zinoviev and Kamenev stood, under the chandeliers and swirling cigarette smoke, to announce the birth of the Bolshevik state. And nowadays, as befits a building of this stature, the Smolny is Party headquarters and the busy, bustling centre of local government.

It is to the Smolny that Natasha comes flushed with cold and the exertion of her walk, striding vigorously. She's known to the Smolny guards who wave her through the imposing wrought-iron gates.

Singing a tune plundered from a jazz musical that has recently swept through Russia, 'Thank you, heart, that you know how to live', humming over the words she can't remember, she can hear her *valenkis* crunching against the compacted snow.

Soon it will be dark but for the moment the sky, viewed through a feathery lattice of velvet brown branches, looks almost white. If it were summer there'd be stretches of clipped green and sparkling fountains but now the fountains are boxed in against the cold, and the lawns and flower beds are covered by uninterrupted beds of snow.

On the occasions when she was young, when her father would come and pick her up from the pioneers, she had loved to sail through the empty streets, then to come here and make her imprint in the snow, Papa waiting patiently for her, before the warmth of the Smolny embraced them both, and she would spend hours quietly drawing, as he finished what he had to do. But now she is no longer young and Boris is much busier.

To the left, rising above a screen of trees, she can see the exquisite cupolas of the white cathedral and, standing in the Smolny grounds and screened from the cathedral by those same trees, the bust of a man, with its bullish head, long beard, sweeping moustache and ferocious eyebrows. It's Friedrich Engels and opposite him, on the other side of the path, his match, his friend, the much more benign-looking, bushy-bearded Karl Marx. Natasha knows the statues well. She throws each a casual nod.

Quickening her step, she goes past the statue of Vladimir Ilyich Lenin and his pointing arm. In summer, he will be ringed by flowers – red tulips – but now he has only snow for his carpet, and a sprinkling of powdery snow on the back of his head and inside the folds of his cap.

'Thank you, heart . . .,' she sings. She is happy. Kolya wants her and, as for her father, well, he'll help her work out what she should do.

What Natasha doesn't like about winter is the way it smells indoors: damp fur, rotting felt, untreated rubber and the stink of bodies after all those garments have been removed. She stands on the grey marbled floor by the cloakroom having handed in her outdoor shoes, almost gagging. She's even considering going out again when someone comes to tell her that her father, who has been delayed, has given her permission to wait upstairs.

She hands her identity document to a guard, a handsome policeman who can't be that much older than Kolya. He smiles at her, his brow lifting to suggest that what he'd really like to do is wink. Flattered, she nevertheless tilts up her chin to demonstrate disapproval – for all he knows she could be a married woman. Or a nearly married one. She says: 'My pass, please, comrade,' but sees that his eyes have now swivelled past and beyond her and that he is standing to attention.

She turns.

Like everybody in Leningrad, she recognises Kirov. His squat, confident figure is unmistakeable and, besides, she's seen him close up many times, with her father or at the Marinsky, a place that Kirov, an opera fan (and a fan of ballerinas, or so gossip goes), likes to frequent.

Sergei Mironovich, Comrade Kirov, is dressed as ever in his outdoor garb of a calf-length, shabby black overcoat and visored Finnish cap. He's not a man to stand on ceremony. The fuss that attends his entrance emanates not from him but from the bulk of bodyguards that surround him. According to Papa, Kirov hates this recent increase in security. What he longs to do is walk in the city on his own, or stop his car to chat to a stranger without having his muscled members of the NKVD pressing close, or hold a conversation, any conversation, even a private one about his health, without always being conscious of these men (there to protect him) listening in. Just shows you, her father tells her, that power and position have their drawbacks, although, Natasha thinks, Sergei Mironovich certainly doesn't look as if he's suffering now. Dark though the rings beneath his eyes might be, he's full of energy. A stocky man with a chubby, smiling face, he draws on a cigarette as he strides past the guards and up the stairs. So much energy: it's almost as if he takes the air with him. People sag when he has gone, amongst them Natasha's guard, who, setting aside flirtation, holds out her document.

She follows in Kirov's wake. While he and his men had gone up the right-hand branch of the white marble steps, she chooses the left. They were hurrying: she meanders. By the time she reaches the second floor their convoy has long since swept past. She hands her permit to a second guard and when he says:

'Boris Aleksandrovich left word that he'll meet you in ten minutes, in the Assembly Hall,' she turns and walks off, the parquet squeaking under her shoes.

The corridor is long and dark, a veritable cove, the same length as Rossi's Street behind Pushkin Square, with every detail correspondingly oversize, including the many doors that, evenly spaced, are each more than ten feet high. If she were to keep on walking she'd end up at the Assembly Hall but, with ten minutes' grace, she decides instead to take a sudden left. She walks into a kind of cul-de-sac, going to its end where there is another door, this one much lower and signposted 'Head Teacher'. Head teacher – that's funny. How come they never took it down? She pushes open the door.

It's very light, this corner room, with windows overlooking the winding Neva. And it's perfect. Like a stage set but at the same time perfectly real for this is Vladimir Ilyich's – Lenin's – room: the office from which he orchestrated the first six months of the revolution.

It's a Spartan space. Lenin's table is in the middle of the room. His green framed light and telephone with wooden receiver sit on the table. And on the walls, those early posters, decrees on peace, decrees on land. And there – most wonderful of all: the hat stand.

There are two hats hanging on two separate branches, and two umbrellas underneath, as if the occupants of the room have just stepped out and will soon be back. Lenin's cap, a little like Kirov's, Natasha thinks, and that other one: that round felt, Krupskaya's hat, so small, so delicate and at the same time so workmanlike.

Natasha would love to try it on. She has always wanted to, and always desisted, but this time she does. She sees her hand smooth and white, reaching out and plucking the blue hat off the stand as if it is a stranger's hand, and she feels that stranger placing it gently on her head. And is that her, whirling round? She cannot tell. She has lost herself in imagining how it must have been. So much to do: so much happening. People running in and out, information to be gathered, orders to be given, problems solved. Heady days, dangerous days, exciting days. A tyranny overthrown: a new idealism reaching for the light. Being here brings back the stories her father used to tell her when she was a child.

He doesn't tell those stories now, she thinks, slowing

down. He's too busy. Or perhaps she's just too old. But how wonderful to have been part of all that, to have helped bring new hope into the world. She does one last 360-degree turn and then pulls off Krupskaya's hat and, taking aim, hurls it back. Perfect: it lands on target. She walks over, adjusting its tilt, making sure it hangs exactly as it did when she arrived and then quietly pulls the door to again.

As Boris Aleksandrovich makes his way along the corridor he sees Stepan Vasilyevich lumbering towards him. The two men, having drawn abreast, stop and greet each other, and follow this with a quick glance, each man over the other's shoulder and then behind himself. Checking. A very modern ritual.

The corridor is empty but for a guard leaning against the wall, his eyes closed. He's too far away, and too half-asleep, to bother listening but nevertheless Stepan Vasilyevich edges closer, his fat jowls wobbling as he says in a low voice:

'Have you thought about the matter we discussed?'

The matter we discussed, Boris Aleksandrovich hears, thinking that this is conversation, Smolny-style, where cryptic questions must be answered indirectly as Boris Aleksandrovich is doing now by saying:

'Yes,' and then, for form's sake and to show he hasn't entirely abandoned speech, adding a relatively garrulous:

'Yes. I thought about it.'

'And?'

Boris Aleskandrovich shrugs. 'It's difficult.'

Which is both a truism and an understatement. Of course it's ·difficult, everything is these days, but to contemplate putting up a candidate (even if it is someone as well established as Kirov) against Stalin as General Secretary which is what Stepan Vasilyevich is proposing: well, this could be beyond difficult. No matter that things are better, that the war is over, the countryside subdued, the economy on its feet, fear still lingers. That's why they're talking about it in the corridor and in lowered voices. And that's why Boris Aleksandrovich still needs to weigh up all the options before committing himself. He stalls for time. For information. Asking:

'What's the general consensus?'

'Hard to tell.' Stepan Vasilyevich throws his own version of a shrug. 'You know how it is.'

'And Sergei Mironovich, Comrade Kirov himself? Is he willing?'

'We think it better if some of the Congress delegates were to suggest it.'

Which means they haven't yet even asked Kirov whether he would stand as General Secretary. Boris Aleksandrovich was right to have been cautious.

'You're not against it, are you Boris Aleksandrovich?' Stepan Vasilyevich asks.

A simple question for which a simple answer, yes or no, would suffice. But how does Boris Aleksandrovich respond? Like this:

'No, on balance no, I'm not against it . . .,' and frowns as if to say, well, no, I'm not against it, you understand, but don't spread this around because I'm not exactly for it either, and to underline this, he adds, '. . . but, Stepan Vasilyevich, we must take into account the fragility of our situation. We mustn't give succour to our enemies. We must think carefully, we must do what's right. We must preserve unity,' which will just about do it, will keep him in the middle of the river, not stranded on either bank.

Stepan certainly seems to think so. He looks carefully at Boris and when he sees his colleague standing there calmly, his face at one with his bland words, he nods as if to say he understands and having shaken Boris's Aleksandrovich's hand – farewell – walks off while Boris Aleksandrovich stands a moment, watching Stepan Vasilyevich's vast retreating back, and then he turns and also continues on his way, the things he is thinking belying his apparent calm. Questions hit at him. Questions like: how did this happen? How did I become this man I would once have despised? Why can't I just say what I really think? What everybody thinks? And as his inner voice takes wing, he wonders what would happen if he'd been braver, if he'd said, quite casually:

'Yes, of course we should put Kirov up as candidate for General Secretary. It's our right. If we're dissatisfied, if we want a change, then we *must* put him up. This is our organisation. Our Party. We wrote the rules: we can help unwrite them. We can ask people to cross off Comrade Stalin's name: what is the harm in that?'

And then he feels like laughing because, of course, there was no way he could risk saying that. Not in public. Not here. And not to a consummate caucuser like Stepan Vasilyevich.

And so the man who has just told himself that he feels like laughing, continues down the corridor, the expression on his face quite grim.

In the Assembly Hall Natasha sees rows of red velvet chairs facing the front; high and regularly spaced windows; a plain, square stage; a mural of V. I. Lenin so large that he towers over oil wells and factories; lights that hang from every point along the ceiling that look like marble but are in fact made of specially polished alabaster. This hall is the site of Smolny schoolgirls' infrequent reunions with their parents. It must have been chaos, Natasha thinks, girls coming through one entrance, princes and princesses through the other, and all of them talking at once, making polite conversation, saying very little because what can you talk about with a member of your family that you hardly even know? And after the girls had been banished from this place, it was reborn as the Hall of the Soviets where delegates cheered the birth of their new nation. How much better, Natasha thinks, to have been outside, celebrating in the streets, rather than shut up in this place and subject to the kind of interminable speeches that bored her to distraction.

'Natasha?'

She spins round, expecting to see her father, but it's not Papa, it's Dmitry Fedorovich Anninsky, her father's underling, although not so much his underling, she thinks, as Papa's frequent, if silent, companion who had come in so quietly (could he have been following her?) that she missed both his opening of the door and his walking down the aisle, so that by the time he calls her name and she turns, he's already so close she can hear him breathing, hard as if he has been running.

'Dmitry Fedorovich, you gave me such a fright.'

Seeing how his face darkens and how he takes a hasty backward step as if he's affronted, she thinks how sensitive he is and how easily put off, and she walks towards him, taking his hands in hers to make up for her abruptness, and says, without forethought:

'My, how cold your hands are, you need warming up.'

And now she sees his face reddening and there's part of her that's inclined to laugh and part that knows how much this would hurt him, and so instead she holds on to his hands longer than she might otherwise have done.

What Boris Aleksandrovich sees when he walks in is this: his daughter hand in hand with Dmitry Fedorovich. And furthermore, he also sees Dmitry Fedorovich gazing in red-faced admiration into Natasha's eyes, and Natasha smiling back. The sight disturbs so that he calls out:

'Natasha,' much more abrasively than he'd intended, for the spectacle has brought back Lina's night-time insinuations, his misgivings increased by the way that, at the sound of his voice, the two break guiltily apart, and so he says even more abrasively:

'Was there something that you wanted, Dmitry Fedorovich?' looking sternly at the other to indicate that it would be unwise for him to give expression to any such desire, no matter how mundane it might turn out to be, and Dmitry Fedorovich, no fool he, just shakes his head – no – and quickly leaves.

Boris Aleksandrovich looks at his daughter, thinking, *you silly fool, don't you know better than to waste your affections on a man like that?* and so he snaps out:

'Natasha, what were you thinking of?'

But when in response Natasha steps back, he reads in her expression not anger, as he'd anticipated, but bewilderment. He hadn't, he realises, caught her in a compromising position. Look at her, she's far too much the child to have led Dmitry Fedorovich on. He should never have spoken so harshly.

I let myself be poisoned by Lina's suspicions, he tells himself, but he must admit Lina has a point and the point is this: Natasha is eighteen, no longer just a child. She should know better than to let a man like Dmitry Fedorovich in so close, never mind to take her hand, and he says:

'Your mother asked me to have a word with you.'

Your mother, Natasha hears. So that explains her father's anger. If her mother had asked him to speak to her, it must be because of something she's done wrong. This, she thinks, is the main reason these days why her father speaks to her: because her mother asked him to.

She says:

'What have I done?'

'Done?' She sees his face softening. 'You haven't done anything,' he adds, although to her ears he sounds hesitant as if he doesn't entirely believe this. 'She's worried about the growing familiarity between you and Kolya,' he says.

Boris Aleksandrovich is watching carefully as he says this, to see how Natasha will react, but the light is now so dim that he can't be sure whether what he thinks he sees – Natasha's colour draining from her face – is real and not illusion. He walks back to the door and there, at the flick of a switch, lights up a score of alabaster holders. By the time he comes back, she is smiling. Brightly. Perhaps too brightly? He says much more gently:

'I know Kolya is your friend, Natasha,' and he's rewarded by her answering nod so that now he asks: 'Is there anything you'd like to tell me?' and hears her answer, rushed out:

'He says he loves me,' before she immediately looks down.

'He?'

'Kolya.'

Kolya. So Lina's right: Natasha's friendship with Kolya has got out of hand. But then, given what he's just seen, Boris Aleksandrovich thinks, is that such a bad thing? He uses a gentle hand to tilt up his daughter's face: 'And do you also love Kolya?'

Do I love Kolya is what she wants to say: how would I know? I'm only eighteen – all of this she thinks although what she says is:

'He wants to marry me,' hoping for . . .

Hoping for she knows not what and not getting it either because although her father nods he doesn't actually say anything and so the silence stretches between them until it is she who breaks it.

'Should I?'

She's looking up at him.

Her pleading eyes make him want to talk to her, openly, as he used to. He wants to say: instinct tells me no. Don't marry Kolya, that's what he wants to say, wait a while. But can he trust his instinct any longer? And how does he know that Lina's objections haven't affected the way he is reacting? And besides: does any father ever want another man to possess the love of his only daughter? Instead of giving in to instinct, all he can do is repeat: 'Do you love him?

Of course, she thinks, I must love him and yet: 'How would I know?'

He sighs. 'You'd know, Natasha.'

She thinks of Kolya on the bridge, looking back, checking she hadn't disappeared. Kolya needs me, she thinks: with Kolya I am strong. She imagines how it will be if they are married. The two of them together, cosy, unbothered by misunderstanding or harsh words. Kolya and she will never argue: they never do.

'Yes, Papa,' she says, 'I love Kolya,' blurting out the words and then looking up at her beloved father, whose opinion she cares about above all others: 'Is that all right?'

His daughter looking up at him, wanting his approval. He can't withhold it. She's always had this effect on him: of all his children, hers is the strongest pull. Besides, he thinks, Kolya is a good boy. A real proletarian: a man of the future. Sure, Lina has a point – Kolya can be dull – but who says excitement is what makes a marriage work? And besides, Kolya is no Dmitry Fedorovich. Kolya's ambition won't endanger her. Granted Kolya's naïve but Boris Aleksandrovich, in his position, can help him. Protect him. See that he progresses. And Natasha is asking for his approval: how can he withhold it? How can I, he thinks, and thinks again: Kolya is no Dmitry Fedorovich.

He reaches out and pulls her to him, hugging her, saying:
'Of course, Natasha, if you love Kolya, then that's all that
matters. I'm happy for you. Really I am happy,' and this
time, when Natasha smiles, he knows she's not pretending.
This was all she wanted: her father's reassuring arms. Her
father giving her permission, and so, surely, it must be right.

Radio Link

Before I came on the *Chelyuskin*, I thought I knew everything there was to know about snow and ice. I am a child of
the north. I have lived through winters so cold that my
breath has turned to slivers that shatter when they hit the
ground. I have seen slabs of marble cracked by frost, I have
pulled sledges across the solid surface of a lake and I have
watched stalactites grow from Peter's great stone buildings.
But here in the Arctic, snow and ice are different. Everything
is. Even space. In this whiteness, a ship can grow enormous
in a clearing fog then shrink down to nothing; or an ice field
that you know for sure is flat can seem to rear up like a
towering giant; or a dull sky that was once at one with the
land can suddenly shine more brightly than a polished
mirror. As for the ice: well, it is a living, breathing, menacing
thing. I have heard its crystals whisper in the air, I have
watched its diamond jags shaft into the snow, and I have
even heard it scream.

It's February. Another month passed by and I am – we all
are – still here. Not much to do but think. And what I have
been thinking is that our ship, the *Chelyuskin*, is not an
icebreaker. Everybody from our captain and Comrade

Schmidt, our political commander, to the lowliest of the cabin stewardesses like me knows this. It's part of our daily talk. It was the first thing said after we passed through the Straits of Matochkin Shar into the Kara Sea – the one our sailors call the ice cellar – and our ship suffered her first mishap: as her 2,500-horsepower engine strained to shift her 4,000 tons through the ice, her bow was damaged and her plates bent in. It wasn't much of a problem (not compared to what's happened since) and it was easily fixed, but that's when the sentence started doing the rounds. Each word separated to show its weight. The. *Chelyuskin*. Is. Not. (That word underlined: <u>Not</u>.) An. Ice. Breaker.

It's obvious. You only have to use your eyes. Icebreakers like the *Krassin* or the *Littke* are narrow-bottomed and angled; they're made to ram through the archipelago of Arctic floes. Our *Chelyuskin* is different. She's big and fat, a basic cargo ship, even if she has been thoroughly (although, as it has turned out, not thoroughly enough) reinforced.

But even though she's not an icebreaker, she's still in the furthest north. This is because her hold is much bigger than an icebreaker's which means she can carry more supplies. That was part of our mission: to relieve some of the people on our scientific station on Wrangel Island and to deliver to those that were staying everything they needed to survive another winter. And we did it. We delivered the supplies. Pity, now I come to think of it. If we hadn't reached Wrangel Island and unloaded, we wouldn't now be down to our last 400 pounds of coal.

That last was an unworthy thought, and it was selfish. Worse than that, it was also anti-Soviet. What would be the fate of the Wrangel Islanders if we hadn't stocked them up?

Our not being on an icebreaker didn't bother us at first. We had the *Krassin* to accompany us and the *Littke* in reserve, both of them real icebreakers. Our protectors. With them we were safe. Invulnerable. Or so we thought.

Some protectors they turned out to be. Winter had just set in when the *Krassin* broke a shaft in one of its engines and had to turn back. As for the *Littke*: well, her crew had already spent too long in the Arctic. They had to leave. They had to see the sun or die; Comrade Schmidt understood and he released them. So goodbye you ice ships *Littke* and *Krassin*, and over to the *Chelyuskin*.

What not being in an ice ship might really mean became clear three months after we'd left Leningrad. We were all confident, or at least I was. I didn't know then about the ice. I didn't know that as winter comes on the ice increases so that the gaps between floes grow smaller. And I certainly didn't know how much power that ice could pack, power not only to hold tight to a ship but also to destroy it.

That kind of ignorance doesn't last long in the Arctic. It was mid-September when the weather first closed in. Nothing to do but to sit it out. So that's what we did, all of us, me included. I sat inside my cabin hearing the thrashing about of a wild blizzard that we'd already been told had been carried in on the tail of a hurricane. It was bad but I'd heard worse – or so I thought.

But then there was another sound. A new one. It started like whispering, as if there was something trying to get attention. Soft it was at first but as it continued it grew louder. I couldn't work out what it was, not in the beginning, but, gradually, it came to me. It was the ice and it was hissing as it pressed against our bow. Ice, elastic but, at the same time, unbending.

I left the cabin and went outside. I wasn't the only one. All of us, the whole ship, clutching the rails as the wind tore at us, silent as we stared into the deep night's blackness at this white foe moving down below. Unfeeling ice. It

surged against our ship's (reinforced) metal plates. If it carries on, I remember thinking, we'll be ground up. But no. I
put the thought away. Our ship was strong, I told myself,
stronger than any ice.

I wasn't the only one who thought like this. All of us,
even our captain, positive that we would beat the ice. Men
crowded in the boiler room, heaping on coal, feeding the
engines, sending them to battle, all three engines near bursting with steam, fighting against the onrush, trying to free us
from the ice, turning the ship's screw so we watched it beating down, swirling, hitting, blow after blow, so that the deck
shuddered and splinters of ice kept flying free . . . and all of
it no use. The ice was stronger than any number of our
engines. Our screw was in danger of being mashed up. The
captain had no choice: he called off the attack.

And that, as it turned out, was not the end of it. The ice
isn't static, it keeps moving even though not all of it moves
at the self-same time. This I learned some days later when
one mass of ice pushed against our port side, twisting and
almost overtaking the ship, crushing her against the solid,
stagnant ice on the starboard side. The floor tilted, the ship
groaned. That's when I understood the might of the forces
that could bear down, and that's also when I understood
how easily we could be sunk.

We weren't. Not then. Our ship swung round and that
way escaped the pressure of the moving mass. Now we
were just stuck tight.

Did we give up? No, we did not. Remember who we
are – members of the glorious Soviet Union, ambassadors,
even on the ice, of our revolution. If the engines couldn't
free us then, our experts said, they would blast the ice away.
They set to work with their ammonal. Black they were, sil-
houettes skidding over all that whiteness, laying charges,
lighting fuses, moving away, covering their ears. Blasting. It

was noisy, and spectacular, the explosions seeming to shake the very foundations of the earth. Not the ice, though. It just absorbed the shock. All the force that we could muster, and still it held us in its grip.

That's when the truth dawned. We were stranded. The *Krassin* and the *Littke* could not reach us. Our plane, that machine which was supposed to make our expedition safer than any that had gone before, was damaged beyond any repair. Nothing to do but hold tight.

A lesson in life, I guess: you set out on one course, and the course just plucks you up, and carries you, and puts you down in a place where the things that drove you there in the first place no longer seem to add up.

As if to make this point, on 5 October, that ice played another party trick. It did easily what we hadn't been able to: it set us free. One day we were stuck and on the next, when our boilers turned over, they moved us forward. Cheering we watched as our captain steered through the dark lines of still water that lay between the ice. We saw ourselves through different eyes: as explorers, not sitting ducks. All of us through the worst. Even me, a cleaner.

But as it turns out our celebrations were too hasty. The ice was only playing with us. Soon, too soon, it came on again, and this time in deadly earnest. It surrounded and entrapped us and now it holds us tight. It will not let go until next summer. If we're still here to be let go of, that is.

At the same time the ice keeps moving, constantly north, carrying us along. We have been drifting since October. Drifting and waiting for the end. Stuck in ice, hundreds of miles from human habitation.

We have our radio, of course, our link to the world. We must save its crystals but Comrade Schmidt says that contact with land is good for morale so each night for a short time we sit and listen. From this we know of the efforts being made on our behalf, of our brave airman Anatoly Lyadersky who, having set out on 20 December – yes, that's right: December! – is still battling to reach us. We can also follow the progress of the fearless Sigismund Levansky, travelling in the opposite direction, flying to Berlin and then to London and onwards to New York so as to circle the globe and reach Fairbanks from where he will fly on to us. Oh, the things we hear. We, and our undaunted spirit, are an important item on the news, as important as the Don production fields fulfilling their quota a full two years ahead of plan, and almost as important as the Victors' Congress even now taking place in Moscow.

Yes, we're up there amongst the greats. The world watching us. Waiting. Of course, they're not praying for us – people no longer pray – but they are working to come and get us.

In the meantime we follow doctor's orders. We keep lethargy and defeatism away by exercising daily on the ice. We keep busy in other ways as well. Our scientists continue to do what they have been put on this ship to do – they take measurements – and so do I: I clean.

Some of us have special tasks. The Party members, naturally, Comrade Schmidt's inner circle. At the moment what they are doing is moving our ship's stores. Secretly. They work at night, taking from the hold to the deck the stuff of life – fur breeches, thick shirts, warm underclothing and sleeping bags to port, food, enough for two months, to starboard – so that if, so that when, the ice squeezes our ship so hard she sinks, we'll have time to get off our supplies. We all know this but since the knowledge might panic us, we're not supposed to know. So they hide the goods under canvas, pretending we can't see it. And we? We do the same.

But there is a limit to the things you can hide from yourself and my own limit has recently got smaller. I've learned to read, you see. Better that I had not, for now I can read about those other Arctic expeditions and about those many Arctic deaths. My reading tells me that, no matter how bad things get, some of us will live. Some always do. The only question is how many. On Valerian Albanov's expedition, out of a crew of twenty-three, two made it home. Maybe it will go better for us: maybe we'll be as lucky as the crew of the *Jeanette* – twenty of their thirty-three survived.

There's no way of knowing. What we do know, though, is that if we die we won't go like those others, walking across the ice. Comrade Schmidt has made this clear. He will not walk. None of us will. We will not walk, he says, because that would mean leaving the weak behind, and this he will never permit. Such courage. Comrade Schmidt is a true leader: a true Communist.

Pity he's not in command of an ice ship.

There I go again. At home, such sarcasm would have got me smacked. Not here. Which is a comfort, I suppose. My husband is far away, back in Leningrad: not even his voice can reach me here. I peer out, out at the long, low line of the horizon. In truth, I still think that it's been good to get away. I might even like him better when I return.

When I return, not if. I am improving. I might even become an optimist. And I'm changing in other ways. I've learned to interest myself in the radio report of our Congress. There's not much else to do, of course, but that's not the only reason. I can read, you see, and if you can read you can also try discussing. Not that I have. Not yet, you understand. The people around me are far too smart.

But I can listen. That's possible. And I can think. Although what I think I keep to myself. Take our city's leader: Sergei Mironovich Kirov. If I happen to find myself worrying about him, I keep that worry quiet. I may have conquered the alphabet but I am still ignorant. What do I know of power? Of conquest? Of position? I should not have opinions: I should not judge. What I should do instead is watch.

I was watching my compatriots last night when the radio talked about Comrade Kirov. Rumours were that he was going to stand for the post of General Secretary but no, he didn't. Stalin must have liked that. He is to reward Sergei Mironovich by making him the last but one to speak: the place of honour just before our father, Stalin. I was watching when they told us this: I saw my fellow Leningraders swell with pride. I heard their cry: 'Long live our Mironych.'

And I? I am a stupid woman. What I thought was: careful, Sergei Mironovich. Kirov, who is such a powerful speaker, coming just before Stalin, who is not.

Will Kirov rein himself in? Does he understand that no good can come from outshining a powerful man?

Can the Dead Speak (1)?

Can the dead speak? Can their cries be heard? Have those countless serfs and prisoners of war who died in the building of Peter's folly been speaking out through his city's marshy foundations? Is it their suffering that makes the city so unquiet? Or is it just this place? This St Petersburg, Peter, Petrograd, and once more born again: this Leningrad. Russia's Paris. Its Venice. Its Prague. This 'rotten slimy' city as Dostoyevsky called it.

Yet what, in 1934, would Leningrad care about Dostoyevsky's opinion? The city has a much more modern detractor. A dangerous enemy by anybody's standards. A man who sits at the centre of his country. Russia's leader, whom his friends call Koba. Born Iosif Vissarionovich Dzhugashvili, now changed into that man of steel: Joseph Stalin.

Stalin has never liked the city. How he applauded the decision in 1918 to move Russia's capital to Moscow and how fiercely he resisted any suggestion that, with the Civil War over, it should move back. What would Stalin care about a Paris, a Venice, or a Prague? He's a Georgian, a country boy, his references to east not west. Not for him the egotistic self-regard of the city's famed intelligentsia, its boasting of its music, art and poetry. Stalin likes folksongs, he likes the technical brilliance of V. I. Repin or the solidity of a realist poster, and he likes his language plain, ordinary and clear. When he looks to history, the history he most embraces is the medieval world, and when he looks to the imagination what stirs him are not those constructivist flights of fancy that fuelled a revolution, but the picturesque folksongs of illiterate tribal bards.

And now, as Stalin sits broodingly behind the Kremlin's walls, sucking up power, and as he waits for his 17th Congress to begin, his distrust and dislike of Leningrad seem only to increase. No matter that he recently scored a victory over the city, that by slow politicking, enticement and manoeuvre, of which he is the master, he has made Leningrad ditch Zinoviev for his friend Kirov.

Sergei Mironovich Kirov, Stalin's choice. Born Sergei Kostrikov, and then renamed after a saint and a Persian warrior. Kirov, Stalin's friend, is no Leningrader. He doesn't even like the place. It's too cold for him, too damp. He's from the Urals: he's a real Russian, a real muzhik, a son of the soil, at home in Russia's Muslim east, not its ersatz Europe. But just as Kirov learns to tolerate Leningrad, so are the people of Leningrad beginning to realise that having Kirov at their head could be good for them. For Kirov throws his heart into everything he does and Stalin likes Kirov.

Kirov means so much to Stalin that, when Kirov dies, Stalin will drop everything and rush to Leningrad and, emerging from the train, will, without removing his gloves, slap the face of the boss of Leningrad's secret police. And later, white and shaking, he'll bend over his friend's coffin and kiss him on the forehead and, later still, will carry Kirov's ashes to Red Square, mounting the mausoleum, not last as is his habit, but first, his head turning side to side, sharing his grief with the crowd. Stalin's tribute to his friend.

But at the moment there is no need for grief. Kirov is very much alive and Stalin, solicitous about his health, sends him telegrams of greetings, posts him books and signs them with affection, invites him to his Moscow residence and his holiday home in Sochi by the Black Sea. He, a man so ashamed of the imperfections of his skin that few are allowed to see him naked, is even prepared to take a sauna in the presence of Sergei Mironovich. For Kirov is Stalin's man. His ally, the one Stalin put in charge of the Soviet Union's most ambitious project to date: the building of a canal to join the Baltic to the White Sea. One and a half years it took to dig out the 227 kilometres, and when, in July 1933, Stalin sailed the canal for days on end, it was Kirov who stood beside him. A triumph for Soviet Russia. Who cares that it was built on prison labour and never deep enough to take anything but the most shallow bottomed ship? A triumph it was for Kirov and at the same time Koba gave to his Kirov another gift: this pesky Leningrad.

Kirov: Stalin's trusted man. But even a Kirov sometimes breaks rank. As he did when Stalin made it clear that, since the two five-year plans were finally bearing fruit, he knew what the next step should be. The grip of the rich peasants, the kulaks, Stalin said, has been broken. Food is flowing into the cities. So why not end bread rationing, make it freely available? Who could dream of resisting that?

Who? None other, it seems, than the very same Sergei Mironovich Kirov who sees it as his job to take Leningrad's side and who thus tells his General Secretary of the workers' fears that the end of rationing will bring a rise in the cost of bread. As if anybody is better qualified than the General Secretary to know what the proletariat fears!

And there is worse, or so the rumour goes. Can it be true? Did Kirov stand up to his Koba once before? Did he actually invoke the name of Lenin to argue against the execution of Ryutin? Did he say, as Lenin once had said, that we Bolsheviks must not go down the Jacobin path to self-destruction, that we must never kill our own?

Watch out, Kirov. Don't you know that tides both wax and wane? Lenin's body lies restless in a mausoleum he never wanted, and when the gods are restless, man must suffer. For if Lenin is God, then Stalin is his high priest. Who would dare invoke the name of God against his priest, his pope, his Grand Inquisitor? If Lenin was immortalised by death, Stalin is still alive: if Lenin is a God, Stalin is a Man, and while gods pronounce, Man must act; while gods judge, Man must make his own mistakes.

Watch out, Kirov. These are dangerous times. The 17th Party Congress is on. Never mind you chose not to stand against the leader: you thought of it and now they – your enemies – are everywhere. Be on your guard. Look left, look right – and look both ways when crossing Red Square in case the onward momentum of a government limousine, or a government initiative, should run you over. And if they do, they'll take your city, and the people who live in it, down with you.

Part Two

The Rescue

I will start over again, and change my life's
pattern,
Will put my naiveté to shame.

(Yevgeny Yevtushenko,
The Snow Will Begin Again)

The Orphan

She weaves in and out of the crowd, thinking to herself: small. She makes herself small. Small is better: small stops her being noticed.

It's cold. So very cold.

Everywhere she looks around the railway station there are people walking, or seated, or sprawled on the ground, sleeping with their mouths wide open. All of them bundled up, their breath steaming out of their open mouths like some beast she must once have known or been told about but has long since forgotten. She sniffs the air. She smells: stale breath and roasted chicken; rotting sores and the vinegar of pickled vegetables. The sour whiff of eggs. She's hungry but this food is not for her. Not here. Not in open view.

She is a whole world in herself. Completely self-sufficient. A world where only some things matter. Not many. She can name them if she has to: food, warmth, somewhere to lay her head when she is weary. Everything else, the stuff of the life she had once led, its memories and its bonds and even the language she once used, are now dispensable. And vanishing.

Her thoughts are plain. Clear. She thinks: trains. They matter. They keep you moving. They take you away from danger. But trains can also bring on danger. You can drop on the rails and be sliced into pieces. You can freeze. Or, just as dangerous, you can run into a uniform.

Time was when the trains were stuffed with uniforms. Two to each carriage. Hard men, looking out for the *bezprizornie*, the homeless kids, like her. You could know them by the red stars on their caps, by their swagger and the swinging of their guns. And then: trouble. You must jump.

Not as many uniforms these days.

Or kids. Once they swarmed the railway stations, hungry like her, elbowing her out of the way. Pushing, shoving: some of them were strong. They would steal your bread or knock you off a moving train if you didn't hold on tight. But no longer. These days she is mostly alone.

What happened to the others? She doesn't know. Finding out means sticking around, asking questions. Talking. All dangerous. She doesn't put herself in danger, not on purpose, not unless there is something to be gained. And anyway she really doesn't care. Without the others there is more food, better places to sleep.

Much more food. Recently, yesterday perhaps if she knew what yesterday was, she had experienced a sensation she didn't fully understand, at least not at first. Then she had remembered. Full – that's what she felt. No nagging ache to keep her going: no sharp edge that stopped her from sleep. Full, she wanted to lie down. Close her eyes. Relax.

Full is dangerous. It makes you less aware. It makes you soft. Time to move on. To run. Running. She is good at that.

She wasn't always. Once in the hungriest time, they caught up with her, first trapping her, then holding her and finally sending her on a different journey. A thousands *versts* she must have travelled, shut up with the others. A thousand. She heard them saying that. A number that stuck even if it has no meaning. All she knows is that she didn't like it there in the thousands. Too cold. The steppe's no good: you need a city to survive. She came back. Slowly. Working her way forward, so as not to be caught again. Oh, she was good at what she did. At surviving.

She mustn't stay out in the open, she needs to find a train. A goods train? They are the best. Not so many uniforms. Too many red stars on the other ones. Red. For danger. But no, tonight there are no goods trains except the one, over there, and that is guarded. Something special being taken. Not that one then. Not worth the risk . . .

On any other night, she would go away and come back when things had moved on. But not tonight. Something's happening in the city. Things moving too fast. Not good. Not good for her. Even this station. It's crowded, much more crowded than it should be.

Crowds can give safety but they can also be dangerous. They attract uniforms, call them close. Something in her tells her: wait. Leave another time. But she cannot listen to that voice, for it has come too late. She survives by deciding and then acting. She has to leave. Tonight. She has already decided. She can't delay. She'll take a passenger train. That is her decision. This is how she always makes decisions. She thinks out the one thing, then the other. In order. Slowly and with care. Then she decides and she doesn't have to think.

To choose a train is a simple thing. She only has to watch out for the movement of the samovars, and to use her eyes to follow the coal trucks jolting down the track, to see the engine already belching, the wheels steaming, the long aprons running backwards and forwards, backwards and forwards as if they are important.

There. That's the one there on a platform at the end. That one. She will get on that.

Where is she going to? She doesn't know. She doesn't care. Another place. That's all that matters. And why is she going? What does it matter? She's going, that's all. Moving on. Instinct told her to and on instinct is how she exists.

On balance she decides she likes a crowded station. That way she can flitter, like a shadow, between the groups and not be noticed. That's the trick. To make as if she isn't there. To disappear. She walks. Not fast. Not slow. Queues of women. Crying babies. Why do they bother? Won't they just shut up?

There: she is almost by the platform. This is the hard part. Only people with a permit allowed. She sticks out. Careful. Two fat boots, thick coats, fur helmets over there. Red stars. Danger.

Danger but she has to take a risk. The city is too busy. Something happening. Something that won't like her. Now is the time. She has to go.

A long apron. A porter. She falls in step with him. On his other side, there's a red star but he's looking the other way and doesn't see her. The porter's different: he knows that she is there. She knows he knows, she saw his eyes on her. He, however, gives no sign of it. She knows his type which means she knows he won't give her away. He'll boast about it later – how he didn't call the authorities. 'I didn't have the heart,' he'll tell his fat cow of a wife. Probably thinks she's grateful. Grateful. Huh! People like that don't fool her. They're like all the rest: they just don't want to draw trouble, even somebody else's, to themselves.

She uses him. That's what he's there for. For cover until they've passed the uniforms. Then, as the train belches steam, she leaps, holding tight to her small satchel by its leather straps, going between two carriages, leaping up. Hidden. Holding on.

And waits.

She is woken when her satchel falls. It jolts down but not all the way. She has wound the strap around her wrist and now, as the bag drops into the darkness of the rushing rails and is almost carried away, it tugs at her. She thinks: a bad mistake. She fell asleep. Not holding on.

She grabs for the door. She can barely move: her limbs and her fingers brittle. Cold. So very cold. It burns. Something, she doesn't know what, tells her to tighten her grip, even though every muscle in her body is aching to let go. Danger. She has watched this happen. Once, when she was travelling on another train, she saw another child let go. She watched as he fell on to the tracks. Soundlessly and without a trace that she could see because the train went rushing on. But before he fell she saw his face. She saw how the muscles round his jaw grew slack, how his eyes sagged and, without even being able to name it for herself, she knew what she was seeing. He was giving up, that's what, and in doing so she saw relief.

A rush of air. Is it her turn? Is she also falling? The relief moves in on her. She feels herself go limp.

The air is warm. The end, rushing to meet her. Yes, here it comes.

But. She is going up, not down. She feels: arms. She smells: the acrid, clinging stink of makhorka tobacco. She hears a voice:

'What have we here?'

She closes her eyes. She doesn't want to know.

The Scholar

It was dark when Boris Aleksandrovich left for work and dark on his way home and in between there has passed one of those thick, grey, winter days, glutinous not only with fog but also with murky speculation as to what effect Sergei Mironovich's refusal to stand for General Secretary might have on Leningrad. Now, arriving outside his front door, Boris Aleksandrovich stops a moment, and lets wash over him those exquisite velvet notes that issue from Ilya's violin.

Boris Aleksandrovich often listens like this – sneakily and from a distance – to his youngest son's playing and when he does he always finds himself conjuring up an image of grace and power and beauty completely at odds with the reality of that clumsy, bespectacled, fat boy who would be sure to dissolve into helpless stutters should Boris Aleksandrovich make the mistake of addressing him directly. Perhaps Lina's right, Boris thinks, as he pushes open the door: perhaps they should have let Ilya study in Moscow rather than making him stay at the Leningrad Conservatory.

He steps into the hallway, and as he does he finds himself pulled back into his own childhood when, coming home from school, he would be met by this same, unmistakeably pungent tang of cabbage soup and stewing marrow bones. In those days, this aroma only ever signified one thing – soup: but now it presages something much more complicated, for nowadays his mother only ever cooks like this either when they're expecting guests or when something has disturbed her. Boris Aleksandrovich sighs. Since he hasn't invited anyone to supper, the smell means there's trouble brewing. He bends down and removes his galoshes as quietly as he can. Not quietly enough, however. The music stops abruptly and in mid-coda, Ilya sensing, as he often does, that Boris Aleksandrovich must be back.

Before he has time to wonder how it got to be this way with his middle child, there erupts into the hallway a fiery demon of a woman – his mother, her tiny body enveloped in her long apron. She's muttering and crossing herself; there has indeed been trouble, although Boris Aleksandrovich notes with relief that her expression is redolent more of outrage than alarm. In answer to Boris Aleksandrovich's greeting, all she says is:

'None of you seem to have any common sense,' before moving off.

He follows, the two of them going into the dining room where he fully expects to find his wife and daughter locked in the conflict that has been simmering ever since Natasha announced her impending marriage. But although Natasha is there, she's on her own and sitting peaceably at the table, her head bent down in concentration. Hearing him enter she does two things almost simultaneously. She looks up and smiles and she lays down one arm so that it hides whatever it was that she is drawing.

The gesture pains him. She never used to hide her work from me, he thinks, but then he tells himself it's only natural. She's no longer his little girl; she'll soon be married, she has a right to privacy, and so instead of commenting he greets her with a kiss and a question:

'Mama not home yet?'

'She was,' Natasha slips the drawing into a large cardboard folder, 'but she went out again. To Anton Antonovich's.'

That name is the trigger Boris's mother is waiting for.

'Exactly so,' she says. 'As hard working as Lina is and as tired, what does she do? She goes haring off to Anton Antonovich's, that's what.' She clicks her tongue in angry disapproval: 'Anton Antonovich indeed!' she says and even though her affection for her son's childhood friend, Anton, is well known, each mention of his name seems to further tighten up her lips: 'A bachelor like that, a man no longer young. Anton Antonovich can barely feed himself, never mind a child. And what kind of child will she turn out to be? A savage, that's what. Filthy. Full of lice. Mark my words, Borya, I know what I'm talking about, I've lived through more epidemics than you could dream of; she'll infect us all with typhus.'

'She?' Boris Aleksandrovich tries.

But once his mother's tongue has picked up momentum there is no stopping it. 'She'll certainly be the end of Anton Antonovich,' she says. 'You'll have to go over there, right now, Borya, and talk some sense into him.'

And with that, having thrown up her hands in a combination of excitement and despair, she marches out of the room, leaving Boris to ask, but this time of Natasha:

'What is she talking about?'

'Anton Antonovich found an orphan on the Moscow train. He brought her home and now he has asked Mama to look her over.'

Why Lina? Boris Aleksandrovich thinks, but bites back the question because the answer is obvious. Lina was a practising doctor long before she turned her hand to medical research. It's a fact that Boris Aleksandrovich often seems to forget although he's not quite sure why. But there's no time to think about that now. Lina is back. She drops her worn black doctor's bag in the corner before going to an easy chair into which she wearily lowers herself. Then, she looks up at Boris's mother who, having returned, is now standing in the doorway, her hands on her hips for emphasis.

'Well?'

'The child's malnourished and dirty,' Lina says, 'and she needed warming up. She hasn't talked yet but I think that's voluntary. Apart from that, she's bound to be a host to parasites but they're easy enough to treat – he'll take her to the clinic tomorrow. Otherwise she seems constitutionally strong.'

'But does he still mean to keep her?'

'So he says.'

'What's got into the man?'

'Who knows?' Lina shoots her husband a furious look. 'Maybe he, like most men, thinks parenthood is just a matter of saying yes.'

As Boris Aleksandrovich reaches the top of the stairs, Anton Antonovich comes out, and for a moment the two men, Borya and Anton, stand on the landing, clapping each other on the back. The warmth of their greeting suggests an easy friendship although perhaps there was a moment's hesitation? No: there could not have been. The embrace that now ensues is too heartfelt, an exchange between two old friends who share a lifetime's familiarity and who don't get to see each other as often as they would like. That moment of equivocation was something that can happen in any friendship, their history catching up with them perhaps, the history of a healthy rivalry between two young boys and the divergence of choices between two grown men. None of which really matters, except, that is, if you happen to be a historian like Anton.

This same Anton Antonovich who now leads his friend Boris Aleksandrovich into his home. Although he's much taller than Boris Aleksandrovich, Anton Antonovich would never attract the same attention, for while Borya carries his sturdy physique with confidence, Anton's most notable characteristic is his tentativeness. He is a gaunt, balding, pale-faced, reticent man who, without those thick-lensed, wire-framed spectacles, can hardly see a thing. He's a studious man as well: this you can see by that pronounced stoop, the kind achieved by years of poring over books.

Anton Antonovich's personal space comprises two rooms, a cramped cubicle that serves as a bedroom and a larger room where all other functions (save those reserved for the communal toilet on the stairway and the communal kitchen opposite) are performed. And it is here in this living, breathing, eating area into which Anton and Borya step, that the books seem to have taken over, jam-packed, at least two deep in the glass fronted cabinets, and stacked up on top of three of the room's four walls, and piled high on every other available surface as well. So many different kinds of books: novels in their originals; in English, French and Russian; volumes of poetry and esoteric reference books; books about ancient cultures and modern dilemmas, and, of course, history books, a seemingly limitless selection but each so lovingly preserved that, of this multitude, should you pick out any one, you'd be bound to find its spine unbent and its pages recently dusted.

Amongst this chaotic erudition sits an incongruous figure. A skinny slip of a girl, with straggly, mouse-brown hair and dark eyes that are far too big for her emaciated face. She is balanced on the very edge of a hard, wooden chair and dressed in a faded cotton dress several sizes too big for her ('My kind neighbour lent it to us,' Anton explains). Her skin is angry red as if someone has been scrubbing it, and, although the room is cold, she doesn't seem to care. Her bare legs dangle down, thin and scratched and covered with scabs.

It's hard to guess her age – she looks wise beyond her years. Eight or nine was Lina's estimation, although Lina had also said that she could be younger or, more likely, as much as two years older. She sits listlessly, looking down as if she hasn't registered Boris's presence and making no sign when Anton goes up to her and crouches down beside her, his knee bones cracking as he levels his head with hers to say gently:

'Anya,' and then, looking briefly at Boris, he says:

'She won't tell me her name and so, for the moment, I will call her Anya,' before turning his attention back to the girl:

'This is my good friend Boris Aleksandrovich.'

The girl, who says nothing in response, continues to hold herself so still that Boris Aleksandrovich might have thought she didn't understand if not for the fact that he suddenly sees her eyes darting first in Anton's direction, then in his, and finally back down again. A tiny, almost imperceptible motion but as her gaze flits over his face, her scrutiny, as brief as it is, seems at the same time so sly, so calculating and so devoid of warmth, it almost sets him shivering. My mother's right, he thinks: this is a ferocious child.

But Anton Antonovich is talking to her gently, as if she is a tiny, fragile thing:

'Boris Aleksandrovich is my oldest friend,' he's saying.

'He's a big man and a loud one but he is also very kind. He will help us.'

It's an assurance that the girl either doesn't understand or doesn't care about because she merely continues to sit and, as if in explanation, Anton now turns to Boris:

'She hasn't said a word but you should see the way she eats. She's so hungry – a thing possessed,' saying it of this girl, this thing, who seems set to sit for ever, but when Anton adds:

'Come, Anya, time for bed', she's immediately up and on the move, although rather than going in the direction of the bedroom she heads away from it, moving to the door that leads out to the hall. To get there, she has to pass by Boris Aleksandrovich and, when that happens, he finds himself taken aback by the way she walks, so carefully, so delicately, so quietly, as if she's found a way to propel herself forward without displacing any air. As if she isn't here at all, he thinks.

She's already by the door. Waiting. For what? To be let out?

'No, Anya.' Having followed her Anton Antonovich now gently turns her, taking hold of one of her hands, saying, 'The bedroom's this way,' leading her, perfectly expressionless and utterly compliant, past Boris Aleksandrovich again, her hand so bony, Boris sees, it's more like a claw.

'I won't be long,' Anton says.

Alone in the living room, Boris Aleksandrovich can hear the sounds of movement through the partition wall and he can also hear, if not the actual words, then at least the soft stream of Anton Antonovich's conversation that overrides the girl's persistent silence; Anton, usually so diffident, now speaking ceaselessly as if he aims to bore her into sleep. Boris Aleksandrovich wanders round the room aimlessly, goes over to the window to look out into the darkness and then, finally, sitting down, picks up a book from the top of a nearby pile and opens it at random. It's no distraction: he cannot understand a word.

'It's fifteenth-century Armenian,' Anton Antonovich says as he walks back in. 'T'ovma Metsobels'i's history of the Turko-Mongol invasions of Timur Leng. Fascinating and, at the same time, suspect, full of repetition and historical inaccuracies. T'ovma himself casts doubt on its veracity, saying he wrote it from memory when he was already old.' Taking hold of the chair the girl has vacated, Anton sets it down opposite Borya who says:

'Timur Leng's a bit out of your period, isn't he?'

Anton nods. 'He's an insurance policy.'

'Since when have historians needed insurance?'

'Since politicians decided that history needs – how can I put it – oh yes, a different line. A more proletarian line. You can imagine what this new class conscious interpretation will do to my study of the French Revolution. The Jacobins without reference to the Girondins, perhaps, or Marat without his Corday. Bit like the Bolsheviks without the Mensheviks, don't you think? Or the revolution without Trotsky?' Anton looks across at Borya, daring out of him an answer, the two men sitting, their eyes locked, their history standing between them and the things they no longer say to each other, the silence stretching out until Anton breaks it:

'Remember how we used to boast that ours would be the generation to change history? I always assumed we were talking about changing the historical future. Now it seems like I was wrong. Seems like we were planning to change the historical past as well.'

Boris Aleksandrovich lays the book down, carefully, on the floor. 'Is the child asleep?'

'She will be soon. I put her in my bed.'

'And where will you sleep?'

'Oh,' Anton gestures vaguely. 'In here somewhere. I'll clear a space . . .'

Boris looks pointedly around the room, the movement of his eyes marking just how difficult that's going to be, and, that done, he looks across at Anton: 'Lina's mistaken, isn't she?'

Anton takes off his spectacles. 'I don't know. What did she say?'

'That you mean to keep the child.'

'Then no – she's not mistaken.' Anton uses the tail of his blue shirt to polish the thick glass.

'You're joking.'

'No. I'm not joking. I've never been more serious.'

'You'll not get permission.'

'I will. If you help me.'

'What help can I give?'

'You can move mountains.' Anton smiles then as if to make it clear that this, his evocation from deep within their childhood, is deliberate, this summoning up of a phrase the young Borya would use when about to embark on some foolhardy venture of which the more conventional Anton was bound to disapprove, an echo that Anton now reinforces by repeating: 'You can move mountains, Borya,' to which he adds, 'but will you move them for me?'

'How?'

'By using your influence. Will you?'

'No.' Boris shakes his head. ' I will not,' expecting that his refusal, so plainly stated, will be the end of it, at the same time as he also knows that it probably won't. Anton is a strange combination of timidity and persistence, a judgement confirmed when he says:

'Why not?'

'It's impossible.'

'Is it?'

'You can't just pick up a stray child and adopt her.'

'Others have.'

'Yes, but that was some years ago, during the height of the collectivisation, when there were many more of those orphans around. That time is gone. The countryside is settled now and there is plenty of food. Things have changed.'

'Not for her they haven't.'

'Look, I'll tell you what I will do. I'll check out the orphanages – make sure she gets into the very best available,' Boris says, but if he was hoping that this would placate Anton, then he's forgotten just how stubborn Anton is.

Anton continues to sit perfectly passively, as he always used to in the past, Boris now remembers, this man Anton who uses his considerable intellectual ability not for the good of others, but to separate himself from the world around. This Anton Antonovich who has become so disconnected from reality that he actually believes he can raise his head from his book long enough to adopt a child. It's incredible. No, it's worse than that. Boris's mother is right: Anton *has* lost his mind.

Boris Aleksandrovich drops his gaze.

'I gather that there were only five votes against Kirov for the Central Committee.'

His head snaps up.

'I also heard that over two hundred people crossed out Stalin's name.'

'Well, you heard wrong. The official results are that only a handful of people crossed out Comrade Stalin's name.'

'Ah, but that's, as rumour has it, after a sheaf of ballot papers, including all but this handful to give the thumbs down to Stalin, were, how should we say it, deliberately disappeared.'

'If they were disappeared, as you call it, either deliberately or otherwise, how would anybody know what was written on them?' Boris Aleksandrovich's eyes are blazing now. 'It was a secret ballot.'

'Which someone had to count,' Anton retorts, looking at Boris straight: 'But perhaps you don't care? As your Boss is so fond of saying: you can't make an omelette without breaking eggs, can you, Borya?'

'And how would you know? You never even learned to cook,' Boris Aleksandrovich answers and then he watches his words hitting home. He knows it's not so much the words but the manner of their delivery, that harsh punch he uses against difficult underlings. Now this same punch finds its target in Anton Antonovich's weak belly. Anton blinks with the force of the blow and looks down. In the silence that ensues Borya is reminded of a time when they were young and when things were simpler, when a drunken Anton had suddenly insisted that, 'History proves' (Anton was always making claims for history then as well) 'history proves,' lurching across the room to fetch a fresh bottle, 'that when a new politician is made, a score of individuals lose their friend,' and remembering this, Boris Aleksandrovich thinks that what history has proved is that Anton was right. This schism in their working lives, and in the choices they have made, means they no longer have much in common.

And what of it? Just because they started out as friends is no reason to hold on to something that no longer suits. Better to make the break before they become further entangled. Better to get up, without another word, and walk across the room and leave. Better, he thinks.

But . . . I'm not ready to lose Anton. That's all it is, a simple thought. He isn't ready. He looks across at Anton. 'You're not really serious about keeping her, are you?' providing an opening which Anton seizes:

'About keeping Anya? Yes, I am.'

Their eyes meet and Boris sees how tired Anton looks. How pale. He says: 'Are things that bad at work?'

'Depends how you define bad. I'm no longer a historian, I'm a transmitter of historical materialism, but I guess there are compensations, I'm not required to teach my students to think – which, let's face it, was always the most challenging part of the job. I only have to drum the catechism into them which leaves me plenty of time for my own research, if, that is, any research I was interested in was on the list of permitted topics.' Making a stab at a smile Anton succeeds only in a baring of his teeth. 'Yes,' he says. 'Things are bad.'

'So how can taking on this child possibly help?'

'It will help her. And it will help me to think I'm doing something. I'm not like you, Borya. You've always had a surfeit of courage: you've always known that you could take on anything, even the whole world. People like me – we're not that ambitious. Mostly what we try to do is endure . . . And, occasionally, we do what we can to help,' Anton leaning forward then to say:

'Please, Borya, help me. Do it for me,' that phrasing calling back the past and that time in the past when it was Borya who had asked this of his friend, not once but in a long sequence of similar requests:

'*Please, Anton, please do this for me;*

Please . . .

Hide this document;

Lend me your apartment;

Lie to the police for me;

Hide me . . .;

Please, Anton, if not for the revolution, do it for me . . .'

Never once had Anton Antonovich ever hesitated or asked how he might be punished if he was caught. And never once, Boris Aleksandrovich also now remembers, had Anton ever referred to the favours he had so generously delivered. Never until this moment, this same Anton on his feet now and saying:

'Come and look at her.'

The two men go into the tiny cubicle that passes as a bedroom. The child is lying fully clothed on top of the counterpane, curled in on herself, tightly in a ball, eyes shut, breathing slow and regular.

'She must have fallen asleep as soon as I left the room. She's so exhausted. Please, Borya . . . ,' Anton Antonovich says.

And Boris Aleksandrovich? What does he do? He says, 'All right, Anton . . . I'll do my best,' not because he owes Anton anything, or because he wants to annoy his womenfolk, or because he wants to court trouble, but because he reckons that, on balance, it's probably the right thing to do.

The Nightclub

In the time since arriving in this nightclub Jack Brandon has drunk so much, and so fast, that the only phrase that comes close to describing what he is doing is drinking with mean intent. Yes: he'll also drink to that. With mean intent he pours himself another shot and with mean intent he slugs it down.

'Cheers, Jack.' This from his drinking partner.

'Cheers.' Putting down his glass Jack tries to recollect the other's name. It's Sergei, isn't it? Or Vladimir? Or Andrei. Yes, that's it: Andrei. Except. Maybe he's Timofei? One or the other. Who cares which? Even without a name, the man with his hefty gut, his long astrakhan coat and the primped and dyed beauty draped over him, is identifiably a type, one of those rare breed of modern Russians with either the influence or the money to pay the bribe (or both) that will get him in here.

This club is underground. A cellar. A dungeon. To get in Jack had first to be inspected by (and hand over dollars to) a guard who then opened the gate so Jack could make his way down a set of steep stairs. The door at the bottom gave a warning peal reminiscent of a whorehouse that the teenage Jack had once visited, and after that he found himself in a tunnel lined by swathes of brocade and satin in maroons and pinks flowing so densely from the ceiling that, passing through, he felt himself in danger of being smothered by the fabric.

How had Marya Demyanovichna, his Masha, with her quirky English, described it? Oh yes – she had said that walking in here made her feel as if she was being 'fabricated'. An appropriate enough description, Jack thinks, since everything in this godforsaken country ends up being fabricated: unless, of course, you plan to have something made in a factory, in which case you might as well give up on the idea of any fabrication.

But that's another matter. He will not dwell either on Masha, or on his production problems. Tonight is for one thing and one thing only: getting drunk.

He'd walked along the tunnel to the coat check where he handed in his coat. All very efficient (checking in vast quantities of outer garments at great speed is one of the things at which Russians excel). After that he'd pushed through a second door and into this plush cavern that is decked out in deeper, darker velvet shadows – purples and heavy reds. At one extreme there's a small and badly lit stage on which different acts perform although the entertainment is a fairly tangential affair for this is a nightclub – Russian style – that specialises in hard liquor, hard men and their decorative companions.

Take the woman opposite who's busy uncoiling herself from her Sergei or her Timofei, so that she can suck up caviar through those luscious red lips of hers. In the real Soviet Union, the one that exists beyond this place, women have badly shorn hair hidden under scarves, and big muscles that can make them seem almost indistinguishable from men. Not this one, however. She's a glorious

concoction of crimped hair, dark lipstick, a heavily powdered face and she smells the way women are meant to
smell. Watch her now, stretching out one red-painted
finger to say:

'Here, Jack. Taste this,' in English, practising it on him
just the way Masha used to.

Not that Masha is anything like this gangster's moll on
whose outstretched finger rests a lump of the finest, pearly-
grey caviar. But what does it matter? Masha isn't here.
Leaning across the table, Jacks lets this other insert the
caviar, finger and all, into his open mouth, and then he lets
her hold it there so that the salt of the sturgeon blends with
the salt of her skin until eventually she decides to slide her
finger out, slowly, over his closing lips, the performance
watched by a laughing Sergei. Jack swallows. It's Beluga.
Bad alcohol and the best Beluga: typical Russian logic. He
reaches for the bottle.

'No, Jack: that's as rough as *samogon*. Drink this instead.'
Sergei flourishes his silver hip flask. 'Brandy from the
Caucasus. The best. As good as the finest of fine wines.'

Jack is not interested in fine wines tonight, only in getting
drunk, but since it would be a waste of valuable drinking
time to share this information with Sergei, he merely offers
up his shot glass.

Sergei, for that's his name – Sergei Grigorevich Ilyan to be
exact – deals in tulips from Turkestan and gossip from anywhere. The tulips go to the Dutch, the gossip most likely to
the NKVD. He's a man with connections, a privileged man
who has permission to drink with Americans, the kind who
leaks bonhomie and deceitful smiles. Not an apparatchik –
Jesus, no, you couldn't get drunk with one of those, they're
far too tight-lipped – but the sort of manipulator who is not
meant to exist any more and who exists anyway, in
Leningrad's burgeoning nightclub world.

Sergei, who has lifted up his glass: 'To the radiofication of our country,' he says.

Which Jacks drinks to, though not because he thinks that radiofication is actually possible.

Sergei replenishes Jack's glass. 'Is something worrying you, Jack?'

'Worrying me?' Jack raises his glass high: 'To a worry-free world,' and, throwing back his head, drains it, setting down the empty all in one practised movement, as he says: 'Why should I be worried? I've got a whole factory at my command. Looks great. Great on paper that is. Who cares that I can't get the bastards to follow the simplest of instructions?'

'You're not by any chance talking about the Soviet worker?' As he says this, Sergei's face is set to smile but the lowering of his voice indicates that even a man like Sergei must be on his guard. While Jack understands and notes this anew, he ignores it, for he's too drunk and, besides, is losing patience with the suspicion that contaminates every aspect of Soviet life. And so, in response to Sergei's whispering, he raises his own voice to say:

'Let me tell you about your Soviet worker. Your new Soviet man who always turns up for work. Sure he does. Somebody might notice if he didn't. But work when he gets there? Why bother?' which proves too much for Sergei, who lifts his glass and says loudly enough to drown out anything else that Jack might have been about to add:

'A toast. To our glorious Soviet worker,' so loudly in fact that his words, overriding the general raucousness, are carried to the neighbouring table where they are taken up and sent on, a ricocheting toast that shimmies through the nightclub, that phrase table-hopping:

'The Soviet worker,' saluted, according to differing degrees of drunkenness, in irony or enthusiasm, the words producing an echo that, instead of dying out, gains strength:

'The Soviet worker. The Soviet worker,' like some mad motto washing over the inebriated. And as it circulates, Jack keeps thinking about how much he has begun to hate the Soviet worker, or anything Soviet, workers and these parasites (that the Party line says don't exist) alike. He hates them for so many things. For their vigour and their lack of energy; their drunken celebrations and their tight-fisted privacy; their humour that skitters wildly between the naïve and the downright sick; their ingratiating obsequiousness towards those in command and their uncontrollable disrespect for authority; their bloody-minded anarchy dressed up in the coat of conformity; and, on top of all that, he hates their arrogance, their lack of self-confidence, their culture, their stupidity . . .

'The Soviet worker . . .'

On and on in an endless sequence of contradictions in a country that has made a science of contradiction and called it dialectics and tried to hawk it round the world although they must know it isn't working in this backward place of theirs. It's like some crazed experiment in thermodynamics, the one about reactions and their opposites, this balancing of Russian natures so that what the stranger experiences is not so much a kind of schizophrenia (because in the Russian character each contradictory trait seems seamlessly to blend) but a sense of the inevitability of drama and of death, of opulence and abject poverty, of Russian history carried on the backs of the Russian people although that same history is no longer said to exist, the Russian forced to join the Soviet, and all the time that Jack is thinking this, the refrain:

'The Soviet worker, the Soviet worker,' . . . goes on. The Soviet worker, constantly capitalised, underfed and undereducated, motivated not by the need to make money but by the need to be seen to be working (because that – the work he does – is what defines a worker?) even if he does no work at all . . . and as his thoughts veer wildly, Jack begins to register that the toast is finally dying out and that a man, oh no, not another accordion player, taps the microphone to check that it's working (although why wouldn't it be? – everything in the Soviet Union always works) and, in the silence that accompanies the fading of the feedback boom, Jack hears the door opening. And thinks: Marya Demyanovichna.

He turns and sees his Masha. There she is. Masha with her halo of curly hair and yes, she's come at last . . .

But it's not Masha. It's some other woman with coarse, straw coloured hair, not Masha's honey; thin, drawn lips, not Masha's generous ones; tight Oriental eyes, not Masha's full blue pools. It's not Masha – she has gone – and as he thinks this Jack thinks he doesn't really hate Russians at all, what he hates is the fact that Masha has gone and that he doesn't know why and, thinking that, he is seized by an urgent need to leave this place. To go and find Masha.

People don't disappear. Not like that.

And yet she has.

It's his fault. It's that he hasn't looked well enough. He will go and find her now, the thought producing the deed. He's on his feet, muttering his farewell to Sergei and lurching across the floor, moving to the frenzied quavering of the jubilant accordion, making his way to the door and out, not fetching his coat, for he is in too much of a hurry and it's hot anyway, and down the tunnel and up the stairs and outside, into the frigid air.

It's snowing. The cold hits him and he staggers back. An arm. The doorman. Steadying him. Good thing too. He's dizzy.

'You'll need your coat, comrade.'

And, yes, of course he'll need his coat. Cursing, he looks up into the heavens and that unrelenting flow of snow and he thinks: will it never stop snowing?

The Middle of the Night

It is the middle of the night and the girl, the one Anton Antonovich has named Anya, is curled up in bed in that same position she was the first time, when Boris Aleksandrovich and Anton Antonovich came to look at her, and the second time when Anton Antonovich came alone. She didn't move, not once, not even when she felt Anton Antonovich standing close, his warm breath fluttering down, herself lying, and concentrating on lying and on keeping her breathing regular and her eyes shut tight which is what Anton Antonovich had been hoping for, his find, his orphan: securely asleep. Satisfied, he went away.

Now she can hear him pottering about in the other room. Making up a bed. Singing to himself. Silly old fool. Thinks he can save her. Thinks she'll stay. Thinks she needs him.

Well, he can think what he likes: she doesn't care. She knows one thing and one thing only and it is this: she will bide her time and then, when he's not looking and the time is right, she will go. That she knows.

It is the middle of the night but it will be a long time before Anya will allow herself to give in to sleep.

*

It is the middle of the night and Boris Aleksandrovich has been out much longer than he'd intended. He had taken the long way round, weaving his way past Leningrad's complicated system of canals, so absorbed in the physical sensation of walking that he hadn't registered the passing of time. Now, coming to, he realises that he must have been walking for hours.

It is very late. The streets are deserted, sheathed in white and cushioned by snow that lies so thick about the ground that, nothing, not even his footfalls, can now be heard. Snow, the great deceiver: it lights the darkness more effectively than the muddy yellow flaring of street lights ever could, and it also covers over the potholes that are everywhere underfoot. Snow – big flakes of it falling as Boris Aleksandrovich walks on. In the middle of a square he passes, there stands a statue of Pushkin so completely masked by snow that only the jutting out of one of the poet's neatly turned legs serves as identifier. Pushkin, Boris's favourite: Boris Aleksandrovich salutes Aleksandr Pushkin before continuing on his way, walking along a normally jagged, cobbled alleyway now soothed by snow, and through to the Griboedov canal where water must have been recently spilled for the path is slick with ice. Holding on to the railing that runs by the canal, Boris Aleksandrovich walks on until the mass of snow turns powdery again and he can let go. He keeps on, heading away from Leningrad's main thoroughfare, Nevsky Prospect, as large, patchwork tufts of snow pat down, melding into clumps on his fur hat before falling again, obscuring vision. He will not bow to it: he keeps his head erect, tossing it occasionally so as to clear his eyes. He's in no particular hurry and although logic, and the icicles on his eyebrows, tells him he must be very cold, he doesn't feel cold.

Ahead, a break in the canal and beyond it a square on

which, in the daytime, trams turn. Here the Griboedov canal joins the river Moika: to the left is the narrow canal that leads out through the portals of the Winter Palace Square and into the frozen river Neva. Irina Davydovna, Boris remembers, lives somewhere close by here. He can't remember exactly where. Not that it matters. Wherever it is that Irina Davydovna once lived, she isn't there now. She's stuck on the ice. In the Arctic.

Crossing the bridge Boris Aleksandrovich stops and looks back at the Church of the Saviour of the Blood, a nineteenth-century daydream of lurid colours, fantastical domes and ill-fitting spires. It was built to commemorate the stupidity of Tsar Alexander II who, stopping to berate one would-be assassin, got himself assassinated by another. Irina Davydovna and the tsar, Boris Aleksandrovich thinks, both of them endangered not only by their own decision but by that combination of personal volition and impersonal fate.

He turns from the church and into a side street, walking away from the canal and towards a building in the middle of a row. The stairwell is cold and dingy. He wonders, as he often does, why Tanya doesn't take up his offer of better housing. Not that he would dare broach the subject again, for Tanya, so pliable in so many ways, can also be extremely stubborn. Like Polina, Boris Aleksandrovich thinks (although no one could ever call *her* pliable), or Anton Antonovich, and, smiling, he slips his key into the lock.

As the key bites, two things happen. Tanya's opposite neighbour opens her door: checking on him as she always does. Doesn't she ever sleep? Boris wonders, but he puts the thought aside because the second event is unfolding. No need for him to have used his key: Tanya is already pulling the door open as she also always does, almost, he thinks, as if she spends her time listening out for him. But he knows this isn't possible because she has a perfectly satisfying work life and friends and family too numerous to count.

'There you are,' she says simply, holding out her arms.

And there she is, his dear Tanyushka. As soft and round as Polina is hard and angular: her lips as full in the delight that he has come as Lina's are stretched tight in disapproval of his absences. His gorgeous, welcoming Tanyushka, enfolding him in a fragrance that can't possibly be what he thinks it is, because nobody sells it any more, saying again: 'There you are, Boris Aleksandrovich,' saying it with pleasure and with sincerity, not blaming him for what he hasn't done, or for what he hasn't said, or for the way he's been away too long, but displaying her pleasure at seeing him. Which is all he ever wanted.

It's the middle of the night and Polina Konstantinovna is awake. She's lying in bed, trying to work out what it was that had pulled her out of sleep. Not Borya's absence: she's used to that. Natasha, then, moving about? Polina lies listening, but apart from the interminable snoring of Borya's mother, who shares a room with Natasha, and the sound of Ilya turning in his sleep, there's nothing else to hear. It can't have been Natasha.

Natasha, she thinks, who will soon be married.

The thought adds impetus to Lina's wakefulness. Harsh words come back to her: the latest in a string of arguments she's had with Borya. He won't listen to her opinion: he simplifies everything, she says, and ends up accusing her of opposing the match because she's a snob who doesn't want to see her daughter married to a worker. He's wrong. Her objection is not that Kolya is a worker but that he is not Natasha's equal. And then she thinks, lying there: that's what her parents used to say of Borya.

She was twenty-two when they met, the only daughter of

professional parents and about to finish her medical training. She was beautiful then as well. And popular. The
world, and many, many men's arms, were open to her. Not
so for Boris Aleksandrovich: he was a dubious prospect, a
twenty-year-old revolutionary, always in and out of prison.
And yet she chose him and, against her parents' wishes,
she loved him and protected him, bandaging his wounds,
visiting him in exile, lying to the police, feeding and clothing their new family, and all of this she willingly did,
because she loved him.

And now? Now Borya is a somebody, a man with a
chauffeur in a land where few possess automobiles, a man
with power in a country where power is mostly wielded
behind high walls, a man who not only puts food on his
family's table but many varieties of food, a man whom she
still loves, or at least she thinks she does. And if she looks at
him as he lies asleep and remembers the strength of his full
flush of youth, or the touch of his hand against her skin, or
the crinkling of his eyes when he laughed, then, yes, she
loves him. And yet, she wonders: can love be preserved by
memory alone? Can it wait until circumstances change? Can
it withstand the irritations that daily increase? And can it
survive his involvement with his mistress?

It is the middle of the night and Polina Konstantinovna
lies awake, hoping her daughter's marriage will not go the
same way as hers has done.

It is the middle of the night and far away from Nevsky
Prospect a man is keeping vigil. He is a stranger to the
Ivanovs and a strange man by anyone's reckoning, curiously squat, hardly more than five feet high, with a huge
head from which his oversized ears protrude, a large, slack
mouth, long arms and a rolling gait that has earned him his
nickname, the club-footed Lenka.

His real name? Leonid Vasilyevich Nikolaev.

Leonid Nikolaev: a man whom history tells us lived and, having made his mark on history, died, as all men must eventually. Nikolaev: a curious unknown. Thirty years of age he is, or at least he soon will be. Thirty: all the years he'll ever see.

At this moment, in the dead of night, Leonid Vasilyevich is not concerned about his dying. His two children are asleep, his wife as well, while he has stayed awake so that he might write his diary. He's a methodical man and a determined one and that's what he will do: he will write his diary.

The room in which he sits is one of two allocated to his family, or at least it's become one of two since the state housing department divided it. The other half, separated by a rough partition, is where the family sleeps. The one in which Leonid Nikolaev is seated serves as living room, family room, and everything else room. Long and thin it is, much longer than it is wide, with half a window (the other half's in the bedroom) at one end. A piano is wedged against the wall near the window. The room is so narrow that to pass by the piano Leonid needs to squash himself against the opposite wall, but the room is also long. Like a waiting room. Long enough to house a table, two straight-backed chairs (they eat in shifts) and one dilapidated arm-chair.

Leonid Vasilyevich is seated at the table. In front of him: two lined notebooks (both open); one pen (filled, its nib cleaned and blotted); and one pencil (freshly sharpened). All as it should be. All in order. Now he can begin.

He looks down at the first of the books. The light is bad and his handwriting not much better: he leans down, close to the page, his concentration showing in the deep lines that crease his massive brow, and in the slight trembling of his rubbery lips. He reads through his previous entry and, reading, simultaneously changes what is there. Words may come hard to him, but he is determined to get them right. He sets to work, crossing out this phrase here and adding that one there. Only when this is done, and done to his complete satisfaction, does he reread the entry before setting the book aside.

Now for its partner. That second diary. An exact copy of the first.

That's one of the things they'll say one day about this man: that he wrote his diary twice. Identically, in every way. And if that is what they say then that is what he must do.

Here he goes. The second book in place of the first. His nose down again, his pen poised and, there: he cuts out a word that was also previously excised; and there: another added. He always does this, or so they tell us: he – writes his diary twice. In case one goes astray?

They're important, these doubled diaries. History tells us this. One day, they will be the target of much speculation but now, in the privacy of his living room, Leonid Nikolaev ignores the future bearing down on him in order to chronicle his recent past. There – he has finished, checking and changing the previous entry and now he can set to the task of entering his next instalment.

Six years of schooling is all he ever had. He leans over the diary (his diary number one), his right hand shaping out clumsy letters, his left covering what he has written. The language he uses is plain and unadorned.

He has a rule: to stick to the facts. Only what happened: not how he felt about it. But tonight, he is distracted, his mind continually drawn back to that letter he received. His orders. Telling him he is to be relocated to the railways.

Why him? He's settled where he is. He's useful. And he likes it there. Why him? Hasn't he given so much already?

He is disciplined. Devoted. Dedicated. He rose to the challenge. He helped drive out the kulaks: he cleared the
countryside. It wasn't pleasant but it was necessary. And
although his health suffered for what he was asked to do,
still he did what he was told. And now?

And now they think they can move him on again, as if he
is their plaything. Their toy. As if he has no mind. No politics. No . . .

Stop. He has to. When he writes his diary, this is all he
does. Writes. Not thinks. Not imagines. Not rages. Bending
his head he writes, single-mindedly, ignoring the sound of
his youngest son barking out that dry, unrelenting cough
he's had all winter, writing until finally he has written to the
end.

And then? And then he reads through what he's written,
just once (he never makes changes until he's ready with the
next instalment, at which point he can be objective), and
then he takes the second book and – how many times has he
done this? – copies out the text. So it proceeds. His pen
scratching against the paper, his son coughing in the background, his own breath wheezing (his health is no longer as
good since he went away) until completion.

Finally. Both books completed. Both books closed. He
takes one, just the one, over to the piano. His family is
asleep and the walls transmit every noise to his neighbours.
He must be careful. Avoiding the piano keys and the strings,
he lifts the lid and lays the diary gently against its lines of
wires and hammers.

This is Leonid Vasilyevich Nikolaev. Hiding his diary. Or
at least hiding one version of it. The other he picks up.
Closes it. Puts it in his briefcase. That's the kind of man
Leonid Nikolaev is: his diary always comes with him.

Could this have happened or did someone dream it up?
Would any man write two diaries? Two identical diaries?

And if he did, would he carry one with him? And . . . this kind of questioning is infectious . . . would a man like Leonid Nikolaev, poorly educated, the son of a dead alcoholic, a boy whose childhood rickets delayed the point at which he could walk . . . could such a man make history?

If these are the thoughts troubling Leonid, he gives no sign of them. Now that the diaries are hidden from sight he will, tired as he is, write a letter. He will tell them. That he will not be moved. He won't.

Limping back to the table he sets himself down, pulls a sheet of paper to him and begins:

'Dear Comrade Sergei Mironovich,' he writes.

To School

The blizzard that had swept across Leningrad has finally abated and now the sky hangs low and dark (it will surely snow again soon) although here and there a shaft of light cuts through the pendulous grey. A limpid, almost translucent light it is, that burnishes all it touches.

Such a light is shining on a front door as it opens to disgorge two figures from its shadowy interior. It's a man and a young girl. A father accompanying his daughter to school? Perhaps – but if so, they make an uneasy duo. He's tall and stooped and pale and, as he walks beside the girl, he throws her anxious glances as if he can't quite believe she's there. As for the girl herself: well, she, a skinny, wiry, dark-haired beauty, keeps edging away from him as if she can barely tolerate his presence. And so they make their way along the uneven sidewalk, together but somehow both alone, reaching the end of the block to stop and wait, silently, together but still alone, for an overcrowded tram to jolt past.

The man – Anton Antonovich Abramov – is absorbed in thought. Nothing unusual in that – he always would have been in the past as well – although then, in the pre-Anya period, he would have been thinking about his writing, or his students, or his most recent research proposal. These days he finds himself instead increasingly, and almost exclusively, preoccupied by the child. Take this moment, as they wait for the tram to pass. He's thinking of her again, albeit indirectly. What he's thinking is that if in the time before she'd come into his life he'd tried to imagine what it would be like to walk a child to school, he'd probably have conjured up a small, warm, sticky hand, clutching his for comfort. How very different the reality: when he offers her his hand after the tram has gone, she, compliant in the manner in which she is in all things compliant, does what's required of her: she lets him take her hand for the duration of the road crossing. But the hand that rests in his isn't sticky and it certainly doesn't clutch: it's dry, cold and uninvolved. And unprotected as well, which is his fault: she'll put on her mittens if he tells her to but should he forget (and he's new at this, he often does forget) she won't. Not that this bothers her: if she never warms up entirely, then neither does she seem to really register the cold.

They cross, this man and child, holding hands, Anton Antonovich breaking the silence at the other end to ask:

'Did you bring your reading book?'

Her hand slips out of his. 'Yes, Anton Antonovich,' she says. She always speaks to him this way, as Anton Antonovich, refusing his wish that she call him Uncle Anton as if stressing the difference in their ages in a manner that implies that, of the two, she is the more mature.

Well, perhaps she is. Despite the fact that she never actually initiates anything, he can't help thinking that, of the two, she is the one in charge. It's something to do with the measured way she looks at him, as if to say that nothing he does can surprise her and something also in the way that, in the weeks since she's been with him, he has hardly ever caught her off guard. Only at meal times, when she's prone to attack the food, does her composure seem even partly to crack. For the rest, she's instantly alert and obediently compliant.

When he goes into her bedroom in the morning, she's wide awake. At his first, tentative suggestion that she might think of getting up, that's what she'll do, and then she'll wash and dress herself as he has taught her to, before sitting down to devour her porridge: all these actions taken precisely and in that same order. And later in the day, when he arrives home, she'll be there, waiting, with the table laid, her school work finished and her hands folded neatly in her lap. She's a model child. A child who makes no trouble.

Add to that her remarkable adaptability. Take her name. She answers to it and she has done from the first although, in hindsight, he regrets the haste with which he gave it to her. Even though he's the kind of historian (a rarity these days) who likes to deal with what was and not with what should have been, he realises it would have been better for him to have waited to take his cue from her before pinning her down with Anya. Now there is no going back. Should he try to coax anything from her about her former life, including her real name, her patronymic or her surname, he is met by that deadly and impenetrable vacancy of expression she can so effortlessly assume. When that happens all he can see in her eyes is himself, and his own ineptitude, reflected back.

She's a strange child. So frail and simultaneously so strong. Take the way she's walking now, doggedly to school. It's as if he isn't even there, as if she's walking on her own. And she's so perfectly turned out, so very neat and clean, her striped apron spotless, her young pioneer tie done up in a perfect bow. Looking at her, you'd never guess how her features were, until recently, caked in dirt.

The dirt has gone now and with it, it seems, her past.

She's a survivor, a casualty of the revolution, in her case of the Soviet Union's rapid industrialisation, but, unlike those other casualties, always yearning for that life they lost, she absolutely refuses to look back. She will not talk of her past, of what she endured, how long she was on the road, whether she had siblings, or even what happened to her parents. He assumes they must be dead, victims of the forced collectivisation and the famine that followed. He also assumes they must have been better off than the mass of the peasantry for she is such a fast learner; it is her teachers' opinion that she must previously have been taught the basics of literacy.

He doesn't ask about her past. He doesn't want to push her. He doesn't want to scare her. He doesn't want to lose her.

In the beginning, he'd never even thought she'd stay. He'd wake up expecting to find that she'd crept out, or he'd come back from work anticipating an empty apartment. In those difficult, early days before they hit upon a routine that suits them both, he might even have welcomed her disappearance. Despite the enduring kindness of neighbours, and Boris Aleksandrovich's help, the responsibility of bringing up a child had weighed heavily. But now he's used to having her around and he no longer wants her to go. So he's careful – he doesn't want to scare her off – and he thinks his care is bearing fruit. Although she gives few signs of enthusiasm for the life he has provided, he no longer fears her abrupt departure.

Thus do the two exist. Side by side if not together. Anya and Anton Antonovich, the waif and the odd professor. So different from each other. So . . .

'Anton Antonovich.'

He comes to with a start, wondering how she manages to say his name so blankly and yet with such reproach? He looks at her. She is merely standing there. Waiting. But for what?

Oh. He sees that they've reached the school. Which means she's waiting for him to say goodbye.

'Goodbye, Anya,' he says.

She nods – that's all she ever does – and then, turning, walks through the gate. She is so straight-backed, so self-contained. And he? As he stands and watches her he is thinking how little he understands her.

He'll be standing where she left him. Standing and watching her. This she knows. It's all he ever does. He stands. He watches. Every single day. Without fail. He stands and watches until she has gone inside and, for all she knows, after that as well.

She knows why he stands like that. He's checking up on her. Making sure she doesn't run away. He's irrational. He thinks that, by standing at the gate, he can stop her. As if! If she wants to go, she will. If not now, then later. He can't be with her all the time.

She knows other things as well. She knows that he stands there every morning, that he wishes she'd turn back and look at him. She won't: on the one occasion when she had, he'd smiled so gratefully it had made her want to kick him, and he'd waved as well, so she'd had no choice but to wave back. Never again. When she goes, she goes: there is no waving permitted. So now, although she knows he'll still be standing there, she will not look back. She walks, not slow, not fast. At a regular pace. As the teachers want them to.

She always obeys her teachers. She likes to. That's why she learns so well: because she listens. And that's why they like her. Especially this one, here, waiting at the door. The brunette.

Anya won't remember the brunette's name. She doesn't want to learn any of her teachers' names. But she knows that this one, the brunette, is particularly fond of her. Look at her welcoming smile, broader than for the other children. The brunette likes Anya. She likes a model student. And Anya likes the brunette. She likes the way she speaks to them in the Red Corner. She likes her discipline. Her neatness. Her general uprightness. And that map the brunette made, showing the position of the ice ship *Chelyuskin*. So Anya returns the brunette's smile. Or at least she assumes she does. She's not quite sure. She makes a mental note – she'll check it out. Later. In front of a looking glass. When she has time.

'Good morning, Anna Antonovna.'

She knows that the brunette is probably joking (she has learned, if not to understand a joke, then at least to identify one when it comes) by using her patronymic, as if she were all grown, but even knowing that it was meant as a joke, she feels her smile, if that's what it really is, icing over. She regrets the change: she didn't mean to let it show. She doesn't like to display emotion. She doesn't like to show she cares. She shouldn't have done it anyway: the brunette made a mistake, that's all.

It's a mistake the brunette should not have made. They all know who she is. All of them. They know not to call her that. She's Anya. Just Anya. Not Anton Antonovich's. She says as much: 'I am just Anya,' she says.

She sees the brunette nod. 'Of course, I forgot. Good morning, Anya.'

The brunette is smiling. Her smiles says that she won't make the same mistake again. She is forgiven. She hadn't meant to do it, it was just routine. It's because Anya is weak. Because she stays with Anton Antonovich. Because he walks her to the door.

She'll stay with him. For the moment. For as long as it suits her. The one thing she won't do is take on his name.

Anton Antonovich registers how different is Anya's behaviour from that of the other children. They tend to skip through the doorway, accepting their teacher's greeting as their due. Not his Anya. She stops and, looking up, says something that in turn seems to demand its own reply, and thus ensues a short exchange that Anton Antonovich cannot hear but he can see the teacher nodding and smiling and responding, eagerly, almost as if she's trying to win the child's approval. Watching, Anton Antonovich sees his judgement confirmed. The teacher knows it too: Anya is different. She is special.

Now the exchange is over, and he watches her walking through the door. She doesn't look back. He's proud of that as well. She trusts him: she doesn't need to check he's there.

Time for him to move on. He turns, reluctantly. His Institute isn't far but he spins out the time of his journey (he's early anyway), his pale head bobbing up in the crowd and then descending, his thin forehead frowning as he tries to organise his thoughts for the coming day. All to no avail. Riffling aimlessly through the things he has to do, he can't stop himself from being drawn back into thinking about Anya.

He remembers her in different situations. The sight of her last night, for example, her small head delicately poised above her unbending back, her eyes down, for she is reading not, as it seems to him, for pleasure, but with that same methodical determination she brings to everything. And then he remembers how she had suddenly looked up and, seeing his eyes on her, had closed the book, setting it aside. She got up then, as if he'd asked her to, and she'd started to clear the table. Regretting that his scrutiny had unnerved her but knowing better than to say anything, he had also got up and cleared the plates with her, the two of them working silently in their undomestic space; she weaving elegantly and he clumsily past the piles of books, so as to gain access to the communal kitchen. It was then he realised that if she's here to stay he must do something about this place which he can suddenly see is more a holding bay for a library than a home. He needs more space, that's what he thought last night, and that's what he's thinking now. Space and a woman. Not for him. For Anya. She should have a woman's touch. Space and help – those two unattainables, unless he changes his status in the Institute, unless he proves his worth.

He's nearly at the Institute, this Anton Antonovich, who would formerly have come here, his head full of the history he was working on, but who now dwells increasingly on domestic matters and on a way he can improve his domestic situation. For Anya I will do it, he thinks: I will not disdain the things I must do in order to get promotion. I will prove my worth, and then, raising his head, he realises that he has reached the Institute, and that there is a knot of his fellow workers gathered together, talking excitedly. While the old Anton would have passed them by, assuming that whatever they were talking of wouldn't interest him, this new Anton, who will now be born, walks up to them and asks:

'What happened?'

'How could you have missed it, Anton Antonovich? It's all over the loudspeakers. A terrible thing. The *Chelyuskin*'s about to go down'

The Sinking

I am asleep when it begins: or – to be more accurate –
when it begins to end. It's daytime if not daylight (in this
deepest part of winter, a watery sun shows itself for only a
few hours if, that is, it shows itself at all). The bell is sounding. Our ship's bell – her alarm – ringing as it has done
many times before. It's loud – our engineers have made sure
of that – so that the sound will always shock us out of sleep.
Which is what happens to me.

I sit up. Added to the shrill of the alarm I can hear that
other noise – running footsteps – that always comes with it.
There are raised voices as well, but I can't make out what's
being said. I am still half-asleep. Another false alarm, I
think, and reach out of my bunk for I know not what.

Which is when it dawns on me that this might not be just
another false alarm. Our ship, our *Chelyuskin*, shudders.
Once – twice – she shakes and then she groans. Like an
animal in pain. And then I hear the screaming.

I've already heard the way moving ice can scream.
Many times have I listened to it, this ice shriek, so many
that I have become used to it, or at least thought I had. But
this time it's different. Louder. More inhumane.

Triumphant. Scenting victory. An enemy that knows its time has come.

Our ship, our *Chelyuskin*, reacts, not consciously, but through her body, just as my father must have reacted when those menacing hooves came crunching down. She tries to get away. She rolls. She bucks. She dips and rises, straining herself against the onrush of the ice.

The voices are by now much closer. I hear people shouting. Calls: 'Hurry', 'Come on, comrades', 'Move it', by which I know that this one can be no false alarm.

I throw myself out of bed and, in the half-darkness, stumble to my feet. The paraffin lamp is swaying, casting wild shadows around my cabin. I grasp the lamp. No time to get dressed. No need either. I've slept in my clothes. No need, even, to pull on my coat: I've slept in that as well.

One tug and the door pitches open, unbalancing me, its draught blowing out my lamp. Darkness.

I am in the narrow corridor. There are many people there. I join their flow, all of us moving as a pack, streaming up towards the surface. I along with all the others. I can smell them – I can smell their fear.

Our ship is restless. She shifts this way and that. She rises, taking us with her, and then she falls back, and we end up jumbled all together. There is no way that we can tell what she's going to do next.

She had seemed so much a part of us: now she is other. Separate. Maybe she knows her time is near and maybe, after all the false alarms and her efforts to keep us safe, she is eager for it to be done with. Maybe she wants to embrace her fate, and ours as well.

The ice mountain moving closer.

Lessons that I have so far learned in life. Lesson number one: expect nothing and nothing will surprise you. But here I am and here I am surprised.

Strange, the thoughts that come when it's no longer the time for thinking. What I think now is that, in teaching me to read, the *Chelyuskin* comrades have also taught me how to worry and also how to fear. I, who was so unimportant that the troubles upsetting the rest of all humanity couldn't touch me, now understand that I am no different from the rest.

I am finally on deck. Our world so small. I stand, just like the rest. My mouth falls open. As theirs do.

Lesson number two: regret is a waste of breath and time. I tell myself: no matter that you now can read, that you can understand. That doesn't mean anything. Set it to one side. Which is what I try to do.

I stand and what I think instead is that, after all these months, I know the Arctic. I know its nature. This I can understand.

The mistake, as it turns out, has been to try to make the ice seem normal. That is lesson number three, that I learn out there on deck. What the ice plans to do cannot be known and, on top of that, it won't ever stay the same.

Its voice is deafening. Not a scream so much as a roar. As loud as the salute of cannons, or a stampede, as loud even as the sound that must have filled my brother's ears on the battlefields just before the world went black. As for the sight that meets my eyes: I will remember it until my own last gasp. The ice gigantic. A huge monster on the move. Towering crests of it, wave upon wave, sliding forward, each layer folding itself into the one that follows as they move closer so that, even as they grow bigger, bits of them also break off, fat boulders clumping down, sharp pieces splintering and whining.

Vengeful ice. Shuddering at our ship. Pressing her. Squeezing her. Breaking her. Our ship, our home, our *Chelyuskin*, hasn't got a chance. She shivers. She is shaken with metallic shocks. She rears up as the ice comes closer.

She tries to get away but it's as if she knows she won't be able to and she's right, the ice is much stronger than she will ever be, so much stronger that it seems incredible that we ever thought she could hold it back. The ice has been playing with her. And with us.

Another sound. The crunch of metal. At first I don't understand – the ice is not metallic – and then I do. The port bows are caving in, easily, as if they were porridge, thick and gluey but tearing apart anyway when a hot spoon slices through. A cry:

'Water in hold number two.'

There are figures darting through the darkness. Ordinary people with extraordinary strength. Mattresses and sacks of coals flying from the portholes. Paraffin and crude oil drums – how far-sighted it was of Comrade Schmidt to stack them out on deck – rolling down. And the pigs. I hear them squealing and then I see why: someone is trying to drive them down the gangplank to the flat ice beyond the ship. Of course, I think. We'll need those pigs for food. If, that is, we get out of here alive.

'Five centimetres.'

Not far from where I'm standing, there's a man acting oddly. Behind him the ice pack rises up: she is almost upon him but he takes no notice. His movements are slow: as if he's in a trance. The ice monster screams while his hands seem to stroke the air. Gently, gently. They are unhurried, smooth and heading down. I can't take my eyes off him. I watch him bending and I watch his right hand lowering down into the well of the ship. I see the hand swallowed up in darkness. Down it goes and up again.

Oh, I see. He is lowering and then raising the water gauge and here it comes again. He holds it up. He looks. And rubs the gauge against his coat. I know what he is doing. He's drying it. Which means it came up wet.

'Ten centimetres.'

Down it goes, the gauge, and up a second time, and for a second time he looks at it. And wipes it. Wet again. Our ship is holed.

'Twenty centimetres.'

The noise is deafening. Not only the ice but the noise of us. Orders bellowed and countermanded. 'To the port, no, to the starboard, hurry, comrades, it is almost too late.'

And the sound of her. Our ship. Our *Chelyuskin*. Her final moment. Now, after all this time, she shakes off the last part of herself and her dignity. Her engines pump so furiously that steam shrieks and rivets fly off the plates, hitting walls, clattering down.

As for the pigs: they push one against the other on the gangplank, a tangled mass of heaving black bodies until one of them is flipped up by the pressure, up into the air, squealing in terror, a flying pig that slams down, hard, on to the ice and then it slips through one of the dark cracks and is gone – so quietly after all that struggling, the life and noise sucked out of it by the same forces that are about to swallow our *Chelyuskin*. The dead silent, the living in a panic, the rest of the pigs pushing, their weight pressing, one body barging at another, their snouts locking, no matter that they're suffocating each other, they clump together, refusing to be driven down. The ice is too loud for them. Too big. Too aggressive. They will not budge.

'Thirty centimetres.'

It's almost over. This I can tell. As can we all. A shout:

'Every man on ice.'

I hear it. Loud. Clear:

'Every man on ice.'

The gangplank slick with blood. How did I miss it, that sailor going about his work? Doing what he had to do. Cutting the throat of each animal before throwing its slack carcass, still warm I suppose, on to the ice. How quickly living things turn from alive to dead, I think. The last of the troop of pigs hurled over. A pile of them. Food for the taking, if, that is, the ice doesn't finish the job before we get to them.

No time to think of that. The pigs are gone, our exit clear. A rush of bodies. Not to the gangplank but away from it. More supplies to be saved, I think, but then I realise that this is no longer the reason for this rush.

'Every man on ice.'

I know what my compatriots are doing. They're running to their cabins; they want to save those things that are dear to them. The stuff of their identity, of their individual lives. I think about doing the same. Why not? I also have my likes. My favourites. I can go back and find the book that I was reading. Take it with me.

'Every man on ice.'

I don't go back. What's in a book? I turn away and, as the cry goes up, again, I obey.

Anya

Every time Anya hangs up her coat on her peg, she thinks about the way she likes that it is *her* peg. It speaks of order and she likes order. It's important not just for her but for all of them. The brunette and the other teachers as well. They like things calm and quiet and clean. Not like Anton Antonovich. If they were to see the chaos in which he keeps his books, well, they would shake their heads, this she knows.

She stands in line. Exercises. She likes exercises. She does them well. They're easy. Too easy. Kids' things. She, who has jumped on trains and over walls, could do much more. Not that she would ever make this known. She likes to be part of the group. The same as them. So what she does to keep herself involved is to concentrate especially hard on the simplicity of the routine. She maps it in her imagination, not herself amongst the rest, but all of them together, one unit. She pretends she can see them from above, seeing them straddle out, their legs wide, their arms shoulder height and stretched level. She makes sure her legs are the same distance apart as the child in front of her and her arms are level as well, and she wills the one behind her to do the same. One unit. If she was in charge they would be only one. They turn together. Their right arms windmill back as the left reaches for the ankle. All together: they're making patterns. She likes that. Clean, clear patterns. She's controlling them.

She's so good that the brunette calls her to the front to demonstrate. Too good. She'll have to be more careful.

The exercises are over and now they are eating. The one, she knows, did not follow on the other. She knows, because she has learned to read a timepiece, and so she knows that time has elapsed, that something must have taken place in the in-between. She doesn't, however, know what. It happens to her, this losing track and only coming to later. She's ashamed of it, although no one else has ever noticed. When she comes out of the dark place into which she has, unknowingly, descended, they treat her as they always do. So at least she doesn't have to worry about their reactions: even so, it does worry her that she doesn't know the dimension of the place to which her mind had gone. She's always calm when she returns – quiescent, which feels almost like others describe happiness – but she knows she must keep these episodes firmly under control. She can't let herself go – it's not normal – and it's not right not to be normal.

They're in the Red Corner. Good. She likes it here. This is where she learns the most. Today they're tracking the *Chelyuskin* and the airmen on their rescue mission. The brunette is using that singsong voice of hers, to tell of how that bold comrade Lyadersky has taken off in his Ant 4 to Cape Dezhunyov and to Lawrence Bay. She's not a good storyteller, not like the ones at the Marinsky, whom Anya listens to whenever Natasha takes her there.

But now the brunette has focused her voice, because she's giving them instructions. You are to draw on the map to show Lyadersky's flight path, she says, looking round. She's going to call on one of them. On Anya, because it is Anya's turn, this Anya knows.

She waits in expectation of the brunette's gaze stopping with her, the brunette calling out her name, so that she can get out and take the outstretched pencil and, going up to the map, make her mark. It certainly is her turn. She always counts. So she knows. And so does Genya, that fat boy over there, who sits, his curly head the target of the brunette's pointing hand.

Anya can't hear right now – that also happens that she loses sound – but she can guess what is going on. Come, the brunette seems to be saying to Genya– Anya can see her lips moving and knows that she is talking and, knowing this, can know what she is saying – the brunette stretching out her hand that holds the pencil, come on, Genya, don't be shy, you come up and draw the flight pass.

Anya knows by the reddening of his neck that Genya can feel her eyes on him. The other children always feel this even though they never seem to look at her. If Genya was like one of the other children he might now ignore her. They do that as well, taking pleasure in the act of thwarting her. But this is Genya. The stutterer, the one who often smiles at her. He's different from the others. Look at him, sitting there, bent in on himself, trying to avoid the brunette's pointing figure. He can feel the things Anya is thinking, her imagining just how hard she'll grab him if he dares to get up, and drag him down and mash his nose. The way she'll punish him, if only in her thoughts.

She sees him. He is shaking his head. Saying something. She knows what. He's telling the brunette that it's Anya's turn. He's doing it, not because he knows what she would like to do to him, but because he wants to be her friend. She sees that when he shyly looks back.

She has no time for friends. For anything. The brunette

offers her the pencil. Her turn. She gets up. Carefully. She doesn't want to tread on the others. Picking her way forward and along the line, she reaches the map. Takes the pencil. Marks the path. Lines in the air. Airmen flying to fetch the stranded. Anya helping.

There. She did it perfectly. That's what the brunette says. She turns and looks along the line. He's there, Genya, smiling. It doesn't make her feel quite right. But she? She gives him what she thinks must be a smile back.

On the Ice

There's always one who thinks he's different. Who thinks the blows of fate that fell us ordinary people won't fell him. The men in my family were a bit like that. My father was, and my brother too. The one, my brother, so principled that he went off to fight a war he didn't agree with, the other, my father, so unconfident he didn't think himself worth thinking about at all.

It turns out there was also a man like that on the *Chelyuskin*. Not our commander, who stayed on board as a commander should, until the last man had left, but a junior seaman who, against orders, had decided to stay as well.

We stand on the ice in front of our ship as she begins to sink. There she rears up, this black beast that has been our home, which now looks tiny against the mass of ice. Our brave *Chelyuskin*. So small, also, are those two figures, the commander and the seaman, on her prow. We watch as the pressure of the oncoming ice makes her dip her bows. It's a kind of dying salute. Some of us salute back, hoping as our hands touch our foreheads that we are wrong and that she will not die, but knowing at the same time that there's no point in hoping this. We see our commander, a miniature against the motion of the ship, ordering the seaman off. Not a moment too soon: the ice mass moves again. We can feel it, shifting beneath our feet. We can see it, almost upon the ship. If those two don't get off, they'll both be killed.

Another surging of the ice, intent on finishing off what it started so long ago. Jump, we shout: jump, as her stern rises. Look at her rearing up, high up in the air. The noise is unbelievable, you can't imagine quite how loud. Jump, we shout, she's going, our seagull cries lost in the roaring of the ice. Jump, we cry, and at last our comrade seaman seems to understand and he's on the move, swinging his one leg up and over, and I can see he means to follow through with the other when – look out – her stern has lifted again, so high this time and so suddenly, it throws the seaman off. There he goes like that pig before him, a stick figure, tossed up into the air, and we watch, helpless, just as is our commander who can't reach him, watching him thrown out, that paper doll that was a man, thrown up high into the whiteness of the sky and then down again to be broken by the onrush of the ice, and sucked into its unfeeling core.

How tight we hold on to our lives: how easy to lose our grip.

No undoing of this moment: no winding back. It's over.

And now again our commander has no choice. We need him. 'Jump,' we shout again and see him, after a hesitation, jumping; he's on the ice now and running hard to the sound of our cries, 'Run, she's going,' and as he runs his ship, our *Chelyuskin*, begins to sink down into the dark waters. A new calling out:

'Back away.'

Back away?

'Back away from her. She'll be sucking.'

And we, who as one had run forward now, as one, run

back and watch as the *Chelyuskin* gives one last, mournful sigh and is forever gone.

The pigs left their blood smeared across the snow. Our lost brother, our seaman, did not. Neither did our ship. Not a bone of our seaman's body. Not a fragment of the *Chelyuskin*. And now, as a fresh blizzard sweeps through the place where we have ended up, the pigs' blood will also soon be gone.

Around me there is furious activity. No sooner do they lose one home than they're busy with the next. They're carving a camp out on the ice. Tent poles are being hammered in, engineers are struggling to tie down their precious radio mast in this whipping wind, provisions are being counted and made safe. Everybody is busy save me. I know that they're right, that without shelter we are lost, but all I want to do is sleep. As soon as our tent is up, the one for us crew members, that's exactly what I will do. I'll crawl inside and I will go to sleep.

The others don't understand. They've seen something up with me but they've put it down to shock which they plan to treat by pouring vodka and tea down my throat. Let them. I won't stand in their way. I've not got the energy to tell them that they're wrong, that I'm not in shock, that I'm just back to normal. My time on board – the camaraderie, the things I learned, the things I wanted to learn – I now can see as what they were: pieces of a useless, and a passing, dream.

A dream which I have all used up. I am awake now, completely so. And yes, I admit that those months during which I floated in an empty-headed fancy of togetherness and equality and self-improvement were lovely, but, when it comes down to it, this is better. Better not to dream because if you don't dream there is no fall from grace.

Even so, I know I'm not completely cured, at least not yet. This I know because of the thing that I find the worst to bear. It's silly: it's that the ice doesn't care. That it bears no ill feeling toward us. That it doesn't think of us at all.

'Course I know that ice can't think, that it just is, that's all. 'Course I do. But what I'm trying to say is this: if we could bring this ice to life and ask it what it thinks of us, what do you think it would say?

I don't even have to think about it: I know. What it would say is that we, humankind, are an obstruction to be easily overridden. Passed by. And you know what? If it said that, it would be right. That's why I'm so tired.

I thought I was gaining in strength on the *Chelyuskin*. Now I know the truth. The opposite happened: I grew weak. The months since we got stuck have softened me as surely as this darkness has drained the colour from my face. I have grown heavy with hope and with belief. I have dared to dream. I actually managed to convince myself that I mattered, that the thoughts I had and the things I wanted were important. Now, at least, I've come back to my senses for which I can thank the ice. It has shown me how little each of us matters, particularly me. I am, I will be, my old self.

Like all the others. They are also as they have always been. They talk. That's what they've always done: talk. Rescue is on its way, or so they keep saying. We'll carry on as before, that's what's been decided, we'll wait for rescue.

Today, our radio technician has informed us, forty dogsleds set off from Wellen and Cape North, that cheery piece of information passed from one mouth to the next as if it makes a difference. Planes, the same ones that hadn't found us while the *Chelyuskin* was still afloat, will guide the dogs. An act of hopelessness. It's got to be. If they thought sleds could reach us they would have sent them months ago, and, if the planes were capable of acting as guides, we would no longer be here. But dogs and planes will be our saviour, that's what we tell each other, and in the meantime we will stay here, camped out in this sheet-white desert, wrapped up in this mist that never seems to lift.

It's so still, so very quiet. No ship to creak, no boards to walk. Not that we need a ship to keep us on the move. We drift anyway, on this pack of ice. East-south-east is our current direction. At 0.29 knots. It's cold, minus 36 degrees, and it can get colder. Even now, as I wait to sleep, I can hear the first flurries of a blizzard on its way.

Do I believe it when they say we'll be rescued? I can't answer that. Thing is: it doesn't matter what I think. Never has. All I want to do is sleep.

The Meeting

'*Comrades.*'

Like the rest of his generation, Boris Aleksandrovich uses the word in a variety of different ways: as reproof, a rallying cry, an exhortation or even, as he is doing now, as a punctuation point. And it works. The meeting had been winding on like any other into which a passing Party dignitary had been invited but now the workers, hearing the load 'comrades', has been made to carry, sit up.

Boris Aleksandrovich is on his feet. Behind him, on a line of chairs, are variously arrayed: the factory director; his four assistants; the Party secretary; and a recorder of minutes, all of them looking out on their full complement of workers from engineers (first, second and third class) to cleaning staff, from cooks to accountants, so many of them that the smell that rises is the musk of unwashed bodies, the sourness of hands blackened by soldering irons and the sharp antiseptic of a nurse's uniform. And there they sit, patiently, while their officials deluge them with slogans, leaving Jack, who is standing to one side, admiring the patience both of Boris Aleksandrovich and the workers, for they seem to listen, carefully, as if there is nowhere they would rather be.

And so it goes, interminably, until Jack begins to regret asking for Boris's intercession although, at the same time, he knows that if he'd tried to sort out the mess himself there would have been no factory meeting and no director and not even one of the director's deputies but rather a deputy of a deputy who would, in all likelihood, be a member of the secret police, his aim to collect enough data to pin the failure in the wireless production line on the foreigner. On Jack.

Now Boris Aleksandrovich says that word again: 'Comrades,' shifting his gaze, methodically, along the serried ranks, and if good timing in speech making is about having all the time in the world, then Boris certainly has good timing. He stretches the moment so far it's almost as if he's registering and remembering each individual face, something that can hardly be practicable because there are too many people in the hall. The tactic works. Nobody stirs. Not a movement: not so much even, in this deep midwinter, as the clearing of a single throat.

'Comrades.' That word is now a metronome and a way of changing direction for, having already covered the generalities of factory targets and society's achievements that are obligatory for any factory speech, Boris now says: 'How did our leaders behave when they were informed of the sinking of our brave *Chelyuskin*?'

There's a quickening of interest at the mention of this icon. A lesser man might have exploited this by upping the volume. Not Boris Aleksandrovich. When he says:

'They didn't sit around blaming the technology,' he says it softly, so softly in fact that those in the back rows lean forward better to catch what he is saying.

'They acted. As early as 20 December they sent our veteran airman Anatoli Lyadersky to Wellen. He flew in storm conditions and, even though he's been forced to make a series of crash landings, Lyadersky has not given up. His engineers, our engineers, worked round the clock to repair the damage and now our comrade is in the air again, flying in temperatures so cold, –37 degrees and 34 degrees of frost, that one in three of his Ant 4's engines continually misfires and yet he keeps on flying, determined to reach the camp. And Lyadersky is not alone. As I speak, our airman Mikhail Vodopyanov . . .'

Is he going to name them all?

'. . . fresh from saving four hundred fishermen and a hundred and ninety horses from an ice floe in the Caspian Sea, is covering the eight hundred and fifty kilometres between Khabarovsk and Vankarem. And Nikolai Kamanin . . .'

Yes, he is going to name them all.

'. . . is leading an arrow formation of five machines, of fifteen men, aimed at the same destination. Amongst them are pilots Ivan Doronin, Galyshev . . .' which means they're here for the duration, Jack thinks, leaning against the wall as Boris Aleksandrovich reels out this roll of honour, 'Vasily Molokov, Sigismund Levansky . . .', the names beginning to merge so that only the staccato delivery of numbers – the fisherman and their horses (what in God's name were fisherman doing with those horses on an ice floe?), the 34 degrees of frost, the 850 kilometres – registers, which, Jack thinks, is typical of this Soviet fixation with the concrete, the countable, the arithmetic, every transaction and every interaction quantified, from the *two million two hundred and forty thousand and twenty* tons of peat delivered to the Leningrad power stations in 1933, to the so many million tons of steel produced by the Don steel-making works on the *third* year of the second *five*-year plan, to the *three* crew members per antiquated aeroplane flying in temperatures cold enough to freeze their instruments in a last-ditch attempt to rescue the *hundred and four* members of a doomed Arctic expedition who have already established their own numerical record by so far losing only *one* of their number, this relentless computation so much part of daily life that even Jack has begun to find it reassuring. Looking round the hall, he sees he's not the only one. The cataloguing of disparate statistics, that always seems to be involved in turning a Russian disaster into a Soviet success, is having a tranquillising effect. Heads nod, beating out each separate stroke of Boris's enumeration as Jack shuts his eyes, letting the numbers roll.

'And there are others of our brave airmen,' he hears, 'heading not to Wellen but to . . .'

A break. A beat. Jack's eyes snap open.

'To Berlin. London. New York . . .'

Now, at last, Jack can guess what Boris Aleksandrovich is up to:

'. . . and finally to Fairbanks on the Alaskan coast,' Boris is saying, 'where the US government – Jack Brandon's government – will loan our airmen their most modern aeroplanes, the American made Fleisters which, with their six-hundred horsepower cyclonic engines, will be flown, by these glorious airmen and under the Soviet flag, to the rescue of the Chelyuskinists. Comrades,' that word, comrade, again, and this time it is a rallying cry, 'comrades, this is a new venture the like of which we have not previously seen. The world's two most modern countries, the United States of America and the Soviet Union, coming together to save Camp Schmidt. The time of enmity is gone. Even as I speak Ambassador Bullitt, the first American ambassador to our glorious Union of Soviet Socialist Republics, is heading for Moscow where he will set up America's first post-revolutionary embassy. A new world is emerging. A new partnership.'

Boris Aleksandrovich pauses. Looks around again. Waits for deeper silence and, when he gets it, says:

'And, comrades, our friend Jack Brandon,' pointing to Jack, 'and his manufacturing process are part of this new order. Our leaders have given Mr Brandon a licence to make wireless sets in our country not out of some bourgeois whim but out of proletarian certainty: because Jack Brandon is the right man for the job. Already the wheels of Soviet industry are turning as never before: we – you – all of us together have pulled our country out of darkness into the modern world, out of a system of domination that was feudal in origin and feudal in practice to a worker's state. In less than twenty years we have done what other countries took centuries to do. Our system is the most modern, the most forward-looking . . .'

And the most bureaucratic, Jack almost says it out loud,

'. . . this Communist system of ours. A system to challenge capitalism. But, comrades, remember this: Mr Jack Brandon has the expertise and he has our leaders' confidence and when he says that the diode tubes in each radio should have a vacuum pressure of a certain number of isobars then, although our Soviet glass is tough, we must understand that it, like American glass, still obeys the laws of nature. The radios produced here have all been defective because the pressure applied to them has been too great. If the pressure on the vacuum is too great, the glass will shatter. If the glass shatters, the radiofication of the Soviet Union will suffer. And so, comrades . . .'

A lowering of the voice accompanied, this time, by a leaning forward as if what Boris Aleksandrovich is about to say is restricted to this privileged gathering, this gathering which Jack can see echoing Boris Aleksandrovich's action and also leaning in, these two halves of a human forest swaying in an oratorical wind as Boris says:

'We all know that the father of radio is our own Aleksandr Stepanovich Popov. In May 1895, Aleksandr

Stepanovich sent the world's first wireless signal six hundred yards and, two years later in 1897, thanks to our Popov, Kronstadt and our navy cruiser, *Africa*, were equipped with the world's first ship-to-shore wireless communications. And this is not the end of Popov's achievements. His wireless was used in the first ever radio communication to help a vessel in distress, saving hundreds of sailors after their battleship, the *General-Admiral Apraskin*, sank in the ice floes off the Gulf of Finland. This same radio system is now being used to locate Schmidt Camp: it will enable the rescuing of the Chelyuskinists. And our achievements do not stop there. Even in the early years of our revolution, in 1922, we possessed the most powerful broadcasting station in the world, a twelve kilowatt transmitter in Moscow . . .'

The audience is comfortable now, their rightful place, their power, their Russia, confirmed by each successive phrase by Boris Aleksandrovich who continues:

'But to the outside world it is not Popov but another man, Guglielmo Marconi, an Italian, whose innovation followed Popov's, who is known throughout the world, quite erroneously, as the man who invented radio. And why is this? I'll tell you why: it's because, unlike Popov, Marconi exploited his knowledge not for mankind but for personal gain.'

Which surely means profits are good, Jack thinks, smiling, waiting to see how Boris Aleksandrovich is going to get out of this one. But Boris is an easy match for this.

'Comrades,' Boris Aleksandrovich says, 'we reject capitalism's edict that only the strong should survive. Like Aleksandr Stepanovich Popov, what we do is not to profit the few but to benefit the many. In the competition for morality between the two systems, there is no contest. In the competition for rationality as well – ours is the system that will eventually triumph. Even so, we must guard against complacency. We must not rest back on our considerable achievements: we must increase them. And we can. We can combine the accomplishments of a Popov and, with Jack Brandon's help, the acumen of a Marconi. Last January, as part of our glorious Five-Year Plan, the Committee of Radiofication and Broadcasting was charged with putting into practice the radiofication of our great country. You are part of this great effort – and the wireless sets you produce are helping to build our better world and you can do this . . .'

. . . Only if you don't overpressurise the vacuum tubes, Jack thinks, and listens as Boris gives expression to his thoughts:

'. . . only if you don't overpressurise the vacuum tubes.'

Although it is no longer snowing such has been the intensity of the previous day's blizzards that the small army of street cleaners that chisels off the newly formed crusts of ice and sweeps away the snow has been temporarily defeated. Tall, soft drifts line the road while the poplars that are set back are weighed down by puffed-out cushions of snow that, growing too heavy, drop to earth.

The sound of this pattering, the swish of tyres against the compacted snow and the interminable sniff-sniff of their adenoidal driver are the only sounds that Jack can hear. Looking out, he thinks, aimlessly, that it's like being in a fairy tale, except that in a fairy tale . . .

'What's that about a fairy tale?' From his seat up front Boris has turned and is looking curiously at Jack who must not only have spoken his thoughts out loud but also done so in Russian, which makes Jack wonder whether he is losing control not only of the factory but also of himself, this thought reinforced by Boris's:

'You look tired, Jack.'

Of course I'm tired – Jack nearly blurts out, but instead he shrugs: 'Do I?'

Meeting Boris's gaze, he remembers how, when they first set out for the factory, Boris had also looked tired, his face thinner and more worn than was customary for him, the area beneath his eyes stained by dark shadows but this, Jack realises, is no longer the case. It's as if the speech that has undoubtedly resuscitated Jack's chance of success has also rejuvenated Boris who now, instead of tired, looks alive – and seeing this, another piece of the mystery that is Boris Aleksandrovich slots into place for Jack. Of course. It's clear. Boris may seem different from his colleagues, he might be prepared to risk a friendship with a foreigner, but he is nevertheless a politician and like all the others he takes delight in the exercise of power. He would have to, wouldn't he, to survive the Smolny?

'Stop over there,' Boris Aleksandrovich suddenly tells the driver who instantly complies, the car slowing down and then pulling up beside a field of snow.

'There's something I'd like to show you.' Boris opens his door, a gesture that Jack echoes so that the two men get out and stand for a moment by the car.

They're in the outskirts of Leningrad. Undulating snow stretches out far into the distance, whitening everything so that even the air, which usually stinks of smoke and unrefined gasoline, now smells fresh and almost clean. A heavy sky, bulging with more snow about to fall, drapes itself over the land, and these two, melding together, saturate the distance with intermingled whites and greys. Jack's first impression – that there's nothing here to see – is reinforced, but when Boris steps over the low wire fence that leads to the empty field, Jack follows. The two walk, Boris Aleksandrovich in front, Jack Brandon behind, their shoes sinking into the virgin snow, their breath as thick as the mist that coats the horizon and all but camouflages a line of distant pines. And still Boris Aleksandrovich walks and still Jack Brandon follows until at last, when they are a long way away from the car, Boris Aleksandrovich stops and, lifting up his hand to indicate the line of trees, says:

'What's the matter, Jack?' his gesture so at odds with his question that it takes a moment for Jack to realise that the pointing of the hand is only pretence, this judgement reinforced by Boris's second question: 'Is it a woman?'

Jack manages only half a smile. 'Isn't it always?'

'What happened to her? '

Good question. If Jack knew the answer he wouldn't be losing so much sleep. He says: 'She left.'

'When?'

'A couple of weeks ago.'

'And you're looking for her?'

'Yes.'

'Had any luck so far?'

Jack shakes his head.

'But you plan to continue looking?'

'Of course.'

The two men are standing, side by side, in the middle of a field of snow and, with Boris's hand now lowered, neither bothers keeping up the make-believe that there's anything interesting to see. Their subject matter has, however, brought them close together, close enough for Jack to see something crossing his friend's face – this politician's face – something that seems almost to be a kind of menace. But even as he catches sight of it, it passes so that Jack might have thought he'd imagined it, save that Boris Aleksandrovich says:

'You must stop it, Jack,' an injunction, not a suggestion, followed by a curt: 'It's wrong.'

That way all Soviet men talk, in absolute rights and wrongs, reds and whites, all of them apparent experts in the art of demonstrating the errors of the foreign way, so that even Boris who, if rumour is to be believed, is no great example of moral rectitude, thinks he can throw his weight about this. Not that Jack intends to stand for it. He's off. He turns.

Except he doesn't. Anticipating movement, Boris has already reached out and grabbed hold of Jack, gripping with more strength than Jack would have credited in the older man, as he says:

'You know the rules, Jack. You've had your fun. Now let her go.'

That contemptuous 'had your fun' enrages Jack, but what stops him wrenching his arm away now is not Boris's strength but his disbelief that the apparently affable Boris can talk like this.

'You have to let her go.'

'You'd do that, would you? You'd let a woman you care about disappear and never find out if she's all right?'

'Yes. I'd do that. If I had to.'

'What kind of man does that make you, Boris?'

Boris shrugs. 'A realist.'

'A bastard.'

Another shrug. 'Well, before you convict me for this crime, tell me Jack: if you find her . . .'

'When I find her.'

'All right. *When* you find her, what exactly do you plan to do with her?'

'I'll help her.'

'You'll help her. I see. You met her in the Astoria. Is that right?'

'Yup. What of it?'

'You are aware, aren't you, that no Russian, and especially

no Russian woman, would go into the Astoria without permission?'

Jack nods.

'So you must know she was working for the NKVD?'

'Not working for them. But, yes, I know she was reporting to them. She had to, and yes, obviously I knew.'

'Then let her go.'

'Because she was reporting on me?'

'No. Because if she was and then she went, well, that's the end of it.'

'I won't let her go. I can't.'

'Goddam it, Jack.' A Soviet citizen, and a well-connected one, invoking the name of God, even in vain, is unexpected and it surprises Jack. As Boris, perhaps, had known it would because now, seizing the moment of Jack's hesitation, he says, more softly:

'Don't you understand? Her time with you was up,' leaning close now, half-beseeching, half-commanding as he continues:

'There are so many different kinds of idiots in this country. There are the idiots who end up with piles of shattered vacuum tubes because they think that if American glass can take a particular pressure, then Russian glass must be capable of withstanding a greater one. They're undoubtedly idiotic, but they at least have an excuse. They were peasants until recently. The mistakes they make are a result of their lack of training. But you – you're a different kind of idiot. The kind who should know better but who falls for the oldest trick in the book.'

'Are you trying to say that Masha . . .?'

'No, I'm not trying to say anything about your Masha. I'm talking about the system that tolerated your liaison with Masha and then capriciously took her away. Who knows why? I don't. But I do know that if you go after Masha, they'll throw you, and her, away just as you had to throw away all that broken glass. That's how it is here.'

'What? Despite your talk of a new world? Of an American ambassador in Moscow? You think the old rules can still apply?'

'Grow up, Jack,' Boris Aleksandrovich says, and saying this he looks so tired. 'This isn't your land of opportunity, it's ours, and if you want to live here, you live by our rules,' so very tired as he goes on:

'And let me tell you something about your William Bullitt. Your new ambassador. He's second husband to Louise Bryant, widow of our great hero, John Reed. I bet you think that this gives Bullitt all the right credentials – a Russian sympathiser who has the ear of FDR. I bet you think this makes him our ideal ambassador? Well, if you do, you couldn't be more wrong. No one here wants Bullit. For a simple reason: a man like him has got too much at stake. He thinks he's going to be Stalin's buddy. He thinks our General Secretary will lay out the red carpet. What rubbish. We – Stalin at our head – are realists. We're serious people: we're in this for the long haul. And we're not stupid. We know we have problems and we know we're bound to disappoint this American idealist, and that once he's disappointed he'll turn against us worse than any sceptic would. That's why it wouldn't be our choice to deal with the likes of Bullitt. We prefer people like you, and yes, I'll use the word – capitalist – we prefer capitalists who come here, not to see their Utopian dreams realised, but because they think there's some profit in it. Which is why we do business with you, because we know where you stand. Ignore that at your peril . . .'

'You're telling me that I should make no attempt to check on her?'

'Yes, Jack, that's exactly what I'm telling you.'

'And if she's in trouble?'

'Believe me, Jack,' Boris shakes his head, 'if Masha is in trouble then your pursuing her will do more harm than good. Forget Masha. Forget your wounded pride. There are forces greater than the individual at work here.'

'And bowing down to them will make me wiser?'

'It will keep you safe. And her, perhaps, as well. Your looking for her will only harm her.'

'And you as well, I guess?' Jack says. But if he expected to get a rise out of Boris with that, his expectation is proved wrong. All Boris Aleksandrovich does is shrug and then, having had his say, he lets go of Jack's arm, so that Jack is now standing on his own, thinking, Boris Aleksandrovich is right, he has to let Masha go, and at the same time he thinks that he was wrong before. She didn't leave without any warning.

Jack stands now, in this field of snow, watching his breath steam out, thinking back to Masha's last kiss, and her last backward glance, both of them delivered with a kind of desperation of which he had taken no notice. But now he realises that this must have been her way of telling him their time was over. Her way of saying goodbye.

So is this what it's all about, he wonders, standing in the loneliness of this vast land: is my anger just a way of camouflaging my damaged pride that I didn't read her signals right? And as he thinks this he sees that Boris has raised his arm again and is pointing, once more, at the line of trees and saying:

'And now, Jack, do me a favour: let your eyes follow the direction of my hand and nod as if what I'm telling you is really interesting and then we'll walk back to the car talking about trees so that I can pretend to be fooling that particular idiot who is both my loyal driver and the person who reports on me.' And so saying Boris Aleksandrovich wheels round, aiming for the car, still speaking, but so softly that

Jack surely only thinks that what Boris Aleksandrovich says
is:

'Look at it this way, Jack. It could have been worse. You
could have been on the *Chelyuskin*.'

Luck

In the time before I ever heard of the *Chelyuskin* I never thought about the future. Why bother? Something either happened or it didn't, luck touched or else passed by, death came or was put off for a few more years, so what was the point of knowing what might happen next? But then everything changed: I got educated and stranded on the ice. Which is when I started in the prediction business.

As it turns out, I wasn't very good at it. I thought we were all done for. I not only thought it: I was sure of it. But it turns out I was wrong: it wasn't over. Six weeks later and I am still alive. We all are. And on our way to Leningrad.

They rescued us, those airmen did. Not right away but in the end. We helped, of course: we are not victims, we are activists of our own fate, or at least that's what those in charge kept saying as they ordered the carving of an airfield out of the ice. Our new battle: every day we dug out the ice and snow. Mostly by hand we dug, carrying away the loose stuff, hundreds of tons of it, smoothing and levelling what was left, and every day, when the planes didn't come, the elements, that terrible duo of wind and ice, tried their hardest to destroy our landing place. Us Chelyuskinists were no longer conquering nature, but trying to keep her at bay.

Is this the same for every grand project, I wonder, that it starts with big gestures (in our case to prove that Soviet man could travel through the Arctic), but always ends up worrying about its own survival?

There were three work brigades at our home-made aero-drome, at least in the beginning, and only one in our camp four miles away. Between these two bases, we spoke to each other by Morse code flags when, that is, the weather was bright enough for anybody to see even as far their own nose, which wasn't often. Base camp was called Schmidt Camp, and that's how it was known throughout the world, after Schmidt, our commander.

The world was watching us. Our story was a regular part of the Tass report that Comrade Schmidt would listen to at 4.30 p.m. on Krenkel's radio. He heard other news as well which he relayed to us: news of Adolf Hitler's coming to power in Germany: of the opening of navigation on the Dnepr; of Spain gearing up for war; of Kalanchevsky Square dug up in this, the final stages of Moscow's glorious under-ground railway construction. All of this he told us about and then set us to discussing, each evening, in the study circle.

We even got a telegram from the Politburo. Our very own message. Telling us how proud they were of us.

But hark at me: the way I talk about those days on the ice. I used that word 'we'. Not me. Not I alone. We. That's what being part of the *Chelyuskin* expedition did to me. It was like an invitation to join 'us'– the collective – if only in my mind.

It wasn't like this just after we were sunk. That was my lowest time. I've been a worker all my life, but when we sank I didn't see the point of working. I, with my energy, was tired, so tired, I never wanted to get up again. When I lay down in the tent that somebody else put up, and curled tight into the bedclothes that somebody else had given me, I prayed – yes, I admit it, prayed – that this would be the last time. It was as if my whole life had been one mind-numbing trudge towards this sleep which was all I craved. A final, silent, numbing sleep.

The others didn't think like me. I was alone just as I had been before I ever came on board. Except this time it was worse: I couldn't see the point of working and so I slept while the others carried on, their lives governed by those old stand-bys, rote, regulation and decree. I lay in my tent, trying to ignore their banter, revolutionary songs and cheery statements – in sum, their unrelenting, bloody optimism. They even named their newspaper, the one they produced on the ice (although there was no one but us to read it): *We won't give in.*

We won't give in! As if 'we' had a choice. Or at least that's how I thought about it then. Now, of course, I see it differently but back then if I'd had the strength to hit out at this cheerfulness somebody might have got hurt. But in those days I had no strength at all. All I wanted to do was sleep.

Or worse. On my way to the cookhouse (the only thing they made me do was eat) I would play with the idea of heading off into all that whiteness. I thought about how it would feel: me leaving camp, alone, and when I could no longer see or hear anyone, lying down alone, in all that snow – alone at last – and sinking into sleep. They say that in your final moments you feel quite warm: well, I was more than ready for some warmth.

It was tempting. I almost went. What stopped me was not that I thought it wasn't right, or that it might upset somebody, and it wasn't even that I couldn't be bothered. It was none of those: what really stopped me going was that I knew that, with my luck, I would just be sinking into happy sleep when some jolly, singing comrade would stumble across my half-dead body and revive me and drag me back, and I would never hear the end of it.

So I didn't take steps to die but nor did I do much of anything else. Not that anybody seemed to care. They made sure I ate but other than that they mostly left me on my own. I don't think this was part of any plan, I think it was more likely they weren't really used to noticing me. Well, you don't, do you? Not people like me. Not if we're your cleaners and there's not much cleaning to do.

I don't mean to sound bitter. I'm not bitter. I understand the way the world works, how some things never change. And I did come out of it. Eventually.

I'm not sure why. The pressure of 'we', maybe, or the boredom of me? And that baby. That one Karina, that was born in the Kara Sea. She helped. Now don't get me wrong. This is not some gooey baby story. That wouldn't have worked for me: I don't like babies, but even if I had, Karina isn't that kind of baby. Even the word – baby – makes you think of chubby cheeks and dimples, but babies who haven't had enough to eat, and I've seen plenty, aren't a pretty sight. And that's the kind Karina is – not a kissable baby. She didn't get my attention by smiling either – I don't think that child will ever learn to smile. No – what shook me from my laziness was her wailing.

Could that child cry. She bawled her way through day and night. There was no getting away from her. We'd been moved out of tents by then, into one big area they called the Northern Palace of Culture, a barracks it was, built by our carpenters to accommodate forty-five. It was high enough to take a person standing (not that I ever felt like standing) and it had windows made from bottles and petrol glimmers of copper tubing and wick. A palace on the ice: or so they never stopped boasting. Even I, in all my misery, thought it was okay as long as I could sleep. But that was the trouble. That awful baby cried, and cried, and cried, keeping me awake.

What had she to do with me? I ignored her.

She cried.

What had she to do with me? I turned away to face the wall.

She cried.

What had she to do with me? I closed my eyes.

She cried.

What did she have to do with me?

She cried until I couldn't stand it any longer and so I got out of my bunk, not thinking, just needing to do something, and once I'd picked her up, I wrapped her up against my skin, and then I went out. I didn't have a plan. I just wanted to walk away from her crying which makes no sense because I ended up walking with her and as I walked, she cried, her tears first wetting my skin and then turning to tiny frozen droplets on their way to join the ice. I could feel the wretchedness of her – her beating heart, her thumping anger, her misery – and that, I guess, is what changed me.

It came to me, suddenly, that I was not the only one. That's all. A simple thought. Not that she could understand me (what baby ever bothers to understand an adult?) but that I could understand her, that I knew what she was feeling. And then, oh wonderful relief, she stopped crying and went to sleep. Maybe that helped as well – that I had done something.

Back in the Palace I laid her in her mother's arms and then, instead of going to my bunk, I went over to the cookhouse and signed myself up on a rota. I don't know why: I just know that I did it. There was no fuss: if the others hadn't much cared that I was gone, then they also didn't mind me being back. That's the good thing, I guess, about not being important. Nobody much bothers to feel too strongly about you.

That's how my long sulk, as my husband will call it if I ever bother to tell him about it, ended. My husband, Fyodor Maksimovich – Fedya, with whom I'm back. In a kind of way.

I'd got better and I'd also learned a lesson. I knew what I'd done wrong: I'd counted on the *Chelyuskin*. In doing that I discovered the risk of risking too much. I'll be more careful in the future. More watchful. I won't commit myself again.

But that's the best thing. There is going to be a future – an 'again'. We have been rescued.

The stories I could tell about the heroics. So many of them: the way eight of our comrades lay down on the ice to make a cross to guide one of the aeroplanes in; or those seven airmen who managed to reach us even though their instruments had stopped working and they had to fly by instinct and through air blackened by walls of fog and heavy snow over a landscape bleached white, and who, after all this, landed without runners on ground so badly rucked that their undercarriages broke. Amazing stories: it's almost as if, having gone to the limit of human endurance and human ability, the airmen and the Chelyuskinists joined forces to prove that, with Soviet willpower, there would be no limit. But I won't go on about all this, not because it's wrong but because it's in the newspapers or the history books. Not me: I'm not there. But the details of the way they got us out. Women and children first. And then the others, in groups of only four sometimes, or larger groups, some of them travelling in the bomb carriages below the planes, until at the very last, as the Arctic spring was coming on and the pack ice melting so fast that there would soon be no place to land, they took our last man off. One hundred and four of us ferried out of there by air. We only lost one, the one who went down with our ship.

What followed was our homecoming. Triumphant. First we sailed to Vladivostok and then a special train shunted us through Russia, stopping at each and every station so the young pioneers could sing and shout their hurrahs, and give us flowers, and speeches, and their hopes. There were high spirits on the train: some of the former non-Party members of the expedition even found themselves signing up for Party membership. To Moscow we went, into the very heart of Red Square, and to the Kremlin where our brave airmen were made Heroes of the Soviet Union. We even had the honour of a meeting with our great leader Stalin, by which I mean 'we' in the collective sense. Not me, of course. But some of us did. And, now, we are on our way to Leningrad where they tell us that a model of our wrecked *Chelyuskin* has been laid out in front of Kazan Cathedral. That's where I am going now, I, a cleaner, now to march at the front of a procession that will, in four days' time, celebrate not only our, but also my, glorious return.

And what a Leningrad it will be. We left in the balmy sweetness of the white nights but now nine months have passed and it's April and they say an early spring has come. They say the skies are blue and it's warm. For someone who's been in the Arctic so long, it will probably feel too warm, especially since the blizzards that will greet us will not be late snow but a snowstorm of confetti. The banquet tables will be made of wood not ice and they will be groaning with fruit. Do you know how long it is since I have tasted fruit? And there are other changes as well, or so I've been told. There's food in the stores, they say. Gaiety in the streets. It's not just us. In the months since we left, things have got better.

Even my husband managed a smile when they sent him all the way to Moscow to meet me. He – that brute – he smiled. In that moment, I saw myself through his eyes: no longer his unloved wife but one of the heroes of the *Chelyuskin*. He still doesn't know the half of it. I haven't told him I can read because he thinks reading's a sickness that first creeps up on you and then it takes you over. And he's right in that. Once you learn what it is to read, you also learn to think. To speak. To act. And that's why I'm keeping quiet. First I'll think about what I'm going to do and only after that will I actually do it.

My husband did ask me something, though, that shows even he's noticed how much I've changed. He asked me: did I also join the Party?

'Course not, I said. I haven't changed that much. I told him: I'm not a joiner. That's not what I do. What I do is watch.

Celebration (1)

To one pupil, and one pupil only, will go the honour of being part of the official delegation to greet the returning Chelyuskinists. Anya is convinced she'll be the one. She deserves the honour. She's earned it. She's the best: the neatest (never once sent to wash after morning inspection), the most reliable (to her most frequently go the merit badges for promptness and good behaviour) and the most alert (always ahead of the others). It will be her, of this she is certain. All that remains is for the brunette – it's her in charge again – to tell them the criteria for the choice. Then Anya will have her conviction confirmed.

The brunette is, as always, extremely slow. Listen to the way she retells the story of the ship and her passengers as if they haven't heard it a thousand times. She's no natural storyteller either: one trip to the Marinsky was enough to tell Anya that the brunette doesn't possess a fraction of the necessary talent to hold an audience. There she sits, up high, up front, talking slowly in that singsong voice of hers as if they're idiots.

'Think of it, children,' she's saying: 'how they must have felt, stranded in all that cold.'

Well, they're not idiots – especially not Anya. She is three steps ahead of the rest, not only the other pupils but most of the teachers as well. She's so quick-witted, in fact, and so good at predicting what's about to happen, that it seems unimaginable that she once understood so little of what was going on. Not that Anya thinks about that time. Her past is gone. It is better gone. She focuses only on the now and on the future when she will be the one to go on the parade.

'And so . . .'

The brunette has wound herself up tight enough to deliver the punch line. And, yes, here it comes:

'The honour of representing our school on the delegation will go to the pupil whose map of the Arctic area is the best.'

The map. Good. Anya's drawings are always the best and this one in particular. She'd spent hours on it, making sure to pin down every detail. She thinks in satisfaction of its neat, clear lines, its perfect symmetry, its precise measurements, all of these carefully placed at the centre of a piece of paper that is now scrolled up (because folding would have ruined the layout) and slotted in her pigeonhole awaiting inspection.

'I'll judge the maps after the rest period,' the brunette says.

Which means Anya still has to wait to have her place confirmed. No matter. Since she knows she will be the one, she can wait. She smiles – she's learned to do that also – and, getting up, joins the orderly queue for soup.

After they have eaten, Anya, on her way to wash, happens to pass by Genya. He's standing, tousle-haired and awkward as he always is, beside his cubbyhole, his podgy fingers clumsily trying to unfurl a large rolled up piece of paper. She's not particularly interested in what it contains –

nothing Genya does particularly interests her – but one almost absent-minded glance in its direction is enough to bring her to a sudden stop.

He is unfolding his map and is now looking at it. She is as well although he doesn't register her presence (he never notices anything unless it's shoved right in his face). Looking at it, she sees how good it is. As good as hers? She looks more closely. Genya used colour. She'd thought about doing that but had opted for pencil. Now, seeing the way his blues and greens and whites give his picture an Arctic hue, she wonders whether she'd made the right decision. And there's more. His coastline is curved like the real coast and not a set of straight lines as neatness had dictated hers should be. She chose precision – everything fitting perfectly and to scale – while he has gone for realism. And finally the *coup de grâce*: he's done as she has done, he has a drawing of the *Chelyuskin* on the place where it went down, but whereas her ship is half-sunken his still stands tall.

This last detail, the fact that, in Genya's version, his ship looks proud, will be the decisive, the winning factor. This Anya knows. Genya has given the *Chelyuskin* dignity. The brunette will like that. And besides the brunette likes Genya and feels sorry for him. There's no doubt in Anya's mind: in the competition between the two drawings, Genya's will be the one to win. Fat, stuttering, clumsy Genya will be the one to greet Comrade Kirov in the name of all of the children of Leningrad. Genya, not me, she thinks, but even as she squares up to this inevitability, something in her refuses to accept it. It can't be, she thinks. Genya can't have done a better piece of work than her: someone must have done it for him. Ah. Now it's clear. His drawings are never this good: he can't have done this one. He must have cheated. Her brow smoothes out. She knows she's right. That's it.

She stands, caught up in her conviction, nodding to herself, and thinking that of course this is what must have happened although, at the same time, she also knows that Genya, who has no mother and whose father spends his spare time drunk, and whose grandmother can't read, is unlikely to have found anybody to help him. And yet, knowing this and knowing that on top of this he has few friends and none who'd put themselves out for him, Anya is positive he cheated. Yes. She stamps her foot. First he cheated and now he's about to steal her prize. Another stamp. She can't let him get away with it. She won't.

'Anya?' The corridor has long been emptied of the other children and now the brunette has come to find her. The brunette who as she demands, 'Anya. What's keeping you?', shakes her head and adds impatiently (although she's never impatient with Anya because Anya never gives her cause), 'Come now,' reinforcing this expression of irritation by adding, 'This isn't like you. You're late,' as she forcibly steers Anya away.

As if Anya is an animal. Or a loser.

The cry sounds out faintly from far below. 'Pull the left hand corner tight.'

Standing high up on the scaffolding that has been put up especially for the occasion, Natasha tugs the left-hand strings that hold up the poster of Comrade Stalin, her action rewarded by another cry:

'That's perfect. You can come down now.'

She doesn't feel like coming down, at least not yet. She loves to be so high – that's why she was the one who volunteered to climb the scaffold.

It's a stunning day. A rare Leningrad day, a few feathery white clouds chasing across a sapphire blue sky clear of the smog that so often dulls the atmosphere. It's warming up as well: although the air is still chilled by winter she can feel, in the touch of the sun's faint rays, the coming of the new season.

Like distant seagulls their cries reach her. 'Take care, Natasha.'

She doesn't need to take care. She's fine.

'You'll hurt yourself.'

She wishes they'd leave her alone, if only for a moment, in this spacious peace.

'Natasha,' they cry, their anxiety fuelled by the fact that none of them likes heights, a fact made apparent in their alarm when they were discussing the need to adjust the poster. With the workmen who had erected the scaffolding gone, only the volunteers from the Marinsky, Natasha's best friends, were available, and they, as it turns out, all seem prone to vertigo. All except Natasha, that is. She isn't scared of heights. Or anything. Not any more.

Holding on, ostentatiously, to one of the bars (perhaps this will comfort them) she gazes out over the roof tops. She's so high she can see into Winter Palace Square, where as high as she is, the angel on its seemingly unsupported pedestal is higher. She's glad they haven't covered up the angel as they have done on other, official occasions. She likes the statue. She thinks it's funny that it has the face of one in a succession of long-dead tsars.

From down below another cry: 'Come down.'

She should go down. One final look, she decides, and so she will. She looks out over the top of the Hermitage to the dark glinting of the viscous Neva and beyond it to the burnished dome of the Peter and Paul Fortress. Such a beautiful city, ours, she thinks and yet, caught up in daily life, she so rarely looks at it. None of them does, especially in the winter. But now summer is coming and, with it, her new life. The joy of it makes her want to swing from the scaffolding, or else execute a perfect pirouette. Experimentally she lets one leg sway free, to be greeted as she should have known she would by an extended: 'Natasha.'

Her friends tilt back their heads and stare up aghast so that from this vantage point, and this angle, she can't make out their features, only the vague pink blush of their mouths, opening and closing, like hungry chicks anxious for the return of their foraging mother.

What they want is her safe return but she knows that when she finally comes down, their relief will turn to anger, this anger fuelled by the fact that, despite their protestations about equality between the sexes, they're ashamed that she, a girl, would go where they, a group of four boys, wouldn't dare. The thought makes her want to stay.

'Natasha.'

But she knows she can't. They're only looking out for me, she tells herself, and she swings herself under, her grip light and sure as she sways herself down the descending levels of interlinked iron poles, until, at the last, she jumps, landing as elegantly as a gymnast, and there to stand while, as she had predicted, her friends cluck round her.

'What did you think you were playing at, Natalya Borisovna?' This from Pyotr. 'Don't you have a social conscience?'

'Why a social conscience?' Pyotr's disapproving expression always makes her laugh. 'You think I might have fallen and flattened you?'

'If she had fallen, she'd have flattened a house,' Vanya chips in, in reference to the weight she's put on recently.

She throws a playful punch at him which he parries before moving out of range. She tries to keep a straight face but she can't entirely rid herself of the smile that has recently become a permanent fixture. She's in such a good mood nothing can spoil it and she doesn't mind his reference to her size. She knows she's got fatter recently but she likes it. She feels less a girl, more a woman: less breakable, more secure. And all because of Kolya.

'Talking about weight, I could see that they're selling Eskimo pies and sodas round the corner . . .'

A general murmuring of enthusiasm and approval tells Natasha she's not the only one in a good mood. After the dingy corridors of the Marinsky theatre where most of the backstage work takes place, this being out in the open, and in working hours, is a tremendous release. They will get ice creams, they agree, but before they do they step into Nevsky, standing back to admire their handiwork. And there, at the feet of the Kazan Cathedral under the watchful eye of the poster of Stalin that Natasha has just straightened, sits their huge tableau, their model of the wrecked *Chelyuskin*, not only the ship itself but a scale aeroplane and some of the ships' inhabitants as well, all of these on a bed of ersatz ice and snow. It is, they all agree, as good as anything they've done on stage. A work of art. A piece of theatre sprung to life.

'And it gets us in the perfect position to watch the procession,' Ivan says as they wheel round and, arm in arm, walk on, almost skipping with the fever of their liberation and the joy of spring and not least of all Natasha. She's so happy. She can't remember when she was quite this happy.

It's like being a child again, she thinks, and all because of Kolya. Her sweet Kolya who, with his easy manner and his loving ways, has even begun to win over her mother. Not that Mama has said so but, when Kolya came round the other day bearing the first of the season's daffodils for Mama, Natasha knows the pleasure she saw crossing her mother's face was genuine. She didn't imagine, either, the way that, after her father had made some loving reference to Natasha's new womanly look, Mama had smiled again, the two parents standing side by side in harmony as they hardly ever seem to do these days. And that – Natasha thinks – is the power of Kolya. Her friend. Her husband to be who has the gift of cutting through and clarifying any tangle, and the power also to cure Natasha of her doubts and her childhood fears. Yes. Of heights and even of her nightmares.

A tug on her arm hauls Natasha into the present. A half-impatient 'What's the matter with you, Natasha?'

'She's daydreaming about her Kolyenka again.'

When another of the group repeats the name 'Kolyenka' in a teasing voice, Natasha can guess what's coming next: they're going to break into song. Well, she's not about to stick around for that: they have terrible voices. Lifting out her arms, she detaches herself from the chain and begins to run, her feet pounding along the sidewalk, dodging the crevices of winter, feeling the sun of spring heating her up. It's so good to run, to feel her limbs so free, she wants to keep on going. And she's fast. Hearing her friends' hammering breath behind, she lengthens her stride, easily outdistancing them, running hard and fast both to prove herself and for the joy of it. And so they go, Natasha leading, pressed on by her friends who bump against each other like puppies, all of them racing towards the ice-cream stand and then back again because none of them wants to miss the procession. Especially not Natasha: Kolya will be there, marching with his factory contingent. And so will Anya because Anya said she would, and what Anya promises will happen always does.

The moment has arrived. Rest over: which means their maps will now be judged. The brunette tells them to form a line and to go, in an orderly fashion, to fetch their maps. Anya does as she always does, standing in her usual place, not too far forward, not too far back, standing patiently as ever, her scrawny body at the ready, her back steel-rod straight. Although she's eager for this moment to be done so they can move on to the next, she gives no sign of this. Only after permission has been given does she walk (the briskness of her pace the only indication that she has been straining for this moment), with her hair and ribbons swinging, to her cubbyhole.

Back again she comes, her rolled-up map under her arm, as contained and as uninterested in joining the general speculation as ever, showing neither elation nor unhappiness. She's recovered her equanimity. It's going to be all right. She knows it will.

And so begins the tedious process of the brunette's version of show-and-tell. Each child called by name. Each map unfurled. Each displayed. Each commented on. Such a time it takes. Such a waste of time. There are only two maps worth looking at – Anya's and Genya's – but Anya already knows: it will turn out well.

Now, finally, her turn.

'Anya?'

She gets up as promptly and smartly as she always does and goes to the front of the room, turning to face her classmates. Slowly, without expression, she unfolds her map and holds it up to show the class, holding it so that they can all see it and while they comment with their usual drawn-out 'ooh', and then turning to display it to the brunette. Who smiles in the same way as she always does when Anya shows her work.

'Very good, Anya,' she says.

Back Anya goes, map under arm, to sit back down again, ramrod straight, and wait for the moment when she will be chosen, and sitting, she suspends the passing of time, this thing that used to happen to her involuntarily, but which she now manages by force of will until it is Genya's turn.

Genya is always last. When his name is finally called, he bumbles his way up and shambles forward. Reaching the front, he continues to face forward until the brunette takes hold of him by the shoulder and steers him round. A titter runs through the ranks of Genya's classmates, a sound he doesn't seem to register because now, tongue out in his habitually self-absorbed concentration, he's busy in the seemingly unending task of the unfolding of his map.

The class sees what has happened before he does. Ink. A huge, dark, bloated ink stain spreads out across the page. Wet ink that even now continues to seep through the paper. They see it and they are wondering why he's bothering to display the map even as they watch his realisation dawning. Through the back side of the paper he can see the stain. He blinks. Looks at the class. He can't believe his eyes. Down again goes his gaze, taking in the ink that has destroyed his drawing. He seems to shiver now and then he turns to look at the brunette.

The brunette's smile has frozen on her face while Genya blinks. He's trying but he can't hold back his tears. They spill out, splashes of his despair rolling over his long black eyelashes and down his podgy cheeks like liquefied rolls of fat. He doesn't even try to speak. If he did, he'd only stutter wildly. He raises his head.

'That's fine, Genya.' He's embarrassing the brunette. 'Another time.' He's embarrassing them all. And, more dangerous than that, somewhere in the ranks of the class, a girl begins to sniff. If the brunette doesn't act, and quickly, this thing will spread. She's dumb but not that dumb. Sensing the impending chaos she takes measures to avoid it. She's already on her feet and steering Genya away as she says, over her shoulder: 'Anya. Yours was the best. You will go to the procession.'

*

Natasha has taken part in previous processions – on every 7 November and on other occasions as well – but this one is special because it's about something that happened, not in her parents' lifetime, not in history before her birth, but in the now. In her time. Her consciousness. And look at them, marching past the model – her model – led by the sturdy figure of Sergei Mironovich.

In front the seven heroes, airmen, so handsome in their uniforms, with their red stars polished bright and glinting in the sunlight, and the Order of Lenin, hanging there, in pride of place amongst their other medals. And behind them, just as heroic, the ordinary people of the *Chelyuskin*. Ordinary people who have performed extraordinary feats of endurance.

'Hurrah.'

The crowd doesn't stop yelling and neither does Natasha.

'Hurrah,' she shouts, so loudly that if she's not careful she's going to lose her voice. She was so looking forward to today and it hasn't disappointed. Nothing can spoil this day. Nothing except . . .

Out of the corner of her eye, she sees a movement. So much to celebrate and she has to notice this! She's doesn't want to think about it: she won't let it blight her happiness. But even so, she owns up to herself: it's bothering her, this presence of Dmitry Fedorovich.

Look at him, no, she mustn't show she's looking, just flick her eyes to the right and she'll see him over there, skulking behind the colonnades of the cathedral. He's thinner than he used to be, and less tidy, but he moves through the ranks of guards of honour and security men with a confidence and an arrogance that shows he's doing well. Well, if he is, good luck to him. She doesn't begrudge him his success. She's got nothing against him. In fact, she even used to like him.

In the old days: when he was kind to her. She might even have gone as far, then, as calling him friend. But no longer. He's changed. The way he looks at her! She can't describe it but she knows how it makes her feel. Ugly. Naked. And guilty. He glares at her, you see. Not only now but every time she crosses his path. He doesn't say anything. He just glares.

He can't be jealous, can he? Surely not. It's absurd. Even if she didn't love Kolya so much, she would certainly not have considered marrying Dmitry Fedorovich. He's too old. Too serious. Too grim. And she'd never marry someone who looks at her like that. Besides he can't be jealous. He doesn't believe in jealousy. He told her so, once; he said it was a bourgeois concept.

That was when he used to talk to her. He doesn't any longer, he merely stares, as he is doing now. It upsets her, so much so that she even thought of telling her father, but what can she possibly say? That Dmitry Fedorovich glares at her and she doesn't like it? If she said that, he'd laugh, she knows he would, and then he'd go back to treating her like a kid. Well, she can't have that. She's no longer his child. She'll be married soon: she'll be leaving home.

Which means she is perfectly capable of coping with Dmitry Fedorovich's black looks. She'll ignore him. That's what she will do and having thought that, she looks out again, on to the procession just in time to see little Anya, marching there, so tall, so proud, so well.

'Hurrah,' she shouts again.

Celebration (2)

'Hurrah,' I *hear.*

That roar for me as I pass by. Not me alone, of course. A better way of putting it is to say it's for us, which is the same thing because the us now includes the me, Irina Davydovna Arbatova, a woman who once saw herself only as a daughter of a failure and the wife of a wife-beater.

Me. I still can't really believe it, but then I tell myself it's got to be true because nobody could make this up. The crowd's so big it feels as if the whole city is out to honour us. The whole city *is* out. Even the sun.

I look up and around. I see this city, my city, with fresh eyes. Educated eyes. Eyes that have seen the world or at least some of it. But I am not only looking at St Petersburg, I'm sorry – I mean Leningrad – I am also looking for a person. For my old self.

For a moment I think I see her in the face of a passing woman reflected in that window over there but then I see that this woman is smiling which means, since my old self never used to smile, she can't be me. Which brings home something that I have to understand which is that what I once was no longer exists. I am reborn.

The crowd's excitement keeps us on the march. Fast and furious we go. We are not military trained, but being the focus of so much attention makes you walk in military style, me as well, in step with all the others. I had no sleep last night but I don't feel tired.

It wasn't only last night that I didn't sleep. I haven't slept for days. My first days home. Strange days. Each evening after the visitors have gone – yes, we keep a crowded house these days, another change – my habit has been to lie in bed beside my husband. When he has finished with his business he goes, as always, straight to sleep. He snores – he always has – while I lie there. And I – yes, me, Irina Davydovna Arbatova – of what do I think? Well, I think about the things I've seen and the things I've learned and on top of that I think about the way my husband has been behaving since he came to meet me in Moscow.

The word that describes the way he's been is tentative. It's a new word to me – I learned it recently and I like to use my new vocabulary – but, last night, as I lay by his side, my face turned aside from the stink of his foul breath, it came to me that an old word and a simple one – scared – was better. That's it. My husband is scared of me. Because I'm different from the way I used to be. Because I'm different from him.

Not that he would ever put this into words. He doesn't put much into words. Never has.

How would I, then, me with my bigger vocabulary, describe the way I've changed? Would I say, as I know he believes, that I have hardened?

Well, yes, maybe I would. Maybe I have been hardened.

Although, if I think about it some more, and if I think about the way I was before I set foot on board ship – without hope, or even emotion – then I don't think you can get much harder than that.

Maybe a better way of describing my changes would be to

say that I've become more hard-eyed. Less confused. I never was one for pretence but now those two other veils – ignorance and apathy – have been lifted. At least for the moment, for I am still a realist. I know that this new confidence of mine won't last much longer than the fraction of time it took to come into being – the same time, in fact, that it will take for my husband's fear of me to wear off, for the visitors to stop coming, and for the present to be turned into memory. And all of this will happen for the simplest of reasons: ordinary life will take over. Dreams are for the old, the idle or for artists. For the rest of us, ordinary people like me, reality soon stretches out its tentacles to fill the space of any dream.

Which is why I have decided to take matters into my own hands before it is too late. I won't sit waiting for reality to interfere or for my husband to find a way to slot me back into his world. I'm leaving. Him. His mother. His sisters. This part of Leningrad.

I've already taken the first steps, although I haven't told them. Today, before the procession, I went out and got myself a divorce. It was easy. Since we don't have children, all that was asked of me was my name and his, before and after marriage, our occupations, social positions and addresses, my identification document and my signature. My signature, not my mark. My first ever signature: I signed it with a fanfare and did I enjoy that. And then it was over.

I am no longer a wife. Or a daughter-in-law. Or, even, a daughter. I have another life to live. My own.

I haven't entirely lost my mind. I've kept some safeguards. I'm going back to work at the Smolny, at least part-time. I fit in there: I've been there all my adult life. It's my security, the thing that never lets me down. So I'll stay at the Smolny, but I've also got myself another job, and this one comes with its own accommodation.

Boris Aleksandrovich Ivanov found it for me.

Boris Aleksandrovich was sheepish when he came to greet me. Shamefaced about his part in getting me on the *Chelyuskin*. He acted as if he owed me. I didn't think he did, what happened was not his fault, but I didn't bother saying so. After all, if Boris Aleksandrovich insists on taking the blame then who am I to stop him? That way, I thought, I might even get something from him. And sure enough, so it turned out.

Boris Aleksandrovich introduced me to a professor. A lanky, white dormouse of a man who looks as if he's never seen the sun. He has a daughter. She's not exactly his daughter, she looks nothing like him, but she somehow also is. I didn't ask for details. I don't need them. No point in knowing everything: that I've always understood. But what I did learn is that this professor needs someone to cook and clean and keep the daughter company. I can do all that. I've been doing it all my life.

I'll move in there today. But before I do, I have one job left. I must tell the man who thinks he is my husband that he is my ex-husband. I'll tell him privately but I'll make sure we're in a public space. That will be safer. His pride is bound to be hurt, and when Fedya's pride is hurt his fists lash out. (When anything occurs that he can't control – which in his case is almost everything – that happens as a matter of course.)

I sound unfeeling but I'm not: I'm just controlled. As I lay in bed last night, as his fetid grunting passed itself through the feathers of our shared mattress and into me, I even found myself wondering whether, behind the anger he so often shows me, my husband doesn't nurse some other, more tender feelings for me. I couldn't decide. No matter how long I continued to lie there, long after he had rolled away and gone to sleep, I couldn't figure it. The thing is: I don't know this man I married. How strange to think that now but not before.

As for me: will I feel the loss of him? Will I miss him? Did I love him? Do I still? These are not questions I could ever answer. For ordinary people like me, love is a luxury. Although, perhaps that's dishonest, using the collective to back up what I believe: that love is a luxury. So I'll take responsibility and I'll say it boldly: I cannot afford love and I don't particularly want to. I've always been this way.

This doesn't mean that everything must stay the same. I'm not a clever woman and I never will be, no matter how many books I read, but one thing I know: I'm no longer just any other woman. I am a survivor of the *Chelyuskin*.

It's not nostalgia for the ship that makes me see myself that way. No, what matters is not what the *Chelyuskin* did, but the fact that I turned out to be different from her. She sank. I did not. Which makes me a survivor, something no one in my family (apart from my mother, who hasn't really ever lived) ever managed. I have broken the mould. I did not become a victim. I will not.

Every decision follows, naturally, from this. If I have the chance, then I must take it. And so, when they cheer, I hold my head up high. I know I'm not a hero but if for this one moment in my life they want to treat me as if I am, why not?

We are no longer marching. We have stopped. We are standing. We are listening.

In front of us a man, stout and stocky, his high boots planted astride the platform. One corner of his long grey coat lifts in the wind but his peaked hat is wedged on top of his square face and it doesn't move. In another time he might seem like an unattractive man, his skin pock-marked and his face a little too broad and too coarse to be called handsome, but this man has presence and he has power. He is Sergei Mironovich Kirov and he can talk. I knew that already; hadn't I listened to him endlessly on the wireless? What I didn't know until this moment is how much power and how much authority, and how much conviction, Sergei Mironovich carries when he talks, not only to you, but also about you.

Listen to the things he's saying. If I were to believe the half of it, I'd blush. He's calling us the vanguard. Us, and that includes me: the vanguard! He says we are ambassadors of this glorious Soviet society, that we are the proof of it. And you know what? Kirov is right. Ask yourself: which other country would have put so much into rescuing such a small band of people? Which other Arctic expedition has been rescued with so many of its people alive?

They say it's aeroplanes and radio that made the difference, and I know there's truth in that, but I also know there *is* something different about us. About our leadership. About Comrade Schmidt who refused to leave the weak behind. Who made us stick together. Who made us whole. And thinking this, as our Sergei Mironovich finishes his speech and as the crowd responds, and one of our number steps forward and presents him with the polar bear pelt that we brought back, I join the crowd, this my first time ever, raising my voice as I, too, shout:

'Hurrah.'

The Stinging

'*There.*'

That clear child's voice cuts through the still, hot afternoon and into Boris Aleksandrovich's reverie. He looks up, startled, and, following the direction of Anya's hand, sees the makeshift box shaking while from inside there issues the buzz of a stray bee which has found its way through the narrow opening and, picking through traces of the honey and anise syrup that shouldn't be there but are, can't quite believe its luck. Boris Aleksandrovich puts one finger to his lips, signalling quiet. Unnecessary really: Anya's hardly the greatest of conversationalists.

The buzzing is growing more frenetic: the bee looking for a way out.

Boris Aleksandrovich says: 'Watch carefully.'

Anya nods. That's all. It's a nod, so precise and composed and so different, Boris Aleksandrovich thinks, from the response that a similarly aged Natasha might have produced.

Natasha used to love collecting honey just as Anya seems to be liking it, but whereas Natasha used to throw herself into the project (so much so that she had once knocked over

the box in her eagerness) Anya sits quietly, her furious concentration stiffening her elfin face, this concentration she
applies to everything that touches her, this child who is so
undersize, so frail and yet so strong. Sometimes, very occasionally, when she smiles, her face lights up as if she's only
just discovered how to smile, but for the most part she
exudes this quality of absorption, of watchfulness.

'There,' she suddenly says. She's right. The bee is out of
the box and off.

Boris Aleksandrovich glances at his watch, registering
the time and then saying: 'Did you see its colouring?'

She just looks back at him. Of course she saw its colouring. She saw it, didn't she?

'It was almost all lead-grey. The mark of the true
Caucasian bee. *Apies mellifera caucasica.*'

This time, Anya's dismissive nod tells him that she's not
interested in the classification but only in the task in hand:
the location of the hive, the collection of its honey. Having
fixed the direction of its flight path with her gaze, she takes
a twig and marks it. Just to be sure.

'Good. Now we'll time how long it takes for the next one
to arrive.'

Another impatient nod as if this is nothing new. Well,
perhaps it isn't. There's got to be information stored in her
memory from the time before Anton found her even if she
never lets it slip. Such a mystery this child, Boris
Aleksandrovich thinks, looking to where she sits on the
grass, her bare, thin legs crossed. Even relaxing, she looks
watchful.

She's certainly vigilant enough for two. Settling himself
into his wicker chair, Boris Aleksandrovich yawns. From
somewhere in the middle distance, he can hear the sound of
Natasha's laughing voice. They're by the lake, she and
Kolya, entertaining Misha's two little boys, as they have

been for hours. And so the generations turn, Boris Aleksandrovich thinks, as he sits unusually relaxed and relaxedly contented, sitting heavy eyed with food and with the idleness of this hot, still summer's afternoon. He's not the only one. Through half-closed eyes, he can just make out the prone shapes of his eldest son, Misha, and Misha's wife, Nina, flat out, both of them, on a rug under the birch tree. To their right, Lina has been pretending to read but now the book is in her lap and her head keeps lolling down to her chest from where she jerkily fetches it up only to have it gradually droop again. Even Boris's mother has got as close to relaxation as she will ever let herself. Ignoring the mound of dirty plates and muslin-shrouded leftovers strewn all over the long, wooden outdoor table, she's sitting in the shade cast by the sloping roof of their green-painted dacha, her legs gnarled and knobbed and splayed out in front of her, as her needle dips lazily in and out of the blouse she's embroidering.

It's hot and still and yet every now and then the soft breeze, scented by pine and fir, that riffles at the pages of Lina's book, carries with it an unexpected, chilly edge: the first, faint hint of the beginning of the end of summer. There are other signs as well: although the trees that surround the dacha are decked in their dark summer's green, look carefully, look down, and you will see the first sprouting of those spongy mushroom clusters that will eventually carpet the forest floor, while the sunset colours of gold and purple and russet are already showing themselves on the leaves of the great lindens that line the road out. Perhaps this is why Boris's mother has allowed herself a rest: because the season of jam making will soon be upon her, her cherry-dyed hands busy weaving unending circles, her huge, wooden spoon ploughing its way through those huge copper vats overflowing with fruits and simmering sugars.

All this, however, for the future. In the now, as the breeze drops, the warning of a winter to come also fades and now Boris Aleksandrovich is conscious only of the heat of the sun through his shirt sleeves. Settling further into his chair, he listens absently to the insistent, thickening rasping of a great tit sounding above the fast, high-pitched warbling of a pair of greenfinches, and above both, but melodically, as if in harmony, Natasha's laughter. Natasha, whose marriage to Kolya, and whose thickening of her waist, the sign of the child she is carrying, seems to have brought a contentment that Boris Aleksandrovich doesn't usually associate with his normally impatient daughter. And, more astonishingly perhaps, this ease has been visited, not only on Natasha but on her parents as well, with the summer bringing a sense of acceptance and of companionship between himself and Lina, that Boris had assumed forever disappeared. In fact, Boris Aleksandrovich thinks, in all aspects life is good, and thinking that he closes his eyes, sealing out the light.

'A perfect moment.'

That voice startles Boris into opening his eyes again in time to see Anton Antonovich, his face flushed from the exertion of his walk, dropping down to the ground beside Anya. When Anton reaches out, affectionately, to tousle Anya's hair, Boris is pleased to note that, though the child makes no move to acknowledge the affection, at least she doesn't flinch away as she would once have done.

'A day away from history,' Anton says.

'Why away from it?'

'Because as Hegel says: times of happiness are history's empty pages.'

For Anton to mention that word – happiness, and with a smile on his face – even in the context of Hegel, shows how much Anya's presence in his life has transformed him. Anya, and the satisfaction of the long summer as well, that seem to have worked their way even below the surface of his skin so it is no longer its usually unhealthy, chalky white, and into his limbs as well, which, normally ungainly and unbending, now stretch out like any other lithe human being's as Anton lies back, resting on his elbows.

Those days of winter, those cold, anxious days that seemed in memory to have been punctuated by sharp, raised voices and aggressive uncertainty, come back to Boris Aleksandrovich, like an unreal dream which cannot be properly caught or examined during daylight hours. How seriously we took ourselves, Boris Aleksandrovich thinks, and thinks as well that, just as Lina has been proved wrong about Kolya – and admitted as much – so had Boris Aleksandrovich failed to understand how very lonely Anton must have been and how good it would be for him to have something, somebody, to care for.

'There.'

Boris Aleksandrovich opens his eyes in time to see that Anya is right again. That first bee, the forager, has done its job and danced its dance and now the box is the target for the second wave, three or four bees this time, that are busy circling it before working their way inside.

A glance at his watch and: 'Twelve minutes,' he says. 'Which means their hive is just under a mile away. Let them take their fill and then, after they're gone, we'll move the box.'

Which they do, not only once, but twice, walking through the woods, the three of them, setting the box down and timing how long it takes for the bees to come and go, and then following the angle of their flight, walking in single file and silent companionship, Anya, intent, serious Anya, leading the way as if her life depended on it, her gravity broken only, for a brief moment, when they've been walking for a while and the sun has just gone behind a cloud, turning the sky gloomy, and Anya suddenly points, and shouts excitedly: 'There. I see it. There.'

Following the line of her pointing finger, Boris Aleksandrovich can also see a beehive hanging out of the hollow of a middle branch of a tree near by. But it's too soon, he thinks and besides . . . motioning to the others to keep back, he walks towards it, carefully and in roundabout fashion, but the closer he gets, the more convinced he is that this cannot be the one, and he climbs a lower branch, and, positive now that this hive must be empty, he takes only the most rudimentary of precautions, hauling his bulk up and looking inside and then, shaking his head and jumping down, landing heavily on the ground to say: 'No good. It's a queenless hive.'

Anya doesn't say anything, but Boris Aleksandrovich is struck by the disappointment in her face, and struck also by the way that Anton Antonovich doesn't seem to notice his ward's response as he starts blithely reciting:

'A queenless hive, where no life is left. Gone is the low, even hum, the throb of activity, like the singing of boiling water, and in its place is the fitful, discordant uproar of disorder. Instead of a neatly glued floor . . .'

Boris Aleksandrovich listens to Anton Antonovich absently as he witnesses that startling transition of Anya's expressions, a series of three, from excitement to disappointment, and then, finally, a closing down into emptiness before she turns away, as if turning from Anton's voice that continues:

'. . . swept by winnowing wings, the beekeeper sees a floor littered with bits of wax, excrement, dying bees feebly kicking their legs and dead bees that have not been cleared away.'

Anton Antonovich in full flood as his ward now walk determinedly in the direction of the bees, and Boris Aleksandrovich stands a moment, hearing Anton Antonovich's:

'All is neglected and befouled . . .', wondering whether Anton is going to quote the book in all its entirety and at the same time feeling impatient with his friend for failing to register Anya's behaviour. But then he tells himself he's overreacting, it was just a disappointment followed by a childish tantrum like other children have, not fit for noticing and so, instead of drawing Anya's hunched back to Anton's attention, he says, as Anton runs out of steam:

'Hegel and Tolstoy in one afternoon. Impressive.'

'Oh, yes. I am the master of words,' Anton says and beams and at that moment the cloud moves away from the sun so that, as Anton's face lights up, so does the day, the dappled shadows taking the place of dullness, and warmth the place of the foretaste of next season's cold.

Boris Aleksandovich returns Anton Antonovich's smile, both of them standing, knowing each other well enough to know that each of them has been pulled back into that time so long ago before Borya had got so serious about politics, that time when politics was still a kind of a game and they'd just done something together – what was it? – something adolescent, most likely, like painting a revolutionary slogan on a church wall, or scattering pebbles to trip up the Cossack hooves, and running fast away from some terrible danger that was probably imaginary, running upstairs to Anton's small room and landing, both of them together, in a puffing exhausted heap which was when Anton Antonovich had pronounced that phrase, 'I am the master of words,' and this had set them off laughing and they had laughed as if they couldn't stop, laughing until they turned red and tears streamed down their faces, until they clutched their stomachs from their desperation of not wanting to laugh any more and on and on until it finally happened that they really could laugh no more and the laugh became a splutter and then an exhausted silence. And remembering all this, it comes to Boris Aleksandrovich once again, the joy of being alive, the carefreeness of youth, the time when they thought they could do anything, be anything.

And now?

And now, he thinks, I'm already a grandfather to Misha's two, and Natasha's about to give me another. Which is only right and only what he would have wanted. The natural order asserting itself. He and Anton now members of the waning generation where the challenge of breaking with the old, their youth-time project, has been turned into the routine of making the new work, of meetings and compromises, of calculated contributions, discreet words and watchful silences, and although Boris Aleksandrovich knows all this is natural, and all of it necessary, sometimes it rankles, although today he feels it less because he's realised that the youth in him, that part of his life that he and Anton Antonovich shared together, still exists and can still be conjured up by a summer's day, and that moment as he is thinking this, he hears Anya's strangled cry.

That Anya should cry out: it must be serious. She must have found the hive. Boris Aleksandrovich starts to run. And she must have gone up to it, not in the way that he had told her to, but stumbled upon it, angering the bees.

He's pounding through the trees, Anton Antonovich beside him, thinking that he warned her to be careful. He distinctly remembered doing so: both the telling her and her response. She nodded gravely, that's what he remembers, to show that she understood.

Another cry. Their four feet beating down on the ground, cracking up twigs and destroying ferns as they run, Boris Aleksandrovich thinking that he should have warned her again, that if it had been any other child, he would have done and continued to do so at judicious intervals, but that's the thing about Anya, it doesn't occur to him to treat her like other children because, once you say anything to her, you expect it to stick fast.

He did warn her though, he thinks and thinks again but they were so close to the beehive, this he'd known. It's his fault. He hadn't been watching properly.

'Anya?'

Anton calling out as he runs.

'Anya?'

But no answer comes and so the two men run harder, Boris Aleksandrovich thinking that, even if he wasn't there to witness it, he knows what must have happened. She must have blundered on, humiliated by her excitement at the abandoned hive and determined to find the genuine article. Everything he told her must have registered in her mind – the way the foraging bee goes back to the hive to perform its waggle dance, giving its fellows instructions as to how they reach the box, so that their timing of the bee's return told them their distance from the hive, their moving of the box ever closer confirming their calculations. And one more thing he had told her, of this he is sure: he'd told her to take extra care when approaching an active hive. Skirt it, he remembered telling her, and he remembers drawing out the picture, illustrating the way you must walk up to a hive in a roundabout way because the bees don't know you're there and, leaving their home as fast as they always do, they won't try to avoid you and if they hit you, they'll sting, and if one stings you so close to its hive, the others will smell the danger and if that happens . . .

There he can see her. She is standing. Motionless. Standing. A fragile figure at the centre of a mist of swelling, buzzing, darting grey. Why doesn't she run? A human twig enveloped by a swarm of bees. Standing. Being stung. Standing as the bees devour her. So close to the hive, stupid girl, enveloped in all that fury.

They're stinging her, they're stinging her, and yet she is so still. He shouts a warning to Anton:

'Keep away,' but Anton Antonovich moves in anyway, running straight at Anya, his arm flailing to try to brush the bees away, while Boris Aleksandrovich, ignoring them both, is on his hands and knees, scrabbling, collecting a pile of leaves and kindling, working fast, snatching up their dryness, and crumpling them together, constructing a makeshift flare that he ties with a length of vine, then standing and, giving thanks that he has matches in his pocket, lighting the flare, all in one motion, and holding it high, waving it, blowing on it also, as he moves in, shoving Anton Antonovich away with his elbow, shoulder pushing her down (she's so strong, see how she resists: he can only get her to her knees) and waving the flare, his eyes stinging, waving it around until the bees have gone – have gone – and how much time has passed?

He has no idea. All he knows is that she has pushed herself upright and is standing there. He nudges her into motion, turning her away from the hive. Her face is red, already swelling. He can't read her expression.

He says: 'The stings give off a chemical that will attract more bees: we have to get them out,' saying to Anton, 'here like this. Don't pull. Rub them off . . .' eventually Anton Antonovich begins to understand, the two of them working together, rubbing along Anya's thin, scratched, swelling arms, her crimson neck, her cheeks puffed out by bee venom, rubbing off the stings until there are no more to rub off, and all the time she tolerates what they do to her.

After those first two cries of hers, not a single other sound. She must have been terrified but she didn't run. And now as well she must be in terrible pain and yet it is down Anton Antonovich's cheeks that the tears are running.

As for Anya: she's expressionless, vacant of word or gesture, her lips tight sealed and straight as always and, seeing this, and seeing how she shifts away from the comforting arm Anton Antonovich offers her, the worry that has been nudging at Boris Aleksandrovich during this whole idle summer's day, and that he has, until this moment, successfully kept at bay, now takes shape and he recognises where it first began, even if he didn't fully understand it then.

It started when he went to pick them up. Irina Davydovna had opened the door, smiling, and there, close by her, her charge, Anya, scowling as if she couldn't believe that they were really going to the country or that if they were, they might forget her. Looking at her Boris Aleksandrovich thought there was something about Anya that reminded him less of a little girl than of a force of nature that surges to the surface, whether she wants it to or not. And then Irina Davydovna had welcomed Boris Aleksandrovich into this larger apartment that Anton Antonovich's new appointment had earned him, and Boris Aleksandrovich had noticed how the place smelled not of musty books or food standing overlong in the pot as it would formerly have done, but of flowers and of newly risen bread, so pleasantly it smelt that Boris Aleksandrovich dismissed his foreboding and thought instead of the way Anton Antonovich's life had been transformed. But now, as he stands looking at this unnatural child, his apprehension returns to him and, brushing the last of the bee stings away, thinks: what if I was wrong?

What if he was wrong to have helped Anton Antonovich? What if, instead of saving Anton, he has doomed him? After all, it nearly happened with Irina Davydovna. Putting her on the *Chelyuskin* was a whim. Ignoring everything that politics had taught him, the most important thing being that true goodness resides in changing the conditions of the collective and not the individual, he broke rules, changed lists, added her name, all of this through some misguided feeling of pity, and what happened? The ship sank, that's what. And she nearly died. That's also what. What price pity then? One random act, he thought, that, trivial as it is, can trigger a reaction, transforming what was into what might be, on and on in a kind of chemical chain that cannot be extinguished. He should have known better. He should have left Irina Davydovna alone. And now he's gone one further. He's added Anton Antonovich to his life. And Anya. This strange child. This curious child.

'Borya. Be careful. You're burning.' Anton's voice.

He looks up to find Anton Antonovich pointing at his hand and he sees that Anton's right, the flare that he was still holding in one hand as he took the stings out with the other, has burned down and scorched his skin. He drops it, stamping it down, and flexes his hand. It hurts. He really did burn himself, and didn't notice, and seeing this he gives a wry smile and thinks, Anya and I are no different, we are all children of our time, but what he says out loud is: 'We'll collect the honey another time. Come now,' and bending he grabs Anya, wincing at the pressure on his hand, and at her stiff resistance, ignoring these both and hoisting her up, high up on his shoulders, saying:

'Lucky we have a doctor in the family,' and walking along with her, that way, he wonders whether she's smiling because, although she resists it, she likes to be so high, and taking her back towards the dacha.

Part Three

History

As the future ripens in the past,
so the past rots in the future –

(Anna Akhmatova,
Poem Without a Hero)

Celebration (3)

The seventh of November 1934 and the country marches in celebration of the revolution. From their factories and farms, schools and hospitals, shops and railways, they march, comrades and citizens, workers and peasants, soldiers, sailors, airmen, not just in Leningrad and Winter Palace Square, but in all those other squares, in all those other Soviet cities. In Moscow they high-step, their boots stamping as they parade past the generals and general members of the Politburo standing on the granite of the Lenin mausoleum, first the army and then the ranks of the fresh-faced, red scarves tied tight, red flags fluttering while those other, newfangled accessories, posters of their leader, Stalin, loop through the crowd. In those other cities as well, in Kiev and Kazan, Rostov and Stalingrad, Minsk, Odessa and Tashkent, these many peoples united in celebration of their grandiose undertaking – man-made but not man-sized – to transform the world. And as in the rest of the country, so in Leningrad. No matter that the centre of government has moved to Moscow: St Petersburg, Peter, Petrograd, Leningrad still has its special place in history's forward march. These boots, *valenki*, galoshes and leaking shoes are marching across the cobblestones of a square, once the play-ground of a tsar, that became the site of his defeat. And there on the platform, Leningrad's Sergei Mironovich Kirov, so talented that he's got two jobs, secretary of the Central Committee and head of Leningrad, so cherished by the Boss that soon he will be gone, snatched up by greedy Moscow.

Kirov, one-time stranger whom the people of Leningrad have now taken as their own. A real Russian, he is a man to boast of, larger than life, an orator, hunter, man of the people, opera-lover, womaniser. Seventeen years have passed since the revolution and now, after all that depriva-tion, there is fuel and even food. At seven in the morning, when the *leningradtsy* set off for work, in winter's darkness, each person joining the heaving, shuffling mass that makes its way along sidewalks and on to trams, there will be buck-wheat *kasha*, turned violet by the frost, in every stomach. And when they come back, again in darkness, there will be the ingredients of a meal, and for this they thank their Kirov.

He stands on the dais, booted, feet planted square, his Finnish cap peaked over his pitted face, the edge of his ragged long coat flaring in the wind, sturdy, a man unyield-ing, dominating that limpid line of freezing foreign dignitaries, those whitelings in their fashion garments who will never know what it is to feel this passion, to love their homeland as a Kirov does, to dare everything, his family, his past, his very being for his country.

The square is packed tight; the band strikes up. Thousands remade as one, Kirov at their head. A people, one vast collective, singing the Internationale.

'Arise ye workers from your slumber,' they sing:

'Arise ye prisoners of want,' singing it not as they would once have done, as an injunction to revolt, but in honour of their revolution.

*

Out of this fabric a single thread is drawn. One man: Leonid Vasilyevich Nikolaev, who sees it as his destiny to unravel the whole. While the crowd lifts its smiling face to Kirov, Nikolaev turns his scowl away; while they sing, he inwardly berates them. And he goes, an awkward figure in clumsy boots, his head jerking up and down, moving as fast as his misshapen legs will carry him.

Listen to them, he thinks: they belt out those words they barely understand. With their strong limbs, robust health and shining eyes, they have sucked up the lies of their false prophet, Kirov. All of them, blinded by his honeyed words.

Alone in his understanding, Leonid Vasilyevich is suffocated by their ignorance. He pushes through the crowd, out of the square. Away from all that cant. Limping, he walks down the wide road and to the river. As he goes his contempt for that mass intensifies. He thinks: straight Kirov commands of them and straight they go. Straight. Straight. Unthinking. Unquestioning. Following their Kirov even unto the death knell of their revolution. On track even while the track wends its way to the very edge of a steep ravine. All they care about is being joined: all they want is to be told what to do, and what to think. All of them but Leonid Vasilyevich: only he is different.

He is a block away now, out of sight but not of earshot. He can hear them still, raucous in their spurious faith, belting out the chorus:

'So comrades, come rally.

For the last fight we shall fight . . .'

What do they know of fighting? The closest most got to battle was a bread queue and, even then, these huddled masses did as they are doing now – they obeyed. They wanted bread? They queued. Simple as that. It never occurred to them to ask how the bread had got there, or imagine what it was like for people such as him, yes, he,

Leonid Vasilyevich Nikolaev, to wrest from the stubborn, sabotaging peasantry that grain that made their bread. Only sixteen when he joined the Party but when they asked him to help in the dekulakisation campaign he went. He went so as to feed the workers. To assure the revolution. He, amongst the few, who made the difference.

And now? How have they rewarded him?

By threatening everything – his livelihood, his standing in society, his honour – that is how. Soon he will have nothing. In the meantime they, those who gave nothing, steal his revolution and his revolutionary songs. Listen to their fading voices, softened not by the impact of the wind's rush over the cooling water, but by their ignorance of the words. Not like Leonid. He can sing them all.

'And if those cannibals keep trying,' he sings:

'To sacrifice us to their pride,' his voice grating loud and tuneless. He, alone, knows what it is that he sings:

'They soon shall hear the bullets flying,
We'll shoot the generals on our side.'

Yes. That's right. The very generals. If they block the way. They'll be shot.

The Man Upstairs

Having woken up at the same time as his family, Leonid Vasilyevich then stayed in bed. He kept out of the way as Milda chivvied the boys, intending to rise as soon as they had left. He remembers the murmuring of his wife and his boys as they hurried about their day's beginning. As if life were continuing as it always had, as if they were talking softly and considerately so as not to disturb him, their man, their breadwinner, in his well-earned rest. Some breadwinner! He hasn't worked since May and he will not work again. He's tainted. He cannot get another job. And so he lay there, feeling the falsehood stretch from his bed to the table where they were seated.

He knows Milda prefers him up so she can pretend that nothing has changed. It doesn't matter what she wants. There is no going back. And so he lay in bed, waiting until the time came for her to take herself and their two boys away.

He remembers their going, the sound of the door closing: thinking that he could now get up. So what had happened? Had he gone back to sleep? No: he can't have done. He was thinking. That must be it. Thinking. But why then can't he remember the subject of his thoughts?

Oh yes, he remembers now: he had been assailed by doubts. By imaginings. Bloodied, they had invaded his mind, staining certainty. Of these he still retains a few disconnected images: a head severed from a body, a body dangling, kicking, unable to die, a heart in an urn. And images of victory: a speaker so powerful that he must be drowned by a thousand drums, a triumphant procession into history, a vision of courage soaked through by the red of a murderess's smock.

As the tide of her pregnancy rolls on, Natasha, who once cleaved to activity, who used to stay on, eagerly, at the theatre for as long as she was needed, now finds herself seizing the first excuse to go home. To rest. To be with herself.

And when she is calm and truly quiet, she realises that the life growing inside her has already half taken over, nestling beneath her swelling abdomen, its constantly expanding self joined to, and fed by, hers. As she sits quietly beside her dozing grandmother, she is conscious of that curled-up creature with its translucent skin inside her and yet quite separate. Blood-thick, blood-sucking, bloodthirsty for life, once it had obeyed her tempo: now she is tuned to it. It drifts, a pulsing, transforming being, fed and lulled by the motion of her beating heart, and when it turns, part of her is also turned so she can its trace its movement, shifting there, below the surface of her skin. It kicks, and she watches a moving bubble along her tightened belly, tangible and at the same time inexplicable for even as she moves her hand to touch it, this imprint of a leg, a foot, an arm vanishes, sucked back into its liquefied world.

Natasha, who has always existed in her senses, in the sights, the smells, and the sounds of the world around her, is now possessed by a self-involvement whose source is an unexpected kind of selflessness. She hears her own breath, timed to the rise and fall of the old woman's sleep. She thinks about the way that, after her father's junior, Dmitry Fedorovich, had come to drop something off and stayed a while to talk to her, her grandmother had issued strange warnings. That Natasha should beware of him. Her grandmother growing fanciful, she thinks, sinking into old age as Natasha's baby grows. She sees that soft yellow skein of wool, her grandmother's half-finished baby blanket, unravelling on the floor where it has fallen. Letting it lie she thinks of this thing that will soon emerge from her. Life's movement, she thinks, life's growing . . . even unto death and she closes her eyes and lets the sleep that's waiting to take over, engulf.

Leonid Vasilyevich is shaking. His teeth are chattering. He is afraid. Not of what he might do but of what he might not be brave enough to do. He wonders whether he is going mad.

He must not give in to fear. He must change his thoughts. He tries to think about normality. About what he usually does.

After the others leave, his sons to crèche and school and his wife to work, that's when he usually gets up. He dresses (although sometimes he doesn't bother). He washes. (sometimes that is, most times not). Tea. He always has his tea. He pours a little, strong cold tea into the glass and then lets water flow, steaming from the samovar, and then he gulps down the result, sucking its bitter blackness through the filter of a sugar lump he holds between his teeth. His gums hurt as the hot liquid attacks, the same way they hurt when the cold air hits, but still he drinks it hot. Once. Twice. Many times a day. He exists on tea.

While the others have lunch he must make do with a chunk of stale bread and the memory of the two glasses of sour, clotted milk that constituted last night's, his whole of yesterday's, meal. Of course, he thinks, he isn't going mad.

He is merely hungry, his wandering mind a symptom of his body's rebellion. There are other signs as well: although he cannot sleep at night, in the daytime he can hardly stay awake. Sometimes he even falls asleep in the morning before he has the chance to rise. Hunger and inaction: they both erode his soul. No – not his soul, of course not, for that's an old word and a meaningless one as well: they erode his intention.

Three weeks have passed since Revolution Day and the month is soon to turn again, and still he hasn't acted. He has written. That, apart from walking, is how he mostly spends his time.

When he walks, he sees the dismal streets packed with people trudging grim-faced, stone-hearted, blinkered. Doggedly from home to work they tramp, and back again, workers in a workers' state, once a slogan to be proud of, now a terrible reality. That's all they are: dumb workers. Not the glorious proletariat marching into their country's future, but cogs in a machine. Kirov's machine. Kirov, the thief, who, having snatched the people's power, is now intent on undermining their most precious jewel – their very revolution.

When Leonid Vasilyevich isn't walking, he writes. His diary – every day he writes it now, and every day copies it anew; and letters – to the Central Control Commission, to Kirov, to Stalin, as well as many to his mother; also pieces for his own private use – most of which he soon destroys. In the old days before that great unfairness, his fall from grace, he worked in the Institute of Party History and there he was trained in the primacy of evidence. And now his self-chosen job is to register how fundamentally history is being changed. He, alone. He, the archivist, holding on to memories that the rest discard; he, the standard-bearer, noting how the past, and thus the future, is being warped; he, the redeemer, his task to call a halt to this decline.

Sources are important, he had learned, and equally, if not more, important in their absence. He must decide not only what to leave behind but also what to destroy because, one day, when – not if, no, never that, it has to be when – *when* he has acted, what he leaves will be all that is left of him, each fragment weighed, disputed and used to draw conclusions.

His bed smells of sweat, sour breath and flatulence. Finally getting up, he goes into the other room. He has no watch. He registers the grey light of a fading winter's day and the fact that it is snowing. It's late: probably late afternoon.

Pulling clothes over his tattered underwear, he opens the tap of the samovar, watching as the water streams into the cracked cup. A welcome warmth makes him realise how cold it is. He looks down at the stove. It's out: he has slept past the time when he should have stoked it up. He should light it before Milda returns.

He won't light the stove – he won't even remember that he promised himself he would – because now he hears a voice, grating, harsh:

'Who's in charge?'

It's not often he bothers to listen to what people outside say. It's a waste of concentration. But this voice commands attention. It is answered by a score of other voices leapfrogging over each other in their anxiety to be heard. He strains to work out what they're saying.

'Where is he?'

Going over to the window and looking down, Leonid Vasilyevich sees a cluster of hats, cloth for his neighbours, and one dark grey peaked militia cap and then he sees a hand pointed up and hears that voice again:

'Let's go.'

Another sound: the creaking of the outside door and the

silvered flash of a gold and red badge, the edge of a long greatcoat before the last of the militia squad vanishes from view.

He can hear footsteps. They are coming. For him.

The blood, not of panic but of failure, rushes to his head. Dark thoughts. Pumping. He teeters, almost topples, throws out a hand and, by luck, manages to grab hold of the table and steady himself. He will not fall. He will not lose his dignity. He will be standing when they come in through the door. And so he stands thinking, what a waste – he hasn't done anything – and thinking also what a wastrel he has become.

The footsteps move closer, drumming up the stairs.

Opening her eyes, the first thing Natasha sees is Kolya. His face hovering, his breath against her skin, his lips grazing hers before he draws back and she sees that he is smiling. She's hot and slow: still half immersed in sleep. She lifts a hand, meaning to clear her vision, but he is already, gently, wiping the strands of stray hair from her forehead.

She says: 'What time is it?'

He shrugs to show he doesn't know, casually, because he doesn't care, not as long as he's with her.

It's dark outside, she sees, which could mean that it is night. But then, she sees that her grandmother is hauling herself slowly from the chair. Which means it must still be afternoon.

Her thoughts come slowly. She looks at Kolya: 'Is your shift over?'

'My double shift, you mean?' Of course – it's coming back to her – he had taken on an extra shift so that he could spend the next two days at home with her. That's where he's been and that's why she is here in her old room.

She says: 'You must be hungry,' and, pushing with her

elbows on the arms of the chair, begins the process of shifting her bulk.

He anticipates her, his arm around her waist, guiding her up, almost as if she is as frail as her wizened grandmother. Once she would have laughed away his cosseting; now she revels in it. He's so strong, and so gentle. The smell of his sweat and an undercurrent of what can only be machine oil sends a wave of nausea through her.

He steadies her. 'We don't have to go home,' he says. 'We could stay here if you like,' which is typical of him. Of his generosity. Although her family (even mama) have accepted him, he is never as much at ease here as he is at their home, the one papa managed to organise for them, a tiny space carved out of a collective apartment not far from here. Their home. Their kingdom. She looks at him, smiling.

'Let's not stay here. Let's go home.'

Hearing the sound of drumming footsteps, Leonid Vasilyevich imagines another kind of drumming. By the Neva's edge it was, many years ago, when a detachment of drummers had beaten out their roll as the revolutionary, Zhelyabov, and his four companions were dragged, shackled, from their fortress cells. Twelve thousand troops to accompany five tsar-killers on their final journey, the drumming not of triumph but to drown out the last words of that perfect revolutionary who never lost his nerve. Drumming as Zhelyabov and his companions were pushed up on to a high tumbrel and drumming as the tumbrel jolted along the road while that man, so strong, so charismatic, they call him Taras, sat straight, blue-green eyes steady, long beard flowing. So fearless, so unafraid to die.

Drumming as they strung him up. No doubts for Zhelyabov. No failure of nerve. He knew he was making this journey not unto death but into history. History moves too slowly, that's what Zhelyabov once said: it needs a push. And he, no theorist but an actor, no coward but a revolutionary, was the man to give that push.

Leonid Vasilyevich knows he could also have been that man if someone – who was it? – had not betrayed him. Drumming. They will also drown him out. Louder are the footsteps closing on his door. Leonid Vasilyevich should act. Make a last stand as Zhelyabov would have done if he'd had the time. As Charlotte Corday would have done. He should grab a weapon. A knife. A gun. He thinks. He must act. Now. He turns.

And hears not the banging on his door but the continuation of those running feet. Going up. It can't be and yet it is. They're after someone else. A shout and they increase their pace. Feet stamping on the stairwell. Where are they going? He stands, expectant, and sees another vision: the executioner's rope breaking, the body falling, limp but not in that ultimate limpness from which there can be no return and a voice, callous, ordering: 'String 'em up again.' He feels that he will swoon. He closes his eyes and feels the darkness descend.

'Leonid Vasilyevich.'

It's Milda. What's she doing on the floor, scrabbling about? She's on her hands and knees: she's collecting up shards of china. His cup. He must have dropped his cup. He hauls himself upright and, standing, looks down at her.

'Get up.' His voice harsh. 'I'll do it.' It's always harsh these days.

'I don't mind.' She smiles. She always smiles as well.

'I said get up.'

She's up. But not still. What's she doing now? Why's she reaching into the pocket of her coat?

'I brought you this.' She holds out a package. It is greasy and it stinks of fat.

Food. 'Did you steal it?'

'No. I . . .'

'I won't have you stealing.'

'I didn't steal it. It's from my lunch.'

'I don't want your food.'

She holds it out. Her hand. So small and still so white with cold. That hand he used to cherish, he has learned to despise for what it does, so innocent, outstretched. Pleading.

'Put it away.'

She keeps the hand level.

He grabs the package.

'The food's cold, Leonid. Let me warm it.'

'I told you.' Ripping off the paper. 'I don't need your food.' Cold dumplings; is that all she thinks he's worth? He stuffs them in his mouth.

She's looking. Always looking. He wolfs the dumplings down, chewing furiously. He could vomit with the taste of them. He does not want her food. Or her concern.

'Where are the boys?'

'They're with Mother. I'll fetch them later.'

The way she looks at him. He hates her for it, for that expression on her dumpling face not of fear, which he could bear, but something worse. Pity.

How could he have expected anything else? How could he have hoped that anybody, any woman, could love a cripple? And yet he did. Before. When he was a some-body. A Party employee. Did they know how much they were taking away when they gave him back his membership but not his job?

Well, if they didn't know, then they soon will. Since those drumming footsteps weren't for him, he has a second chance. He will seize it: he'll show her and all the rest. Oh yes: it will happen. He'll make sure of it. The drums they used to drown out Zhelyabov didn't work. As for

Zhelyabov, so for Leonid Vasilyevich Nikolaev. One day he, too, will be remembered not for the job he lost but for the sacrifice he made.

'He got his comeuppance then,' he hears. Startled, he looks down.

She's on the bloody floor again. What's she doing? Oh. The stove. She's lighting it. He says:

'I'll do that.'

She shrugs as she chatters on: 'I knew they'd get him.'

'Get who?'

'That no-good upstairs. He beat her once too often.'

Oh. So that's who the militia were after.

'Didn't you hear?'

Does she think he's deaf as well as crippled? 'Of course I heard. I was here, wasn't I?'

'Yes, Leonid,' she says meekly. 'You were here.'

Sometimes he wants to hit her, not for what she says, but for the way she accepts the things he says to her. And listen to her prattling on:

'About time too. I was saying as much to Tatyana Grigoryevna. If that man's not careful, I said to Tanya, he'll end up killing her.'

Gossip, that's all it is, about a man she doesn't know and a woman she doesn't even like. She's the same as all the rest: while their beliefs are annihilated, they absorb themselves in tittle-tattle.

'He was never sober, not when I saw him. I told Tanya. I said, Tanya, something ugly is bound to happen.'

That's all she cares about: some minor domestic incident. Meanwhile, their country will be ruined unless he acts.

'What do you think they'll do to him?'

He knows what they will do to him. Oh yes, he knows.

'Leonid?'

'What is it?'

'What will they do to him?'

'To who?'

'The man upstairs.'

What does he care about the man upstairs? He grabs his coat. 'I'm going out,' he says. Or maybe he doesn't. Maybe he only says it after he has already gone.

Kirov

Sometimes, when I have the time, I think about the way
my life has changed and what I, Ira, have become. I would-
n't have before. Then I never thought, I just was. Even now
I ration myself. One thing I learned in the days following
the sinking: too much thinking brings despair. But I sometimes let myself think about the distance that I've come. I
don't mean to the Arctic and back, I mean how far I've come
in life.

It's the deep of night. I am awake and will be until day's
dawning. It's my job, occasional night relief, hired to sit at
this table in this kitchen in Kamennoostrovsky Prospect. No
ordinary kitchen this: it's in the apartment belonging to
Sergei Mironovich, member of the Central Committee, and
leader of Leningrad. Our hero, that same one: Kirov.

I like it here. I like the quiet. The cleanliness. The loneliness.

I was recommended for this privilege, probably by that
man, Boris Aleksandrovich, who had already changed by
life, first by sending me on the *Chelyuskin*, and then by finding me a job with his friend Anton Antonovich. Boris
Aleksandrovich hasn't actually told me that he was the one

who had also suggested me for this job, but I know it must have been him. That's the way things work in his circles. Like an echo: first one person mentions your name and then another takes it up, and soon you are well known enough to end up on a special list where you find yourself asked to do all kinds of things that draw you closer to the centre of power. If only, in my case, to its kitchens.

I'm only called upon to do this work every now and then. Which suits me. Full-time would have been too solitary: although I like some quiet, I had more than enough isolation in the Arctic. These days I like to get about, something I manage well. I have a number of different jobs. I continue to clean at the Smolny (I don't think I'll ever give that up), I keep house for Anton Antonovich, and, on top of that, I come here when needs be. When the permanent staff are off.

The work's light. The apartment is already cleaned and dark when I'm let in up the stairs and through the back door. I always come here late at night, and it's always very quiet. That's almost the best part. The rest of Leningrad is bursting but here everything is restrained. No neighbours breathing heavily through makeshift walls, no drunken rows, no tipsy fights outside. They've even immobilised the loudspeakers in the street (he practically writes the bulletins, he doesn't need to hear them). It makes a change, I can tell you, and I appreciate the quiet – I have done ever since my time on board.

There's not much for me to do: just stay alert in case I'm called upon. Sergei Mironovich is an important man, and a man also of irregular habits. Sometimes he sleeps through the night, but mostly he does not. He's in so much daytime demand, I guess, that the loneliest hours are the only times he has left in which to read, smoke and generally pace about, which is mostly what he seems to do. And all this activity often makes him peckish. That's where I come in. I provide the food and drink should he ring for me.

Tonight, so far, I've not been needed. I think he's sleeping. I hope he is. He's not been looking good of late: he's not been very well.

I'm glad I'm not important. I couldn't take the strain. Our leaders are all so busy: the speeches they have to give, the travelling, the meetings, the decisions and the telephone calls. From the outside it may look easy; not so close up.

There are things I've seen here, I'd never have guessed at. Take the speeches. Sergei Mironovich is an orator, that's well known: didn't we all hear, on the radio, how the delegates cheered his closing words at the Congress? I've also heard him talk in person, and seen for myself how well he stirs a crowd. Watching him, you would think it all comes naturally, that he speaks without a note. I certainly used to think so; everybody does. But these days I know better. He thinks before he speaks (unless he's drunk, of course, which is another matter). I have seen him, hard at work, planning exactly what he'll say and I have seen how, after he's given a speech, his work goes on. Many times in the Smolny I've seen him standing by his stenographer (he leaves his door open: he can't bear to be confined) as she types out what he says. He's a stickler, changing a word here, a phrase there, checking each full stop before *Pravda* can print the thing.

How tiring to have to issue so many words and then rein them in. And Kirov's showing the strain. When first I came across him (by which I mean when he first passed me while I was cleaning in the corridor), he was vigorous. Sure of himself, an outdoor type who liked nothing better than to hunt or climb mountains. A real daredevil, he even pilots his own aeroplane, when they let him. But now something's wrong. He's lost his zest, and so, it seems, has his wife, Marya Lvovna, who spends more time in sanatoriums than she ever does at home. She's in one, her third this month, at the moment.

A problem in their marriage? No – in my opinion, it's not the marriage, it's the calls.

He has five telephones on his desk – two ordinary ones, one direct line to the Smolny, one Red Star for conferences, and the one that causes most of the trouble – the hot line to the Kremlin. The calls he gets on that: they dog him day and night. In fact this shift has only been restful because the telephone has been still. I hope it will continue so – let the poor man sleep.

It's been so quiet, in fact, I'm safe to leave the kitchen. Not for the outside (I'd wake the guards and they can be touchy when roused) but for the rest of the apartment. I sit in the kitchen if he's up (it wouldn't do to get in his way) but if he's not, if he's safely tucked up in bed, I like to walk about. It does no harm and, besides, I reckon that if you can survive the Arctic and better yourself in the process, then it's worth taking the occasional risk.

I don't go anywhere I shouldn't, or look in private places. I just wander around and look. That's what I've always liked to do: I like to look.

They keep a light on in the hall, so it's easy to find my way. I have a route I mostly stick to. Out of the kitchen, past the new refrigerator they brought all the way from America, and down the hall to my left, his special room.

No politics here. Something better: an aquarium. I like to stand in front of it, watching mirror carp weave their way around as if they're really going somewhere. They calm me down, and then, when I've had enough, I do a quick inspection of the rest of the room. There's a billiard table – Chinese – and, in pride of place, the things that don't much interest me but which Sergei Mironovich himself values – his work bench with his tools. He's a practical man: he likes to make things and to fix them too. Even though tools do nothing for me, I admire Sergei Mironovich for his hobby (I'm not the only one. It's what gives him his popularity – the fact he's so down to earth). Would have been a workman in another life, I guess, if, that is, he believed in another life.

After the workroom, I double back on myself, making my way down the corridor and left again into the living room.

His books. I love the sight of them. So many, so neatly packed. He's a big reader. He has book cabinets all the way up to the ceiling, and he also keeps bringing more from the Smolny. He reads them, secretly it looks to me, when things are really bad.

I don't get much time for reading but I like to keep in practice. Now I walk along the shelves, reading off the names. I don't pick up the books (I think he'd notice, I'm sure somebody else would) but even so, I can admire them, can't I?

Makes me feel good to be close to so much knowledge. Having never had books around me, now I'm surrounded, what with this job and with what I have at my new home, Anton Antonovich himself being a keen reader. Although these books can seem more attractive since they're not mine to dust.

I look at the books and then I do the thing I really like to do. I slip off my slippers. My socks as well.

I walk forward and soon I am standing on it. It's warm no matter what the weather. And soft. Luxurious. I look down. Even in the semi-darkness it shines out white – this polar bear pelt he uses as a rug.

We presented it to him (not me, of course, the collective we, our expedition), and every time I'm here, I like to pay my tribute. Don't ask me why. I'm not moved by those other dead things, eagles, foxes, pheasants, and all manner of other birds, framed and glassed-in trophies of Kirov's shooting expeditions that adorn the walls. In my view, there's something boastful about all that stuffed, dead meat. But for me, the pelt is different. Its power reduced, it's so small, and so unthreatening, compared to the fury of the animal in the wild, but it pleases me. I love to touch it. It reminds me of that other time which I sometimes believe I dreamed up.

I stand on the rug and try to bring it back. But there's nowhere like the Arctic for nothingness. That's what I most remember. That landscape in black and white. That solitude. Nothing to hear, nothing to smell, nothing to do. Strange how hard it seemed then, how tempting now.

I may have changed, though, especially in my circumstances, but longing for that time that nearly killed me will never do. Off the rug.

It's late. I yawn. I go over to the window. I often do this, just to stand. That's all. I like the view of the gardens opposite.

I think about my new life. Not about my ex-husband who weaves his drunken way into our apartment every now and then to insult me. I don't waste time on him. The person I most often find myself thinking about is that man: Anton Antonovich.

Is it love? Not likely. Even if Anton Antonovich were on the hunt for love, I would hardly be the woman to supply it. But I have been known to slip into his bed. Why not? He's gentle and he's grateful (and I have needs as well) and we both make sure that what happens there, between the sheets, stays there. Easy come; easy go. No more than that.

Although, if I was going to be really truthful, one of the reasons for my occasional sex with Anton Antonovich is to annoy the child.

It's not as if I have anything big against Anya. She's hard, but so what? Life has been hard to her. In truth, I admire her spirit. She's fierce that one, a true survivor; she'll go far and she deserves to. But knowing this doesn't stop me from wanting to annoy her.

It's not the way she looks at me, with those narrowed eyes of hers, that stern impatience, as if she were the adult and I the child. That kind of witchcraft might work on a sensitive soul like Anton Antonovich, but not on me. What I most detest is not the way she looks at him, but the way *he* looks at *her*.

There's so much gentleness in his regard and so much longing. He's an innocent, without a clue as to how someone like Anya will despise him for his need of her. That's why I give him my body: to shift the balance and to toughen him up as well. Another example, you might say, of my political education on the *Chelyuskin* paying off: 'from him according to his ability, to him according to his needs'.

That thought makes me want to laugh.

But wait. Was that a movement in the dark? Can't be: it's far too late. I press my nose against the cold window. I love the cold (my husband says that the Arctic froze my blood and I will never warm it up again). I could be out there now, but not anybody else, surely not?

Down in the street the lamps are dimly lit, blearing yellow in the darkness. It's snowing, thick flakes curling down, and the streets are virgin white, no tracks even. It's all empty and all very quiet. Nobody there.

I shouldn't be here in this room. I might get caught.

The telephone's ringing. Pealing loud. I should have known it would: not a night has passed recently when it hasn't rung. Ring ring. On and on. It's not one of the links to the Smolny or any of the other lines (Sergei Mironovich's temper is enough to ensure they stay mute at night) but the *vertushka*: the special telephone. Which means it's never going to stop, not until it has been answered. For this telephone is connected to our leader's chambers. Our highest leader in the land. Our boss – Kirov's boss – Iosif Vissarionovich Stalin himself – and he expects an answer.

No need to call Sergei Mironovich. He's already up. I hear the bedroom door wrenched open. I step back. My slippers. Mustn't leave them here. I grab them up, socks and all, before beating a fast retreat.

Not a moment too soon. Kirov's out of the bedroom. He finds it hard to sleep and hard to wake as well. I can hear him make his stumbling way in the direction of the ringing telephone. I know it would be better if I could have been in the kitchen when he picks up, but I also know I won't manage it. He's too close: he'll hear me. No choice. I stop. Now I must make sure not to move again, until this is over.

'Hello?' I hear his voice, thick with sleep.

I still my breathing.

A pause. 'No, Koba.'

It *is* his Stalin then . . .

'. . . not dreaming. But, yes, I was asleep.'

Another pause, this one much longer, and at its end what comes out of Sergei Mironovich's voice box is a strange rumbling. Like a winding of his chest, a closing of his throat. A laugh, I guess, even though it sounds more like a death rattle. Which is understandable, when you're pulled from your deepest sleep to listen to a joke.

But now. 'Yes, Koba,' he says. 'Yes, I am.'

A beat.

'We are.'

Then, carried on the deepest sigh:

'I see.'

And again: 'I see.'

And finally. Last words:

'Yes. All right. Goodbye.'

That is what I hear which makes it sound as if the conversation is short. Not true: it goes on for quite a while, with what Sergei Mironovich says coming between long pauses.

That's what happens, I suppose, when you have not just your wife, or your mother, or your daughter, but your whole country listening to your every word – you're bound to become talkative.

The telephone goes down. I mustn't move. I stand and still my breathing further. And listen.

He's talking to himself. 'My marriage!' he says.

His marriage? That makes no sense.

He says it again. 'My marriage! He wakes me up at four o'clock in the morning to ask about my marriage!'

It makes no sense at all.

'What the hell does he think he's playing at? Drunk again. No doubt about it. Drunk and sleepless. Wonder why. The bastard.'

I can't have heard that right either. Can I?

'Bastard. Just because his wife killed herself, does he have to try and kill me and mine?'

I'm hearing things. It has to be. I need to go. I turn.

'A suit. A bloody suit!'

I hear a thump, 'Shit,' and a rustling of papers.

I know that room so well, I also know I'm safe. I begin to tiptoe off. No point in being spotted as a witness. Never is.

'Irina Davydovna.'

The way he says my name, so softly, tells me he must know how close I am.

'Irina Davydovna.'

'Course he knows. He's got more sense than most, that one. And he's used to being watched.

'Irina Davydovna.'

'Yes, Sergei Mironovich?'

'When you looked out of the window,' he says.

So he knew I was there as well. He's a clever man.

'Did you see anybody?'

He sounds so sad. So tired. What can I say? That I think I might have? But no. That wouldn't help. There are ghosts everywhere these days. Better to ignore them.

'I thought there might have been a movement out there a moment ago but now it's quiet. Did you see anyone, Irina Davydovna?'

I give him the answer I think is sensible which, come to think of it, is all we can ever give each other. 'No, Sergei Mironovich, nothing I can be sure of.'

He doesn't reply.

I wait.

A sigh. Such a sigh. 'Well,' he says, 'doesn't make any difference: my goose is already cooked,' or at least that's what I think he says.

But when he speaks again, his voice is raised, awake, clear. Much more like him in fact. As is his request:

'Bring me an arak, will you please, Irina Davydovna?'

'Yes. Of course.'

'And after that, you'd better go and tell Misha Gerardovich we're off to Moscow again tomorrow.'

'Yes,' I say.

I'm sorry to have been caught eavesdropping, and relieved to be let off the hook. 'I'll do that,' I say, pulling open the kitchen door.

'Glorious Stalin, magnanimous Stalin, is going to fit me with a new suit.'

Or at least, that's what I think I hear. Can't be right, can it? Poor man, I think. He'll not sleep again tonight.

Shadows

In the gardens, following Kirov, all Leonid Vasilyevich Nikolaev had wanted was to be heard. He never got the chance and, worse than that, this time they didn't only shove off, they also arrested him. Getting no reply to his letters, he thought that if he could only have an audience with Kirov, then the wrong that had been done to him would be righted. Naïve Nikolaev who went to the station to wait as Kirov strode down from the high *Red Arrow*. How stupid: before he had the chance to say a word, that knot of sycophants had whisked their god away.

Even then Leonid Vasilyevich would not give up. He tried again, going to Kamennoostrovsky Prospect and waiting outside Kirov's lair so as to beard him there. No luck again: they took their Kirov out the back, sneaking him away like the crook he really is. Like soiled goods he was treated, manhandled, dragged from the sight of this pretender Kirov, handed over to the NKVD, bundled into a basement room.

What happened then?

He doesn't exactly know.

Two men: he's almost sure of that. He can summon up, if

not their features, then their outlines. They are seated. They are bored, the one picking his nails with the edge of a folder, the other with his crossed legs, feet upturned, his unblemished soles a reproach to Leonid Vasilyevich's holes. This is the sight that Leonid Vasilyevich remembers.

He remembers the beginning or he's almost certain that he does. A voice:

'What did you think you were doing, my fine fellow?'

In this ghost world of Nikolaev's remembering, there's now a light, so dazzling that the rest of the room is cast in darkness, so bright that he can make out only the edges of a table and the shadow of the men. And their voices hammering.

'What were you doing, following Sergei Mironovich as if you were his shadow?'

He can see their teeth. Smiling. Their smiles that stretch and freeze. Death masks. He shuts his eyes.

It comes to him, occasionally, in the dead of night, when he cannot sleep. Splintered fragments of a conversation. Half-remembered phrases, washed in on a fever of restlessness. What really happened?

They're gone. He is alone. It didn't happen. They never spoke to him. It's only a dream he conjured up.

A dream more real than life itself. Here it comes again. Those voices:

'Eyes open.'

Those heads turning in unspoken synchrony. Nodding. Without a word they nod. Did he make them up? Could he have?

'Answer the question, Nikolaev.'

'What were you doing in the gardens?'

'Answer.'

They're trying to scare him, vanishing like that. Well, he will not be scared. Not by phantoms that don't exist. He tests his voice. If this is a real encounter he will hear it. He says, 'Is it a crime to try and speak to Comrade Kirov?'

'A crime? Under which article?'

'I have a right to speak to Comrade Kirov.'

'Comrade, he calls our leader.'

'How dare he?'

'How dare he call our Sergei Mironovich his comrade?'

'How dare you, citizen?'

'Thinks he's special.'

'What right hàs he?'

'Destroyer.'

'Spoiler.'

'Degenerate.'

'What right?'

He knows their game. They're trying to bury him under the welter of their accusations. He refuses that. He *has* a right. He will find his voice. Will tell them.

'I have the right by virtue of my Party card,' he says and, oh, that's satisfying: he sees them startled, both of them (or was there only one of them? He can't remember). He didn't do what they expected. Didn't tremble. Quake. Touch his forelock like a serf. They're impressed. They say as much.

'A Party card?'

'Very fancy.'

And mute their voices: 'Show it to us then, my fine young man.'

'My little fellow.'

'Don't be shy.'

'Bring it out.'

'Don't hold back.'

'Cough it up, my consumptive one.'

His Party card. He had it with him. Here. He knows he did. But where?

'He looks around.'

'No card appears.'

'Won't show it to us.'

'Can't.'

'Doesn't have one.'

'Him! A Party member!'

'Huh!'

Is he standing? Seated? In that room? He can't remember. All he knows is that he must show his card. It's there – see over there – in the briefcase he was carrying. The one they confiscated. Lying on the table. He points.

'Pointing.'

'Where's he pointing?'

'Nowhere. There is nothing there.'

They're right again. The briefcase isn't there. He must have imagined it just as he is imagining this.

'He's mad.'

'Not mad. He's bad.'

'Saboteur.'

'Spoiler.'

'Counter-revolutionary.'

'Thinks he's more important than our Kirov. More important than the revolution.'

That last. It saves him from being sucked into the vortex of their accusations. He is clumsy but he is strong – dogged – and that he cannot have. He says:

'No one is more important than the Revolution,' not only saying it but shouting, for if there is one conviction he holds most dear, it is this – his baseline – that no one is more important than the Revolution. 'No one, not even Kirov,' and he watches their closing mouths and hears their silence and sees their surprise.

A beat. He's more than they'd expected. Better. A challenge. They return to safer ground.

'You? A Party member?' Speaking in unison. 'Don't make us laugh.'

He says: 'I am a member.'

'You were, you mean.'

'Expelled in March.'

Which means they've already looked him up. He feels himself confirmed. Strengthened.

He says: 'The expulsion was a mistake.'

'A mistake!'

'The Party doesn't make mistakes.'

'I was reinstated in May.'

'Expelled in March. Reinstated in May. What is he, a jack-in-the-box?'

'Jack-in-the-box . . . don't be funny. Look at him, sitting on the floor. He can't jump. He can hardly walk.'

They're right. He's on the floor. How did he get there?

'Stand up, cripple.'

He's on his feet. Was he ever really down?

'How did you get your membership back?'

'Answer that, our misshapen little comrade.'

'How did you get it back?'

He answers. With the truth: 'They took the strain of my time in Murmansk into account.'

'The strain of Murmansk!'

'Lah-di-dah!'

'He's a weakling.'

'Not just a weakling. A deviationist.'

'A sheep.'

'Traitor.'

'Follower of Zinoviev.'

That angers him It does. He's shouting now: 'How can you say that?' His voice ricocheting around the room. 'Ask anybody. Ask around. I backed Comrade Kirov when the time came to replace Zinoviev. I persecuted Zinoviev, it's a well-known thing.'

And heard himself using that word: persecuted. It's the way they talked but not in public. Not in interrogation.

'You?'

They're roaring now.

'You persecuted Zinoviev?'

'You!'

'What right do you, you with your blemished record, have to speak against a member of our great Central Committee?'

But now he hears them truly. Not the words they use but the way they say that name – Zinoviev. They spit it out. They don't like Zinoviev any more than he does. Now he knows for sure: he is being tested.

Well, so be it. He will pass the test. Time for bold words. Like: 'Zinoviev was destroying Leningrad: he had to go. Our great Stalin said so.'

'So why do you now trail after Stalin's choice, Comrade Kirov?'

'To speak to him.'

'If you are a Party member as you allege, you know the way to operate. Why not go through the channels?'

'Because Kirov owns those channels.'

'First Zinoviev . . .'

'Now Kirov . . .'

'Knows everything, does he?'

'Will nothing satisfy this man?'

Mocking. Teasing. Testing. No matter. From his awareness of their contempt of him springs his determination. Zhelyabov would not have failed the test. Charlotte Corday would not. Leonid Nikolaev will not fail it either.

'You know better than the Party, do you?'

'Planning to bag yourself your own Marat?'

To bag his own Marat? Is that what he had planned to do?

'Yes, he is,' they say. 'I can see it now. He takes on the role of his precious Charlotte Corday.'

'She killed Marat.'

'Or he sees himself as Zhelyabov who masterminded the death of a tsar.'

'Him: a Zhelyabov! Ha! How would he do it?'

Do what? Kill Kirov? Could this be what they mean?

'With a knife?'

The knife. Charlotte used the knife.

'A bomb?'

And Zhelyabov the bomb.

'Oh no . . . he's an original this one. Not a knife, or a bomb. He's got himself a gun.'

'Confess.'

'That's what you were doing in the garden, wasn't it?'

'Confess.'

'Trying to shoot our Kirov.'

He'd never thought of that before. He drops his head. Holds it in his hand. Thinks. Stop it. Stop it.

They will not stop.

'That's why you had this gun.'

This gun. What can they mean?

'Look up.'

'Look here . . .'

His briefcase. They have it there.

'His briefcase?'

'Has to be. His precious Party card. Inside this hole he cut.'

That's not a hole, it's more a slit. That slit. He never made it. Or at least he doesn't think he did.

'Where did you get this gun?'

How would he know? He never had a gun.

'Is this his fate?'

'Murder?'

Are they asking him? Or goading him? Do they also see what this Kirov is? Do they also want him gone?

'Assassination?'

'Is this his fate?'

Holding on to sanity. He says, 'To Napoleon, fate is politics.'

'Napoleon he's quoting now.'

'Get him out of here.'

Out? Into the open? They accuse him of planning murder and then they turf him out?

'Out.'

'Out.'

Delirium. How could that have happened? They talk to him of murder and then they let him go? How is it possible?

'Out.'

He hears the echo of their command and feels himself expelled and then he is outside. In the cold. Alone.

Did it happen? Could it ever have?

They gave him back his briefcase. They must have done because he has it now. He feels its cold solidity. It tells him he didn't dream it up. That gun and the slit that has been made for it. He had no gun before but now he has. It could not have been a dream. Those voices. They told him what to do. Not clearly – they didn't say, you got rid of Zinoviev, now do the same for Kirov – but he read their meaning. They told him and he will act. The time for dreams is over, that's what Zhelyabov said: 'From dreamers we became workers. We took to deeds not words.'

Now it is Nikolaev's turn to follow Zhelyabov. He will. Do the deed. If fate is politics, then Kirov's fate is death, and Nikolaev's to be his executioner.

1 December

The first of December 1934 and Sergei Mironovich Kirov is awake. He has been almost all night, this night that could turn out to be, if Leonid Nikolaev has his way, his last on earth.

Sergei Mironovich is not, however, thinking about the time that might remain to him. For if he was would he have chosen to polish the report he's due to deliver at the Tauride Palace at 6 p.m.? And would he still be working now, on this day that might turn out to be his last, churning out instructions to push into the greedy hands of the courier who will return, once, twice, three times and a fourth, before he tells her, at 2.30 p.m., not to bother coming back? No, he wouldn't. If he really knew his end was near (if any of us ever knew), he wouldn't ignore his beloved dog, Strelka, as she lies at his feet beneath his desk, her breaths puffing out messages of her dreams. If he really understood how little time might remain to him, he'd lean down and nuzzle that silky, grey head. And then he would pick up the phone – surely he'd do that as well – and ring Marusya (his Marusya) in her sanatorium and find a way to tell her how, despite the years, his work, and other women, she will always be his wife.

And there are other calls that Sergei Mironovich might reasonably be expected to place. He might choose to ring his sister, Liza, whose letter, received some two years previously, he hasn't yet found time to answer. Or he might call his friend, his friend, Sergo, whose recent illness prevented him from accompanying Sergei Mironovich on the *Red Arrow* as he usually does. Contacting the sister is probably doubtful (more than twenty years have passed since he was last in touch with her) but he would most certainly call his Sergo to wish him well, and tell him, jokingly of course, that, given the timing of Sergo's illness, he should think twice before he dines again at Beria's table.

There is, of course, one last call that he would most likely make. Long distance again: to Moscow. He'd have no trouble getting through: he's earned his leader's, his friend's, his Koba's, attention. But if he were to make that call, what exactly would he say? Would he ask that question – why? – that history would later ask for him? Or would he avoid all mention of himself (what, after all, does an individual, any individual, really matter?) and use his last moments to argue about the lifting of the bread subsidies, due in January, that he opposes? Or would he steer clear of both these options to use the precious time remaining to him to wish his leader good health, and swear his allegiance as those others, on the verge of death, would one day also do?

None of these perhaps. Sergei Mironovich has always been a dedicated drinker – perhaps he'd just get drunk. Or perhaps he'd do exactly as he is doing now – press on with normal life. Why not? To men like Sergei Mironovich, products of the tsar's end and of revolution, civil war and its bloody aftermath, death is not so special. Like the rest of his generation, he has long lived within its reach.

Besides. All this talk of death is just the result of some

insignificant's, some madman's, fantasy. Sergei Mironovich cannot know, as few of us can ever know, whether this will really be his last day on earth.

It is 1 December 1934, and Sergei Mironovich Kirov can't waste time in speculation: he has too much to do.

It is 1 December 1934 and Leonid Nikolaev is coming out of sleep. The transition is unusually abrupt: one moment he is wrapped in oblivion and in the next, opening his eyes, he is instantly alert. He thinks, clearly and with conviction: today's the day.

He is calm. So calm in fact that he managed to sleep the whole night through, something he hasn't done for months. Just one thought possesses him: that this, the last day of his ordinary life as he has known it, might also turn out to be his last. In which case he must savour it. And talk to Milda.

There isn't much space in the room, not with the four of them on camp beds and sofas. He doesn't want to wake the boys and so he is careful as he turns to face his wife, his intention to reach out, gently, and pull her to him. But then . . . he hesitates. She has contrived, he sees, to turn herself away from him as she almost always does, so that all that is left to him is her back, curved and lumpy. Like congealed pudding. Even her limbs she keeps away from him. She has one arm tucked under her and the other abandoned and outstretched as if reaching out to the sleeping boys, as if she is protecting them from me, he thinks.

Desire has fled and with it the impulse to wake her. He turns away to face the wall. His wall. His place. Needing to clear his mind of her (he will not permit himself the distraction of even righteous anger), he concentrates on the sounds of the city stirring. Directly outside, he can hear the banging of the toilet door as one of their neighbours is early to beat the morning queue. He won't listen to that – it will only annoy him further – so he stretches his auditory antennae to embrace the world outside.

It must have snowed again last night, he thinks: instead of the tapping of early morning feet, all he can hear is the soft slurring of boots. Soon, he thinks, Milda will be getting up. Soon life will appear to go on as normal. But soon . . .

He shuts his eyes. He will lie here, quietly, as she wakes the boys. He will not speak nor get up. Not yet.

Later he has something to accomplish. For the moment he must conserve his strength.

It is 1 December 1934 and so cold outside that, stepping into the warmth, Kolya finds his vision almost completely misting over. As he waits for it to clear he stretches, easing out the tendrils of damp that have penetrated his bones. He looks across the room.

After first removing his boots so as not to wake Natasha (that's the reason he volunteers for the night shift, so she can be more comfortable in the small bed they share), he sees she's already up and dressed and that she's standing, full-bellied, by the window, gazing out. It's almost as if she was watching out for him but if she was, she seems to have missed his arrival. She keeps standing. Staring.

She amazes him, she always has, and more now with her shifting female form. When he's directly behind her, as he is now, she looks almost as slender as she was on the day he first declared his love. All he has to do is change position, however, and she is radically transformed. He moves, one step to the right, and sees what she has become: her once small breasts plumped and rounded, her once flat stomach swelling with new life, her adult thighs firmer and stouter than the girl's had ever been. And that's not where the changes end, for although it's true that pregnancy has physically overtaken her, this transformation in appearance is trivial when compared to those other changes. The Natasha of old had existed only within a blur of frenzied movement. Now, however, the word 'tranquil' can even be applied. To be a bystander to this developing body and this personality shift – well, this often leaves him speechless and not a little afraid.

She makes him feel so clumsy.

It's always been this way. He who is lauded in the factory for his precision work has always felt too big, too gauche around her, and at no time more so than at the present. As she gets larger, she also seems to get more graceful.

She's so different from him. So much better educated and accustomed to privilege – the dacha, the apartment on Nevsky, the mammoth meals her grandmother always provided – all of which she exchanged for him, this wretched room and the adequate but monotonous diet which is all they can afford. Sometimes it worries him and that happens when he can find himself assailed by doubt. And now the girl he married, his girl who teased him and who, perhaps more importantly, needed him, is being overtaken. Her point of focus has shifted, so much so that sometimes he thinks he has already half-lost her to their unborn child, and then he can't help thinking: when the child comes, will there be any room for me?

'Kolya.' She has turned, and perhaps she had seen him coming into the house because she's seemingly unsurprised to find him there. She's also smiling, so radiantly he's ashamed of doubting her.

'Natyushka. You should still be sleeping.'

'I wanted to be up for you.'

Stepping over the pile of washed clothes that she hadn't yet got round to packing away (she never does), she's soon in his arms, and he's holding her, feeling the swell of her and his own strength to contain it, and thinking how silly he has been. She loves him, his Natasha. There is no doubt of that. And, besides, she hasn't really changed. She's as undomesticated as she ever was, this wife of his, and she needs him just as much. More, even, he thinks, looking round the room and seeing the chaos that seems to have overtaken it since he left for work.

She sees him looking. She laughs: 'I know. I'm completely hopeless.'

'No you're not,' his voice gruff compared to hers and to cover up the confusion, 'I doubled my quota last night,' and then finds himself doubly discomfited as he sees the flash of her eyes – a sure sign that something has amused her – but she doesn't laugh again, she merely says:

'My brave worker,' and he knows he has misjudged her, she hadn't been about to laugh at him, his thought confirmed when she adds:

'I bet you're hungry after that. Let me make you some *kasha.*'

'No. I'm fine. I ate at the factory,' blurting out the lie because he's not got the heart to tell the truth, which is that she has the knack of making even the simplest of foodstuffs utterly unpalatable.

She laughs again – she knows what a bad cook she is – but doesn't pursue it. 'I'll let you sleep then,' she says. 'I'll go out for a walk.'

He wants to say no, tell her that it's too cold outside, and too slippery, that she should wait for his help, but he doesn't. She's right: he needs to sleep and he knows how much she enjoys the snow and how the fresh air is good for her and, anyway, he's never been able to stop his Natasha, even this new, grown-up manifestation of her, from doing anything once she's set her mind to it. So he kisses her and goes over to the bed and sits down, keeping out of her way as she pulls on her coat, tugging at it to draw the two sides together.

But then, instead of going out, she seems to hesitate, and comes quickly over to him and kisses him, full on the lips, and says:

'Be careful, won't you?'

This time she leaves abruptly, the imprint of her lips lingering as he thinks: now, why did she say that?

It is 1 December 1934, a crisp and forceful day in which Natasha delights. She walks briskly through the snow-filled streets, walking without purpose, just for walking's sake.

She loves to walk, her limbs, her flesh, feeling the sharp sting of winter. She is a match for anything: even the cold. She tilts her head back and the first feathery pat, forerunner of a fresh flurry to come, alights on her skin, caressing her forehead and then melting as if that passion that she has inside her is turned outwards, causing her skin's surface to burn.

At times like this she feels as if she could keep walking, going straight, walking into her future without a break, walking on forever.

'Natalya Borisovna.'

Someone calling her? She stops.

'Natasha.' A familiar voice although at first she cannot place it.

'Natasha.'

There, she's spotted him, that figure over the road who is even now breaking away from the knot of bunched pedestrians. It's the American, Jack Brandon, muffled in a glorious, floor-length astrakhan coat, Jack whose Russian is so perfect but whose appearance so foreign: she hasn't seen him for quite a while.

'Jack.'

Later, much later, she will wonder: is this when it began? Was it this, her chance meeting with Jack, that condemned Kolya? Was it her fault? That's what she will think in the dark times to come, but at the moment all she feels is pleasure as Jack Brandon strides to meet her.

'Jack.'

He's close now, close enough to think that either he had forgotten how beautiful she was, or else she's grown more beautiful, and then he sees how high her coat has ridden, its straining buttons, and he remembers, of course, that she's pregnant, Boris Aleksandrovich had told him that.

'You didn't know?'

'I did. Your father told me. Congratulations. You look well on it.'

'Do I?' She does something then, this married woman. She executes an almost perfect pirouette, a full circle, there in the snow, twirling on tiptoes and coming to rest in front of him but closer than she was before, and looking up she obviously decides she has come too close because she steps back a little, as if ashamed, this girl struggling with a new womanly consciousness of her dignity and saying in a slightly strained voice: 'And you? Are you also well?'

'Yes.' Her confusion is endearing, he can't stop smiling: 'Thank you. Very well. And pleased to be back. I've been in the States.'

'The States! Did you see the Statue of Liberty? Or the Brooklyn Bridge?' She pronounces the unfamiliar names with such enthusiasm (so uncharacteristic in this country that disparages all things American) that he almost bursts out laughing as he answers:

'No. Afraid not. I was only in Boston,' and as soon as the words are out of his mouth he regrets not pretending that he had seen them, if only to give her the satisfaction of it, and regrets also that the laughter is obvious in his voice because he sees her face flooded by uncertainty, and when she speaks again her voice is dulled.

'You're back here for work?' she says, finding refuge in this, her country's obsession with labour and quotas and production achievements, and adding dutifully: 'How's the factory?' As she asks this, she starts to walk, perhaps because by standing in this constantly flowing mêlée she thinks they would be too noticeable or perhaps because it's just too cold to stand, and he keeps pace with her. She finishes with: 'Have you solved your production problems?'

'Yes. I have. The production line's moving smoothly thanks to your father's efforts,' and then he adds: 'Boris Aleksandrovich is a miracle-maker,' because this is what he really thinks of Boris and also because he thinks it will give Natasha pleasure. And it's true his words manage to draw a smile from her, but it's not as open as he'd anticipated and it occurs to him that, although she's still a free spirit, she is also changed and no longer so enamoured of her father. Which, he thinks, is only right for a married woman. 'Are you heading anywhere in particular?' he says.

'No. Just walking. Giving Kolya time to sleep.' She pulls her coat tighter. 'But I didn't realise how cold it was.'

And he sees how she does indeed look cold, her skin not so much white as blue in this half-light and he finds himself putting an arm around her, as a friend might do, and saying:

'There's a café round the corner: why don't you let me buy you a hot drink?' and seeing her hesitate and draw away he says, quickly:

'Come on, Natasha, I'm not going to hurt you.'

The words spring out unbidden but he's glad they do because now he's named what must have been on her mind (she's just an ordinary girl, like any other). She laughs and says:

'A chocolate would be lovely', and then she lets him guide her across the road and towards the light.

It is dark outside and inside as well but Leonid Nikolaev doesn't bother turning on the light. There is no need to. He is leaving. Soon. And, besides, he doesn't need a light. He can see without it: not the stuff of everyday life, of course, the position of the table, for example, with his pen beside his inkwell, or the piano with his diary safely ensconced, or the door to their bedded cubicle, but beyond all that. He can see the things he needs to do. He can see: his future. His country's future. The things that must be done. That only he can do.

His phantoms, his heroes, his Corday and his Zhelyabov, who have been with him so long, are no longer in the forefront of his mind. No need to look for them. Soon another name will be added to their ranks: Leonid Vasilyevich Nikolaev.

He hasn't eaten. Although that's inaccurate. Better to say that he has eaten but not retained his food. He sat at the table chewing at a chunk of heavy rye bread, hard even after he had dipped it in water, and then he swallowed it but couldn't keep it down. It had come churning out so fast he had no time for the basin, all he could do was watch helplessly as that grey lumpy starch flavoured by bile flowed out of his mouth in one gelatinous stream, so that he could feel parts of it passing through his lips even as he watched the remainder landing on the floor, so noxious it made him retch, over and over again, until he thought that he was even going to spew up his very guts and so he'd waited, too weak to do anything else, for the dark redness to ensue. But all that happened was that the waves of nausea gradually subsided until what churned out of him was no longer food but air, and he began to cough, dryly and so hard he felt his chest might cave in, and he could hear his own wheezing, distant, as the world seemed to shake and he must have blacked out, for the next thing he knew he was lying on the floor.

Time is passing. He cannot let it go. Up he gets. On his feet. Straightens himself as best he can. Washes his face. Wipes his clothes. Clears up his own disorder. He cleans up his vomit, too. He almost didn't: he almost left it where it was, an inheritance to his family. But then he remembered that what he would leave them would most likely turn out to be more bitter than that vomit, at least in the short term, and so he gets down on his hands and knees and scrubs the floor, scrubbing out his traces. Scrubbing out himself.

There's satisfaction in that.

And now he's ready, even though the traces of what he spewed up linger on. No matter how often he rinses his mouth, and scrubs his tongue as well, he cannot rid himself of the taste. And now it is as if his tongue has swelled, as if it is hanging out of his mouth, lolling slack and purple, like the idiot that people wrongly assume him to be. For a moment he imagines stuffing his mouth, not with food but with leaves and bark and dried herbs, those rich aromas of country remedies his babushka used to feed to him when he had a fever, and, imagining this, he feels himself filling with her wisdom in this inhalation of the very earth, his taking it in, his dying in order that all the rest shall live, and he finds himself gagging again but there is nothing left to regurgitate and he stops himself by force of will for nobody would ever again say of him, as they told him in that meeting when he lost his job: 'You have no concentration, no energy to carry what is needed to its inevitable conclusion.'

He stands, and thinks, I'll show them now. He thinks, how wrong they were.

Oh yes, he will show them. He puts on his leather jacket.

No matter that it's snowing. That he will be cold. That people will notice him for what he wears. He likes its animal smell. Its softness. His only garment that improved with age. And what does he care about the cold? He doesn't feel it. He won't.

And so he goes. For the last time, out of his door. For the last time, into his street. For the last time. Or at least he hopes that it is so.

In another part of town, in Leningrad, someone else is also on the move. Sergei Mironovich Kirov, who, having already phoned down to warn his men that he is leaving, now steps out and waits for his black car to draw up. When it does, however, he doesn't climb in beside the driver but rather leans down and, speaking through the open window, tells the man that he plans to walk at least as far as the Troitsky bridge. Why not? Sergei Mironovich is a physical man who spends far too long at desks and in meetings. And besides – he's due at the Tauride only later. At 6 p.m. He has ample time in which to stretch his legs, to walk, breathing in the air. So there he goes, a stocky figure striding out, unremarkable in these parts and largely unremarked on although later, when everything has come to pass, those who were here this day will tell their loved ones how they saw him, if not then, then many other times before. A kind man, Sergei Mironovich, they will say. A good man. One of us. Man of the people. See how he chose to walk. He liked to be with us.

It is 1 December 1934 and Sergei Mironovich Kirov pushes his way through the falling snow, ignoring the car that glides beside him. As he reaches the bridge he stops a moment, under a lamppost, and turns his wrist, squinting into the lowering dark to catch the numbers on the watch face. It's later than he thinks, but not too late. He looks up.

The car door is already open, waiting to receive him. He gets in, slamming the door shut, and facing forward says:

'The Smolny.'

He takes his driver by surprise, for Kirov's due at the Tauride, not the Smolny; it's written in the schedule, plain for all to see. They're probably filing in already, so they'll be there when he arrives. Besides, there's not much time, no time at all, and the schedule needs fulfilling for without it they are lost.

None of this does the driver actually say. He's not the boss, and if Kirov says the Smolny then the Smolny it will be, and so the driver puts his foot down, his tyres spinning momentarily in the gathered snow, and then they grip, and Sergei Mironovich Kirov is off.

It is still 1 December 1934, this Kolya has now worked out, but when he first awakened he had no idea what time it was. What day even. Surfacing was hard enough. Heavily he had lumbered from a place too dark and musty to bear recalling only to find himself lying on a bed (their bed) in a room (their room) in darkness. All he knows is that he has slept but for how long he cannot tell. Some hours perhaps. Some days even. It feels like months.

Another thing he knows: he is alone. He had not expected that. He lets his eyes range around the room hoping he'd find Natasha sitting quietly so as not to wake him, but even in the darkness he can sense her absence. Must still be out, he thinks. He throws off the eiderdown and rolls himself out of bed. His limbs are sluggish as he walks the two steps to the window and looks out. It's dark but not quite night: too many people for that. Afternoon then. This afternoon. It has to be. Otherwise, where would Natasha be? It was morning when he went to sleep. It's dark now. Hours since she left.

A walk, she said. He remembers that. A walk. But how can a person walk this long, especially one who's pregnant? He thinks. Gone out, come back and out again. Oh yes. That must be it. She wouldn't leave him this long: she must have returned and then left again to run some errands. She'll soon be back, he thinks. Of course she will. He sits down on the bed, setting himself to wait.

Four p.m. and, although it's long since stopped snowing, beds of snow still line the Smolny path, a dark gash in a sea of white along which Leonid Nikolaev progresses. His jacket crackles in the cold. His feet (his boots are leaking) are numb. He takes no notice, he keeps walking, too briskly to be strolling, too slowly for a run. A briefcase, that briefcase, under his arm. His hands, ungloved, in pockets. His thoughts unmasked – for he has no thoughts. Only intention.

How does he know to come here? That he cannot tell. This he will not tell. Ever. Or, if he does, it doesn't bear repeating.

But all that's for the future. Now Leonid Nikolaev walks. Deliberately. Up the path. Past Lenin. To the building. Up the few short stairs. Through the doors.

There are people queueing. Some he knows, some not. They eye him, drawn by his leather jacket, but say nothing or at least they say nothing that either he or they retain. When his turn comes, he hands his briefcase over and it passes muster as he knew it would. He hands over his Party card and it proves its worth. He's through the security check. Passed with flying colours. As he knew he would. And now: three flights to climb.

He climbs. Up and up, trudging up to his fate. On the way he passes a man he knows. Who says:

'Leonid Vasilyevich, where are you headed? The meeting's on the second floor.'

What meeting? Nikolaev thinks, the time for meetings is gone, and says:

'Don't wait for me. I'll join you soon,' this the first in a series of lies he will tell not only to his friends but also about his friends, layer upon layer of untruth that will sound out in the cellars of police headquarters, and stretch out, overlaid by other lies, right on into the future so that no one will ever know what really happened save for the fact that Leonid Nikolaev looks at this man he knows and says it anew, so innocently, you'd never know what he was up to:

'I'll catch up with you later,' and goes on.

Third floor. There he is. Rounding the corner. Disappearing.

He must have disappeared, for how else could he have passed through that special guard station where a Party card alone would never be sufficient? To enable him to walk on, a special employee's pass was required. This is a fact, just as it is a fact that Leonid Vasilyevich Nikolaev did not possess such a pass, and yet when he's next spotted he's on the third floor, past the guard. And disappeared. Into the toilet, or that's the story that is later spread around, so he can watch through the window for the arrival of his Kirov's car.

He doesn't have long to wait.

There he comes – Kirov – through the main entrance of the Smolny, this well-known face, no need to show his pass. Up the stairs, following in his would-be assassin's footsteps, no man to question him, however, just a posse of five – four secret police and his faithful Borisov – who accompany Kirov as he climbs up and then goes past the guard who did not, who could not, have granted admission to Nikolaev (for who would ever admit to that) and then his bodyguards peel off, save one, old and slow Borisov, much beloved, who follows his boss, and who is witnessed to be following, even as Kirov rounds the corner.

What happens then?

Kirov walks towards his office. His no-nonsense office with its monumental desk littered with workaday models of oil tanks and details of machines. His office where he keeps the book Stalin gave him, Stalin's *Problems of Leninism*, inscribed to a brother and a friend. The office he doesn't like for they moved him here without first asking his permission. It's for your own security, they told him, never told him why the room he had liked had suddenly become so unsafe. Well, never mind: you don't get to be a Kirov by worrying about things you can't control. This new office has a use value identical to the one before. It's an office. For work. And so he goes down the corridor and through his reception room towards his office, not to make decisions but merely to pick up some statistical material for his talk, and then be on his way.

Later there will be rumours. Interrogations. Files. Questions. Cells. Graves. And a song:

Hey, fresh tomatoes.
Hey, want a cucumber.
Stalin killed Kirov
Got him in the corridor.

But later, if this song circulates, it will be denied, and later, when there is time for speculation, there will be no speculation. Not, at least, in public.

What happened?

Ask Borisov.

But Borisov wasn't there.

How is it possible? Watch them, those two men, one behind the other, Kirov and his faithful Borisov, Kirov safe because, with Borisov accompanying him, nothing can go wrong. And yet, when it happened, when danger loomed, Borisov was nowhere to be seen.

Did something delay him? Did someone stop him? Ask him, you say. Good idea. Except he didn't live long enough to be asked.

But all this is for the future.

For the now, there goes Kirov. Alone. Round the corner. Alone?

No. Not alone. There are two men in that place. At least two men. The one an electrician. Up a ladder. Or not. As the case may be. The other, Nikolaev. Coward Nikolaev who shoots, not from the front, but from behind. Who raises his revolver as Kirov passes and who shoots his Kirov dead.

There, it is said. It is done. That bullet passing from the Nagan pistol into Sergei Mironovich's brain. That message to a people.

A shot. There was a shot – there had to be, for blood appeared – and soon Kirov will be gone, although for him what happens next takes an age, a lifetime, for when life is almost gone, the time remaining is itself a lifetime.

Is he thinking as he goes? Of course he is. He never stops thinking.

A thud and perhaps he thinks, without surprise: shot; and thinks then: blood. He feels no pain, just what it is: that it is done. His body falling, cased in red. Those images, gashed by blood. A bullet in his brain. His brain fleeing to the past. Backwards reeling. The sounds of the Marseillaise, those many years ago, Iosif, that other Iosif of his childhood, lying there and Kirov, pressing forward with his precious Party's standard soaked in the blood of his dead friend. I'm dying, he thinks, without surprise.

A thud. Another shot? Perhaps. They say that there were two. But if there were, he cannot hear them. His body on the ground. A mountain ahead. One that he would like to climb. So cold though. Cold carried on a kiss. His mother's half-dead lips grazing his.

She kissed him, all of them, he and his sisters, that day before she died, kissed him goodbye as he is no longer capable of kissing anybody ever again. Who would want to kiss those lips, anyway, with that pink froth bubbling out? Who would want to touch him now?

Smoke. He can smell it long after he can no longer see. Acrid smoke, familiar, the product of a gun. Well, what is it to him? He has smelled worse.

Red. It flares up. Red. The colour of a revolution. He lies there. Slack and still.

'Sergei Mironovich.'

His name. A useless rallying cry. He cannot answer. He will not answer. He lies there, slack and still.

It's obvious he's already dead but this is a country where the obvious can be changed, where the obvious has obviously been changed. They won't let him go. They're determined. He must see his future. They will not let him die.

They lift their Kirov. Blood leaking from the neck. No matter, he can no longer feel. They carry his dead weight, his head lolling so they must hold it up, to an office. Not his office. Chudov's. Lay him on a conference table, the indignity of death. He doesn't care. He is beyond caring. Let him be. He is dead.

We suffered too much, Kirov was once heard to say, from war and civil war that wiped out the value of human life, hardening our people. The right to spill blood, he said, to take away life, ceased to be a tragic problem. This is what their Kirov said, in public, for all to hear. And yet, in the name of this same Kirov, they defy him. In his name, they defile him. He might be immune to death, not they. They cannot, they will not, let him die. He is theirs now. They work on him. When oxygen has no effect, they pump him full of drugs. Of adrenalin. Ether. Camphor. Caffeine.

Fighting a death that has already had its victory. Shooting liquids into veins that cannot respond.

While outside there is shouting:

'What have I done?' as they drag that other one away. He shouts: What have I done, his cry rebounding.

'What have I done?'

What has he done?

He has killed a man, that's what, and not only killed a man but also severed an artery. Unleashed a plague, a blood-letting to which there will be no easy end.

Love

She comes hurrying back, pushing the street door open and launching herself at the stairs, taking them two at a time. She can hear her breath wheezing hard – she ran all the way – and can feel the heat rising within her but she ignores them both. She's late. Kolya will be worried. And angry. Except, of course, that Kolya never does get angry.

All the way back she was imagining his waking to find her absent. It had never happened before: he would be wild with worry. She thought she could see his apprehension reflected in those she passed: people, grim-faced on the streets who gazed askance as she ran on. They were judging her and they were right to judge: she'd been gone far too long.

She wonders how it happened, and why, but there's no reason to wonder because she knows the answer. She did it by not watching the time, and she did that because she was enjoying herself. Unusually.

Catching that thought, she renounces it. It's not that she doesn't usually enjoy herself. Far from it. She loves Kolya. She loves his company and she loves making a home, as best as she can, for him. And yet . . . sometimes – and this she can admit because there is no harm in it – sometimes she does feel herself a bit constrained.

It's natural. She knows it has to be. When the baby comes, it will be different. But meanwhile, when Kolya thinks she's too big to work but she's not big enough to produce the baby, the echo of old feelings can invade. Feelings of impatience. Of irritation.

Not that they last long. She loves Kolya. That is not in doubt. With him she feels a sense of rightness in the world, of rightness in herself. He has done what her parents never could do: he has stilled the beast in her.

And yet with Jack Brandon for a moment there it was different. He's a stranger, that's part of it, she knows, and a stranger as well who will never stay and so with him she can indulge in that make-believe that she, from her married vantage point, can see was once her daily fare. With Jack she sensed what it might be like to be like him and fly. He has a way with women that she, safely ensconced in pregnancy, can now enjoy. How wonderful to feel herself admired again. And then, of course, there was the comfort, those deep, plush chairs, that rich velveted brocade, muted yellow light, and more than that all those delicacies that Jack kept offering. Cakes. Light and airy, made from white flour, as many as she could fit in, and chocolate as well, made with real milk. The kind of food she eats no more, that she thought she didn't miss, but now, as her taste buds continue to tingle with the hot sweetness of what she has consumed, she realises how deprived their monotonous diet can sometimes make her feel.

But it's late. She's late. And Kolya will be worried. Reaching the landing, she pushes open the door.

Dark. The room in total darkness. Kolya's gone, this she knows, without needing to look round, as she also knows where he is: he is searching for her.

She stands, her breath coming hard, trying to work out what she should do. While her good sense tells her to stay here, to wait for his return and make sure she doesn't miss him, instinct has her heading out again. She thinks: I have to go, thinking how worried he must be, and how cold, the impact of her absence and of her neglect carried in on a wave of guilt that is quickly turned to anger.

How dare he? she thinks, stopping abruptly: he who spends most of his time, most of his life, at his precious factory. He's even there at night these days. Which is his choice: he doesn't have to take that shift. But take it he does, so that she, who no longer sleeps so well, finds herself waking often to an empty bed. To a lonely bed. And when he comes back, he's always tired. He boasts continually of strength at work, of his speed, and yet, coming home, he is always spent.

Her self-righteousness and, with it, her indignation, swell. What does he expect? That she will sit in this tiny room motionless in the dark while he lies insensible on the bed? Or that she will quietly tidy up around him so that, when he deigns to wake, he will do so in a room of which he can approve? Is that what he expects?

Well, she's tired of waiting for him. That's why she's been gone so long. It isn't the comfort or the cakes, it's because, in Jack's company, she's allowed to talk. Oh, precious freedom, for she knows her future. She knows how soon it is that she will spend most of her time waiting silently for that other's cry, for those other needs. Soon. Not yet. In the meantime, she will not wait. She wrenches open the door.

And hears a sound. The speaker from the street squawking loud. A voice:

'Comrades, we have grave news.'

Still thinking that she will find Kolya and give him a piece of her mind, she listens absently:

'Today the first of December at 16.30, in the city of Leningrad, in the building of the Leningrad Soviet (formerly Smolny), a murderer, a concealed enemy of the working class, killed Comrade Sergei Mironovich Kirov,' and stops abruptly, in her tracks as the voice continues:

'The Secretary of the Central Committee and Leningrad Committees of the All Union Communist Party (Bolshevik) and member of the Presidium of the Central Executive Committee of the USSR. The gunman has been arrested. His identity is being established.'

Burial

As the pageant of Kirov's death grinds on, there is no one in the Union of Soviet Socialist Republics who doesn't hear of it.

First the wife, Marya Lvovna, Kirov's Marusya. A Party secretary goes up those stairs, his lips moving in practice of the words he thinks he has to say, but there is no need because she is already standing on the threshold of her apartment, as she is simultaneously beyond the threshold of her married life, and seeing this junior of her husband's, she who is accustomed, when she's in town, to watching from the window for her husband's safe return, knows.

'Something has happened to Seryozha,' she says.

And in another part of town, that other Leningrad, another wife also learns of her husband's fate. Thirty minutes is all it takes to send those men up the stairwell, their fists hammering against the door, their faces set not in the delicacy of grief but staged in fury, as they push their way in, too many to fit in the room, heading straight to the piano to flush out that diary, knowing already half an hour after the murder that it would be there, and then wheeling round they shout, 'Where is the other?' as if they also knew he kept two diaries as if anybody ever would keep two.

So the unmasking of Leonid Vasilyevich Nikolaev begins, the dismantling of his life, his children banished, his family arrested, his wife pawed over by those blazing eyes, her connections to the Smolny exposed and then dissected until rumours fly that she and Kirov, you know, you know what Kirov was like (and that's why Nikolaev did it). As if Kirov, who could have had the pick of Leningrad, who did have it, would ever have alighted here.

No matter. History's moving on. Wheels are turning, a country turning over, and here he comes, carried by those wheels, to guide the process, the man himself.

That man who has lost his friend. Travelling on the *Red Arrow*, saying faster, faster, because Leningrad has been orphaned and he, the father of a country, the great, the one, Stalin, must be there.

And here it comes, his train, steaming into the station this dank morning, this 2 December, and out he steps, this man wrapped up in grief but not grief-stricken enough to neglect what he knows must now be done, and as the words of the song start spreading:

Hey, fresh tomatoes.
Hey, want a cucumber . . .

This man acts; keeping on his glove, does what any man who has lost a friend might choose to do: he slaps the face of that failure, that Medved, head of the Leningrad NKVD, who should have stopped this from coming to pass. And then, without a break, Kirov's friend moves on, riding through the sombre streets, past those pictures of Kirov's face edged in black in black-lined windows over which water runs, snow melting as if even the very buildings are weeping, and here he is, this man, stepping, going without a break to Kirov's office, there on the third floor, where he takes over, hauling out files, scouring the past, shredding it as he goes, and then squeezing Nikolaev until he vomits up not only the beer that they have given him but also names. Names of friends, enemies, those he doesn't even know, all of them joined together in this knock-kneed, hunchbacked conspiracy that points eventually to Zinoviev, a conspiracy that Kirov could have told everyone makes little sense. But Kirov cannot speak, will never speak again, for he lies, laid out in the Tauride Palace (he got there in the end), blackened by his fall, bloodied by the shot, more still than could ever be dreamed as crowds, held in check by bands of militiamen, traipse past, here in the Tauride, and in the Smolny as well, they go, there to view that symbol, the thing that Kirov never would be parted from, his cap, stained by blood, his blood, and by the blood to come. As all the while one question does the rounds:

'What happened?'

> Stalin killed Kirov
> Got him in the corridor.

Is that what really happened?

Why not ask the bodyguard? Borisov, who loved Kirov, who would have laid down his life for Kirov, but who never got the chance, because although he was there, following close, he wasn't present, at least that's what he first says, or so it was reported, at the crucial moment when the shot (except there were two shots) was fired. And he never gets to answer why. He dies before he can speak again, on his way to give evidence in the truck in which they fetched him. He dies, the truck skidding, hitting a wall, and Borisov, alone amongst all those others in that vehicle, is injured, dead. No one can say what really happened, not the doctors whose post-mortem report of injuries consistent with an accident is contradicted by a different medic who sees the evidence of many blows, nor the driver, whose tales of steering wheels wrenched from his hands could, after all, be just that, a tale to cover up the fact that he drove badly, that, in skidding, he caused this witness's death.

Only one thing is clear. Two down. Many more to go.

Soon it will come to pass but, for now, Kirov must be buried.

Two days are allowed for Leningrad to view its leader and then it's Moscow's turn. There it goes, his coffin carried in that freezing damp through the crowd-lined streets, into that train garlanded by sorrow, to that other city and that other place of mourning, that House of Soviets, where he lies in that heavy aroma of loam and evergreens for two more days, until finally the moment arrives.

The funeral march plays as Kirov's friend, his leader, his Koba, mounts the platform and leans over that casket and delivers that one last kiss and then it is finished. The coffin closed, the remains combusted and carried through the streets strewn with white sand. That long parade of leaders, commissars, officials, directors, technicians, tanks and what seems to be the whole Red Army, a vast shuffling of feet, a threshing of the dead, can be heard until that moment when the music starts and the planes flow overheard. The speeches begin, hours of railing against Kirov's killer, those voices magnified a thousand times as if to drown out the echo of thirty-nine cut down by NKVD guns in Leningrad the day before or the twenty-nine in Moscow, or the ones to come: the nine in Minsk, the Kiev twenty-eight, on and on in an endless flow of blood. As Kirov's friend bows his head and his wife faints, other wives begin the process of bowing their own heads, of grieving and fainting from their losses, the wailing of this crowd magnified and then suppressed as it spreads throughout the country, the silent grieving for the losses yet to come and all because Kirov has been killed.

A Joke

Today I heard the first line of a joke or at least I think it was a joke. It started as a question:

'How many people does it take to kill a Kirov?' it began. I can't say how it went on. I didn't wait to hear. It's not wise to be caught eavesdropping, not these days it isn't, to be seen to want to know.

But after I'd moved away I couldn't get it out of my mind. I kept asking myself that same thing: how many people does it take to kill a Kirov?

I started to count the ones we'd heard of.

First off: there's Nikolaev. He pulled the trigger, or so they say. It must be true: they found him (didn't they?) in the corridor with Sergei Mironovich, Kirov breathing his last, Nikolaev just out cold.

Nikolaev named thirteen of his associates, so that makes fourteen, all of them tried in secret and quickly shot. What kind of people they must have been to believe that they could get away with it, I can't imagine. Followers of Zinoviev, or so we're told, which, given Sergei Mironovich had got Zinoviev's job in Leningrad, makes some kind of sense. But what I don't understand is, if they were the ones, how did the White Guards fit in? They were also caught in that opening trawl. Hundreds of them punished for Kirov's death, some shot, others just moved out of the city. You could see them, extended families of the former aristocracy, bundled up in railway stations, on their way to who knows where. You could find their possessions polished and piled up in the special currency shops, soon to be relocated in apartments like the Ivanovs' on Nevsky, now upgraded to include a White Guard chandelier, where it continues to cause trouble, with Boris Aleksandrovich's mother complaining about having to clean it, while those who like to whisper in the Smolny mutter about the pretensions of Boris Aleksandrovich (didn't they always know he had aristocratic leanings?).

If you ask me, both are wrong. Boris Aleksandrovich works hard: why shouldn't he have a chandelier? As for the cleaning of it, well, take it from someone who knows: far better to use your energy polishing up those finely carved crystal pieces than passing a mop down corridors over which a detachment of dirty-booted militia is soon bound to tramp.

Hark at me. My husband, my former husband (he's caught himself another woman and so, mercifully, no longer bothers me), is right: I never could stick to any subject. Or, come to mention it, to keep away from cleaning.

Back to Kirov and his string of murderers. The White Guards weren't the end of it. Others were also soon accused. Two men in particular: Medved, the head of the Leningrad NKVD, and his deputy, Zaporozhets.

I've not heard anybody accusing them of direct involvement in the murder, but it stands to reason, doesn't it, that they had to shoulder some of the blame. How else would Nikolaev have got so close to Kirov if they hadn't slipped up? And how else did it happen that not only had the secret police guard peeled off, but even Kirov's favourite, Borisov, was not there when it happened? And so, of course, the two men had to go.

Where they went to was the Arctic (my Arctic, as I like to think of it) to the Kolyma gold mines. Also of interest, if only to me: the ship that took them was accompanied by the icebreaker *Krassin*. Yes, that's right, that same which wasn't around when we, the Chelyuskinists, had desperate need of her.

From this fact some people might think it's safer to be a failure in the secret police than a member of our most important scientific expedition, but not me. I know the Arctic: I know its treachery and I certainly don't believe the rumours that those two have got special treatment in exchange for silence. Their silence? Over what?

To continue. If we thought Medved and Zaporozhets would be the end of it, if we imagined that the punishment of the murderer and his accomplices, the ideological remnants that needed clearing out, and the secret policemen who slipped up, if we thought getting rid of them would close the case on Kirov's death, then we were wrong. So many people did it take to kill our Sergei Mironovich, from the left and from the right, that if they'd held a meeting they'd have had to book a hall, no, not a hall, a town, a city. These people who confessed to what they did, so many linked in a conspiracy so vast it almost beggars belief . . . although who am I to disbelieve what I am told? No longer just monarchists or White Guards now, but actual one-time members of our highest body, our Politburo. First Zinoviev and Kamenev shot, with the sixteen others of the Trotskyite–Zinovievite centre, and then those seventeen of the anti-Soviet Trotskyite centre, followed by the generals (tried in private and also shot) and now there's another trial in full swing: the twenty-one members of the anti-Soviet blocs of Rightists and Trotskyites that include two men, Bukharin and Rykov, who stood alongside Lenin and Stalin.

An ignorant person such as myself might wonder what kind of comradeship it was that had bound them together if this is the way they now behave, but then I know I'm ignorant and that this has nothing to do with comradeship or personal whim. It is about the obligation of a revolution that must be preserved at all costs, which it seems is the only principle on which all these former comrades can agree. And meanwhile people talk, not openly but in soft voices further softened should a stranger pass by, and all the while those rumours and those jokes – how many people does it take to kill a Kirov? – do the rounds.

I also often think about it. Why not? Kirov is not just some name that they have put instead of Marinsky's on the headboard of our opera house; or given to one of our city's summer islands; or to the biggest factory – now the Kirov Works – in Leningrad; or to a score of streets across our Soviet Union. No, to me Kirov is not this figurehead – this martyr – Sergei Mironovich Kirov. To me he is the real man. The man I knew. Who was kind to me and who suffered as ordinary men can and who died as we all must do.

In my lifetime I've known much death and most of it of men, and time has hidden them, the months and then the years wiping them from memory as surely as worms have devoured their flesh. But with Sergei Mironovich, it's different: his face has stuck. I picture it often, that laughing face, or that high-browed face bent in concentration, or that angry face urging someone to action. And, yes, I know he's been ground into our lives, his portrait everywhere (although less so now than when it had just happened) but I also know that it isn't his likeness I remember: it's him.

Strange. I wonder sometimes: could this be because his death changed everything? Because change everything it did. But then I think of something else. I think that maybe the reason he won't leave my head is that I was one of the people who betrayed him.

After he was killed, when I was questioned then, well, I also gave only those answers of which I could be sure. No fantasies. No talk of ghosts in the dead of night, or of his feeling that somebody was after him. Sergei Mironovich was dead and so I stuck to my motto: keep your head down (or else a horse might trample you). Not a bad motto, now I come to think of it, for our whole nation. We are a people of lowered heads. Eyes that turn away. Lips that tighten. Ears that close. Straight looking we are, aimed straight ahead, no deviation. A new era is upon us and we must all adjust. It happens. We are Russians. We are used to change. We don't think about it. We just get on and do.

Can the Dead Speak (2)?

The catch is now begun. They are taken out in the dead of night, vans speeding through the city while the wakeful lie in bed hoping that this visit, this future and this fate will not be theirs. And then, as feet pound up the stairs and fists smash open doors, the time for hope is gone. People are taken from their jobs, their neighbourhoods and homes; from their wives' embraces and their children's memories; expunged from the records; excised from history.

All on the orders of one man. Their leader. Their Boss. Their *Gensek*. Iosif Vissarionovich, that same whom his closest call Koba and whose other names – the Jesuit, Genghis Khan of the Politburo and Ivan the Terrible Reborn – also given by his friends, are intoned in muted, private whispers.

This man. This Stalin.

This trickster who, with one hand, summons up his comrades to his side on the podium in Red Square and, with the other, dispatches hard men to pick them off. This calm man who sits in the highest office, colouring red the eyes of the wolves that he has already doodled. This avenger who scrawls profanities on petitions sent to him for clemency.

From General I. E. Yakir, one-time commander of two military districts and a one-time member the Central Committee, Stalin receives this promise:

'All my conscious life has been spent in selfless and honest work before the Party and its leaders,' Yakir has written, to which he adds:

'I shall die with the words of love for you, the Party, and the country, and with a boundless faith in the victory of Communism.'

In response to which Stalin scrawls:

'Scoundrel and prostitute,' while a handful of his comrades – the ones he hasn't killed – Voroshilov, Molotov and Kaganovich – queue up to add their insults – 'traitor, swine' – to their leader's.

Their leader, Stalin.

This time traveller, capable of speeding himself far into the future to see where danger lies not only to himself but also to his fatherland (for are not the two the same?), and then, on his return, to take action in the present, cutting off conspiracies that only he is wise enough to guess will surely one day come to pass.

This administrator who is driven to kill those who, if he doesn't rid himself of them, might later find him guilty of their murders.

This devious man whose finger settles on his former comrades each in turn.

One by one they go, these lifelong Bolsheviks. Unwillingly they go – for who would choose a traitor's death? – but willingly enough, for what they have in common is that they will do anything, even give their lives, to stop a split developing in their movement, these clever men never asking who, after they have gone, will keep their Party in one piece, or what this Party has become.

Watch them as they make their obeisance and then pass

on. These educated Russians who let a wily Georgian slowly pick them off. These people whose imaginations are strong enough to conjure up their revolution but whose insight fails them when it comes to Him.

These men, once Lenin's closest, now speechless in the face of multi-barrelled accusations that Stalin's prosecutors let fly. Political contortionists, they are called: traitor-terrorist-conspirators; faithless dismemberers of their motherland, and in longhand:
severers of their country from the Ukraine,
and Belorussia,
and the Central Asiatic Republics,
and Georgia ,
and Armenia,
and Azerbaijan
and also, don't forget,
the Maritime Region of the Far East.

And more than that as well: Communist allies of German fascists, or Bolsheviks who murdered, or at least tried to (it makes no difference which), their Boss, their Stalin, as well as their friend, Kirov, their beloved, Lenin, and even the writer, Maxim Gorky, who sometimes took their side. Doctors are found guilty of poisoning their patients, engineers of destroying their factories and theorists of forsaking their intellects; secret policemen are shot as children denounce their parents. A world turned upside down. Disputes eradicated through strange dock-side pairings as those age-old opponents – Rightists and Trotskyites – accused of membership of the self-same anti-Soviet bloc.

All in this blood frenzy. This final cleansing of a nation. Of an ideal.

For a moment they might raise their heads and cry 'Enough' – and then the moment lapses. They have gone too far, these men of principle in whose name all principle has been killed. These activists, once brave enough to renounce the old world, now forced by logic to renounce themselves.

Could they have stopped Him? In that moment after Lenin's death, should they have publicised his last judgement that Stalin could not be trusted? Or in those many other moments: when there was a victory against the whites; or the kulaks; or the Trotskyist left?

Were they so busy being against, they forgot what they were for?

Could they have stood together? Faced Stalin down? Held fast and stopped Him in His tracks? Stripped Him of His power?

But no, they never could, and they cannot, for even on the edge of death they do not understand. They write to him, their Stalin, and they ring him up. He cannot know, they tell themselves. He cannot know.

Thus does Radek, on the eve of his incarceration, plead with Bukharin to write to Stalin on his behalf.

And so does Bukharin, who, once the Revolution's golden boy and now himself waiting, in Stalin's former bedroom, for his own arrest, decides to phone his Stalin, once and once again, his Stalin who cannot listen to his pleas because Stalin has gone to Sochi and can't be reached.

And thus as well does Iona Yakir, the Jew found guilty of being a German fascist hireling, that same Yakir, that man whose leader labels him a 'scoundrel' and a 'prostitute', thus does this Yakir still keep his promise:

'Long live the Party,' he calls before they shoot him, and then, as a bullet flies towards his brain, that final rallying cry:

'Long live Stalin!' and he is gone.

What is known is simultaneously not known. What is

unbelievable becomes commonplace as shots ring out. In the basements of Leningrad, of Moscow and Kiev, of every city in this great Soviet Union, they sound, the unbearable now being born.

Part Four

Under the Red Wall

And I pray not only for myself,
But also for those who stood there,
In the bitter cold, or in the July heat,
Under that red blind prison wall

(Anna Akhamatova, *Requiem*)

The Seal

On the rare occasions when Natasha allows herself to think about that time in 1937 when everything was changed, two images recur. Two opposites. Light. And dark. The one before, the other afterwards.

The ritual of her remembering never changes. She remembers: herself, alone on stage at the Marinsky (except it's the Kirov now). She can't remember exactly what she was doing, putting the finishing touches to the backdrop probably, but she has exact recall of the moment when the stage lights were suddenly switched on. She wasn't expecting that. Blinded, she throws up one hand to try to shade her eyes and the other out for balance as a voice calls:

'Now.'

This instruction is followed by the muffled clunk of a familiar lever, the lights going off again, and, although Natasha is familiar with the sound and knows exactly what it heralds, the darkness nevertheless hits her unprepared, enveloping her like a shroud, blacker than the deepest night.

She blinks and staggers back, panicked, although her rational mind tells her she is safe and there is nothing here to panic her, and in confirmation she hears that voice again issuing from the highest gallery:

'Thank you, comrades. Gently now.'

The stage lights begin to come up, bringing with them the gradual lifting of the darkness and of her blindness, as the voice continues:

'Did you see how Natalya Borisovna nearly fell?' and is answered from deep backstage by one sentence:

'We did, Comrade Director.'

If all of this had happened on any other day it would have been forgotten. But because of the timing she remembers it. She remembers her sheepish smile (that she could have been so easily caught out) and her relief. She can even see herself from that gallery's vantage point, herself uncertain, standing centre stage, wrong-footed by a trick of light.

'So you see, comrades,' the disembodied voice continues, 'if that's the effect a sudden change of lighting has on Natalya Borisovna – and remember, she's accustomed to working on stage during lighting changes – you can imagine what it would do to this season's inexperienced chorus members. Timing, comrades. Everything is in the timing.'

A trivial incident – the opera director using her reaction to teach the lighting crew a lesson – nailed in memory. In hindsight she sees it in two ways: as the moment when she felt that first fragment of a dread that would soon envelop her and, at the same time, as almost the last moment of her former life. But if she removes what happened afterwards from the equation, the dread she remembers experiencing is either neutralised or turned into a seemingly overblown exaggeration that hindsight has invented.

She sees herself centre stage, Natalya Borisovna Kozlova, mother of her beloved Katya, wife of a valued worker, daughter of a Party activist and a brilliant scientist, and, in her own right, a respected member of the Kirov theatre's backstage team, secure in what she is, happy with what she's got, intent on continuing with whatever it was she had been doing (although she still can't remember what that was) except that the voice from the gallery sounds out:

'Don't worry, Natashka . . . you can finish that tomorrow', and looking at the clock she sees that he is right, it's her time to go.

She walks briskly across the stage, taking care to lift her feet so she won't trip on a half-completed piece of scenery (she remembers it clearly, could reproduce its exact shade of sapphire blue if need be), and, going out, makes her way through the warren of tunnels that connects one section of the basement to the other.

Fragments of dislocated sound – a soprano warming up, a trumpet blaring, the insistent tapping of a single piano key – rise to meet her as she passes by rehearsal rooms, fetching her coat, pulling on her galoshes, saying goodbye to her friends (so many she had then), and finally emerging into the late afternoon.

In this segment of her memory she is smiling although she's not entirely sure whether this is accurate or whether she just assumes she was smiling because that's what she mostly remembers doing in those days. See her, this young self, this stranger, all bright efficiency as, pulling her coat tight against the biting cold, she makes her way to the trolley stop, her mind caught up in aimless anticipation: the pleasure, for example, she will feel when it's time to tell Katya her bedtime story; or her wondering about the timing of Kolya's shift and her realising it was an early one so he'll be at home; and finally the touch of an errant flake of snow, that, floating down, comes to rest on her upper lip. She uses her tongue to lap it up, tasting her own skin's saltiness.

She was always happy in those days. Waking up each morning with her husband Kolya beside her and their baby, Katya, in easy reach, she was filled with joy. It was as if her whole life has been lived in anticipation of this moment when she would understand what it was to feel so wanted and so loved. No – it was even better than that: she had discovered a feeling that she hadn't known before, that wonderful sensation of being the active one, the one who feels privileged to be allowed to love so well.

She recollected how just yesterday, she was ironing and, at the same time, watching as Katya reached out for Kolya, the baby's dimpled hands beckoning on his callused ones, demanding to be picked up, which would certainly occur because Kolya could never resist his daughter. And then, as Natalya flicked water on to Kolya's much-darned shirt, she watched Kolya tossing their Katya up, high into the air, the child's laughter increasing to the sounds of her mother's mock alarm, which Natasha shouldn't have bothered with since she knew how powerful were those arms of Kolya's, and how safe, waiting to receive their daughter, so strong that when he caught her and threw her up again, she seemed as light as the snow that now begins to fall in earnest on Natasha.

A cold wind has also come up, whipping the snow forward. Natasha bends her head against its impact.

From lightness into dark. A man, tilting against that same wind, coming in her direction, not watching where he's going, careens into her and almost knocks her over. It wouldn't have mattered, she would never have remembered it, save for the fact that it happened then and that not only does the stranger not stop to check that she's all right but, by the time she's regained her balance and has turned to look after his black-coated outline, his voice barks out over the wind:

'Why don't you look where you're going, you stinking piece of dung?'

The violence of those words, so shocking they almost knock the breath from her so that, as he staggers off, she, who would never normally allow anything to stop her from speaking out, holds her tongue and then it's too late anyway because the trolley has arrived, its bell jangling.

It stops for her and she climbs in.

Out of the darkness, into light.

The trolley is crowded: she has to push her way in. No need to hold on – the press of people keeps them all upright. It's only a short journey to Katya's crèche but long enough to set aside that unpleasant encounter (the man, she tells herself, was just an angry drunk), and she's soon smiling again.

Her stop. She pushes through the crowd of unwashed bodies and damp coats and jumps down. Standing for a moment to catch her breath she looks up. The sky seems strangely clear (that was a snow flurry before, not a storm), almost opaque, a white night almost to match high summer. Light and dark, she thinks, as she crosses the road, walking through the darkness towards the light.

Katya open-armed, wide-eyed, laughing as she croons her special baby version of hello. There's a moment also in the crèche, Natasha listening to the account of what Katya has consumed that day, and how she slept and when, and saying yes, she's really beautiful, the best baby in the world, and it doesn't matter that the crèche workers probably say the same thing to all the mothers, Natasha knows how, in Katya's case, it's true. And then the two are off, Katya bundled up in Natasha's arms, only the tip of her nose poking out which Natasha holds against herself to keep it warm and feels her baby chortling and then into the tram they go with Natasha thinking idly that she is always on the move

but thinking also that she's a mother now and her movements have a purpose and that's part of what she loves
about her life, so many things to do, so many demands, and
people looking at her, a mother, with respect, even her own
mother, welcoming her into womanhood.

And there. The last stop or at least the one nearest home.
She and Katya off the tram. Carelessly she walks from the
tram stop to their building, pushing the front door open
and going in.

'Don't be silly,' she croons as she takes the stairs two at a
time: 'Don't be silly, we'll soon be there,' while, snuggled in
her arms, Katya looks up, hungry but not desperately so, on
the point of fussing, but she's still a baby and although there
is little she can do yet, her options are nevertheless infinite:
she could cry and make her mother hurry, or she could do
as she suddenly decides to, unwrinkle that perfect brow of
hers and beam, her chubby face lighting up, bright enough
it seems to Natasha, to light up the dingy stairway.

Natasha starts to sing.

Years later she will remember all of this in detail, will
picture herself singing as she transports a delightedly smiling Katya up the stairs. It's happening elsewhere, in a score
of other streets in Leningrad, a young mother and her child,
a happy mother (even if a tired one) back from work and
on her way has fetched her baby from the crèche and now
she is almost home, their home, where she will feed her
baby and then cook for herself and for her husband as she,
once the most undomesticated of young girls, has learned
to do and then . . . who knows. The evening stretches out.
An evening at home. The kind, these days, she likes the
best.

She remembers other things as well. A piece of paper on
the first landing. No, not quite, the landing before that, on
the top step of that first flight of stairs, that's where it was.

She remembers how it took her by surprise – the staircase is usually spotless – and how she picked it up and looked at it, soon losing interest for there's nothing to look at, just some indecipherable scrawl and a few random numbers, a scrap of paper someone accidentally had dropped. She holds it up, away from Katya's grasp, says: 'No darling, it's dirty,' distracting her baby by pointing to the next flight, 'Papa's waiting for us up there,' and simultaneously slipping the paper into her pocket with the intention of throwing it away once she gets upstairs.

It will still be there weeks later: she'll throw it away then.

There are other things as well that she remembers. A heap of piled-up snow on the sidewalk, waiting for disposal, as she jumped off the tram; the merest fragment of a passing conversation, the words 'two tons', she overheard as she passed two men; the creak of the front door as she pushed it open; the fraction of a second it took her to adjust her eyes from the brightness outside to the gloom within; and the way her neighbour looked at her – and just as quickly looked away – as she began to climb the stairs (something she didn't even realise she had registered until later), all these trivialities burned in memory by what happened next so that, in the months that followed, she would wake up and, opening her eyes, would relive that same sequence in its most basic detail until, that is, she trained herself on waking to keep her eyes firmly shut.

But there are things as well she can't remember. The song she was singing, for example: it has vanished. The picture of herself is mute. No matter how hard she tries, she cannot bring back the sound, cannot ever know what she, in her innocence, could have been singing out.

She climbs the stairs. Singing. She's hungry. So is the baby. So will Kolya be. She idly weighs the odds that he will have remembered to clear away the breakfast things (not good: he hardly ever remembers this although he said he'd try) and to fill the samovar.

In that moment when it should have been clear that life as she has so far known it has ended, she does not understand.

The door has been locked. Why bother? It's also hanging off its hinge. She doesn't understand. It's broken but it's closed.

Sealed by wax. The initials NKVD. A police seal.

Another Woman

One glimpse of Natasha is all Boris Aleksandrovich needs to know they've taken Kolya. She's his daughter, his most beloved, and he only has to look at her to know. But in the fraction of a second after he registers the sound of the door opening and glances up, annoyed that whoever it was hadn't bothered knocking, and in that moment before he is almost undone by her wretchedness, he sees her, dispassionately, as he has begun to see that stream of other women who have taken to coming here for help, using his office as a stopping point on their pilgrimage of sorrow, muting their voices so as not to offend, pleading for an explanation they know he can't provide, wondering out loud, hopeful in their utter hopelessness, whether there isn't something, anything, he might be able to do to clear up this misunderstanding, for misunderstanding it always is. And so they sit because they have no energy to stand, humbled in the chair he offers them, heads lowered in submission as out of their disbelieving mouths come forth clotted sentences of rage and of despair, disbelief and half-acceptance, clogging up the air until it begins to feel as if they are also clogging up his arteries, although whether this will lead eventually to his heart's failure, or merely to its hardening, he is at a loss to know.

And now his daughter is standing in these women's place and all she says is that one word, her husband's name:

'Kolya.'

This is not one of that stream of women. This is his daughter for whom he would lay down his life, and he is already up and by her side, instinct telling him to take her in his arms, but instinct defied, because she's no longer a child, his little girl whose sorrows he can hug away. And so, instead of embracing her, he leads her over to a chair, helping her down into it, standing by her a moment, uneasily, for he is conscious of how he's towering over her, and yet he doesn't want to do as he would normally and use his desk as a divider by sitting at its other side. And then he thinks, of course, and he fetches the chair from behind the desk and sets it down, close but not too close, and reaches out to take her hand.

She lets him have it.

He feels her hand lying, passively, in his, but the sudden look she throws him, as well as the tilt of her chin as she then looks away, speak neither of passivity nor of the humble manner of the women who have preceded her, but of a challenge and he finds himself wondering whether the cold determination he can read in her profile is a sign of what widowhood might do to her, and then, shocked at the thought (for Kolya is alive: he has to be), he says:

'Where's Katya?'

'I took her home.' Her voice is flat.

'Our home?'

A nod.

He says: 'Good,' and waits to hear what else she has to say. She doesn't speak. She keeps her face averted.

He sits beside her, watching how she bites her lip, and then gradually he finds his gaze drawn, as is hers, to the window and outside and he sees to his surprise that it has long since grown dark.

'What happened?' he asks although he doesn't really need to, for he already knows what happened.

He's heard it all before, endlessly, monotonous tales of police raids, usually in the dead of night, of neighbours hauled from sleep and taken to the target's home, given a chair so that they might bear witness, although what they usually do is nod off and who can blame them for the dramatic has become routinised, the unexpected commonplace, as night stretches into dawn and wardrobes, bookshelves, floorboards, and even the materials that make up the very walls, are disassembled, despoiled, their contents strewn about, papers confiscated, suitcases packed, children hugged, and very little spoken except for that one, enduring question. The inevitable question:

'*Why?*' which has no answer save for the cursory:

'*You should know,*' spat out of the mouths of those whose skins bear the pallor of their dark work, their manner thick with fury that this is what they have to do, night after night, raid the homes of those whose behaviour has stripped them of the protection of the law and also, apparently, of their originality, for all this succession of idiots can ever seem to ask is that same, dull, repeated question: '*Why?*'

'They took him away,' Natasha says.

'Do you know where?'

'No. They sealed the flat.'

'You didn't go inside?'

A shake of her head.

'Good.' Boris Aleksandrovich sits, waiting for Natasha to continue, but she doesn't. She merely holds the silence, the two of them sitting there, wrongly, in the circumstances, without a word, so that the urge to fill the emptiness builds up in him, until he finds he can't stop himself, but like all those others before him, he, even knowing how futile is the question, finds himself impelled to ask:

'Have you any idea why they took him?'

She turns her head then, sharply, and looks at him and then she does begin to speak.

He concentrates on what she's saying in a monotone so uncharacteristic of her. She is speaking of her husband, her Kolya, describing him to her papa as if he were some stranger, relating in a singsong voice how Kolya is the best of husbands, the most inoffensive, undisruptive and good-natured of men; who, as far as Natasha knows (and she knows him well), has never held an unkind thought or a disloyal one; who cannot be accused of shirking for he has never once arrived late, nor missed a single day of work; and neither can he be guilty of sabotage because his targets are always fulfilled (earlier than most); and as for a possible lack of diligence, well, when it comes to the *subotniks*, he goes to all of those, even ones he doesn't need to go to. In summary, Kolya is a man who does more than is required of him. As a matter of fact, if anything, he's too good, it some-times annoys Natasha, now she happens to mention this, the way he puts others' needs before his own, but, wait a minute – what's she saying? – she has nothing to complain of. He's the perfect husband and the perfect father, who, unlike most other men, will pick up their daughter, Katya, when Natasha's working late, and make sure she eats and even, on occasions, puts Katya to bed, for that's his life, his factory and his family, no time for caucusing or anti-Soviet activity or even making enemies, because that's not his way . . .

All of which Boris Aleksandrovich knows to be the truth, for isn't Kolya his son-in-law, and wasn't it with his support that Natasha married him?

He wants to stop her, to say what she must already know, that whether Kolya is a good man or not is hardly the point, but Boris doesn't interrupt her flow. He has come to understand that this compulsion by the woman to bear testimony to her husband is part of the process that must also be endured. It's as if, by naming their husbands, and by describing them, these wives can keep their men, or perhaps only their hopes about their men, alive. So they come here to use Boris Aleksandrovich as their sounding board, a witness to their need to convince themselves that if this is the good they see within their men, then surely the interrogators, or whoever it is who holds the power of life or death over their husbands, will find it too, and thus will this misunderstanding be resolved. As if, Boris Aleksandrovich thinks, their husbands' fate has anything at all to do with the individual interrogator or the individual accused. This is what Boris Aleksandrovich always thinks as he hears them out, but doesn't ever say, for he also knows that what these women can't afford to acknowledge is that the events that have visited their homes have nothing to do either with their individual husbands or with mercy, but are about the demands history makes and history's need for change. And that when this happens, onlookers – even innocent ones – are sometimes sacrificed.

He cannot tell them this. They don't give a fig for history, all they want is their husbands back, and who can blame them? And so he doesn't try to argue, but only hears them out and promises to do his best (and often he does, and sometimes it pays off) but after that, he has no choice, he has to work. He has to show them out.

'I don't know what to do,' he hears Natasha saying.

He says: 'What you must do right now is look after yourself. Go home.'

'I can't go home.'

'Go to our home on Nevsky.'

'I can't.'

'You must.'

'I can't just sit there doing nothing.'

He squeezes her hand: 'Looking after yourself isn't nothing, Natasha. You must keep strong. For Katya's sake. For Kolya's.'

'I have to find him.'

'Go home, Natasha. Rest. Look after Katya. I'll make inquiries. Find out what happened.'

She nods and sighs and he sees that her eyes are dry and realises that, unlike those others, she hasn't cried at all, registering this with a kind of pleasure for she is his, strong as he is, and no matter what happens she will survive. She looks at him. Deep into his eyes.

'Will it be all right?' she asks.

There it is: the other question that he always dreads. No matter how they might try to hold it back – and the wisest of them know he can't predict their husbands' fate – it invariably escapes their lips. He always tries to answer truthfully – that he doesn't know – although he also tries to deliver his answer gently, with a smile, trying not to strip them of their hope – and it's true, he doesn't know, and some will be all right – and when he does this, he always sees how the really intelligent ones read his hesitation for what it is, and he can see their disappointment flaring, as their heads dip, almost in appreciation that he has not lied to them.

This situation is, however, different. This is his daughter, not some half-known woman, some partial stranger's wife.

'Yes,' he tells Natasha. 'It will be all right.'

She makes her way along the corridor. She is crying, tears rolling down her cheeks. She takes no notice: she would, in fact, be utterly astonished if somebody were to draw her attention to her tears.

She hears his voice again. What he had to say.

'Yes, it will be all right,' she hears and she knows, as she did then, that he was lying.

And after that, she thinks, it's as if he wanted to get rid of her, insisting she go home to rest (as if she could), saying he will take care of it, and though she wants to believe him, with all her heart she does, she finds herself walking down the corridor with her tears streaming down, and she's thinking not only that Papa has let her down but that something else is badly wrong because always, when Kolya was away, at work, or even that time when he went to the country to help bring in the harvest, she has felt him with her, inside of her, has known that he was safe. But now: she cannot feel him. It's as if the wax seal they used to keep her from their home has also sealed up her instinct and her understanding, so that the only thing that's left to her is the enormity of his absence.

The Black Crow

Kolya sits on the floor of the black crow, jolted and bumped about as the van races through the darkened streets of Leningrad, and all the time he sits, he thinks he doesn't understand. That's the first thing, he thinks. It's a mistake: that's the second.

He decides to think of something safe: Natasha. He thinks about the shock she'll get when she comes back from work and sees the door sealed, and he thinks about who will help her, and where she and Katya will go. But then he thinks, that's stupid. She'll go to her parents – naturally – and they'll take her in. Besides. This is a mistake. He'll soon be back. This is all he thinks. Nothing else. In their family, Natasha is the one with the imagination. Not him.

The van stops, so abruptly that he's bounced against the walls. Before he has time to right himself, the door opens and two of them are at him, dragging him out, swearing as they set him on his feet and push him forward. He can't understand why they're so rough. He's a worker, isn't he? One of them.

They push him through the gates. He knows where he is – in prison – but that's the limit of his knowledge. Not that he matters. He's reduced to meat. Line fodder. Put in a queue. Told to wait. To be processed. Or at least he thinks that this is what he's been told. They speak so fast, he can barely understand.

Of the men who have brought him here, one seems less belligerent than his fellows. Seems to know Kolya is innocent. That he's done nothing wrong. When, just before leaving home, Kolya had reached for his coat, this man asked if it was his warmest, and, on Kolya's assent, told him to bring an extra jerkin. He even took the jerkin when Kolya, not bothering because this is a mistake and he'd soon be out, left it behind, and threw it into the black crow. Now, waiting in line, Kolya sees this man close by and calls to him:

'Can I get a message to my wife?'

But it seems he has misjudged his man, for the policeman turns puce and after saying, 'Don't try snivelling up to me, citizen,' loudly, much louder than is necessary, adds:

'I'm not your nursemaid,' and walks off.

Standing, watching the man's retreating back, Kolya registers the use of that word: citizen. Kolya's no mere citizen, hasn't been for years. He's a comrade. A Komsomol member. Destined for the Party. Everybody knows that.

Well, he tells himself, that proves it. It's a mix-up. Has to be. They've confused him with someone else. Yes. Just as mistakes can happen, so they can be remedied. He'll be out of here. All in good time.

But now. Concentrate. Do as you're told. That's what they keep telling him and they are right. No point in making trouble. His turn has come, he must do as he is told. Except they're yelling at him. Too slow, they yell, and yell at him to remove his clothes, no, not tomorrow, citizen, now, think you're in a rest home, do you? And move it, citizen, shift your indolent self to one side, no not there, here, you reptile you, gangrenous piece of pestilence, and don't you ever stop fiddling, need delousing do you? And all the while they keep picking through his clothes, turning them inside out, rifling through every corner, even the seams. He is embarrassed. That he is naked. That his clothes are dirty.

'Hark at this one, blushing like a girl.'

'Calls himself a worker!'

He wants to say: comrades, why treat me like this? I am a worker, an honest man, who does my best, gives my all, a man like you, no other, but he holds his tongue. He's a plain man, not a clever one, but he knows when to keep quiet. They're too busy to hear him out, working on his clothes, ripping out his bootlaces and his buttons, taking away his belt and then throwing back what's left, shouting, what are you waiting for? Get a move on, you carrion, get dressed, we don't have all day, and he does as they tell him, doesn't want to make trouble, they're only doing what they must, it's not up to them, whoever is in charge will soon sort out this mess, and he dresses, or at least he thinks that's what he does, he can't think, it's all too sudden, too incomprehensible. But he must have got dressed, for he is fully clothed now as he follows a warder down a long, grey corridor.

Sluggish thoughts. He is very tired. Doesn't know what to think. He hears: clicking. Doesn't understand it. Wonders why the walls are quilted grey.

'Hurry up.'

Bunching his trousers in one hand. He walks faster. And straighter. He will not hunch. Nor be treated as an animal. He is innocent. And a man.

A stop. Heavy key turning in a lock.

'Won't take long to wipe that look off your face.'

The warder puts his hand on Kolya's back and then, mightily, shoves him forward.

'In you go.'

Kolya stumbles. Into darkness. Throws out an arm to steady himself, finds himself flailing in the stench, his hands hitting at something soft and pulpy. Flesh and the sounds of someone swearing. And then a voice, quite gentle:

'Hey. Easy now.'

He staggers backwards. 'I'm sorry, comrade.'

A hand on his back. Steadying him.

That gentle voice again. 'It's all right, comrade, take your time. Let your eyes adjust.'

A friendly voice. He stands and takes his time.

It's cold. The kind of cold that is also wet. And dark as well. He swivels his head round, trying at least to get a sizing of this cell. Can't see much at first. The outline of high windows. Securely shuttered. Not that it matters. Dark outside as well. Well, never mind. He is strong. Not easily panicked. He continues to stand. Waiting until his patience pays off and he begins to see.

But first the smell. Rank, human smells. Festering excrement and piss. And something else – nature at its worst: rotting damp. He stops himself from breathing deeply and stands, and the darkness begins to take shape.

Men. He counts. Six in all. He thinks. Each seated but off the floor. On bunks then. No room between them: his first impression a continuum, a mattress of men, unbroken wave of feral humanity. Six pairs of eyes. Must be six then. Watching. To see what he will do. He draws himself up. Full height again (when did he slump back?). Hears voices:

'My! Look what we have here!'

'The genuine article. A real Stakhanovite.'

'The unguilty type. Case of mistaken identity, I bet.'

'He can't understand why he's ended up with us subversives.'

'Hey, watch who you're calling a subversive. I'm a degenerate, me.'

Laughter – so they can laugh in this hell – followed by that gentle voice: 'Don't take any notice, comrade: in this place we have to make our own entertainment. And don't be shy either. See – over there. Your bunk. Go on, sit down, make yourself comfortable. And then tell us what is happening in the world.'

Memory (1)

Boris Aleksandrovich makes his way along the Smolny's high-domed corridor, along the parquet floor past a succession of grand wooden doors that stand sentry on either side. His eyes are facing forward, as if he's searching out something in the layers of snow that cushion the window at the corridor's end. He is not, however, looking at the snow. He is instead concentrating on an inner voice. Although that isn't quite accurate. The voice he hears is not inner, but remembered. It's Lina's voice.

What was it she'd asked him last night as they'd lain together?

'Will you do anything to hold on to power?'

Yes. That was it.

Or was it? Boris Aleksandrovich sleeps badly these days and hardly at all that previous night. He thinks less fast as well. Things are slipping. In the past, he would have had exact recall, not only of Lina's tone, but also of her words, but, in these times of shifts and changes, it's increasingly difficult for him to be exact about anything (even though he also knows how dangerous it is not to be). He is forty-eight, no longer a young man, and yet his whole existence demands a kind of mental agility, and a flexibility, that has already defeated many a younger man.

Walking, he takes himself in hand. He will make an effort to conjure up precisely the form of words that Lina had used and, that way, refocus his mind.

He was wrong, he decides. Lina wouldn't have bothered with a question. That's not her style. She would have shot out some furious accusation, something like:

'You will do anything to hold on to power.'

The anger that Boris Aleksandrovich kept at bay last night now floods over him. Lina had indeed thrown down that statement, and, in the fashion of their times, made herself prosecutor and judge. His was to be the double role of accused and already convicted, his options either a plea of mitigation or, most likely, of confession, both of which he refused and so instead he continued to lie there, silently, willing himself not to lift a hand against her as he felt inclined to do.

Now, in the light of day, he remembers the things he'd wanted to say – his rage swelling – and the things he should have said. A question of his own, hovering, on the edge of being enunciated. His question:

'Don't you understand?'

That's what he'd wanted to ask. No: that's wrong. Not ask. That's too mild. He'd wanted to make it his demand.

'Don't you understand?'

He wants her here, right now, so he can say it.

'Don't you understand, you stupid woman? It's not power I'm holding on to. It's my life. And yours. And Ilya's and Natasha's: are you too stupid to see that, Lina?'

In fact, he is seized by the desire to go home and say it to her now, loudly, loud enough so that she, his mother, his son, even their neighbours, will hear, so these innocents who think it's a matter of choice what people like him do, so that these guiltless simpletons who by their inaction hold on to their precious sainthood, so that they will see it from his point of view, as it really is. Then they will finally understand that their innocence is bought at the cost of his complicity, their passiveness allowed rein only because men like him are not too scared to act, their safety bought with his daily risk. And more than that he wants to shout:

'You want somebody to draw a line, why not you?'

But as the words sound in his mind, he feels himself deflate: what would be the point? She doesn't understand. She and Anton, both, so dumb it hasn't dawned on them, and never will, that only those who commit themselves, who actually take a risk, stand any chance of changing anything.

He hears a voice. 'Good morning, comrade.'

He sees a tall young man who, having greeted him, is already passing by. Protocol demands that Boris Aleksandrovich answers the man, and quickly, and so he says:

'Comrade,' saying it as pleasantly as he can, hoping he hasn't given away a symptom of his age, himself so preoccupied he didn't notice the man and, on top of that, doesn't recognise him, although, he thinks, this lapse is not necessarily age-related. The man might really be a stranger. It's more than likely: there are many newcomers to the Smolny these days. And many disappearances.

Boris Aleksandrovich half-turns to watch the man's retreating back.

The man walks straight and fast, but not too fast, his long limbs thinned by distance, stretching out but then almost immediately reined in as if, feeling Boris Aleksandrovich's gaze on him, he's trying to show that the last thing he wants to do is get away. Or that is Boris Aleksandrovich's first assumption. Could be wrong though: could be that this particular young man doesn't care. Could be that he's one of those fearless unmaskers who take it upon themselves to watch who comes and goes, self-assured in his special status, unbothered by Boris Aleksandrovich's gaze.

The man stumbles and almost falls. Catching himself and straightening up, he can't help one desperate backward glance. That says it all. He's not a watcher. He's just some poor sod who's worried about the way that Boris Aleksandrovich has been watching him. Boris Aleksandrovich should have known better: no NKVD man would have bothered with a greeting, he'd have just walked on. Boris Aleksandrovich should have let the poor man walk down the corridor unobserved, should not have given in to the spirit of the times that is making sadists of them all.

He turns. Now where was he? Oh yes. On his way to his office. Past that room there.

There are no name plates on the doors. Another symptom: the current turnover of staff being so fast that the Smolny administration has decided to forgo them. Even so, that particular door looks familiar.

Boris Aleksandrovich stops. Of course it looks familiar. He often comes here.

Correction – he used to come here often.

No point in thinking about that. Boris Aleksandrovich has work to do. He must get moving.

And yet he doesn't. Standing, he finds himself drawn back into the past.

He sees the name that once adorned this door: Stepan Vasilyevich Filatov. He sees himself standing in front of it and knocking. He hears a gruff voice calling out:

'*Come.*'

It was two years ago, July 1935, when this happened. Seven months after Kirov's death. High summer. Standing by that door, Boris Aleksandrovich sees . . .

'*Come.*'

He sees himself walking into Stepan Vasilyevich's office. Stepan Vasilyevich's new office: he has recently been moved as have most of the Smolny's workers in the months that followed Kirov's murder. As a matter of fact, Boris Aleksandrovich remembers thinking as he closed the door that he and Stepan Vasilyevich could count themselves amongst the lucky ones: they only had to move floors. Not so the majority of their comrades, who have disappeared from the Smolny corridors, some of them moved to Moscow, while others had to go further afield, to Sverdlovsk and Novosibirsk, Tashkent and Baku, Kharkov and Arkhangelsk, or to a score of other smaller towns that lie somewhere in this vast Soviet Union of theirs, and some, or so it is whispered, have even vanished behind the heavy gates of Leningrad's Shpalerny prison or the Kresti, or even to Moscow's Lubyanka, and from there on to who knows where.

'Come in,' Stepan Vasilyevich says to Boris Aleksandrovich who is already in.

Light floods through the bank of windows. Stepan Vasilyevich might have been moved down a floor but this large office, and the assistants who scurry to do his bidding, show that he hasn't suffered a corresponding drop in his prestige. His huge plain desk, littered by files and memoranda, confirms this.

'Please, comrade,' Stepan Vasilyevich says. 'Take a seat.'

As Boris Aleskandrovich does so, he sees the way that Stepan Vasilyevich continues to look down at a document that seems to require all his concentration. His jowls, are fat, fatter than before: he has put on a lot of weight. His fleshy hand grips his fat fountain pen, poised above the paper, and now it starts to move, determinedly, along the page, as if what he is writing is more important than anything Boris Aleksandrovich could ever say. Which it probably is. Boris Aleksandrovich wonders why Stepan Vasilyevich bothered to send an assistant down the Smolny corridors to ask Boris personally to deliver a set of every-day statistics that the assistant could either have taken back himself or have got Boris Aleksandrovich to phone through.

'You have the figures?'

'Yes.' Boris lays the paper down.

Stepan Vasilyevich continues writing. The rolls of fat that spill all the way down his neck quiver as his hand moves along the page. This man, who has always undoubtedly liked his food and has a reputation, even amongst Russians, as a prodigious drinker, looks as if he's now trying to stifle himself in consumption, the apparent proof of this lying on his desk, close at hand, where a package is leaking the vinegary thick odour of herrings and dark rye bread that Boris could smell as soon as he had opened the door.

Sitting in that scratching silence with nothing else to do, Boris finds himself wondering what it feels like to be a Stepan Vasilyevich who, once so close to Kirov, must now be anxious for his position.

'Thank you, comrade. I will consider your report. In the meantime,' Stepan Vasilyevich looks up, long enough for Boris Aleksandrovich to see the dark rings that underline his eyes, but not long enough to read his expression before his head bends down again, 'you might want to look at this.'

'This' is slid across the desk, and 'this' is unmistakeably a dossier, and, what's more, Boris sees, it's a restricted doc-ument, aimed at the highest ranks of the *obkom*, the Party regional committee, headed 'top secret', for the eyes of only five named people, of whom Stepan Vasilyevich is one and Boris Aleksandrovich is not. And yet here it is, being pushed at Boris, without explanation, and without a further word, for Stepan Vasilyevich continues writing furiously.

It's a document to change perception. Now Boris Aleksandrovich views Stepan Vasilyevich's new bulk not as a signal of distress but as the man's visible layering of success. Fat born not of desperation but of deception. How else could a man like Stepan Vasilyevich, a Kirov loyalist, have kept his position as the purge sliced through the Smolny, excising not only oppositionists but also Kirov's closest, unless he'd helped to run those purges?

And here he sits, larger than life, using his thick fingers to push a dossier across his desk to a man who shouldn't see it and who is being allowed to, Boris knows, for only one reason: so it will compromise him.

Boris Aleksandrovich shifts in his chair, planting his feet more securely on the carpet. He is determined. He will not lose his dignity, no matter what ensues. He looks down.

He is looking at a report on the public's reaction to the new constitution. That's how it's labelled. There's another label also. For the eyes only, this one reads, of Stepan Vasilyevich Filatov and four others. Not for the eyes of Boris Aleksandrovich Ivanov – it doesn't say that – but this is what it means. He reads the date. 1 June 1935. The report is two weeks old.

Boris Aleksandrovich has seen its like before, not top secret like this one is, but aimed at men of his rank, digests of such reports after their secrets have been removed. Reading them was routine, and Boris Aleksandrovich had always known why he was doing it. But then he thinks: well, I also know why I'm reading this secret one. He is – he is very sure of this – he is reading, or is about to, of his impending downfall.

It can happen this way. While most are taken suddenly, others, and he's going to be one of them, are given notice either by a demotion or an unexpected move, or like this, through a written accusation.

Boris Aleksandrovich has rarely been so sure of anything as he is of this: that if he reads it, slowly and carefully, confirmation will come. His own name: that's what he's looking for.

He begins to read, his eyes moving down the page. He wonders what it is that he has said, carelessly, about the constitution. What offhand remark that, having issued from his unwary lips, had developed a life all of its own, plucked up by one of those who bear him ill because they want his job, or because he had slighted them or a wife, or a brother, or a neighbour, or none of these; perhaps just because they don't like the way he walked down the corridor, or looked at them as they walked down a corridor, his offhand sentence savoured, committed to memory and, eventually, carried down the stairs into the basement where men search for the slightest deviation or provocation over which they will be certain to take action?

He reads slowly.

'The vast majority of the people of Leningrad have reacted to the drawing up of the new constitution in a positive and healthy way,' he reads.

Yes. He thinks. He even nods. That's true.

'The workers in the Kirov Works hailed this era of civil peace and of legality,' he reads. 'One of these workers, Zavlavskaya Katerina, machinist, aged twenty-three, was overheard in the canteen saying that the glorious Soviet proletariat can now no longer be pushed aside. "People will have more room under this new constitution," she said. Engineer Orlov, Party member, of the Tr— Works, was also heard to say . . .'

Boris Aleksandrovich seems to register the name Tr—
Works as familiar, but he doesn't know why. He tells himself that all factories in Leningrad are known to him, and
he turns the page and continues to read, this time about
the manner in which the workers of Leningrad are united
in their endorsement of this new era of Soviet prosperity
and Soviet freedom, and of their new constitution which,
in these happy times, will provide new civil rights for all
the many peoples of the glorious Soviet Union. On he
reads, anticipating the imminent change in tone, for,
despite the optimistic framework in which these reports
are always set, they also serve a more serious purpose, to
warn the authorities of any dissent, and so those negative,
those backward, those unhealthy comments, like the one
Boris must inadvertently have let slip, will also be written
down. And so Boris Aleksandrovich reads, in expectation
of his name, and at the same time wondering how the
report writers will manage the transition from the factory
into the Smolny corridors of power. But then, that's
stupid; those who write such reports move without
restraint: what matters to them is not an unbroken narrative, but a proper accounting which requires no normalised
narration, and here it comes, he sees it signalled in the usual
way:

'However, alongside this healthy reaction on the part of
the majority of peace-loving people,' he reads, 'there are
certain cases of anti-Soviet, counter-revolutionary statements . . .'

He wants to stop and set the report aside. To pretend, if
only for a short time, that the die has not already been cast.

As if by stopping before he finds his name, he can actually hold back what he knows is about to unfold, not only
the loss of his position, his freedom, perhaps even his life,
but that much greater loss, his family. He wonders what

will happen to Lina and to Natasha and her family, and to Ilya, and even his eldest, Misha, not safe enough these days in Moscow, and he thinks how foolish he has been to assume that his position has protected them, for when people like him fall, great are the consequences. He has done the opposite of protecting them. He has exposed them to deportation and exile, or even, if they really decide to go after him, to eight years' imprisonment as the members of a family of a traitor to the fatherland:

'Worker Kozlov, Nikolai Vladimirovich,' he reads, and, in his absolute his astonishment, he says:

'Kolya,' out loud.

Stepan Vasilyevich looks up and for a moment the two men's eyes lock. And then Boris Aleksandrovich continues reading:

'Worker Kozlov, Nikolai Vladimirovich,' he reads, 'engineer second grade, aged twenty years, suspected counter revolutionary infiltrator of the Komsomol, son of an evangelist . . .' and draws up short, unable to believe it, reading it a third time, these words written for the NKVD and for five important people, but not for Boris Aleksandrovich who nevertheless reads:

'Worker Kozlov, Nikolai Vladimirovich, engineer second grade, aged twenty years, suspected counter-revolutionary infiltrator of the Komsomol, son of an evangelist, was heard to pass negative comments on the subject of the constitution, alleging that it is a charade instigated by our leader, Stalin, to mask the increasing lack of democratisation in the country . . .' and Boris Aleksandrovich thinks this can't be. Kolya, sweet, ignorant, innocent Kolya, puppy dog Kolya, would never dream of saying any of this, Boris Aleksandrovich thinks as he reads those words that Kolya must have said, to their conclusion and to the final judgement:

'Further investigation is being carried out on this sus-pected anti-Soviet element. SI?'

Kolya an SI? It's absurd. Kolya having contacts abroad! It's enough to make him laugh.

He doesn't laugh. He looks up. Stepan Vasilyevich has put his work aside, and is sitting, eyes bulging in their regard of Boris Aleksandrovich, and Boris wants to say: 'What are you looking at, you bastard?' but holds his tongue.

He closes the report, his thoughts come so fast that, in the moment it takes him to effect this simple action, there is time enough for him to tell himself why Stepan Vasilyevich showed him the report. It's a test. And a provocation. Kolya is not in danger. Stepan Vasilyevich is merely telling Boris Aleksandrovich that Boris's days are numbered. More devi-ously than that, Stepan Vasilyevich is daring Boris Aleksandrovich to try to protect Kolya, an attempt that, if he falls for it, will bring down the furies on Boris's head.

Boris Aleksandrovich slides the report over the desk. 'What is this to me?'

Stepan Vasilyevich blinks. 'Sometimes it is better to be forewarned.'

Forewarned, yes, Boris Aleksandrovich certainly is fore-warned. He lays a hand, carefully, on his chair.

'As our great leader, Comrade Stalin, said,' Stepan Vasilyevich begins.

But the loud scraping of Boris Aleksandrovich's chair stops Stepan Vasilyevich from carrying on with whatever it was that Comrade Stalin had said. He sits, flabby-mouthed, a fat gawking fish breathing heavily in and out in his relief that he is on his side of the desk and Boris on the other, as Boris Aleksandrovich says:

'If there's nothing else, comrade?'

'No.' The mouth shuts. The trap sprung. 'I will forward these statistics to the relevant committee, comrade.'

Boris Aleksandrovich smiles. He's still a comrade then –
if only for the moment. 'As you will,' he says and walking
out he closes the door.

*

And now, three years later, Boris comes to consciousness to
find himself standing outside Stepan Vasilyevich's former
office.

It's a waste of time. They have taken Kolya. He must act.
With determination, he leaves behind Stepan Vasilyevich's
former office and goes downstairs, to his own little cubicle.

The voice on the other end of the line says: 'Pyotr
Maksimovich is gravely ill. He's unlikely to be back.'

'I see,' Boris Aleksandrovich says. 'Thank you, comrade,
for your kind attention.'

He puts down the phone and clasps his hands together,
making of them a dome on which to rest his chin. He must
stay calm. He must sit here and think it out. But before he
can stop himself he's up because he can't stay down, and in
motion because not to move seems far too difficult, and so
he goes to the window and stands there looking out, his
mind caught up in admiration of the flexibility of the
Russian people who have adapted so easily to this new language, codified to fit their times, where 'ill' serves as
stand-in for 'arrested' and as for that rote phrase – 'unlikely
to be back' – well, that requires no explanation, does it?

And then he has another thought – how did it come to
this? – and, catching the thought, almost laughs out loud.
That he, who has so much to do (and should, by now, be
home), is also indulging in this flatulence of their times, this
nonsensical naiveté that stinks up the air! What kind of
question is: how did it come to this? As if he doesn't know
that there can be no one answer, only a string of truisms like,
'each decision leads inexorably to the next'; or, 'each action
to its own reaction'; or, yes, here comes a favourite, 'if there

are distortions, well, that is only to be expected, for this vast project of ours is bound to have its setbacks'; and finally, this handy short cut, 'the system must find its balance, it needs more time'.

Not that Boris would argue with any of the above: it's more that he can see little point in their reiteration. For a stranger it might be useful. For someone like the American, Jack, whose interpretation of history seems to derive almost exclusively from whatever it was that the person he last spoke to has just told him, it might make sense. But Boris is no greenhorn who, at the first faint sign of difficulty, feels he must draw back. He already knows it came to this because of those forces ranged against them. If people like him hadn't acted, their whole country would have collapsed.

Even so, it seems, it has still come to this. To him, Boris Aleksandrovich Ivanov, uselessly standing here, arguing with himself. You're not on the podium now, Borya, he says, actually speaking the sentence out loud, and even as his voice sounds out in the room, he knows that this is all diversion, and that the question he should have asked is not how *it* came to this, but how *he* did.

He should have seen it coming.

There. It's out. He is to blame. He, and his silence, are responsible for Kolya's arrest, this admission bringing with it a sense of rightfulness.

Once again he finds himself thinking back.

He remembers leaving Stepan Vasilyevich's office, and going to his own, and shutting the door. And there he stayed, for hours on end. He'd considered all the possibilities, weighing each one up, until finally he came to the same conclusion to which instinct had initially led him, namely that it was he, Boris, and not Kolya, who was threatened.

With hindsight, now that Kolya has been arrested, this

seems absurd, but how else was Boris then supposed to have made sense of Stepan Vasilyevich's apparent insubordination in showing him the file? This was the same Stepan Vasilyevich Filatov, remember, who was one of the most committed yes-men Boris had ever come across (and he's come across a multitude of those; you do in politics). And it was also the same Stepan Vasilyevich who, Boris knew, would never have risked his own security for someone else. And say even, for the sake of argument, that Stepan Vasilyevich had decided to step out of line, it stands to reason, doesn't it, that he'd not have done this to save a nonentity like Kolya? Of course he wouldn't. It's laughable anyway (or at least it seemed laughable back then) to think the authorities would waste their time on Kolya: Kolya's an innocent, a cog in a machine, a well-meaning boy, and harmless, not the kind to merit their attention, all of which led Boris to one conclusion: that Stepan Vasilyevich was following orders.

They were testing Boris Aleksandrovich's loyalty. That's what he decided then. The more he thought about it, the clearer it became. The report was bait. They were watching him. They wanted to see whether his loyalty to his family was more important than his loyalty to his state. And that's, finally, how Boris Aleksandrovich accounted for Stepan Vasilyevich's showing him the text.

He's thought about it since. Has lain awake wondering if there is something he should do, in case he's mistaken. He's discussed it with Tanya, but his Tanyushka is not a political person – she didn't know what to say. He even considered asking Polina's opinion, although this he soon dismissed because Lina no longer tells him what she really thinks but only what she thinks will punish him. In his solitude, however, he did come up with one possible solution – to send the two away: even if Kolya had made enemies, he reasoned, he could hardly be considered a big enough threat to warrant them tracking him to another city. But this option Boris eventually discarded. He couldn't imagine Natasha happy without the job she loved, in a distant city with only Kolya for company and, besides, if Boris was the target rather than Kolya, his sending them away would be all the excuse his enemies required. And he was the target, of this he was convinced, his conviction growing as the months rolled by and nothing happened, right until the day when he heard the news that Stepan Vasilyevich had been arrested.

That shook him. It made him wonder whether he'd got it wrong, whether Stepan Vasilyevich had shown him that report not in order to betray him but to help. He weighed up all the odds, more than once, but in the end he decided the fact that Stepan Vasilyevich himself had fallen didn't mean Boris Aleksandrovich had been wrong. On the contrary. Everybody knew Stepan Vasilyevich, a Kirovite, must always have been under threat. What better way to prove his loyalty than by testing Boris Aleksandrovich? That might actually have been a factor in Stepan Vasilyevich's downfall, his desperate stepping out of line, his showing a top secret report to Boris Aleskandrovich and, come to think of it, to others, one of whom most probably took the obvious next step of reporting on him. Yes. That had to be the explanation. There was no connection between Stepan Vasilyevich's arrest and Kolya's fate. Over the uneventful months that passed, Boris grew sure of it. Kolya was safe. He always had been.

And now. What has happened has cut through all this twisted logic. They have taken Kolya. That is clear. That pathetic, and now jailed (if the rumours are to be believed, also disappeared), Stepan Vasilyevich must indeed have done the unexpected, must have stepped out of line to warn

Boris Aleksandrovich that his son-in-law was threatened. That is also clear.

What isn't clear is what, if anything, Boris would have been able to do about it.

The Cell (1)

How long has Kolya been waiting for this moment? He doesn't know. A day? Two? More? It's hard to tell, encased as he is in this same cell with its shutters, unmoveable on the pain of punishment, blocking out the light of day. He does know it has been long enough for him to grow used to the stench of the slop bucket that lies beside his bunk (the newcomer always gets that bunk, he's told: don't worry, stay long enough, you'll get a promotion); long enough to tussle with his memory, trying to figure out how he of all people has ended up in jail, and long enough also, having failed to come up with anything he could have done in contravention of the law, to rekindle hope.

This flickering of hope he keeps quietly to himself. Those six other men in the cell with him – well, they're not the worst companions. Sure they tease him but what's a little teasing? He's used to it, people are always joshing him, and he can see why his cellmates could think him a figure of fun. He's so much younger than they are, for a start, and not nearly as clever – they're intellectuals.

Natasha would be at home in their conversations. Not he. Everything about him is too different, even his complexion, ruddy in comparison to their skins that are greyed by age and lack of contact with the light. But given that, and given that a man can't ever be at his best in prison, they're not so bad. If their mockery often stings, well, he knows it's because they're scared. And just because they're in here, because they've done something, well, it's not for him to judge. They're still human, aren't they?

He has even begun to count one of them, Aleksei Yakovlevich, the most senior, as a friend. Aleksei Yakovlevich is a good man, who has taken Kolya under his protection, fussing over him almost as if he's a son, teaching him the ropes, telling him to put on his extra jerkin, to keep warm and dry or else he'll get sick, something Kolya can well believe, given Aleksei Yakovlevich's nasty, racking cough.

Kolya has told Aleksei Yakovlevich almost everything about his life, his love for Natasha and Katya, and his arrest. One thing only has he kept from Aleksei Yakovlevich and that is hope. He might not have been incarcerated for long (not when you compare him with the others), but it has been long enough to learn that hope is a precious commodity, needing private nurture.

And now the door opens, and this time when the warder calls out it is to say:

'Surname beginning with K.'

Kolya can feel this same hope rising. He has also been here long enough to understand what's required of him. He's immediately on his feet, making his way over to the door, there he goes, at long last, and offers up his name, in full:

'Kozlov, Nikolai Vladimirovich,' with an eagerness that takes his cell companions aback, but hasn't he been waiting for this moment? At last his time has come.

The grubby room into which he is taken is not as he

expected. Neither is this grubby man who points almost
languidly at a chair, who stinks of stale tobacco and of alcohol, and who looks at him with bloodshot eyes, not
unkindly Kolya thinks, in fact almost with indifference, as if
Kolya is not really worthy of his regard, and who says in a
voice monotonous enough to confirm this impression:

'Name?' and, having listened impatiently to Kolya's
reply, adds:

'History?'

Now this at last is something Kolya had expected, this
recitation of the details that make up his life. His date and
place of birth, the class origins of his parents, their political
involvement, affiliations and places of employment, his job,
wife (along with her class history), participation in voluntary *subotniks* and factory meetings, date of acceptance into
the Komsomol, in short that litany that will tell the interrogator exactly who Kolya is, not that he really needs to be
told, or that he is even listening, for he has Kolya's file in
which that same history must surely be inscribed. But
there's comfort in the ritual, and by the time Kolya finishes
hope has risen. This seems a reasonable enough man, he
thinks, he'll clear up this mess, a thought corroborated
when the interrogator leans back, making himself comfortable before asking, in a softened voice:

'Do you know where you are?'

It is an easy enough question to which Kolya answers,
yes, he knows, he's in prison, and is corrected, softly once
again (so softly that Kolya has to strain to hear him), that the
building is unimportant, what matters is that he is in the
heart of Soviet Intelligence. Kolya says, yes, he can see that
as well, which seems to please the interrogator, who leans
forward and asks:

'Have you formed any hypothesis of the reasons for your
arrest?'

A question after Kolya's heart for he has thought of nothing else, turning it over and over again, trying to figure out what he could have done to land up here, and so can now say, his conscience clear:

'No, comrade, I . . .'

He is interrupted with a single word, barked out: 'Citizen.'

That word again, telling him the rules have changed; that in this place, and even if unjustly accused, he has forfeited his right to be a comrade, and so he says:

'No, citizen, I . . .'

'Citizen examiner.'

To which he can only take a deep breath, and tries again, this time saying:

'No, citizen examiner.'

By this time he has half-forgotten the question, or, if not the question, then at least the way he was planning to answer it: not that it matters, for the citizen examiner isn't interested in what Kolya has to say, but is too busy belching, his breath foul-smelling, to ask then:

'What do you think of the constitution?'

'The constitution?'

'Correct. Our Soviet constitution. Heard of it, have you?'

'Yes, citizen examiner. Of course I've heard of it.'

'What's the problem?'

'There is no problem, citizen examiner.'

'Is it beneath you to tell the likes of me what you think of it?'

'No, citizen examiner, I . . .'

'Or perhaps you think I was talking about another constitution. The American constitution?'

'No, citizen.'

'Or the British constitution. Like the British, do you?'

'Of course not, comrade examiner.'

'I am not your comrade, you stinking piece of carrion, you heap of human excrement, can't you even understand that? I am not your comrade.'

'I'm sorry, citizen examiner.'

'I am not interested in whether you're sorry. I'm not even interested in you. All I want is for you to answer my question and tell me what you think of the constitution and I want you to tell me now, not in five minutes, not in a day, nor in a month, although make no mistake about it, you're not going anywhere, we can sit here for as long as it takes, you swine, you dregs, you pygmy, tell me.'

Those words resound, *swine, dregs, pygmy*, and more to come, *you snot-nose, you filthy lickspittle, you, you scoundrel*, countless others roaring through his head, the interrogator going at Kolya, dissatisfied with everything that Kolya tries to say, interrupting until he ties up Kolya's tongue in knots, and then demanding to know why Kolya is being so stubbornly silent, pleading sometimes and hectoring at others, telling Kolya to imagine the charge against him but Kolya can't, he truly can't, his strengths are practical, not within the realms of the imagination, he has always left that to Natasha, and in the moment that this occurs to him, there comes a lull and he says:

'Citizen examiner, what will happen to my wife?'

And hears the man's reply:

'If your wife's got any brains, she'll disown you.'

The Queue (1)

The wooden shutter clatters up.

'Name?'

This is the fourth day she's been asked this self-same question. The right day. It has to be. She cannot be turned away again. This must be the day for the Ks.

'Kozlov,' she says.

And yes, finally, it is the right day, for instead of slamming down the window the clerk says:

'First name, no short forms, patronymic, surname?'

'Nikolai Vladimirovich Kozlov.'

The clerk looks down at a list. Says without looking up: 'Who are you? Sister? Wife?'

'I'm his wife.'

'Papers?'

She pushes her permit forward and then is forced to jump back as he grabs it and, almost in the same movement, slams the shutter down so fast it nearly catches her hand.

Conscious of the line of women behind her, she stands. Standing and waiting, at first in patience and then less patiently, but it doesn't matter how she feels, for she has no power over him, no power over anybody any more, and he still does not return. So standing, she thinks this must be another trick, like yesterday's when she was told she'd come at the wrong point in the alphabet; or the day before when they insisted they'd not heard of Kolya; or the day before that when they were inexplicably closed. Now she thinks she hasn't got much time. If she doesn't go back to work, she'll be in trouble. She can't afford to stand here any more, she must leave and try another avenue and she turns and hears a voice:

'Stay where you are. He'll be back.'

She looks back down the line of women but can only see lips shut tight, unfriendly features, grey faces set in disappointment and in pain; snivelling children, whining babies. So many of them. So very tired. She wonders whether that's the way she looks as well and wonders also how long they've been queueing here.

'Your papers.'

The clerk is back, the shutter up. He shoves her permit across the divide.

She says: 'Ko—'

'The case of your husband, Kozlov, Nikolai Vladimirovich, is being looked into,' and the shutter goes down again.

The Cell (2)

The door closes behind him but he doesn't move. He stands there. Silent. Frozen in the moment. Hears:

'What happened to you, diddums?'

'Did the nasty man swear at you?'

What harm has he ever done them?

'Should we tell him to leave you alone?'

''Course we should. You've done nothing wrong.'

His eyes fill with tears.

'Ooh . . . now he's crying.'

He feels himself filling up with rage. How dare they? Just because he's good-natured, because he's sorry for them, for the way they look, their ill health, their prison pallor, their stench, their hopelessness, just because of all that, because he doesn't try to get the best of them, they think they can use the only weapon they ever had, their smart words, on him, all without redress. Well, let's see how they'll like being on the receiving end of his weapons. He bunches up his fists. Let them speak now. Let them try.

'Watch out. He's getting angry.'

What's he got to lose? He's going to give them hell. He takes one step.

And hears another voice. 'Come on, comrades,' Aleksei Yakovlevich's voice. 'Leave the boy alone.'

'Who do you think you are? His keeper?'

They are rotten, all of them, all except Aleksei Yakovlevich, and Kolya's had enough. He's going to get them, can already imagine the satisfying crunch as his worker's fists make contact with their aristocratic noses. Their blood will spurt, make no mistake, even though they are so pale, and he doesn't care what happens to him after that. At least he would have done something to leave his mark, something he is impelled to do. So he takes another step, and would have done it, he knows he would, save for the fact that he hears Aleksei Yakovlevich's voice:

'What's to be gained from this? It's what they want. Can't you see that?'

A pause and then:

'You're right, Aleksei Yakovlevich. We're sorry for the boy as well, but he can get on your nerves. He's such an innocent.'

The Queue (2)

How many times has Natasha been through this? She can't rightly remember. Too many.

Not enough.

'Name?'

'Kozlov, Nikolai Vladimirovich.'

Here it goes, this unchanging and unchangeable ritual, the question about her relationship with Kolya, the demand for her identity papers and then the shutter. No need to jump back this time: it's all routine. The wait is no longer of any concern. Why does it matter? She's got all the time in the world.

'The case of your husband, Kozlov, Nikolai Vladimir-ovich, is being looked into,' she hears. That's all. Today complete.

She turns and walks slowly, as she always does, down the long line of waiting women. They are always waiting, just as she is, and many of them she has come to recognise and yet of this she gives no sign. They have all learned the same lesson, that contact is dangerous and that keeping yourself open to strangers (or even, when it comes down to it, to friends) is to open yourself up to rejection. Theirs is a queue like no other. A queue into nothingness. A sisterhood of despair where the very thing they hold in common is the thing that must drive them apart.

She is out in the open. It's snowing. It always is these days. No matter. She doesn't feel the cold – hasn't since they took Kolya away. She walks looking neither to left nor right, but straight ahead. Walking without thinking where she's going. Doesn't need to. She's going nowhere. Katya's at home – no longer welcome in the crèche – so she's safe, but as for Natasha, she has no job, not any more.

They told her one day, not long ago, although maybe it was – time slides past her these days. Told her. Go. Get out. Said: what do you think you're doing here? Turned their backs. Not her enemies. Her friends. Her one-time friends. Which leaves her nothing.

Stop. That isn't right. She has plenty. The important things. She has Katya. And she has Kolya and she will have him again for, most important of all, she also has hope. Her father is going to help. He has promised that he will. Told her that he can. Gone to Moscow to see what he can do. She starts up again and walks because not to walk is to risk frostbite, or worse than that, notice. She walks for walking's sake, and all the time she tells herself it will be all right.

Papa will get Kolya out.

Moscow

'*Name?*'

'Boris Aleksandrovich Ivanov.'

'Papers?'

He lays his Party card on the table. His card, his passport not to another country but to something much more important, a whole way of life, lies there untouched and it exerts a fascination on him, a compulsion which will not let go its hold, he stands staring at this scrap of paper, battered from its years of use, such a precious thing and so easily lost. This was brought home during that time in the Ministries when each member was made to wait before finding out whether he was worthy of its return, and it didn't matter what you had, or hadn't, done, it was impossible not to feel apprehensive – for isn't there always something that could have been better done? It was one of the very few times that Boris Aleksandrovich found himself possessed by imaginings he would normally discount, and he found himself conjuring up an image of what life might become without his Party card, thinking then that what Polina had once said, in fury, was correct, the Party is more powerful than a family for it is not something you can leave, nor something you would ever want to . . .

'What brings you here?'

Careful. This isn't Leningrad, it's Moscow, the big city, the centre of power. He must be on his guard. 'It's a personal matter, comrade.'

'You think that the Commissar has nothing better to do than attend to your personal life?'

'I think that Comrade Yezhov, the People's Commissar for Internal Affairs, busy as he is, unwavering in his diligence, a Communist of the highest principles, who has rightfully earned the trust of our great leader, our father, Comrade Stalin, does still, out of the generosity of spirit for which he is renowned, make the time to meet with longstanding comrades in order to hear them out.'

'Wait here.' The policeman gets up – Boris Aleksandrovich watching – his hand moving, it seems to Boris, in slow motion, down towards the table – Boris knowing he's going to – picking up what Boris has only just laid down, those stubby fingers gripping the document, that stolid body turning away, and Boris watches as his Party card, his lifeline, disappears.

The sound of handclapping reaches Kolya as he walks down the corridor. It's a familiar sound, the warning of the approach of another prisoner (some guards clap, others click their fingers), and it produces from Kolya's warder a hissed:

'Against the wall,' to which Kolya responds by stopping and turning to face the wall, keeping his head down and his gaze averted as he's required to do, waiting for that other prisoner and his escort to pass. That's what prison has been, a gradual closing of vision, the things Kolya is permitted to see reduced to three inanimates – his shadowed cell, this

corridor and the interrogation room – and three corresponding categories of animates – his cell companions, warders
and interrogators – although these restrictions have facili-
tated the extension of his optical range so that standing this
way against the wall, his head bent, his eyes apparently
shut, he still manages, somehow, to take in the spectacle of
this passing prisoner, some poor soul Kolya's not come
across before and will most likely never come across again,
some unnamed wretch who's in much worse shape than
Kolya, his ashen skin slick with sweat, his trousers stained
by something darker than sweat, so unsteady on his feet
that his guard has hold of him and, bearing most of his
weight, propels him forward, the two merged into some
strange, four-legged creature that does a slow, sideways
crawl down the corridor until eventually it disappears. And
when this happens Kolya's warder says:

'Get going,' and Kolya turns, and continues along the
path from which, in this place at least, there is no diverging.

How long before he becomes that man? This is the
thought that runs through his mind. The prospect of physical violence doesn't frighten him. The opposite in fact. He
would far better withstand a physical attack than the inces-
sant verbal abuse thrown at him, questions boomeranging
around the room, none of which he can answer because
even he, as slow as he is, understands that when they shout
at him to tell the truth, what they want is that he tell their
truth, the truth that makes of him a double-dealer, a man
who, masquerading as a worker, mocks that great victory of
the working class (the constitution), and who, worse, con-
sorts with foreigners and spies, or who would do, given the
opportunity. In short, their truth is that he is a serpent in the
midst of the revolution, an anti-Party oppositionist dis-
guised as an aspirant Communist.

'Confess.'

That's the extent of their refrain.

'Confess. Tell the truth.'

And he would; in fact, if the truth were to be told, there's nothing he'd rather do. But they don't want him just to confess, to say, yes, I did all that of which I stand accused. No, they want more, they want him to embroider the narrative they've invented for him, to breathe life into it, in short, they want him to prove them right and he can't do that, not because he doesn't want to, but because he can't imagine how he might have gone about committing the crimes of which he stands accused. For the real truth, and this he knows he can never let slip, is that he is exactly what he seems to be, or at least used to be, a contented worker, happy with his job, his country and his life, who wouldn't spend much time thinking about the new constitution or any of those complex other issues that he leaves to Natasha, preferring to be guided by her opinions or, if the real truth is to be told, not to have to think of them at all.

'Who do you think can possibly benefit from your pigheadedness?' Kolya hears, and comes to with a start at the realisation that he's no longer on the move. He's here again. In an interrogation room. Doesn't matter which. They're all the same.

He has no memory of getting here which happens with increasing frequency, long stretches of time when nothing seems to change followed by a sudden jolt, the disappearance of one of his cellmates, for example, or the addition of another, or this magical translocation from the corridor to this place, standing in the middle of the room as he, for all he can tell, might have been standing for hours. A better-educated man might suggest that this strange dislocation echoes that earlier one, when a sleight of hand transformed a model worker into a treacherous destroyer. But he thinks it's probably more to do with diet, and fatigue, for never once since he's been here has he slept the whole night through, and as for food – well, better not to think of that.

'Your wife?'

He looks across, peering into the brightness. What about Natasha?

'Do you think your attitude is helping her?'

His legs are aching although he will not let that show, just as he will not allow himself to think of Natasha. Not here at least. She is his strength outside this room. His memories of her sustain him there. But here – well, he has taken a decision, that he will not think of her in here, will not let her face, her voice, her entirety, be contaminated by this place.

'You know the law, do you?'

He thinks: which law?

'The one you've broken, you scoundrel. Article 58 of the penal code. You know what you stand to lose? PhS – suspicion of espionage, eight years. KRD – counter-revolutionary activity, five years plus. KRA – counter-revolutionary agitation . . .'

Five years. He thinks. Eight years. For nothing. It no longer surprises him.

'What about your wife? Do you know the sentence she will receive just for her misfortune in marrying scum like you?'

No, that he doesn't know.

'. . . for being a family member of a traitor to the fatherland . . .'

How can he have betrayed the fatherland? What was it they really think he did?

'Five to eight years. That's what she will get.'

He stands and looks and doesn't move, neither his features nor his legs. It doesn't matter what they say. He will not fall for it. Will not think of Natasha. Not in this room.

'You think your wife will be allowed to keep your baby? Think that, do you?'

And he won't think of Katya either.

'Your Katerina, Katerinka, Katya, Katyushka, your little girl. What do you think is going to be done to her?'

He stands. Legs so tired but rooted on the floor. What other choice does he have?

The path that leads to the office of Commissar Yezhov, head of the NKVD, Prosecutor Vyshinsky's bloodhound, Stalin's courier, is almost as convoluted as the layers of intrigue that Yezhov himself must daily cut through. The journey is the stuff of legend, so much so that Boris Aleksandrovich already knows how it will go.

It starts like this: his papers returned. Dropped on to the table. He picks them up, carefully, so as not to stain them with his relief. Hears a voice: 'You know the way?' Nods and then he's through.

First off: the lift to the fifth floor. Steps out. Another barrier. Hands over his papers, waits for them to be returned. Thinks: I could go back, nobody would be the wiser. But does not turn back. Walks instead. Along the corridor to the staircase at the building's other extreme. Another demand: papers. The ritual re-enacted, his papers more carefully scrutinised this time, so much so that long after they are returned his palms retain their moisture. Down the steps, sweaty-fingered, heavy-hearted, trying to convince himself that this is right. That it must be done. All the way down to the first floor, an internal monologue of doubt interrupted by that relentless demand: 'Papers,' always his papers, not once, but twice in that one corridor alone and now it's too late, he can't go back, he must keep moving, along the corridor to that other lift, stopping for that other inspection, and then it's up, Boris Aleksandrovich and an NKVD officer in full dress uniform, whose woollen tunic is the colour of fresh laid snow, the gold braid on his shoulders glints in the mirror of his bloodshot eyes, and then the doors open at the third floor and Boris has arrived. At Yezhov's secretariat. Stepping out, papers at the ready and then . . .

And then what happens? This he can't foresee.

That place on that inaccessible third floor is the place to which imagination will not extend. Where vision ends and possibly also Boris's career. If not his life. He stands, Boris Aleksandrovich Ivanov, a good man, who has done his best, who has made his contribution, nobody can deny that, who is standing: thinking. What am I going to say when he asks why I have come? Will I vomit up the words before my time is up? And if I do, what words will be the right ones? How to summon up Kolya in a sentence, and, at the same time, exonerate him? Perhaps use that word – mistake – but what are individual mistakes to Yezhov? Maybe that other word then, distortions, for Yezhov's job it is to grapple with this word, his task to look into even the minds of members of the Politburo, so distorted they disdain their revolution. But how, he thinks, can this same Yezhov also care for Kolya? And all of this for what? To fulfil a promise to Natasha he should not have made, because he should have known it was a promise he could not keep? In the past, perhaps, if he'd got Kolya out of Leningrad, that might have made a difference, but the past is done with and it cannot be undone. Kolya will gain nothing from Boris's regrets, neither will Natasha if she ends up losing not only her husband but her father too.

'Comrade Ivanov?'

He looks up, startled. He was lost in thought. In his imaginings. And now – what's this? His papers, landing not on the table as he had imagined it, but passed into his hands as the policeman says: 'The Commissar cannot be disturbed this morning. But if you were to come back this afternoon . . .'

His mind made up.

'I apologise, comrade.'

His voice certain.

'I'm sorry for wasting your valuable time. You are right. The Commissar has too many important matters to attend to: he should not be distracted by the likes of me,' and, saying that, he turns and goes.

Another dislocation. Kolya back in his cell, on his bunk, stretched out as best he can on this stinking horse-hair mattress, his only private space in this mildewed cell, with its dampened air and sticky odour of unwashed men, this place that now defines his world. No matter. Necessity is the best teacher: he has found a way of existing here.

First of all he sleeps, or tries to, or, at the very least, closes his eyes. He does this for as long as he can manage; he needs his sleep.

Should sleep elude him he will move on to his next level of activity. He will make lists. He's not particular about what he lists, anything will do as long as it is in general compliance with his rules which are that the targets of the list-making must be material and not ethereal, tangible but not verbose. He has so far listed: the ages of the people in his work brigade; the tools in the factory storeroom; the locations, and number, of the flights of stairs he climbs in an average week; the names of each of his former teachers in alphabetical order; the number of hours he has worked in each year of his working life; and the years in ascending order that he has slept the most, and anything else when it occurs to him to list it. And then, and only then, not ever before, when this listing can no longer hold his attention, well, that's when he gives himself permission to think of her. Of Natasha.

He guards her carefully, not only from his interrogators and that place of his interrogation, but also from himself. Doesn't want to overuse her. Needs her too much to risk that. He needs the memory of her face, of the way she talks, of the things she does, to sustain him. He knows he can't afford to wring what's left of the good in him into lifelessness. And so, deliberately, he rations himself.

But now her time has come. He has done with listing: he can think of her. He closes his eyes.

There are two ways he's found of doing this. The first, the most rewarding, is for him to lie quietly and open himself up to her, inviting her in, waiting to see what form she'll take. At its best, this method has the power to transport him as a memory of Natasha he didn't even realise he had, gradually filters in: the sight, for example, of Natasha nursing Katya in the moment when their baby unexpectedly breaks off her suckling and looks up at her mother and, and this is the very first time Katya has done this, smiles, gazing up, slack-necked and toothless, to bestow on her mother her first, joyous smile, and now Natasha's calling excitedly to Kolya to come at once and see, Katya's discovered how to smile, but even though Kolya does come, he can't at first bring himself to look at Katya for it's the sight of Natasha that mesmerises, her face lit up with pleasure and love, her astonishment that she has accomplished this, not only produced a baby but produced one who can smile so brilliantly, that pride and wonder in her achievement lighting up her face as dazzlingly as all the lighting in the theatres could have. And standing, looking at her, he is bowled over, caught in his own delight, so that even a year after the event, when that memory comes to him, he can feel himself light up, no longer cold or damp, but warmed by the glow of that sight come back to him. And now he lies back, lies unmoving, keeping his breathing even, cutting out all extraneous sounds, and waiting for another memory to return.

He waits but nothing happens. His mind a blank. No matter: he has time. All the time in the world. He shifts in the bunk, settling himself in, and then waits some more. Once again he draws a blank. No. It's worse. His mind begins to fill. That voice. Invariably. *Confess.* He shakes his head. It comes again: *Confess.* That same voice he keeps separate from his Natasha now has insinuated itself as, talking of Natasha, it demands to know whether Kolya realises what he's done to Natasha, and insisting that his fate will be hers, his treachery her undoing, his action, and his refusal to own that action, the betrayal not only of his fatherland but of his wife, his Natasha, those accusations, reverberating round his head, spreading out, taking over the void into which his memories of Natasha used to slip.

Enough. He sits up. Opens his eyes. The voice annihilated. That's better. He lies back but stays alert. This time he'll keep his eyes open and he'll also choose the second option. Not try for originality, that's too much to ask, he's tried, but instead recall a memory he has already stored for just such an occasion. He thinks: I will remember my first sight of her.

His first sight of Natasha. He thinks back. He was what? Oh yes . . . he was five years old. He's . . . let's see, he's drawing. That's it. Drawing. Something (one of the many things) she is much better at than he. A podgy boy he is. Stolid, they call him, strong but socially hesitant. As for her . . . well, her he'll leave for later in the memory. He stretches out for a coloured pencil at the same time as she . . .

Stop. This isn't right. It's not memory, it's just a story he's telling to himself. He can't really see her: he's just pretending he can and that's against the rules. He thinks: well, never mind. Perhaps going so far back was expecting too much. He'll choose another incident. A more recent one. He thinks: which one shall I choose?

Natasha . . .? No. Not that one. How about . . .?

It's no good. For the first time since he's been in here, she will not come to him. He cannot summon her.

Natasha.

She's gone.

The cold air has the effect not only of making Boris Aleksandrovich gasp but also of bringing him to his senses. It was a madness what he'd planned. To think he'd almost carried through with it, had almost confronted Yezhov in his inner sanctuary. To ask him what? That he, the head of the NKVD, make an exception for Kolya? For a young man with whom Boris Aleksandrovich, if the truth is to be told, is not intimate, and who might perfectly well have done what he's been accused of, not out of malice, for there's no malice in the boy, but he's not the brightest either (is he?), and, if his performance at the supper table is anything to go by, he doesn't pay much attention to what's going on, so it's conceivable, no more than that, it's even probable, that he could have let slip some unguarded and unthought out anti-constitution sentiment. Not that Boris Aleksandrovich is actually in favour of jailing people for a moment's carelessness (and he can't believe Kolya, of all people, would have had anything to do with a foreigner or a spy), but he is, above all, a realist. There's a lot that happens of which he doesn't necessarily approve but can't do anything about and, besides, he knows that, just as the civil war, and the collectivisation, and the shock industrialisation are now memory, this phase too will one day pass. It needs working through, that's all, and in the meantime people like him, the middle ranks, must keep their nerve, and choose when they speak out. Besides, one thing is very clear: to keep on with the plan of facing down Yezhov, that would bring down disaster not only on his own head, but on all their heads.

And so he continues walking through the snow-laden Moscow streets, thankful that instinct drove him from that place. He's not entirely sanguine, however. He keeps remembering that look on Polina's face after he had told her that he was planning to go to Moscow and confront Yezhov. Her face had lit up, then, as it so rarely does these days, and then she'd looked at him, if not in love then at least in admiration. It felt wonderful. It truly did. That's a large part of what had propelled him on to the Moscow train . . . that and Natasha's misery.

And now? What's he going to tell her on his return? That he changed his mind? Came all this way and didn't go in?

No, he can't do that. Telling that truth to Lina and Natasha will only increase the sum of their unhappiness. He'll spare them that (and yes, he knows, himself as well) by telling them that, yes, he did go to Moscow, which is true, and, yes, to Yezhov's office as well, which is also true, but that Yezhov refused to see him, which, now he comes to think of it, is most probably what would have happened if he'd stayed.

But then he thinks: no, again. He can't say that. What's most important is Natasha and her survival and for Natasha to keep holding on she needs hope. He must give her that. He must tell her that he saw Yezhov, and that Yezhov promised to look into the matter. That sounds right: extends expectation without promising too much. It will all turn out all right in the end, anyway. They'll release Kolya, of course they will.

He can now relax. He stops and looks around It's a glorious winter's day, the sky a crystalline, ice-white blue, startlingly bright in contrast to the greyness that seems to have overtaken Leningrad. His feet, he realises, have led him unerringly to this most renowned of Moscow locations, Red Square. It stretches out, magnificently, smoothed down by white and lined by the rose-red brick of the Kremlin walls, and in the centre a long, snaking queue of people waiting to pay their respects at the tomb of Vladimir Ilyich. Boris plays with the idea of joining them; why not, he has time, his train doesn't leave until midnight, but before he does he lifts his eyes up beyond the queue and over the walls to the Kremlin, that scaled-down city that is the centre of Soviet government. This sight has the same effect on him as it always does: it brings home to him the immensity of their achievement that they, and yes, he counts himself amongst the people who made it possible, have so trans-formed their country not only in its government but in every other way as well. In its very nature.

'Borya.'

What's that? Someone calling him?

'Boris Aleksandrovich.'

It is him they're after. Must be. But this is not a voice he recognises.

He turns and looks around. Tries not to panic. Sees a man, it must be him for he's waving now, a man whose face he doesn't recognise either but, wait a minute, that's not correct, now that Boris thinks about it, he realises that this man might not be a stranger, Boris might even know him, although he can't quite work out from where, this man who is now striding over, rosy-cheeked, his breath fogging up the air as he vigorously proclaims: 'Boris Aleksandrovich,' as if Boris were his best friend: 'What a surprise. And what brings you to Moscow?'

Boris Aleksandrovich shrugs. Casual. World-weary. Says: 'A meeting.'

'Isn't it always that? I even meet people in my sleep these days.'

The man, ah, now it's coming back to Boris Aleksandrovich, the man's some minor functionary in the railways, or at least he used to be. By the looks of his expansive chest and his fur coat and his high fur hat he's doing well now, he must have been promoted. And now he has caught up with Boris Aleksandrovich and is hugging him, kissing him, heartily, and perhaps a little drunkenly, on both cheeks and saying: 'Got time, have you? Why don't you come with me – have a drink.'

Boris Aleksandrovich thinks, why not, he could do with a drink, and besides, he's visited Lenin's tomb often enough, why make the queue longer and take the place of somebody who hasn't?

'Aleksei Yakovlevich.' Kolya keeps his voice low, hissing across the space that divides their bunks: 'Aleksei Yakovlevich.'

'Yes?'

'Are you awake?'

Aleksei Yakovlevich shrugs, or that, at least, is how it looks from the back.

'Can I ask you something?'

Aleksei Yakovlevich turns, painstakingly, to face Kolya. 'Of course you can.'

Now, Kolya thinks, ask him now, and breathes in deeply, wondering how he should phrase his question and then, on the out breath, comes out, quickly, with: 'I've been thinking about cities. To pass the time. Are all the foreign embassies in Moscow?'

'Yes. That's right. 'Aleksei Yakovlevich frowns. 'In Moscow.'

That's what Kolya thought. 'Not in Leningrad?' he says, checking anyway.

'No. Although some countries did have consulates here.'

'So they have consulates?'

'Had,' Aleksei Yakovlevich says: 'You do know Leningrad has been closed to foreigners, don't you?'

No. He didn't know that. Or maybe he did – but didn't register it. 'Was it closed a year ago?'

'No. Not a year ago. Quite recently.'

'So a year ago, say, if you wanted to meet an American, would you go to the American consulate?'

'If the Americans had one here. I don't know if they did.'

'Where else would you go then? If you wanted to meet an American?'

Aleksei Yakovlevich frowns. 'Umm . . . I don't know. To one of the big hotels, I suppose. The Astoria perhaps? Or the . . .' Aleksei Yakovlevich, who has so far been dealing with each question in his usual professorial manner, weighing each answer before delivering it, now cuts off what he was about to say to look across at Kolya, his expression darkening, his whole face tightening, even the watery blue of his eyes seeming to deepen, along with his voice, which sounds out harshly: 'Why do you want to know?'

'I told you. I was just thinking.'

'No one just thinks about foreigners. Especially not in here. Why are you asking me this, Kolya?'

What can Kolya say? He looks away.

'You're doing this for them, aren't you?'

For them? Yes, he supposes that he is.

'Using me as your bargaining chip.'

Using Aleksei Yakovlevich?

'Worth that much, am I?'

What?

'Exactly how many years did they promise to take off your sentence for giving evidence against me?'

How could Aleksei Yakovlevich think that? 'No,' Kolya

stammers. 'No. Aleksei Yakovlevich, I would never . . .'

'Planning to tell them how I boasted about my meetings with foreigners, are you?'

'No.' How could Aleksei Yakovlevich think like that? 'No. Of course not.'

'Why ask such questions then?'

How can he explain?

'Come on, Kolya. Tell me. Why did you ask me about foreigners if not to . . .' and then, all at once, the fight seems to go out of Aleksei Yakovlevich, the flush draining from the skin, the energy from his voice, as he says:

'Oh. I see. You're doing this yourself, aren't you?'

Kolya nods.

'You're planning to tell them what they want to hear? Is that it?'

Kolya's eyes go down.

'And you think I can help you fill in the details of your confession?'

Yes. That's exactly what he's been thinking.

'Look up, Kolya. Look up, damn you.'

He looks up.

'Is that what you really think? That you're the only inno-cent here?'

No. Of course not. That's not what he thinks.

'That the rest of us in here, well, we must have done something. Stands to reason. They'd never do that, the authorities, would they, arrest an innocent? Oh yes, of course, in your case, but that's different, mistakes can happen. As for us: we must have done something to attract their attention. Is that what you think?'

No. Of course not. It's not what he's been thinking.

'You thought that, didn't you? You thought: ask Aleksei, he'll know how a real traitor operates? Is that it, Kolya?'

Is it?

'Oh, Kolya.' That's all Aleksei Yakovlevich says, before he sighs, and makes as if to turn away and, watching, Kolya wants to shout: don't, don't turn away, for he knows if Aleksei Yakovlevich does, this heralds the end, the death, of their friendship, and how would Kolya, who has already lost Natasha, once in reality and the second time in memory, survive that? And yet how can he stop Aleksei Yakovlevich from withdrawing, when this is all his fault?

He had told them, yes, I admit it, I am guilty, I spread anti-Soviet propaganda, I spoke out against our glorious constitution, thinking that if he did this they would leave him, or at least his family, alone, and once that occurred to him it built up until confessing became not just a thing that he could do but the thing he must do, and anyway each day that passes it becomes increasingly more likely that he actually could have committed those crimes of which he is accused, that he must have committed them, for they have witnesses to prove it, fellow workers who will come to court and testify to this, and why would they do this if it wasn't true?

And then, finally, when he decided to confess and when he did, what happened? They heard him out in silence, and then, when he'd finished, they mocked him. Called him insincere, a coward who was speaking to make them stop, and when he denied this, they told him that if he really meant what he'd said, if he really was contrite, then he had to prove this by relating the details, like where he'd met the foreigners, what he'd said to them, how much he was paid, and then it had started up again, their voices:

'Tell us, you swine, you reprobate, you traitor. Tell us . . .', but how can he tell them, if he has no idea? He is an uneducated man. An unsophisticated man. All he knows is he must find a way to make them stop. That he must save

Natasha and their daughter. Must give his interrogators all they're after, because that will be his only way out.

And now?

And now he has managed to alienate his only friend.

He says, 'Aleksei Yakovlevich.'

And looking across sees that Aleksei Yakovlevich has not turned away but is merely lying there.

'I'm sorry.'

In fact Aleksei Yakovlevich is smiling as he says, quietly: 'It's all right.'

'I'm sorry, Aleksei Yakovlevich. You're right. I didn't think. I don't . . .'

'It's all right, Kolya.'

Aleksei Yakovlevich's tone is so soft. Without resonance. So exhausted. It makes Kolya look more closely and when he does he sees, as if for the first time, how thin Aleksei Yakovlevich has become and how that quivering of his hands that was barely visible when Kolya first arrived has turned into an emphatic tremor. A man diminished, that's what Kolya sees, this old man whose fortitude and gentleness had made him seem so strong. Now, however, his decline is plain, his broad shoulders, testimony to his former athletic prowess, all caved in, his graceful movements, the evidence of the truth of his stories of waltzing with a succession of beauties far into the night, reduced to this shifting to and fro, Aleksei Yakovlevich constantly repositioning himself as if he can't get comfortable and on top of that his lips are blue. He must be very cold. Of course he must, he's badly dressed while there sits Kolya half his age, no more than half his age, doubly insulated, and all this time it hasn't even occurred to him to . . . The thought produces action. Kolya gets up, takes off the jerkin, the spare one, the one he doesn't really need and . . .

But Aleksei Yakovlevich, understanding what Kolya is

about to do as he understands everything about Kolya, shakes his head. Says: 'No.'

'Please.'

Aleksei Yakovlevich's lips tweak up. A smile? 'I'm happy in my own stink: what would I want with yours?'

Kolya stretches out the jerkin.

Aleksei Yakovlevich shifts, trying to get away from it, but slowly as if even this one, small realignment hurts.

Kolya lays the jerkin down.

And receives from Aleksei Yakovlevich the loudest flow of words that he has yet directed at Kolya, perhaps the loudest Aleksei Yakovlevich will ever direct, a speech that starts softly enough:

'No, Kolya, I'm absolutely serious. Take it back,' but soon increases the volume, the man who tolerated, with near equanimity, Kolya asking him about foreigners in this place where mere mention of foreigners can bring death, now enraged at the prospect of a gift:

'You should know better than to try and force that obligation on me. If you continue, I'm giving you due warning, you'll forfeit my friendship, for what's the use of having a friend who cannot learn?'

That gentle voice reaching fever pitch:

'Haven't you understood what I've been telling you? Haven't you even been listening? Because if you had you would know that this is not the time for stupidity or self-sacrifice, that there never is a place for those, not unless they have a goal, and there is no goal to be served by empty gestures, especially not here.'

Aleksei Yakovlevich's voice is loud enough now to attract the attention of everyone in the cell. He's in full flood, using words that Kolya can barely understand, not only because they are the words of an older man, of a man with learning and experience, Aleksei Yakovlevich talking himself out so that, finally, the torrent of his words begins to slow and he is calm again and saying, softly:

'I will talk to you, Kolya, I will put up with your naïveté, your foolish innocence, I will listen to your confusions, I will even do my best, such as it is, to help you. But I will never take your jerkin.'

Natasha makes her way slowly along the road. It's snowing, a soft downfall swirling around her head but not yet settling, sinking instead on to the pavement where her feet, and the feet of all those around her, quickly melts them. She looks down, watching the pattern of her undershoe imprinted briefly, before it vanishes. She is walking slowly, a small island of seeming composure in the midst of a bustling crowd.

She has no need to keep up with them. No need to hurry.

She has nothing else to do. Just this. This ritual that has taken the place of what used to be a life. This walking down this road so as to reach its end and then to go inside. This going inside so she can join the queue. This queueing so she can reach the front. This arriving at the front so she can produce her papers. This producing her papers so she can be told that there is nothing to be told.

Sometimes she wonders why she keeps making the journey, doggedly, to this place. It's certainly not the prospect of hearing any news: she no longer waits in the expectation of that. And it can't be the camaraderie: there's no alliance possible between those families of the damned.

To pass the time then? No. Not that either. The waiting doesn't pass the time. It engorges it, each minute distending until it seems to occupy its very own lifetime punctuated by the noise of a baby whimpering, or a consumptive cough, or an involuntary howling of despair, abruptly cut off, and, always, by that slow tramp towards a shutter that always will bang down. And when it's over and she makes the journey in reverse, coming out into the everyday world that is the whole world to most people, she finds it unchanged, as if no time at all has passed.

She is unwelcome in this normal world. Uninvited. An unperson.

No one will take the risk of employing her. No work then. And no social life. She gets no invitations and has no friends. No visitors, or hardly any. Only one in fact: her father's former assistant, Dmitry Fedorovich, who still comes by. Odd. If she'd made a list, in ranked order, of which of her numerous friends and acquaintances would be most likely to stand by her, Dmitry Fedorovich (if she even remembered to include him, which is doubtful) would have come right at its very end. He's so strait-laced and conformist, the kind more likely to justify convention than to flout it, but while her innovative, convention-defying friends have run as far as their sharp-witted, artistic legs will carry them, he alone has remained a friend.

Perhaps he's really coming to visit my father instead of me, she thinks: although he doesn't often manage that, because Papa is rarely home. He spends more time at work than ever, returning late at night to eat quickly, to sleep, and then he's out again, often before anybody else has risen.

It's been worse, she realises, since Papa came back from Moscow. Since then, he's been working harder, drinking more. She wonders if something happened to him in Yezhov's office, some humiliation endured for her sake. Whatever it was, he came back haunted. Told her that Yezhov had promised to investigate, but the fact that he couldn't look her in the eyes while he was saying this confirmed her first impression: that he did not believe an important man like Yezhov would bother with a Kolya any more than she did. She knew it wouldn't work. She shouldn't have put him in that position.

She walks. Dully through the streets. Sees that the snow has begun to settle. Greyed as yet, still mixed with sidewalk grit, but as it thickens she knows it will turn white. A picture postcard world – that's what she'll see when she comes out.

She pushes open the door. Steps in. Sees the queue snaking its way towards that shutter. Thinks: perhaps this is why I keep making this pilgrimage. Because in this vast, unheated room, where the rules of normal exchange have been reversed, where normality itself has been discarded, in this room what I feel is – normal.

Again they come. Always again.

'Surname beginning with K.'

It will never end. Wearily, Kolya hauls himself on to his feet.

Again the wooden shutter and that same refrain:

'First name, no short forms, patronymic, surname?'

'Nikolai Vladimirovich Kozlov.'

'Who are you?'

'His wife.'

'Papers?'

The routine that never changes. Papers taken. And papers returned:

'The case of your husband, Kozlov, Nikolai Vladimirovich, is being looked into.'

And then that shutter banging down again.

Kolya

When the door opens, Kolya looks up, but only briefly. There's no point in looking for longer, they can't have come for him. They only do that at night, and even in this shuttered place he can tell the difference between night and day.

Not for him then. He doesn't look up. He is, for once, quite busy, making a list. He's listing the colours and the types of shoes he's ever worn. He knows that won't take him long so after that he'll add on socks, not the colour of course, because there's not much variation there, but the number and the length of time they lasted before first darning, and then he'll develop the theme by listing the number of undarned socks worn per pair of shoes.

Except. There's something in the quality of the silence that makes him look up. He looks towards the door. Sees it's still ajar. Doesn't take much notice. It's not for him. Can't be. Instead, he wonders vaguely why they've come. A search perhaps? That happens sometimes. Or a court appearance? Even that's been known.

Whatever it is, he doesn't care. He's tired. Let him get on with it, quickly, so he can go back to his list and perhaps that way lull himself to sleep. They might come for him, again, tonight: he needs his rest.

He hears a voice:

'Surname beginning with K.'

Is that what sits him up? Must have been – his is the only K. Except he knows it isn't only that. It's that unwavering, sharp, uneasy silence. It's watchfulness. Here, in this place of dulled routine, something new is taking place.

'Surname beginning with K.'

He puts his feet down on the wooden slats that line the stone floor. Carefully: mustn't put them too near the slop bucket. Looks towards the door. Presses his feet down. Sees not just the one warder, but two men, one, the warder who is concentrating on his boots as if he's found something nasty there, the other, his eyes quite level, unmistakeably NKVD.

'Get a move on. Surname beginning with K.'

He rises but doesn't walk, answers: 'Nikolai Vladimirovich Kozlov,' and repeats it: 'Nikolai Vladimirovich Kozlov.'

Let them hear his name. Let him say it.

'Come with us.'

His eyes move, slowly, round the cell. From one bunk to the next. Taking in each of his companions. He notices: how they seem to hold themselves suspended, to be alive without the need to breathe. They are almost perfectly motionless. He chooses a plainer word. They are . . . still. Still as stone, he thinks, as ice, as . . . but, no, he won't think that. Time is precious. He must use it well. He slows down the movement of his head, looks straight at each in turn, seeing how each in turn looks back. He thinks he knows what they are thinking. They think he doesn't understand. He is their muzhik, no, not their muzhik, their pet worker, well-meaning, simple-minded, uneducated, down-to-earth. They are fond of him but have no faith in his ability. They have no idea that he can read faces as well as – no, better than – the next man. And hearts: these he can also read, especially of those he loves.

He looks at Aleksei Yakovlevich and although Aleksei Yakovlevich merely looks back blankly, as if his mind is otherwise engaged, Kolya can see that his heart is breaking.

That's what gets Kolya moving. That sight. Not much time left but time enough to spare Aleksei Yakovlevich further pain. He walks over to the door, this surname beginning with K, this young man all but stripped of youth, this hope of a nation dashed, this Kolya. Walks to the door and stops.

That takes the guards aback. They look at each other, he sees the involuntary mutual movement of their heads and reads the question that flashes between them: what's this? That almost makes him smile. He can read their thoughts as well. Their thoughts: are we going to have to drag him out?

Now he does smile, if only to himself. He is strong, they can't know how strong, if he does make them drag him, they'll need to fetch more than two.

But he won't make them drag him out. Not in front of Aleksei Yakovlevich.

'I'm coming,' he says and then he turns away. There's still something he has to do.

His limbs are heavy. More lethargic than they have ever been. What an effort to do this, this that he knows he has to. That, more than anything, he wants to do. Slowly he grips hold of the edge of his jerkin and then raises up his arms, above his head, lifting it off. There. It's done. He puts it down, carefully, on the nearest bunk. Says – yes, he still can speak – says:

'I'm hot. They'll steal it from me if I take it off. Look after it, will you, Aleksei Yakovlevich?' saying this in as even a tone as he can muster, seeing Aleksei beginning to shake his head, and he thinks Aleksei must not speak, for if he does Kolya will be unmanned and so he bursts out, 'Please, Aleksei Yakovlevich, this is all I will ever ask of you,' and that's it, he wants out of here, to be done, he can't keep this up, not any longer, not in front of Aleksei Yakovlevich, and so he turns and starts to walk, doesn't care whether they are with him or not, let them worry about that. Let them follow him.

Door closing. The finality of that sound. He hears footsteps. His? Theirs? Their breathing – or is it his? The perfect fusion of their steps. For a moment he is seized by the urge to go back and ask Aleksei Yakovlevich: is this the sensation of a waltz? This slowed-down precision, limbs moving to another's beat, body harmonised so as to re-enact this age-old ritual. And then the impulse dies away.

So many things he wants to do. That he will never do. The moment magnified, each second an age, a lifetime, but all too short, so in one breath he is intensely calm and in the next gripped by terror. Images. Not of those he loves – where have they gone, he cannot find them – but picture-book images, the diagram Natasha's mother kept close, that bloodied network of veins and arteries in the outline of a man, those pathways that he feels inside him, nerves fluttering, tendril-thin, wisps of energy firing as he walks, thinking, let it be quick, and almost immediately its opposite, let it be slow, willing himself to stay on his feet, he will not falter no matter what comes next, his legs about to give under him, but walk he must, walking towards a future in which there will be no future, something pushed against his head, cold, against his ear.

Then at last he sees her. Natasha. She's back. His Natasha. He can even hear that lilting voice of hers, her singing as she seems to have sung her way through the best part of his life, the only part of which he is truly proud, Natasha's voice full of love, of thwarted love, and he sees her smiling, not a construct but the real Natasha, the way he will always remember her, smiling as he hears a click, the chamber open and . . .

'Brave, that one. Embraced his fate with dignity.'
'Don't be stupid. He didn't have a clue . . .'

Article of the Law

Natasha can almost read herself in the posture of the woman in front of her in the queue. She watches as the woman stands, not hunched exactly, but closed in, as if that way she can protect herself from her own expectation. She is waiting. For the shutter to open. For those words to issue forth. Those words:

'*The case of your husband . . .*' and then whatever her husband's name is:

'*Vasily or Ivan or Solomon or Pavlov or David or Grigory*' or any one of that other litany of names that parents found to give their infant sons, gazing down in love at their darling, helpless mite, saying what shall we call him, Vasily or Ivan or Solomon, this son of ours whom we will nurture and protect and help grow, saying this and then one day (hopefully when the parents are already gone) his name will be called again and with that name, that sentence:

'*The case of your husband is being looked into.*'

And then the shutter closed.

Except this time, as Natasha waits in line, the clerk delivers a different sentence to the woman in front.

'Your husband has been found guilty of contravening

Article 58 of the penal code,' the clerk says. 'Ten years. You will be informed, in due course, of where you may to write to him', and only then it comes, the shutter going down.

The woman totters. Looks as if she might be about to fall. Natasha makes no move to help: experience has taught her that any such offer is more likely to be greeted with a curse than a thank you so she stands, waiting, as a woman turns and, wearily, begins to walk away.

'Ten years,' the woman mutters, passing Natasha by. She is pale, grey-white like the first sprinkle of that settled snow outside. Bone-thin. Greyed by malnutrition. She walks, unsteadily, listing to one side, almost swooning and yet she doesn't, for what would be the point of swooning here? She walks away. A lucky woman, Natasha thinks (a thought that will later come back to haunt her), for at least she knows.

'Next.'

The shutter rolling up. If Natasha doesn't hurry she'll miss her turn. She forgets the woman (only remembers her later). Crosses the emptiness. Goes up, close up, to that shutter. To another world. Sees that clerk. Same one. Doesn't greet him. Doesn't get greeted either save by that peremptory:

'Name?'

'Nikolai Vladimirovich Kozlov.'

'Who?'

'His wife.'

'Papers?'

The routine that never changes. Papers taken. And papers returned and then that sentence, now with Kolya's name:

'*The case of your husband, Kozlov, Nikolai Vladimirovich, is being looked into.*'

Except this time, it isn't so. The clerk hasn't gone. Her

papers held out but not taken. The clerk busy. Reading. Down the list go his eyes. As they usually do. Down, and then, unusually, impossibly, up again.

Natasha, watching, sees those cold eyes moving, sees them start at the top and scroll through the list again and then . . . Ritual over. The clerk looks up, but this time not so as to deliver that other part of his ritual:

'Who are you? Sister? Wife?' the answer to which she has already given.

Not to take her permit.

Not to pull the shutter down.

None of that.

Just to transmit one sentence. Six words.

'No one of that name here.'

Part Five

Personal Fates

Remember that the great cause of the USSR lives on, and *this* is the most important thing. Personal fates are transitory and wretched by comparison.

(Bukharin to his wife, on the eve of his trial and execution, from Anna Larina, *This I Cannot Forget*)

Celebration (4)

Nineteen thirty-eight, and the first thing Natasha does on waking is open her eyes. A natural enough reflex, save for the fact that Natasha habitually keeps them shut when surfacing. It's something she taught herself to do in those terrible first days, a year ago, and something that has become second nature until, that is, this morning when, needing the protection of this new-found control more than ever, she finds her routine unexpectedly reversed.

It's dark. These days it always does seem dark. She looks across the bed. Her grandmother is sleeping as is Katya beside her. Holding herself quiet, Natasha hears the soft in and out of Katya's sweetness, and, droning above this, her grandmother's exhausted snore, and while she listens to their counterpoint she also takes in the sight of Katya's milky whiteness nuzzled into the parched wrinkling of the other, those two, even at this near end of night, clinging to each other as they so often do, life's beginnings and its endings joined in an embrace of mutual need and love.

Not for much longer. Today will be witness to Natasha's new beginning. The severing of her past.

The thought is enough to get her moving.

The crust of ice that has misted the window tells her that the room is very cold. She doesn't feel it – she hardly ever does these days – although she puts on a dressing gown because that's what's expected of her and she's found that doing what's expected saves time and trouble.

By the door, on top of the dresser, there's a looking glass. Her grandmother, who in the past would often be heard bemoaning the vanity of young women who spend too much time fussing over their appearance, insisted on the mirror when Natasha moved back. She thought it might help, might revive Natasha's interest in the world; and, to please her grandmother, Natasha does occasionally look in it, although rarely when unobserved. This, at least, is not a new beginning. She was never vain, even before, when checking her reflection was something she only bothered with if she'd been drawing and wanted to make sure she'd got rid of the last vestiges of smeared charcoal from her face. But today she decides to make an exception even though her grandmother isn't awake to see it, for today is Natasha's wedding day, and isn't looking in the mirror something you're supposed to do on your wedding day?

She picks up the glass and goes with it to the window where she can use the white-reflected snow as lighting. She sees: a woman. Well, that's a start. She can no longer be called a girl. She's twenty-one. No, that's not right, she had her name-day two weeks ago: she's twenty-two. Her skin. Pale. Another continuity: she always was pale. What's different now is the way her skin is so uniformly pale – no pink flush of exertion to redden up her cheeks – but that's probably because she's just got up or because she hardly has the energy to exert herself. To continue: she sees: a brow. Smooth. That's a surprise: she frowns so much these days, she had assumed it would have marked her. Not yet apparently. Thin. She also sees that. Her face much thinner than it used to be. Drawn as well.

Her gaze moves downwards so that she is now concentrating on her face's lower half. Lips. Ripe pink. Pulled meaner than they used to be but if she parts them, as she does now, clinically to see what happens, they plump up as before. Chin. Small. Pert. Pointed. That's it: the full inventory. All of it just as she expected if, that is, she'd bothered to expect anything.

Except – she's wrong – that's not quite all. She hasn't examined the eyes. She raises her head, looks at herself straight. Sees: blank stranger's eyes. Drained. Not dead exactly – more like indifferent. Nothing of what was once there, that sparkle that she had supposed would still be there because, whenever she looks into Katya's glistening innocence, she imagines she's also seeing herself reflected back. But this real face of hers, this face of Katya's mother, that watches as she watches back, is completely other. A face framed, not as Katya's is, by joy, but by Natasha's especial and most tightly held emotion – by hatred.

She holds out the mirror, at arm's length as if that way she can somehow deny what she has seen. To no avail. She thinks: whom is it I hate? Her life and her world are both so circumscribed, there aren't many people from which to choose. Nobody from amongst her old associates, that's for sure, that multitude she can no longer count as friends. They have become too distant and insubstantial to be targets for her hatred, like phantoms, just as they must think of her (if, that is, they think of her at all) as a long-vanished ghost. Not them, then. So who?

How about Dmitry Fedorovich? No. She cannot think that. She carries the mirror back over to the dresser. Not Mitya. She props the mirror up. She cannot hate her saviour. Katya's saviour.

Her own father then? No. She shakes her head and watches its shaking in the mirror. Not Papa. Papa has done nothing wrong. Nothing that he could have done differently.

Who then? Herself? She stands suspended. Perhaps myself, she thinks: on the rare occasions when she thinks about herself, she certainly doesn't find much to like. But then – she shakes her head again – even in her case, everything she has done, that she is doing, she does for love, if not of the man, then for his child. Not herself then.

That name. Kolya.

'Kolya.'

She whispers it, now for this once, and then whispers it again.

'Kolya.'

She will let it out. She hears it in the now and in her memory also. Hears it louder. Herself calling him. Sees him turning. Her Kolya. Smiling. That boy-child, that innocent, frozen for all time as a young man, never to change, to age, to learn, as she has had to learn, what it feels like to be left. Kolya. She thinks: could it be Kolya that I hate?

Why not? She smiles: her thin lips tweaking up in the dim light. Why shouldn't Kolya take the blame? It's his role. In life. In death as well.

But stop. She must not think of him, especially not today. The belt of her dressing gown is awry: she straightens it, pulling hard on its two ends, tugging at them, hard and tight, as if that way she could wring herself of Kolya. She can't understand why he's coming to her. He doesn't normally. She speaks of him to nobody, not even to her daughter Katya – his daughter Katya – so why today?

Today her mind is full of him. Think, she sends this instruction to herself: think. Not of Kolya. Of something else. Anything else.

Katya.

Katya still a baby. Katya sitting on the floor, playing with some pieces of wood and burbling, trying out new syllables as babies do, hitting on a repetition:

pa pa . . . pa pa

which that younger Natasha, still in the grip of the shock of Kolya's death but more level-headed than she used to be, ignores, expecting the moment to pass as it usually does, but Katya seizes on the sound and starts lilting it out, a kind of rising drum beat . . .

pa pa. . . pa pa . . .

tasting its resonance with her tongue and her cherub mouth. . .

pa pa pa pa . . .

unremitting in its mad persistence, repeating the sound (because it annoys her mother?) laughing and shouting as one gloriously, unending string . . .

pa pa pa pa pa pa . . .

hits the air, louder because Natasha has demanded that she stop, the baby revelling in her power to make her mother mad . . .

pa pa pa pa pa pa pa pa pa pa pa pa pa . . .

on and on for so long that Natasha wants to shake her.

Strike that. The truth. It really happened.

The truth: Natasha picks Katya up and shakes her, shaking out that rattled papa papa, so that the outraged child lets loose a yell, and then, as if it has only just dawned on her, the full extent of the outrage her mother is committing, opens her mouth and begins to bawl, shaking now not at the motion but at the intensity of her mother's response, her mother whose tears are falling, merging with the child's, her wet cheeks struggling to rest against those chunky ones of Katya who has gone rigid, arching backwards, trying to wrench herself from her mother's grasp, screaming as her mother smothers her with kisses, and murmurs her own, useless repetition:

'I'm sorry, I'm sorry.'

That sound competes with the wailing of the child and that other sound, the hammering of a fist against the wall, from their neighbour who managed to keep his silent counsel as the police vans drew up, or the militia thundered up the stairs, or Natasha struggled to manoeuvre herself and Katya and her shopping and the books she has to sell through the narrow corridor. But this same neighbour will not keep silent now and wait for Natasha to calm her baby, and he aims to make it worse by yelling. She can hear his shouts resounding: the whole building must be able to hear them, hears him shouting that if Natasha doesn't keep it down, he's going to do something and something she, the traitor, counter-revolutionary, double-dealing she, he's going to make sure that something happens that she of all people cannot afford and even in her desperation and her anger she knows how he can harm her.

She puts a hand across her baby's mouth. Bites her own tongue. Waits. For the baby to stop her whimpering. To fall asleep in shock. For her tears to dry. For her neighbour to shut his bastard mouth. For life to go on.

And now she comes to, drawn out of memory with a start, thinking that life has gone on. She thinks: what will I say when Katya asks about Kolya?

What can she say? It suddenly seems important. She must work it out. Not in the future when it might happen but now before her day unfolds. She conjures up a scene to be enacted in that future. Having imagined it she watches it unfold. She sees herself at the stove, stirring porridge, no, not at the stove, she is on her hands and knees, scrubbing the floor, while her daughter, say eight, no, better, nine, years old, reading at the table, looks up suddenly and, apropos of nothing, says: 'What happened to my father?'

Natasha, this old-hand, remarried Natasha, will be prepared. She will have been anticipating this moment for many years. She knows what she will say. She tries it out now, says it out loud but softly so as not to wake the sleepers. She says:

'Don't think of him, he's gone, my Katyushka,' but then she thinks those words just don't ring true. It's stupid, what she's doing, thinking of this now, but she does it anyway. In her imagination she tries a different version. A more abrupt one. Like:

'Your father? He's right here. He is your father now.'

She shakes her head. That won't do either. Dmitry Fedorovich has been kindness itself, has proved himself her only friend when all the rest had vanished, and he'll learn to love Katya, this she knows, because everybody does, but even so she can't really see him in the role of father.

A third option then. She walks back over to the mirror and sees herself, once more, in its reflection. Straightens up. Brings out another voice. The one her own mother would have used. Her sternest voice. Her coldest.

'Don't be silly. Take your elbows off the table, Katya, and eat up,' and sees herself, a mother and her own mother merged, nodding to herself in the present, thinking, yes, that'll be the phrase I'd better use: 'don't be silly'.

Bagrat and Timur

If I shift myself to the right, I can watch Anton Antonovich. He is sitting at his desk. His thin, domed head is bent, his round wire glasses teeter on the end of his nose. He's writing as usual, so fast it's as if he's frightened that if he stopped, what he means to say will disappear. I can hear him as well – that's another change. Him talking to himself. He does that a lot these days. He writes and he mutters, red blotches on his pale face, as he sicks up his ideas, scrawling them out, page after page of them, strange symbols I can't make sense of, so that sometimes I think the pile of manuscript that keeps growing is nothing more than nonsense, created out of madness, but it doesn't matter what I think because there's nothing I can do to tempt him from his desk. He, always scrawny, has grown even thinner, so bound up in his work that he will hardly eat, will not come to the table, ever, unless his precious Anya is there, for he has eyes for nothing but his work and her.

He lays down his pen and starts to read what he has just written, and so fierce is his concentration that I know there's nothing I could do to draw him from it. But, suddenly, he stops and then he does look up and why? Because of Anya.

She's singing. Or at least, it's what these two would call singing. Listen to that eerie little voice:

'Stalin will come to our parade,' singing out in that flat way she has:
'And give us his good greeting,' bawling it out now because she knows we're listening, as if it's some fine tune that is suitable for her age:

'For all the children, all of us,
He's our own true father.'

Anya is so clear-sighted that when she looks at you it's as if she can see right through you, but she can't tell when she's off key. And she's not the only one: Anton Antonovich doesn't know it either. See how he takes off his glasses, his eyes lighting up, his smile widening even as she underlines that last word – father – showing (I know her well and I know this is what she's doing) that she has no other father. But Anton Antonovich comes alive at the thought of his Anya happy enough to break into song, for where Anya is concerned he is blind. He can't see that she's only doing this to annoy me, to show me that she can still lure him in.

As if I was ever in any doubt of that.

Which says everything about the way things stand between her and me, not that this is ever expressed. We have an understanding. We tolerate each other as best we can and try not to involve our patron (or at least in any way that he might notice).

I have things to do. I must prepare myself for the wedding. Say what you like about whether Natasha should or shouldn't do it, at least we're going to try to celebrate. Which doesn't happen much these days.

Sometimes I wonder: could it have been different? If Kirov hadn't died? If the degenerate, parasitic, White

Guard, double-dealing, left extremist, right opposition, Trotskyite–Zinovievite foreign spies hadn't done for Kirov, and Kolya had died of natural causes, would Natasha still make the same decision? Would Boris Aleksandrovich let her?

Enough. I made a resolution on the ice and I will stick by it. I will not live my life with ifs. I will go now. If Anton Antonovich can't be bothered, I will at least try to smarten myself up for this wedding (and mercifully, at the same time, take myself out of earshot of this awful caterwauling).

The work that Anton Antonovich had set himself, some few months back, is now complete. It lies there on his desk. At the Institute they're expecting it. The day has come for him to deliver on his promise.

He thinks: what have I done?

Too late to ask that, he tells himself sternly: far too late. He begins to read:

'*Now after Bagrat and his queen, Anna Commena, had been made prisoner by Timur, the* sarang *of Timur came to them and using not threats but sweet talk,*' impressed, despite himself, by that turn of phrase 'sweet talk'.

'*And using sweet talk, the sarang mediated with King Bagrat, passing on his master's message that if King Bagrat embraced the Muslim faith for which Timur was full of zeal then Timur, the merciful, would set his captive free and allow him to reign in peace over the entire domain of Kartli and Kakheti. And Bagrat, fearing for his people, did as Timur demanded and apostatised and Timur kept his promise, allowing King Bagrat and his Queen to depart from the fortress in peace and bearing many gifts. Great was the joy at the return of the wise King Bagrat, beloved of all his country, and as he travelled on he was accompanied by all his didebulis and the sound of trumpets and tambourines and much rejoicing.*

But when Bagrat who had ruled with such wisdom and lack of rancour came upon his son, Giorgy, who had, in his father's imprisonment, become master of the country, Giorgy turned away, saying, "Father, I pity you for what you have done no King must ever do, yielding to this Timur." And Giorgy pleaded that Bagrat should take back his word and unite with Giorgy to drive the infidel from the land. Long did Bagrat, with wise words and arguments, resist his son for Bagrat had seen the power of Timur, respecter of his honest enemies, ravager of those who defied him, and he had seen as well the strength and determination of all Timur's troops. But Giorgy would not listen to his father. He refuted everything his father said, over and over again, until Bagrat could no longer deny this son whom he loved even beyond his country . . . and so it was that Bagrat, joining forces with Giorgy, renounced his apostasy and, bearing the honourable cross, attacked the enemy and soon were . . .'

No, that's wrong, Anton Antonovich thinks, picking up his pen and changing that last to . . .

'and soon it was that lamentation was heard right across the land even unto the far borders of Abhkazeti which is the end of Bagrat's kingdom . . .'

And as he writes, that question – what am I doing? – comes again, before a voice intercepts it:

'Stalin will come to our parade,' and the lunacy in which he has enmeshed himself has blurred the boundary between work and imagination, between life and fiction, and he wonders what Stalin and a parade have to do with anything, but then he comes to and realises that all he's hearing is Anya singing.

'To give us his good greeting,' he hears.

Looking up, he thinks that once the banalities of that would have been enough to enrage him, wrecking his concentration and thus his morning's work, but not any more. Now he keeps his door open precisely so he can listen out, if not for the words themselves (even in his newfound state, he finds it hard to tolerate such clichés), then for the miracle of Anya's singing them.

Her singing fills him with wellbeing and with pride. It always does. That the child he took in and fed and clothed and housed and, yes, he can take credit for this as well, whom he has fathered these past four years, has been turned from that distrustful, wild thing into this carefree young girl who revels in the simple joy of singing, is a miracle, his miracle, and, what's more, it's a transformation that has impacted not just on her but on him as well so that he can divide his entire existence into two distinct parts – pre- and post-Anya.

This is what I've done, he tells himself: I have dared to change.

The old Anton Antonovich was a man prematurely aged and permanently disappointed, a man who valued accuracy above imagination, precision over insight, and who kept himself apart from his fellow men for the sole purpose of passing judgement. This new Anton Antonovich, post-Anya, is completely different.

Thinking back on that lonely, other man, the new is filled with incredulity. How could he, how could anybody, have chosen to exist in isolation, caught up not by life but in the dutiful cataloguing of lives long past? What Borya used to accuse him of and what he used so vehemently to deny, this reformed Anton now knows to be correct. The old Anton was, as Borya said, a snob, a voyeur, and, worse, he was a man who refused to commit himself not because he was pure, or because he knew better, but because he was afraid.

That's the truth to which the new Anton Antonovich, on the brink of this great risk, can admit: that in the time before he let Anya into his life, he was always afraid. Ever since he was a boy, in fact, when he grew not broad and strong as the other boys, but long and thin and myopic – a target – and he'd had to learn to use his mind, his sharp tongue, his friendship with Borya, and his own isolation to try to stay the hands of bullies. Even after he left the gymnasium and was no longer in physical danger from his peers, he continued to be frightened of so many things. Of belonging and of not belonging, of succeeding and of failing, of commitment and of a failure to commit. He was also afraid of bees until that day when, seeing them attacking Anya, he had thrown off his fear and rushed in.

That incident, he thinks, is symbolic of all his changes. It was the moment when he saw the person he had become: a man with the courage to set aside his fear in order to save someone he loved. A man who deserved a home rather than just a set of lodgings; a life rather than a series of dislocated encounters; a family that now includes, not only Anya, but also the indispensable Irina Davydovna; and an attachment to an institution which, instead of grudgingly tolerating him, will soon include him as a fully fledged and highly appreciated member.

What he has done is clear. He has made a choice. He has decided not only to survive, but to live and to live well. To find a way, in these uncertain times, of keeping his child, his housekeeper, his apartment. There was only one way he could find to do all that, and here it is, lying on his desk, waiting for him to hand it in. That's what he has to do: no going back.

No more questions. No more doubts. He is committed.

Despite what I meant to do, I have actually kept my place in the kitchen. I watch Anton Antonovich's head dipping. He's going back to reading.

Having finished her caterwauling, Anya is on the move. I watch her as she comes out of her room and walks down the corridor. Fierce little girl with that fierce little face of hers, screwed up in concentration. She doesn't so much walk this one, she marches. Thin arms swinging, thin legs striding out. Marching as they teach them to do these days.

Funny that this girl, who has so much of her past hidden, should be so bad at hiding her desire. Her eyes are fixed on me, unblinking. Those pooled brown eyes far too big for that long, pinched face. Doesn't matter how much she eats, she never puts on weight. She has grown of course, but gangly, like Anton Antonovich I suppose, not that she's like him in any other way. He's so timid; she so sure. Or at least, she pretends to be.

She's certainly single-minded. So much energy she spends on everything she does: her determination put on ice only briefly when at last she falls asleep. She looks so different when that happens, innocent, like the child I don't believe she ever really was. But even then, breathing as deeply as she does, her lips slack and plump and almost sweet instead of set in that usual grimace, even then, I soon discovered, she doesn't really drop her guard. I found this out on the one occasion when I made the mistake of standing over her as she slept. I thought that because she seemed so fast asleep, she would not easily awaken. It's not a mistake I'd ever make again. She might sleep deeply but she wakes like a cat, as soon as you come near. And what an awakening it is: her eyes snap open and she looks up as if she is about to pounce.

Now she stops in front of me. No words, of course, to ask for what she wants. But then I tell myself I'm not such a great believer either in the power of words or in form, and so all I say is:

'You forgot the brush.'

I should have known better. No sooner have I said that than she brings out the brush. Don't ask me how she hid something quite so awkward on her flimsy person. I certainly know better than to ask her.

She smiles slyly at this victory over me. I let her. Why not? It's so important to her to win. I take the brush.

Her response is to turn until she has her back to me. She stands.

I say, 'If you stand, I won't be able to get a proper grip.'

I always say that and I always get the same answer. Without so much as a look in my direction (might be taken as her asking permission) she backs up until she is tight against my knees and then climbs on. She's in my lap.

This is how I always brush her hair. Every time the same ritual. She stands with her back to me. I tell her I can't do it like that. She sits. If I didn't know better I'd think this is why she, who does everything for herself, still involves me in this part of her toilette: so she can get this close. But the fact is, I do know better and I know that it's more likely she knows that, of the two of us, I am by far the best at plaiting.

To tell the truth, this is a ritual I even half-enjoy. Thin she might be but her hair is not: it's as if all her growing strength has been sealed up in those long, shiny tresses of hers, so much sleeker than mine have ever been. And besides. When she sits on me like this and I brush her hair, she's so good, so still, no longer a spitting cat but a child with that delicate child's nape of neck, and that soft, rounded, yielding, half-bent child's head that makes me wonder whether we might have all got her true age wrong, whether she has been on this earth for fewer than the twelve years that we all think she has.

Can't be right. She's top of her class. Couldn't do that if she was much younger than the others, could she?

In silence, and always in silence, I brush gently down her hair, from the crown of her head to her mid-back where her hair finally tapers off. I get a rhythm going. It's almost comfortable, her weight in mine against the soothing glide-down of the brush. She also finds it comfortable: she sits completely still.

If a stranger were to walk in now, he'd mistake us for that everyday coupling – mother brushing her daughter's hair – and although this is far both from the truth and from what either of us would wish for, in all honesty I do admit that there might be some make-believe at play.

I like the brushing, also, because when I'm doing it I think.

I think about the way things are. They're different. It has to be said. Take those two old friends Boris Aleksandrovich and Anton Antonovich. On the surface, their friendship might look the same, but I know better. I have heard them in the past, arguing when they came together, and so I know that this politeness that has sprung up between them isn't natural. It's as if each of them thinks it too dangerous to hint at those things that might drive them even further apart, for each has troubles of his own.

First Boris Aleksandrovich. He suffers for what happened to Kolya. Terrible to have spent so much time getting power and then, when it really matters, not to be able to use it. As for Natasha's marrying Dmitry Fedorovich: well, without being too judgemental all I can say is that Dmitry Fedorovich, good as he's been to her, is a cold one and not a man I'd ever happily matchmake with any of mine. And she doesn't love him – that's clear – although, come to think of it, that's not necessarily a problem. She married for love once (as did I) and look at where it got her. And anyway, who says that love can't grow out of necessity? Even so, I can't imagine that Boris Aleksandrovich is best pleased.

As for Anton Antonovich. Well, he's a queer one, always has been and no more than at present. He keeps saying he's happy which is odd in itself – he never used to feel the need. And what, I ask you, is this kind of happiness? He's worse than ever, keeping himself to himself, burying himself in books.

A cough. I look up, startled, and see that Anton Antonovich has joined us, or that he almost has. He's standing by the kitchen door, coughing to get our attention.

Anya doesn't even bother looking up.

He coughs again.

I could leave them to it, wait until their stupidity plays itself out to its conclusion, but I am the go-between, my job to ease the distance between these two.

'Did you want something, Anton Antonovich?' I say.

He gives a half-smile. 'I have to drop something off at the Institute on my way to the Ivanovs'.'

I nod.

'I won't be there long.'

I carry on brushing.

'You could come with me,' he continues, 'and we could go on to the Ivanovs' together.'

I know full well to whom that 'you' refers. She, too.

I hold my tongue. She doesn't bother speaking either.

What a brat she is, I think, and for a moment I consider turning her over, right here, right now, and subjecting her backside to a proper battering with the flat end of the brush. Not that I, who knows what it's like to be beaten, would ever carry it through, but even so the thought pays off because she who, unlike Anton Antonovich, can always tell what I'm thinking, looks up and says, in a bored kind of voice:

'We will meet you there.'

The itch to hit her comes flooding back especially when I see the disappointment in Anton Antonovich's pale face.

'I could come with you,' I say, knowing that it's not me he wants and having this borne out in the shake of his head.

'That's all right, Irina Davydovna. You travel with Anya when she's ready.'

He smiles then, as if it's all one to him. As if he's strong. Pathetic really. My heart goes out to him. (But he's not interested in my heart, is he?) Turning, he walks back down the corridor, as hunched as ever.

She dips her head. She expects me to carry on, and that's what I do. I brush her hair as I watch Anton Antonovich walking to his study. I can still see him as he goes in. He is stooping over his desk, picking something up. Even from this distance, I think I can see how his hands are shaking.

My anger returns. Enough, I think, and give the child a push. She doesn't budge. Thin she might be, but weak she isn't. Getting her off before her time would take a lot more determination than I put into that one push.

I haven't even started the plaiting. I go on with my brushing.

Anton Antonovich's papers are all in one rough pile. He tries to shove it in one of those folders he uses, but the papers aren't straight enough and so he doesn't manage. Seems to change his mind anyway. Lays them on the desk, straightening them again, and then picks them up, in a bunch, just like that, and brings them out with him. Standing at the end of the corridor he says:

'I'll drop these off then.'

That sentence was meant for me. I nod and continue brushing.

I can hear him in the hallway. He's fumbling: I guess it must be with his coat. He's like a big kid, I think: can't even get dressed without a performance.

But then I hear a sound that freezes my smile. A curse. It's not like him to curse, I think, and then I hear the curse cut off and a thud. As if he's fallen.

'Anton Antonovich?'

No answer.

'Anton Antonovich?'

I am flooded by alarm. I try it a third time:

'Anton Antonovich,' and this time, when again I get no answer, I do shove her off.

I make my way down the corridor and into the entrance hall. My heart is beating. I am half-running.

It doesn't take me long to reach the hall and, when I do, my fear is changed into irritation. He hasn't fainted, or had a heart attack, or even tripped and fallen down; he's just done his usual, dropped his papers and then sat down, heavily, and now he is trying to gather them together. Didn't bother answering me. Had other things on his mind. Got himself into a terrible mess: his coat half on and one of his boots as well as he sits there, in all those papers, like a clumsy child who's given up all hope of being able to extract himself from this mess of his own making.

'Come on, Anton Antonovich,' I say, hearing my voice, like a clucking hen, which I dislike. So I don't say anything more but I do take over. I'm used to that. It's my job. I make sure his other arm finds its way safely into its sleeve and then, while he pulls on both boots, I sort out his papers. It's not difficult: they're numbered on the bottom and, ever since the *Chelyuskin*, I have known what it is to count. I put them all in order, concentrating on the numbers, not the writing. Wouldn't help if I did: I can't make head nor tail of what's written there. I straighten up.

He's standing now. I hand them over.

He says: 'Thank you, Irina.'

There's something in his voice, his saying my name without the patronymic, that makes me look at him again. He looks tired, I think, although that's not unusual: he's a man who always looks tired. He's pale as well – but then, again, that's Anton Antonovich for you.

So what worries me is not in his appearance. Nothing I could put my finger on. Something in his expression, I guess, in his way of holding himself which makes me think there's something wrong, but before I can think of a way of asking him, he's saying:

'I'll see you at the Ivanovs'.'

Making my way towards the kitchen, I think I could drop off at his study and go over to the window to watch him coming out of the building and making his way to the tram stop. But then I see Anya still standing, there, in the same position where I had left her, and I know she will carry on doing this until I come back. So I decide to give any window gazing a miss and instead return to my place in the kitchen, and, setting her, quite roughly I'm sorry to report, back on my lap, I continue to plait her hair.

The Institute

Outside it is bitingly, breathtakingly, staggeringly cold, so cold that Anton Antonovich's breath, when it mists out, turns almost immediately and visibly gummy. Pulling his coat tighter, he makes his way towards the tram stop, walking gingerly like a old man, although this owes less to the coating of ice that has overlaid the surface of the sidewalk and more to his thoughts that in one moment propel him forwards, and, in the next, counsel him back, a push-pull that increases in intensity as he walks on.

Such a waste of his energy. He knows full well that what he told himself before is true, that there is no going back. And yet he is still assailed by doubt. That's why he tried to persuade Anya to come with him.

As if her presence could somehow reduce his risk! Stupid. If everything he has done has been to protect her, how can he dream of using her as his protection? He's weak, that's how, or at least the old Anton is weak and the new Anton not securely enough entrenched to win over the old.

In the apartment after he dropped his papers, he nearly changed his mind again. If Irina Davydovna hadn't joined him in the hallway, he would have done. Even now, with the tram stop in sight, he's toying with the prospect of going back. Tomorrow will be soon enough, he thinks. Yes. He nods. He'll go back, toss this piece of dynamite back on his desk, and wait for Anya and Irina Davydovna to get ready, before setting out with them.

He doesn't yield to this temptation. What stops him is the thought of Anya's contemptuous look (she hates it when he changes his mind) and, he tells himself, she's right. He is committed: he must act. Now. Not tomorrow. Now. No more vacillations.

It's not even as if this kind of anxiety is unfamiliar. The old Anton used to feel it as well, in the run-up to his handing over even the most trivial piece of research. He was notorious then for making editors wait as he added a full stop there, a comma here, or requalified a fact. Unbearably pernickety is what they used to say of him, loudly enough for him to hear. Only reason he kept some influence in the Institute was that even his worst enemies had to concede that when he finally deigned to hand over his material, you could be sure it would have been checked, double-checked and thoroughly cross-referenced. Not for nothing was his work on the Jacobins quoted as arbitrator in any disagreement (in those days, of course, when it was still modish to argue about the Jacobins).

And now, with the study of the Jacobins consigned to the dustbin of history, Anton Antonovich must hand in this new paper.

He glances down at it, viewing it as advertised: his painstaking translation of an early fifteenth-century Georgian manuscript that he had accidentally stumbled across in the archives. A unique, and hitherto unknown, document, or so his propaganda had run, of a dark moment in Georgian history that heralded the end of the independent Georgian nation. Anton's lucky find, a diamond enough discovery to secure the reputation (and therefore the position) of any scholar.

Except that it is none of this. It is a lie. His lie.

His history. His fiction. His imaginary translation of a bogus manuscript that he himself has authored.

Madness. He will never get away with it. He must turn back.

He doesn't. He doesn't really have that choice. It's true that if his forgery is uncovered, he'll be done for; it's also true that if he doesn't hand it in, the same thing will happen. Only sooner. The signs are everywhere. He is superfluous to requirements. He has made enemies. There's no doubt in his mind – he is next for purging.

He stands shivering in the glacial dusk of this deep midwinter, the streets deadened by layers of settled snow, while ice fringes, laced and intricate, decorate window ledges, pipes and roofs, and he thinks of the months it took him to get to this point. Months during which his position in the Institute has grown increasingly precarious.

It all started, as it always does, with a chain of muttering.

'What's the use of Anton Antonovich?' that question loud enough to reach him:

'What's the use of Anton Antonovich?' confirming that his turn had come. He, who had sat quiescent through the series of expulsions that had rocked their Institute in the past two years, was about to be targeted. Without allies to speak up for him (and who spoke out these days?) he would be ousted. The *modus operandi* was a well-worn path. First, a meeting called, everybody to attend. He walking along with all the rest, into the hall and taking his seat. Those same grim-faced men seating themselves on the stage, behind the table, those same slogans, flags and portraits embellishing their power. The meeting beginning with that death knell:

'On the agenda tonight we have only one person . . .'

which can be heard in purge meetings like this one, not only in the Institute but throughout the length and breadth of their land, those same words: 'on the agenda tonight we have only one person,' with a name. His turn, his name:

'Anton Antonovich Abramov,' and that will seal his fate, for what will follow is also laid down.

A commotion in the room, as anybody unlucky enough to have sat down in his close proximity will develop a boisterous coughing fit, or the urge to smoke, both of which will draw them away so that on their return they can sit elsewhere, anywhere, as long as they are far from him. And then? The accusations.

There is some latitude allowed here: they could accuse him of multiple sins or of a single one, of academism for example, or bourgeois objectivism, or, at its most basic, just being a class enemy, any one of these enough to lose him his job and everything else that follows: his home, his freedom, perhaps, but if not, certainly his place in Leningrad. Next step: his daughter?

What's the use of Anton Antonovich? That question reverberating. That answer, repeating. No use. Not unless he can find a way to save himself. To save them all.

So hopeless does it seem that the old Anton Antonovich would have given up. Not so the new. He now has something, somebody, at stake. He needs to reinvent himself, and quickly, to come up with an offering that will give his enemies pause. That will make him seem useful. No, he needs more than that: he needs to make himself indispensable. And more on top: untouchable. But how?

First off: the parameters. He needs to stop being known as an expert on the French Revolution. He needs to choose a period that isn't a contradiction of anything Marx, Engels or Lenin might have ever, even casually, let slip, or, of course, that could be seen as a challenging of Stalin's often-changing view of history. Nothing too fancy, either (doesn't want to open himself up to the charge of dilettantism), or too off beam (obscurantism). He sets himself to work, scrolling back through history.

Not the first thirty years of the twentieth century: too dangerous. The nineteenth? Not the Romanovs, they're dynamite. Not the Napoleonic campaign, for this would entail an analysis of the Russian military response that, in this current climate, would be tempting fate. Further back then? The seventeenth century? How about that crossover tsar, Leningrad's founder – Peter the Great?

Peter was tempting, for, with his grand territorial ambitions and his administrative finesse, he was coming back in vogue. Except: this very fact is what discounted him. Too much expectation. Ditto for that other tsar of the sixteenth century, Ivan the Terrible, another moderniser (albeit by blood), who is also now being subjected to a materialist re-evaluation, the end product of which, Anton suspects, will make him seem not so terrible after all. As for the fifteenth century: well, since that was the preserve of Anton's Director, it was also ruled out.

The fourteenth century? The fourteenth in Russia? No, not that either: arguments about the way the principality of Moscow became the nucleus of the Greater Russian state, and how much the Tartar khans helped in this process, were already making the kind of waves that Anton knows he must avoid. The thirteenth century, then? The twelfth? Eleventh? No – none of them, for to delve into Kievan Rus meant embroiling himself in the debate as to when feudalism began or ended that had already disposed of Pokrovskii's reputation and was now set to do the same to other favoured historians.

Paralysis. No subject. No place in the Institute. No use.

That was the prospect facing him, that he had all but

accepted, the old Anton leaking back, his imminent defeat luminous in the zone of exclusion, until the day when the new Anton reasserted himself and he made the leap.

It happened in a meeting. He was sitting with his head averted in order to avoid a colleague's scrutiny, when his gaze snagged a picture of their leader, Stalin. Nothing unusual in that: Stalin's portrait is increasingly ubiquitous. But this time the sight made Anton take another tack. Not Russia, he thought, staring at the Soviet's Union's most famous Georgian: but why not Georgia? The state of Georgia in the fourteenth century. Georgia: Stalin's birthplace. It was madness, and yet in that very madness might lie salvation. If it was dangerous for Anton Antonovich to consider studying Georgia, then wouldn't it be doubly dangerous for any of his colleagues to try to stop him?

Nothing wrong in exploring the idea, he thought, and he began to read it up. What a liberation to move away from that distortion of liberty that his study of the French Revolution had become. Not that Georgia in the fourteenth century, or the Mongol invasion which ravaged it, was any the less bloody than Jacobean France.

Caught up in this whirlwind, Anton kept on reading. At the centre of his attention, one man, Timur Aksak. Timur, crippled in his right leg and renamed the lame. Timur i lang. Timurlane, Christopher Marlowe's Tamburlaine, Handel's Tamerlano. Son of a tribal leader, Timur claimed a noble lineage: a descendant, or so he said, of the greatest of all Mongols: Genghis Khan. Timur the merciless, Timur the cruel, his armies sweeping across Eurasia from Delhi to Moscow, from the T'ien Shan mountains of Central Asia to the Taurus mountains in Anatolia. Timur, the illiterate, who turned Samarkand into a centre of culture and learning: Timur the barbarian whose knowledge of medicine, astronomy and history was legend. Timur, Georgia's scourge. Timur, who walked with a limp.

This is it, he thought, Georgia in the fourteenth century. But how? Merely studying an epoch was not enough. To achieve what he most desired – untouchability – he must also make his mark.

He didn't have much time. Spending too long in the archives was to risk being seen as that most despised of bourgeois remnants – a member of the archival rat pack. Plagiarising what was readily available was too risky.

Then it came to him. If history is the history of the victor, why not assume the pose of victor and make it up? Madness, and yet the more he thought of it, the more sense it seemed to make. Madness, and yet it gripped him so hard that he, who had spent his life wrapped in thought, didn't think but acted. The next time he was challenged to give details of his current research, he boasted about the document he'd found. It's a new addition to the *Kartis Tshkovrebva*, the history of Georgia, he heard himself saying, similar to the one published by Academician Brosset in 1849, amazed to hear himself saying this and at the same time thinking: why not? It's a special edition, he elaborated, a new *Matiane Kartlisa*, a Georgian chronicle written in the fifteenth century but covering the political developments of the last twenty years of the fourteenth. And then, as if this was not dangerous enough, he went on further, adding another piece of bait, saying that the document he had found would be of interest, not only to the historian, but to their whole society, illuminating as it does the decisions a leader must take when faced by the threat of foreign invasion.

As soon as the words left his mouth, he saw the gleam in the eyes of the Institute Director. Anton Antonovich's courage had turned to hubris. It had taken him too far. To find a new document that might throw light on the past, well, that would be a prize indeed – but to do so in a way that illuminated the present, well, if the document failed to follow every twist and turn of Party policy, therein lay disaster. And yet, having committed this act of verbal bravado, he could not unsay it.

'Interesting, Anton Antonovich,' came the Director's immediate response: 'I await, with enthusiasm, the completion of your translation,' the words pronounced with such glee that they said two things: first, that the Director wanted rid of Anton Antonovich, and second, he thought his chance has come.

'And when exactly will you be finished?' the Director said.

How could Anton Antonovich ever have thought that this system of theirs, which was built on a foundation of arrant disbelief, would take what he said on trust? He stuttered. 'It ... it ... it might take some time, Comrade Director.'

'Of course it might, Anton Antonovich. But if it were to take too much of your precious time, we could provide you with some help.'

Which meant that if he didn't deliver this translation in which the Director did not, for a single moment, believe, then they would wrest the original (which he didn't have) from him. Which meant he had to follow through. He had to produce his chronicle. A lesson – in history as much as anything else: action leads on to reaction. There is no turning back. That's what Borya always said. And it's true. Anton Antonovich has no option. He must set to, no longer a recorder of history or an assessor, but its creator.

So it was that Anton was forced to breathe life into his unreality, to sit in his study, hearing the street loudspeakers spit out insults, their reproduction of the poison that issues daily from Prosecutor Vyshinsky's mouth, Vyshinsky who, in Moscow, is making his own demand: 'To a Mad Dog, a Mad Dog's Death'. He is doing what Anton also aims to do – inventing history – while amongst Vyshinsky's accused sit two former members of the Politburo, Bukharin and Rykov, whose knowledge of history is gleaned from their own control of it. Those two once-powerful men, seated now in submission, await history's judgement, and in Leningrad that timid man Anton Antonovich is finding his own way forward, writing, unstoppably, in an invented Georgian voice, of Timur, the treacherous, the wicked dragon, precursor of the anti-Christ. The victor: Timur i'lang.

And now, as Bukharin and Rykov face death, Anton's time is also up. He must show his document.

The jangle of the approaching tram. He hurries across the road. As he arrives so does the tram, its upward connecting arm slicing through a pattern of jagged icicles that have jammed themselves along the wire. The tip of one lands on Anton's paper. He brushes it away, while thinking it's probably too late to stop it from leaving a faint watermark. He should have stayed to fit the lot into the file, but then he thinks: no matter. The smear will give the whole a look of authenticity. Not, he reminds himself, that a copy in translation, which is what this purports to be, needs to have an authentic appearance.

It's warm inside the tram, the heat generated as much as anything else by the press of bodies. The old Anton Antonovich would have found this proximity distasteful; the new enjoys it.

That's what Anya has done for him: she has helped him, not so much to find his own humanity as to join the rest of humankind for it has taken him this long to understand that conformity is not a giving in to control, but a giving up of an inhibition that he previously mistook for control. Now he understands that in ceding some of his separation from the rest of his society what he has gained is not enslavement but a kind of freedom.

He looks down at the document: his only hope of securing this newfound freedom. He was right before: there will be a faint water mark. No matter. There are processes to come. Colleagues to assess and pass it on. Editors to read it. Typesetters to lay it down. Printers to roll their ink along it. By the time they have finished, the mark would, long ago, have been obliterated not only from reality but from memory as well.

The Party

Anya and I have already been at Nevsky for an hour while Anton Antonovich has not yet turned up. He's normally punctual to a fault, and especially so when Anya bothers to grace us with her presence. But now, finally, I hear him coming. It's got to be him: no one I've ever met makes quite such a fuss of climbing up stairs. There's a sequence of thuds and then a bang, as if he's either tripped up or careered into a wall. Or both. The bulb in the stair light must have broken, I think, and I play with the idea of going to the hall to open the door and light his way but then I decide against this. It's not my business if he brings the neighbours out.

As it turns out, he didn't need my help. He must have been taking the stairs three at a time. That explains the noise and his speed, for in the next moment I hear him bursting into the hall.

'Hurrah.'

Hurrah? That's not like Anton Antonovich. Hurrah, as if he's going into battle.

He's stumbling around the hall, and it crosses my mind that he's drunk but it can't be that: Anton Antonovich is no great drinker. And then, here he is breezing in (he's not normally much of a breezer either), smiling so widely that his face looks almost broad. He's full of, what's the word he'd use for it? Oh yes. Full of bonhomie. He's carrying flowers. Flowers, I ask you, in the dead of winter. Red roses, piles of them, a bouquet for Natasha, Polina Konstantinovna and the old babushka. I even get one. Not a bunch you understand. A rose.

I will press it between the folds of that big dictionary of his when we get home.

He's also carrying other gifts. Bread, a big loaf of sour, dark rye which he insists on cutting up and handing out. To help soak up the alcohol, he says, for he's also brought a bottle of vodka, and no sooner is he in the room and stripped of his burdens than he's pouring it out, a shot for everyone, even Anya. She, I'm pleased to see, puts hers aside. Always keeps her wits about her, that one.

'A toast,' Anton Antonovich says.

Anton Antonovich giving a toast! Well, that's another first.

But a good toast it turns out to be, not because of the long words he uses (that's only to be expected), but for the way he talks about those two, Dmitry Fedorovich and Natasha. Things had been sticky in the room until this moment, which is no great surprise: stands to reason when there're ghosts around. But Anton Antonovich saves the occasion by speaking of the newly marrieds as if they're any normal young couple, setting out on their life together in hope, he says, and rightfully so for isn't this world the world of youngsters like them, full of vigour, full of life and, as he goes on to draw a picture of what they could do, reminds us that although Dmitry Fedorovich might not be everybody's idea of a perfect husband, he has proved himself a friend to Natasha, perhaps her only friend. In fact, without him, she probably wouldn't be here in Leningrad but exiled (if she was lucky) or jailed (if she wasn't), the poison of her connection to the dead Kolya spreading through the family. So Anton Antonovich is right, although, of course, he doesn't put it quite this baldly. The truth is, though, that by taking Natasha and Katya on Dmitry Fedorovich has lanced a nasty boil, the boil of suspicion that had affected Natasha and all the family Ivanov, and, besides, everyone can see he loves her. It's clear in the way he looks at her like a cat which has stumbled into the creamery and how, when he's with her, he doesn't ever want to leave. And, I'm sure, he'll grow to love the child as well: that's only human nature.

By the time he's finished, everybody's smiling and when Anton Antonovich says it again,

'A toast,' glasses are lifted, and the evening that had started so slowly takes off and becomes what it always should have been: a celebration.

I sit on the sidelines watching as it all unfolds. Anton Antonovich continues to be the life of the party. I was right though: he's not drunk. He's loud, that's all, uncommonly loud, and surprisingly active. In one moment he's squeezing Boris Aleksandrovich's wizened mother until she squeaks with pleasure, in the other, picking up an accordion and playing a tune (I never even knew that he could play), or crouching down and kicking up his legs in a Cossack dance that, of course, ends up in him in a tangle on the floor. He doesn't seem to care, this is a new Anton Antonovich, wilder and much more carefree. Soon he's up again and laughing at himself in a way that invites us all to laugh with him and then, putting on the gramophone, pulls Polina Konstantinovna up and sets her dancing.

I watch, thinking that this is what our century has taught me: that anything is possible. I've already seen a lot – war, revolution and the Arctic – and now this new bewildering sight: Anton Antonovich the social animal. It's as if those two old friends, Anton and Borya, have switched positions, for while Anton Antonovich grows louder, Boris Aleksandrovich seems to shrink, Boris Aleksandrovich taking Anton Antonovich's place, morosely by the table, and I begin to notice how much Boris Aleksandrovich is drinking, as if there's no tomorrow, or, if there is, he doesn't care, the drunk man taciturn, the sober one ecstatic.

And now Anton Antonovich, puffing with the effort of his exertion, is standing by the window, telling stories. He's no natural storyteller, too interested in the details, but I, for one, have little trouble following his thread. He gets going with the exploits of the lame one, Timur, and his one-time protégé, Tokhtamysch. I find myself caught up in what he says. It's a good story about how the lesser man, Tokhtamysch, growing arrogant with the power Timur has given him, turns on his master and starts a war. I get caught up by his enthusiasm even as I marvel at it, and I see how the others of our party are also enjoying it because, while the story might be strange, what matters is the keenness of its telling. This is enough to lift our attention away from what we were all thinking before and for that moment the ghost of Kolya and the times in which we live are made to retreat, and I'm left thinking that although this society of ours is harsh, no doubt about it, what we must never forget is that it is no harsher than the one that came before. And I think as well of the changes it allows, thinking: why not?

Why shouldn't Anton Antonovich throw off his reserve?

Why wouldn't Dmitry Fedorovich be the best of husbands?

And why can't Boris Aleksandrovich get drunk?

A Parade of Ghosts

Anton Antonovich's first thought on waking is how much his head is pounding. His second is to wonder why. He wasn't drunk the previous night, he was merry and not from vodka but from his relief at finally having handed in his paper. In truth, he thinks, he'd never been so sober. Or alive.

Four hours later he is walking, gingerly, along the corridor. Four hours of pushing paper from one pile on to the other, and his headache has returned. The vengeance of vodka, he thinks, or of his own excess. Except maybe it's not a hangover, maybe he's ill. He thinks. Perhaps I should go home. If I did I could avoid . . .

Too late.

'Comrade.' The Director of the Institute is ahead, his lugubrious figure blocking the corridor.

Where did he come from? That's the first thing Anton Antonovich thinks. The second: it doesn't matter. The new Anton Antonovich must join him. He walks forward, saying:

'Comrade Director,' at the same time wiping his forehead because he's sweating despite the fact that it's not particularly warm in the corridor.

The Director makes no small talk. Never does. Says instead, abruptly, 'I have examined, in some detail, the document you submitted, Anton Antonovich.'

Already?

'Interesting,' the Director says.

I'm sure it is, Anton Antonovich thinks, and waits. No longer nervous. Too late for that.

'I have some questions,' the Director says, his vast, domed forehead wrinkling into so many folds it looks as if it has been pleated.

'Questions?'

'About the merit of the translation.'

It's over, Anton Antonovich thinks.

'At certain junctures,' the Director says, 'the phraseology seems modern.'

Me and my ambitions, he thinks. Me and my freedom.

'You've never translated anything before, have you?'

'No.' Shaking his head as if to deny that no. 'Not before.'

'Well,' the Director sniffs, like a bloodhound, and then he sucks in breath through the gap in his stained front teeth. 'That explains it,' he says, baring those teeth, but not in anger, in a twisted smile. 'That's all detail, and it can be remedied.'

Detail. That word, repeating on Anton as he stands there, overcome by a sensation of relief. I've got away with it, he thinks: I've got away with it, as he hears himself on automatic saying: 'I would value your undoubted expertise to remedy this problem, Comrade Director.'

'I have made some suggestions.' The Director holds out the paper, and Anton Antonovich receives it, seeing the watermark and flipping through the rest, noting the occasional directorial mark.

'You found the original where?' the Director says.

Anton Antonovich looks up. 'In the archives, comrade.'

'The archives. Yes. I see. You made a copy and left the original there, of course?'

'Yes, comrade. Of course.'

'Strange that this manuscript should end up here in Leningrad.'

'My very thought, Comrade Director.' Last night Anton Antonovich played the accordion for the first time in public. Today he's learned to act. 'Incomprehensible really,' he says, wondering whether he might be overdoing it.

The Director doesn't seem to think so. 'There are no others there?'

'Not that I came across, Comrade Director,' Anton Antonovich says, thinking: nor will you ever, you're far too indolent, but then adding as an extra disincentive: 'After I found this one, I did search well, of course. To see.'

'Of course. The committee have also all read the document, naturally.'

Them as well? So soon? The calm he had felt before was mere mirage. There are rivulets of sweat, now, massing on his forehead. He can feel them slick, ready to run.

'We are unanimous in our opinion,' the Director says. 'This document must be published. No need to wait for a journal. It can go out on its own.'

Anton Antonovich breathes out. Hard. He needs that breath out so that he can take in one more.

'We all agree, however, that it requires an introduction. A piece that would put this important find into its proper historical context. We want you to write it. Would two weeks suffice?'

What's happening to him? He can't see properly. Nor hear. All he can do is speak, his voice coming from a great distance. 'But surely . . .'

'Surely what, comrade?'

He makes an effort to pull himself together. 'Surely,

comrade: you know how new I am to this arena. Shouldn't the honour of writing the introduction go to an experienced historian such as yourself?'

'No, comrade.' When the Director shakes his head, both his forehead and his long jowls shiver. 'We must all be ready to admit to our own mistakes, even a Director such as myself. I take responsibility for the fact that I doubted you, Anton Antonovich, and that you have proved my doubts unfounded. You have done well, Anton Antonovich. Very well. We know how expert is our leader, Comrade Stalin, in all fields of study but we also know of his considerable expertise in this field of medieval history. He will be presented with a special edition of this paper.'

A special edition, Anton Antonovich hears, and for a moment, feeling as if he's about to keel over, he reaches out, grabbing hold of the Director's arm.

'Comrade. Are you all right?' he hears and says:

'Yes,' his voice coming to him as distantly as the Director's had, his mind concentrated on keeping his balance, his hearing gradually improving as the Director continues:

'Do you need some help?'

'No.' He lets go of the other's arm. 'Thank you, comrade,' and turns away, hearing the other's voice:

'You don't look well, Anton Antonovich.'

'I'm fine,' he says, walking to show that he is fine, making his way down the corridor and up the stairs, so slowly he feels as if he's been walking for an age, and arriving finally in his office, sitting himself down, sitting, just that, for a long time, until his head sinks down, into his arms that are, without his conscious volition, there to receive it, and then he thinks: What have I done?

Bathed in sweat, he lies, eyes closed, oblivious to the wet cloth that Irina Davydovna keeps on his forehead to cool him down and to the comings and goings of doctors, oblivious of anything save that imaginary hand of his moving over the lines of a non-existent exercise book, eons passing as he uses up its pages and calls out for another:

'More.'

Irina Davydovna, who has been at his bedside for days, fetches water, curving her arm around his back and guiding him up, lifts the cup to his closed lips, urging:

'Come on now, Anton Antonovich, make an effort. For me. Have a little.'

Eventually he does, swallowing not for her but to rid himself of her so that she will let him sink back into the embrace of those soft pillows and back into this project which is consuming him as surely as the fever that is coursing through his body.

History enacted before his insentient gaze. Wraiths from the past: a parade of ghosts. Timur limping, or is it someone else? A shadow that becomes a man. Broad-faced and grey-haired, ruddily complexioned with cruel hypnotic eyes: a famous man. The prosecutor, Vyshinsky.

Andrei Yanuaryevich Vyshinsky, who jumps up, his agility belying his brute force and, seizing a shadowed partner, begins to waltz, graceful, gliding through the bars of a prison but stopping suddenly to turn back and point the finger of accusation. Vyshinsky lets loose a string of curses, naming Anton, branding him a liar, fraudster and a spineless cheat. Vyshinsky thunders as he calls up judgement on this milksop pygmy, summoning up that cursed line of dead, Kirov, Zinoviev, Bukharin, Rykov and Yagoda, to come forward, making the dead speak in condemnation of this nonentity, Anton Antonovich Abramov, this Anton who cries out in despair:

'What have I done?' and hears Irina's voice:

'Ssshh now. Ssshh. It will be all right.'

He is awake, his voice calling, not in a dream space, but in greyed reality. 'Where am I?'

A soft reply. 'At home.'

He tries to raise himself but doesn't have the strength. 'Ssshh. Lie still.'

He says: 'It's dark.'

'It's night.' A light clicked on. Irina Davydovna, ghostly, getting up.

'How long have I been here?'

Her face looming. 'Five days. They brought you here from work.'

He closes his eyes.

'Anton Antonovich . . .'

Why won't she let him be? He tries to turn away.

'Anton Antonovich.'

He opens his eyes. Time has been advanced: now light streams through the window. He's tired. Doesn't want to be awake. Wants to sleep. Without dreaming. Never to wake again. He shuts his eyes.

'Anton Antonovich. Come on. You need to eat.'

He doesn't want to eat. He wants to die. Not because of pain, but for the absence of pain that death will surely bring, to die not from passion but from its lack. This is what he wants to do. To die.

'Anton Antonovich.'

He tries to turn away but she, outguessing him, hauls him back. Her hands like steel. He's too weak to resist them.

'I told you, you need to eat.'

He is puppeted by her, she rearranging his limbs to suit her whim, propping him up and repositioning him until, at long last, she lets him be.

He says: 'Anya?'

'At school. Come on now. You need to eat.'

He opens his mouth – what else to do? – and she spoons in beef broth. He swallows as she sits waiting with another spoonful. Always another.

'How long have I been here?'

'Six days. Eat.'

Eat. That's all she ever seems to say. 'Eat.' He begins to dread that voice wrenching him reluctantly from sleep, and he begins to hate her for her invariable injunction: 'Eat.'

'How long?'

'Seven days. Come on now: eat.'

Seven days. Too long. He only has another seven.

'Don't worry, Anton Antonovich. For the first time since you took to your bed, the doctor left here with a smile on his face. You'll soon be well.'

To get up, he thinks, and go on with my forgery.

'The Director of your Institute came and left his good greetings. Said, don't worry, they will wait until you are strong enough to write the introduction.'

Wait, he hears, and, closing his eyes, falls back to sleep.

While he has been lying insensate on his bed, Irina Davydovna had cleaned his study.

On the first occasion that he re-enters it he is not only taken aback by the unaccustomed order she has imposed but he is also furious. He stands in the doorway, frozen by the sight of shelves of the cabinets not only dusted (which he has always permitted) but also perfectly regimented; by books that had previously littered almost every available surface now neatly stacked; by the newspapers that used practically to obscure the floor now bundled together and tied up with string. As for his desk: it is so tidy it looks as if it belongs to an altogether different man. A bureaucrat.

How dare she? All he's ever asked of her in here is to

keep the dust at bay and that's all she's ever done. And now? Has his illness made her think that he's no longer master of this place? If so: well, that's a dangerous path for her to tread. She should know this: he's her employer, could easily rid himself of her.

He never says so though. He's too weak to sustain such rage (and besides, a clear sense of righteousness has never come easily to him). He owes so much to her. She's tired – he can see that, and all because she has been looking after him and Anya. Anya, who, come to think of it, has hardly been to see him. No matter. He understands. Anya has lost too much already, she cannot afford to open herself up to the possibility of another loss.

As for Irina Davydovna's reordering of his study. Maybe it was a cleansing: that's the way he now thinks of it. A new start, not only for his work space, but also for him.

His fever has served a purpose, burning up doubt and resistance in the furnace of delirium. No need any longer for him to keep comparing old and new. He has become one, the two Antons joined. His act of transformation is complete: he has rebuilt himself.

On the eighth day Anton Antonovich – both the old and the new – sits down at his blank desk, picks up a pen and begins to write.

'*It is my honorary duty,*' he writes but immediately thinks: no, this will not do. Too personal. Scratching out the sentence, he starts the piece anew:

'*It is the honorary duty of the historian . . .*', which is better but still too individualistic. He tears the paper from the notebook and, crumpling it up, drops it in the new waste bin that Irina has thoughtfully provided. A new page: his third attempt:

'*It is the honorary duty of* all *historians,*' yes, this has promise, '*to assist in the building up of a comprehensive view of the history of a country such as Georgia which ranks amongst the most ancient in the world. This document is a new, and a (perhaps) surprising, addition to the* Kartis Tshkovreba, *the history of Georgia, that corpus that, compiled in the twelfth century, stands as an invaluable source for the study of Georgian history, the development of the Georgian feudal monarchy and the political unification of Georgia.'*

He's rolling now. He leans back, stretching his arms above his head. A good start. Even time to take a further risk. Rocking forward, he bends over the page and continues:

'The analysis presented here suggests that it represents a minority view, a view that was perhaps subsequently suppressed. The document concentrates on that period of the Mongol invasion of Timur i lang (1386–1403). This is the first moment since the Arab imperialist invasions of the mid-seventh century deferred the unification of Georgia until the second half of the tenth century (when the principalities on Georgian territory united to form an all-Georgian feudal monarchy) that the Georgian nation was subjected to such intense external pressure. The style of this anonymous . . .'

'Anton Antonovich?'

He looks up, startled. Irina Davydovna, standing in the doorway. He didn't hear her coming. How long has she been there?

'It's late,' she says.

Is it?

'You mustn't overdo it.'

It *is* late, he sees. Has long been dark. 'Is Anya back yet?'

'Yes. She has already gone to bed.'

Without a word to me, he thinks and then withdraws the thought. Of course she wouldn't have come in: she never disturbs him when he's working.

'You should go to bed as well.'

Yes. That as well. He has time. No need to overdo it. He gets up, yawning, and says:

'Thank you, Irina Davydovna, that I will.'

He must still be weak; he oversleeps, waking only after Anya has already left for school. No point in hurrying to get up then. He lies in bed, revelling in his newfound calm. For the first time in he doesn't know how long (he has lost count) his sleep was empty both of any dream that he might remember and of the hallucinations that had been his companion in delirium. He gets up slowly, has a leisurely breakfast, and then ambles along the corridor to his study.

Now, where was he? Oh yes. He was in the middle of writing a fraudulent introduction to a forgery. Unhesitating, he picks up his pen, turns over the page, and continues:

'*The author looks backwards without nostalgia. It is his assertion that the historical conditions necessary for the recreation of a strong and stable Georgian state were in place in 1382 before Timur invaded.*'

He's coming to the point of which he is most justifiably proud and, at the same time, most justifiably afraid. The link: past and present united:

'*In the second and more contentious part of his account, the author argues that the king would have been better served by a temporary alliance with Timur. Then Timur would not have waged war and Georgia would not eventually have been broken up. In this, the chronicler shows a remarkable understanding of the forces at work.*'

Even Anton's Director, slow as he is, will be able to see the parallel, that in this late fourteenth-century Georgia Anton has partly reconstructed and partly created, the rulers are facing the same dilemma as the modern Soviet Union: although, of course, in the contemporary example, the threat comes not from Mongols but from German fascists who are even now talking of war. And here, as well, is an unknown historical figure wrestling with the very same dilemma which will confront Stalin, the decision over whether to send the army to the borders and risk this war, or, instead, make peace with the potential invader and so build up his country's strength. Dangerous ground – if Anton doesn't pull it off, he's lost.

The Appointment

It is done. His introduction completed and handed in, he is back at work. Thinner than ever, and more stooped and always walking through the corridors. No change then? But yes, there is a change. To his colleagues he has become someone of note, a man of worth, a scholar whose work will bring great prestige to their Institute, a person whose presence must be acknowledged. As he walks the corridors, he is greeted. Enthusiastically. He is their comrade, their Anton Antonovich. His name resounding. His name:

'Anton Antonovich,' most often just in greeting, but sometimes accompanied by a request:

'Anton Antonovich. A word, comrade, if you please.'

He turns and stops and waits for the Director to draw up abreast and, as he is doing this, he thinks: is it time?

But no. It is not time.

'I have taken the liberty of further defining certain of the terms you have used in your introduction,' the Director says. 'I trust you do not object?'

He shakes his head. 'No, Comrade Director, of course I do not object.'

'Given my contribution, I have also added my name.'

'Of course, Comrade Director,' he says and of course he should have known that would happen next, the noose tightening, not only around him but around the whole Institute, and for a moment he is sorry to have drawn them into this, but only for a moment as he is too tired – no longer sleeping – and, besides, here comes another to claim his attention, all those voices tugging at him, those voices pursuing him down the corridor, those things they want him to do, those demands, comrade, Anton Antonovich, he hears them calling to him, comrade, would you be so kind, comrade, as to look over this monograph I have written, Anton Antonovich, please, a moment of your time, I'd value your opinion on a student, comrade, I know how busy you are, Anton Antonovich, but if you would honour me with your signature on this . . . on and on . . . a non-stop chain of supplication and demand and running underneath this a progress report, his paper (his and the Director's) being proof-read, printed, bound, and now, it's on its way to Moscow, Comrade Anton Antonovich, the honour of it, even now, comrade, heading for the Kremlin, and on top of all these voices he is visited by dreams.

Waking dreams they are, filled, not with visions of Vyshinsky or Bukharin or Timur the lame, but with phrases that repeat on him when he's least expecting them. When he's shaving, for example, or saying goodbye to Anya, or walking into the Institute. Phrases not of his invention, but those that he has used, deliberately, in the corruption not just of history, but of language itself. *Battle for hegemony*; that's one, but it's not particularly notable for there are also many others, a multitude from which to choose and any one will do, any expression, even *medieval Georgian nation*, will be enough to suck him into this waking delirium. Each one embedded in the text he has faked, enough to build a killing case. The case against Anton Antonovich provoked not by a colleague's jealousy, or an offhand remark, or a change in line, but by Anton Antonovich himself.

How could he have dreamed he would get away with it? It was arrogance. And, yes: it was surely arrogance but it was worse than that as well. Absurdity. Yes – and worse again. Criminality. All of this done not just to himself, but to Anya and Irina Davydovna both. His history destroyed. His life, and the lives of those he loves, discarded and all because he had convinced himself that he would be the next target of an Institute purge.

Now he doesn't even think that's true. There has been no purge meeting for some weeks now, and only the other day something Borya let slip made him wonder whether there ever would be again: Borya muttering in that cryptic manner which, these days, he's prone to use, that the near disaster of the trial of twenty-one and the death of Bukharin were the end of it and although he never specified the end of what, Anton thinks he knows that what he meant was the end of this systematic flushing out of every structure.

The ritual enacted since Kirov's death heading to its final conclusion. Enough. Enough disruption. Enough old Bolsheviks who, marching to their deaths, say: *Ave, Caesar, morituri te salutant* as they pass their leader. Those same old Bolsheviks who now have new graves. Enough. There is no need for more. Everything has been reordered. Enough. To the Party has come a new generation of recruits. To the Komsomol: new blood. To the army: new generals. To the state: new administrators. To the NKVD: New Man. Enough.

This tidal wave of purges was never aimed at the Antons of this world. All they had to do was lie low, guard their ordinariness, make allies for themselves, all of which Anton should have done. But what did he do instead? He decided to play Stalin, and thus the Party (for aren't the two synonymous?), at his own game. Crazy. This is him – Anton Antonovich – remember. The cautious man. That man whose world was once defined by the learning world. That protector of the written word. That same Anton Antonovich who has single-mindedly transformed himself into a liar, a cheat, a forger, a failed gambler who has lost the courage to continue along his risk-laden path. A Gogol who, so afraid of death, has brought his own death on himself. An Onegin who doesn't have to ask that question – *will I fall, pierced by the arrow, or will it fly past me?* – because he already knows the answer. Yes, he will fall. This he knows.

The courage he put into every page he wrote is all used up. He is plagued by terror that each day strengthens. He goes into the Institute because he cannot stay away, a creeping thing, reading into every casual glance and comment, his own impending doom. By night, however, it is worse. He cannot sleep.

It doesn't matter now how tired he is. He has only to lay down his head, in fact, and sleep flees. Deep, dark, merciful, silent sleep, he calls it to him. Sleep. That's all he wants to do, sleep, but instead he must rise to the pretence that he wants to live, this soon-to-be-dead, walking dead man, who dresses and breakfasts and walks the corridors of his place of work, nodding as others pass him with their smiling greeting:

'Comrade.'

Each time they call to him his terror increases, each sound of his name adds to an accumulation of dread. Yet he must get up each day and go to work; be greeted and greet back; see students or not; push paper or not; all of this depending on what's required. These are the repetitions he performs, not so much a sleepwalker – if he were sleeping he wouldn't be so scared – as the outer shell of a man who concentrates on the moment when he can be released to go home and there at home be persecuted by his lack of sleep.

Each day one question: will it be today? Each day when he leaves home to walk the corridors, or sit in his office, or talk to his students, he does all this in anticipation of his Director's summons and each day that this doesn't happen his fear increases, the expectation growing so intense that he begins to wish for that moment that will herald the beginning of his end.

And finally it comes.

'My office. Tomorrow. Ten a.m.'

A note there on his desk.

Nothing else – my office. Tomorrow. Ten a.m. – and the Director's initials scrawled below. No other explanation. No need for it. No marching of boots across a parquet floor. No need for that either. Anton Antonovich's fate has been pronounced and simultaneously postponed until the morrow when he must deliver himself up to it.

He leaves the note lying there. Each time he returns in the day it's the first thing that he sees and each time he leaves his office it's the last. The day stretches on. Moments last a lifetime and then are over – each one its own discrete death.

And then at last his working day is ended. For the last time in his office, he picks up the note intending to take it with him. But why, he asks himself – he knows what it contains. He puts it down. Hesitates. Picks it up again. Puts it down and then, before he can change his mind, leaves the office and goes home.

Not to sleep. That will come soon enough. No – he goes home to live. For this one last evening of his former life. To sit at the table with Anya and Irina Davydovna and listen to the things they say. Not that they talk much: they have that in common, all three of them, a certain reticence. But in their silence, in their parallel lives, the sound of the hallway clock after they have eaten, its pendulum marking off the hours while Irina Davydovna cleans the kitchen, and Anya stays in her room, and he reads, or at least he pretends to, in all of this normality lies more contentment than he has ever known. And now its time has almost come.

Anya off to bed. He can hear her moving. And then he hears her door closing. He cannot go to her. This he knows.

Soon. Irina Davydovna's turn. Irina Davydovna switching out the lights. Irina Davydovna's head popping round his door. Her question:

'You're not going to bed, Anton Antonovich?'

Irina Davydovna smiling, offering him her company. If only. To be held: oh, how he yearns for it. But it is no longer his for the taking. He says:

'There is some work I must do, Irina Davydovna.'

She knows there's something wrong. She always does. She can read his face. His being. She stands there, hesitating, on the verge of saying something more. He needs to stop her. To rid himself of her.

'Please,' he says, 'don't wait up for me.' An order that: one of the few he has ever given.

Her face closing down. He has hurt her. 'Goodnight then.' She turns.

He says, 'Ira.'

'Yes, Anton Antonovich.' Her beloved figure frozen.

'Goodnight.'

He sees her hesitating. Thinks. She knows. And yet she doesn't know. She can't. 'Goodnight,' she says again and goes.

He waits. For the hall light to go out. For her door to close. For Irina Davydovna and Anya to stop moving. For the clock to strike.

Ten.

Time to sleep. He goes to his bedroom and, fully clothed, lies down. If only he could sleep.

Eleven.

If he can sleep it may not happen.

Twelve.

Sleep: he wills it on.

One.

He cannot sleep. In its place, instead – despair. He wants to cry out, rend his clothes, call out to the God of his youth who has long ago forsaken them. He wants.

He wants . . .

He wants to sleep.

Any way he can.

He gets up. No option now. Goes back to his study. He is calm. Has never felt so calm. Sits down at his desk. He knows what he must do. Picks up his pen. A note. He must leave a note.

Should I quote Mayokovsky, he thinks:

'The incident is closed.'

Or Mandelstam:

'A leap and my mind is whole,' knowing that he will quote neither of these men, not even himself, he draws the pad closer and then begins to write.

Memory (2)

The memory comes. I watch as it unrolls. I see that sight I would rather have forgotten. I push it away, if only for a moment, and in its place I call up the time before. I see myself . . .

I see myself: waking. Something ordinary, something I just do, that everybody does. Regular I am and have always been, waking at the stroke of six. Regular I was then, waking into darkness.

I've never been one for lying in bed. Up I got and quickly dressed. That's another thing I also always do. It's a rule I made when I first moved in, and a rule I've stuck to. My night clothes and my dressing gown I keep for the privacy of my bedroom. For the rest of the apartment that exists outside my closed bedroom door I am always fully dressed. I will not be spotted in the hallway, passing between my room and Anton Antonovich's, unclothed.

A thought. If I hadn't been so rigid, if I'd changed my routine, could I have changed what happened next?

Foolish thought. By then he was already gone. My Anton, beyond my saving.

Fully dressed, I leave my bedroom. It's very quiet. They're both asleep (well, actually, they weren't, but I didn't know that then). I walk down the hallway. It's very dark. Not that it matters: I could walk this easily, even in my sleep. It's also cold: ice slithers shining against the window panes.

Into the kitchen. The stove gone out. It happens sometimes when I'm careless. Not often. I wasn't concentrating before I went to bed, I remember thinking as I went to the stove and opened up its door. There was a basket of pine sticks lying close. I put a handful in the stove and as I did this I was thinking, and, yes, I can remember thinking this as well, how I was worried about Anton Antonovich. I lit the sticks and closed the door and waited for them to flare and then die down again, and as I waited I thought about the way Anton Antonovich had recently been acting. He'd not been himself, that's what I was thinking. I remember thinking he hadn't been himself, not since he was taken ill and even after he recovered he had remained thinner and more withdrawn – both of which I could understand – but also prone to mood swings, sometimes laughing out loud for no reason and when he did that, and when I looked at him, I saw how sad he looked. In fact, I kept thinking (and I'm almost sure this is what I was thinking) of how I hadn't wanted to leave him on his own the night before, how something in the way he looked told me not to go. Or at least I think this is true. I'm almost sure of it, in fact. I certainly remembered offering him my company, something I hadn't done since he was taken ill, and I also remembered his refusal.

I was thinking about all this on that morning. Yes. Now I'm sure I must have been. I was thinking about it so hard I nearly let the sticks burn out. Just in time I caught myself – and them. I opened the door, added the next load in and there, with the stove lit and its door shut tight, I could get on with my other duties.

Even today I have to tell myself: if I had not done this, if I had gone straight to him instead, it would still have been too late.

I wasn't thinking this then. I wasn't thinking anything in particular. My concentration had moved on, caught up by my routine. I mixed grains and added milk and salt and, while the *kasha* was simmering, I fetched a cabbage from the cold cupboard. I was going to make *shchi*: I had the stock prepared. I remember that feeling of satisfaction as I began to shred the cabbage, watching the knife working fast across its hard green surface reducing it to slivers, and I remember also thinking about my hands as they chopped, those workaday hands, scarred by years of labour, those hands that are no longer made for caresses although, of course, I didn't know that then. The speed at which I worked. That's what I remember. And that familiar sound: Anya's door opening and Anya coming out.

I guess it must have occurred to me to wonder where Anton Antonovich was although I don't remember that. But I imagine it must have crossed my mind for he was usually up before her (he couldn't bear to miss even a second of the time she spared for him). That's the odd thing about my memory which is usually so reliable. Not this time, however, for this time, although I remember all those details, my waking up, walking down the hall, lighting the stove, preparing the porridge, chopping the cabbage, I don't remember wondering where he was, and nor do I remember how it was that I found him.

All I see is this: Anton Antonovich's door open. I see. Him.

Was it me? Did I find him?

Did I?

Or did she?

I don't know. Honestly. I don't remember.

What I do remember is Anya eating. I think it was before. I'm almost sure it was. I remember it particularly because she, who has never had particularly good table manners, this time outshone herself. She was eating like a thing possessed. Like an animal. It must have been before. She couldn't have eaten like that afterwards. Except. I don't think the *kasha* was ready then, not mushed as she likes it to be.

Whether she ate before or after doesn't matter. It's time.

Anton Antonovich's study door. That door, open already or being opened by me, it doesn't matter which, for what I can remember, what I can never forget no matter how hard I try, is me looking in. Anya there beside me. Standing. Mute. I remember that. And Anton Antonovich as well. I remember him, or at least I remember seeing what he had become.

He was hanging from a beam. Dead. No doubt. Dead. His eyes bulging. His tongue: oh, how much downy tongue he had, swelling out from deep down in that blackened, open mouth of his. As for what was left of what had been his face: well, it was now blood red.

Silly man, I thought, dead as he was, while Anya stood there staring. Silly man. What a thing to think and yet, I remember it, that this is what I thought. Silly man, as I moved forward, as I took a decision and acted on it, something that Anton Antonovich, I was thinking as I did it, that Anton Antonovich, when he was alive, had never liked to do.

Did I go for help? No. Not then I didn't. I knew, you see, even through my shock that there was no help for the likes of me. I remember thinking that. I knew I had to act.

I cut the rope. Sawed through those strands that had

carried him to death. I can remember doing that. I can even remember picking up the chair that he must have kicked over, climbing up on it, thinking that's the last place he had ever stood, trying not to look into his face, as I cut him down. I had the knife in my hand, or I had gone back for it, I don't know which. It doesn't matter. What I do know is that I used the knife until I cut right through.

I wasn't trying to save him – he was dead. Maybe I was just being spineless, just didn't want him hanging there, or maybe I already knew he shouldn't be. Whichever it was, as the last thread of the rope was cut, I bore that dead weight of him. Of what he had become. I held it. That stink. That chill of waxy, yellowed skin. That welt around his neck, dried blood there was, I remember that as well. Those dead eyes bulging. Staring. I laid him down and then, leaning over what he had become, I closed those eyes.

I looked up. Saw the child. Standing. She hadn't moved an inch.

I thought: why did he do it? And then I thought: the desk.

I understood Anton Antonovich. I knew him well and I knew he wouldn't be like the men in my family all of whom had slipped so silently away. Not he. An educated man like him. A man so proud of all his learning. Even in his despair, he would be bound to have left his mark. I got up. Went over to the desk.

I was right. He had left a note.

'*I have taken my own life,*' it began:

'*. . . in the hope that I can save the lives of those I love. What I have done, I did without their knowledge. Without their consent. May they forgive me.*'

Forgive him!

There was more. It being Anton Antonovich of course there would be. Two pages of the stuff. I read the whole once and once again as the child continued just to stand. I read those plain phrases. His last will. Phrases like:

'*I made up history*,' and, reading this, I couldn't help thinking about my brothers who had died, all three of them, the first of hunger, the second of disease, the third of war, all of them in the company of thousands who also met with death, all of them dead, I guess you could say, by the hand of history, and now I was standing in this room with this thing, this Anton Antonovich, on the floor, dead by his own hand and all because (or so he wrote) he made up history.

I read what he had done – I, the only person – reading it until the end, and then read it through again, a confession of the way he'd forged a document and passed it off as real, how he did this knowingly (but without our knowledge, he kept saying) to keep his position in the Institute, how all of this he had done, my eyes moving over the words, and when finally I had read it a third time, I took it to the kitchen.

I could hear Anya behind me. I didn't look back. I opened the oven door meaning to feed Anton Antonovich's nonsense to the flames, but found I couldn't. It was his. His last. I couldn't burn it up. So I hid it. First in my pocket and later somewhere else. I may not be like Anton Antonovich, I may be uneducated and lacking his knowledge, but one thing I knew – if his note saw the light of day then all of us, not just Anton Antonovich, but Anya and I, those Anton Antonovich professed to love, all three of us would be finished.

I turned. I saw Anya. Standing. I said: 'Don't you dare ever say a word,' dropping my head to indicate my pocket, and she didn't. She held her tongue, although whether this was because she was obeying my order or because she had nothing to say, I will never know.

Thinking it over now, I think that must have been when she ate. Greedily. Like a thing possessed.

And I? I did the only thing I could. I phoned Boris Aleksandrovich.

Boris Aleksandrovich didn't ask a single question. A habit I guess. Either that or he could hear how serious it was from my tone of voice. Before I knew it he was at the door, standing there, that big bear of a man, Boris Aleksandrovich, wanting to know what had happened, although at the same time I could read in his expression that he didn't really want to know.

I led him to the study. I watched him seeing Anton Antonovich, watching how his face paled and watched him swallowing, hard, as if he was swallowing down the truth of what he was seeing, swallowing it fast and at the same time facing up to it before he turned to me to ask:

'What are we going to do?'

What are we going to do, I heard, and for a moment I was flattered. That it should come to this, I thought, that this man, Boris Aleksandrovich Ivanov, powerful Boris Aleksandrovich with his car and his driver and his office in the Smolny, should ask me, ordinary Ira, what *we* were going to do. But then I felt my pleasure turn to something darker. A wave of anger it was that swept over me and almost had me shouting out: '*Me?*' That's what I wanted to shout: you're asking *me* what *we* should do? You who play so carelessly with other people's lives? Who comes across a woman in a broom cupboard, and sends her without a moment's hesitation, not only through the ice in a ship that wasn't built to handle ice but into a whole new world, knowing as you must have known that her old life would collapse and with it her marriage (which is probably why you did it: you're a revolutionary, aren't you, good at overthrowing the old order) and when all that you must have known would happen did happen, what did you do then? You set her up with your friend Anton, that's what you did, easy it was, after all she was just some piece in a game that took your fancy, her life yours for the changing. And now when it's all gone wrong, what do you do? You turn to her, that's what you do, and you ask for her opinion, as if this were something that you ever sought, as if it were your life in danger not hers, as it was her job to protect you just as you put her here to protect your friend from his own stupidity. And even as these thoughts rolled through my mind, I knew that it wasn't Boris Aleksandrovich who should rightfully be the target for my anger, but Boris's friend, Anton Antonovich. Anton, who had done this to me, to all of us. So clever he thought himself, he couldn't do it like any other, ordinary man, no, not him, he wouldn't dream of killing himself by jumping off a bridge on a winter's night, so we could say he died the ordinary death of an ordinary drunk. Oh no, Anton Antonovich couldn't do that, could he, he had to go and die in front of us and leave a note as well to boast of it, with all his brains, that is what he had to do, putting us in danger and now, to make things worse, here stands his friend, another clever man, in front of me and asks:

'What are we going to do?'

And I know: I can't let my anger out because Boris Aleksandrovich really doesn't know what to do and it is up to me to find a way and so, instead of shouting, I answer quietly:

'You must find a doctor who will testify to a natural death.'

He hears me, I know he does although he gives no sign of it. He is looking at Anton, and this time he is frowning as he says:

'Where's the rope?' his frown working its way deep into his broad forehead as he turns to look at me again, and when I answer:

'I burned it', this clever man, this Boris Aleksandrovich asks:

'Why did you do that?' adding, before I've got time to answer him:

'And why did you cut him down in the first place?'

This question tells me, if I hadn't already known, how very lost he is. I stand, forcing myself into calm, as I say:

'Listen, comrade', using that word that is normally strange to me, but knowing if there is ever a time for it, then its time has come, and using it again, speaking slowly so he could follow me:

'Listen, Comrade Boris,' I say, 'that rope Anton Antonovich used to kill himself would have wound itself round my throat as well. And around the child's. I had to cut him down. And burn it. Now think, Boris Aleksandrovich; which doctor will you call?'

It works, because when he says:

'I can certainly find the right doctor,' I can almost hear his mind turning over:

'But what will I do about the workers who come for the body? How can I make sure of their silence?'

And even though I know he's really talking to himself, I also know that I must answer or lose him, so what I do is borrow a phrase our beloved Comrade Schmidt of the *Chelyuskin* used in those dark days. I say:

'You will find a way, comrade,' (although, of course, Schmidt would have said that *we* would find a way), adding to make his duty clear:

'You, Boris Aleksandrovich: you will find a way.'

And, of course, he did.

A simple way as it turned out. I've noticed that: the

really clever people always choose the simplest. Not so much a solution, this one, as a man: Boris Aleksandrovich phoned his son-in-law and soon he came, Dmitry Fedorovich Anninsky, sidling weasel-eyed into our apartment, taking command, making threats in that way that only men like him can do. It worked. The doctor signed the papers and the workers took Anton Antonovich Abramov (unfortunate early death from heart failure) away, and all we had to do was watch them going and accept their fine condolences. All of us: me, Anya, Boris Aleksandrovich, Dmitry Fedorovich and Natasha, who had come along as well.

Now one thing I know about Dmitry Fedorovich: he is not a man to put himself out for others. It's a mystery how Boris Aleksandrovich managed to persuade him to use his influence on such a personal matter. I would never dream of asking how he did it, a piece of advice I might also have offered Natasha, who was watching her husband with suspicious eyes, taking in this exercise of his power as if it had only just dawned on her who he was and what he was capable of doing, and then looking at her father. I knew she was wondering what power Boris Aleksandrovich had over Dmitry Fedorovich to make him do this, and it occurred to me to give her this one piece of advice – let it go, Natasha – but I didn't, because who am I to give advice, and who is she to listen to what I say? And anyway, I had other things to worry about and other things to do: Anton Antonovich's work to tidy and the child to get ready and that question to answer that I knew would be coming soon:

'Will you keep her?' asked in the confidence of my answer. What choice did I have? I had to keep her if only to protect her and myself from what she might say to someone else, and, anyway, I had grown used to her. And there. It was all settled, save for that other question I was also expecting.

'Did he leave a note?' Boris Aleksandrovich asked.

I did not hesitate. I looked him in the eye. 'No,' I said. 'Anton Antonovich did not leave a note.'

Can the Dead Speak (3)?

And now it sounds out again. That question:

Can the Dead Speak? this time in the interrogation chambers of Stalin's police.

'Can the dead give evidence?' ask Konstantin Rokossovsky, once a division commander and now a prisoner charged with membership of a present-day, counter revolutionary centre, the evidence against him apparently supplied by a man who is already dead and has been for some fifteen years.

And, yes, it does seem that the dead can give evidence, for as this festival of death continues, someone must be giving something up. A wholesale cleansing, it is, a leaching, a harvesting of blood. A nation bled and its army too, so many of them that Stalin must be getting writer's cramp signing death sentences (5,000 in one sitting).

A new high in Soviet achievement. The top ranks of an army culled. A growing list of Red Army seniors cut down.

A summary of the dead:

Marshals – three of five;

Army commissars, 1st rank – both (one to suicide);

Army commissars, 2nd rank – all fifteen;

Army commanders – three of five;
2nd rank army commanders – all twelve;
1st class flagmen of the fleet – both;
Both 2nd class flagmen too;
Flagmen (not of the fleet), 1st rank: all six;
Flagmen, 2nd rank (not of the fleet) – nine of fifteen;
Corps commanders: fifty-seven of sixty-seven (and three imprisoned);
Division commanders: 125 of 199 (eleven imprisoned);
Brigade commanders: 200 of 397 (and twenty-one imprisoned);

On goes the list, down the ranks, tens of thousands, arrested or killed or held captive and sent to the gulags, a military denuded of its head and shoulders and sometimes, even, of its feet, while beyond the borders . . .

But no. This is no time to speak of life outside the borders. What is important is the revolution and the man – Stalin – who has become the revolution. Which means, conversely, that the revolution has become the man, and only he and the ones he chooses can be trusted.

See those others as they march on by. Not only the military, but also the civilian dead. Stalin's men all of them, for those who were never numbered amongst his comrades have long been vanquished and now it is the turn of his closest to make the transition to that other place.

Those individual deaths that add up to a slow massacre of an entire collective.

There goes Stalin's man, for example, Yagoda, who was head of the secret police at the time of Kirov's murder and who later stands condemned for being one of Kirov's killers. Yagoda, who is sentenced to death as co-conspirator with that same Bukharin whose arrest Yagoda himself must once have sanctioned.

And then after Yagoda, that man who helped seal his

fate, his deputy and his successor, the dwarf Yezhov, so bloodthirsty that they named that period of the greatest purge – the *yeshovshina* – after him, and yet his turn must also come and although he disappears without a trial, his fate is not in doubt, especially when his place is taken by his deputy. By Beria.

There they sit in the Kremlin, Stalin and his Beria, wiping out their own Red Army at the point of war. Closing their ears to the callings of the dead. Signing pacts they are, their newspapers denying rumours of a military build-up on their borders.

'Lies and provocations,' their organs steadfastly insist, 'lies and provocation,' while not far from Russia's borders three million German troops, bolstered by Romanians to the south and Finns to the north, and by 2,000 aircraft and 3,350 tanks, move into battle stations.

Lies and provocations.

Part Six

What Lies Ahead

Ahead of us lay Leningrad, but in our thoughts
we were already there.

(Adolf Hitler)

Domestic Life

1941. Outside, as summer draws on, day pushes into night and heads that have been bent against the winter's cold straighten, coats are discarded, smiles and greetings exchanged; in short, the pace of life is escalating and with it the general clamour.

Inside, however, in a second-floor apartment in Kamennoostrovsky Prospect, a stone's throw from the Kirov museum on the Petrograd side of Leningrad, it is almost completely mute.

Two people – Natasha and Dmitry Fedorovich – sit together in a small, neat room, Natasha keeping company with her husband, Dima, as she does every single evening. He is marking up a report, as he also almost always does, while Natasha, who normally draws or sews or reads, is for once without distraction. She sits and watches as the light shimmers through the off-white curtains, watching as, dulled by the final onset of night, it fades and still she continues to sit, thinking that she should probably get up and switch on the light but remaining in her chair, just sitting and listening.

She can hear: footsteps in the street below and a cheerful

greeting and then, as the steps grow distant, silence returns and all she can now hear is the tick of the hallway clock; Katya's sleeping breath filtering through the half-open door; the scratching of Dima's pen; the occasional turning of his pages; all of that, and the beating of her heart. A peaceful moment although Natasha is very far from peace.

Three years have passed since she married Dmitry Fedorovich. Three years that, looking back, she seems to have spent almost entirely indoors. Three years, days in the kitchen, preparing for Dima's return, and nights keeping him company in this room.

The apartment she shares with him is so much bigger than the one she had before. Bigger and much more vacant. Even the furniture is spare, consisting of three matching and straight-backed chairs pushed into a well-polished and well-cleaned table and two armchairs swivelled at an angle to the stove, so that if their occupants (Dima in his and Natasha in hers) were simultaneously to look forward their gaze would intersect in the middle of that thick-weave rug that Natasha's parents gave them as a wedding present, this rug supplying the only splash of colour to the room. There are no other decorative touches – Dima likes to keep things plain – no pictures, nothing on the walls.

Three years with only Ira and Anya to visit and Katya, when she is not at school, for company. Three years of sparse conversation – Dmitry Fedorovich is not one for talk. Three years of emptiness.

And now, for a reason she doesn't fully understand, she feels she can no longer do what she has done these three long years. And so, even though she knows no good can come from what she has to say, she addresses herself to the focal point of the room – the rug of her former life – saying in an almost conversational tone:

'Would you have saved him, Dima?' although this is not

part of any conversation she and Dmitry Fedorovich were having or have ever had.

The question startles him. Astonishment crosses his gaunt face before he pulls himself together, adjusting his expression, toning it to disapproval (he doesn't like to be interrupted when he's working).

'Not now, Natasha. I'm busy,' before dropping his head and readdressing himself to his text.

He's working, which is what he always does. He is a man of strict routine: she his dutiful wife. She should leave him to get on with it, she thinks, but her voice sounds out again:

'Would you have, Dmitry Fedorovich?'

He looks up, sharply, his annoyance obvious, designed to shut her up, but, when meeting her unwavering gaze, he changes his mind, leaning forward and laying down his report on the floor, adjusting it so it's lined up with the foot of his chair, and then, straightening, looks at her again, sighing a second time and saying, mock patiently:

'Would I have done what, Natasha?'

'Saved him.'

'Saved who?'

'Kolya.'

His name. Out loud. For the first time in three years.

'Would you have saved him?' she says.

He blinks. 'Why are you asking me this?'

'Because I want to know.'

'You never asked before.'

'Would you have, Dima? Would you have saved him?'

'You didn't ask me to. Not when it happened.'

'But if I had asked, Dima, would you have saved him?'

He says: 'Is this your idea of a joke?'

She shakes her head – no – but he has clearly decided that it is and, to this effect, he lifts the corners of his mouth, the closest he ever gets to a smile.

Now, finally, he deigns to speak:

'You think I'm that influential?' he says. 'You think I could actually pluck a man from death? How very flattering,' except he isn't flattered. His voice is hard and cold and warning her what she should already know, that he is dangerous when roused. But even knowing this and understanding that for her own good, and for Katya's, she should stop, she says:

'I know you might not have been able to save Kolya, Dima, but what I'm asking is, if I'd asked you then, would you have tried?'

'I hardly knew you then, Natasha.'

'But would you have? If I'd asked?'

'Why bring it up, now, after all this time?'

And she thinks he's right. So much time gone by. So many mornings of her surfacing from sleep to Kolya's absence, and after that, her decision to marry this man she can never love, sentencing herself to this apartment and to sitting here, registering the ticking of the hallway clock. An age passing by, the future so unimportant, the present so measured, and the past so very distant that she barely holds any memory of what came before, almost as if life with Dima is the only life she's known, as if Kolya had never existed, and yet, at the same time, when on the rare occasions she allows herself to think of him, she thinks of her loss of him as if it is happening now, in the moment of each heartbeat.

She closes her eyes. Squeezes them. She will not cry. She never does.

His voice reaches out to her. It is hard, cold: 'What's got into you, Natasha?'

She doesn't know what's got into her.

'Why are you asking this now?'

She opens her eyes. 'Because I want an answer.'

He shakes his head. 'Drop it, Natasha.'

There. He. Her husband, Dmitry Fedorovich Anninsky. He has spoken and, having spoken, he is confident she will obey as she always does and so he bends down, reaching out for his papers, when her sharp injunction:

'Don't, Dmitry,' puts a break on movement.

He looks up, doubly shaken. She never tells him *don't* and neither does she ever raise her voice to him as she is raising it now, saying:

'Kolya might be dead, Dima, but he still existed.'

'Ssshh . . . you'll wake the child,' he says, an injunction that, in any other circumstance, would have quietened her, but in this one only has the effect of inciting her:

'His child, Dima,' she says, 'Kolya's child,' and hearing his reply:

'She is my daughter now,' she raises her voice another notch: 'No, she is not yours. She is his. She's Kolya's.'

'Come on, Natasha, what's the point of this? He's dead.'

Dead, she hears, and looks at him: 'Who, Dima? Who is it that is dead?'

'Don't be childish. You know who.'

'Say it.'

'This is silly . . .'

'Go on, Dima: say his name.' She stares at him, fiercely, and, staring, she sees him swallowing and it occurs to her that he's about to turn away and end this conversation and there is part of her that even hopes that this is what he will do, but when he says:

'All right: if it means so much to you, I will say his name,' he says it with clipped precision, adding, clearly:

'I have never said that Kolya,' and with studied calm, 'or shall I give him his full name? Why not? To repeat: I have never said that your former husband, Nikolai Vladimirovich Kozlov, was not the biological father of our child. Will that do?'

And seeing her, sitting frozen in his sights, he says:

'And now, Natasha, if you don't mind, I have work to finish.'

His tone serves to underline his anger, this man who so rarely loses his temper, this bloodless man which is the way she thinks of him, this husband of hers who she has always known must not be pushed too far. And yet knowing this, and recognising it anew, she cannot stop herself. She says:

'You think he was guilty,' speaking the thoughts she has so long suppressed. Her second husband thinks her first was guilty.

What did she expect? That he would deny it? Is that what she'd hoped? And if he had, would it have ended there?

It doesn't matter what she was hoping: what he does is give a short, unamused bark of laughter and say: 'What does it matter what I think?'

'It matters, Dima. You're my husband. Say it.'

'Come now, N—'

'Say it.'

'All right.' His voice is level, and looking at him she sees in his face an expression that she has only seen once before – in Anton Antonovich's apartment. 'All right, Natasha,' he says. 'If this is what you want.' His eyes are on her.

She has always feared those eyes, but this is no time for fear. Dmitry Fedorovich is already on his feet, crossing the space between their chairs, before stopping to stand and look down on her as he says:

'Yes, you're right, Natasha. I do think he was guilty and, just to be clear, by he I mean your Kolya, Nikolai Kozlov. I not only think he was guilty, I also know it for a fact. Kozlov was an enemy of the state. He got his just deserts. And now that is enough: I am going to finish my work in the bedroom,' and with that he turns and leaves the room.

*

She sits in darkness.

And in silence.

After a while she hears the familiar sound of Dmitry Fedorovich readying himself for bed. She doesn't have to be there to know what he is doing. She knows his routine by heart. She knows the order in which he removes each item of his clothing and lays them neatly on the chair. She can visualise the almost dainty motion of his feet pushing into his pyjama legs and his precise hands pulling at the drawstring before they move upwards for their careful fastening of his long flannel shirt. Then she hears him moving, just two steps, and she knows the brush must be in his hand and that he must be sweeping it across the top of his head, always in the same direction, always two strokes, before he lays it down, carefully, on the dresser beside his cufflinks. A pause. Which means he's pulling back the cover. And then. Another pause. He will come out now, tiptoeing as he always does if she doesn't follow him, to request her presence.

She sits, knowing that she will go to him. How can she not? She has never refused him, has never even contemplated doing so. She sits. Waiting for him to come.

Except – a break with tradition – he does not appear. She waits. She is sure that he will come. Silence. He can't have gone to bed, she thinks, and she wonders whether he could be standing behind the half-closed door, listening to her with the same attention as she is listening out for him, but then she dismisses the thought and decides she must have been wrong before. He's probably long in bed. He could even be asleep, he who has the capacity to fall instantly into unconsciousness.

Not her. She doesn't sleep easily: she hasn't, not for a long time, not since . . .

She thinks: is that what's got into me? Am I just overtired?

It's possible. She is very tired. Bone-tired. Dead tired.

Even so, she thinks, tiredness is no excuse. She should not have provoked her husband. It's too risky and, besides, what was the point, to have confirmed what she already knew: that he thinks Kolya was guilty? It's no surprise and neither is it unusual. Almost everybody would agree: her friends, her so-called friends, the people with whom she used to work, Kolya's comrades from the factory and, for all she knows, her father. Kolya himself would likely have thought it as well for Kolya held fast, just as Dmitry Fedorovich does, to his faith in a system that can do no wrong. If a man was convicted, so the logic ran, then he must be guilty. That's the way the Kolyas – and Dmitrys – of this world think. That's all there is to it. This she has always known.

What she doesn't know, however, is why she brought it up.

Celebration (5)

It was different for me than for Natasha.

When Kolya died, she had to face the danger that led her into Dmitry Fedorovich's bed. In my case, thanks to that same Dmitry Fedorovich, everything was covered up. The authorities actually honoured Anton Antonovich and, since he was gone, I became the target of the honouring. Me and the child, both of us put on the train to Moscow.

Quite a journey it was. She was even less forthcoming than normal. Wouldn't have thought that was possible, would you, but it's true: she lay in the compartment that was ours alone, curled in tight on herself, refusing to join me at the window. She cheered up though when we got to Moscow, and after we had left the railway station she actually went as far as to treat me to one of her rare smiles.

So there we were, both of us, in the Moscow subway, taking advantage of the spare time we had, for once in perfect accord in our eagerness to get out at each and every stop. The sights we saw: it's enough to make you believe in the power of Soviet society. Such underground visions: mosaics on the ceiling in Mayakovsky; pink marble and bronze at Komsomolskaya; a floor decorated to look exactly like a carpet at Belorusskaya; huge and green-streaked marble walls at Kurskaya; and, when we finally got out at Red Square, those bronze sculptures, scores of them, hundreds it seemed although we couldn't stop to count them for by now we were almost out of time.

So out we went, my head spinning from everything I'd seen, although I couldn't help thinking how hard someone must have to work to keep those miles of marble and bronze clean – what water can do to marble – but then I took myself in hand, telling myself that for this once I must stop thinking like a cleaner (which I am) and act my new, if short-lived, part as the wife of a hero (which I, of course, am not).

They took charge of us when we came out, polite men who treated us really nicely. They took us, first of all, to pay tribute to Vladimir Ilyich in his mausoleum. We skipped the queues, us treated as even more important than the brides who, decked out and beaming, had come to mark their wedding days. Past Vladimir Ilyich we filed, with his high wax cheeks and pointed chin. Can't say I'd like to be kept like that, but then I'm not a leader, and there was no time to think of it, because through those high gates into the Kremlin they led us, my first time (they didn't have us unimportant players in for the *Chelyuskin* ceremony) and I daresay my last. Anya and I were centre stage, all eyes on us, people wondering what it was that we'd done to be so honoured, taken to the Hall of Soviets and presented, along with scores of others (the different nationalities that were there, I could hardly believe my eyes), to other men who made speeches about us, or, in our case, about Anton Antonovich.

What they actually said I can't tell you, not because it was private but because I have never been one for paying much attention to speeches. Anya made up for my wandering mind, her face staring straight ahead and shining, she who usually seems so dull. And then it was over and back we went, Anya once again returned to her disapproving presence and me with a medal that I do not deserve and that Anton Antonovich did not rightfully earn. Although now I come to think of it, that's not true. Anton Antonovich ought to have a medal, I reckon, posthumous or not, for the way he fooled all those other clever people.

Nobody knows what he did but me. Nobody ever will. I have hidden his letter where no one will ever find it.

But, come to think of it, I can't be the only one who knows. Those historians he worked with: they've got to know. Stands to reason.

Not many people are content, as I am, to wait and see what life delivers: most of them want to get on, to make their mark. So it stands to reason that, if Anton Antonovich's colleagues at the Institute had really thought his work was an advancement in the revolutionary under-standing of our nation's history, as they kept telling us in the People's Hall, well, then they'd have been round here like a shot, taking his papers away and trying to find out whether we knew anything that might help them and not some other colleague, continuing Anton Antonovich's work and so earning themselves their own little trip to Moscow. But none of this happened. The opposite in fact. Nobody came round at all, not since the day of the funeral. All communication – the reallocation of the apartment to me, the transfer of the guardianship of Anya – has been conducted by post.

Not that I'm complaining. I've got what I want without having to fight for it. A home, some independence, and, I guess, for Anton Antonovich's sake, the child – all of these the legacy Anton Antonovich left to me.

To be truthful, it's not a legacy I would have chosen. Truth is, I miss him. Yes, I know he was a timid man whose one act of bravery turned out to be the height of folly, and, yes, I know that he probably thought of me not as his equal but as a convenience to service his household and, if I was willing, his bodily needs as well. But I didn't mind. I might even have felt similarly about him. I miss him. I miss the comfort of his body and I miss that quirky way he had of looking through me, not out of nastiness, but because his mind was caught up in another century and another way of life.

And all that tormented stuff about making up history in his letter. About lying. Shows how out of touch Anton Antonovich really was: didn't he see that we're all liars now? That life has made us so? As for the part where he said that what he did, he did without our knowledge and consent: well, since when did knowledge and consent have anything to do with anything?

What I can't remember, though, is if I knew it then, if I tried to say so, to offer to keep him company, for example, and if I did, if he refused me . . . in short if I could have done anything to prevent what happened next.

Enough. To think like this is to ditch the code by which I've always lived which is that 'what ifs' are a waste of breath. I said as much to Natasha today. I said: it doesn't matter what Boris Aleksandrovich could have done or your new husband either: what's done is done, I said. Accept it. That's what I told her, but even though she nodded, I know she didn't really understand. She has a long way to go, that one.

Not that I blame her. There are few people in this world who stand above the others but Kolya was such a one. A real innocent he was and, yes, I know innocence is overrated especially in these times of ours, but Kolya's innocence was genuine and he was also genuinely sweet. As a matter of fact I used to think that Natasha (another innocent but one whose innocence expressed itself in her paying no attention to anybody that didn't interest her) wasn't good enough for him. But recently, since I've got to know her better, my hopes for her have risen. She could amount to something, that one, not a hero of the Soviet Union, perhaps, but a decent person and there are precious few of them around.

A little more growing up is what she needs. And a lot of luck. She's too strong-willed. She sits here, in my kitchen, for the most part barely speaking, but she doesn't need to speak to reveal some of the dark thoughts passing through her mind. I worry about her. I worry that, once she's come out of the hole of her grief, something she's showing every sign of, she'll do something that will get her into trouble.

I've made a promise to myself. I'll keep watch on her. A careful watch. That's what I've learned from Anton Antonovich's death.

The End of Spring

Catching hold of the corner of the page Natasha's grand-mother carefully turns it over, and there at last is the picture for which she has been searching. Stretching out a finger that is gnarled by arthritis and trembling with age, she lightly touches the album.

'There.' She is drawing Natasha's attention to a sepia-stained daguerreotype, a portrait of a man whose well-starched shirt ends high up on a stout, strong neck, and whose face is dominated by his twirled moustache, his high cheekbones, his broad forehead and his hard staring eyes: 'That's your papa,' she says.

'Not my Papa.' Sitting at the table close to the old woman, Natasha smiles at her: 'Yours.'

Her grandmother starts, her rheumy eyes blinking in confusion. 'Yes,' she says and repeats it: 'Yes,' as if she's trying to convince herself and it seems to work for her voice sounds out stronger when as she says: 'You're right, of course. Papa. Your great-grandfather.' Closing the book she begins slowly to stand up. 'Don't take any notice of me, Natashka, I am a foolish old woman who grows increas-ingly more stupid with age.'

'You'll never be stupid.' Natasha hugs her grandmother, thinking as she does so how thin her grandmother feels and how frail. 'Why don't you rest in your chair?'

They move together, arm in arm, a reversal of another duo when it was the grandmother who used to lead the child. And now, Natasha thinks as she helps her grandmother into her favourite easy chair, Natasha is herself a mother and twice married while her grandmother, despite Natasha's denial, does seem to be sinking into a state of dependency and childishness, this woman who has always lived by the seasons, by the need to plant in spring, hoe in summer, harvest and bottle in the autumn and, in winter, to warm and clean, and who is now moving into her own twilight, for which there will one day be no further spring.

'There.' Having plumped up the pillows, Natasha settles herself down at her grandmother's feet, and for a while all they do is sit.

Time passes, Natasha sitting, thinking that here at last she can feel herself at peace. She lets her gaze range round this living room on Nevsky, this place where she grew up, taking in the sumptuousness of its accumulated possessions, thinking what a contrast it makes to her own spartan surroundings. And then she just sits without further thought, feeling her grandmother's bird-like fingers gently stroking her hair, until her grandmother finally breaks the silence to say:

'You are good to me, Natasha.'

Natasha smiles. It's a long time since she has felt so calm.

'He was good to me as well,' she hears. 'My father was. In his own fashion. He was a handsome man. And a stern one. He kept a tight rein on us girls. But he was decent. He always put his family first.' The old woman's eyes mist over, perhaps with tears, perhaps merely with the effort of conjuring up the past. 'All dead now,' she says.

Natasha's eyes seem also to be smarting. She shuts them tight, she who never cries, and swallows hard but now for the second time in as many days she doesn't succeed in stopping the words that spring to her tongue so she says:

'Do you think the dead can speak?' and hearing her grandmother's bewildered: 'Hmm?' she tries to explain what she doesn't herself understand. She says:

'Do you think it's possible that I can hear Kolya's voice?' as she thinks that in this idea – Kolya's talking from the grave – might lie the explanation for her disrupted nights and anxious days, and, thinking that her grandmother, who is closest to the grave, might know whether this could be true, and so she wills her grandmother to answer, not just the question, but all that the question implies.

But she has asked too much. Her grandmother just continues to look down on her, smiling so kindly that Natasha really does want to cry, and then her grandmother holds one bony finger up to her own lips, saying:

'Ssshh now . . .'

When her husband tried to shush Natasha, he just managed to provoke her. Now she finds herself comforted by the sound that, issuing from her grandmother's lips, summons up a childhood of her grandmother rocking her to sleep, or holding her after a bad dream, and she is seized by a desire once again to enfold herself in that embrace and be lulled by the serenity that comes from the abrogation of all responsibility and even as she wishes for this she knows it cannot be.

Her grandmother is too old. Natasha is as well. She, who now has a child, can no longer be the child she was. And besides: looking back she sees that her grandmother, having shut her eyes, has sunk immediately into sleep, as only the very old or the very young can do.

Natasha can no longer remember what it felt like to be a child. Something is happening to her. That rationality that has recently ruled her life is disintegrating. Rationality told her to marry Dmitry Fedorovich, a man she didn't love, in order to save a child she did and she had obeyed it – she had married Dmitry. And that same rationality forbade her from broaching the subject of Kolya with Dmitry, and for three long years she listened to it, that rationality that no longer works. It had made her pack her memories of Kolya away, and for a while she did, but now she finds his image sketched in her mind's eye and she cannot stop herself from thinking not only about the things he did and the way he was when he was alive, but also about the things he might have done and the person he would have become if he hadn't died. As if the dead Kolya has come back; as if he were talking to her now; as if the dead could speak.

She has learned about the dead. Since Kolya died, she has been caught up in that dark place. Going through the motions of living, she cut off all feeling save that small piece she reserved for Katya. And now, suddenly, for no reason she can understand, the shroud that enveloped her has lifted and she sees herself anew, a stranger, irrevocably changed and living with a stranger, a woman whom Kolya, who had only ever known the girl, would not have recognised, a woman with neither the power to move on nor the strength to hold back the past, a woman who, realising all this, sits at her sleeping grandmother's feet, her head touching her knees, her shoulders shaking with the effort of keeping back the onslaught of her dammed-up grief.

She is no longer drawn to this family. Her grandmother – yes – for her grandmother is old and might not be with them long and Natasha knows what it is to lose someone without having the chance to say goodbye. But as to the rest of the family: well, Ilya, never the most communicative of brothers, is now almost totally wrapped up in his music, while Mama, who was initially so outspoken in her opposition to Kolya, seems to dislike Natasha's alliance with Dmitry even more and as for Papa: well, there's something about the way he looks at her these days, or, perhaps more accurately, about the way he doesn't look at her, that unsettles her. And so she visits only in the daytime, when they're all likely to be out.

Which means she must leave now, before they all return. She gets up quietly and hears a door open and then her father's voice.

'Yes. That's right,' she hears. 'She ended up marrying Dmitry Fedorovich.'

Her father talking about her, but to whom? She stands and holds her breath, listening to the murmured reply of another man, but it's no good, she can't make out his identity.

Papa sounds out again: 'Not at all. The arrangement seems to suit her.'

That galvanises her. She takes another step at the same time as she wonders what kind of an arrangement Papa thinks her marriage is, listening to him saying:

'And now, Jack . . .'

Jack, she thinks. The American? Jack Brandon?

'. . . to get back to what you were saying. I realise it must be frustrating . . .'

Yes, it must be the American, and yes, it is, for the two men have moved closer and when Jack speaks not only does she recognise his accent and his voice, but she can also make out what he is saying:

'It's not just frustrating – it's criminal. We've been warning your lot for more than a year, and now the Germans are just across the border at Memel. Their tanks are massing. And yet nothing is being done . . .'

What's Jack doing here, she thinks, as she hears her father:

'Of course there's something being done.' Papa is speaking in that voice, loud and simultaneously expressionless. She hates it when he talks that way. It reminds her how, unlike most of his comrades, he has managed to survive and even prosper, and this despite the impediment of a daughter who was married to an enemy of the people, and, thinking this, she remembers how it was when she had gone to ask whether she should marry Dmitry Fedorovich. She remembers that moment of his shocked reaction and then, quickly, his change in expression that she had then thought indecipherable but now, reliving it, she sees it as a kind of calculation – his working out what her alliance with Dmitry Fedorovich would do for him? – and thinking this she keeps on walking, forward into the present, as she hears her father saying:

'But you have to understand how we got to this point. Don't forget: we did try for an alliance with Britain and France. They treated us with contempt. Britain didn't even bother to send a politician to the talks, just some functionary of the King's that nobody's ever heard of. They forced us into this uneasy truce with Hitler. But that doesn't mean we can't see what kind of man this Hitler is. In fact . . .'

And there she is, walking into the vestibule, tripping forward, dissembling, smiling as she has learned to do even when there is nothing for her to smile about, and saying:

'Jack: when did you get back?' passing her father to go up to the American and kiss him on the cheek, and then stepping back to say:

'My, you look smart. Did you get your factory back?'

Both men are made awkward by her appearance, her father bearing that familiar look of shock, while Jack, who also appears stunned by the sight of her, pushes back the edge of his hat to say:

'No. Some people in the States asked me to talk to some people here,' and then taking one step back he looks her up and down and says, between his teeth as if what he'd really like to do is whistle:

'You're looking good, Natasha,' which pleases her perhaps because she suspects it will annoy her father, her playing the coquette like this with Jack, something she never thought she could do, but after all she is twice married and independent of a father's control, and so she says:

'Thank you, Jack. And now I'm afraid I've got to go.'

'You won't stay, even for moment?' This from Papa who's looking at her with such sad longing that it makes her wonder whether he misses her, and for a moment she feels her attitude to him softening, but then she thinks, that's the problem with 'arrangements', they have effects. And she says, breezily:

'Sorry, I can't. I'm in a hurry,' and, saying that, she whirls past both men, thankful that it is almost summer and her outdoor shoes are easy to put on. She wrenches open the door and, lets herself out, and, closing it, stands leaning against it, because she is, oddly, trembling.

On the Neva

Of all the buildings in Leningrad, St Isaac's Cathedral is the most clearly visible from any point in town. Grandly it sits, its hefty brown marble columns rising high, its dome heavy above two dozen tall statues greened by age and neglected, as is this whole construction which, once designed for the worship of God, is now a monument to atheism, dominating not only the city but also its own elegant square not far from Nevsky. And it is in this square, on one side of the cathedral, that the Astoria hotel is sited.

Standing by the window of his Astoria room, Jack Brandon is looking out on St Isaac's Square in summer. The square he seems to see, however, rather than being saturated by the brilliant light of summer is lit by the memory of an altogether different season – by winter – and by the hard reflected white blue of piled-up snow, a vista that dates back to the last time Jack stood here in this place. Then he had been waiting for Masha. In vain: she never did turn up. Now, standing in the same spot, he remembers how devastated he'd believed himself to be, and how convinced that what he felt for her was, if not real love, then at least real passion. But now, seven years later, he sees his reaction for what it more likely was: wounded pride, or (as Boris Aleksandrovich presumed) misguided chivalry. Not that he wishes Masha ill. He hopes she's well and living somewhere in the Soviet Union with a husband and three plump children, not, he can't help thinking, that Masha, with her taste for Parisian fashion and expensive stockings, was an obvious candidate for contented matriarch. But goodwill aside, he neither misses nor yearns for Masha.

For Natalya Borisovna, however, his feelings seem completely different. Since he bumped into her at Boris's apartment, he hasn't been able to get her out of his mind. That he found her attractive is no surprise: he was always much taken by Natasha. But this time the sight of her provoked two thoughts: the first, that Natasha was no longer a girl, and the second, that it didn't matter where they met or how much she changed, he would always know her.

Even now, as he looks out with newly focused eyes, he sees a small figure darting through the knots of people in St Isaac's Square, and although the figure is very distant he immediately thinks: Natasha. He tells himself it cannot be – wishful thinking must have conjured her up – but as he thinks this he is simultaneously pushing against the window, meaning to open it and call to her.

The window's stuck: he can't get it to budge. Fortuitously, he thinks, as he stands watching the figure disappearing round the corner, knowing that to call to a Russian woman from the Astoria window would be ill advised. Probably it wasn't Natasha anyway, he thinks; it can't have been, but even as this thought occurs he has already turned from the window and is moving quickly across the room, making for the door.

She is far enough away. She makes herself slow down. She had been walking fast, almost on the point of running through the square but now she's turned the corner there is no need. She stops and takes a few long breaths.

All around are people strolling in the sunshine, or sitting to drink brightly coloured sodas and eat Eskimo pies. The chill with its apparently interminable fog that gripped Leningrad through winter and long into spring has finally lifted, and the June sky is a clear, light blue and almost entirely free of clouds.

June: once her favourite month and yet when did she last feel this good? Not for a long time. Nor for the past four years. And now life is beginning to return.

She has spent the morning walking happily outdoors, caught up in the physical sensation of movement and in the scents of summer, the sweetness of flowering jasmine, the heady smell of lilacs on the brink of decay. Now she heads for the river, thinking what an act of lunacy it was for her to have contemplated stepping into the Astoria to see if Jack Brandon was staying there. Such an act of folly would have brought her to the attention of the authorities. It was lucky that something, Irina Davydovna's internalised voice perhaps, for Ira is always warning her to be careful, or the conspicuous disapproval on the faces of the men who guard the Astoria doors, was enough to turn her off course and send her scurrying across the square.

She didn't actually set out with the intention of calling on Jack. She was walking aimlessly, her feet going where her mind would not, leaving the Moika and leading her through the streets to St Isaac's Square and, almost, into the Astoria. And now as she hurries away, the relief that she knows she should feel at having saved herself from doing anything so foolhardy is tinged by a sensation of regret she doesn't fully understand.

It is Natasha. He follows her, keeping pace while still

maintaining a respectable distance. She's headed in the general direction of the Aleksandrovsky Gardens, or at least that's what he first assumes, but when she continues on through Decembrist Square, he realises she must be making for the Neva. He watches her as she weaves through the crowd, seeing how she walks, straight-backed but with her head slightly dipped as if she's hoping she won't be noticed. So different from the Natasha of old, he thinks, who, although she never appeared to be pushing herself forward, always seemed to be in view.

He almost calls her then, but something stays his tongue. A foreboding, perhaps. A consciousness that she, who's had enough trouble, doesn't need to get into any more. Let her go, he tells himself.

He stands and watches as the distance between them grows wider.

At the oversize statue of the Bronze Horseman she pauses to glance up at its imposing bulk. In a moment, he knows, she'll be off again, crossing the wide road and then walking along the banks of the Neva. When that happens, he thinks, I won't follow any more. He stands, watching her, willing her to turn round.

She doesn't turn.

She's about to go on. He doesn't stop to think. Stepping forward, he calls:

'Natasha.'

The sight of Jack Brandon makes Natasha shiver, although she would be at a loss to explain why.

He leans forward, about to kiss her on the cheek. She averts her face. Whereas she was happy to kiss him in front of her father, out here in the open feels too exposed. She offers him her hand instead, following it with the first words that come to her: 'You're not so smart today.'

He shrugs. 'That was only to impress.'

'To impress who? Me?'

'No.' Although he intended to laugh what comes out of his mouth sounds more like embarrassment than laughter. 'It was put on specially for a meeting. I don't dress like that all the time.'

'I see. And what are you doing here?'

'I saw you and . . .'

'No. I mean what are you doing here in Leningrad?'

'Oh.' He is awkward: thrown off balance. He had followed partly because of her familiarity, but now having her close makes him understand that she's no longer quite the person he knew. She's a woman and one who has survived, not only childbirth, but also a deeper pain.

'Jack?' She is looking at him quizzically.

He has held on to the silence too long.

'I'm here for – what's the official name for them? – oh yes . . . you call them consultations. There's a war in Europe and it will come here,' garbling out those same sentences that have issued from his mouth continually since he's been back and that have been met by a variety of responses ranging from rank denial on the part of the most blinkered, to guilty acknowledgement by men like Boris who know that war is coming but who, because of official dogma, cannot risk saying so. Natasha's reaction, however, stands out from all the others', not because of what she says, because she doesn't actually say anything, but because she does nothing to suppress the flashing of her eyes that seems to signal either defiance or wilfulness, as if, he thinks, what she'd really like to say is: well, then, let there be war, and thinking this, he blurts out:

'I was sorry to hear about Kolya.'

There: he has done what his embassy had warned him

not to do – named an unperson – and now he watches Natasha for her reaction.

She doesn't have one. Not at first. She looks at him, her face so immobile he marvels at the sight. She looks for so long, he begins to grow conscious of the sun beating through his jacket and then, finally, when he is beginning to think that their conversation must be over, she gives the faintest nod, before saying, in a voice every bit as blank as her expression:

'That's my most favourite section of the Neva, over there, just beyond the Admiralty. Come, I'll show it to you,' and, without waiting for a reply, turns and walks away.

He follows.

At the edge of the road she stops. So does he. They wait for a car to pass, and, waiting, he feels the force of her, radiating out more strongly than this early summer's sun.

'Now,' she says and she steps out.

Reaching the embankment on the other side, instead of going right towards what is conventionally regarded as the most beautiful section of Leningrad, she turns left, heading away from the centre, and away from the crowds, walking with determination, her head held high.

He follows.

Down a set of steps near the bridge that links this part of the city to Vasilevskiy Island they go, until, finally, at the bottom, by the water's edge, she stops.

He also stops and stands there, his gaze taking its lead from her, the two of them staring at the waters of the Neva, the syrupy ink of its viscous water, its top layer ruffled by a warm wind, its quilted surface smelling strongly of the open sea, and he almost feels himself pulled down into its oily depths.

'That's where Kolya proposed to me,' he hears and, wrenched up from the river's depths, he sees Natasha is pointing at the nearby bridge, their eyes meeting in the moment of his astonishment, before she says:

'Or don't you think Soviet citizens would ever do anything so romantic?'

The way she phrases the questions sounds as if she's teasing but there is no laughter in her voice. 'Kolya,' she says, 'asked me to marry him up there,' before dropping her hand, limply, to her side.

He was wrong before. It is not that Natasha has been changed because she is now a woman, or because she has been marked by grief; what's happened is she has lost that easy exterior of hers, or perhaps, he thinks, what she has really lost is her innocence, and, thinking this, he feels terrible sadness. He reaches out and gently touches her on the cheek.

She pulls him to her.

Is this what happened? Did she pull him to her and, in the gesture's aftermath, forget what she had done?

Thinking about it afterwards, she can't remember how it happened. What she can remember is that they were close. So close – almost unbearably so.

And she can remember something else as well, the press of her body against him, her mouth exploring his, her breasts against his chest, her nipples pressed against her clothes and his, and she feels her connection to him hard enough to burn but it is a burning that draws her in, feeling him grow big, his tongue opening up the cavern of her mouth, and she wants to go even deeper, to burrow inside him if she can, to lose herself in the intensity of this sensation she has not experienced for what feels to be longer than a lifetime but which she knows is just the time that has elapsed since Kolya's life was ended, this thing that is much more than passion, this thing that she had buried, this thing called feeling. It is a feeling that can no longer be held back and it overrides Jack's effort to pull away and so she draws him closer, pushing down her trousers and unbuttoning his, seeing her wild disregard reflected in his eyes, and then feeling him inside her, this stranger pumping life, herself jammed by him against the wall, his head blocking out the light, both of them driven as much now by passion as by the knowledge of the danger they are in, carried forward by the storm of a grief that is as animal as this coupling, so that she calls out, her voice eerie in this open space, his face wet like hers, she rocking him and being rocked until at last what they have done is over and the sound subsides.

Married Life

She sees Jack when she can, the two of them searching out dark crevices in the city where they can be alone and unobserved. It isn't easy, especially when the sun is out – for the first time in her life, she finds herself wishing for rain – and yet somehow they have managed it.

She knows the danger she is running, if not from Dmitry then from his state. She knows that she should stop. She can't. With Jack she is different. With him she feels alive not only when they're making love, but also when they just sit together watching the slant of this gentle summer's rain and seeing the shafts of watery light that gradually filter through its mist.

For the rest of the time, when she's not with Jack, she continues with a way of life that, until recently, she considered normal but that she now sees is anything but normal. She looks after Katya, laughing with her more than she used to, and she also performs her other duties, keeping the house and, most importantly of all, servicing Dmitry Fedorovich (which is the way she thinks of it). And here she is again, standing by the stove, stirring *kasha*, as she has done almost every morning during the last three years. Her

husband is sitting where he also always does – by the table –
while Katya, who has already been fed, is waiting patiently
in the other room. And so Natasha stirs the pot without
looking at Dmitry, not because experience had taught her
to avert her gaze, but rather to conceal the flush that she
knows must light up her expression when she thinks, as
she is thinking now, of Jack.

She thinks about the places she could show Jack, thinking
that if the sun keeps shining they could go walking, no need
to talk or draw attention to themselves, but walk compan-
ionably together and then, as she is thinking this, Dmitry
changes the habit of his married life never to speak at breakfast, by suddenly saying:

'I'll be away for a few days.'

She's so surprised she looks up and she can't stop herself,
she smiles, and then, to cover up her smile says: 'I see,'
before quickly looking down again, thinking that she will
not think of what she can do while he's away, or at least, she
will not think of it now.

'Don't you want to know where I'm going?' His tone
puts her on guard. She raises her head and sees he is looking intently in her direction, his thin face set in an even
more forbidding frown than usual and she thinks – does he
know? – and thinking this she wants to shrink away, to
leave the room. But of one thing she is certain: she must not
show him that she is scared, not when it comes to this, and
so, instead, she says, even-toned:

'You don't usually like questions about your movements.'

He gives a quick nod, adding verbal confirmation: 'That's
true.' Subject closed. He picks up his empty plate.

For a man who does so little domestic labour he is always
very neat about the house. He walks over to the counter
and puts the bowl carefully down in the sink before moving

on to the next section of his daily routine. It's something that he always does, and something she's learned to ignore, but now she finds herself mesmerised by this habitual pouring out of water into another bowl, and by the way he proceeds to wash his hands, carefully, as he always does, and so she stands, watching the broad span of his thick fingers spread wide as he soaps them, each in order and in turn, and as she does so she continues to stand, she, Natalya Borisovna Anninskaya, watching her husband's, those stranger's, hands, at the same time as she also seems to be seeing a reprise of another's hands. Jack's hands. Jack caressing her, tracing the line of her neck, and down again to her breasts, his fingers grazing her skin, not claiming it as Dmitry Fedorovich does, but exploring it, guided as much by her reaction as by his instinct, his hand not stopping abruptly as Dima's does as if duty has been served, but going where the feeling leads her, him following the line of her belly and of her hips until the pleasure for which her body reaches out takes on its own life and takes her with it as well, so that for once what she is conscious of is not what happened and what cannot be undone but only this moment.

'Natasha!'

Startled, she refocuses her eyes to find that Dima, who has finished his ablutions, is standing and holding out his hands. She knows exactly what he is after – this, too, is part of his routine – and she knows he expects her to supply it.

She picks up the towel and takes it to him, handing it over and continuing to stand close but not too close as he also likes her to do, waiting for him to dry his hands. He does this meticulously as well, while she stands, mesmerised again, wondering whether he washes and dries his hands like this before coming home from work, and thinking that he must, for his hands are always clean by the time he gets back, and then she hears his voice again:

'What's the matter with you?' those words barked out so ferociously that she says automatically: 'I'm sorry,' although she's not sure what she's done wrong, but then she sees that he is holding out the towel as he has probably been doing for a while and she thinks, as she reaches for it, that she must be more careful.

She takes hold of the towel and as she does she hears him saying:

'You're not yourself these days,' and although she was expecting him to yield up the towel, he keeps his grip on it as he continues:

'You need to get a job.'

'A job?' She looks up, across the piece of material that fastens them together. 'A job?'

'You don't think you should work?'

'But you were the one who told me not to.'

'That was then,' he says. 'This is now,' which is vintage Dmitry Fedorovich, the notion that he might have been wrong in prohibiting her from working transmuted into the objective reality of 'then' and 'now', and for a moment she wants to shout out and tell him, at least this once, how difficult he is but then she tells herself he's offering her something she would dearly love, it's not in her interests to give him an excuse to take it back, and so instead she says:

'At the Marinsky?'

'The Kirov, you mean.'

'Of course. I'm sorry, Dima,' she says eagerly. 'Can I go back to the Kirov?' too eagerly, she realises, as she hears his firm:

'No. Not the Kirov.'

'But, Dima . . .'

'A theatre is not a suitable venue for the mother of a young child. You cannot work at night,'

And, of course, he's right.

'You could find some other useful work,' he says, and she knows what 'useful' is to him, this thought confirmed as he adds: 'In an office. Or a factory,' and then, as if he can read her thoughts, says, icy-voiced: 'There is dignity in such labour.'

She knows that tone. She has heard it often. It's his way of telling her what he thinks about her, that she's been too indulged. What made him marry her, this man who seems to hate not only the Marinsky but also everything else she has ever loved, and not only everything but everybody as well, including, she sometimes even thinks, her father, for she has caught Dmitry looking at Papa. To a stranger's eye Dmitry Fedorovich's expression might have seemed set at neutral; she knows him well enough by now to read in its appearance not only his contempt but also something stronger – another version of his hatred, the kind the strong may feel towards the weak. Papa has indeed been weakened and is showing signs of struggling to hold on to his position – that's why he can't look her in the face these days – and thinking this she comes to, to see Dmitry Fedorovich still standing close, connected by a towel.

She tries to take it.

He resists.

She gives a tug. He holds hard his grip and, aware not only of his strength but also of his will, she knows she won't be able to wrest it from him, and so she just lets go.

For a moment he stands there, towel hanging limply, and she thinks, I've won – a tiny victory but nevertheless victory – but then he releases the towel and it drops and there it lies between them on the floor, both of them looking down, until that moment when she hears his voice:

'Pick it up,' commanding her as he has done, incessantly, throughout these last few years, instructing her not only how to behave but also what to feel, that voice which she has had no choice but to hear and to obey, and to do so gratefully.

'Pick it up,' and she, who has done everything he has told her to, now wonders what it would be like to refuse, to shake her head, and say:

'*You dropped it. You pick it up,*' hearing her own voice sounding out, strong, as it hasn't done for years. She imagines his astonishment and his standing there, open-mouthed, the towel something much more than a towel, lying between them at their feet, her gaze the one to burn into his, her force the one to be felt and . . .

And thinking this, she is engulfed by a fear the like of which she has not felt since those early days, just after Kolya's death, when every knock on the door, every stranger's gaze and every snatch of conversation had seemed to herald danger. This fear has gradually abated since her marriage to Dmitry Fedorovich, to be replaced by an emotion which she once took for a sense of security but which she now thinks was merely the absence of all emotion. She feels for him not gratitude but hatred for all his kind, for what they have done to her and to Kolya. Possessed by this emotion more ferocious than any she has ever felt, she stands, feeling this, but when he says:

'Pick it up.'

She does what he demands. She bends down, and picks up the towel.

That pleases him. He smiles and then he nods and, without a word, he turns and walks over to the door while, watching him, she wonders whether he can feel her hatred, and just before he is about to go out, she says:

'Dima,' and sees how he turns, abruptly, but no, he is Dmitry Fedorovich, ignorant of her needs, he cannot know how she is feeling, and he looks at her, as he normally does, without expression, his face unaltered as she says:

'I'll stay with Irina Davydovna while you're away.'

'Not with your parents?'

'No. At Ira's. Katya will benefit from Anya's company.'

Visitors (1)

There is a question that keeps repeating itself in my mind. It hits when I'm least expecting it. When I'm on all fours, for example, polishing a corridor; or when I'm queueing for meat and trying to make sure the best cuts aren't all gone before my turn; or even, strangely enough for someone who is such a good sleeper, when I'm asleep. Then I wake up with a question pressing down on me. A question: What was I supposed to do?

What was I supposed to do?

It started with a visit from Natasha. About two weeks ago it was when she turned up, out of the blue. Hearing a loud knock at the door, I called out, 'Who is it?' When I heard her voice I didn't think anything of it. She has the habit of dropping in. But after I opened up the door, I should have known she was up to something. To be honest I did kind of know – I just didn't guess how it would affect me.

One glance was all it took to tell me she'd been changed. She looked alive, you see, no longer sealed up in that dark place. Her head was raised as it hasn't been since Kolya was taken. As for those deep brown eyes of hers: well, they met my questioning gaze straight on and not in that beaten manner which I always dread. I remember thinking: good, it has finally happened.

I had always hoped it would. I had seen her strength. I knew that, given time and the right push, she would find her own way of coming to the light. What I'd never have guessed, however, is the route she'd take.

Would I have turned her away if I'd had an idea both of what had changed her and what she was about to ask? I have no answer for that and, now I think about it, I realise that it doesn't matter. As I am in the habit of repeating, both to myself and to Natasha: there's nothing to be gained by hindsight. In plain language: *what ifs* are a waste of breath.

She came into the kitchen – that's where we always talk – and after we'd drunk tea and made small talk about our children (funny that, me thinking of Anya as mine), and sat in companionable silence as we often do, Natasha gradually got to the point.

She came at it in a roundabout way. For a start, she asked if she and Katya could stay with me while her husband was away.

I liked the sound of that – some adult company – so I said: 'Of course you can. The company will do Anya good,' saying it carelessly even though I don't actually believe that anything – good or bad – ever makes much impression on that child.

'Thank you,' Natasha said.

I got up then. I can't remember what I did, poured water into the samovar maybe or just as likely polished it, as I often do when I'm relaxing, but after a while it dawned on me that there was something strained about the way she was holding on to the silence. It gave me notice that she had something else to say. I looked across at her.

I was right. Catching my gaze she also seized her opportunity. She said:

'Can I ask you something else?'

How did I reply? Well, to tell the truth, it makes me laugh now to think how gaily I replied. I mean, I'd already had the clue in the way she'd carried herself in and, with that in mind, only a fool would had given her permission to go on. But I am a fool and so I did:

'Ask anything you want,' I said.

Which is exactly what she did. She asked me anything, or in this case:

'Can I come here with Jack?'

That's all. No explanation. None needed. There is only one Jack in her life, and that is the American. As for the reason why she would want to spend time with him in my apartment: well, since just fraternising with an American without official permission would be (even if you were to keep on all your clothes and have me and the entire bulk of my family, dead and alive, as chaperone) every bit as dangerous as anything two people might choose to do alone, what does it matter what her reasons were?

'Can we?' she said, and, hearing the determination in her voice, I knew she understood exactly how much she was asking of me and I also knew that she wasn't going to make it easy for me to refuse.

I thought: danger.

It's a new thought, that, for me. I never used to dwell on danger's prospects. You don't, do you, when your time is taken up in maintaining life, in getting to work and back again, or wondering whether you have enough meat to add to the soup or whether your husband has drunk just enough to lose interest in you but not too much to mistake you for a punching bag? But once your horizons expand, well, then you get to see a whole new class of danger. Not that everyday danger that comes from a natural span of life, or even a dose of bad luck that might kill a man after a horse charge is done, but a much more sinister danger that hits at whole factories and neighbourhoods as well. The kind that spreads. The kind that took Kolya and, they say, thousands of other Kolyas.

And so when Natasha asked me if she and Jack Brandon could use my apartment, I'd be an even greater fool than I actually am not to answer exactly as I did, which was to say:

'I'm sorry, Natasha, but no, you can't,' and while I said this I made sure to keep my voice determined and to look at her, straight, so as to show her that I meant it.

She didn't argue. She nodded and looked down.

I told myself she was taking my 'no' well even though she couldn't hide how depressed it made her. What I should have also told myself was: well, so what? Depressed is one thing: arrested in the middle of the night and taken to who knows where, another. I should have let it lie.

I tried to. I changed the subject, rattling on for a while about the strange weather we were having, but even to my own ears it didn't sound as if I really cared.

The thing is, I had a problem, and it was this: I'd been waiting for the moment when Natasha would come alive and, now it had happened and she had mentioned Jack, I knew he must have been the reason. And it made sense: with Dmitry Fedorovich in your bed, who wouldn't think of looking somewhere else?

That's why I didn't manage to let it lie as I knew I should: I didn't want to be the excuse for her shrivelling up again. I didn't want the Dmitrys of this world to win, not hands down as they have so far won. So instead of closing down the subject as I should have done I stopped wittering on about the weather and then trapped myself by trying to justify my 'no'.

I said: 'You know what Anya's like. First sight of Jack, and she'll be reporting us all to the authorities.'

I had given Natasha a way in and she grabbed at it: 'I'll only bring him here when she's at school.'

I shook my head. I was trying to make it clear, to her and probably to myself as well, that my answer was: no. A real no.

She answered by saying:

'I understand, Ira,' and on top of that she smiled, as if to say she really did understand and was letting me off the hook.

Clever Natasha. In hindsight (the kind of which I don't approve) I know she wasn't letting me off any hook at all. She was just pretending to. She knew me so well, you see, better it seems than I knew her. She was reeling me in and I, with mouth wide open, came easily.

I said: 'But where else will you meet?'

'Don't worry,' she said: 'we'll find somewhere,' although she and I both know that there are no 'somewheres' in our city – not if you don't count the outdoors and even Natasha isn't foolhardy enough to allow herself to be so exposed. But apart from some deserted open space – and at this time in summer nowhere is deserted – there is no place where a Russian woman might take an American man: not without their every move being noted down.

Her apartment, you say, if Dmitry Fedorovich is away? Absolutely not. In such a poky place there would be no chance of escaping detection.

Her parents' apartment then? No again: if Boris Aleksandrovich ever found out, he would personally kill Jack Brandon. Which left only my apartment: and I could see her point. My place is ideal. I have a front entrance that is mostly used and another one at the back – a bit like Kirov's place, now I come to think about it – which is much more hidden.

'It shouldn't become your problem, Ira,' Natasha said.

Clever girl, she who used to be so naïve. She's learned some cunning since – anybody would, I guess, being married to Dmitry Fedorovich – and the mark of this is, as it was beginning to dawn on me, that despite what she had just said, it actually was my problem.

In the past it wouldn't have been. In the past I would have just said: nothing to do with me, and having said that I would have let the whole thing go.

Nothing to do with me. That's the way I used to think: I had no power and therefore no right to act. But somewhere along the line – a combination of the *Chelyuskin* and Anton Antonovich, I guess – I have lost that ability and instead find myself hamstrung by what might happen.

I stood and I thought: if Natasha and Jack went where there was no one to watch out for them, then disaster would follow. And if that happened, I thought, Katya would lose a mother, just as she has already lost a father. She might even lose her life: it's been known. And where would all that leave me?

In the same place that Anton Antonovich's suicide had left me, that's where. Wondering.

That's what I was thinking as Natasha sat patiently, waiting for my answer (smart girl, she didn't try to prompt me). I was thinking about Anton Antonovich first of all and, after that, I had a different thought.

There's war in Europe, that's what I thought, and furthermore, I thought, if the rumours are to be believed war will eventually come here. And then what? And then I thought: if nobody in our society can find the courage to defy, how will we survive?

Yes. Exactly. It surprised me, as well, to catch myself thinking such grand thoughts. That's not the way I, who used to think of myself as somebody who watches and never acts, once thought. And now look at me: deciding on what to do about Natasha by thinking of a distant war! Just shows what they say is true: your circumstances do decide your consciousness. And my circumstances have changed. I've come a long way. The fact that I now have charge of an apartment that anybody might want to use to put us all in danger is testimony to this. So:

'Yes,' I said.

She, wanting more than a simple yes, continued to look at me. Told you she was clever. She wanted confirmation.

Which I gave to her. 'Yes,' I said, 'you can bring Jack here.'

That was it. Decision made. Decision acted on. And so she and Katya came to stay, and Jack Brandon to visit when the children were gone, and, now, as we move towards the third week in June and Dmitry Fedorovich is back, they come to visit, she and Jack Brandon, during the day.

They're here now. I thump the iron down on to the board and hear it hissing, and thump it again, covering any sound that might be coming from my bedroom. Yes – that's where I put them. It was that, or Anton Antonovich's room, and I could hardly put them there.

Could I?

They lie together, side by side.

Natasha is still, her eyes closed, her breathing so soft and regular she could be asleep.

Propped up on an elbow, Jack drinks in the sight of her. He can feel the touch of her, not yet a memory but still a felt reality that lingers on his skin, and he can also taste her on his lips. For a moment, he shuts his eyes, and thinks of making love to her as he has just done, and then he thinks that being with her has forever changed the experience of what making love could be.

Each time they meet it is different, each moment unlike

the one that preceded it. They talk sometimes but most often they communicate by feel. Occasionally they will repeat the ferocity of that first sexual encounter by the Neva, but in the main they are gentle with each other. As they have just been, his body inside hers, her widening eyes fastened on to his, the two made one, and now that they are separate again, Jack thinks, he can taste her, not only on his lips, but in his heart as well. He opens his eyes.

She was not asleep before. Now, as if they are still joined, her body tuned to his movements, even the flicker of his lashes, she looks up. Her gaze is clear and sure and fearless, and seeing this and seeing her smiling, it comes to him what he has always known but not expressed, even to himself, that he loves her, and has done from the start although he didn't realise it until this moment, now, and thinking this, he straightaway puts the thought into words, saying:

'I love you,' and when she answers, easily: 'I love you too, Jack,' he adds: 'I mean it.'

A pause. She swallows. He can see her throat fluttering. Her gaze stays fixed to his, unwavering, and he thinks: I want to spend my life with her as he hears her saying:

'Do you?'

He nods. And whispers: 'Yes.'

She doesn't speak. Not that it matters. He has put what he knows to be the truth into words. For the moment, that's all that matters.

He leans towards her and kisses her, feeling her arms coming up around him, and her mouth opening, the two of them moving together again.

They never arrive together. They don't leave together either. That's part of our agreement. She comes and goes through the front entrance, while he uses the back. She always leaves first: he waits until she's gone and then he waits a little longer so that if anybody was watching both exits they'd find it hard to connect the two.

I walk her out. I always do that as well. Can't have them standing on the doorstep, can I, for one of my neighbours to see? And, besides, I like taking her to the door. Even though she's usually in a hurry to get back home, it gives us at least a little time to chat, something we don't do much of these days: she's far too busy with Jack Brandon. Not that I'm complaining. I miss her company, that's certainly true, and her conversation, but I don't miss what she was. I prefer what she has become – the liveliness returned to her.

Now I hold the door open as I always do. I expect her to go – she is later than usual and I know she must pick Katya up – but instead of walking through, she stops. I can guess why. There is something she wants to tell me.

Some things I no longer want to know, I think, and jump in quickly with:

'Be careful you're not late, Natasha. You don't want to give Dmitry Fedorovich any reason to be suspicious,' and hearing myself saying that, I wonder at it. It's not like me to interfere or to tell her how to safeguard herself against Dmitry Fedorovich. I wonder: did I just warn her off because I had a clue of what she is about to say?

Maybe so – but if I had thought I could, that way, stop her saying it, I was wrong.

'He says he loves me.'

I know she means Jack Brandon and not her husband although I also know that this statement could equally apply to both. I am suddenly quite cold and yet, despite this, and despite the mournful tone of her voice, I can't stop myself from smiling. Silly girl, is what I'm thinking: as if I needed to be told. She shouldn't either: it's been obvious both in the way Jack Brandon looks at her and in the gentleness of his touch, even when I am present, that his feelings are strong. Just sex, maybe? I'd say not. I know a thing or two about men and their needs – you can't help that if you've lived my kind of life – and I can see that for Jack Brandon, the sex part of it is both a pleasure and a shaming thing, that they have to meet like this, in private, the bed calling because of lack of space and time. He wants her, this I can see, not only bodily but in everything.

She, however, hasn't noticed.

I look at her to see her watching me. She's waiting for my reply. I don't really know what to say, so I stick to the obvious. To convention. I say:

'And do you love him?' even though I could have bet my life on how she'd answer that and I would have been right for here she is saying what I predicted:

'I don't know.'

I know she doesn't know. That she can't know. And I know something else as well: if she can bring herself to love again, if she can open herself up to it, then it will be Jack Brandon that she loves. This I know.

None of this do I say out loud.

I have three good reasons for my caginess. One: I know it's none of my business. Two: I can see she's not ready to understand. And three, and most importantly of all: I fear for her. I fear that if she ever faces the fact she loves Jack Brandon, well, that's where real danger lies.

The Announcement

Natasha has stayed too long with Jack and now she and Katya are very late. Gripping the child tightly, Natasha hurries along.

'Mama,' she hears.

She looks down to see Katya crying and, by the look of the dark streaks running almost the length of her face, she must have been crying for some time. Natasha stops and, crouching down, her face level with her daughter's, resists the urge to cry also, not just for Katya's pain but for the fact that she, and her self preoccupation, have been its cause.

'Come, my Katyenka, I'll carry you.'

Seeing the flaring of Katya's eyes (there's an amber fleck in one of them, just as there used to be in one of Kolya's), she knows Katya is worried about what her new papa will say for Dmitry Fedorovich has, amongst his other household decrees, made it clear that the carrying of a six-year-old, no matter how tired she might be, fosters dependence and is therefore wrong, Natasha whispers:

'It's okay. We won't tell him,' before scooping up the child.

Katya immediately snuggles in. She's solid (she has Kolya's build as well) and Natasha staggers slightly as she sets off, shifting Katya to redistribute her weight. Seeing how Katya is now smiling, she thinks it's good to be so close and to feel Katya's solidity and her bulk and so she goes until she is within hailing distance of their building, when she stops to let Katya down.

In that moment her mood is changed. It's as if the light which she knows will continue to shine long into this white summer's night has suddenly gone out and she is left in darkness to face the reality of her own tardiness and the fact that Dmitry Fedorovich would already have long been home. Parcelling all thoughts of Jack away, she grips Katya and they proceed together hand in hand to the front door, Natasha urging Katya in and up the stairs at the same time as she tries to work out what she's going to say to Dima Fedorovich when he asks where she has been, as he always does when she is late. She could tell him a story, she thinks, something about Katya's expedition from the coast being late, for Katya's so scared of Dima, she'd never dream of contradicting the lie, but then she thinks if she uses Katya as her alibi that would stoke the antagonism between her husband and her child. Instead, she decides to say she was out walking and had lost track of the time. Dima, despite his dutiful reiteration of his belief in the importance of cultural workers in a workers' state, actually regards all artists, Natasha included, as impractical wastrels. He will surely swallow that.

Natasha pushes open the door, and, walking through, greets her husband: 'Good evening, Dima.'

He is in his chair. Hearing her coming in and registering her greeting, he glances up briefly to say a brisk hello and that's all he bothers saying. He doesn't ask her why she's late or where she's been. She was wrong before, she realises,

he never asks her that. Not any more. Not since he came
back from his trip.

Can he know?

His head goes down again, back to his report, and she
thinks, of course not, he cannot know. She has been too careful. She gives Katya a gentle push.

'Go on. Go and get yourself ready for bed,' she says, and she
goes into the kitchen and prepares the meal.

Supper disposed of and Katya in bed, time once more
begins to slow.

Dmitry Fedorovich in his chair and Natasha in hers. He is
reading. She is pretending to. His high forehead is knitted in
concentration, his lips moving as if he is not only reading,
but also memorising the contents of his report while she
moves her eyes deliberately along the pages, her fingers
turning them over at appropriate intervals. If someone were
to ask her, however, about the book in which she is apparently so engrossed, she wouldn't know its name.

She is too busy thinking. She thinks about the contrast
between her secret life and her married one. She thinks
about the way she feels alive with Jack whereas, in her husband's company, she seems to become almost completely
inert, and then she thinks about the way time flies with Jack
while with Dima it edges forward, painstakingly slow, sitting in this chair counting the progress of each separate
moment until the time comes when she can retreat to the
solitude of their bed.

That's another recent change. She goes to bed early these
days, and alone, and is asleep, not just pretending but genuinely asleep, by the time he joins her, and, thinking this,
she thinks again: does he know?

No. It isn't possible. Dmitry Fedorovich wouldn't stand
idly by to be cuckolded by another man, especially if that

man turned out to be a foreigner. If he knew, he would have done something to stop it. Which means he cannot know.

And yet, she thinks, something in Dima has been changed.

No. It cannot be. She turns another page.

Another minute disposed of. She hears: the ticking of the clock; the clearing of Dima's throat. She looks up. He is sitting perfectly still, concentrating so hard on his report that she is free to sit and watch him and so she does, seeing him hunched up in his chair and frowning. He looks so small, she thinks, this the first time that such a thought occurs. He *is* small, she realises, or at least he is when compared to Jack. His face is thin, as well, and pale, especially in contrast to Jack's hearty complexion. Even their teeth are different: Dima's are sharp and pointed and uneven, an impoverished imitation of Jack's regular white lattice.

Another minute.

What would it be like to live with Jack, she thinks, to sit by his side at night?

Jack also imagines it. He said as much. Today. After he told her he loved her.

'Come away with me,' he'd said.

Away. It had sounded so lovely as she lay there in his arms, half-drifting into sleep, as his voice came at her again, asking:

'Will you? Will you come away with me?'

He sounded so solemn and so intent. She remembers thinking that. And she also remembers herself smiling. Her voice saying: 'Of course I will.'

'It's not a joke, Natasha.'

But not a reality either, she had thought. 'You know I can't. The moment we set out on any trip, no matter how short, somebody would be sure to tell Dmitry Fedorovich.'

'I don't mean a short trip.'

'Hmm?'

'I meant come with me. Forever. To America.'

'Me and you in America?' The absurdity made her laugh out loud.

But Jack was serious. 'Yes: you and me, Natasha. Katya as well.'

'How can you offer that? You've never even met her.'

'I don't need to meet her,' he said. 'I already know how lovely she is. I know her mother, don't I? And I knew her father. That's good enough for me.'

I knew her father. She must not cry. Not now. Not with Dmitry Fedorovich.

These tears were summonsed then, not by the pain of Kolya's loss, but by something so much sweeter. To hear Kolya's name spoken as recommendation! Kolya pronounced not in disapproval but as an endorsement; Kolya's life given value, and not only his life but the man himself, his daughter vouched for not because her stepfather had taken pity on her mother but because of her father, because of Kolya!

She looks up and she sees that other man, Dmitry Fedorovich. Sitting. He is so . . . He is so unknowing, she thinks, so ignorant of her thoughts. She sees: that furrow on his thin face. His frown of concentration. His eyes half-closed. Those lashes, the only soft thing about him, almost girlish, they are, in their thickness and cast down. He looks tired, she thinks, dead tired, and it occurs to her that she no longer senses him in bed for the simple reason that he only joins her when she is fast asleep, and thinking this, and looking at him some more, she feels neither anger nor a sense of indebtedness, but something so much softer. Pity.

To find herself pitying this man whom she has always feared? Can it be true?

Yes, she thinks, it is. Although she still does fear him, she also pities him. She pities him for her hatred and his coldness, for her betrayal and his loneliness, for his inability to feel and that blinkered superiority that seals him off from human contact. She pities him for the way he is.

How terrible to be such a man, she thinks, how desolate, and with that thought she gets up and, saying goodnight, she goes to bed.

She lies awake. Long into the night. It is too early for her to sleep. She is restless, full of desire. Light streams through the flimsy window curtains just as it will continue to do throughout the night. She cannot fight her wakefulness. She lies, consumed by energy which has no focus, lying aimlessly and impatiently, lying alone and, lying perhaps, to see when it is that Dmitry does actually come to bed. And then she can't lie any more. She gets up and goes over to the window, drawing back the curtains, and there she stands, feeling the late night air warm and still.

It is very late, the streets lit by that hazy half-light that passes for the high point of night. There are still people out, lightly dressed, and strolling easily, speaking softly to each other so that she catches a half-sentence here or a snatch of laughter there, both of them wafting up like distant memory. She leans out a little further, her gaze snagged by a couple – a young boy and a girl – on the pavement opposite, and watching them walk past, she thinks she was once such a girl, carefree and in a summer frock, her arm linked in friendship and in love, with Kolya, and it comes to her that this is the first time since he was taken that she has thought of Kolya without that deep anguish that she had thought would never go.

The boy has sensed her presence. He glances up, quickly, in her direction and then away; at the same time as he pulls his companion into the shadow of the building, saying something to hurry her, the two of them now separate from each other and scurrying anxiously away. She is sorry that she has been responsible for breaking their companionship. Stepping away from the window she goes back to bed.

For the hours that follow she continues to lie there, half-sleeping, half-awake, and in all that time Dima doesn't come. She lies, her eyes closed, wondering how he knows that she is still awake, how he senses it. She cannot understand it – Dmitry Fedorovich is not that sensitive – and then it occurs to her that perhaps he spends the night in that chair to which he has become so peculiarly attached, and thinking so, she finally, in the early morning hours, drifts slowly into sleep.

She is jolted suddenly from her unconsciousness. Her eyes open. She sees: Dima. She hears:

'Attention!'

He is by the window, a rigid silhouette against the bright light that comes streaming in. She blinks and refocuses her gaze, looking up and over his head. The sky is a clear untrammelled blue. She has overslept.

'Attention!'

What's he doing there? No matter that it is Sunday – he always goes to work.

That squawk again: 'Attention!'

Something wrong. She calls out:

'Katya?'

No answer.

A burst of music. She is out of bed, running to the door, wrenching it open, calling again: 'Katya?'

'Katya isn't there.'

'What have you done with her?'

'I haven't done anything. She went to the picnic. You were still asleep so I took her there.'

She turns, moving slowly in the certainty of her dread. She sees Dmitry Fedorovich watching her. She says: 'What happened?'

He doesn't tell her. He doesn't have to, for at that moment the music stops and a man, not Dmitry, begins to speak, his voice sounding out both in the street and from the wireless Dmitry has left on. A familiar voice it is, but strangely tentative, this voice of one of Stalin's closest, Comrade Molotov:

'Men and women, citizens of the Soviet Union, the Soviet government and its head, Comrade Stalin, have instructed me to make the following announcement. At four a.m. without declaration of war and without any claims being made on the Soviet Union, German troops attacked our country, attacked our frontier in many places . . .'

The voice telling of an invasion that Jack has long predicted. The voice urging the Soviet people to resist, this call pouring out from the loudspeakers into those shocked streets and apartments, sounding all over this vast territory of theirs, that is now overrun by German troops. That voice trembling as it relates what has happened at the same time as it tries to stir them all to action, his voice calling:

'Our cause is just. The enemy will be beaten. We shall triumph.'

Departures

Leningrad is in turmoil, the enemy close by.

Nothing, not the sharp-edged tank traps that ring the city and its surrounds, or those miles of trenches on the Luga line dug by the *leningradtsy* as bombs thudded down, or those young men who, armed with spades and hammers and homemade swords, marched straight from their factories into death, helped to slow down the invaders. And now, in this moment towards the end of August, the Germans are drawing in on one side while Finnish troops block the escape route on the other. The roads are almost completely impassable, the fighting for Mga at its height: if the Germans win the battle there, as rumour says they must, then Leningrad's last railway link to the outside world will be cut. Then the enemy can encircle her and, having secured her, deal with her at their convenience.

It is Natasha's last day in Leningrad. More than that: it is almost her last hour. She is going. She and Katya and Jack, who has already arranged three seats for them on the aeroplane to Moscow.

After that, she doesn't know. She hasn't asked. Jack will see to it.

She has told nobody she is going. Not Dmitry Fedorovich, of course not him, but not her parents either or her grandmother, or her friends. Not even Ira.

Jack has gone to the aerodrome to secure their places. She and Katya will follow only at the last minute. The other passengers will be panicked by then, Jack said; they won't dare make trouble in case it delays their going.

For the last time Natasha walks down Nevsky, on her way to pick up Katya. For the last time. Once she goes, there is no turning back. She cannot return, either in war or in peace time, for once she goes she is a traitor. An outcast. A potential source of pain and danger to everyone she knows.

She is going.

All around she sees: shops empty save for those plaster replicas of provisions that, having done good service during the famine of the early thirties, are back again, giving off a desultory air, an air of resignation and of normal life not only suspended but also in peril. The city, gearing up for war, knowing from everything it has heard that it faces a future even more terrible than its past, this prospect settling on those who are resigned to stay.

It wasn't like this when the invasion first began. Then there was energy in consumption, the shops stocked and crowded, as were the banks, with people hastening to lay in stores and money. But now that time is over, the shelves and safes unfilled, and the queues that inch forward are dulled by the knowledge that all they can acquire are those rations that have been imposed throughout the Soviet Union: 800 grams of bread a day for a worker, 400 for a dependant, and 2,200 grams of meat that is supposed to last a month.

With her morning's bread inside her, Natasha cleaves close to the edge of the pavement as she hurries through the crowd. This is all the space that is left to civilians: troops have taken over the central section of the prospect. There they go, marching to the blare of martial music, some veterans of the Finnish war, the rest raw recruits. Natasha's eyes are drawn to those young and fresh-faced men, some of them properly in step while others struggle to learn to march just as they will, soon, have to learn to fight. And also learn to die. Straight-backed they go, these braves, faces pinched in fearful anticipation and in pride, their arms swinging high in the hope perhaps that this motion will propel them, body and mind, into the part that they must play. Straight they march, eyes looking to the future and not the past which, like a bedraggled counterflow, comes limping in the opposite direction. This gaggle of the defeated and displaced is fleeing before a conquering army. They pass by, ragged families driving on the few animals that they have saved. Their faces are frozen by their losses, by their children vanished, carts overturned, limbs severed, corpses abandoned, old people dropping from exhaustion, while their eyes cannot let go of the things – shots ringing out as lines of people fall into graves that the Germans have made them dig, young men flayed before their mothers, girls hanged in public squares, villages put to fire – that they have witnessed.

War. More furious than nature. More violent when aroused. Thus have the Germans driven forward, and thus do they drive Leningrad before them. Already Hoth's Panzers are moving in, twenty-nine of Germany's best divisions ready to face fifteen weak Soviet divisions and that cannon fodder of Zhdanov's People's Draft.

Through the agony of this defeat and the certainty of the losses yet to come, Natasha keeps walking. She is heading for the river and the bridge that will lead her over to the Petrogradsky side. For the last time.

For the last time, she passes the snub solidity of the

Kazan Cathedral, now ringed by troops, steps leading down to its vast cellars, where Nevsky's most prominent air raid shelter is sited. Behind a barrier she sees girls standing, resolutely, holding their AA guns, their eyes shining at the spectacle of the military march past, their feet tapping out its rhythm, and, passing them, Natasha knows that she should be amongst their number, protecting her beloved city from its enemy. And yet she cannot. She is leaving.

Over the road she hastens, to the embankment, looking to its opposite side. She sees: traffic piling up in all directions, mangy dogs running through a heaving throng; and the spire of the Peter and Paul Fortress, no longer gleaming as it has done ever since she can remember it, but dulled by the camouflage netting that has been thrown over each one of Peter's glorious buildings, the city dimmed and blunted not by the absence of sun but by the greys and dark greens and sandbags that protect the buildings and those sculptures too big to move.

She is on her way. Leaving. Forever.

Last night, her last in the city, she climbed, after curfew, to the top of her building and there she stood – until Dmitry Fedorovich came to get her – beside the watchman and together they had watched the war.

In the beginning, she remembers, it almost felt like peace. The night was overcast and the city more sunk in silence than she can remember, and shrouded by a darkness of such intensity that it was only when she felt the watchman's arm lifting that she realised he was trying to draw her attention to something in the sky. It didn't take long for her to find out what. Following the direction of his pointing, she saw a blurring, a spreading scarlet sky, a false sunset, a dusk created not by nature but by man. By war: the black night now severed by that distant reddened burning.

The air was warm and full of smoke, that hint of

destruction, of death, far away and coming closer. And then: a sound cut through the calm. A hum that, gathering force, soon became a loud drone. Up went Natasha's gaze and the watchman's also, up into the night, as the sound intensified, and then a concentrated beam of light slashed through the blackened sky, lighting up a narrow corridor, sweeping over until it had trapped that flying thing, an ungainly insect caught in a flare, that moved in time to the movement of the aeroplane so that for a moment both made a tableau and a stream of sparkles came floating down from the aeroplane, leaflets, words blossoming out, a thing of beauty and, it seemed, of peace. Then the clouds shifted and the darkness lifted, and as the watchman cursed the depravity of the full moon, the bowels of the plane unleashed its other, much more deadly cargo which, no longer floating, fell, and falling shook the earth, a hard booming against the feeble crackle of answering AA guns, the bomb's impact far away, and yet their building seemed to shake or at least Natasha and the watchman reached out to steady each other while down in the street a whistle sounded out, and then Dmitry Fedorovich appeared and ordered Natasha in.

Inside heavy drapes mask windows crisscrossed by paper. The air is still, the room very warm.

Natasha and Dima sit together for the last time, although he doesn't know it.

They are waiting. For what? For nothing perhaps or for something: for the planes to come this way, the air raid siren to sound, the thundering to begin, and, finally, if they are lucky, for the all-clear to ring out.

Natasha sits in her chair. Dima isn't reading: he's too tired these days. He sits, quietly, seeming to gaze into nothingness and, watching him, she wonders how he will react when he discovers she is gone. Will he cry out, she wonders, in fury or in pain? Or will he summon up that cold, sure, calculating part of himself, and use it to stop her getting to Moscow and then on, across the border, and if he does that, could he possibly succeed?

Jack says not: he says the authorities have better things to occupy them than stopping one Soviet citizen from crossing over into the capitalist West. She doesn't know if Jack is right: she only knows that she must try and, knowing this, knows how much she will wound this man, her husband. She distracts herself by saying to him:

'When I was on the roof, I saw the aeroplane drop leaflets before it started dropping bombs.'

Dima nods. He knows this is what they do. It's his job to know, which means that, although the rest of the *leningradtsy* would not pick up a leaflet from the street, when Dima brought one home the other day, she was able to read it when he left the room.

'*Beat the Jews*,' she read: '*Beat the Commissars. Their mugs beg to be bashed in. Wait for the full moon. Bayonets in the earth! Surrender.*'

Reading this she thought she understood the darkening of Dima's face as he had looked upon this text, that pent-up rage targeted at those beasts, those Germans, and thinking that she saw a different Dmitry. She saw his passion for his country, his determination, and she felt it too and she thought: how can I leave?

'There was a new leaflet telling women and children to wear white so as not to be bombed,' Dima says. 'And then, do you know what the fascists did? They deliberately targeted all the old women wearing white kerchiefs in the fields. The Junkers flew specially low so as to get them. To show that they will stop at nothing.'

Saying this, he looks at her, so furiously that even though

she knows his anger is aimed not at her, she finds it difficult to withstand his gaze, especially when he continues:

'You had no right to be on the roof, Natasha, subjecting yourself like that to such unnecessary danger. You are a mother and a Soviet citizen, it is your duty to take care.'

And hearing that she thinks: how can I stay?

This morning, after she had dropped Katya off, she went back home.

Dima had already left. Alone she sat, in this place that had never really felt like home, and wrote a letter, drafting and redrafting it, trying to put the inexplicable into words and failing, so that in the end all that was left were a few curt words of explanation and two final ones: forgive me.

'Forgive me,' she wrote, and then she signed her name:

'Natasha,' and placed the letter far back on a shelf, beside the stove.

He will find it. Eventually. After it has dawned on him that she is gone.

She didn't pack. No need to, Jack said, and, besides, there would be no room on the plane. The things she needs, that Katya needs, he will buy for them. She took only photographs, pulling them from the album and putting them in an envelope: all the few she had of Kolya; the best of herself, as a young girl, standing with her parents and her brothers; one of Ira when Anton Antonovich was alive and one of Anya after Anton Antonovich's death. None of Dmitry Fedorovich. He always turns away from the camera. He does not photograph well, he says.

Her history in her pocket. Only one more thing to do. Someone she has to see. Her grandmother. That's what she's doing on Nevsky, saying goodbye not only to the city she loves but also to the old woman who had always been her constant.

She went to her parents' apartment and sat, uninterrupted since her parents were both at work, with her grandmother, clasping those bruised and parchment hands, not saying goodbye to the old woman because she couldn't tell her she was going, but listening to her murmurings. Her grandmother was talkative, savouring disaster, full of stories of an autumn prematurely arrived, of bunches of leaves, still green and moist, dropping, unready, to the ground and landing there amongst a carpet of spreading mushrooms, ahead of time. All of this was nature's way, her grandmother had insisted, of prophesying doom that, if only her grandmother had realised, does not need to be predicted for it is already upon them.

Listening to this chatter, Natasha thought about the hurt her grandmother would experience when she learned of Natasha's leaving, and she thought again – can I go?

She could not leave. Her grandmother held on to her.

Natasha will remember this moment for as long as she draws breath. Herself half-risen and half-restrained, looking down on that diminished figure, seeing those faded blue and watering eyes, heavily hooded and misted over, clouded by a lack of understanding and yet seeming nevertheless to understand what nobody else has realised: that this is her final parting from her grandchild. As Natasha bites her lip, the impulse to restrain her seems to fade from her grandmother's consciousness and now she is just smiling, vaguely, and letting go, and Natasha can straighten herself and having straightened and kissed the old lady on the top of her head, she can walk, as she does, walking to the door and saying softly to herself:

Forgive me.

She is over the bridge. On the Petrogradsky side. Not far to go and then she will pick up Katya and they will be on their way.

A convoy passes, queues of slow-moving lorries making for the bridge and from there towards the front. In the opposite direction come other vehicles, laden down with the hastily gathered possessions of those who are being moved from the outlying districts of Leningrad on to this more sheltered island. The sounds of banging, boards going up, instructions shouted through loudhailers, bursts of military song, almost entirely mask that more gentle sound where, at the edges of the green that looks out on to the netted fortress, a gang of women is digging into the lawn. Another line follows the first, this one removing the top layer of grass, digging trenches, and beyond them, a group of workers practises some obscure military drill. A dishevelled bunch they are, almost comical in the determined set of their jaws, so young most of them they are not yet shaven, although it isn't funny because, like those who went before, they too will most likely soon be dead. Passing them, Natasha thinks only one thing:

Forgive me.

The sound of laughter, and there, finally, she sees what she has been searching for: a group of children, further reduced each day, and yet still there, because in the midst of their city's torment, old women will continue to gabble and children to play, and she can see them circling in the distance, their mouths screaming in delight, as at their centre, her eyes covered, a small girl stretches out blind hands to catch those flitting past, seizing the air, and eventually the plait of one who has grown too brave and come too close, pulling her, shouting 'got you', as the nursery workers watch laughing and Natasha half-laughs as well as now, close, her gaze moves from one onto the next.

She can always pick Katya out from amongst the crowd of her fellows, almost as if the sameness of their aprons and their smocks conceals what they have in common and lets shine out that special beauty that belongs to Katya. But not this time. Natasha's gaze, that, at first roves easily through the knots of children, becomes increasingly more urgent, as the beating of her heart is amplified and she looks again and then again, telling herself that it is because she is nervous that she has failed to pinpoint Katya, knowing, at the same time, that it isn't so, that Katya is not to be seen, her certainty confirmed when she hears a question:

'Natalya Borisovna: have you come to say goodbye?' and thinking – goodbye? – whirls round to find one of the workers, Katya's favourite, looking puzzled in her direction and saying:

'I thought you were going with Katya.'

Going, Natasha hears and thinks: how do they know? thinking that if they know then she is finished, as she says: 'Where is she?'

'Where is who, Natalya Borisovna?'

'Katya. Where is Katya?'

'But she has already gone. Your husband, Dmitry Fedorovich, he came at least an hour ago to fetch her. She is being evacuated, he said, while the railway still functions.'

She has no memory of getting to the station.

One moment she remembers running in the park. The next she has arrived. One thought: that she must find her daughter. One explanation: that Dmitry went back home, found her letter and, in revenge, took Katya.

The station is flooded with people and with noise. She calls out: 'Katya,' as loud as she can, but her breath is coming hard and her voice too soft to surmount this chaos, babies wailing, wounded groaning, women yelling out, orders issued and countermanded, engines belching, people shoved into railway carriages while others push in the opposite direction. As Natasha runs, calling for her Katya, her voice is only one amongst many. Please give her back to me, she promises: give her back, and I won't go. Give her back: I won't go. Running forward, blindly, she almost falls over a soldier who, slumped on the ground, blood leaking from a bandaged arm, shouts out:

'Have you no respect?' and she knows she should apologise but instead she shouts at him:

'Excuse me, comrade, do you know which train is leaving next?'

She can see his lips moving but it is too noisy in the station, she cannot hear what he is saying and so she leans down and says: 'Which train?' and hears his answer that is not an answer:

'Don't they know that it's too late?' and she wants to shake him but instead she shouts into his ear: 'Please, comrade: I have lost my daughter.'

'As we are all lost.'

'Please, comrade. Think of your own daughter. Of your mother. Tell me: which train goes next?'

And now finally she is rewarded, as he points into the distance: 'That one over there.'

She is already up and running, his voice pursuing her:

'Why do they evacuate only now when it is too late?' as she runs to the platform and pushing through, stronger than she has ever been, making people who are also trying to push through move out of her way, running and shouting, hoarsely: 'Katya,' running, thinking, what if Katya is already gone, and shouting it again: 'Katya,' knowing she has come too late, she and her selfishness, she and her desertion, calling: 'Katya,' and then . . .

And then she sees Dmitry Fedorovich. He is by the train. A picture of tranquillity. Calmly looking up. Smiling in that way of his. Holding something aloft. A piece of bread which he is handing in.

She is beside him, now, and there she sees, framed, in the window: Katya's terrified face, Katya shouting:

'Mama.'

She shouts at Dmitry: 'Get her out of there.'

'Mama.'

'Get her out of there, Dima.'

No longer scared of him, no longer feeling anything but a rage that burns as surely as that village that last night she saw burning in the distance, saying it a third time:

'Get her out of there,' and watching as he obeys, pushing through the door, the crowds dissolving as they see him coming, and now he's in and lifting Katya, and handing her through the window, so that Natasha grabs her daughter, and, holding her, buries her head in the child's hair, thinking: thank you, thank you, and, confirming the promise she has made.

I will not go.

Air Raid

Today, when I went to the bread shop to take over the queueing from Anya, the ground was glistening with the first faint signs of frost, a forewarning of much more to come. I had already seen its patterns on what glass was still visible beneath the tape, but I'd pretended to myself that I had not. That's not like me, I know, ignoring reality, but there are now many things that are not like me. I am changed. We all are. While we pray (something, after they reopened the churches, we are now officially allowed to do) that our city's boundaries, or what now remains of them, will be preserved, we also know they cannot stay the same. The thing that I have already learned – in the forty-one years I have lived through a revolution and three wars, four if you count the recent one with Finland – is that death can come at any time. We, the living, are proof of that. We, once the *leningradtsy*, have become the *blokadniki*: our only undertaking to survive.

Natasha is now working in a factory, making bullets for machine guns; Anya is out of school and mostly on the roof, watching out for bombs; and as for me: well, funnily enough, my lifelong passage into respectability has taken another upward turn. I have been made our building's head of defence. Me! Voted for by all the other residents, even the ones I thought had never noticed me.

It's an honour and a responsibility. I am kept busy ensuring that the building's safe – or as safe as it can be – that the entrances and exits are clear, all the garrets emptied, the windows covered and, that there is an adequate supply of water and of sand. And, of course, I check the windows, my own as well, as I am doing now.

There's no more room for tape. I get off the chair and, stepping back, make sure the heavy drapes are properly closed before I think of turning on the light.

Darkness has now almost completely fallen. It is danger amplified, for they especially like to bomb at night. Or maybe that isn't true: maybe they just like to bomb, and it only feels worse at night. It happens in the day as well, increasingly, those murdering Germans growing more violent, or so it seems to me, as each day passes.

Today there was the biggest attack I've so far seen. I was out when it began. I was collecting supplies, or at least I had been, but having as much as I could carry, I was about to cross the Troitsky bridge and head home. It was a wild day, dry and cold as it has been for some time now, but the wind that had blown away the frost was now whirling off the last remaining reddened autumn leaves, and whipping foaming, grey waves off the Neva. Us pedestrians, weighed down by burdens we would once have thought light, seemed to have been stained different shades of matching grey. Looking about me, I could see my own faltering steps mirrored by my compatriots'. A threadbare procession we must have made, muffled human beings, scarves wound around our heads, fragile human remnants plagued by hunger. We shuffled on past worker guards with their barricades made from rusty springs, bits of bedsteads, barbed wire, and anything sharp that came to hand, and, standing close, a pile of Molotov cocktails, for we have become a city of cardboard tanks and crude explosives, both of which we must use to fight the massed ranks of the Panzers should they break through.

They are there on the hills near Pushkin. At certain points in the city, you can even see them. And, of course, if we can see them it stands to reason that they can also see us.

You'd think that, with all this going on, the focus of our thoughts as we trudged about our business would be war. But it isn't. Those soldiers and sailors in their uniforms of khaki and blue, well, maybe they think of war, especially the ones whose right-arm ribbons show they've already been wounded. But as to the rest of us, the real *blokadniki*, who are on fewer rations than the military and whose staple is bread that, since the burning of the Badayev warehouses, is more floor shavings than flour, what we mostly think about is food.

Not that anybody says so – there's precious little conversation – but there is no need to say it. It's obvious in tongues that lick out suddenly at the sight of a half-starved worker carrying a yellow cardboard box containing the porridge she has kept for her fully starved child at home. And you can see it in that dreamy look that comes over the features of a passing stranger, that look that tells you, because it happens to you too, that this person is daydreaming, not about his love, but about a meal he once had or a feast the future might deliver. If, that is, there is a future.

The first shell, the one we're not expecting, is the worst. It comes from nowhere, and what it lands on it wipes out. After that it's easier. You know where they are aiming and you can get out of the way. Or not. As can also happen.

So it was that on this ordinary day, we, the besieged, were going about our business when the siren sounded. I was out in the open. No shelter near to hand. Nowhere to run to. All around I saw people doing what I was doing, standing and waiting for that first shell to fall. Waiting and hoping. And then it fell, destroying hope, because it fell close by, close to the bridge and so to us, the noise changing from near silence into the wailing of the air raid siren, the thumping of another bomb, and that eerie scream of death.

I'm a slow thinker. Funny. Never thought I was. But I am, and I was still trying to work out where to go, and whether that white-shrouded thing that was floating down was real or some imagining, when I realised that things had changed and that I was hearing: nothing. Me standing there, wrapped up in a silence so total, so absolute I knew it couldn't be real, watching as the ground began first to shake and then to undulate, me standing frozen as a visible wave seemed to travel below its surface, the earth now pitching and rolling in separate folds as if it had dissolved to water, my legs leaden as I watched mouths open. A part of me knew I must also be shouting but still I could hear no sound, not my own voice nor any others as I saw earth spray up, cobblestones flying as if weightless, and for a moment, I thought calmly, well, this is it and then . . . Darkness.

Darkness from which I, out of the blue, awoke.

I had no idea how long it took. There was dust in the air, still settling. I thought: I am on the ground, I must have fallen. And I was right: I was lying on the ground. I couldn't have been unconscious for long, I thought, or else they would have taken me. I raised my head. I was lying on my own at the very edge of a yawning hole. A bomb just fell there, I thought, thinking this calmly, as I noticed something else. A bloodied hand, it was. Just that. One hand. Four fingers.

I thought: I'm seeing things, but no, I looked again and there it was. A hand. Four fingers. A gash where the thumb should be. I looked some more, expecting, hoping to find the arm to which the hand belonged, but there was no arm, just that hand where I had fallen, me, looking at it, wondering if it was mine, and then suddenly, just as suddenly as it had earlier gone, my hearing came back and I could hear the shriek of a warden's whistle and, above that, high-pitched screaming and I raised myself, using my two, whole hands, thinking that other wasn't mine, and looking to the bridge where an engineer was winding frantically at its mechanism. Those wheels turning as another bomb came cannonading down, hitting the water, water spraying up and then a torrent splashing down, the pavement awash as the teeth of the bridge cogs bit one against the other, the engineer winding, his responsibility, his bridge being raised, winding against the falling of more bombs and the screams of those who, caught on the bridge, were fighting to hold on, even as more bombs fell, and me, kneeling there, unable to tear my eyes from the sight of that engineer who, winding with all his might, had tears coursing down his cheeks, winding because he had to raise the bridge or lose it, crying because he could see that same woman as I could, that one, over there, with the dark red scarf, her fingernails scrabbling vainly at the surface of the now almost vertical bridge, her grip slipping, herself silent now as slowly she slid off, and still the engineer kept winding. He had to save the bridge.

Whether we saved the woman, even though we eventually managed to fish her from the river, is anybody's guess. The water was cold and she, like all of us, malnourished. She was shivering when we brought her up, and for a long time afterwards, even though we poured cups of hot water down her throat.

That's all it takes these days – a chill – to snuff out a human life. That's the lottery we endure. The first shell falls on you – you die; you get wet – you die; you slip and can't get up: you die; and if it isn't you, then it's somebody else, somebody you have never seen before, somebody you don't necessarily ever see, but only their unattached hand.

Death. In all its many variations.

And here it comes again: impending death. That monotonous knocking of the metronome, that pulse of wireless life, has been disrupted. Listen to its speeding up: a warning. And now, into the silence created by the absence of the metronome travels a wailing siren and a voice calling out through loudspeakers, that unchanging piece of agitation, rising above the siren and the tolling of church bells:

'This is the local air-defence headquarters. Air raid! Air raid!'

'Air raid! Air raid!' Anya hears.

She is on the roof and has been there for a while. She has been checking everything is in place, intending when that is done to go inside. Now, however, hearing the loudspeaker, she pulls her coat to. She will not leave. Not until the air raid is over: not until her job is done.

She stands. Waiting. From a distance she looks to be a slim, almost fragile figure. Close up, however, she does not look so frail. There's a toughness about the way she holds herself, a wiriness displayed not so much in her muscle definition, although she does have some of that, as in her expression. She's a plain girl whose features are evenly spaced and unexceptional, as if the whole has been put together to escape attention, everything that is except her eyes and it isn't even the eyes themselves, for they are also ordinary, a common brown and sized to match her inoffensive nose and conventional mouth. No, what makes her, if not beautiful, then at least striking, is the expression in those eyes, for no matter where she looks and for how long, she never blinks, her gaze remaining hard-edged, impenetrable and, at the same time, startlingly ferocious. She stands, a stick figure on the roof tops, glaring, as if that fierce gaze could hold back war.

'Air raid! Air raid!' The fourth in as many hours and yet she doesn't flinch.

How old is she? Fourteen? Fifteen? Sixteen? There is no way of knowing. She is grown, that's all that can be confidently said. She is no longer at school and hasn't been since the outbreak of war. She doesn't mind. She, who had been the most diligent of students and the most successful, always top of her class, no longer even thinks of school. This is the way she lives, that stern gaze of hers focused not on what has gone, but on what needs doing next. And so she stands, as darkness falls, solitary in her place, on the roof top of her building. Her domain. Hers. She chose it or it chose her: it doesn't matter which. All that matters is that she is there.

'Air raid! Air raid!

She has been guarding this place almost since the start of the war. She knew, you see – she always does – that this is where she had to be. She was here through August and into this September, standing in this same place as the Germans bombed and burned the Badayev warehouses down. She stood, unflinching, watching the conflagration from her high vantage point, the sky brightened by a full moon, lit blue by falling bombs, sirens ringing, and she watched as the fire took hold, tongues of yellow flames licking almost delicately over the distant roof tops before they began to darken and shoot up, burning more fiercely, reddening the horizon until the heavens turned crimson, that blood-red taint of a city half-ablaze, that flush in time driven out and in its place a mountain of thick black smoke, clouds of it billowing, darkening the night and filling it with the smell of burning meat and the acrid aftertaste of caramelised sugar, Leningrad bleeding out its food supply. And all this time, Anya had stood, waiting, for her turn to come.

'Air raid! Air raid!'

And now, with the moon a dim sliver in the darkness, she hears that sound and still she waits. She is ready to do what is required.

To risk her life?

Yes, perhaps to risk her life, although this is not the way she thinks of it. Not for her such grandiosity. She is a Soviet child. A materialist. A young woman without a past: a comrade constructed by the present, her concentration on the tangible and on the things that are required.

And here it begins again. No need for any loudspeaker. Through the wall of darkness there are sporadic flashes of distant light: the German guns, and the jagged reply of the AA stations. The time has arrived.

If Anya were to lean over the edge, she knows she would see the occupants of her building, Irina Davydovna included, agitated ants, fleeing their building in search of shelter. Not her. She never flees. She never wants protection. She is not frightened. She will stay here until her task is done.

'Here they come,' she hears, a fragile human voice reaching out over the roof tops and, yes, here they do come, the planes, that far-off buzzing, an irritation it might seem, if you didn't know what the sound prefigured, and, yes, again, the noise changing, no longer a distant annoyance but a droning that intensifies until it saturates the air, so loud they must be very close. Yes, here they are, the first, black, shadowed forms in the darkest night, a knot of them swooping, their movement jagged from the upflung panels of light so they seem to be flying in staccato bursts, their deadly choreography driven forward by the gunfire that pursues them, bombs falling. Then the riposte, the crackle of masonry and glass, bricks and windows, breaking up and there, as a cloud of dust precedes them, the planes are almost overhead, the building shaking with the impact of another building's fall, and she can hear a despairing shout, the jangle of a fire engine, but she takes no notice for she must make sure to keep her footing and to ignore anything but the job in hand. The one she knows so well. That she does so well.

Time distorts as it always seems to do up here. Already the planes have moved on, the sound of their engines fading, and yet what they have dropped is only now floating down, blizzarding the sky, before it lands and drifts along the roof tops. She looks across, watching as this lethal rain of phosphorus bombs begins.

At first there are only small darts of isolated blue that fall, but as they fall they seem to increase in numbers and intensity, small rivulets that interweave until they are merged into one indistinguishable mass, a river of fire, sapphire and white, that dances across the tiles, almost playful in the way it dives and soars, that warmth that burns and that, burning, destroys, and all across the roof tops are other figures, Anya's compatriots, frenetically at work, trying to stop their buildings burning down, and there, a man has lost the battle, himself alight, rolling across his roof top with the fire, away from it if he can, pursued by fire and bringing fire with him, an unearthly screaming that Anya ignores because her turn has come, the storm lighting up her domain, and she puts away extraneous thought which in this case is any thought at all.

She is fine-tuned, her makeshift pincers catching up a firebomb and, carrying it across the roof so as to drop it in a waiting tin, herself turning away but registering the sound of water spluttering and of the bomb inscribing its angry, dying circles, boiling until eventually it fizzles out, but she is already elsewhere on the roof top, catching up another and, at almost the same time, returning, using her pincers to pick out the used-up remains and throw them off so as to make room in the tin.

Leningrad is burning as bombs continue to rain down, rescue bells clanging desperately, and all the while, this young woman who, with her stiff body and her unassailable consciousness, can often look clumsy but now moves without a pause, stretching up, swooping down, a graceful dancer on the roof tops, caught up in the wildness of necessity, explosives lighting up the sky, planes battling now for the air space above the city, while her intensity is channelled into this one activity, not this saving of this building, but this thing that she must do because . . .

Because she knows she must?

Yes, perhaps, but it's not only that. It's because . . .

Because she likes it, yes, the thought pushing through, herself alone, in this moment of her frenzy and she registers the reality that here she can be different because here she feels . . .

She feels herself to be something, such an alien feeling that she has to grope to find the word to describe it, and here, in this moment of her distraction, the word comes to her, a strange word for her to think of at this time, at any time, a strange word for her . . .

Happy.

Yes. That is it. She is happy, that stretch of her mouth not the grimace of her endeavour that she has been telling herself it is, but a smile. A real smile. Her own. That nobody will ever see.

*

Down in the shelter we wait for the moment when the all-clear sounds. We are packed together on long benches

ranged against the walls. We are women, mostly, young and
old with our children, or like me: on my own.

What conversation there is is thin. In the beginning, when
war broke out, we would talk to break the tension, but this
is all now so normal that some amongst us on the surface
don't even bother coming down. I wouldn't either, if I had
the choice, but as head of our building's defence I have to
set an example. So I lean back against the wall. I am tired:
oh, to sleep in my own bed. I close my eyes.

Just as I am dropping off, I hear a voice sounding in my
ear:

'She's brave, your girl.'

I straighten up, and look to my left. There's an old
woman there who smiles, a toothless grin, and says:

'We rely on her.'

'Yes. She's brave.'

Me smiling back, although what I would rather be
inclined to say is that Anya isn't brave, it's just that she has
no fear, never has, which is not the same. But I don't say it.
I hold my tongue.

And so I sit in silence.

It's a long raid and a noisy one. No chance of any sleep.
The conversation gradually picks up. I half-listen. I hear
about a new bomb they're using, a magnetic, naval mine,
especially powerful, that they send down on a long para-
chute, and, hearing that, I think that's what I must have
seen today, and that's why its impact was so great. But I'm
not really listening any more, not just because the latest
advances, especially when it comes to things that can blow
me up, never have impressed me but also because I'm
thinking.

What am I thinking?

When it dawns on me what it is, it surprises me. I'm
thinking about Anya. Now, I grant you, this itself is not

unusual. She's kept me on my toes, that one, over the years. What's different, though, is the way I am thinking about her now.

I am thinking of her with fondness. Yes, that's the way I'd put it. Not with love, but definitely with fondness. She's difficult, no doubt about it. Impossible some might say, either to know or to like. But one thing about her: at least she is consistent. No two sides to her. If she doesn't seem to like me much, well then, at least I know it isn't personal: she doesn't much like anyone. And the thing is, and come on, I might as well spit it out, I've got nothing else to do as I sit here, breathing in stale air, the thing is, I am used to her. I am.

'Your girl' they call her, and, if anybody were to ask my opinion, I wouldn't say they're wrong. In spite of her resistance, and mine as well, she has become my girl. I worry about her on the roof. She has no feeling for her own security. No drive for self-protection. A fanatic, she is, this I have always known, but now she has become my fanatic. I worry. I sit here, worrying, waiting for the all-clear to sound, so I can go out and make sure that she's survived and thinking all the time, dreaming up a way of making her come down.

Memory (3)

On the way back from a visit to the front, Boris Aleksandrovich emerges from a reverie whose focus was the intricacies of the allocation of food to find himself being driven past a series of snow-covered fields. He looks out absently through the window, watching the fields rolling by. They stretch out, far into the distance, vast and vacant in this section of Leningrad's suburbs that have been completely evacuated. A picture of tranquillity, it seems, an undisturbed and uniform winterscape, promising the kind of peace that can no longer be found in any other part of life. Taking in the sight, Boris Aleksandrovich thinks that there's something familiar about that field coming up over there, and before he has time to think about what he's doing, he hears himself saying:

'Pull up, comrade.'

They're at the edge of the front in a place that, if the Germans manage to gain any further ground, will soon also be occupied. Occasional gashes in the snow mounds bear testimony to the way that shells, falling short of the city, have the habit of landing here. Hearing Boris Aleksandrovich's instruction, however, the driver doesn't even blink. He's seen so much danger it no longer frightens him, and, besides, pulling up will give him the chance he's been wanting to roll a clump of makhorka tobacco along with a sprinkling of nicotine seasoning dust into a piece of *Pravda* that he's specially saved, and there to set light to the ungainly, homemade cigarette in the open where the stink and crackling of ersatz tobacco will not bother Boris Aleksandrovich, who has anyway stepped away from the car and is already clambering over a low fence.

It's so quiet: after the clamour of the front line and the desperation of the city it feels intoxicating. Boris keeps walking, his boots sinking deep, walking for the joy of the moment and for its solitude, and as he goes it comes back to him that the reason he recognised this place is that he was here, once, years ago, with Jack Brandon.

A line of trees, their branches weighed down by heavy clumps of snow, stands stark against the whitened land just beyond the point where Boris stops. To make his way towards them, or to any other point that could conceal the stalking shadow of a man, would be madness, so he continues to stand in place as he tries to remember what it was he could have been doing here with Jack all those years ago.

Jack's factory, he remembers, was close by – they must have come from there – but that's as much detail as his memory will release. To work out why they'd settled on that previous stop, or what they could have been talking about in this same field, is to summon back another life, one that took place so long before the onset of war it's completely out of reach. The only way that Boris Aleksandrovich can even half-recall it is through his senses as he is doing now, standing and remembering the familiarity of the field, how quiet it had also seemed then, and how fresh it had smelled, a contrast he registers with the present because now this emptiness is heavy with the stink of battle, of cordite and the acrid stench of heavy gasoline, of burning meat and rotting flesh, this mixture of odours, although whether it's being carried to him by the wind or has so effectively penetrated his clothes that it travels with him wherever he might go, he doesn't rightly know.

What he does know, and of this he is completely certain, is that there is no going back. He can't stand and remember what he had said to Jack, or Jack to him. He can't bring back that time. It's gone, driven away not only by war but by the years leading up to it, by the things Boris Aleksandrovich has had to do, and the things he didn't manage.

As has Jack. He's no longer part of the picture. He has gone. Somewhere. Caught up, probably, as Boris Aleksandrovich is, by war.

There is little prospect that they will ever meet again. And little prospect either, Boris thinks, that he and many more of the *leningradtsy* will survive the war. That any of them will.

That's what Boris Aleksandrovich was thinking before the familiarity of the field attracted his attention. He was thinking of the people trapped inside the city and of the dwindling food stocks; of the diminishing fuel supplies; of the engineers, hovering at the edges of Lake Ladoga, waiting for the ice to thicken up sufficiently to take the weight of even the lightest horse. All of them are mindful of the fact that an ice road across the lake will probably only become possible after it is already too late to save great sections of the population.

The number of people now collapsing in their schools and streets, their factories and government offices and their apartments, is growing. The corpses are beginning to pile up as the ground hardens, hunger turned to malnutrition and then starvation and finally death, and in the midst of this there's nothing that men like Boris Aleksandrovich can

do but make sure that this deprivation is as evenly distrib-
uted as is possible, the city functioning long after the time
when the materials that are necessary to keep such a city on
its feet have disappeared.

Here they are, the compromises that once obsessed if not
a nation then at least those men, like Boris Aleksandrovich,
who thought they could reshape the nation, now reduced to
this: survival. And the irony is that it's easier in some ways,
at least for Boris Aleksandrovich, than it ever was before.
Now the decisions he must take are clear and for the good
of all the city. Now he is one of them. Also hungry. Also
determined to survive.

He must soon go: the cold is eating into his bones. He
looks around. Dusk is already on its way, the grey of a pendulous sky tinged a vague pink glow, either a sunset or a
distant battle, he can't tell which. He knows they should
get going, that they must be back by dark. He turns and
begins to retrace his steps, thinking as he does so that with
his mother dead, Lina at the front and Ilya evacuated, he
could move in with Tanya, but knowing that he won't –
why change the habit of a lifetime? – and then, climbing
the fence, he gives brief thanks that Natasha has Dmitry
Fedorovich to look after her. Then it's back into the car, and
he's off.

A Promise Delivered

It took a war to get Natasha into a factory. A war to get her to do Dmitry Fedorovich's bidding (his wife at last a living example of Soviet womanhood, a worker), although it wasn't Dima who had made her volunteer: it was entirely her decision.

She could have gone elsewhere. With most of the able-bodied men out of the city and the proscription against employing the wife of an enemy of the people cancelled by the requirements of unity, even the Kirov theatre would have had her back. And if she had opted for the Kirov, Dmitry Fedorovich wouldn't have stopped her. Since that moment in the station when he pulled Katya out at her command, he seems more scared of her than she of him.

She didn't, however, choose the Kirov. As part of the unspoken bargain she had made with an unnamed deity (in whom, of course, she does not believe), in return for his sparing of Katya, she chose one of Leningrad's newly established small munitions factories.

A bargain delivered: Katya was spared while the train in which she would have left was bombed, the survivors being eventually returned, battered, to the city.

A fair bargain then? Of course: Katya is alive. For the moment. And anyway, the passion Natasha once felt for the Kirov – for anything other than her daughter – has drained away. She has learned what it is just to make do.

There is comfort in this life of set routine, in getting up to lay out the breakfast and to eat, in making the journey on foot to work and thus increase her rations and their food, to stand all day in the makeshift munitions factory, her hands pushed through two holes in the protective mesh screen while she, carefully, carefully, threads fuses into the noses of 45mm artillery shells. Hers is an exclusive task, those nimble fingers that once constructed fantastical models from soft materials – damasks, crêpes, satins and velvets – having been remarked on and selected for the factory's especially dangerous top floor.

It doesn't bother her. She has little sense of personal danger. Unthinking she mostly is at work, insensate, an automaton whom few can rival for the speed and accuracy with which she arms each shell. She has become like Kolya, both of them Stakhanovites, although in his case he worked zealously to achieve his status, while what she does, she does almost by default. She has a talent for this work, a talent, if not for killing, then at least for the arming of those who do.

Her work is now over for the day and she must hurry. Katya, who spends most of the day alone indoors, is waiting.

Thinking about Katya is something she will not allow herself to do at work in case it makes her fingers slip. Now, as she walks towards the exit, her heart starts beating faster. What if there had been an air raid? Or, just as dangerous, what if the stove went out?

No. She will not think like that. She will not panic. Panic is destructive. She breathes in, carefully, to calm herself but not so deeply as to bring on a fainting fit.

It will be dark outside. These days it mostly is. And cold as well. Deathly cold. She winds her long scarf first around her head, then her neck and, finally, she uses it to overlay her mouth, tucking it in so only her eyes and nose are left exposed. Her boots she has already stuffed with paper: now she pulls them on. Next her gloves: they have been frozen, defrosted and dried out twice today (she collected her ration in her break). They also go on. Only one more task, one that she almost forgot, before she can step out. She slips a gloved hand into her coat pocket and – yes – precautions confirmed for there it is, that hard piece of bread, a makeweight that she has saved for the journey home. Preparations complete. She pushes at the door.

It's as she expected: cold and dark. Not completely dark, however: the moon is rising, its soft yellow light turned an electric blue by the undulating layers of snow that envelop the pavements and the road. It is very quiet, deathly quiet, the drifts of untouched snow deadening any sound from those flitting figures who, like black and muffled bats, go about their business. A whitened world. A world passed by.

This snow has lain untouched for some three weeks, only the main roads being now kept clear. Without the man-power to shift the others, these high drifts will remain either until the blockade is lifted or until the spring thaws arrive. Whichever is sooner.

Inhaling sharply against the bite of cold, Natasha steps out. Her boots sink in but only to ankle depth. She takes another step. The snow has compacted, a hard crust form-ing, which makes it easier to walk, snow crunching underfoot. It's colder even than she expected. It always is these days, a result either of the hunger she permanently feels or of an especially savage winter: she can't tell which.

It has been a terrible winter so far, a legendary winter, although the freezing temperatures have at least brought one benefit: the relative absence of disease. Despite the continued bombing which has left large sections of the city without water or functioning drains, there has been no outbreak of cholera and little typhus. There isn't much disease at all in fact, only death brought about by bombing or through that syndrome – dystrophy – that has insinuated itself into the collective vocabulary. Dystrophy – the effects of starvation, that along with dysentery, diphtheria and bronchopneumonia, comes, like a medal, in first and second classes. There is no third class. Only death.

A biting wind. Her eyes water as she feels its sting against her nose. Pulling the scarf tighter, she speeds up, but not too much: if she were to slip, she might not be able to summon up the strength to drag herself out. And so she walks in this hushed and whitened world, still enough of the romantic to see the beauty in the rolling snowdrifts that make such contrast to the stalactites of sharp ice that cling to every surface. She loves its serenity, and the vastness of its canvas, and she also loves the silence that, when there is no bombardment, is almost total.

The city has been like this before, in her parents' and her grandmother's time. The old woman never tired of telling Natasha of one such period, after the revolution, when the roads were also left unswept. Her grandmother who has herself now been relegated to memory for, despite the extra rations Papa's position generated, his mother was one of the earliest victims of this modern, dystrophic plague.

A lucky victim. She died before the ground had hardened. Not for her the fate of countless others who were to follow, their bodies either remaining where they fell, buried by the snow, or else taken in one of those pine-scented lorries to the Piskarovskoye cemetery and there piled up in preparation for a lessening of the cold that might allow the digging of one deep, communal grave.

Death. In all its manifestations and extremes. In private, behind closed doors, death by starvation, old people's beds turned into their hidden tombs, or half-dead children discovered cradling their fully dead mothers, or bodies sinking without trace under drifts of snow. Or a much more public death, people blown from sleep, their dying selves hurled out, flesh shredded or turned to brittle stone as they lie, abandoned, the iced-up shell of human beings, while around them their possessions, clues to a life ended, litter the street, exposed for all to see .

That's what must have happened in that building over there. Natasha stops to look. Only for a moment, or so she tells herself. She looks. One whole wall has been blown away. Two floors annihilated although one remains, so that there sits, half-exposed, a three-walled room, stranded up in space, like a stage set whose play is a testimony to the end of life if not of all possessions for there, in front of a textbook window, a samovar stands neatly on a small table on which a white, embroidered cloth is laid, and, beside it, on a divan bed, are pillows piled in orderly fashion as if the bed has just been made. A stage set whose actors might be imminently expected except for the fact that, directly above the bed, the ceiling has been blown away, the wallpaper droops down low enough to cover a picture, and there, a little further along, is a pile of bricks that once made up a wall.

Strange. Natasha doesn't remember noticing this destruction on her way to work. Which means the damage must be recent. So was there an air raid so close to the factory today? An air raid? That didn't register with her? She can't believe it. No matter that she has grown used to working through sirens and the thundering of bombs, a bombardment strong enough to fell a building could not have seemed so insignificant that it slipped her notice. Could it? No. It isn't possible.

There must be another explanation. Perhaps the building was already like this and she hadn't noticed, or perhaps, memory lapses being a side-effect of near starvation, she had noticed and has since forgotten.

She comes to. Time has elapsed. Danger. She doesn't know how much time she's wasted but she knows that it is far too much: she is beginning to feel sleepy and, more frightening, also warm. She must get going. She has to. For Katya's sake.

She takes the hard bread from her pocket and, having moistened its tip with her saliva, bites off a tiny piece. It isn't really bread. Not as they once knew bread to be. It has a muddy flavour and is hard to chew, baked with more wood cellulose than flour. She feels it in her mouth, gumming up. She swallows hard.

Despite the way her feet are hurting, she forces them forward. Hurting is good: danger in these snow-filled wastes lies not in pain but in its absence. She walks, steadily, without enthusiasm, driven by her need to reach Katya, trudging down the street. Her head is lowered, and her ears alert, not to the threats from the skies, but to that twin of dystrophy – cannibalism – that stalks the streets. Even though rumour has it that it is children who, with their sweeter flesh, are the target for roving cannibals, who knows whether she, hungry but not yet starving, might not, now that parents keep their children in, make an acceptable substitute. Granted she is much bonier than she used to be, but she still has flesh on her, a result not of her father's beneficence but of her husband's.

Dmitry Fedorovich will be wondering where she is. She speeds up a little, turning the corner. She is in a main road now: the going is much easier, for although its centre has been cleared of snow, fuel shortages ensure that what traffic passes is only sporadic. She walks beside the abandoned tram line, past the dark hulk of a burnt-out tram and another one that, although undamaged, is utterly iced up.

It's been some weeks now – she can't remember how many – since the trams stopped running. Since then, what activity survives, its impetus and focus being the maintenance of life, is carried on by foot, the only other method of transportation being a sled like that one over there, a child's sled which, hauled behind a slowly trudging woman, contains a bundled, lumpy form, the child herself, perhaps, or her corpse, or just a pile of wood.

Natasha keeps moving, slowly following the tram lines until they bend to the right, when she parts ways with them, going to the left. Her journey nearly over.

One glance towards the frozen Neva. There is no water on its surface, only a long sweep of snow and ice out of which the occasional dark outline of a sunken boat extrudes, and there, by the bank, a queue of dark-shawled women, ignoring the shrouded corpses of the dead, waiting to fish water out of an ice hole. Natasha turns away, walking a few more blocks. And then finally she is: home.

Home. Either the outside door is iced up or else she is weaker than she'd thought. It takes an effort to push through and when she does she's met by a darkness and cold almost as intense as outside. No lamp to light her progress. No fire, either, in the hallway. She walks gingerly and with great attention, feeling her way not only because it is dark but also because the floor is bound to be slick with ice – the result of water spilling from buckets as they're carried in. And in addition to these reasons, slowly is the manner in which she always walks when on her way to Dmitry.

Katya. She reminds herself: Katya will be there. That's why she goes home. For Katya whom she loves.

As to her feelings for Dmitry Fedorovich: it's not only that she no longer fears him. It is more than that. It is, she says it to herself: it is that she hates him, when, that is, she has the strength to summon up her hatred.

Her hatred is irrational. What Dima did to her and Katya she knows to have been inadvertent: his taking of the child to the station was not his way of making sure she didn't leave. It couldn't have been. She'd found her letter where she'd left it. Unopened. He hadn't known of her intentions.

Nevertheless she hates him. She hates him for . . . For everything he represents. For being alive when Kolya is dead. For being there when Jack is gone. She hates that twisted smile of his, that unchanging plainsong of his instruction that is his only form of conversation and she also hates his silence. She hates him. Full stop. She is consumed by her hatred, as if that slogan: *Death for death. Blood for blood* . . . that is everywhere in Leningrad has wormed its way inside of her, turning her detestation of her husband into something live. She hates the Germans, yes, of course she does, for everything they have done and everything they want to do, but on top of that she hates an individual. She hates Dmitry Fedorovich. With all her strength. All her waning strength: She. Hates. Him. And hates herself for being with him.

She is at the inner door, pushing it open, carrying her hatred in and then setting it aside to call:

'Katya,' for which she is almost instantly rewarded. Katya, all bundled up as Natasha makes sure she always is, comes running from the kitchen, Katya squealing in excitement, wrapping her arms around Natasha's legs, this undersized six-year-old who, like six-year-olds all over Leningrad, has learned to stay alone all day.

Natasha leans down and, with an effort that daily increases, picks up Katya, hugging her, kissing her repeatedly, until finally she stops long enough to say: 'Is Dyadya Dmitry home?'

Katya's answer is a nod.

Pleasure dispensed with. Natasha puts Katya down. They go into the kitchen. The place where life is lived.

Dmitry Fedorovich is sitting at the table, a living testimony to correctness who says,

'Good evening, Natasha,' as he always does, while she answers, with equal and habitual formality:

'Good evening, Dmitry Fedorovich,' before taking off her gloves and boots and coat and unwinding her scarf, laying them all close to the fire to ensure that they will be dried by the morrow.

He has fuelled the stove as he always does. He hasn't, however, bothered to start the food. He never does. She hates him for that also. She sets to.

Thanks to this same intolerable man there is on the table the makings of a feast the like of which few people in Leningrad can these days boast. Apart from what's left of his bread ration to which she adds her own, he has brought back (has scavenged is the way she thinks of it) a couple of turnips, a few slivers of compressed meat, some discoloured potatoes, a dried herring, some small spoonfuls of powdered egg, a portion of sheep-gut jelly, and there, wonder of wonders, a half-tin of condensed milk.

So that's why Katya was so excited, Natasha thinks, looking at her daughter, thinking also that it's not that Katya's eyes have enlarged, it's that her face has shrunk and then she thinks that it's just like Dmitry to leave the condensed milk under Katya's nose, making the poor child wait. She says: 'Do you want some?'

That's all the permission Katya needs. She grabs the tin, gripping it with both hands and, throwing back her head, sucks up the thick syrup so greedily and so fast that Natasha is forced to grip hold of her daughter and to straighten her up, saying: 'Gently, Katya, gently,' before

removing the tin not because she begrudges Katya this treat
(although, by the look on Dmitry Fedorovich's face, he
does) but because, in this time of death, vomiting on your
own gluttony is just one of many ways to go.

'I'll make something equally delicious,' she promises
Katya, picking her up and depositing her in a chair by the
stove, before setting to work.

The herring and powdered egg she sets aside. Although
Dmitry Fedorovich never comes home empty-handed
(where does he get it all?) she is careful to preserve their
stocks. That's the thing about a siege: you never know. His
supplies might dry up, or one of them might get sick or
even (and she watches this thought passing almost wist-
fully) he might get himself killed. But then she smiles at the
absurdity of this, for he is the type who always survives.

'Mama?'

Katya's voice pulls her back from hatred, and Katya is
right. She needs to cook. They need to eat. She uses a small
portion of the jelly as an oil in which to fry some of the vegetables and a half-portion of the meat, which she serves
along with a kind of porridge she makes from bread.

A feast indeed.

They sit together at the table which has been pushed near
to the stove. This is the way it also goes: their living space
depleted day by day. First, the retreat into the kitchen, and
then, gradually, this homing in on the circle of maximum
heat around the stove, where everything, cooking, eating
and sleeping, is accomplished. Which brings her to another
way in which to hate Dmitry Fedorovich. She hates his
body, hates its proximity that after such a long period of
separation stays close to hers in sleep. She hates him for the
way he lies, instantly asleep, and the way he sleeps, as still
as stone, and for the way he wakes, quietly, like a thief and
the way, awake, he is so predictable for she knows that any

moment now he'll say those same words, 'very good'. He always says it at this point in the evening, and she mouths the two words to herself, 'very good', as his voice confirms her expectation:

'Very good.'

She wants to get up, kick the table over, ask him what he's doing here, but she holds her tongue, she has a more elaborate plan and so she answers:

'Yes, Dmitry Fedorovich,' her hatred smothered by civility.

And now. That other time has come. Those thin lips parting (to think she once had kissed those lips).

His ritualised 'very good' having been dispensed, she knows what's coming next: war talk. Something uplifting, she thinks. Something positive.

And yes. She's right.

'Comrade General Boldin's force is holding out in Tula,' he says, and she realises that she hates him even when what he tells her something she knows to be right and something that also gives her pleasure, she hates him just for being there, for being him, thinking this, as he continues,

'Moscow will be saved,' boastfully, as if when that happens it will be the result of something he has done.

But she, who has learned to hug her hatred close, does not say any of this, saying instead:

'Yes, Dmitry Fedorovich,' sugaring up her voice to lay her trap as her father would use honey to coax in wild bees as she continues:

'Moscow will be saved – and Russia too – thanks to those ordinary men,' men like Kolya, she thinks, not saying his name but pausing long enough, thinking it and knowing that Dmitry Fedorovich will think it also, before she adds:

'Brave men, soldiers and partisans and members of the people's militias, who left their cities,' as Kolya would certainly have done, 'to lay down their lives for their country.'

She knows how hard her praise of other men sits with Dmitry, for her hatred has brought her close, and it has helped her to understand him as she has not done before. So she continues:

'And did you hear about the political instructor Kochkov who, armed only with a few grenades, threw himself under a tank to stop a Panzer advance?'

She looks at Dmitry Fedorovich's face, thin and pale, which, she thinks in his case, is not a sign of encroaching malnutrition but how he's always been, his bloodless emotions seeming to fuel his blood-free complexion, so that now, in his discomfort with her admiration for another man (even a bona fide Soviet hero), he doesn't colour but whitens as she finishes (mustn't overdo it):

'Sacrificing himself for his motherland.'

Her words have struck home. She can see this in the opening and closing of his thin mouth, this cold fish whom she has the power to wound. He knows himself to be deliberately belittled. For a brief moment she feels sorry for him, but then she asks herself: what good is pity in these piteous times? And so she continues to hold her tongue, eating in the silence that always does descend, that silence of hunger temporarily assuaged and, in Katya's case, of timidity (her chattering being certain to bring on one of her new father's everlasting scowls).

Such a short duration of their eating time, though, an epoch is now opening up before the next meal can be consumed. Katya looks up longingly at the condensed milk.

'You can have some more tomorrow,' Natasha promises, stowing the tin high out of reach, before sitting down with Katya to read.

She does this faithfully each evening not because she's thinking to the future, the hurdle of the present being as much as she can manage, but because, since one symptom of the almost dead is that they lie down as soon as they have eaten, Katya must naturally be encouraged to stay up. And so she sits there with her daughter, sterner than she feels, correcting Katya's halting reading at the same time as she wonders what portion of the dark shadows under Katya's eyes has been cast, not by the oil lamp or fatigue, but by a creeping starvation.

'Mama, I'm tired,' Katya says, more than once, each time to be met by Natasha's coaxed:

'Just a little more, darling.'

Eventually, however, Katya's drooping prompts Natasha to take pity on her and so, having made her drink the infusion of pine leaves that are said these days to stave off scurvy, Natasha tucks Katya up in bed.

That time has arrived – her worst. The hours before she can permit herself to sleep. Her time with Dmitry Fedorovich.

Perhaps that's why she keeps Katya awake so long: so as to delay this moment. Now, however, it is upon her. She sits. Opposite Dmitry. A tableau of their married life. A man, a woman, brought close together not by any feeling but by the dimness of the light. She reads. Her aim to get through one more chapter of *The Red and the Black*, to keep her mind alive.

'*In bold and proud natures,*' she reads, '*it is only a step from anger with oneself to fury with other people.*'

The words swim, for she is too conscious of his presence to make meaning out of what she is reading and so she tries again:

'*In bold and proud natures, it is only a step from anger with oneself to fury with other people; one's transports of rage are in such circumstances a source of keen pleasure.*'

But it's no good, none of this has any meaning for her. She cannot concentrate.

It isn't just his presence. It is something else.

His eyes on her perhaps? Yes. She can feel them, boring into her.

She will not have him watching her. She will not. She looks up.

He is looking at her now but wasn't before: in the actual moment of her glancing up, she had caught the flickering movement of his gaze. She follows it in hindsight. He wasn't looking at her: he was looking up. Towards the shelf. This husband. This greedy man.

She says: 'Would you also like some condensed milk, Dmitry Fedorovich?'

He shakes his head. 'No.' That's all, that one word, a blank denial, but the speed with which it is delivered by one who is usually so measured feeds her mistrust. Not the condensed milk, she decides: if he had wanted that he never would have brought it home. What else then? The sack of dried beans? The few precious pickled mushrooms? Or . . .

Or the letter that bears his name. The one she wrote. The one he never opened and that she had hidden, pushing it, when they returned, back, deep into the shelf, out of sight.

The letter that meant to tell him she was going. The reminder of a time that seems not only improbable but impossible, and of the person she no longer is.

To think: she had actually believed that she and Katya could just get up and go; that the fairy tale she'd dreamed up with Jack could actually come true; that Jack could really take them out; that Dmitry Fedorovich, and all those other Dmitrys of their world, wouldn't find some way to cut off her escape. That she could start again.

Now she sees that plan for what it was, childish, foolhardy, ridiculous. War has changed her sensibility, has discarded all her dreams.

And yet, even now, she can't help thinking, if Jack were

to come back and offer her that same way out, she'd go. Without a second thought or one look back. I'd go, she thinks, thinking this as Dmitry Fedorovich says something to her, thinking it with such intensity that the thought obliterates his words, and it is only with a great effort that she pulls herself out of her imaginings to say:

'I'm sorry: what did you say?'

He answers quietly: 'You wouldn't have all this.'

This?

'If I was at the front.'

His eyes are narrowed, his face closed tight. He hates me as much as I hate him, she thinks, and then his gaze moves off her and up and, following the direction of his glance, she realises that the 'this' he was referring to (that she couldn't live without) is the food he brings. And yes, it is, his voice sounding out again, confirming this:

'You'd find it hard to survive without these little treats.'

She shrugs. Says contemptuously (knowing how her derision hurts): 'Well, I don't have to, do I?'

'You would. If I volunteered for the front.'

Trap baited. She holds her breath.

'It would be hard on you,' she hears him saying while she looks down at her lap, concentrating on it at the same time, in a bid to keep the excitement she feels out of her voice, and she answers softly:

'If you were needed at the front' (careful, she tells herself, don't carry this too far) 'I would accept that sacrifice. If you were needed.'

And, yes, it's working, she can hear his defensiveness:

'It would be hard on Katya as well,' he says.

This husband of hers, using the daughter with whom he has had so little to do, save for that one attempt of his to pack her off on a train of death.

'You wouldn't want to take that risk,' he says.

What would he know of risk? She answers, briefly: 'My father would help,' at the same time thinking that it's been an age since she last saw Papa.

'With Polina Konstantinovna at the front, your father has barely enough to feed himself. I saw him a few days ago. He is looking very thin.'

So Dmitry does see Papa and doesn't bother telling her. Dmitry, who has cars at his disposal to take him through this frozen city to her father.

'You wouldn't get any help from that direction,' he says.

And haven't for a while, she thinks. Not really. Not since Kolya was taken. Or since she married Dmitry Fedorovich. 'We'd manage,' she says.

'How?'

'We would have to. And it would be . . .'

Here it comes, this moment for which she has so long been planning. She will be word-perfect, feeding him back his own brand of poison, saying:

'. . . it would be our duty,' stressing that word – duty – he can't deny, and it works as she had hoped it would, entrapping him, she can hear it in his voice as he replies:

'My work is valued here.'

As if he doesn't fully believe this and at the same time as if he is pleading with her to help him, to let him off the hook, he adds, 'I can't go to the front.'

She looks at him. Straight. 'You are right, Dmitry Fedorovich,' she says.

'I am no coward.'

'Of course not. No one could accuse you of that.' And now she treats him to her most innocent of smiles: 'Could they?'

Survival

I finally got Anya off the roof. As it turns out, it wasn't difficult. If there's one thing I've learned in my journey through life it's the necessity of knowing who to speak to and how to speak to them. So I found a comrade in the local defence structure who's also known as a devoted father. I didn't say I wanted Anya off the roof. I just told him what she was doing, and then I gave him my opinion of her age (the date of her birth being, after all, a mystery that will never be solved). That's all it took. He immediately said, she must come down.

I knew Anya wouldn't like it, but I also knew that it had to happen. She's already been exposed to too much risk. Now that deep winter has set in she won't survive much longer, especially not after our latest ration cut – the third within as many weeks.

When I broke the news to her, I didn't beat about the bush – I don't believe in that. I said it straight. I said: 'Anya: you've been ordered off the roof.'

Her reply was that usual bunching of her fists and tightening of her lips. Not that she followed through with words. Never does. Bides her time, that one, and holds her tongue, although she did use those fiercely narrowed eyes of hers to glare at me, daring me to carry on.

I don't let her frighten me: or at least not so as to make it show. I carried on. I said: 'You've been allocated to an orphanage, Anya, you are needed there,' saying it without emotion, acting as if it was all the same to me. Shouldn't have bothered. She knew I'd had something to do with the change. 'Course she did. She always does know everything, even if she won't admit it.

That's Anya. Nothing seems to alter her, not even war.

Take the bombardment of mid-September. It lasted over fourteen hours, and all that time she was up there on the roof. She must have been scared and she must certainly have seen sights, as did we all, horrible enough to disturb even a battle-hardened comrade general. But when the raid was over and she came down, she was her usual controlled and unforthcoming self almost as if she had just come back from somewhere as everyday as school. Odd, I know. Odd enough to put most people off.

Thing is, I no longer think of her as odd. I've grown used to her, I suppose. And more than that: she suits me. I've even taken to appreciating her good points, the main one being that she never wastes her breath, or mine, on argument. She looks at me, of course, as she did then, and if looks could burn like the incendiary bombs around which she loves to dance, I would have shrivelled up completely. But looks can't burn, can they? And so I faced her down. I said:

'You will go tomorrow. They're expecting you.'

Matter closed.

If we hadn't been at war, she would then have taken to her room there to nurse her grievances in the isolation she seems to prefer. But we are at war, and that past we used to know is gone. Everything is changed including our apartment whose unused rooms are far too cold, even for someone as stoically inclined as Anya. Besides, she wouldn't have been able to gain access to her room, for as part of our continued retreat (in order to regroup and that way survive) we've stripped out the rooms we no longer use. We continue to do our living here, in the kitchen, its windows blocked out, our only light a wick burning in a dwindling pool of oil, the two of us so used to twilight that if the sun were to show itself, which it doesn't now winter is upon us, all we would do is blink.

A deadly winter it has turned out to be. Colder than most have ever known.

Not me, of course, since I have also known the Arctic, although even on the *Chelyuskin* I don't remember feeling quite as cold as this. It's the hunger that wears us down, that hunger that stalks our city, although hunger is the wrong way of putting it: it's starvation. There's so little to go around, and even the ice road they are building over Lake Ladoga won't be able to solve the problem. And so we stay here and starve, our hunger made worse by stories of trenches turned to tombs of ice, and birds frozen on the wing.

I myself have noticed the lack of birds but whether, in this city of rumour, fear and official assurances, this is because they have fallen down in flight or because they have been shot and eaten is anybody's guess. It doesn't matter. Only one thing is clear: there are no birds. And no food. And on top of that, another factor adds to our plight: the lack of fuel. So little is there that when I'm not guarding the building I am out foraging for wood. Not from the trees, of course, unless a branch should happen to fall, because how will our beloved city look, once the war is over, without its trees?

Like nothing and we can't have that, can we? So the trees,

by mutual if unspoken consent, we leave alone and instead we snatch up anything else that isn't being used. Anything that can be burned – sections of picket fences, wooden slats from abandoned homes, furniture, and even books – is fair game.

Anya and I, Anton Antonovich's inheritors, are well off for books, so much so that if they were able to burn longer, we'd be toasty here, what with the size of Anton Antonovich's collection.

I started on his library weeks ago. Unwillingly at first I opened up the room and carried books through the hall and fed them to the stove, but my conscience soon stopped bothering me. I said to myself, I said: burning of books might be a betrayal of everything for which Anton Antonovich stood but then, given how he chose to end his life, so is survival.

I have parted ways with him. It took a long time and a siege but now I know: I will not choose his path. I am determined: Anya and I must live. That is my goal: that we will live. We'll show those murdering Germans. Yes – she and I, a cleaner and an orphan.

We.

Will.

Live.

To this end: the orphanage. Not only will Anya be safer there but she'll also be better off in other ways. They'll feed her properly or at least they will when she is there.

She'll come back home at night. Her choice. They said she could move in permanently with them (to save travelling back and forth) but she refused and they bowed to her refusal. I know exactly why: they thought, and I tell you, I could even see them thinking this, that the reason she wanted to come home at night was to keep an eye on me. They liked that. Her, caring so much for me, her guardian, that she was ready to risk the to and fro through frozen streets: it confirmed their faith in human nature.

I, of course, know better. I know her and I know how partial she is to her own company: far better, she must have thought, to be boxed up in a kitchen with me, rather than having to endure a whole household of sleeping strangers.

Not that I mind. On the contrary. She's grown on me, she has. In this time when there is so little pleasure to be had, I look forward to her coming home. Not for the conversation: if she stays true to type (and when does she not?), she'll tell me nothing of her day. But the company's enough.

And I like having somebody to care for: it gives me purpose. I think about her, and how to feed her. I think I'll make us something special – a cake from the greens I have left, or a cutlet from the herrings – something that will have the feeling of a proper meal.

We'll eat slowly. We're not the type to gollop down our food: we try to stretch out that moment when we have something in our mouths, and something promised to our aching stomachs. And after we have eaten? I'll do the rounds, I guess, as I always do and then I'll come back to sit here, and sew a little or, if I don't feel like that, I'll just sit. As for Anya, I know what she will do. She'll whittle. She always does. Using our sharpest kitchen knife (our only kitchen knife: I traded the others for extra bread) she'll slowly whittle down a piece of wood.

When she first took this up, I thought she might be showing an artistic bent but it turned out I was wrong. She wasn't carving out a statue and she didn't mean to. All she ever aims to do is whittle away until all the wood's gone.

It got on my nerves in the beginning, all that hard work for no result. Now, however, I admire it. I admire the sheer contrariness of a girl who, in a city frantically caught up in producing feasts from no ingredients and fires from materials that were never meant to burn, has chosen to spend her free time making nothing out of something. Well, not exactly nothing: there are always shavings left over which she takes care to gather up and save.

And it isn't only that I admire her eccentricity. In these days, when nothing can be certain, I have begun to find comfort in her routine. I have even grown to like the sound, that slick of the knife against the wood, the inflection of its downward stroke, and the soft scrape of slivers coming off.

I look forward to it, in fact, tonight, when she gets home.

Note the deliberate use of that word: *when*. When: not if. I am convinced of it. She will come back.

She has to.

She'll live.

I know she will.

To War

In his lifetime, or at least his adult lifetime, there are only two things Dmitry Fedorovich has done without first weighing up all the consequences. Two things, he thinks, as he stands waiting for the barracks door to be opened but before he can specify them to himself, he finds himself drawn back to that moment when he told Natasha that he was going to war.

He had gone home after signing up. Not straight away. First he'd endured the incomprehension of his comrades when he told them what he'd done, and – and there's no point in denying it – also their contempt. Only after that had he gone to Natasha, to stand in front of her.

He remembers it as it unfolded.

There he was, standing tall.

'I am going,' he said.

And she?

She looked up. Not in surprise, as he had expected, but frowning as if annoyed by this disruption in her concentration.

'Going?'

'To fight,' he said.

There. He had finally got her attention. She even put down her book.

'Have you been ordered to the front?'

That was better. More what he had expected.

'No,' he said, and, having planned what he would say after that, he said it loudly and with pride: 'I volunteered,' he said, adding, and this,. he thought, was a nice touch that would go down well: 'It's my duty.'

What had he expected? That she would shower him with praise? With kisses? Or, better still, take hold of him and beg him not to go?

He hadn't expected anything. He disdains expectations. They are useless. He had merely waited to see what she would do.

She'd smiled. That's all she did. Smiled and sealed her lips.

Which had made the silence that stretched between them his responsibility.

Well, he had never been a man to shirk responsibility.

'I'm going tomorrow,' he'd said.

That produced another smile: 'I'll make you some food.'

He didn't want her food. He didn't need it. He said as much.

'The Red Army will provide,' he said. 'You keep your food. With me gone, you'll have need of it,' hearing her meek reply:

'Yes, Dmitry Fedorovich,' that no longer sounded meek to him.

And now, as he stands here, in the barracks, he knows.

He knows what she was thinking. He knows. More than she could dream. He knows what she'd been planning to do with the American. What she would have done if he hadn't found a way of stopping her.

He knew it then as well. He had stood there, watching her fake smile and he had listened to her words:

'If that's what you prefer.'

And he had thought: well, let her smile.

He thinks it now again. Let her smile. He'll show her.

Let her. He'll go to war and, after it is over, he will come back. And when that happens, this is what he thinks, then he will have her and he will bind her tight, and thinking this again it is he who smiles, so freely that he almost loses consciousness of his surroundings and he is taken by surprise by the sliding back of the barracks doors, and by the shout:

'Be quick about it, comrades. We have a war to fight,' and then he puts all thoughts of Natasha to one side, as he is driven forward with the other men.

Out they come, these new volunteers of the people's militia, hungry men, disordered and confused, trying to be what they are not, spilling out, a hurrah issuing from their collective as if they were already on the point of battle rather than just about to march the few miles to the front. Fresh-faced, they are, not the hardened (and now dead) workers of the first wave but younger, many of them yet to need a daily shave, and although some walk out with exaggerated swagger, they are all, if not scared, then at least full of foreboding. Given their prospects, who would not be?

Dmitry Fedorovich Anninsky, that's who, or at least that's how he makes it seem. As he walks forward, he is an island of certainty in the midst of self-doubt, an unimpeachable imitation of a comrade soldier who, having laid the strap of his bread knapsack flat against his greatcoat, holds his Mosin-Nagant rifle at the prescribed angle, marching if not yet with authority then at least with the sense of knowing what it is that authority might require and his example begins to take hold, his orderliness spreading through the ranks until they are all marching, eyes forward, in almost perfect synchrony. It is as if rather than having been given the most rudimentary of trainings before being hurriedly dispatched, they have been drilled for many months.

'Forward.'

Forward they go, their boots tramping over hardened snow, their feet moving faster and with more determination than they have done since the hunger first descended, their advance applauded by those few who have the strength to watch them as they go, this new wave of the *leningradtsy*, volunteers all, passionate men driven by the deaths they have witnessed and the stories heard, by love of their country and by government exhortation, forward into battle, not one step back, and amongst them Dmitry Fedorovich, not a member of the elite as he could easily have been, but a common soldier marching to defend his city, his face grim as if in anticipation of the battles soon to come, this Dmitry Fedorovich Anninsky, marching single-mindedly to war.

With her husband gone Natasha is driven by a compulsion with which she cannot argue to also quit this place. No matter that it is dark, and that it's snowing: no matter that she could wait until the morning. She wants to go. She has to go. It is distasteful to her, more than that it is unbearable, this place holding as it does not only the memory of what she has forced her husband to do, but continually reminding her of it. She'd like to be out now, immediately, without a backward glance but this she knows she cannot do, for first she must pack.

Tucking Katya in on the shelf above the stove, hoping that the child might this way store up some heat, she sets to. She can only take what she, with the help of Katya's sled, can drag. A difficult decision, especially given her mind's confusion.

She is very hungry: she hasn't eaten since Dmitry left. (Since she dispatched him.) She stands and wonders: how to begin?

Oh yes. She will separate out those items – fuel – food – warm clothes – without which life cannot be maintained. Although her impulse is still to flee this apartment and what it has come to mean, and to do so quickly, she makes herself slow down. She is a mother, with responsibilities. So many things can kill these days and ill-considered haste is amongst them. She has to take herself in hand. And so, in the hope that the performance will turn into reality, she acts out the role of someone who feels no urgency, as methodically she separates each category of necessity into its own separate pile. It takes a while, and going through the motions of efficiency is like wading through glue, but eventually it's done. Everything they need laid out on the kitchen floor. Standing back, she surveys the whole.

Her mistake is immediately apparent. She has laid out far too much. It will be too heavy. She has to lighten the load.

To this effect she sets the clothes aside: what they can't now wear they will not take. A pause as she looks again. Still too much, thanks, in part, to Dmitry Fedorovich's diligence in bringing back a huge bundle of firewood before going.

(Dima whom she knowingly sent to war.)

Stop it. She will not allow herself to dwell on his fate or the part that she has played in it. Concentration is what's required, the preservation of reason being necessary to prolong her own, and therefore Katya's, life.

She reapplies herself to her packing. Fuel first, she decides: for stability. She bundles up a portion of the logs, adds some kindling, enfolds the result in an old tarpaulin which she then ropes up, pulling it tight, before tying the bundle to the sled.

There. Fuel allocated. Now to the food.

Of this, she knows, she should take all. But because of the quantity of wood that she has piled up on the sled, she doesn't have room. And so she must begin again, undoing, reducing and reattaching the fuel bundle to the sled and, that done, parcelling up the food, wrapping and double-wrapping, working clumsily because since outside the stove's ring of heat the room is freezing, her hands are gloved. But there at last: she is nearly ready.

Only one more item to add: the photograph.

That time before when she had been about to leave she'd taken a whole set of pictures. Now, however, this siege being the probable final chapter in a life that has been gradually reduced, all she will permit herself is one. She pulls the album off the shelf and extracts the loose bunch she had so recently (in that other life) returned. She splays them out, face up, on the table, and looks along the line-up. She doesn't need to look for long. She will take that picture of Kolya. Naturally. The one of him smiling as he always used to do, this man who had no aptitude either for hatred or for malice.

(Unlike her.)

No picture of that other man. Of Jack.

She shakes her head. Tells herself again: I will not think of it. Then, gently, she takes up the photograph and tucks it under her shirt before she turns to Katya to say: 'Come now,' and, having fetched Katya down, begins to dress her, not that Katya wasn't already dressed, but what Natasha now does is add more layers. Picking garments from the heaps on the floor she piles them on, thick socks and dungarees and sweaters, heaving Katya's limbs through, the child's eyes wide and her face serious as Natasha yanks and tugs and stretches each layer over the preceding one, Katya's physical boundaries spreading until, with the addition of her coat, she has broadened immeasurably and also rounded like a butter ball, or an ersatz copy of the chubby youngster she once had really been.

There: Katya's ready. Now for Natasha. She must also add more clothes.

She weighs up her future need of a wardrobe against the fear of impeding her progress and then she chooses what to wear, taking not what she is fond of, but what will do, the warmest clothes and the ones that will fit over them. And there. She is done.

Almost time. She lets hot water run out of the samovar into two cups where she has already placed small portions of burnt molasses. She stirs vigorously, the liquid turning a dirty shade of grey, and then she hands one cup to Katya and drinks down the other. Finally, she gestures to the chairs.

She and Katya both sit down, and for a moment that's all they do: sit.

Silence, the two side by side (as Dima and Natasha used to sit). Heads bowed in this familiar ritual of leave-taking. A moment of contemplation, Natasha wondering what on earth Katya could be thinking and . . .

As for herself: does she think about the time she has spent in this apartment? Or about the journey that lies ahead? No. Better not to think. Instead:

'Quick,' she says. 'It's time,' and, rising with her daughter, hauls the sled, not the child, downstairs.

The sled is very heavy. The child must walk.

'Hurry,' she says, telling herself that Katya's sluggishness must be the result of lack of practice rather than a sign of encroaching illness and ignoring that part of her that wants to send them both back upstairs, to the safety of the apartment. She can't stay there. It is too full of Dmitry.

She sets the sled outside the door and then, taking Katya by the hand, she gives the stairway one last glance. She will not go back. She cannot. She must leave this life of hers which was only ever half a life: she must press forward into a future even though it might herald the very end of life.

With forced determination and an optimism she hardly feels, she says: 'Here we go,' before stepping out.

Into the midst of a wild snowstorm they go, huge, soft flakes swirling furiously or, as the wind lets go its hold, pattering down, and there for a moment all they do is stand. Natasha stands looking first at the ferocious flurry, and then at the ground where she sees a perfect stillness of downy, settled snow, seeing how cosy it looks and, knowing how dangerous such a thought is, continues to stand, enveloped by this churning whiteness, as her gaze is drawn up and outwards. Now she sees how, because the sky is the same shade as the snow-drifting streets, the distant horizon seems to melt into the air, a sight so magical that Katya, who hasn't been out for some time, claps her hands, the successive layers of her mittens slapping dully, as she laughs out loud.

Laughter. So long since Natasha has heard that sound. And she's not the only one. Katya's laughter acts like a siren on those few people who are struggling through the snow: they stop, immediately, and turn their heads and, who knows, perhaps when it dawns on them that this is no looming air raid but a normal child or at least the echo of what a child used to be, they may also have relaxed, their faces breaking into smiles, although they're all so bundled up there would be no way of telling even if this were true.

A moment's lightness soon cut short. They must get moving.

'It's not far,' Natasha says and, taking hold of Katya's hand, she begins to walk.

She drags the heavy sled behind her, driving forward, her body straining as she struggles to keep herself and Katya separate from the falling and the fallen snow and from those unimaginable things that lie hidden beneath it.

Two dark and insignificant blemishes they are in this vast, wintry landscape. Two unprotected figures, the snow too high for Katya, and her layers of clothes too constricting, so that soon Natasha must stop and take off Katya's coat and unpeel some of the layers which at first she also tries to carry, but as Katya grows increasingly tired Natasha has to face the prospect of carrying her as well, and so she begins to discard the clothes, dropping them as she hauls herself and Katya and the sled forward, a human packhorse driven by the most basic of needs, by shelter, food and warmth, while behind her snow continues to fall over the clothes-strewn path, covering up their trail.

'Dig, you fuckers,' the sergeant shouts as the artillery barrage intensifies, shells thudding down, the ground shaking with the impact, snow spurting, and all the while, above the noise, the sergeant's voice: 'Dig, you fuckers, dig.'

Dmitry Fedorovich swings up his puny arm, his pickaxe inscribing an arch through the driving snow to bite down into the ground as the sergeant continues to walk along the labouring ranks, his order rising over the bombardment:

'Dig, you fuckers.'

The profanity grows faint as he passes along the line and then, reaching its end, he wheels round, his hectoring voice escalating as the distant darkness is lit by those juddering flashes of white light that are the signal that the line of enemy artillery has been discharged. Not that any signal is required for the noise and the spraying up of snow is clue enough, the very earth seeming to explode while Dmitry Fedorovich and the newly arrived soldiers continue to do as they are exhorted. Having already fired the ground to soften it, they dig, at first furiously, driven by terror and by the onslaught of the sound. But after a while they cannot keep up the momentum, and indifference starts to ride in on exhaustion as they continue digging much more slowly, but nevertheless digging through this blizzard, snow cascading down and simultaneously churned up, flying up, slapping down, so they are already whiter than they would have been if they'd been issued with camouflage like the regular troops. That cold, powdery substance insinuates itself into eyes and noses and mouths and boots and backs of necks, an endless cycle, snow hitting skin and turning to water and later, when this activity's over, back to ice. There is nothing they can do to stop the ingress, nothing save obey that command:

'Dig, you fuckers, dig,' the ground slowly yielding to their effort, the trench, their new home, opening up as poles are thumped in and laced together with thick wire. Still the sergeant walks along the line of sweating, heaving, winded men, and then, as the guns suddenly stop firing, his language mutates to match the sudden silence:

'Keep digging, comrades: this is your new home: all that stands between you and death,' his voice more yielding than it has been or at least it is more yielding until he is about to bypass Dmitry Fedorovich at which point he deliberately raises it, redirecting the full force of his rage, shouting:

'Come on, you bastard, you can do better than that. Put your weight into it.'

As Dmitry's pick goes up, his aching shoulder swinging, that same sergeant's voice sounds, but this time softly (and directly) in his ear: 'How does it feel, *comrade*, to have to do the hard labour instead of always sentencing others to it?' before the sergeant moves along the line.

Dmitry Fedorovich acts as if he hasn't heard, his pick thumping down as it was intended to. He will not stop, neither for the guns nor for this anti-Soviet degenerate whose probable only escape from execution was the front.

He will not think about the sergeant's goading or about the effect it might have on the other men, popularity being, in Dmitry Fedorovich's opinion, a much-overrated virtue. So what if some disillusioned and disreputable *frontoviki* have recognised Dmitry Fedorovich for who, or rather, what he is (or what he has been). He is not ashamed of it. He is pleased that the sergeant recognised him for what he is, even during a snowstorm and an enemy attack. It is a tribute, both to himself and to all his kind.

'Dig, you fuckers. Might as well fire at least one shot before you're killed. To do that, you need a trench. Keep digging.'

And Dmitry Fedorovich will keep digging, his resolve so strong (he will show this double-dealing renegade the kind of man he is), his resolve stronger in fact than a man of twice his bulk, and yet suddenly, despite this resolution, he finds he cannot dig, for when he tugs at the pick to pull it out of the earth, it doesn't budge. .

What's happened? Is it possible . . .? Has he been hit?

'Get that pick out now.'

No. Not hit. The guns are far away. And they have stopped. Of course not hit. There's a more trivial reason for the ineffectiveness of his actions. The pick's stuck fast. He yanks at it, trying to pull it out. Without result.

His legs are shaking. He is tired. Hungry. Cold. He thinks that he can't go on but hearing the return of the sergeant's mocking voice:

'Weakening, are you? Who's the bourgeois now, *comrade*?' he tells himself, it doesn't matter how tired he is, he will not give up but will continue and live to see this sergeant shot, if it is the last thing he does. By his persistence and his ultimate will to prevail, he will show this tyrant what men like Dmitry Fedorovich Anninsky can do. He will demonstrate exactly why he is amongst the chosen watchmen of the nation.

Repositioning his feet, legs astraddle, determination evident in his straining muscles he hauls on the pick. There: his feet planted, he uses all his strength to dislodge the pick, and yes, it works, Dmitry Fedorovich staggering back as the pick comes free, his neck now slick with sweat, his muscles demanding a rest that his willpower will not allow, as he steadies himself for the downward motion, telling himself he is not ashamed of who he is, he will show Natasha, who thought she could leave not only him but also their motherland, and not only Natasha, he'll also show the others what it is that men like he, dedicated Communists, unwavering cadre, can accomplish, the handle slipping in a hand which, beneath the glove, is also wet, his grip hardening despite the blisters he can feel as he hears that voice again:

'That's right, desk boy: dig, you fucker, dig.'

Natasha is lost. In this city where she was born, this city that she has never left. She trudges on through streets whose names and numbers have either been concealed below the billowing layers of freshly fallen snow or whitewashed out in case the Germans should break through. Is she really lost? Perhaps. Or perhaps not. At this point in her journey, it is entirely immaterial. All that matters is that she has lost her forward drive; her strength; her capacity to think apart from one clear thought: that she doesn't know how far away she is.

Time has passed. She has no idea how much. An age it feels, a lifetime, that she has been tramping through these streets.

Something – ? pulls at her. What? She looks down. Of course. It's Katya. Katya, tugging at her coat, half slumped against her, her snow-heavy lashes beginning to close. The moment Natasha has been dreading: Katya can't go on.

Natasha is already far too weak. She cannot carry Katya. She thinks: what can I do?

Should she retrace her steps? No: they've come too far. They'll never make it back. Should she call out then? No, not that either: her voice is too weak to reach across the muffling snow. Knock at the nearest door? Again, no. She cannot leave the sled.

Her thoughts slowing. Her mind closing. Except that word intrudes, one word. Sled.

The sled. Of course. That's what she has to do. The thought turned into action, it has to be, before it flits away, her bending down, slowly (don't sink) and gesturing to Katya, who, eventually understanding, totters over to the sled there to sit awkwardly on top of all the bundles, while Natasha struggles up and turns, ignoring the sound of Katya who has begun to whimper.

She's only gone a few steps when she sees in her mind's eye a picture more vivid than reality. She sees herself plodding through the snow, pulling at the sled, so exhausted she doesn't feel the jolt and then the lessening of the load as Katya loses her grip and slides off, Natasha, so tired she doesn't even register how much her burden has been lightened, moving forward, leaving behind Katya sprawled, Katya's eyes closed, no longer feeling cold . . . no longer feeling anything . . .

Now Natasha shakes herself, snow falling, but she cannot shake off the image. Her thoughts come slowly, jagged words floating through her mind that are seemingly separate from consciousness but once they have occurred, they cannot be disputed.

Dragging Katya by sled is far too dangerous.

Weak or not, Natasha must carry her.

Now.

Before she forgets.

She turns back, struggling over to the sled, bending down to lift Katya off. Katya comes, numbly, a dead weight in Natasha's arms. Her arms that seem too heavy: without sensation. Something else she has to do. But what?

Oh yes. She puts Katya down, signing to her to stand, and then she fumbles awkwardly with the rope, an age passing, a lifetime it feels, before she manages to tie its free end round her waist.

The sled secured: she must get going.

She picks Katya up, staggering under the weight of her, righting herself to indicate to Katya how she should wrap her legs around her mother's waist and her arms around her neck. That done, Natasha launches forward thinking that if this, the last fraction of her strength, also gives out, she will abandon the sled, but thinking, no, she can't do that for the loss of the sled would condemn them both to death (this the second time she has risked Katya's life, the first being the baiting of Dmitry Fedorovich and thus depriving Katya of his privilege and his protection). And as she thinks this, she wills her right leg to lift and fall and the left to follow through, her left knee buckling so that she sinks into the snow and only just manages to keep hold of Katya, her jaw grinding in the effort to extract them both, swaying as she tries to find her balance, and haul herself forward.

One step. That's all she's managed. She must do better. She strains forward.

It's no good, she isn't even moving any longer, her feet just sinking further, requiring an ever-increasing amount of energy to suck them out. If this continues, she and Katya will die, here, on this spot. She must rid herself of her burden.

The sled.

She has to do it, to rid them of the drain of their possessions.

She fumbles with the rope, tearing at it in her desperation to sever their connection, and at last succeeding, and taking another step, this time a successful one, the sled, silent, unmoving and abandoned behind her.

She's near Irina Davydovna's apartment. She must be. Has to be. Ira will find the sled. Ira will . . .

At that moment as if by magic she sees a dark door yawning open across the road. Someone coming, she thinks, thinking that she will call to them, and that they will help her drag the sled, of course they would, especially if she offers them a share, but all of this she, even in her dulled condition, knows to be wishful thinking, as she sees an old woman emerging.

A desperate woman she has to be, to brave this weather. She is certainly painfully thin, a tremulous black-shawled figure making her way, haltingly, along the pavement, and watching, Natasha thinks of calling out at least to ask if this is Irina Davydovna's street, or somewhere close. But in her weakened state she knows her voice would not even bridge the pavement never mind the road, and at that moment the woman disappears.

One moment she was there and in the next she sank, so fast and so far that it cannot just be a drift that has snagged her, but must be something worse, her legs giving way perhaps, and yes, from that place where the woman used to be a tiny bundle of thin twigs which Natasha knows must be a hand, flutters, feebly, above the snow, once, twice, before flickering down, and all Natasha can do is stand and bear witness, thinking that if the woman doesn't rise, as she is now unlikely to do, then she is finished, and thinking also that if Natasha, in her own enfeebled state, were to start across to try to give the woman help, the end point would be not one, but three, deaths, and knowing this she forces herself to start up, leaving the sled behind, as the tears that have leaked out of her eyes turn to slivers of diamond ice.

The snowstorm has abated. The firing also and the digging: the trench is built. In the silence that now seems to have enveloped the whole world, Dmitry Fedorovich crouches down in it. He is tired. More tired than he has ever been. And hungry.

The bread and piece of dried herring that are his full day's issue are both rock hard. The bread's no problem, its condition easily modified, the addition of some snow being enough to make it chewable. The herring, however, presents an altogether different challenge: it is so stiff that no teeth, or at least no teeth that Dmitry possesses, can dent its surface. And yet others have managed: one glance along the trench is all it takes to reveal the fat mitts of one of his fellow soldiers clumsily slipping a small piece of herring into a portion of his bread, before shoving the lot into his gaping mouth.

Dmitry tries again, biting down, but once again without effect. Another method then? There has to be one.

Dmitry Fedorovich Anninsky is a persistent man. And a hungry one. He will not be defeated. Not by a fish.

There has to be a technique: there always is, for every problem. Once again he looks along the line-up, all those others soldiers crouched like him but in groups of twos and threes. He is looking for something that the veterans (a mere two months at this front being ample qualification for veteran status) might have passed on to those freshly arrived. Not to him. They are all avoiding him, even the ones with whom he marched.

Although they were previously content to take their beat from him, now they're here they've turned like sheep, the lot of him, to take their cues from others.

He is alone. As he always used to be. Before Natasha.

Not that this bothers him. What does he care, either for their conversation or their approval? Not a jot. If this had ever been his requirement he would not, in his own small way, have been able to ensure the continued progress of their revolution. Let the others mock his dedication, he will not be deterred (although he will, of course, at the first available opportunity, report this counter-revolutionary behaviour to the political commissar, not because of any personal slight – for once again he asks himself, what does this ever matter? – but because of principle). Discipline is necessary for morale, and morale is vital for the successful prosecution of this, their great patriotic war.

In the meantime: the herring. There at last: his vigilance rewarded. He sees a soldier slapping something against the underside of his boot. Of course. That's how it is done. Of course. Dmitry Fedorovich should have guessed. And, of course, in a short time, he would have worked it out. In fact he has. Nobody told him, did they?

Ready now: picking up the herring, he turns his foot and slams the fish, hard, against the sole.

In the moment when she had thought that all was lost, some force acted as her guide. Some instinct, if not for her own, then at least for Katya's preservation, prompted her to look up, which is when she notices a set of chimneys that, even smothered as they are by snow, look oddly spaced and different from all those around them, and she remembers remarking on this fact when recently with Irina. Which means: there, that one over there. That is Ira's building. She has arrived.

She strains forward.

Careful now. She can't afford a slip.

She speaks to herself as if she were a child. She says:

'Careful.'

And:

'A few more steps.'

'Come on, Natasha.'

'That's right. Push.'

And so she does, pushing against a door she hopes will be Ira's, pushing so hard that when it yields, she pitches forward, she and Katya, falling, the two of them, sprawled across the flagstones.

He huddles in his greatcoat in the trench. The storm is done, the sky clearing, the cold settling in. He shrinks into the coat, pulling its collar up and his hat down and tells himself that he must get some sleep.

His part of the trench is empty but even in this solitude he feels the presence of those others. How could he not? Every sound is magnified so he can hear the soft murmur of two men talking, and a rackety cough starting up. Dmitry Fedorovich lies curled in on himself, listening to the way the sound metamorphoses from a cough into the convulsions of a man gasping for breath, this sound in turn shot through by something more mellow, distant, the strains of an accordion, and a man's melodic voice:

'*Daleko* . . . *daleko* . . .' Far away . . .' singing of a love far away at home, and hearing that Dmitry Fedorovich thinks: there are only two things that he's ever done, without first figuring out all the consequences.

The first was to marry Natasha.

The second to go to war.

The Orphanage

Anya sits and as she sits she just keeps looking out. She hates it here – she hates sitting – and yet this is all she ever seems to do.

It was different on the roof. There she was always on the move: either putting out fires or else struggling to maintain her body heat. Here there's no need. It's warm. Not by normal standards perhaps, frost continues to etch out intricate patterns on the inside of the window panes, but in a blockade where everything is relative, this counts as warm. And on top of that, there isn't much for her to do.

She volunteers for all the menial jobs, for the cleaning of the bathrooms, the wiping up of vomit, the scrubbing of soiled linen or the unloading of supplies. Anything rather than this task they have assigned her: to keep this one child company.

Look at him, the way he sits there in his orange smock, silently, upon his bunk, one of an increasing band of children who have no family. He was found in a room of frozen corpses, he, the only one of five to survive. It's possible he has a father who is still alive and at the front but as yet no word has come. He is a thin child. A mangy child. A child devoid of both charm and inspiration. He is a numbskull. A void. He doesn't do anything other than sit . . . in fact, if they let him, he would sit all day looking out and for all she knows all night as well. His eyes, too big for his narrow, sunken face, are so unblinking that he might be blind, except for the way that, when his breath fogs up the glass, he reaches out with an emaciated arm and wipes it clear.

He was so malnourished when he arrived this misting didn't happen for his breath, even in the coldest environment, came out translucent. But now he has been given food supplements and the warmth generated by his body shows itself against the glass, so he is continually reaching out, like a nervous tic, to wipe it off, as he also continues to sit, watching . . . nothing. His eyes are fixed on a bombed-out and abandoned building where nothing ever changes. He has been told, often enough, that all the people have gone, that there is nothing to be seen, and yet still he keeps on looking.

He is an unresponsive boy, an unlikeable boy who registers nobody but himself, and yet the myth has been deliberately spread not only that he likes her but that he also chose her. It's ridiculous: he barely bothers sparing her a passing glance. He doesn't like her. He tolerates her, that's what he does, opening his mouth when she wants to feed him, and arranging his limbs in such a way that she can dress him, all of this as long as she is careful not to obstruct his view.

'Look at how good he is with you,' the others tell her, for the only time he ever makes a sound is when he screams, should they come close.

'You have a gift for this,' they say.

She doesn't think she has a gift. A gift would make her feel good about what she does: would make her want to do it. A gift is what she had up there, on the roof. She liked it there and she was good at it.

Which is hardly the way she experiences this child. As for liking him – well, that she never can. She keeps him company, not out of pity, but because it's her job and she has always done her job. But as she sits with him she counts the hours until her release when she can go home and there embrace a different kind of silence, one that she controls, cutting down wood, her knife stroking against the grain as keenly as if she were cutting into this parentless child.

Not that she wants to hurt him. Not that. She has nothing against him. He is nothing to her.

What she can't stand, however, is his desperate need.

She understands, you see. Not so the others. They are kind people, but they are also stupid. They have a prescription they want to fill. They have saved him from dying: now he must embrace their life.

This is exactly what she understands: why it is that he will not.

They think he should join in: she knows he cannot. They think he should come away from the window: she knows he should stay here. They think he should listen to music: she knows why he must close his ears. They think he should sing with the other children: she knows that even to open his mouth would be betrayal.

She knows, you see. She knows what he is looking for as he looks out. He's looking for his past, keeping watch for those he loves long after they have gone. It doesn't matter that he knows they will not come. He still keeps looking. Keeping faith.

Was she also like this once? Is that why she understands? Does she remember herself, like him, on a train, keeping watch? Or herself at Anton's, keeping silent?

No. She will not think of that, ever. She will sit here, with this boy, because it is her job. She will sit, that's all. Until it's time for her to go.

Visitors (2)

Each day that passes sees a lessening, either by death or by departure to another building, of the people in my building but I don't let that excuse me from my warden's rounds. I take my duties seriously. This is not a boast: it's just a fact that fits with my theory that in this time of death we must find meaning in our lives so as to survive. My particular meanings have settled on those two responsibilities: Anya and the building.

And it pays off in ways I hadn't reckoned on. Who knows what would have happened to Natasha and Katya if I hadn't done my rounds and found them when I did. Except that's wrong. I know. They would have died: frozen to death, there, in my hallway.

Even thinking about it now can stir me up to anger. Yes that's right, I, Irina Davydovna Arbatova, who doesn't normally allow herself to be rattled by anything, am brought to the point of rage by the behaviour of that other woman, Natasha, who is my only friend.

A bundle of soggy rags is what I thought they were at first, some leftovers of the passing storm. I was irritated by the sight: as if I didn't have enough to do without having to dispose of other people's messes. But going closer in the darkness, I saw it was a body, no, not one but two, and not any bodies, but Natasha and Katya, the one lying in the other's arms.

I was at once upon them, feeling for their pulses, calling out their names, slapping them to try to shake them into wakefulness, but even caught up in this action, I was angry. I kneeled down by Natasha, shouting:

'Wake up, Natasha,' shaking her and her daughter, too:

'Come on, Katya: you can't sleep now,' while all the time what I was thinking was: how dare you, Natasha?

'Wake up.'

How dare she take a chance like this, coming out not only in the middle of a snowstorm but also just as dark was falling? How dare she land on me like this?

'Come on, my darling,' willing her to wake, saying this in real concern, for she is my darling, but at the same time what I also felt like saying was: How dare you leave my finding you to chance?

'Get up. That's all you have to do, get up.'

It was shock, I know, that fed my anger, and the fear that I might be too late to shake them into life. But it was more than that as well, for as I continued to work at them I couldn't help thinking that it wasn't enough that Natasha had already risked my life by bringing Jack Brandon, a foreigner no less, to my apartment, an anti-Soviet act if ever there was one that, if uncovered, would have meant the end of me. But now she also has to land on me like this, without warning and with no provisions, trusting that I would find her, warm her, bring her back to life because that's what I do – don't I? – I rescue people, educated people with opportunities, people like Natasha and Anton Antonovich who leave to me the act of rescuing them from themselves, and if I don't manage it, well, what does it matter, they're already gone, and it's me, the onlooker, who's left to bear the consequences . . .

Even as these thoughts were racing through my mind, I saw her eyelids flutter, my friend, Natasha, alive, and her daughter also coming round, and relief took anger's place, as well as action and the need to get them warm. I dragged them, the child first and then her mother, up the stairs (I don't know where I found the strength), and propped them as close to the stove as they could get, rubbing their feet and their hands to set their circulation going, swapping their wet clothes for dry ones, the first that came to hand, before coaxing warm water down their throats, and what food I had (knowing that this is all we had until the ration queue tomorrow), until I could hear Natasha's muttered refrain:

'I'm sorry.'

I'm sorry, that's all she kept on saying, those two words stuttered out although whether she was apologising to me or someone else, Katya perhaps, or even Dmitry Fedorovich, whom she seems to have just sent off to war, is anybody's guess.

I had them both tucked in by the time Anya got home. I was by then much calmer. There were things that I had remembered, like the way that, ever since the blockade began, Natasha has shared with us the fruits of her husband's favour. She was always dropping by with gifts of food that a less generous friend might have kept entirely to herself. And, I also told myself, although it was stupid of her to set off in such conditions, this is what starvation's doing: making us all stupid.

I gave Anya time to warm herself up and then I sent her out to look for Natasha's sled. I told her not to stay too long, just to take a look. Maybe I shouldn't have. She's already tired and still cold, but if the sled contained even half of what Natasha said it did, then I thought it worth the risk.

To be honest, though, I had another motive. I wanted a minute on my own. There's something I have to do.

Natasha and Katya are dozing by the stove. I put on my gloves and hat (even indoors we never take off our coats) and, leaving the kitchen, feel my way along the corridor. I know this place so well by now, in lightness and in dark, and I soon have my hand on the door of Anton Antonovich's study. Since we started on his books, we've unblocked the entrance, hanging a blanket there to keep out the cold. Pushing it aside, I now go in.

It's so dark in here, I can't see a thing, not even the outline of a shelf. No matter. I don't really need to see. I know it by touch as well as sight, this frozen remainder of a room coated by ice that covers everything, even the dust that had started to accumulate.

It is a study only now in name. A room almost completely taken apart. The easy chair is in the kitchen and the rest of the furniture was burned before we started on the books. And now Anton Antonovich's library is also in the process of being destroyed. We started in one corner, top shelf, extreme left, and have been working our way down and along ever since.

Don't think that just because I'm no great reader the destruction of Anton Antonovich's collection comes easily to me. The truth is that it does not. It hurts. I had just got myself to the point where I didn't think of him as much, but now, every time I take down one of his books, I can't help thinking how much this library meant to him, and it hurts some more. But then I tell myself: Anton Antonovich is dead, and we the living must also tend our needs.

This time, though, I haven't come for books. I've come for something else. I know exactly where it is – last book, bottom shelf, extreme right – because I put it there, deliberately so that it would be the last to burn. Now, for reasons that I don't fully understand, I cannot bear to wait that long. Who knows: perhaps Natasha's foolishness has spread to me.

I've had enough of reasons. All I know is that I must act. I go to the corner, bottom left, and kneeling down take out the book.

It's French.

Before he died Anton Antonovich was teaching me to make out the French alphabet: it's the kind of thing that tickled him. Pity he didn't think it worth sticking around to teach me what it meant, I think, and then, pushing the thought away, I reach out for the book. I can still remember how to spell out its title, and I could show off, if I had more light, but there's no need. I've learned it off by heart. *Charlotte Corday et la Mort du Marat*, it reads, although I can't swear to pronounce it right. Doesn't matter – I'm not about to read the book. Or anything for that matter. What I'm looking for is Anton Antonovich's letter.

Doesn't take me long to find. It's there where I put it: in the book's second half. I flick the pages until my fingers snag against it and then I draw it out. I put back the book and, with the letter, leave the room.

I'm freezing. When you're as empty as I am, a few minutes in unheated spaces is all it takes to set your teeth to chatter. I know I can't afford to lose more strength – not with Natasha and Katya exhausted in the kitchen and Anya out. I hurry, but not so much that I might forget my duties. I make sure the door is properly closed and the blanket spread across any gaps. Then I make my way quickly, but not so quickly that I might fall, to the kitchen.

Its warmth reaches out to me. I am breathing hard: I am tempted to stop and rest, and yet I know that if I really want to get this over with before Anya comes back, I can't stop. I walk quickly to the stove, past Natasha and Katya who are both half-sitting, half-lying, with their eyes closed. They don't seem to realise either that I've been gone or that I've returned. Which suits me fine. What I am about to do, I want to do alone.

I open the stove and then, without another thought, I feed the letter in. No need to look before I do. I won't forget his words. And no desire, either, to see the marks his desperate hand once made.

Once I've let go of it, though, I am driven to take a look. I crouch down, watching the piece of paper flaring and then it's gone, crumpled into ash, and only after that does it occur to me what a peculiar thing to do, to hold on to the letter for so long before, suddenly, giving myself up to its elimination.

Not that I regret it. It feels good. Should have done it years ago.

I hear a voice then. Anya's voice.

'No,' she says.

I look up quickly to find her standing by the door. She's looking at me strangely. Did she know what I was doing, I wonder, as I rise and say:

'You couldn't find the sled?'

She shakes her head. She's scowling. Never likes to lose, that one.

I say: 'It's not your fault,' and it isn't. Given the confused way that Natasha's told her story, it would have taken a miracle to find the sled.

I say: 'No matter. Come. Sit down. Warm yourself up,' hoping, as she obeys me, that the sled hasn't entirely gone to waste. I hope some lucky bastard got hold of it and took it home, although I know it's much more likely that some unlucky bastard tripped on it and died, sled and corpse both buried by this unceasing and infernal snow.

Anya's still scowling. I tell her again that it's not her fault. 'It's not your fault,' I say.

She shrugs. Silly me. She didn't think it was: never does. She is angry though.

I set to work making us a porridge from a few oat crumbs I found and a tiny piece of bread, and out of the corner of my eye I watch her balanced there at the edge of a chair, sulkily striking down a piece of wood. If I didn't know better, I might think she was jealous of the attention that I am showing to our visitors. But that would take for granted that she cares, that she'd rather have me to herself, and I do know better. Her anger must have another source: the unexpectedness of their arrival perhaps.

Yes. That must be it. That's Anya all over. Never has liked changes to her routine.

And now at last Anya is asleep. Funny how innocent she looks and how unguarded. The cold helps. She's sharing her bed with Katya and both of them are curled up and nuzzled close.

Natasha's still awake. I think she has been all along. Her eyes are half-closed but she is awake. Stubbornly. I tell her to get some rest, I say:

'We can talk tomorrow: get some rest.'

But she won't. She seems to need to talk.

Tell you the truth, I'd rather she did not. I don't feel like conversation. I'm tired. I wouldn't mind some sleep. But I tell myself that I must put off sleep. I must continue sitting by her side. I'm worried about her. Her breathing's coming hard. I put a flattened hand across her forehead and when I take it off it's hot. Not a good sign.

I say: 'You need your rest, Natasha.'

She answers with a question clearly put: 'Did he read the letter?'

My heart seems suddenly to be jolted. Does she mean Anton Antonovich's letter? Did she see what I was burning and understand? Does she know of it?

No, I tell myself, no it can't be, and when she speaks again I realise that I'm right.

'He never opened it,' she says, 'he couldn't have', which is when it dawns on me that she is talking, not about Anton Antonovich's letter, but about another one, one, it seems, that she wrote, and one, if I'm understanding what she's saying, she had left out for Dmitry Fedorovich but then wished she hadn't, though I can't be sure because she's really rambling now, and I've lost her.

She's talking not to me but to herself, saying: 'It's still there, on the shelf,' loudly, as if I might have said it wasn't on the shelf, when all I've done is wipe a wet cloth on her forehead, which she ignores, for she is caught up in what she has to say: 'It's not been opened,' she says, and she looks up at me to add, 'That means he didn't read it.'

Her dark, pooled eyes beseech me: 'Doesn't it, Irina Davydovna? He didn't read it, did he? Not if it was sealed. He didn't, did he, Ira?'

Her voice pleads as she repeats my name, and so I choose to answer:

'Yes, Natasha: if it was sealed that means he didn't read it,' although what I'm really thinking is that there couldn't be anything simpler for the likes of Dmitry Fedorovich than to open up an envelope and never leave a trace of what he's done – I bet this is the sort of thing he does the whole day long – and I'm glad I didn't say so because she's off again, all over the place, not talking about things she might have written and Dmitry Fedorovich might have read, but about him, and that other husband, Kolya, whose name she hardly ever says, now repeated in her softly muttered voice, so I can hear only fragments:

'. . . and what if I'd been there . . .' and 'you think he thought of me, when they did it. 'Course he did. That's what love does,' and finally:

'I shouldn't have forgotten . . . it's my fault. My fault . . . I should never . . .'

And then, suddenly she says something I do manage to catch clearly, something which, by looking up at me again, demands its own reply:

'He won't die, will he?'

For a moment I think she's so far gone she's doesn't know Kolya's dead, but then I realise, no, of course not, even in the deepest fever how could she ever forget the fate that had taken Kolya, which means she must be asking me about Dmitry Fedorovich, that other man, that poor, sad sack who loves her, but not well enough to fasten down her love, and she's asking me whether Dmitry Fedorovich will also die, and, in the spirit of trying to comfort her, I say:

'No. He won't die,' although once more what I'm thinking is the opposite. For the odds are against anybody surviving at the front, and for Dmitry Fedorovich, who has never known how to arouse much loyalty, the odds will be even lower, but none of this do I share with her, I just lay my hand again on her burning forehead and talk to her as if she were a child:

'He'll be fine. Hush now, get some rest.'

To Live

Dmitry Fedorovich is feeling good. He is.

He has survived the night. Not so some of his fellows. As the trenches begin to stir, they lie there, the dead, stiffened into ice.

Carefully he moves his fingers and his toes, urging them to life.

That done, he shifts away the piece of tarpaulin that he'd pulled over his head as protection from the falling snow and shakes it out and then for a moment he continues to sit in this whitened world, his immediate surroundings and the distance folded up in layers of billowing snow, the distant tree line standing stark against it.

He has no idea what time it is. Early, he thinks. He looks up at the sky, searching out a clue. It's very still but, although it is also still dark, the sky isn't the inky black he'd expected but a shining navy blue. It's beautiful, he thinks, tilting back his head, and there, moving almost visibly downwards, a perfectly formed crescent of a moon. It's beautiful, he thinks again, and as he continues sitting he is awed by the enormity of these heavens, and by their quiet, appreciating them in a way in which the urgent bustle of his life has always disallowed.

He is cold. Or at least he knows that he should be. Sitting in this place, however, and looking up, he doesn't feel the cold. On the contrary: it's almost as if a warm current is moving through him, bringing him to life. Bringing him to peace.

How strange that he feels harmony, here of all places, on the very edge of one of the world's most bloody battle fronts. And yet he does. He who has spent his adult life, and the time before that also, in calculation, is now no longer driven by his reason. He is instead feeling. He feels himself to be: brave, purposeful, worthy. A soldier like any other soldier whose job is not to give orders but to obey them, his role no longer to lead (except by example) but to follow. In short, he is no longer special and, to his great surprise, there is joy in that.

Dropping his gaze, he directs it at the trenches. He sees a first aid worker slapping yellow frostbite ointment on translucent skin; a corpse brigade hauling out the dead; and a group of four towing a howitzer into place just beyond the trench. And there, behind him, in the ruins of a village, figures also stirring in the snow. Orders sounding in the distance. Engines revving. The trappings of war, and of more to come, and yet he is calm.

He thinks: Natasha would be proud of me.

Natasha would be proud of him, not only for the fact that he is here, but for the way that he can finally see the world not as something to be moulded and improved, but as it is, in all its splendour. He sees it in her dream space, and seeing that, gets an inkling of what it is to live by her imagination.

It took a war and a night inside a trench but now his loving of Natasha, the only irrational thing he has ever done, the only impulse in his life that he was not capable of resisting, has finally come to this. To tranquillity. It was worth it, he thinks, to have kept her from leaving. Just for this and for the moment when he goes back. Then he will tell her, and she'll agree with him: it was worth it, what he did.

He has loved her from his very first sight of her when she was still a girl, and he had continued to love her long after she rejected his overtures for Kozlov's.

Dmitry Fedorovich is not a man who dwells on what he cannot have. When she married Kozlov, he accepted it, closing himself off from his desire. But then, with Kozlov's purging, came his opportunity and without thinking about it, or no – it wasn't like that – he did think, long and hard and then, against his better judgement, he seized his chance, wooing and winning her and also taking on her child.

And now, because he cannot bear to be in the same space as her, knowing that she is comparing him with that other, he is here, and because he is here, he is changed.

It is different now. He is against the fascists, naturally he is, but he is also for something. He is for his motherland. And he is for Natasha.

By his actions he will earn his place inside her life. Of this he is certain.

Of this and one other thing: that he will survive.

To Die

The fight has all gone out of Natasha: she's showing the now familiar symptoms of decline. She has stopped going to her factory. And worse than that: she, once so proud of her appearance, has lost interest in keeping clean; once so energetic, having gobbled her bread, immediately she lies down and worse again: she barely has a smile to spare for Katya. Which tells me all I need to know: the fight's gone out of her.

I've tried reasoning with her, but her reason is all gone. By feeding her I have tried, at least, to stem her body's decay (even though I know that it is her will, and not her body, that has given out) but there's not enough food for that. I've also had a go at threatening her, but what threat can be worse than the fate that has befallen us?

Sometimes when I see her lying down, cluttering up my place (and hogging the heat as well), I am upset by how pale she looks and by those dark rings below her eyes; the way her hair lies, stringy across her face, but more than anything, I hate her passivity, hating her as well only because she is my friend and because her time is running out.

Only three days before the turn of the month is upon us

and when that comes Natasha will be changed from a patient into a terrible responsibility for then it is that our ration cards must personally be renewed. She will not get hers, not unless she rouses herself and goes out and finds a doctor who will testify to her sickness, thus explaining why she hasn't been to work. I have thought about wrapping her up, and taking her myself, but if I do that, as weak as I am, it might be the death not only of us two but also of our dependants.

'Hold on,' I say to her: 'Hold on.'

I say more as well. I tell her, as she lies seemingly unconscious, of the talk of the ice road beginning to pay off, of supplies filtering through and even of the rumoured ration rise. Which may be true, I daresay that it is, although I can't help thinking that any rise will owe as much to the increasing death rate (with the resulting drop in mouths to feed) as it does to that convoy that keeps on rumbling over the frozen lake. I don't, of course, tell her that (not that it really matters what I tell her, she isn't listening). I don't tell her either what I know to be correct, that whatever the source of a rise in rations, if something isn't done she will not be around to share in it.

She lies, day in, day out. She has given up. No: it is actually worse than that. In my opinion (I know I'm not an expert but I, like all the *blokadniki*, have gained experience in this field) she is actually willing herself to death. She, who was once so chatty, doesn't bother talking, by which I mean talking for conversation's sake. She does, however, mutter continually to herself. I try not to listen: what she has to say only serves to further anger me.

She is caught in guilt. She blames herself for everything: for Kolya's death, for Dmitry Fedorovich's going to war, for losing the sled, and, for all I know (and this wouldn't surprise me in the slightest), for the actual onset of war.

I have tried to reason with her. I've tried telling her she's not responsible and that none of this is personally directed. It's random, I tell her: like the ice, out of man's control.

I could just as well save my breath. She will not listen and if I keep on at her, she turns away to face the wall. As I said: the fight's gone out of her.

Well, the fight hasn't gone out of me. I tell myself: I will not let her die.

My mind made up, I turn to Anya who is concentrating as usual in her eternal shaving down of wood, and I say: 'I'm going out,' and even in the waning light I pick up that flaring of her alarm, she who usually has her expression under such control. I think: did I see that, and does she really care? – the question bringing home to me how very fragile I also have become, since what she actually says (in that familiar accusing tone) is:

'You never go out this late,' giving me to understand that what I had seen in her expression was not concern, but shock, at this disturbance in our mutually agreed timetable.

I say: 'But I am going now. I won't be long.'

Having said this, I want already to be gone. But impatience is a killer, so I slow myself down, adding on extra clothes. In the process, I get a whiff of myself – I stink and so do my clothes – and also the flash of movement, the shifting of a colony of lice, when I shake out my jersey. A sign of life, I guess, our especially adapted blockade lice having taken to fleeing corpses in their search for food. I ignore it. I'm not fussy. Can't afford to be. I pull on the jersey, and over that my coat. There. I am set.

'I won't be long,' I say, repeating the phrase as I pass by Anya, when I do something that is both unexpected and unintended: I reach out and stroke my hand across her head, an outlandish act that she at least pays me the respect of not acknowledging.

I think to myself: you're getting soft, Irina Davydovna, and then I leave her, going downstairs and out.

It isn't snowing. Which is some relief although it does mean it is very cold.

Stepping out, I feel the cold stabbing at my chest. I make myself breathe – one long exhale – and then I make myself move. I don't have far to go, although even a few steps is an endurance. But I am determined and I have no choice.

The streets are empty and layered by towering mounds of snow. The sky is clear, lit both by a growing moon and the twinkling of a million stars, something that would, a month ago, have been an extra cause for fear. Recently, however, there's been a fall-off in the number of air raids, a signal both of their intention to wait and starve us out, and also of the difficulties those green devils are encountering as well as their terror at our pilots' tactic of ramming them in mid-air.

I walk, silently, across the silent street, a lone pedestrian in a city that no longer moves. My rasping breath is the only sound I hear, the sky my only source of light. I walk by instinct, trusting myself, sure-footed in my determination to survive. I walk a few blocks west and then I cut across and, there: I have reached my destination.

The outside door opens at my touch. One obstacle overcome. I walk into the darkness. There is a stench about this place. Of damp. And mould. And death. I wonder – is this one of these empty buildings, its former occupants now all of them entombed? – but pushing the thought away, I begin to climb the stairs.

It's hard going and I am soon out of breath, but I keep on until I reach a door in darkness. This is it, I think. Stretching out my hand, I attempt a knock but the material I have wrapped around my mittens muffles the impact so effectively that I have to unwind it, take off the mittens and knock again.

The noise resounds throughout the building. It's almost loud enough to wake the dead, I think, although it can't be, because no one answers.

I wonder: can she be dead?

I knock again, harder this time, feeling the impact of the wood against my knuckles and hearing the echo of my assault, ugly in the emptiness, me thundering on the door, carried away by the motion and by frustration, knocking although there is still no answer until, finally, it dawns on me that what I thought before is right: it is too late.

Stupid, I think, to have hoped.

And stupid to waste my energy.

I am heading down, already on the fourth step, when I hear a muffled voice:

'Who's there?'

I freeze.

It's coming from behind the door. 'Who's there?'

I hurry back, calling out anxiously to keep her at the door: 'My name is Irina Davydovna. You may not have heard of me,' and, of course, she hasn't, because I now hear her reply:

'I haven't any spare food.'

I say: 'I've not come here for food.'

'Well, what is it that you want?'

I am on her doorstep, at a loss for words. Weak as I am, and untutored, how can I possibly tell her what I want?

'I'm warning you,' I hear her saying: 'You'd better tell me or go.'

Although it's clear she's alone and, by the sounds of her, without muscle to back up that menace, I'm frightened that if I don't say something she'll walk away, and, since I have neither the strength nor the will to break down her door, that will be end of it. So I say: 'I've come here for your help,' a risk as in these times of desperation not everybody is prepared to help (although it is surprising how many do) but then I console myself with the memory that she is, by all accounts, a kind woman, and sure enough, the accounts are proved correct, for I hear her fumbling with the lock, and then the door swings open.

She is holding an oil lamp that garishly lights up her face. I see: not the person I have come to see.

The woman I am seeking should be middle-aged: this one is old; that other woman is supposed to have smooth, white skin: this one's skin is wrinkled and yellow; the woman I want is supposed to be quite plump: this one is fragile with the frame of a skeleton.

I am in despair. I say: 'I am looking for Tatyana Morozova,' and hear her reply:

'I am Tanya.'

I can see she isn't lying and I think I should have guessed; none of us looks like ourselves any more, war having aged and reduced us all, but then I cast the thought aside because she is still waiting, but not easily, her hand is trembling, the lamp wavering and casting up great shadows, and I see her lip also quavering as if she is regretting her recklessness in opening the door. To try to put her at her ease I say:

'My name is Irina Davydovna . . .' but I have already told her that, and to no effect, and so now, in a bid to describe who I really am, I pull this out: 'I was once on the *Chelyuskin*', seeing the first vague signs of her recognition. 'Boris Aleksandrovich it was who secured me my place there,' I say.

Which is all that was needed. She nods. That's all. A nod. No pronouncement to the effect that Boris Aleksandrovich is a stranger: no question as to how I know of her relationship to him. Instead:

'What is it that I can do for you, Irina Davydovna of the *Chelyuskin*?'

'I need to get in touch with Boris Aleksandrovich.'

'I see.'

'He's too far away. I'd never manage to reach him. Can you give him a message?'

'And what would that message be?'

'Tell him I have Natasha,' I say. 'That she's in a bad way. Tell him she needs his help.'

That's all I say for I have lost the art of conversation, and besides, I am letting in the cold, and so I turn away from Boris Aleksandrovich's mistress and leave.

There's only thing more to relate about this evening. A small thing but astonishing.

It happened after I had made my slow way back.

Arriving safely at the building, I push open the door. It is then I catch sight of a shape, a darting shadow that flees at the sight of me, running from my voice, up the stairs, turning the corner and disappearing

I am too tired either to be frightened or to give chase. I wearily climb up the stairs and then I go inside. I take off all my extra clothes. I go into the kitchen and see: Natasha in her usual place, Katya asleep beside her, and Anya where she always is, doing what she always does.

An unchanging sight: a sight unaltered from the time I left. You'd think.

But if you thought that you'd be wrong. Something has changed. Anya has. She was up before, I know she was. She walked down the stairs. I'm sure of it. And then, she stood there, in the freezing cold: keeping watch for me. Anya – worried about my wellbeing. Worried that I might need help and running from me when she saw that I did not.

Amazing.

Did I tell her that I'd seen her?

Of course not. I never would.

And Live Again

In the absence of regulation-issue camouflage, Dmitry Fedorovich has whitened his helmet. White is the colour of privilege in the trenches, of the hood, smock and overalls of the elite, of the sappers who lay mines in front of approaching tanks, of the ski divisions making light of the white distances between them and the enemy, and of the snipers who crouch down, endlessly patient, in front of their white-painted walls.

In the absence of any white issue of his own, and also of any proper training, Dmitry Fedorovich has only his courage, and his certainty that he will not die, to tell him what to do.

After days of inaction, the attack has suddenly begun. By sound it first announced itself, in the reverberation of diesel engines revving in the forest, this followed by the heavy clanking of tank tracks and, as orders are issued, men in the trenches taking grim hold of guns, lines of Panzers, two, three, four and more deep, start clambering out of the forest and lumbering forward, snout-nosed as their front ranks fire, the wrecks of buildings behind Dmitry Fedorovich crumbling into dust, the roar of the tanks eating up the ground, their bass blasts wounding those they do not kill, and deafening those they do not wound, this heavy percussion of a battle joined, snow flying, crimsoned by fresh blood, machine guns stuttering above the puny shouts of man, hands turning wildly, as the crane feeds rounds into the howitzer, crews covering their ears, to fire, and still the tanks keep coming, ungainly and seemingly invulnerable as they cover ground, Dmitry Fedorovich firing, his rifle puny against the might of the invaders. It's no good. If he stays here, he will be overrun, himself oblivious to the orders of officers, convinced that he can be a hero, and shouting:

'Hurrah,' he clambers from the trench, the blood roaring in him along with the conviction that he will show Natasha that it's not only those strangers, the Klochkovs of this world, who can make a difference, ignoring the sergeant's bellowing for him to get down and instead grabbing up a grenade and then running forward, this man who is so confident that he won't be killed but so stupid he doesn't know better than to hold the metal with bare flesh, and who ends up stuck to the grenade, throwing, not it, but both himself and it.

If he had a chance to live again, would he have acted differently?

Too late to ask that question. He is already dead.

Darkness

A voice probes down into the darkness that binds her.

'Natasha.'

Calling out her name.

'Natasha.'

Summoning her.

'Open your eyes, Natasha.'

The darkness suits: she will not wrest herself from its embrace.

Her name again:

'Natasha,' and she cannot help herself, she is too weak, unable to resist.

Opening her eyes, she waits as the space above her swims slowly into view. She can see: the ceiling, out of focus, and, between that and her staring eyes: a looming face. Her eyes hurting: she winces and they shut.

'Natasha!'

Why won't he leave her alone, this wizened stranger. He is nobody to her. Let him leave. She's tired. Once more her eyes begin to close, the darkness rushing in.

That voice again: 'Natasha.'

That's all – her name. This time it is enough.

'Papa?'

And, yes, it is her father, her father's voice confirming this:

'Yes, Natasha.'

She opens her eyes. Looks up at him. Is that a smile she sees, or a grimace? She thinks: something is very wrong.

She says: 'Mama?'

'Still at the front.'

'Ilya?'

'He's been evacuated. He's safe in Kuibyshev.'

'Misha?'

A shrug. 'Fighting somewhere. I'm sure he's well.'

'Then what are you doing here?'

'I have come to be with you.'

'To say goodbye?'

'No, Natasha. Not to say goodbye.'

He says this firmly, a copy echo of the man he once was, asserting his authority, but she's not fooled. She thinks: this man. Is not my father. He's too old. Too pale. Too exhausted.

And too late.

She prepares herself to move. She will turn away from him, she thinks, and this is what she tries to do, hefting herself up, but he reaches out one bony hand, his thin finger digging at her shoulder, and easily pulls her back.

'Listen to me, Natasha.'

Not to him. She will not listen. The time is gone. She strains against him.

He is stronger. Always was. Her father, hauling her so she faces out and then half-lifting her, propping her up.

She closes her eyes. She doesn't want to talk with him. She doesn't want . . .

Iron fingers probing. Digging at her face. She cries out but they only seem to dig harder. She feels them, one on each cheek, jabbing as if meaning to pierce flesh. She tries once more to move away, but someone else has her in their grip and keeps her there, those fingers stabbing in so hard that she can no longer resist and her mouth opens and, when that happens, she feels cold metal – a spoon – inserted and then turned, a thick syrup spilling out, flooding the inside of her mouth.

It is sickening. She must purge herself of it, must spit it out. She prepares herself, for even that will need energy, but when she's ready, she finds she cannot for her mouth is forcibly closed at the same moment as someone squeezes her nose, blocking off the air, so that she can't help herself, she swallows, the treacly sludge saturating the capillaries of her throat, so thick it is, she cannot seem to swallow it. She can't breathe either: it is stopping up her air. She starts to cough and then to retch, bile rising up and being swallowed back, and it passes through her mind that the hatred she had felt for Dmitry had been sucked into her rotten and gummy mouth, and spread its poison into this putrefaction of a woman she has turned out to be, she, no better than he for, at the first chance she'd had, she'd mimicked him, letting unexamined whim and undigested bitterness prompt her into sending him off to risk his life. And as she thinks this, she hears a distant sound that she knows must be her own rasping breath, herself gasping, her throat convulsing, and she knows she's choking, panting for breath that will not come. She is dying, angry that she cannot die in peace as she had wanted to, as she feels a hand moving down her back, smoothing it, smoothing her into calm , and gradually her breath returns, and she lies back, and this time, what she feels is: sad.

That voice again: 'That's good,' she hears, 'now try another spoonful.'

She is too exhausted to resist. She opens up her mouth, swallowing to his instruction, this, her father, patiently feeding her the nourishment he had brought and when that's over, he lets her lie back again, although she's not yet left to sleep for, as she starts drifting off, she feels him passing a warm, wet cloth, first over her face and then down her limbs, her gentle father washing her, this father she had long ago thought she'd lost, cleaning her and, with Irina's assistance, changing her clothes and her sheets, until finally, satisfied, they let go of her.

At last. She lies back, her eyes closing.

She wants to sleep. That's all she tells herself she wants.

Her eyes begin, involuntarily, to open. She is checking that he is still here, and checking also if he is real rather than the construct of her longing that, when her eyes are closed, she tells herself he will turn out to be.

No matter what she tells herself: he's there and there he stays, by her side, one of his hands resting lightly on one of hers. She feels her eyelids drooping. She cannot help it: she feels herself sinking into sleep.

Waking later into darkness she can hear the steady breathing of the others fast asleep. She looks up, hopelessly, expecting nothing but once again she's wrong.

He is still there. Her father. Sitting by her side, his hand on hers.

She says, softly so as not to wake the others: 'Why are you doing this?'

'Because you must live.'

Must I? she thinks: 'Why?'

'Because that's what we all have to do. We have to live. Go on. Otherwise, what's the point?'

The Road of Life

Can the dead speak?

Can their voices be heard?

Maybe they can for I, Ira, as I stand here, at the edge of Lake Ladoga, am almost that: the speaking dead.

My feet are rooted deep in a bed of snow that stretches to the edge of the lake and then beyond. The covering of snow is so even that the division between land and lake must be taken all on trust. I let my gaze trace over the boundary that I know exists even if I don't know where it is.

Out on the frozen lake, I can see white and petrified waves that stretch out into the distance. For a moment I think that there might be movement there, but by strengthening my stare I realise that this was only a trick of the light and that the surface of the lake is perfectly still. A white layered sky hangs down, so at one with its surroundings that only that faint greying of the far horizon shows that at some point, somewhere, there might be change.

Along this whiteness lies the Road of Life. It is our escape route to the other side.

It's not a road as such: it's a marked-out and guarded section of the ice. Our only link to the rest of our motherland.

I hear distant roaring. I know it is the convoy of lorries, lurching and tilting and weaving over the ice, making its way to us. The lorries have been travelling for hours, past checkpoints, anti-aircraft and repair and fuelling stations, over thick ice and over thin, driving without lights, to bring in food. When they get here, which by the sounds of it will be soon, they won't stop long. The food quickly unloaded, they will fill up with human cargo and be off.

I am here to say goodbye to Natasha. She is going. She and Katya, across the ice to Novaya Ladoga and then to greater safety.

Boris Aleksandrovich had also got places for me and for Anya on the lorries, but we will not be using them. Anya has refused. I tried, half-heartedly, to change her mind. I told her what was the truth: that most of the orphans have already left, and that she would be just as useful somewhere else in Russia. Her only answer was to say that there will be more orphans, soon, in Leningrad, a fact that is also undeniable. And so, because she is staying, so must I.

To be honest: the decision suits me. This is my city: the city that I love. In my lifetime I have left its borders only twice, the first time into peril and the second to Moscow and deception. Twice is enough for me. I have lived through Leningrad's darkest times. I have seen its pain and I have also seen its heroism. I am part of it. I am like Anya. I do not want to leave.

The sounds of the lorries being unloaded. I tear my eyes away from the outstretched lake. I turn. I am so cold, my joints have stiffened up: it even hurts to bend my hand. I know that if I am to be in time to wave Natasha off, I must get moving, but even knowing this I still keep standing. I look across at a line of fir trees crusted by snow, clumps of it which fall down now and then, and so display the ghostlike mauve-brown tendrils of the spiky leaves, their evidence of life. It's a beautiful sight, that's what I think, standing here: I, Irina Davydovna, who, long ago, had her gaze so focused down, I would never have thought to look for, never mind actually see, such beauty.

I am changed. A different woman. Transformed, as we all have been. We know things, now, more than we used to. And one of things we know is this: we will survive, or that enough of us will. It doesn't matter what the Germans throw at us. Because of our determination, and our resistance, this is a war they can never win.

Grand thoughts, I know, and I mean them. But now I also think that I must hurry or I'll miss Natasha. I walk over the snow, towards the staging post. I can hear doors slamming. I speed up. I feel my feet, plunging down, deep into the snow. It is an effort to suck them out again, but I do this cheerfully, for the extra food Boris Aleksandrovich has brought for all of us helped me build up my strength.

And there he is, Boris Aleksandrovich, standing by a lorry. As I walk closer, I see he is helping Natasha up before handing in her daughter.

They're the last passengers in this particular truck: the driver shoves the tailgate shut.

Katya settles herself on Natasha's lap. Both sit there, wrapped in as many layers as we could fit. Natasha is so well covered that all I can see of her is a tiny section of her face. Although she still looks almost deathly pale, I am secure in the knowledge that she is no longer on the point of death.

Her arm reaches down.

I know what my friend is doing. She is reaching out for me. I stretch up and grab that hand, clasping it tight, and for the moment that's all I do, standing there, holding on to her, no words, for there are no words left, and then the engine kicks into life and I hear a shout, and the convoy starts moving, and I have to let her go.

I will not cry in case my tears should turn to ice.

I stand, waiting as the lorry drives away.

Over the ice road it goes.

The road will soon be over with – spring will come, and the ice will melt – and then it will live on only in our memories. The last of the lorries hisses past. Its tail lights flash, once, before it trundles on to the ice. I watch it, watching as the light begins to fade and the lorry disappears from sight, and after that as well, long after it has gone.

Acknowledgements

History, especially in this world I entered, is not always easy to track. To this, I have added another twist – the shifting of details, of dates, weather and happenings – in an already complex time. The responsibility for this, and for any mistakes, I take on myself.

I am beholden to many contemporaneous and historical accounts. Thanks in particular to the *Matiane Katlisa* (anon.); Valerian Albanov's *In the Land of White Death*; Anthony Beevor's *Stalingrad*; Charles E. Bohlen's *Witness to History*; Reader Bullard's *Inside Stalin's Russia*; E. H. Carr's *Foundations of a Planned Economy*; Otto Preston Chaney's *Zhukov*; Robert Conquest's *The Great Terror* and *Stalin and the Kirov Murder*; Sarah Davies' *Popular Opinion in Russia*; Isaac Deutscher's *The Unfinished Revolution*; Joseph Edward Davies' *Mission to Moscow*; Walter Duranty's *I Write as I Please*; A. V. Gorbatov's *Years of my Life*; Lidiya Ginzburg's *Blockade Diary*; Vasily Grossman's *Life and Fate*; Vera Mikhailovna Inber's *Leningrad Diary*; Amy Knight's *Who Killed Kirov*; Victor Kravchenko's *I Choose Freedom*; Anna Larina's *This I Cannot Forget*; Nadezhda Mandelstam's *Hope Against Hope* and *Hope Abandoned*; B. F. Manz's *The Rise and*

Fall of Tamerlane; Roy Medvedev's *Let History Judge*; Catherine Merridale's *Night of Stone*; Anatoly Nayman's *Remembering Anna Akhmatova*; Boris I. Nicolaevsky's *Power and the Soviet Elite*; Richard Overy's *Russia's War*; Anton Antonov-Ovseyenko's *The Time of Stalin*; Boris Skomorovsky and E. G. Morris's *The Siege of Leningrad*; O. Yu. Schmidt, I. L. Baevsky and L. Z. Mekhlis's (editors) *Voyage of the Chelyuskin*; Andrew Smith's *I Was a Soviet Worker*; Harrison E. Salisbury's *The 900 Days of the Siege of Leningrad*; Dorothy Thompson's *The New Russia*; Nikolai Tikhonov's *The Defence of Leningrad*; Marina Tsetaeva's *Art in the Light of Conscience*; Arkady Vaksberg's *The Prosecutor and the Prey*; Linton Well's *Blood on the Moon*; and Vasily Efimovich Zubakov's *Heroic Leningrad* as well as many other sources too numerous to name.

Many thanks to Moira Forjaz for taking that first, generous journey into the unknown with me; to Joe Schwartz for treating my technical questions as if they had depth; to Sara Wheeler for opening up her library and her knowledge; to Farrukhkhon Polatov for his help in my investigations of Alisher Navoi; to Gerard McBurney for giving me a flavour of his experiences; and to Robert Service for so readily playing along with a stranger's impertinent desire to rewrite Georgian medieval history. Thanks also to Shawn Slovo for her encouragement and to Luise Eichenbaum, Sarah Dunant, Susie Orbach, Caroline Pick, and Jud Stone for their forebearance and support during this long haul.

A special thank you to Tatiana Tihonova, a stranger who opened her home to me, and afterwards spent many hours interviewing survivors of the siege on my behalf. To them, and their stories, I owe an enormous debt of gratitude. And thank you to Victoria Brittain, Linda Grant and Robyn Slovo who read and commented on early drafts, and, afterwards, helped keep me going, to Ronald Segal whose generosity and skill with the pencil knows no bounds, and to Sally Laird for her care and attention to detail.

Thanks, as ever, to Andy Metcalf for his unwavering support and for encouraging me to stay true to my vision and to Cassie for being so good tempered about living with so many strange people for so long. And finally, thank you, Lennie Goodings, my dream editor who gives me permission to dream, and then, unerringly and unflaggingly, helps me polish the result, and my agent, Clare Alexander, who, new to me with this book, has given of her confidence, her composure, her honesty, and her sharp mind to help see it through.

About the Author

Gillian Slovo was a finalist for the Orange Prize for *Ice Road*. She is the author of the novel *Red Dust*, now a major motion picture, as well as eight other novels and a family memoir *Every Secret Thing*. She is coauthor of the play *Guantánamo*, which had highly praised runs in London and New York. Born in South Africa, Slovo and her family were exiled to Britain in 1964. She has lived in London ever since.